Joseph G. Dobesh 1952

D1071169

A History of Norway

A History of
NORWAY

By Karen Larsen

Princeton University Press, Princeton
for the American-Scandinavian Foundation
New York, 1950

Copyright, 1948, by Princeton University Press
London: Geoffrey Cumberlege, Oxford University Press

Second printing, 1950

Printed in the United States of America by Princeton
University Press at Princeton, New Jersey

TO MY SISTER

HANNA ASTRUP LARSEN

1873-1945

PREFACE

With the widespread interest in Norway which has been evinced in our country during recent years, there should be room for a history which strikes a mean between a sketchy popular account and an exhaustive critical study. It is hoped that this volume will in some measure meet such a demand. In trying to combine the many lines of development into one harmonious picture as nearly true as possible, the writer is faced with ever-baffling problems of selection upon which no two authors could agree. It has been my aim not to crowd the pages with too many details, and—to mention but one example—in selecting a few names from a long list of writers or artists, I have been guided not only by the intrinsic value of the work of the individual, but also by the degree to which he typifies the trends of his time. Obviously the scope of the book precludes the discussion of controversial issues.

The footnotes, which have been kept down to a minimum, and the brief bibliography, in which books available in English have been emphasized, give only a slight indication of the many Norwegian historians and other writers to whom I should like to express my gratitude and respectful admiration. Nor is it amiss to say a word of thanks to the visitors to and from Norway whose knowledge of present-day conditions has helped me to bridge the Atlantic. Among them are Mr. Sven Evenson of Oslo, who gave generously of his time, and Dean Norman Nordstrand of Saint Olaf College, who read the last chapter.

I wish to acknowledge with thanks the assistance of every kind which I have received from Mr. Datus C. Smith of the Princeton University Press, and from Dr. Henry Goddard Leach and other members of the Committee of Publications of the American-Scandinavian Foundation. While the manuscript was in preparation, Mr. John B. C. Watkins was ever ready with help and encouragement. Professor Robert Fife of Columbia University was kind enough to read the manuscript, and Professor William Witherle Lawrence, also of Columbia, has read the proof. I am humbly grateful for the criticism of these scholars. Mr. Erik J. Friis, too, has read the proof.

To members of my family also I wish to express my gratitude: to my brothers, Henning Larsen of the University of Illinois and Jakob A. O. Larsen of Chicago University; and, even more, to my sister Ingeborg Larsen, who has aided me immeasurably in whipping the book into shape.

To my sister, Hanna Astrup Larsen, I owe more than words can express. Her initiative and confidence alone gave me the courage to undertake this task, and her incisive criticism and dauntless enthusiasm spurred me on. My thoughts also go back to my childhood home, where Mother imbued me with love for the land of her birth and Father tempered my ardor with his critical judgment.

KAREN LARSEN

Saint Olaf College
Northfield, Minnesota
March 1, 1948

PREFACE TO SECOND PRINTING

As this book goes into a second printing, I wish to express my thanks to reviewers and others who have given me helpful suggestions. To Professor Halvdan Koht I owe a special debt of gratitude. He has been most generous with his time, and given me the benefit of his keen scholarship and wide knowledge. This has been of inestimable value. It has not seemed desirable, however, to make any major changes in the book, and the responsibility for weaknesses which still remain must be wholly mine.

KAREN LARSEN

February 17, 1950

CONTENTS

PART I

The Early Ages

CHAPTER 1

BEFORE IRON CAME TO THE NORTH

ON THE VERY EDGE OF EUROPE LIES NORWAY, to the north facing the cold Arctic and to the west the mild Atlantic warmed by the Gulf Stream. We think of it as a small country, for even in modern times its population has reached only three million, its natural resources are meager, and the amount of land under the plow is not impressive, constituting even today less than three per cent of its soil. Yet Norway is a vast country stretching from 57° 59′ to 71° 11′ north latitude. From Norway's capital it is as far to the North Cape as it is to Sicily, and from the North Cape it takes a long sailing to reach the Finnish border. Norway lies close enough to the rest of Europe to have shared the course of development that has shaped the civilization of the countries farther south, though of necessity these influences have often reached this northern outpost of Europe rather late. There have, however, been compensations for this slower development for, in marked contrast to most of the small states in Europe, Norway lay off the main highways of wandering peoples. In the Balkans, to mention but one striking contrast, innumerable races milling back and forth have produced a history dramatic, but filled with tragedy. The greater degree of isolation together with the nature of the land has given the people of Norway an unusual opportunity for a long unbroken development, as well as comparative security against foreign conquests. Never, before modern warfare turned topsy-turvy all the conditions of the past, has the country as a whole been conquered, or even temporarily occupied by outside forces. Norway's history has been dominated less by conflicts with alien peoples than by struggles with an inhospitable nature, struggles rarely spectacular but nevertheless heroic. "If any people in the world owns its land with honor and right, has conquered it, not from other people, but in obedience to the Creator's stern commandment that man shall eat his bread in the sweat of his brow, it is we Norwegians who call Norway our country."[1] The effort to win a living from a niggardly land has been the basic fact in the development of the Norwegian people, and the topography and climate have to a great extent determined the character of its history.

The country took its form during the Ice Age when glaciers at least three times covered most of the land and again disappeared. The masses of ice split the mountains forming fjords and ravines and leveled down the hills of the great plateau, leaving only the peaks that had risen above the ice, and which still stand out sharply above the surrounding land. As the ice disappeared, the land lay scoured and bare, stark and inhospitable, and the long process of building up soil and vegetation was begun.

Another factor in shaping the country was the sinking of the land which took place after the Ice Age, and its subsequent rise. This phenomenon was most marked in southeastern Norway. As the sea receded, it left in its wake a deep clay sediment which forms the soil of the wide, gently sloping valleys of the Eastland. In Trøndelag, the region about the Trondheim Fjord, the change in the sea level was only slightly less than in the southeast. There, too, rich sediment was left, producing the broad fertile plains which constitute the chief break in the long western coast of narrow valleys between mountains often dropping off abruptly into the ocean.

The smell of the sea has so entered into the very blood of the Norwegians that even in the briefest sketch of the geographic conditions that have helped to shape their development mention of it would have to be made. Throughout Norway's history the greatest economic, political, and cultural advance has been achieved when the people have had untrammeled access to the surrounding ocean and have been able to make use of the opportunities this offers. Their livelihood has in no small degree come from the riches of the sea, and it has been almost their sole highway leading to the outside world. Of greatest importance is perhaps the closed fairway along the coast with its outer barrier of skerries and rocky islands of fantastic shape. It is the roadway that has linked together valleys which would otherwise have been hopelessly separated, thus helping to tie the isolated settlements together into a united country. Long before people ventured out on the open sea, primitive boats plied their way along this shielded fairway, and from this oldest of highways, this "northern way," the name of the country has been derived.

The climate of Norway is largely determined by the ocean. It is not within our province to trace the climatic contrast between the different

[1] Sigrid Undset, *Return to the Future*, 4, New York, 1942.

glacial and interglacial eras with the accompanying changes in plant and animal life. Suffice it to mention that as the ice retreated for the last time, the climate gradually grew warmer until the Arctic period had given way to the so-called "Boreal Age," named from the dry northern winds that prevailed. The climate then was so warm that islands along the northern shore which are now covered only with grass or stunted shrubs were densely wooded, and large stretches of the mainland which are now above the treeline were covered with forests of pine and birch, while animals characteristic of Central Europe, such as the wild boar, roamed the woods. The "Boreal Age" was followed by the "Atlantic Period," which was even warmer and also much damper than the preceding era. The climate was more continental than at present, with more marked contrast between summer and winter, while extensive swamps and dense woods of semi-tropical growth made the interior almost impenetrable.

Gradually all of this changed, and about two thousand years ago present weather conditions became dominant, first on the coast and then in the interior. There is much rough, even cyclonal, weather along the coast, especially in the north, with tumultuous winds, heavy rain, and blinding fog. But the sea has given cool summers; and although a third of the country lies north of the Arctic Circle, the kindly Gulf Stream has bestowed upon Norway remarkably mild winters in spite of Arctic darkness.

¶ When human life first appeared in Norway is a question to which scholars have devoted much attention. During the earlier periods ice had submerged all Northern and Central Europe, but the last Glacial Age covered a smaller area. It is well established that people continued to live, under Arctic conditions of course, in southern France and Germany during this age. Even in Norway, on the northern and northwestern coast, there were spots between the glaciers where the snow disappeared in the summer and where certain hardy forms of plant and animal life continued to exist throughout the age. So human life, too, some scholars believe, might have existed just in the same manner as on the edge of modern Greenland, but whether or not it actually did has not been incontestably established. There are reasons for believing that the oldest traces of human life in Norway are remains from the culture of a race which inhabited the country in the last interglacial period. Some scholars believe, however, that these people came in from the East after the last retreat of the ice, and find in the culture some similarity to that of the

Volga region. The first finds were made not many years ago on the northern coast of Norway, at Komsa in Finmark, and the mode of life these primitive remains represent has been called the Komsa or the Finmark culture.[2] Though it is uncertain who the ancestors of the Komsa people were and when, whence, or by what route they first came into Norway, it seems that they spread along the western coast as the ice disappeared for the last time. For remains similar to those found in Finmark have been discovered along the shore as far south as Bergen, being especially abundant in Møre. Traces of human life of like character are found also in Østfold, or Baahus, the little section of the country east of the Oslo Fjord, or Folden Fjord as it was called in olden times. The people here, it would seem, must have come from the South. It seems extremely unlikely that any descendants of the earliest people in Norway survived into the later ages or that there is any connection between them and the primitive people who became the ancestors of the modern Norwegians. What contribution, if any, they may have made to later civilization is as yet an unanswered question.

As soon as the ice receded for the last time from the southern shore, people began to filter in from the South. Norway was not settled through any large mass migration, but by little scattered groups of people who gradually occupied the coast.

It is difficult to determine the race of these early people with any degree of finality. It cannot be ascertained through the archaeological finds which supply most of our knowledge of the age. The anthropological material so far found is slight and can give little help in drawing any final conclusion, though it has been claimed that even in physical characteristics the Norwegian of the Old Stone Age resembled his descendant of today.[3] Two types have gone into the making of the Norwegian people. The dominant is the tall, fair, dolichocephalic type; but the stockier, shorter, brachycephalic type, found chiefly in the western coastal region, also makes up a considerable element in the population. When the two came to the North is shrouded in mystery, and it is not impossible that they were mingled before they entered Norway. The oldest linguistic evidence is to be found in place names, of which extensive studies have been made.[4] The oldest, which go back into the Bronze Age, show no trace of anything non-Germanic.

[2] Gutorm Gjessing, *Fangstfolk: et streiftog gjennom nordnorsk førhistorie*, Oslo, 1941, embodies late research in this field.

[3] Gustav Heber, *Normennenes historie i førkristen tid*, Oslo, 1936.

[4] Magnus Olsen, *Farms and Fanes of Ancient Norway*, Oslo, 1928.

New people have come into the country and new elements have been added to the population, but in all probability they have not displaced earlier settlers, only become assimilated with them and thereby enriched the culture of the land.

All great advances in the culture of Norway were inaugurated by impulses from the South brought in by commercial contacts or by new groups of people who drifted northward. Newcomers, by adapting themselves to the environment, became in reality natives. At a very early age the people in Norway developed a mode of life suited to their land, and their culture took its form from the means of livelihood that the country offered. "Life took its rhythm from the inexorable dictates of nature."[5] The sea, the forests, the mountains, and the demands of the different seasons have determined the mode of life of the Norwegians from the earliest times, and in many cases they do so even today. In some of the early dwelling sites along the coast there are indications that implements of bone, stone, and iron were in use at the same time. The early methods of fishing and hunting persisted even to a very late age; and when farming, with cattle raising and agriculture, was developed, hunting and fishing were not displaced to anything like the same extent as in Denmark and Sweden. From the Stone Age down to the present the two modes of winning a livelihood have been intertwined and supplementary to each other. Like the fisherman on the coast in the Late Stone Age, his descendant of today has fields and cattle at home.

It is therefore clear that no sharp line of demarcation can be drawn between the different ages. Yet with some reservations the classic names for periods can be used even in tracing the story of Norway.

¶ In general the Stone Age comprises the whole time preceding the middle of the second millennium before Christ, or about 1500 B.C.

The earliest part of the Stone Age might best be called the Bone-Stone Age. It has been mentioned that almost as soon as the ice disappeared from the southern coast of Norway, little groups of people found their way from the South and settled along the shore. They were in a purely food-gathering state of development, depending almost wholly on the sea for their living. As time went on, the climate grew warmer and life became easier. The land from the high central plateau down to the sea was densely wooded with fir and birch, and then came the oak and beech into the southern region. The animal life, too,

[5] A. W. Brøgger, *Det norske folk i oldtiden*, Oslo, 1925.

changed and grew more varied, and the rich vegetation supplied more of that plant food which people whose diet is chiefly meat devour with such ravenous appetites. Using dugout boats or possibly skin canoes similar to the Eskimo kayaks, the people spread northward along the coast finding new hunting and fishing grounds. But it was a long time before they began to push into the interior. Not only were the woods almost impenetrable, but the coast of Norway was particularly well adapted to the type of life they were living. The virgin wealth of sea and land was almost unbelievable. In the famous Viste archaeological finds on Jæren, the southwestern coast of Norway, the bones of about fifty kinds of animals have been identified, among which only the dog was domesticated. Great schools of whales came to shore, seals were so close in the shallows that the hunter's little boat could hardly make its way between them, and of fish there was an unbounded wealth. Islands were literally covered with sea fowl, providing eggs and down in abundance. The streams teemed with salmon, and in the woods roamed wild animals both large and small, which could be caught at the drinking and fording places. The big game hunting was often carried on in some spot where reindeer in great herds could be driven out over a steep cliff or precipice and then slain or left to perish—a most barbaric and wasteful mode of hunting. In such places the early hunters have left the greatest monuments of their art. They are rock tracings of animals in natural size executed in vigorous, rhythmic lines—sketchy, improvised, unplanned pictures, they have been called the first impressionistic art of Norway.[6] The drawings probably had a magic purpose, that of securing good hunting. As time went on they became smaller, less naturalistic and more geometric, losing some of their artistic quality, but, we suppose, of just as strong magic power.

The people of the Bone Age were well equipped for their work. Many of the finds in exposed places on the shore furnish ample evidence of the use made of stone, while most organic matter has disappeared. There are, however, spots which give material for fairly complete reconstruction of the life of the age. One of the most notable examples is a snugly sheltered pocket in the mountain at the mouth of the Voss River, not far from Bergen. There layers of refuse show how life has been carried on from the earliest time down through the Viking Age. In the bottom layer have been found a multitude of bone and horn implements, such as fishhooks, arrowheads, spears, harpoons for catching seal, sewing needles, scrapers used in dressing hides, and the

[6] Leif Østby, *Norges kunsthistorie,* 10, Oslo, 1938.

like, all of good design and remarkable efficiency. It can safely be assumed that wooden implements, too, were used, but no trace of pottery has been found about the stone hearth.

¶ At first stones were used only in their natural form, either as missiles or as aids in making bone and horn implements. The invention of the axe, the first manufactured stone implement, marks a great advance in civilization and ushers in a period which is often called the Middle Stone Age, or the beginning of a true Stone Age. These primitive axes are called Nøstvet axes from the place at the head of the Bunne Fjord near Oslo where they were first discovered, but later thousands of them have been found scattered over a wide area. They had no handle and were roughly hewn with only the edge ground down by using sand and water on a flat sandstone, the same technique as was employed with bone. As in other countries, the first stone used was flint, but for all its mountains Norway yielded only a small and poor supply of flint, consisting mainly of loose blocks found in glacial moraines. The Norwegians, therefore, very early began to use other kinds of stone and to make a search for good material. And so were begun Norway's first stone quarries. Several such quarries have been found, for example one at Bømlo, on a little island off the western coast. Near the quarries, which were really the industrial centers of the age, tools and weapons by the thousands were made; through wanderings and trade they were distributed over a large area. The variety of implements increased, and small tools made of quartz and, especially in the North, of slate gradually took the place of bone. There was a new beauty in the weapons, too, and pottery made its first appearance. The population spread somewhat and there was probably more hunting of large land animals, but otherwise the Middle Stone Age brought no fundamental change in the mode of life.

¶ Immigrants from the South introduced the great changes of the New or Late Stone Age. Farther south the culture of this age has been called megalithic from the massive burial places built of huge stones which characterize the period. Although Norway has only a few small examples of monuments from a late period, found in the southeastern corner, the name has been applied there also, inasmuch as influences spread to Norway from Denmark and Skaane, which were important centers of this culture. Another stream of immigrants of less importance than the megalithic peoples came into eastern Norway and Trøndelag from east-central Europe, a warlike tribe bringing along mighty battle axes far superior to the native product.

This age brought great advance in the making of stone articles. Especially in the use of flint Norway was almost like a province of Denmark, and beautiful implements were imported. The Norwegians, however, mastered the new technique and made very efficient implements of many kinds, from axes which modern experiments have proved could hew down big timber quite efficiently, to little instruments for surgical operations such as trepanning. Sometimes axes were made for beauty perhaps even more than for use, and the material selected was shining black basalt, red porphyry, and lovely green volcanic stones. The axes were smoothly polished, and the flat surfaces covered with artistic designs showing a highly developed sense of beauty. Pottery, too, was more generally used in this age, although the ceramic finds have been rather meager.

The most important influence from the South was the introduction of agriculture, both grain raising and animal husbandry. The interior began to be occupied, no doubt because people were looking for places where they could cultivate fields. Though individual trees could be cut down with stone axes, the clearing of large woods was an almost insuperable task; so the first farmers kept to the open places where little plots of land might be scratched up for seeding. They kept cattle, sheep, and hogs, but as yet farming was of secondary importance. The Stone Age folk were conservative; their land was hard to cultivate, but it still offered boundless game to the huntsman. And so the new did not displace the old, only supplemented it. Sites along the coast which are rich in finds from the Late Stone Age were evidently not permanent dwelling places, but stations occupied during a short season for hunting, fishing, or gathering material for tools and even making them. The permanent homes must have been farther inland, near little plots of cultivated land.

Even when this comparatively high development had been reached, the old methods and old implements of the Bone Age continued in general use. Likewise through the millennium of the Bronze Age and the first centuries of the Iron Age the people in their daily living were still largely in the Stone Age.

❡ The Bronze Age came to the North in the second millennium before Christ, about 1500 B.C. or earlier, and continued for about a thousand years. The art of smelting and casting metal, the great advance in civilization which characterizes the age of metals, had long been known in the Mediterranean lands. In the second millennium, when the Egyptian, the Cretan, and somewhat later the Mycenaean bronze cultures flourished in their greatest splendor, their influence, especially the Mycenaean, reached far to the north traveling over the Alps and by a more easterly route through Austria and Hungary. Thus a fully developed Bronze Age came to the North through commerce with the Mediterranean, carried on indirectly through Central Europe. There was also trade with the regions east of the Baltic and to a smaller extent with England. The development of the whole Bronze Age in the North was dependent on trade, for the metals needed were not found in Scandinavia. Denmark became an important cultural center in this age in spite of the poverty in metals, for there was a wealth of the much-sought amber which could be exchanged for bronze.

Norway, on the other hand, had nothing to give in return for metals. Bronze was expensive and Norway poor. The country was, therefore, culturally more dependent on Denmark than it had been during any earlier time, and bronze was never extensively used. As compared with the thousands of articles unearthed in Denmark, a bare five hundred bronze objects have been found in Norway. Of these only two hundred are tools, so it is clear that implements of other materials must have been generally used. The stone axe made with a hole for a handle is characteristic of this age and marks an advance, but other stone and bone articles have also been found which indicate that the life of the common people underwent no revolutionary change through the introduction of metal.

Nevertheless, the Bronze Age was a notable period in the history of Norway. At no time either before or since have climatic conditions been so favorable. This meant much in comfort and made possible a more expansive and richer life than in times of more severe weather. The remains from this period are so rich and varied that we can know the people of the Bronze Age much better than those of earlier times. There are in the first place the bronze articles which have given the age its name. Though some of these were imported, the Norwegians mastered the art of casting, using Norwegian soapstone for molds, and the archaeological finds make it possible to trace the development in technique till it reached a high degree of perfection. The art in bronze shows refinement, beauty, and variety, and the ornamentation is especially characterized by elegant, graceful spiral lines. It is, however, a somewhat exotic art in which the many strains of foreign influence have not been thoroughly assimilated. It is indicative of a refined upper class culture of southern splendor, yet the people who produced it must have been natives, as there was very little of the foreign influx of population which had characterized the New Stone Age.

The elaborate care bestowed upon the burial of the dead, both men and women, has furnished invaluable material for the study of the age. Massive stone tombs show an almost barbaric love of display on the part of the aristocracy which alone had the power and resources to put up such monuments. More important even are the oak coffins found in Jutland, which contain articles in a remarkably good state of preservation. The men, who were tall and fair, wore a little cap, a short cloak, and sandals. Their needs in the next world were well provided for. Even their toilet articles, including a bronze razor, pincers, and a little stylus, probably used for tattooing, must go with these men of the aristocracy on their long journey. The dress of the women was more varied and more like the modern styles. Sometimes, perhaps in winter, they had long skirts, but more often they wore dresses reaching barely to the knees and with elbow sleeves. They were made of wool; so we know that the arts of spinning and weaving had been developed and that woolen clothing was supplementing skins. Bracelets and other jewelry were common, but the most prominent ornament was a large disk worn at the belt. Their long hair was combed back from the forehead and held in place by a net.

Priceless among Bronze Age archaeological treasures are the many rock tracings. They are not naturalistic sketches, as are the rock pictures from the Stone Age, but mere symbols closely connected with the religion of the age. The sun is indicated often in these tracings, so it can safely be assumed that it occupied a central place in the worship; and other supernatural forces worshiped were spirits who could give fertility and prosperity in the daily occupations. There are pictured large boats indicative of trade with far-off lands and men hunting with bow and arrow; but the occupation most emphasized in the rock symbols is farming, most especially animal husbandry, which was of prime importance. In addition to the domestic animals of the earlier age, the horse was now used. It was a shaggy little animal of protective coloring, brown in summer and white in winter, which was distributed over a large part of Northern Europe but is now extinct. Grain also was more extensively cultivated, oats being added to the earlier rye and wheat. The agricultural regions of the country became more important, and in large sections farming consumed more time than hunting and fishing.

Unique among the rock tracings is a large picture in Hardanger which is painted. The background is a nearly white cliff sheltered by overhanging rocks. "The picture is large and embraces the well-known symbols of the Bronze Age, as well as a goddess of some sort. It is probably the only real symbolic painting relative to agriculture which we have in Northern Europe from the Bronze Age."[7]

Agriculture had brought with it a more settled life and consequently a more organized society. This change, begun in the Late Stone Age, was more marked in the Bronze Age. In some sections there were the beginnings of a political unit larger than the neighborhood settlement, or *bygd*. The leaders were those chieftains who have left their mark in the archaeological finds of the age. In spite of the advance toward political organization, however, the people were not so rooted in the soil as they were in later ages. The climate was such that the flocks could graze in the open through the winter, so there was probably no shelter or fenced-in pen provided for them. The cultivated land was, therefore, not kept productive by application of fertilizer, nor could it be well worked with only wooden tools. The soil became exhausted in a comparatively short time, and then, it seems, the people moved on to new homes. Evidence of this is found in the wide distribution of the implements of the age, and the absence of any traces of permanent farms.

About 500 B.C. the prosperous Bronze Age ebbed out. The Norwegians had, however, developed a mode of living which was so well established that they were able to cope with the problems of the next centuries, perhaps the most difficult time that ever tested the endurance of the people in this outpost of civilization.

[7] Haakon Shetelig in *Tidens Tegn*, July 2, 1940. The picture had been known by the people of the neighborhood long before it came to the attention of scholars.

CHAPTER 2

THE OLD IRON AGE, 500 B.C.–A.D. 780

THE OLD IRON AGE is the name applied to the long period extending from the passing of the Bronze Age, about 500 years before Christ, to the Viking Age, which began approximately at A.D. 780. Only when iron came into general use did Norway have a real metal age, and the changes resulting from its use can be compared in importance only to the earlier introduction of grain culture and animal husbandry or to the later coming of the machine age. In this era Norwegian life assumed the form it was to retain far into historic times. There grew up a rural civilization, a *bonde kultur*, centered upon the method of winning a livelihood which was in its fundamentals to remain the same to the day of firearms, and in some respects much longer, into the nineteenth century and even to our own day. Although the divisions may seem somewhat arbitrary, the age can be divided into four periods.

¶ During the last centuries before the Christian era iron was in general use throughout the greater part of Western Europe. It became known even in Norway, although stone was used there just as generally as in the Bronze Age. While these centuries are classed as the beginning of the Pre-Roman Period of the Iron Age, they appear to be in reality a return to the Stone Age, or perhaps it might be more accurate to say a continuation of the Stone Age with the bronze veneer gradually disappearing. Whatever name we use, the civilization of this time was poorer than that of the Bronze Age. Norway became more isolated. The Celtic peoples, moving toward the west, occupied Central Europe and thus cut off the lively commercial intercourse between Scandinavia and the Mediterranean region which had characterized the earlier age. This meant the end of importation of bronze and other articles of luxury, the end of the golden aristocratic culture based on foreign contacts, and probably the disappearance of the old aristocracy which had dominated the past centuries. Yet it is from this period of isolation that we have the first description of Norway written by a foreign visitor. In the age of Alexander the Great, ca. 330 B.C., a Greek geographer and explorer from Marseilles, named Pytheas, sailed along Great Britain to the islands north of it. There he heard that six days' journey away was the land of Thule, the outermost region of the earth, or Ultima Thule, as the Latin phrase has it.[1] He set sail to the northeast and spent a summer on the western shore of Norway a little above the Arctic Circle. He has left correct geographic descriptions, notably of the most remarkable sight he beheld—the midnight sun. Of the people he tells little. They lacked the finer fruits of the South, he says, but lived on vegetables, wild fruit, roots, and oats. Whether others had sailed to Thule is a matter of conjecture. Somehow information given to Pytheas had been obtained, and perhaps the Norwegians, too, knew that the sea to the west was not boundless, but that beyond dwelt unknown peoples.

The Celts, who had blocked the highways in the south, had themselves very little influence on Norway. They had acquired the knowledge of iron before they moved west, but while they were excellent blacksmiths, they were not good teachers. Moreover, as they came into western lands their interest was directed much more to the south than to the north, and therefore they contributed very little to Scandinavia, especially to Norway. Several hundred graves of this period have been found, most of them in the vicinity of the Oslo Fjord and in southwestern Norway, the region of Jæren, in Rogaland, but they contain only a very few iron objects. Not one of the Celtic axes so common in Central Europe has been found, not one iron tool, and only one sword and helmet. Most of the iron articles are ornaments, long pins, fibulas, or buckles, but even these are very few.

In these last centuries of the pre-Christian era, Norway not only experienced commercial and cultural isolation, but suffered from a change of climate as well. The subtropical conditions of earlier centuries disappeared, the weather became cold and raw, and the amount of snow increased greatly until large stretches of the plateaus were once more covered by glaciers and eternal snow. Some authorities believe that the change was rather sudden and that the weather became extremely cold and wet so that the old Norwegian myth of the terrible fog winter (*fimbulvinter*) had its origin in this age. Other scholars, however, claim

[1] Some authorities hold that the Ultima Thule which Pytheas visited was Iceland. See Vilhjalmur Stefansson, *Ultima Thule: Further Mysteries of the Arctic*, New York, 1940.

that there are no facts to bear out this theory of extreme change, although it is agreed that for a while the weather was probably less favorable than at present. Approximately modern conditions became fixed only toward the opening of the Christian era. Certain it is that the change in the climate forced the people to adapt their mode of life to new conditions.

Agriculture became more difficult and probably people had to return to a greater dependence on hunting and fishing for their sustenance. Yet they could not give up the progress already made, and farming was continued under less favorable conditions. The cattle could no longer shift for themselves throughout the year, but had to be provided with fodder and shelter, and people too needed warmer houses. So they naturally settled down, built houses for themselves and their flocks, and stone fences about their pens and little fields. Thus their life became fixed on one spot. In a few cases the name of a farm, or *gaard*, dates back, it is thought, to this time, as for example Sander, meaning "the sands," near the lower end of Norway's largest lake, Mjøsa. Like other names from that time, it describes a large stretch which now comprises many farms, and is indicative of how sunny dry locations were most sought for settlement. Sander was not an individual farm in those days, but the home of a rather large group comprising quite a number of families. The difficult task of tilling fields with wooden implements and the tremendous undertaking of gathering fodder for a herd of cattle with the aid of stone tools only could best be handled by co-operative, or perhaps we can say communistic, efforts. Life was too hard and meager during this last blossoming of the Stone Age to produce much advance.

¶ The time of the Roman Empire brought to Norway an era of great creative power and tremendous possibilities for the future. The progress was based on the general use of iron. When the Romans established the Rhine-Danube frontier they came into very close contact with the Germanic peoples; the influence of their civilization, particularly as found in the frontier provinces, reached even to Norway. In the first two centuries of our era it came to the North from the upper Danube region and Bohemia, mainly through the then powerful Marcomanni who threatened the Roman Empire in the age of Marcus Aurelius. In the third century the region about the mouth of the Rhine was the chief distributing center of a marked Roman-Gallic influence, which was strongly felt along the western coast of Norway even as far north as Trøndelag.

There was no doubt lively traffic along the shores of the North Sea in these times, as traders from the South sailed around Jutland, probably even visiting southern Norway. For the Romans were decidedly commercially minded, and always aware of the possibilities of opening up new markets even among the most primitive peoples. Norwegian furs were becoming an important article of trade, and rapacious merchants no doubt also brought from northern shores many a slave to be sold in Roman marketplaces. Norwegians visited the Empire in other capacities as well. Some of the unrest of the migrations in later days had already entered into many of the young men of Norway, inducing them to seek adventure and fortune even in Rome itself. As early as the reign of Augustus, the tall fair men of the North were much in demand as soldiers, especially in the praetorian guard. The folk and fashions of the faraway lands became a fad; blond hair, to mention but one example, brought a high price in the shops of Rome. Norwegian soldiers and adventurers often returned home bringing with them not only weapons but ornaments and other objects of Roman manufacture.

A great many imported articles reached Norway in these days, as is shown both in the rich grave finds and in the remains on the dwelling sites. There are pottery and glass, jewelry of gold and of bronze, pendants, buckles, bone combs to be worn in the hair; also textiles and improved implements for their fabrication; and of course weapons. Many of these articles are of Roman make, but more are of Germanic manufacture influenced in pattern and technique by Rome. Roman coins are found not infrequently and ornaments patterned on them. It is interesting to note that the name of the little Norwegian coin, the *øre*, is derived from the Latin *aureus*, the name of a Roman gold coin. The Norwegians, however, were not content only to import.

As the Romans adopted and adapted the skills of all the people with whom they came into contact, so the Norwegians acquired from them various industrial techniques and learned to adapt them to their own use. There was a striking development of native handicrafts imbued with a native character. The ceramic art flourished, and a multitude of articles were made varying from small rather thin pieces to large heavy cooking utensils. But the most distinguished work was in metal, fine filigree work, for which Norway has been famous through the centuries, and inlaid work, such as silver in iron or gold in bronze.

The most epoch-making advance made through Roman influence

was the mastery of the skills necessary to furnish an adequate supply of iron implements. Iron was imported in large quantities, both finished articles and raw iron, and most of the objects in the oldest finds are of foreign origin. As time went on, however, more and more things of home manufacture came into use. The Norwegians discovered that their bogs were rich in ore and learned how to extract the metal. Only toward the close of the Roman Period, however, did this art come into general practice.

The first writing in Norway, the oldest form of runes, also dates from the Roman Period, from the second century. We cannot enter into any discussion of the origin of these runes, which were in general use among the Germanic peoples, but it is worth noticing that, because of their contact with the older Mediterranean civilizations, the northern peoples began to use a form of alphabet writing without having gone through any preliminary stages of picture or syllable writing. Modern scholars agree that the runes are based on some earlier alphabet, but in olden times they were thought to be of supernatural origin: perhaps Odin practiced the art even before man appeared on earth. Mysterious forces might be controlled, it seems, by him who could master the runes; and no doubt there are magic implications back of many inscriptions, even among those from the Christian Middle Ages. The examples of early runic writing that have been discovered are very few. If all Norwegian runic inscriptions antedating A.D. 800 were to be printed in modern form, they would constitute but a meager half page. Yet they indicate a decided intellectual advance and are sufficient to enable scholars to add not a little to our knowledge. In the first place, they give us some idea of the religion of the age, showing that, as in earlier times, the powers controlling fertility were worshiped. The religion of the people was closely associated with their efforts to win a livelihood from their flocks and fields. The runic inscriptions also contain enough words and grammatical forms to enable philologists to reconstruct the grammar of the language, and thereby they have ascertained the character of that early common northern language from which was developed the Old Norse of historic times.

The one phase of this era which is still to be mentioned links the Roman Period closely to the following age. It is the expansion of settlements. We have noticed that in the earlier times the population of Norway had been largely concentrated along the coast. This can be explained by the fact that there was a wealth of food to be obtained near the sea and by the equally significant fact that the country was difficult to penetrate because of the lack of inland highways. There was really only one, Lake Mjøsa and its tributary rivers in eastern Norway. A little penetration into this region had begun earlier, but in the fourth century it assumed proportions never known before. Old communal settlements began to divide up, and a farm appeared here and there held by one family only, though generally a "grandfather family" of three generations. The early farm names from this period are often a combination with the syllable *vin*, meaning an open place in the forest. They show that sites were chosen where tillable land could be found without clearing the forests. The most extensive settlements were in the wide, wooded valleys of eastern Norway. The settlers there were new arrivals in the land, coming in from the East, and hence all the lakes and rivers were first settled on the eastern bank. The newcomers had been perhaps a warlike people, influenced by that general stir which was to cause the great migrations, but as they came upon virgin lands that had to be subdued, not upon hostile tribes to be conquered, they settled as peaceful farmers. Thus folk of another Germanic strain, coming from regions farther east, entered Norway and adapted themselves to the way of living suited to the country. The third and fourth centuries show a marked Gothic influence, and as the Goths had long lived in southern Russia, this brought to the civilization of all Western Europe a Graeco-Scythian influence quite distinct from the Roman. Although neither Norway nor any other part of Scandinavia was Romanized as was for example England, the Roman contact was of such great importance that the whole era is very properly named Roman. The advance of the following centuries was largely a continuation of the beginnings made in this markedly creative period.

¶ In the fifth and sixth centuries, the movements of the Germanic peoples who had harried the Roman Empire during the preceding centuries reached much larger proportions. In the West the Empire was demolished and smaller states, dominated by the invaders, took its place. Even in Norway these vast movements became an important factor in the development, although it is only in the coastal settlements of western Norway that permanent results of the migrations can be ascertained. Besides the constant movement to and from Norway of individual traders and warriors and of small groups, it is quite certain that two whole tribes, Ryger and Horder, settled in western Norway in the fifth century, giving their names to the districts of Hordaland and Rogaland. These migrations were probably in some way connected with the Anglo-Saxon conquest of England. At any rate there was a close contact between England and Norway throughout the period of the migrations. There was a marked change from earlier eras, however. Norway was no longer only the recipient of cultural impulses, but there was a give and take in her intercourse, for by now the country had a rich and vigorous civilization of its own.

The flourishing culture in Norway, which began in the last years of the Roman Era and continued until the late Middle Ages, was based on the smelting of native iron. In certain sections of the country, especially inland in the valleys of Valders, Sogn, Voss, Eidfjord, and Hallingdal, as well as about the Hardanger Plateau, bog iron was found to be plentiful in the soil of the shallow lakes and marshes. When the process had been learned, it was a rather simple matter for the farmers about the country to smelt their own iron. Sod rich in ore was piled up and left to dry. Simple blast furnaces, if they can be called by so pretentious a name, were built in the region where the ore was found. The earliest known smelting places were in the houses, but they soon gave way to furnaces in the open. Charcoal was the fuel and this led to a destructive use of the forests, so that in some places they disappeared almost completely. Archaeologists have discovered hundreds upon hundreds of these simple smelting places dug into the ground, as well as some large hoards of pig iron, in one place as many as 573 ingots. Refining of iron was a seasonal occupation and people moved up from the farm to the smelting site and stayed there until their work was done, just as they did for hunting, fishing, or grazing. The old laws recognized that a family which had obtained its iron in a certain locality from time immemorial acquired a legal right to the place and a monopoly of the use of it, a custom which has prevailed till modern times. Thus it became one of the appurtenances of the farm. Though the iron smelted was generally for home use only, it was produced for trade in the regions where it was especially good and plentiful, and much of this iron was of very fine quality.

The abundance of iron is astounding, and it was used in a profusion such as was not known either before or after this age. Norway was much better supplied than were some of the more important countries in Europe, for example France in the time of the Merovingian or Carolingian rulers. The inventory of one of Charlemagne's large manors, on which there were fifteen houses, lists only twenty articles made of iron, including kettles, kitchen implements, and tools. It would be a poor farm indeed in Norway, even two or three centuries earlier, that was not better equipped. As there were no specialized occupational classes, the men on the farm were their own blacksmiths. They became skillful smiths and produced a great variety of articles, some of which had not been made of iron in earlier times. The knife for cutting twigs, the sickle, and somewhat later, the scythe were of great importance in gathering fodder. But the most epoch-making tool was the iron axe which in this period came into the hands of practically every farmer. Originally it was probably a weapon; and it still served well both in war and in encounters with bear or wolf, but it was more significant as the tool that made possible the two greatest developments of this age, namely the expansion of agriculture and of seafaring. Attachment to the soil and love of the sea have been striking traits in the Norwegian character through the ages.

We have noticed that in the Roman Period the larger settlements were beginning to break up into homesteads for individual families, and in the Age of Migrations this movement reached vast proportions. With his iron axe the pioneer could tackle the primeval forest and clear new fields for himself on land hitherto unoccupied. So the settlements crept up the valleys in the interior even to a high altitude, tending to avoid the low places where frost came early. In the course of a century or so settlements were scattered over a very wide area, although the population was still small. In fact some of the farms in the higher altitudes were later abandoned, and it is chiefly through such places that scholars have been enabled to reconstruct to a large extent the life of these distant times. In this age the *gaard*, or farm as we may call it for want of a more accurate word, assumed in its essentials the form it was to retain until very recent times. It was the basic, almost self-sufficient unit of economic and social life. Many a farm of this time was placed up on the hillsides, for though it might be exposed and windy it was important to have a place with good drainage. No effort was made to level the ground when a house was to be built, and if there happened to be some large rocks on the site selected, they were left to serve as tables, benches, or the base of a fireplace. The walls were solid, built of stone, sometimes three feet thick, and the roof was of wooden beams covered with birch bark on which turf was laid. There were no openings except the doors, preferably placed in the long southern wall, and the outlets in the roof for the smoke that hung heavy under the rafters. The thick beams that supported the roof must have made the eerie light from the hearth even more weird. The fire had to be guarded carefully, for even with practice it was not easy to strike fire with flint or iron. There were many activities going on about the hearth during the long winters. Although there were cooking places out of doors, cooking and baking were generally done in the house. The bread dough was rolled thin and baked on hot stones. The grain was dried on stones near the hearth and ground into flour between rocks. The women also had their spinning, weaving, and sewing to do, and the beautifully made implements for their handwork were among their most treasured possessions. If a farm was so fortunate as to possess good clay, making pottery became quite an industry. The articles were shaped on a board held in the lap, and bartered away in a nearby market or sold to a wandering peddler. There were heavy kettles and pails, but also thin cups, vases, and other containers often of good lines and decorated with designs drawn in while the clay was still damp. If iron was plentiful, the smiths might also make iron articles for sale, such as axes, scythes, scissors for shearing sheep, knives, arrowheads, needles, and many other things. Sometimes they exchanged their iron goods for precious metals, and made brooches of silver, buckles of bronze, and other articles, all of native design. Although we cannot describe all the activities which kept the people—men, women, and children—busy, we might mention cheese making, churning, preparing hides and furs, and carving out wooden dishes which were doubtless used in great numbers.

The houses were sometimes very large, in some cases nearly 200 feet long. They were divided into sections, each with a hearth and a door, and at one end, sometimes separated from the rest of the house by a wall and sometimes not, was the space for the cattle. Such a house was probably the home of a three-generation family, each group occupying one section. As the tendency grew for the smaller family group to become independent, the dwellings were placed farther apart, and new little farms appeared. It took centuries, however, before the large early *gaard* was displaced by the farms of modern dimensions.

The fields lying about the houses and enclosed by a stone fence were small and meager indeed, and the large piles of rock thrown together here and there are witnesses of the back-breaking toil that had gone into clearing them of the largest stones. "At the outskirts of almost all the cultivated land in Norway there lie great heaps of stones, which have been broken up on the fields and carried there. The first men who cleared the soil and settled here laid the under layers—they are sunk down in the sub-soil, overgrown with moss and gray with lichen. The topmost layer of smooth light stones was picked up and carted here after last year's plowing. These heaps are Norway's proudest memorials of ancient times. They are silent witnesses of our right to this land which our forefathers for more than two thousand years have toiled to conquer."[2] Flocks were of more importance than fields. They were provided with an enclosed pen and a fenced-in path leading to the open lands where they could feed. The pastures beyond the enclosed fields and the lands where fodder of grass, leaves, and twigs could be gathered either belonged to the farm or were held as a common. But in Norway it was not easy to live on farming alone. A well equipped *gaard* must have good fishing within reasonable distance, where a part of the population of the farm camped during the height of the season, and use gave a claim to fishing places. Hunting, too, must be available. And especially where the farms were close together it became necessary to take the cattle far up on the mountain to a *seter* for the summer. In the coast settlements the whole household often migrated to the shore in the summer for pasturage, fishing, and hunting, thus making for a less settled life than in the interior.

The development of farm life produced at first a society which, incongruous though it seems, was democratic with an air of aristocracy about it. It was a rural society in which the *bonde* class was dominant. A *bonde* (plural *bønder*) was a free land-owning farmer generally of considerable property and prestige. All the early farms, although differing somewhat in size and resources, were fundamentally on the same level so that they did not form a basis for any class distinction, and community life was therefore democratic. On each farm, however, life was patriarchal, and the head of the family had a position of dignity and importance. His household was made up chiefly of his own kin, and landless dependents were so few that they hardly constituted any separate class. In the interior, in eastern Norway, where land was more abundant, this situation continued for a long time, while in the coastal settlements, where the good sites for large farms were early taken, inferior homesteads were built up whose owners were on a lower social level, sometimes more or less dependent on the master of the neighboring large farm. Unlike any other element in the population, the farmer class has had an unbroken development throughout the history of Norway, and has set its stamp upon the country's culture.

Second in importance only to the great spread of agricultural communities with their characteristic mode of living was the expansion in shipbuilding and seafaring. Boats had plied along the coast as far back

[2] Undset, *Return to the Future*, 3.

as there had been people in the land. We have noticed how life in the Stone Age was intimately tied to the sea. A boat was at least as important as a house, and traffic across the straits to the south, especially with Jutland, brought new cultural impulses. When the far-flung trade of the Bronze Age was broken off, local coastal traffic continued. During the Roman Period it became more extensive, reaching at least as far as to the mouth of the Rhine, but it was only in the fifth and sixth centuries that Norway's own traffic over the seas attained large proportions. The general unrest of the age was a contributing factor. Many foreigners visited Norway and the grave finds indicate that they often became chieftains or at least men of wealth.

But the main reason that the foundations for Norway's seafaring were laid in this age is the iron axe, which made possible a marked advance in the building of boats. With the axe planks could be hewn, and gradually the more primitive types of boats went into disuse, as both the small boats and the larger vessels approached the type of the later viking ships. A valuable find, the Kvalsund boat, probably from about 600, shows great advance in shipbuilding, both in the usefulness and the beauty of the vessel. The Kvalsund boat is almost fifty feet long, is built of narrow oak boards, and has a keel and rudder suggestive of the viking ships. It has lines of real grace, its prow and stern rising boldly high above the surface of the water in strong, noble curves.

Although it is impossible to know how much of the traffic was carried on in Norwegian boats, the contact with other North Sea shores was so lively that the whole civilization of Norway's southwestern coastal regions at this time has been called a North Sea culture. There was a constant interchange both of goods and cultural impulses with England, Norway's chief export being fur. The even older intercourse with the Frisians on the coast near the mouth of the Rhine also made great advances during this period. In return for furs, hides, and perhaps wool, the Norwegians imported metal and glass of Frisian and Frankish make, probably also cloth finer than their own homespun. The center of the trade was Hedeby in southern Slesvig. Ships from the Frisian coast sailed to the narrowest part of the Jutland peninsula and were then hauled up the river and across the portage to Hedeby, then sailed up the straits east of the peninsula. The great wealth of imported articles of luxury formed the basis for the development of an aristocratic chieftain class from which remain imposing graves scattered along the coast from Vestfold to Lofoten. But not content to trade with the more civilized South, the adventurous seamen of the Westland also maintained intercourse with Arctic Norway. They exploited the more primitive natives, obtaining from them furs, dried fish, walrus hides and tusks, and other Arctic products. Tradition tells of Norwegians visiting the White Sea about A.D. 600, when the restless formative period of the migrations was coming to an end.

¶ The Age of the Small States is characterized by different cultural and social factors which in the Viking Age led to the unification of the country and to the expansion into a greater Norway. The dates correspond roughly to the period known in the history of Western Europe as the Merovingian Age, although the rule of the Merovingians in France came to an end somewhat earlier. As the Germanic states which took the place of the Roman Empire in the West had been formed and political conditions slightly stabilized, intercourse between the states was quite lively, reaching even to Norway where civilization now found expression in forms less local and more generally European than in the preceding age.

To western Norway the name Merovingian Age can well be applied. There Merovingian influence dominated in burial customs, ornaments, clothes, and weapons. It is the only region besides northern France which at this time adopted the short one-edged Saxon sword and the heavy lance. The unadorned weapons and the simple ornaments of the women found in the modest graves from this time may indicate a Christian influence from Western Europe, but also a decrease in that exuberant display of wealth characteristic of the chieftains of the preceding period. As sites suitable for the development of large farms were not many on the mountainous western shore, settlements crept far inland and north into Trøndelag. From western Norway of this warlike age dates a wealth of heroic legends, not unlike the family sagas of the following centuries, dealing with deeds of the chieftain families. Piratical expeditions to Danish waters and to Baltic shores were quite the order of the day, shipbuilding and seafaring developed greatly, and the lively North Sea traffic continued. No doubt some sailors settled down in foreign lands and, like Norwegians of all ages, overcame the handicap of a strange language and new ways of living. Many returned home and, in addition to new things and new ideas, brought with them perhaps not only tales of the countries they had visited, but rumors of rich lands farther south and of islands to the north, how far away they knew not, which offered room for new settlements, stimulating the emigration to the Western Islands which, though begun in this age, constitutes the first chapter of the vast expansion of the Viking Age.

Eastern Norway, facing east and south, received its main cultural impulses from regions farther east, through contact with Sweden and Central Europe. The luxurious civilization which developed near the coast, especially in Vestfold, found its best expression in the art of the age. The characteristic art of this section had begun in the Age of Migrations, possibly with some South Russian influence. Its central motif was the use of animal figures interwoven in the most fantastic way. It went through several stages, reaching its most luxuriant form at the close of this period. The Oseberg Ship, perhaps the most remarkable single archaeological find in the North, belongs to the closing years of this era. A very high technical skill had been achieved in wood carving, weaving, and metal work, including filigree, inlaid work, and gilt bronze; and for a short period there was also high achievement in ceramics. It was a wild, luxurious, warlike art. Later it became more restrained, as in the dragon style of the Viking Age, but in general the old type continued until the eleventh century, when it gave way to Christian art. Even then its influence continued as is indicated by the dragon heads on early medieval churches. There was no Merovingian element in the art of eastern Norway and not a trace of Christian influence. It was thoroughly heathen, showing a very materialistic view of death. Men and women of high station were provided for the future existence not only with weapons and lavish adornment, but with all manner of equipment for a life befitting their rank, even to boats. It was the day when the Asa faith had reached its height in the North, and eastern Norway had close connections with Uppsala in Sweden, the center of this worship.

In a third important section of Norway, Trøndelag, was found a combination of the influences that shaped the culture in the eastern agricultural and the western seacoast sections. Trade with the Frisians had very early reached that far north, and later Merovingian influences made themselves felt, mainly through contact with the Norwegian coast regions farther south. But since agriculture was the main means of sustenance of the broad settlements of the interior, their intercourse was more to the south and east, with the Eastland and Sweden.

So the three principal sections of the country faced in different directions and had different social and political, as well as cultural, development. But these regions do not include the whole country, and there was much diversity in the other sections, too.

While Norway's seafaring was becoming bolder and reaching out farther and farther, the farmers of the interior were more and more making use of the mountain regions. The flocks were of prime importance in the economic life of the day, and the land close to the farmhouses could not possibly yield enough fodder. It must be remembered that artificial seeding of grass was not begun before the eighteenth century. But up in the mountains were large stretches of lush pasture lands, and the use of these, which had begun in the Age of Migrations. now became more extensive and more systematic. The custom of driving the cattle up in the mountains in the spring became obligatory, and no one was allowed to keep his flocks at home and use up winter supplies. In spite of all the toil devoted to collecting winter fodder, it was scarce and had to be used with such cruel thrift that the cattle were often so feeble in the spring that they had to be carried out of the barns. All butter and cheese for the winter had to be provided in the summer. Much of the pasture land was held in common, but each farm also came to have its own *seter*, or place up in the mountains, even as today, and laws against moving of the fences are of very ancient origin. It seems that in some cases what is now a *seter* for summer use only was in the Old Iron Age a permanent dwelling which was deserted in the decline of the late Middle Ages.

Even farther up the mountains than the grazing lands were vast stretches affording excellent hunting, which were also more fully utilized in this age than they had been before. The huntsmen from the interior valleys went farther afield than earlier, going up on the great highland stretches where wild reindeer roamed in countless numbers. On the Hardanger Plateau men from the surrounding settlements established camping sites and dug huge trenches into which herds of reindeer plunged headlong as they rushed forward. Similar methods were used in Jotunheim, especially by men from Valders and Gudbrandsdal. The hunters early established claims to certain regions, and when these overlapped there was often a clash of arms. The reindeer hunters were the creators of the earliest roads in Norway and developed that sense for finding the way which was part of the psychology of the Norwegian until the road building of the nineteenth century changed the old ways. To the shut-in settlements these paths became veritable life lines, and men and women, keen and toughened by the endless struggle for a meager livelihood, picked their way up the steep trails with heavy loads of salt or grain on their backs.

The social grades of the later Viking and Middle Ages, too, became marked in this period, and although there was no caste system, stratification of society was rather definite and class feeling strong. At the bottom were the more or less numerous thralls who worked as servants or tenants for the chieftains or for the wealthier farmers. In *Rigsthula* in *The Poetic Edda*[3] the thrall is described as "black" with an "ugly" face, that is as belonging to the brachycephalic type, while the upper classes are described as of the Nordic stock. The ancient poet describes the woman of the upper class as follows:

> Her brows were bright, her breast was shining,
> Whiter her neck than new-fallen snow.

And her son is pictured also:

> Blond was his hair, and bright his cheek,
> Grim as a snake's were his glowing eyes.

The sagas themselves, however, bear testimony that the distinction between free and unfree by no means followed any "color" or type line. Nor was the social system as simple as pictured in the *Edda*, which divides society into the conventional three classes of thralls, freemen, and chieftains. Although the whole social system was tied up with landholding, there were free men who were not connected with the soil, but this group was neither large enough nor homogeneous enough to constitute a class. On the coast there were still people who lived solely from the sea and the chase and had no land. On the farms there were free servants and there were young warrior free-lancers who followed some chieftain. These people might be either freedmen or freemen.

In the grades of the rural society, above the thralls were the freedmen. They were in a somewhat nebulous realm between thralldom and freedom, and it might take three or four generations before the descendants of an emancipated slave were entirely free. It is therefore impossible to draw a sharp line between the unfree and the free among the poorer tillers of the soil. We know little about these people between the thrall and the well-to-do farmer, how many there were or their exact social and economic status. Their position was not unlike that of the peasantry in countries farther south. They were most numerous in the western coast settlements where good land was not plentiful. Some were more or less dependent on a richer farmer, but many were independent owners of small farms and really constituted the lowest group within the class of freemen. There was the *husmann*, or crofter, who had a small place on the outskirts of a large farm and paid his rent in

[3] See below, page 67.

service and kind, and there was the free farmer, who might not be better off economically, but still valued his perfect independence. *Hávamál* in *The Poetic Edda* gives us a glimpse of such a petty farmer:

> Better a house, though a hut it be,
> A man is master at home;
> A pair of goats and a patched-up roof
> Are better far than begging.

The great majority of the people continued to belong to the freehold farmer class, but the difference in prestige within the class was growing, depending on landed wealth and whether the land was held in lease, by purchase, or as old family inheritance.

Most influential in shaping the history of Norway were the substantial large farmers. They generally held their farms under the hereditary odal right. The title to the land belonged in part to the kindred, and if the owner wished to sell, the odalmen had the first right to buy and also the right to redeem land that had been sold out of the family. The owner of a large farm was the lord over his family and group of dependents, and responsible for supporting the household. Women occasionally filled the position of head of a household, as for example, the widow Aud who took land in Iceland. The early Gulathing law[4] recognized the privilege of a widow as nearest in odal right to meet at the *thing*. In general, however, their share in the odal right was of later date. The chief reason for this is probably that the most important responsibility of the head of the household was to provide food, and, even on the richest farms, food-gathering occupied a large place in the household economy. To the women might be left, in addition to the indoor work, the care of flocks and fields, but the master himself must lead the expeditions, each in its proper season, to the seaside, to the salmon stream, to the iron bogs, to the hunting grounds, or to the trout streams in which trout had been planted almost as early as the interior was settled.

The odal farmers were not only important in the social and economic life, but they were a significant factor in the political development, particularly in the movement for unification when their support or resistance would often determine the issue. They became more elevated above the common freemen as the aristocracy of powerful landowners and chieftains became stronger and stronger in every district. The power of the chieftains increased greatly in the last centuries of the Old Iron

[4] See below, page 79.

Age with the greater opportunities offered then for amassing wealth. There was wide diversity in the position of different chiefs. Sometimes the leadership was based on their landed wealth, sometimes on riches acquired through trade and piracy, or on military prowess, often on a combination in varying proportions of these different factors. The story of how they rose to power is part of the political history of the age.

As the building of a political society began very early, the beginnings are obscure. The formation of genuine states can hardly be said to go farther back than the Age of Migrations, and the development was in no way complete before the centuries which have rightly been named the Age of Small States.

Perhaps the first units larger than the family were the groups on the coast that claimed a common hunting ground and were ready to defend their rights. In the New Stone Age, perhaps 4,000 years ago, when people began to move away from the coast and take up farm lands, they formed peaceful settlements with natural boundaries, being separated from others by mountains and woods. Such a settlement, or *bygd*, became a real political unit. The feeling of blood relationship within the larger family group, or kindred, was very strong, and the settlement of any quarrel within the kindred was not a political problem. But when there were more groups in a neighborhood, there was need of some judicial agency to settle disputes, and so arose, just when we do not know, the *thing*, a gathering not unlike the old English moot. This rather democratic local *bygdething* was primarily a judicial body, but customary law grew out of its actions, although the Norwegians, like most primitive people, looked upon law as a divine institution rather than a human enactment.

A primary need was to establish some legal system of compensation, or *bot*, to take the place of the blood revenge that resulted from the principle of an-eye-for-an-eye by which the families had sought satisfaction for an injury to any of their members and upheld the honor of the kindred. Naturally the two methods continued to exist side by side for a long time. Besides the legal bond, common worship drew the settlement together, and a common *hov*, or place of worship, was a strongly unifying element. Sometimes a voluntary religious association was formed which might or might not include the whole population of the settlement. It was called a *sogn*, which today means parish. When need of defense against robbers became urgent, a larger military district generally comprising several settlements was formed and a chieftain elected. Such a district, or shire, was generally called a *herred*. In the

Westland the name *fjordung* and in Trøndelag *fylki* were used to designate similar units.

While some of the organizations mentioned may date even from the Late Stone Age, it was only in the seventh and eighth centuries that political development became more rapid and more marked, and the formation of real states was consummated. It is difficult to generalize about this development for there was a great deal of variety in the character of the government, the size of the states, and the different names used. Yet there were some common features. Thus, with the exception of the two tribes that moved in during the Age of Migrations, people had drifted into Norway unorganized, and the whole political growth took place on Norwegian soil. The smaller units that have been mentioned were found all over the country, and the general unifying influences were the same.

The military shire often became a political, religious, and commercial unit also. Where the *thing* was held, a center of worship might also be established, as well as a market (*kaupang*) to which came traders from afar. A chieftain was chosen, sometimes called *herse*, but among his fellows he continued to be only *primus inter pares*, and thus a democratic farmer state was formed. Often several districts were joined into larger realms forming the principal units in the Age of Small States. There were about thirty such states besides the smaller regions which remained independent. In the most markedly agricultural districts they were free states with their own *thing* and elective chieftains, and perhaps shrine and market places also. The fifth and sixth centuries were primarily the age of the *bonde* chiefs, but in the large interior valleys, as Valders, Gudbrandsdal, and Østerdal, strong *bonde* republics and chieftains held their own and were virtually independent through the Viking Age and beyond. Sometimes the head of such a state might be called king, although he was really only the president of a republic. Along the inner fjords to the south and west also small republics maintained themselves.

These states were based on an agricultural society, and leadership depended on a family's wealth in fields and flocks. Although bloody quarrels might arise, especially about fishing, hunting, and pasture preserves, such a society was fundamentally peaceful, and its warlike activities were chiefly for defense. The need of this in the restless fifth and sixth centuries is attested by the many fortresses. They were placed on inaccessible hills, where there was space enough to seek refuge with flocks and goods, and where there was water. Every chieftain was a military leader. The nearer the coast a settlement was, the greater was the danger of raids, and as time went on many a peaceful rural community found it profitable, sometimes necessary, to pay tribute to some "protector" rather than to be subjected to intermittent robber raids. Thus some of the little free states lost a part of their former independence.

In the districts by the sea there was no democracy and no self-government. Usually one man, whose strength was based on military prowess and whose capital had been amassed in hunting, fishing, or trade, went in for piracy and then for complete political control of a larger or smaller district. The heads of these districts may have formed aristocratic republics among themselves under a common leader. Thus there were a great many chiefs whose position was not primarily based on land ownership, and who did not represent a community of farmers. Some were kings though they had little of the exalted position later associated with that name, but the commonest title was the very indefinite jarl. A jarl was generally at the head of a district either independent or under a stronger jarl or king. He might, however, be a chieftain who had no state to rule, but only gathered about him a group of men who followed him on expeditions of adventure, war, or piracy. Sometimes he had already won so much wealth that he hired his followers; at other times, as with the *comitatus* of Tacitus, he was chosen by an independent group of warriors as their chief. It was these chieftains of the sea and shore who were responsible for making the seventh and eight centuries an age of piracy and war between states. It was against them that the efforts to unite Norway were chiefly directed in the following century, and it was they who terrorized Europe in the Viking Age.

PART II

The Viking Age, 780-1030

CHAPTER 3

A GREATER NORWAY

THE VIKING AGE is the name that we may use to designate the period from 780 to 1030, which lies in the borderland between prehistoric and historic times. This is the only epoch in the history of Norway before the nineteenth century to which much attention has been devoted by students outside of the North itself. At this time the field of Norwegian history suddenly expanded to include a large part of Europe and a bit of America as well, and the Norwegians exerted an influence on Europe that has not been equaled by them in any other era. It is an epoch which stands out with a certain dramatic quality, and it teems with remarkable achievements that might be a source of pride to any people. Moreover, we know the Viking Age better than either the preceding eras or the time immediately following it. We even know individuals, not merely types as from earlier times.

Archaeological remains are the chief source of information. In Norway, and to some extent in the colonies, heathen burial customs continued to prevail, and, as the wealth of the chieftains had increased enormously, the grave finds scattered over the wide area of greater Norway are richer than those from any other time. Literary sources supplement our knowledge. Norwegian literature had its beginnings, or at least began to take definite form, in this age. The poems in *The Poetic Edda* as well as much skaldic poetry were composed then, and many of the sagas took form, to be retained as an oral tradition till a later time. Earlier foreign writers made only few and brief references to Norway and its people, but about the vikings chroniclers and poets of invaded countries furnish a mass of information. While only a few scattered references to them are found in other countries, the literatures of France, England, and perhaps even more of Ireland, are filled with accounts of the unwelcome visitors. The stories are disjointed and, of course, one-sided, as the writers were concerned only with the depredation wrought by the invading hordes, not with their cultural development.

The remarkable, almost fantastic, oversea expansion in this age has so caught the imagination of later times that the whole era has been named after the warriors who sailed the seas and descended upon foreign shores.

No attempt to explain the causes of the sudden outburst which spread with irresistible force over the greater part of Europe can be quite adequate. The beginnings lay in the Old Iron Age, the Viking Age being a logical evolution from the preceding period, but now everything was speeded up to a degree that could never have been foreseen, and the vigor and force increased almost unbelievably. All the activities of the age were, as a Norwegian historian puts it, the expression of "a buoyancy and spirit of unrest in the very soul of the nation."[1] And it did not take the vikings long to discover that Christian Europe was in no condition to offer successful resistance. After a period of glorious advance, Western Christendom was shrinking in the ninth century. In the south, the Mediterranean Sea was virtually a Saracen lake; from the east, Slavic tribes were pushing westward and, even worse, over the Danubian plains horde upon horde of Asiatic Hungarians poured into Germany, northern Italy, and even eastern France, causing a havoc that has seldom been equaled. And from the north came the Scandinavians. There were no unified states with an army, or still less a navy, that could drive back the invaders. It seemed almost as though Christian Europe were to be vanquished, leaving heathen hordes in undisputed control.

¶ Vikings were a product of all three Scandinavian countries, and it is impossible to follow the trails of the Norwegians without sometimes meeting Danes and Swedes as well. The conditions in the three countries were similar, though not identical, and the lines between the nationalities were not so sharply drawn as they later became. The people of the invaded countries therefore often had very vague ideas about the distinction between the three races and did not differentiate between them in the names they used. Sometimes, as in England, all vikings were called by the name of the first comers, in this case the Danes. "Northmen" was conveniently used for them all. The fact that people from the different countries often mingled and cooperated increased the confusion. Although a student might get into a hopeless tangle if

[1] A. W. Brøgger, *Ancient Emigrants*, 19, Oxford, 1929.

he tried to determine the nationality of all vikings, the main spheres of activity of the three groups were somewhat distinct.

There is least difficulty with regard to the Swedes, who followed what was called the "Eastern Way." Long before the Viking Age, probably as far back as in the Bronze Age, there was intercourse between Sweden and the eastern shores of the Baltic. Archaeological finds show that civilization was to some extent transplanted from Sweden, and skaldic poems tell of early expeditions to Estonia and Finland by kings of the famed Yngling family. In the Viking Age Swedes in great numbers crossed the Baltic in their swift, light boats, rowed up the rivers that flowed through dense forests into the Baltic, dragged their boats across the divides, then followed the course of the great streams that flow south through the Russian steppes, the Volga, the Dnieper, and the Don. They were called *Rus*, which is thought to be derived from a word related to "row," and this designation still lives in the name Russia. While this term was applied particularly to the Swedes, a later name, Varangians, was used for all Scandinavian people, meaning those who had pledged themselves by oath as members of a brotherhood. Later the word was applied specifically to the viking bodyguard of the Byzantine emperor.

The viking trade routes from the Scandinavian countries along the Russian rivers to the regions about the Black and Caspian Seas, to Myklegard as they called Constantinople, and the Caliphate of Bagdad, were among the most important in medieval Europe. Saracen and Byzantine luxuries, silks, gold, wine, and southern fruits, found their way to the far North, while in return the vikings gave slaves, furs, hides, honey, and wax, collected as tribute among their Slavic subjects. Along the routes of the *Rus* are scattered coins from the West and the East, even from India. They were not only traders, but often combined commerce and pillage. In 860 they even attacked Myklegard and, though they could not conquer the city, won favorable trade rights.

Over the conglomeration of tribes that occupied Russia the invaders established political control, introducing their own institutions, and maintaining their power by building cities. In the North, Novgorod, or Holmgard, was the center of a state of considerable importance, whose first king was supposed to have been Rurik. The largest part of Russia was included in a kingdom which the Northmen called Gardarike, the land of forts, with its capital at Kiev. This "city of four hundred churches" attained great splendor under King Jaroslav of the family of Rurik. Gardarike was a progressive and strong state, and many northern personal and place names still remain to bear witness that the vikings were not few. Yet they always constituted a small minority of the population, were gradually amalgamated with the Slavs, and, like them, became Christianized from Constantinople. While northern influences held their own longer in Novgorod, the death of Jaroslav in 1045 marks for Russia the passing from the Viking to the Byzantine Age.

Though the vikings from Norway most often followed a western route, many of them joined their Swedish kinsmen along the "Eastern Way," and the East occupies a conspicuous place in the sagas. In the later Viking Age there was especially close contact between Norway and Gardarike. Chieftains of the two countries were often related by blood or marriage, and it was quite usual to make at least one trip to the most eastern viking outpost. Among such visitors were the two heroic Olafs, Olaf Tryggvason and Saint Olaf.

Although Danish and Norwegian vikings not infrequently joined forces, there were definite areas in which the Danes predominated. They held Skaane and other districts of what is now the southern shore of Sweden, thus controlling the Sound. They had a lively trade in the Baltic, or East Sea as they called it, and carried on vigorous viking activities along its southern and even eastern shores, fighting Slavic tribes, particularly the Wends who were repeatedly endangering southern Denmark. On the Frisian coast, which stretched westward from the Danish peninsula of Jutland, the Danes had held important commercial interests at least since the early sixth century, but political control had been prevented by the Frisians. They were the only sea power in the North before the Viking Age, but were ruthlessly and, as history was to show, unwisely crushed by Charlemagne. The region was now defenseless, and through most of the ninth century the Danes dominated the coast and the commercially important mouth of the Rhine. Serious Danish attacks on Western Europe began in the reign of Charlemagne, for Denmark's strong king, Godfred, whose rule extended also into southern Norway, became alarmed when Charlemagne defeated the Saxons and extended his realm to the Eider River, the southern boundary of Denmark. When Charlemagne died, Louis the Pious, who lacked his father's force and genius, was faced with the task of keeping together the vast Empire in the face of insuperable difficulties. He made a treaty with Harald of Denmark by which Harald in return for accepting Christianity was given a little territory south of the Eider, the Danes thereby gaining a foothold in the Empire. After Louis's death in 840, when the Empire was falling to pieces and internecine wars were sapping the strength that might have been used against the invaders, the attacks continued with growing ferocity. In 845, Rouen was taken and Paris plundered. The vikings were bought off, but as was their custom, returned for more. If the peasants rose to defend themselves, they were in turn struck down by the nobles. So they often fled in panic leaving the land almost depopulated. The legal, social, and economic system was broken up, and the people were crushed by taxes levied to buy off the invaders. Only at the close of the century did there seem to be any answer to the petition in the Frankish liturgy: "From the fury of the Northmen deliver us, O Lord!" In 891, the German king Arnulf inflicted a crushing defeat on the vikings at Louvain, and in 911, when Rollo with his Northmen received Normandy as a fief from Charles the Simple, the vikings themselves undertook to protect the Frankish realm from further raids.

The Danish activities in England were closely related to those on the Continent. When the Danes arrived, there was no kingdom of England, although the church had begun its unifying influence, and the names of Boniface, Bede, and Alcuin are indicative of the high achievements in the cultural centers of the North. The larger part of England was occupied by little Anglo-Saxon kingdoms which were in the midst of a shifting period of rivalry, sometimes Kent, then Northumbria, then Mercia or Wessex having the lead. Old English literature is full of stories of how the vikings made good use of the confusion, how the attacks became more frequent and lasting, how the strangers in 854 for the first time wintered on Sheppey Island, how the great fleet, when bought off in France, attacked Northumbria and in ten years won control of much of the land, and how in 871 most of England except Wessex was in the hands of vikings. That year Alfred became king of Wessex. At first he had to buy off the Danes, and, when they returned with new demands, he had to flee and take refuge on Athelney. But the tide turned. Alfred gathered an army, defeated the Danes, and made a treaty drawing a line, largely following the famous old Roman road, Watling Street, from Chester to London, between the Danelaw held by the Danes and his own realm. In 892, when the famous chief Hastings led against England the Great Army which the year before had been defeated at Louvain, Alfred had built up a fleet strong enough to force Hastings to leave and to maintain peace throughout the rest of his reign. In the tenth century the history of England centers upon the successful efforts of the kings of Wessex to continue the work of

Alfred and consolidate the country under their rule, and thus Danish political dominance was brought to an end and the campaigns ceased. Near the close of the tenth century, during a period of weakness in the English government, viking activities were renewed on a large scale, reaching a climax when the Danish kings Svein and Canute won the English throne. This, however, was rather a war of states and ruling houses than a viking attack like those of earlier years.

In Ireland also the Danes made some raids, joining sometimes the Norwegians and sometimes the Irish in their struggle for control, but they gained little foothold in the Emerald Isle.

¶ The Norwegian expansion was more varied in character and affected a wider territory than the viking movements from Denmark or Sweden, and it alone resulted in lasting Northern settlements beyond the sea, which retained the race, language, and civilization of the mother country.

The expansive energy that was generated in Norway during the Old Iron Age reached its climax in the Viking Age. The chief outlet for this energy was to the west, across the seas. This emigration can well be compared to the later movement in the nineteenth century, when Norwegians went to every country on the face of the globe, but principally followed the westward routes to America. In both periods the chief aim of the emigrants was to find new homes and more land. In the earlier age, however, they took by force anything they wanted and could not get by peaceful means. As most of them followed what they called the "Western Way," they came either into unoccupied lands or into the regions held by Celtic people. This gave rise to two types of settlements: the unoccupied lands were settled peaceably and became the seat of enduring Norwegian communities, while the Celtic possessions had to be conquered, and the newcomers eventually mingled with the earlier settlers, thus losing their identity.

Vikings went out from every part of the long Norwegian coast, Vestfold especially contributing a large number of redoubtable warriors. But the great emigration went out chiefly from the Westland. The expansion of agriculture and the growth of the population increased enormously the demand for land, and the narrow valleys and precipitous mountains of the Fjordlands offered little room for new homesteads. Land must be sought elsewhere, and to find it Norwegians set out boldly across the sea. They were pioneers, leaving all shores behind and setting sail into the broad expanse of the ocean.

¶ The region to which the first large migration went was the little groups of islands north of Scotland, the Western Islands, as they were called. Tradition as well as archaeological finds, notably the brochs, impressive round stone towers, tell of seafaring Celtic Picts who had once held sway in these islands; but their strength had vanished and only a very small remnant of the once powerful people remained. A few Irish anchorites who had sought solitude were there when the Norwegians first found the islands. When this was we do not know, but traffic across the North Sea may have been going on for centuries.[2] The main time of settlement, however, occupied approximately the two generations from 780 to 850. The vikings had ships fully as seaworthy as the sailing vessels which brought emigrants of the early nineteenth century across the Atlantic. But in the open viking boats, which carried only one square sail, it was tedious and impractical to beat to windward on a long voyage, and it was therefore customary to wait for spring to bring favorable offshore winds. This was a good season, also, because the stars are particularly clear in early spring, and the early sailors had—aside from their uncanny instinct for finding their way over the deep—no guide but the sun, moon, and stars. Farms in western Norway abandoned at about this time may have belonged to emigrants who set sail with their whole family, their servants and dependents, their farm tools and household goods, and even their stock. In the new lands they built up an agricultural society very much like that from which they came. Their houses, their daily life, and their political institutions were the same as they had been, with, of course, some adaptation to local conditions. The peaceful nature of the settlement is clearly indicated by the scarcity of weapons and the abundance of fishing and farming implements in the finds from the age.

The nearest and the first to be settled were the Shetland Islands, or Hjaltland as they were called. They could be reached in two days' sailing; with a favorable wind the viking boats made about as good time as a steamboat of moderate speed. It would seem that these small, treeless, isolated islands with rocky shores beaten by the sea must offer small inducement to the settlers. Yet the ocean supplied a wealth of fish and whales, the shore teemed with birds, and, though agriculture could never be extensive or particularly successful, the low hills furnished pasturage more lush than the newcomers had ever seen. Sheep, probably brought there by Irish hermits, were found on the islands when the Norwegians arrived and they were the most important stock of the

[2] Nansen, *In Northern Mists*, 1:234.

Shetlanders in early times even as they are today. Communities were established after the pattern of the mother country, with local *things* in several places and one for the whole island group meeting at Thingvollvatn, on Thingholm. Neither sagas nor traditions, however, tell us much about the Shetland settlements; they were too remote to be important in a political or military way. They were not economically independent for they had to import grain and, what was even more important, material for building ships. Therefore, except when occasionally the jarl of the Orkneys claimed a right to rule the islands, the Shetlands were in close contact with Norway.

Farther to the northwest the Norwegians found another smaller, even more remote group of islands, also with a rocky coast lashed by the waves and the interior covered with grass green and damp with the mists of the sea. The Faroes were discovered and settled somewhat later than the Shetland Islands, but the character of the settlement and their history, or lack of it, were much the same. A reliable Irish source from 825, an account written by the monk Dicuil, tells that Irish monks had occupied the islands earlier, but gives no account of the heathen settlers. These islands, too, had their own institutions with their central *thing* at Thorshavn, and their own saga, but other sagas make little mention of the Faroes except as a port of call for ships going to Iceland.

Southeast of the Shetlands, just off the northern shore of Scotland, the Norwegians found the Orkneys. Nature was not quite so chary there, and farming became a more lucrative occupation. A Scottish minister of a much later date summed up the difference: "A Shetlander is a fisherman who owns a farm, whereas an Orkneyman is a farmer who owns a boat."[3] Lumber, however, was lacking, though it could be procured near at hand in Scotland. On the Orkneys the Norwegians established an *althing* which all free men attended, and a representative *lagthing* with an elected lawman as the president. In marked contrast to the islands farther north, there developed a strongly aristocratic and military society, perhaps because of the nearness to Scotland and the resulting need of defense and easy access to conquests. A jarl ruled, surrounded by his chieftains who sat in his council, commanded his ships, and met up to a man at the annual *thing*. The earliest known ruler of the Orkneys was Jarl Ragnvald who in the sagas is identified with the famous Jarl Ragnvald from Møre in western Norway. For three centuries a chief of this family ruled the islands. Among them was Peat Einar, known for his skaldic verses, some of which are extant,

[3] Quoted by Brøgger, *Ancient Emigrants*, 35.

and for teaching his people to use peat as fuel, whence his nickname. Saga writers, forgetful of the common man who built the farms, have in *Orkneyinga Saga* given us a detailed story of the Orkney jarls. A bloody tale it is, filled with viking adventure and conquest, with family feuds and murder. This island group, which had been at the edge of the world, so to speak, became an important center of viking activities. From it expeditions went out to Ireland, England, Scotland, France, and even to the shores of the Mediterranean.

Though the emigrants to the Western Islands brought with them the institutions and customs of their former home, the settlements were politically independent, for Norway had not yet been welded into a united kingdom. But there was a lively intercourse across the sea, a common culture bound mother and daughter communities together; and a loosely defined conception of a North Sea empire was an important factor in Norwegian history throughout the Middle Ages. A really organized empire did not develop before the thirteenth century. In 1468 the two larger groups passed under Scottish rule, the Faroes only remaining united with Norway. It took two more centuries, however, before the old language was displaced by English and the people reduced to tenantry. Yet even today not only archaeological remains, but customs, characteristics of the people, place names, and words adopted into the English language remind us that Norwegians dominated the islands for five centuries.

¶ Beyond the Orkneys to the south the vikings came to lands that had long been settled. Celtic peoples—very different from the Norwegians in race, language, and culture—occupied the greater part of the British Isles. The Irish Sea was a Celtic lake, with all its shores and islands peopled by Celts who kept up a steady traffic over its waters. They occupied all Ireland and the greater part of Scotland, Wales, western England, and the lesser islands even to the northern tip of Great Britain. In southern Scotland and northern England only did the Norwegians come into contact with the Anglo-Saxon peoples, who were most closely related to them, while they left no part of the Celtic world untouched.

The first known landing of Norwegians in England is recorded in the Anglo-Saxon Chronicle and occurred about 790. During the next fifteen years small raids scattered over a wide area took place, but they were not numerous, only ten being mentioned in the chronicles. The first formidable viking raid was the attack in 793 on the famous monastery on the little island of Lindisfarne off the northeastern coast of

England. It made a deep impression on Western Christendom "that heathen men had gruesomely destroyed God's church on Lindisfarne with plunder and murder," so much the more because, as Alcuin says, no one had thought such a trip across the North Sea possible. Next year vikings were repulsed in an attempted attack on Wearmouth, a monastery farther south on the eastern coast of England, and from then on followed the "Western Way" into Celtic waters along old routes that had been used by traders even in the third millennium before Christ, when a highly developed culture based on seafaring spread its influence from Spain over all western Europe. Several noted shrines were attacked, the most famous being the monastery of Saint Columba on Iona, which was twice raided. Churches and cloisters were the chief victims because there great wealth and herds of cattle were concentrated, and because they were conveniently located by the sea in places which hitherto had been considered safe from robbers. Although the horror and consternation roused was great, the attacks were really few and the destruction very limited, for the vikings were not merely pirates, but explorers. Following the custom of the North, they made a landing to forage wherever convenient when they wanted meat and helped themselves to the cattle they needed. As they discovered undreamed of wealth to be had for the taking, plunder, rape, and murder came with every landing. No part of the British Isles had formed a strong central government, nowhere was there adequate military or police force to deal with the unwelcome visitors, and no naval force existed that could dispute viking control of the northern seas.

In the wake of exploration came emigration, settlement, and land-taking. The emigrants came mostly from western Norway, often by way of the Orkneys. Generally they came in large companies under the leadership of chieftains who took land, divided it among their followers, and were the rulers of the settlements. There were, of course, many, especially young men of the upper classes, who went out on brief viking trips lured by the prospect of winning wealth by plunder and trade, and incited by love of adventure, of travel and fighting, and who returned home. But, although these vikings figure as heroes in the sagas, they were not nearly so numerous as the unsung emigrants who went out with their families and possessions to build new homes. In these settled regions the newcomers did not get their land without fighting, nor could they build up purely Norwegian communities as they had done farther north. The relation with the other peoples was first one of bitter conflict gradually giving way to peaceful intercourse and trade, and finally amalgamation. Though in the minority, the Norwegians not only left remains of great richness and significance, but put their mark on the language, place names, and institutions wherever they came. Every region of viking operations, however, has a characteristic history of its own.

On the rocky, barren Hebrides, or Sudreyjar (South Islands) as the Norwegians called them, the folk from the Westland found opportunities to carry on the type of life to which they had been accustomed, winning their living mainly from the sea. In the early ninth century several important families whose names later figure prominently in the settlement of Iceland took land in the Hebrides. The many Norwegian place names indicate that the settlers were numerous and that they were firmly established. Amalgamation of the races seems to have come quite early, with Celtic culture but Norwegian political institutions in the ascendancy.

Farther south the Norwegians came upon the island of Man, which occupies a strategic position between Ireland, England, Scotland, and the Hebrides. The Isle of Man had been settled and Christianized from Ireland, and has a wealth of remains of old Irish primitive stone churches and monuments. In 798 a noted shrine to St. Patrick, just off the shore, suffered a viking attack, and soon after settlement followed, probably at the same time as in Ireland. The northern half of the Isle of Man became Norwegian in race and language and has even today a great many Norse place names, while the southern half was little touched by the invaders and remained Celtic. Yet the two became politically united, and lived harmoniously together under a Norwegian dynasty lasting about two centuries. Runic inscriptions from the tenth and eleventh centuries indicate that Norwegian culture and language were in the lead at that time, but also tell of the peaceful mingling of the races.

On the Isle of Man is found the most interesting example of the persistence of Norwegian elements in political institutions even to modern times. When the island in 1405 recognized the overlordship of the king of England, it was on condition that the people might keep their old legal and governmental usages. The central authority is a council of twenty-four elected members, called the House of Keys, which goes back to old Norwegian usage, and every legal enactment must be announced on Tynwald Hill, an artificial elevation where the old *thing* used to be held at midsummer. For local administration, the island is divided into six sheadings, derived from *skeid*, a small warship. Each sheading furnished one ship manned by twenty-six warriors. The sheadings are divided into treens, generally twenty-six in each. It seems that the island was organized on the basis of the *leidang*, or duty of supporting a fleet.

In Ireland the vikings came upon the most remarkable culture in all Western Europe. Untouched by the leveling influence of the Roman Empire and by the upheavals that disrupted it, Erin had kept fresh its weird and wild old sagas and its passionate, nature-filled songs from heathen times. And the church of Saint Patrick developed a rich culture, centering in the monasteries. There lived artists who embroidered or worked in stone, enamel, and precious metals, producing intricate, lovely patterns, sometimes with an exotic, almost Oriental strain. Even the copiers of manuscripts were artists of high rank. Latin classics were treasured at a time when they were seldom read in continental Western Europe, and Greek was studied when even the illustrious Pope Gregory the Great did not know the language. The chroniclers, of whom there were many, whether they used Latin or their native tongue, wrote with a rare poetic and imaginative sense. So, in contrast to the other Celtic lands, in Ireland every viking deed or misdeed was fully chronicled and lost nothing in the telling. But since individual incidents were recorded without any sense of continuity, modern historians have been confronted with a mass of confusing details.

The influence of Irish culture, and especially of the church, was felt far and wide. Wherever Norwegians came in Celtic lands, and even in the Anglo-Saxon, Irish missionaries had preceded them and established their church. So the Irish church, which was not absorbed by the Roman before the eleventh century, was the form of Christianity with which the vikings first came into contact. Even islands as far north as the Faroes and Iceland had first been discovered by men from Erin, animated both by love of travel and by religious enthusiasm for the hermit's life in the wilderness.

There was a curious contrast between the high culture centered in the monasteries and the primitive society in Ireland. The Irish had retained their early clan and tribal system with petty kings, and, although they had a "high" king of Tara and possessed a certain amount of racial or national feeling, they had not attained any political unity. In "noble Erin, the king's isle, glorious scene of heroic deeds," there raged bitter family feuds with bloody vengeance, wild wars between petty kings, and, most of all, sharp fights about herds and pastures, for the chief livelihood of the Irish was from their flocks. No conditions could have been more favorable for the vikings.

In 795, only two years after the attack on Lindisfarne, vikings landed at Rechra, a little island off the northeastern point of Ireland, plundered, broke open the reliquaries, and burned the church. Twelve years later, they penetrated to the interior and burned Roscommon, the seat of a bishopric. Then began the real invasion of Ireland. No coast was safe, and the danger extended far inland, especially along the rivers and lakes. "The sea spewed forth streams of strangers over Erin" and "there was no harbor or landing place free from the fleets of the pirates," say the chroniclers. In 839 a large fleet arrived commanded by a mighty warrior, Thorgils, or Turgeis, who became the real founder of Norwegian power in Ireland. He built a fort at Dublin and established other well fortified camps which grew into cities, some inland, but most, like Limerick and Waterford, on the shore. Turgeis planned to conquer the land, and was unique among vikings in making the destruction of Christianity a part of his policy. "In every sanctuary and every house of God, heathens from Dublin Fort," says an old poem. Many a church was turned into a heathen shrine, and the worship of Thor was so firmly entrenched that it continued at least until the year 1000 when the Irish burned the grove sacred to him. Even natives reverted to paganism and joined the enemy.

In 851 Olaf the White established himself in Dublin where he ruled for twenty years, while his brothers, Ivar and Sigtrygg, ruled in Limerick and Waterford. Olaf is the first Norwegian in Ireland who is known also from northern sources. He was said to have belonged to the Yngling family, whose story is intertwined with the history of nearly every section of the viking world in the West. For over a century after his time Norwegians played a dominant role in the history of Ireland, leaving the Irish in peace only for a brief period of twelve years. The leaders were the Dublin rulers, able but fierce men whose ambitions extended far beyond Ireland. It was a tragic and confused age in Irish history. Sometimes the Irish fought each other with Norwegian or Danish aid. Occasionally they united sufficiently to defeat the invaders. only to be again conquered by the Norwegians, who were strong enough also to drive out the Danes. Ireland suffered much, and the glory of Irish culture faded. Monasteries were looted and burned, schools closed, books lost, and their bindings carried off among other treasures to make ornaments for the Norwegian women. Scholars followed in the path of their earlier kinsmen and sought refuge on the continent. Noble ladies no longer plied their needle in fine embroidery only to have it become the loot of pirates, and the goldsmith lavished less care on his handiwork.

The most famous of the Dublin kings was Olaf Kvaran whose checkered career is indicative of changing times. For a while he ruled both in northern England and in Erin. He kept the peace with King Brian, the greatest of the Irish leaders, and their families intermarried. The amalgamation of the two races had begun; and the vikings, no longer strangers, had entered into the normal life of the Irish. Kvaran himself married an Irish woman, became a Christian, and in his old age left his kingdom to go on a pilgrimage. He died as a monk at Iona, the shrine of Saint Columba, which vikings in days of yore had twice plundered.

The peace was broken, however, by a new attempt of the Norwegians to regain complete control. They were defeated in the battle of Clontarf, in 1014, and their dominance permanently broken. But the people stayed on, and the Cathedral of Dublin, built by the Norwegians and dedicated in 1038, is a monument to the submission of Thor's clan to the White Christ. The Norwegians kept up their contact and trade with their mother country until 1263, when they asked the king of Norway for help against the English, but after that their story as a separate people is over.

If we try to discover what the Norwegians left in Ireland, the most tangible finds are the rich remains in the viking graves and the many geographical names along the coast, names of skerries and promontories, and—more important—names of cities. The vikings built cities which had not earlier existed in Ireland, developed trade, coined the first money in Ireland, and taught the Irish much about seafaring. Early Irish manuscripts are full of Norse words for things connected with sailing and boats. We cannot estimate the slight, intangible influences on the race and mode of life, but we know that the material for song, legend, and story was much enriched by the men from Norway, "Lochland with the dark ships," as the poets called it. But neither viking nor native had the strength to keep the country from succumbing to the English. "Such sorrow shall come to the Irish people as man never shall forget."

Scotland was almost surrounded by vikings and naturally subjected to a great many attacks. There was no kingdom of Scotland when the vikings first became masters of the western seas. The land south of the firths of Clyde and Forth was part of small states in England, Strathclyde to the west and Northumbria to the east. The region north of the two firths was inhabited by two races, the Picts to the north and east, and southwest of them the Scots who had earlier come from Ireland. When the vikings made the Irish Sea a veritable Norwegian lake, the Scots were cut off from Ireland, and this may have helped to bring on their union with the Picts, who in 844 were forced to submit to the king of the Scots, and the kingdom of Scotland was born.

Little is known of the earliest raids on Scotland, but in 866 began systematic attacks for the conquest of the country. There was a threefold invasion: from Ireland, from the Hebrides, and from the Orkneys, at times invaders from all sides cooperating. The new little kingdom continued to exist, but it had to put up a hard fight for its life, and much of its land was held by invaders.

Three times in the years from 866 to 871, Olaf the White made successful invasions from Ireland, exacted tribute, and held much of the kingdom. The magnitude of his ventures is indicated in the Irish annals which mention that he brought back two hundred ships laden with booty and prisoners, Scots, Britons, and Angles. The later rulers of Olaf's dynasty continued his policy with varied success.

Much of the western coast of Scotland was almost a part of the Hebrides, and Norwegians felt quite at home among its fjords and mountains. They made raids on this shore both from the Hebrides and from the Isle of Man, but more important was the peaceful penetration by many settlers from the west.

Perhaps the greatest Norwegian influence in Scotland came from the north. The militaristic Orkney jarls found the nearest field for conquest directly to the south, in Sutherland, as they called it, and Caithness in northern Scotland, where Norwegian settlers probably had preceded the conquerors. For many years this territory, and sometimes more, was held by jarls of the Orkney family. The saga tells tales of their conflicts with the Scottish kings as well as their friendly intercourse. Most renowned was Jarl Thorfinn, whose mother was a Scottish princess. He took part in the conflicts for the Scottish throne, supporting, it seems, the claims of Macbeth, and his daughter became queen of Scotland as the wife of Malcolm III. Upon the death of Thorfinn in 1065, Caithness and Sutherland passed under the overlordship of the king of Scotland, but for a long time the population was largely Norwegian. In no part of the British Isles have the vikings left a more marked influence on the race, culture, geography, and language than in Scotland. No single monument of the Norwegians in the West is more famous than the exquisitely wrought Iona cross-shaft. Much in the language seems familiar to one who knows Norwegian, and in many quaint customs, charms, and tales, scholars have detected Norse influence.

In the history of England and Wales, also, the Norwegians have a significant part. On the western coast there were still three little Celtic British states separated from each other where the Angles and Saxons had reached the shore. These little kingdoms of Strathclyde, Wales, and Cornwall, became the chief sphere of penetration by vikings who raided the shore from Caithness to Cornwall. Everywhere are names that bear clear evidences of viking settlements. In the Lake District Norwegian names predominate, not only near the sea but far inland among the lovely lakes where the name of many a farm indicates that the vikings occupied the best land while the Celts took to the hills. Two distinct groups of Norse names in Wales indicate trading posts and harbors used by the vikings, and possibly small settlements. Some of the names on the Welsh coast are easily recognized as Norwegian, such as Grassholm, Flatholm, Lundy (earlier written Lundey), and Swansea (which used to be written Sveinsey). Both *holm* and *ey* mean islet or island.

Especially interesting is the settlement around Chester. When Norwegian domination was temporarily lost in the tenth century, a Norwegian chieftain from Ireland received land from the daughter of Alfred the Great, Aethelfled, the Lady of Mercia. There was no attempt to gain political independence. Every farmer received land bordering on the sea and extending inland to the hills, as was the usage in Iceland. The harbor gained new importance, doubtless under Norwegian leadership, and the city was after this ruled by lawmen as was customary among Norwegian colonists.

All ventures were not so peaceful. There were many military expeditions, principally from Ireland, and many of them connected with the family fights of the Dublin dynasty. The most remarkable achievement was that Dublin chieftains won control over the powerful kingdom of Northumbria, which had been in the hands of the Danes but which Norwegian settlers had also penetrated from the west. When Alfred's son Edward, with the help of his sister Aethelfled, was unifying England, he entered into friendly relations with the Norwegian kings in Northumbria. The ties became closer under the following king Aethelstan, who gave his sister in marriage to the old one-eyed viking king Sigtrygg. Upon Sigtrygg's death in 926 Aethelstan moved into

Northumbria with his army and annexed the kingdom to his realm. Years of closer cooperation between the races followed, and jarls of northern stock continued to hold *thing* and have a share in governing England. It was at this time that the king of Norway, Harald Fairhair, sent his son Haakon to be reared at the English court. There he had as his companions a son of the king of Scotland and a prince from France who became Louis IV. But the vikings were not yet ready to abandon control of Northumbria. In 937, Olaf Kvaran, king in Dublin, launched a great attack to win the throne of Northumbria which his father had held. Aethelstan defeated the vikings in the Battle of Brunanburh. The battle has been immortalized both in the Icelandic saga of Egil Skallagrimsson, who fought in the battle on the side of the English, and in Old English song and story. "Greater carnage had not been in this island ever yet, of men slain by the edge of the sword, as the books of old writers tell us, since the Angles and Saxons came to land here from the East, and sought Britain over the broad seas." Olaf was routed and escaped to his ships with a small band, "the bloody relics of the darts." There was peace during the rest of Aethelstan's reign, but in the troublous times that followed his death Olaf Kvaran twice succeeded in making himself king of Northumbria for a short period, both times to be followed by Eirik Blood-Axe, who had been driven from the throne of Norway. These events were purely episodic, however, and with the death of Eirik in the Battle of Stanmoor in 954, fell the last Norwegian king in England.

During the forty years of peace that followed, the Norwegians made themselves felt in the affairs of England. Edgar, the most notable king of the period, followed a policy so strongly favoring the Norwegians that there was much complaint in court circles. Englishmen were shocked because the foreigners had made drunkenness common even in the halls of the king, and were jealous of the "Danes," who were popular with the ladies because they combed their hair every day, bathed every Saturday, and changed their clothes often. Throughout the tenth century the Norwegian language and customs continued, and the influence did not disappear when the amalgamation of races was consummated.

And so in the ninth and tenth centuries there were viking settlements, often close together, all along the shores of the British Isles. In southern and eastern England, Danes were the dominant element, and in northern England Danes and Norwegians vied for control. Otherwise the settlers were predominantly Norwegian. The varied archaeological discoveries of which Norwegian scholars have made a systematic study—graves, weapons, utensils, art objects—all show that the settlers, like emigrants of later date, kept much of their old customs, dress, and mode of living while adapting themselves to their new home and gradually becoming amalgamated with the people of the land. Their northern religion, however, did not take a strong hold in the new soil; and the Norwegians were early influenced by the teachings of the White Christ, chiefly as presented by the Irish church.

¶ When the vikings came to the British Isles, they found much-traveled sea routes to the south open to them and they were not slow to seek adventure across the southern seas. Early in the ninth century, vikings, coming the "Western Way" mostly from Ireland, began to harass the western shore of France. In 836, some years before the building of Dublin, a band of vikings wintered for the first time on the little island of Noirmoutier, at the mouth of the Loire. In 843 they were joined by a fleet of sixty-seven ships directly from Norway, with men from Vestfold, say the old accounts, and the island became a fixed center of viking operations. Vikings went farther along the coast into the Mediterranean, to the mouth of the Rhone and to Italy. In Spain they fought against the Moors, and brought many captives with them to Ireland—"These are the blue men in Erin . . . long indeed did these blue men remain in Erin." They also established trade between Ireland and Spain, buying from the Arabs silk, leather, and costly cloth.

But on the continent, France was the country in which the Norwegians were most active. There is a marked contrast between their history in France and in the British Isles. In the latter their main aim was settlement and the winning of land; but in France they showed little desire to build states. There operations were military and predatory. In no place were the viking thirst for blood, lust for women, and greed for gold more unrestrained. In the disruption and wars of the late Carolingian period the vikings found plenty of opportunity for fighting. They learned military technique from the Franks and formed large mercenary armies that were ready to fight wherever there was gain and loot. And when no one hired them, as is often the case with mercenaries, they operated on their own. This may explain why no other country suffered as much from the vikings as France. Their number has astonished historians both old and new. They were hewn down by the hundreds and the thousands, say old accounts, and still more and yet more came. "No road is too long for them," says an old

French chronicle. Such tall and handsome men they had never seen, but otherwise the chroniclers had little good to say of the fierce, daring men from the North, who kept neither word nor oath, who were cruel for sheer delight, who knew neither fear nor pity, and whose course was marked with dead bodies.

In France it is even more difficult than in the British Isles to distinguish between the Danish and Norwegian vikings. While the Danes extended their raids into northern France, the Norwegians predominated on the islets and the western coast. Often they joined forces to spread terror through the harried land. The commander both at Rouen and Paris is said to have been Ragnar Lodbrok, the most famous, but also the most shadowy of viking chieftains. The sagas and annals are full of stories of Ragnar and his four doughty sons. They are discovered on expeditions in England, Ireland, Spain, Italy, and Africa, often using the Orkneys as their point of departure. Ragnar, a legendary tale says, met his death in England where the king of Northumbria threw him into a snakepit.

Both Danes and Norwegians had a share in winning Normandy, the only viking state on French soil. There are many indications that the leader, Rollo, was of Norwegian descent, but the majority of his followers were probably Danes, and from Normandy contact was kept up with Denmark, not with Norway. As much of the land was practically depopulated, the Northmen had ample opportunity to utilize their capacity for political organization, and the influence of their laws and system of private ownership of land continued long after the people had been amalgamated with the French. Though the Northmen rapidly became Normans, that is French in their language and culture, the successors of Rollo held on to the land. The energy, the seamanship, the military and political capacity of the Northern people contributed greatly to the prominence of the Normans in later medieval history as shown in their leadership in the Crusades, the conquest of England, and the building of the kingdom of the Two Sicilies. Just as important was the cultural preeminence of Northern France, which was best expressed in the *chansons de geste* and the Norman Gothic cathedrals.

¶ During the first five or six decades of the ninth century viking expeditions had been growing ever larger, bolder, and more numerous. Then a gradual decline set in, and through a large part of the tenth century the northern seas were comparatively peaceful. It was natural that an outburst of such tremendous energy as the viking ventures should spend itself, but there were other important reasons for the decline. Many vikings had become colonizers and found plenty of outlet for their surplus energy and fighting propensities within the new lands, and the new settlements furnished openings for further peaceful migration from the homeland. Often the viking states themselves, notably Normandy, gave protection against further raids. Moreover the states in Western Europe became strong enough to resist raids; and the Scandinavian countries, like the others, were forming national states whose kings entered into diplomatic relations with countries farther south. These kings were anxious to protect their own realms from piracy and were also influenced by protests from other countries. There are records of several remonstrances from the emperor to the king of Denmark, and in one case it is stated that the king replied that he had executed some vikings upon their return from France. More curious is the account of a Moslem embassy sent north to protest against viking raids in Spain. The Northmen could hardly excel the Moors in the art of piracy.

In this more settled, peaceful period, the Norwegians turned from plunder to commerce. They had been traders, it is true, from before the Viking Age, and they had often declared a truce in the midst of their warlike raids to give opportunity for peaceful exchange. But now trade became the dominating interest, and the Norwegians contributed greatly to the building of cities and the establishment of trade routes, making the vast territory of their colonization into, we might say, a great empire bound together, not by political but by commercial ties.

Yet the idea that some experience as a viking belonged to the education of an ambitious young man did not disappear, and near the close of the century, about 980, there opened a brief period in which viking activities were renewed with much of their old intensity. It is worth noticing that Olaf Tryggvason and Saint Olaf had both been vikings before they became champions of a united Norway and of Christianity. As a new age was dawning, however, in which war between states took the place of private ventures, the vikings often sold their services to a foreign king. At the same time, they themselves were subdued by the White Christ, and the Viking Age came to an end.

Kingdoms had been built up in the West, as strong as any in the homeland, yet they were destined to vanish, though not before the vikings had exerted an inestimable influence on the great upward swing in civilization which Western Europe experienced in the later

Middle Ages. The Scandinavians had not only contributed new blood and vigor, but they had added to Christian Europe the whole North, which had been practically unknown, and they had built up a vast commercial empire extending from the Caliphate of Bagdad even to the New World, with a trade that was of cardinal importance in bringing about a higher civilization in Europe. Earlier European trade had been more local. The seafaring of the Northmen was the first to embrace the whole continent and beyond, and "sea power, sea law, the art of navigation as developed later in northern waters by the ships of England and of the Hanseatic League, all go back to Norse tradition. It was a goodly heritage."[4]

But even as the Northern peoples were helping to create a larger Europe and contributing to the rapid advance of civilization that was to come, they were themselves being conquered. Christianity and classical civilization had an unquenchable vitality which in the end subdued the invaders. Meanwhile undaunted Norwegians were pushing on to new conquests that taxed their courage and seamanship even more than the exploits to the west and south and took a greater toll in life and hardship.

¶ The last great wave of viking migration carried the Norwegians into the uncharted seas of the North as pioneers in Arctic exploration and settlement. Intrepid sailors visited Baffin's Bay to the west; according to some authorities discovered Svalbard, and extended their voyages eastward to Novaya Zemlya, five hundred years before ships of other nations entered these seas. The first land to be found was Iceland. The discoverer, according to one tradition, was Nadd-Odd, an outlaw who had settled on the Faroes in the middle of the ninth century. At one time when he was to sail for Norway, storms carried him to the northwest, and he came to a large land with high mountains. He landed, but found no people there. Irish hermits had been in Iceland years before, but they were so few that if any remained when the Norwegians arrived they had no influence on the history of the island. Other explorers followed, but the first man who wintered there left after one winter. His cattle had all died because, the saga says, he was so occupied with fishing—for fish was more abundant than he had ever seen—that

[4] James Westfall Thompson, *An Economic and Social History of the Middle Ages*, 283, New York, 1928. Professor Thompson's chapter, "The Expansion and Colonization of the Norse Peoples," is a striking summary of Norwegian influence, which, he says, "it is hardly possible to overestimate" (281).

he neglected to gather fodder for his stock. He returned to Iceland when the great land-taking was in full swing.

The sources that tell the story of the settlement of Iceland are unique in completeness and reliability, in spite of some corruption resulting from years of oral tradition, and throw light also on the little known history of the other settlements in the West. The two chief sources are *Íslendingabók* (The Book of the Icelanders), written by Ari Frodi about 1130, and *Landnámabók* (The Book of Land-Taking).

The settlement of Iceland was a migration movement on a large scale. In a little more than half a century, from 870 to 930, between 15,000 and 20,000 settlers arrived and all usable land was claimed.

The first settlement was led by Ingolv Arnarson from western Norway. He came in his own ship, bringing with him his wife, his children, some kinsmen, thralls, and dependents; also his household goods, his tools, weapons, and stock. Symbolic of the idea that the new homestead was to be a continuation of the old is the story that the carved wooden pillars that had flanked the high-seat of the chieftain in the old home were carried along to be used in the new. As he approached the shore of the unknown land Ingolv cast the pillars into the seas to guide him to the place that was to be his new home. The shoreline was searched with care, and the pillars were found by a little inlet over which floated the vapory cloud from a near-by geyser. Reykjavik, or "Smoky Bay," the settlers called it. There Ingolv built his house, and thus he and his followers became the first settlers on the future site of the capital of Iceland.

So many people left the Fjordlands of western Norway that Harald Fairhair tried to stem the exodus by placing a tax on emigrants. Perhaps just as many came from the colonies. The list of settlers includes names of people—men and some women—from the Shetland Islands, Orkneys, the Hebrides, Scotland, Ireland, and even England. Sometimes emigrants from Norway pulled stakes a second time, and sometimes the second or third generation in the new lands became in turn pioneers. Not a few had Celtic blood in their veins or had married Celtic wives, and many brought with them dependents and thralls from Ireland or Scotland. Although this foreign strain was small and Iceland became thoroughly Norwegian in language and institutions, Irish blood and Irish temperament have no doubt left some impress on the traditions, temperament, and literature of the land of the sagas and perhaps contributed something to make Iceland different from

Norway. It is interesting that the name Njal, one of the best known names in the sagas, is of Celtic origin.

The immigrants came to Iceland in large groups. Often a chieftain, like Ingolv, brought with him in his own ship or ships—one chieftain had four—all his dependents and possessions, and as many followers as his ships and wealth permitted. Sometimes a three-generation or grandfather family formed one group. The chief took the land, kept some for himself, and divided the rest among his followers. So his homestead became the center of a settlement of more or less dependent farmers. Less wealthy and prominent families joined, several engaging one ship together. Before long the demand for land became great, and a rule was established that no man could claim more than a runner could carry fire around in a day. Later comers acquired land by grant or purchase from the earlier arrivals, the distribution being largely controlled by chieftains.

This method of settlement naturally resulted in the formation of communities that were to all purposes little independent states, each dominated by the original leader, and, in most cases, by his heir after him. Economic conditions too, even more than on the western coast of Norway, led to the control of large areas by one man. Food-gathering constituted an important part of the livelihood. Besides his fields, a well-to-do man must have pastures for his sheep up in the hills, a preserve for salmon fishing, and access to iron. Much of his living, moreover, came from the sea, so he needed shore land for fishing, hunting seal, gathering eggs, and collecting driftwood. As Iceland was dependent on the importation of grain and lumber, and only the wealthier men could build ships large enough for ocean traffic, they also had to keep up trade with Norway.

Among the four hundred odd settlers who were prominent enough to have their names recorded in the sagas thirty-nine were chieftains, or *godar*, and each the head of what was virtually a small state, or *godord*. In some cases this corresponded to the original claim, but often more land had been added. There was no jarl or king in Iceland, for there was no need of united preparation for war. Family and clan feeling, on the other hand, was developed more strongly than in any other Norwegian colony, traditions of the family were carefully preserved in the sagas, and family feuds might be relentlessly bitter and bloody.

It was, however, impossible for a local community to continue an entirely isolated life, and the need for a common law was soon felt. A man named Ulvljot was sent to study the laws of Norway, select what was suited to the needs of Iceland, and compile a code for the whole island. In three years he returned with a set of laws based largely on the Gulathing laws of the section from which most of the Icelanders originally hailed. These laws were adopted in 930, at the first meeting of the *althing*, or *thing* for all of the land. Every midsummer the *althing* met at a place set aside for the purpose and hence called Thingvellir. Lava formations provided a natural amphitheater, there were hot and cold springs in the neighborhood, wood was available, and the surrounding land supplied ample grazing for the hardy little horses which carried men and supplies to the meeting. People came in great numbers, sometimes bringing their wives and as many followers as they could gather. Many built booths that could serve them from year to year, and private as well as public business was carried on at the annual gathering. There was no democracy about this government, for the chieftains had full control, and could stretch even the law, which Icelanders revered, to suit their desires. The central government did not become strong enough to enforce the law, for family connection was the strongest force in Icelandic society. Nevertheless the establishment of the *althing* represents a great achievement in the development of government, and the annual gathering at Thingvellir made the Iceland settlers into a people by itself.

Iceland was independent, but in some instances the Norwegian king was recognized as having a position of influence, if not authority, in Icelandic affairs. The island was not formally incorporated into Norway's domain before the thirteenth century, but in the intervening years close contact was maintained between the two. The Icelanders retained their citizenship in Norway, and found there greater economic opportunities and more adventurous living than within the narrow confines of their new home.

The richer events in the mother country supplied also themes for skaldic verse and material for saga writing. Iceland is significant in the history of Norway because of the invaluable contribution this "Land of the Sagas" made to the preservation and writing of this history. Moreover, the Old Norse language and old traditions were there preserved with less change than in the mother country, and Iceland is the one modern state which has had an unbroken development from its foundation as a Norwegian colony.

¶ When the Norwegians came to Iceland they had reached the borderland between the eastern and western hemispheres. Viking enterprise, however, did not stop there, but pushed on to the New World. The first known settlement of white men in the New World was in Greenland. In the age of the great land-taking about 900 a man named Gunnbjørn set sail for Iceland. Carried out of his course far to the west, he saw a large land and many small islands, but fully three quarters of a century passed before Gunnbjørn's land was explored. Eirik the Red, an undaunted old viking, hard and quarrelsome, but born to be a leader, was outlawed in Norway for homicide. He went to Iceland, but after he had committed several murders in his new home, he was again outlawed. Then he fitted out a ship and set sail to look for Gunnbjørn's land. The eastern shore he found uninhabitable, but soon after he had rounded Cape Farewell, he took land and spent three winters there. In the summer he explored the whole coast up to Davis Strait, from the outer skerries to the deepest fjords. This voyage, Nansen says, "is one of the most remarkable in the history of Arctic expeditions, both in itself, on account of the masterly ability it shows, and for the vast consequences it was to have."[5] The land he found is beautiful in the summer, with its many islands, its blue fjords, and the lush meadows dotted with Arctic flowers, berry bushes, and stunted little birches. But the glittering glaciers are menacing in their nearness, and remind the explorer that he is in the land of never melting ice, that only the surface near the shore is thawed out during the brief summer, and that the winter is long and dark.

But Eirik called it Greenland to attract settlers. He returned to Iceland and became the leader of the largest emigration that went to the new land. In 986 twenty-five ships set out from Iceland, of which fourteen reached Greenland, while of the others some were forced to return and some were lost. From his big farm, Brattalid, Eirik and his family after him exercised unquestioned leadership. The colonization proceeded rather rapidly, and it is estimated that the two little settlements which were formed on the southwestern shore had a population of about 2,000. Traces have been found of sixteen churches and 280 homesteads. On the larger farms there were as many as twenty buildings—dwelling houses, storehouses, haylofts, barns, and even *seters* for use during the summer grazing. The houses were built of stone and sod, as in Iceland. At first the frame for the roof was made of driftwood, but later lumber was imported from Markland on the North American mainland.

The Greenland settlement is unique as the only case we know in

[5] Nansen, *In Northern Mists,* 1:268.

which European people have built a farming community in a wholly Arctic land. The experiment was doomed to tragic failure. Much of the livelihood had to be procured through hunting and fishing. Each farm had its boat, and the farmers often had huts along the coast to which they returned every summer, as had long been the custom in Norway, to fish and hunt seal, walrus, and polar bear. Sometimes they visited the eastern shore or the mainland, but generally they went along the western shore, where a rune stone has been discovered as far north as 72° 55′ north latitude. As grazing was good the Greenlanders could depend much on their flocks of sheep and goats, and occasionally cows, and cheese and butter were consumed in large quantities. Grain, however, could not ripen in the short summer, and many of the settlers never saw or tasted bread.

If the colonists were to maintain the mode of living to which they had been accustomed, trade was necessary. Grain was highly desirable, iron was needed for tools and weapons, and lumber and tar were indispensable for shipbuilding. Before long lumber was obtained from Markland, but other articles had to be procured from the Old World. In exchange Greenland exported seal skins, goat and cow hides, walrus hides which were used for ropes, and walrus tusks, which were much in demand for ivory carving, especially for crucifixes, bishop's crosiers, and other articles for the church.

Life must have been a constant struggle for survival, but it went on in about the same way as long as trade was kept up. Gradually commerce fell off, yet some contact with the outside world continued until the fifteenth century. The tragic disappearance of the colony is veiled in mystery, but the most probable explanation is that the settlers were absorbed by the Eskimos, whose mode of life would have to be adopted when the contact with Europe was broken off.[6] Only of late have archaeologists reconstructed the daily life of this colony on the edge of the Arctic ice:

"Far in by the fjords, where people seldom come, forgotten settlements sleep—ruins of farms with many little stone houses on green slopes, foundations and walls of churches—and in the churchyards rest people of long ago who spoke the Norse tongue and traced pious prayers in runes on little wooden crosses that mark the graves."[7]

The little settlement in Greenland became the point of departure of

[6] Nansen, *In Northern Mists*, 2:95-134.

[7] Shetelig, *Det norske folks liv og historie*, 1:363.

the daring Vinland voyages, as the next step in viking expansion naturally led to the mainland of North America. Vinland was a mythical name of uncertain origin that had long been used to designate the unknown lands in the West; and as the word caught the imagination of men of yore as well as of moderns, it has become customary to speak of all the expeditions beyond Greenland as Vinland voyages, although of the newly discovered lands Markland was of most importance to the older colonies.

Just as in the history of Iceland and Greenland, the Vinland voyages went through three successive stages: accidental land-sighting, purposeful exploration, and finally settlement, all in the short period of forty-five years, from 986 to 1030.

The first land-sighting of which there is any record is that of Bjarni Herjulfsson and his men. Bjarni sailed from Norway to Iceland to visit his father, Herjulf, only to find that he had moved to Greenland. Bjarni decided to follow him although, as he said to his men, it might be rash, as none of them had ever been there. The ship was carried out of its course to the south and west, and when land was sighted Bjarni knew, both from its location and its appearance, that it was not Greenland, and therefore turned to the northeast. Twice again he saw land; but in spite of demands from the crew that he go ashore, he continued his course to Greenland and arrived at Herjulfsnes, just outside his father's home. The trip tested the courage and seamanship of the crew to the utmost; but the story is recorded with typical saga restraint and the convincing accuracy of a ship's log. From the description of the land and weather conditions it is almost certain that Bjarni skirted along the coast from Labrador to Baffin's Land.

Soon after, Leif the Lucky, son of Eirik the Red, came to Greenland, sent by King Olaf Tryggvason to bring Greenland the gospel of Christ. Like his king, Leif was youthful, heroic, and daring, and withal keen and able—one of the most striking personages of the age. He already had to his credit one of the great achievements of that remarkable age. He had come to Greenland directly from Norway, without stopping in Iceland, and thus made the first deep-sea voyage over the Atlantic, with no effort to keep the usual course or stay near land.

When he came to Greenland he met Bjarni and obtained from him all possible information about the land he had seen and the course he had followed. Leif, a born explorer, planned carefully for a voyage of exploration. He bought Bjarni's ship and set out to follow his course, but in the opposite direction. First he found the last land sighted by

Bjarni, the flat, barren, rocky shore of Baffin's Land, or Helluland, then he sailed along the shore of Labrador, part of which was wooded. Markland is the Old Norse name. He sailed on, how far is uncertain, but no distance seemed too great for Leif. He landed perhaps on Newfoundland or on the coast of New England, possibly even farther south. There houses were built, the expedition went into winter quarters and explored the surrounding country, and they named the land Vinland.

Not long after this Leif's brother Thorvald borrowed the ship which had made the two voyages, and secured permission to use the houses Leif had built. The nautical skill of the day is shown in the fact that he sailed directly to the place, seemingly with no hesitation. "This place is fair and here I will build my home," he said. But an unlooked-for tragedy occurred. For the first time the explorers clashed with natives, *skraellings* they called them, and Thorvald was mortally wounded. As far as we know, his was the first Christian burial in the New World. Discouraged, the expedition returned home after an absence of a year.

Among the semi-legendary Vinland voyages might be mentioned that of Freydis, the daughter of Eirik the Red, a woman as bold as her half brothers. Hers is a tale of wild romance, treachery, and murder, but it has little historical significance.

The largest Vinland expedition was that of Thorfinn Karlsefni, which consisted of three ships, with about 160 people, among them not a few women. They carried with them cattle, iron, and other things needed for settling. The description of the place of settlement might fit many points on our eastern coast, and the exact location cannot be determined. The little colony roused much interest among the Indians. First they were friendly, but before long they attacked the newcomers and killed several of them. When Karlsefni saw that the colony would have to defend itself against the *skraellings* if it were to be continued, he realized the hopelessness of the situation and prudently abandoned the whole enterprise. With bows and arrows the handful of newcomers could not hold their own against a horde of natives. They would soon have shot away all their iron arrowheads while the Indians' supply of chipped stone was limitless. It was only after the use of firearms had become quite general that Europeans subdued the more backward races. So ended the early Norwegian attempt to colonize North America.

While the main facts of the Vinland voyages are incontestably established and tireless efforts of scholars have thrown much light on the whole subject, much uncertainty about details still remains. How long intrepid seamen continued to brave the tremendous distances of the western seas or how far they penetrated we do not know. The theory that they reached Minnesota[8] has not yet been accepted by scholars. Casual mention of Vinland voyages in the fourteenth century shows that the expeditions were not considered extraordinary. The latest definite mention of a Vinland voyage recorded is from 1121, when a Bishop Eirik set out in search of Vinland, presumably never to return. But an Icelandic annal has an entry for 1347 about the arrival of a small ship from Greenland which had sailed to Markland and on its return voyage been driven from its course and reached Iceland. To the Greenlanders, who depended on Markland for their lumber, the westward voyages doubtless became more important as the trade with Norway declined, and they were probably kept up until the Greenland settlements lost their vigor. With those ill-fated colonies, much knowledge of the New World no doubt perished. Yet the tradition never died completely, and an unbroken chain of knowledge may connect the early Vinland voyages and the explorations of the Northwest in the late fifteenth century.[9]

The Vinland voyages had practically no influence on the history of Norway and were little known there. Other events seemed more important and interesting, and colonies nearer home offered ample outlet for the adventurous, the more so as the tremendous energy of the age had largely spent itself. Nevertheless Leif the Lucky's achievement—the discovery of America by a Norwegian in the year 1000—is a heroic climax of the viking expansion across the sea.

[8] Hjalmar Rued Holand, *The Kensington Stone*, Ephraim, Wis., 1932. *America, 1355-1364*, New York, 1946.

[9] W. Hovgaard, *The Voyages of the Norsemen to America*; A. W. Brøgger, *Vinlandsferdene*, Oslo, 1937.

CHAPTER 4

NORWAY DURING THE EXPANSION

WHILE vikings were active in foreign lands, the indigenous heathen civilization in Norway reached its finest development. Practically the whole country felt the stimulating effect of the viking expeditions, which brought to the homeland new ideas, new articles, and new outlets for excessive energy. The thrill of adventure and fresh breezes from across the seas pervaded the age. Though it is difficult to evaluate accurately this influence, it certainly was a potent factor in the life of the time. A constant communication was kept up with the emigrants to hitherto unsettled lands as well as to regions with older civilizations, and it is probably safe to say that something was brought home from every shore visited by Norwegians. The liveliest intercourse was with the Celtic world of which Ireland was the cultural center. The most marked foreign influence was, therefore, Irish with the English and French also significant. Many Irish ornaments, probably loot from raids, are found in the viking graves, especially in western Norway. But more widely scattered over the country were other Irish articles, such as bronze kettles and scales, acquired in trade rather than by pillage. Anglo-Saxon and Frankish ornaments and weapons are also found, but not in so great number.

It must be remembered, however, that Norway had a conservative, rural society with its roots in the distant past, and that fundamentally life at home during the Viking Age was a continuation of the past, subject to much less change than in the settlements in foreign lands. Even the tremendous ferment of the age, which speeded up development in every line, antedated the viking voyages.

¶ Religion was a powerful force in old Norwegian society, and some of the beliefs and practices of the Viking Age, especially those connected with the worship of the forces of fertility and growth, go back to the dim past, even to the Stone Age, it seems. But in the Viking Age the Asa mythology, with its many complex stories of gods, giants, and numerous other strange creatures, assumed the form in which it has come down to us. Though the majority of the gods were not extensively worshiped, the wealth of allusions in the poems of the skalds show that the myths and legends were very generally known; and the warmth and dignity which pervade the religious literature indicate that there was much personal belief in the gods, who influenced the fate of every human being. Sometimes a person carried with him a little image of a god made of precious metal, thus selecting one divinity in whom he placed his complete trust, but the many amulets show that this religious faith often degenerated into crude superstition.

Our knowledge of the form of worship is very meager compared to the rich mythology that has been preserved. Every householder was a priest for the family, and the women kept up the belief in the household sprites that lived on the hearth. There were also a great many sanctuaries, centers of the local community or of the larger shire, early small stone altars in the open, and houses of worship combining rooms for the statues of the gods and halls for the gathering of the worshipers at the sacrifices.

At the larger sanctuaries, or *hov*, the local chieftain usually performed the sacrificial functions. The priest-chief would place the bowl containing the blood of the sacrificial animals on the altar and then sprinkle blood on the images of the gods and the people present. The meat would then be boiled and consumed by the assembled worshipers.

At the height of the Viking Age there may have been thousands of temples in Norway. It was quite common for a well-to-do farmer, a *herse*, or a *jarl* to have his own private *hov* on his property. This was exclusively the case in Iceland, where every *godi* (plural, *godar*) was both priest and ruler of his own *godord*. In addition to the private temples it was quite common in Norway for each community to erect a *hov*, usually dedicated to one single god. Some of these may still be traced through modern place names, such as Norderhov (Njord's Hov) and Torshov (Thor's Hov). A few of the *hovs* achieved in time national importance, although none became a national shrine like Leire in Denmark or Uppsala in Sweden. The most influential were perhaps the one at Skiringssal in Vestfold, the *hovs* at Lade and Mæren in Trøndelag, and one or two temples on the Westland. The big public *blots* were held three times a year: October 14, *haustblot*, to welcome the winter season; January 14, *midvintersblot*, to induce the gods to give a good harvest;

and April 14, *sommerblot*, at which the gods were asked to grant victory in battle.

In Snorri's *Saga of Haakon the Good* there is a description of a banquet to which the people came from far and wide, their sleds loaded with food and mead. All shared in the sacrificial feast, the chieftain in this case being both host and priest. Snorri leaves us to imagine the wild scene that might result when the people were gorged with mead and meat, and he does not mention the brutal human sacrifices which were not uncommon. The gods demanded cruel payment in return for their gifts to man. The divinities most worshiped were Odin, god of combat and wisdom; Thor, protector against diseases, sorcery, and other dangers, as well as god of agriculture; Frey, god of fruitfulness; Njord, god of seafaring and prosperity, worshiped mainly in coastal regions; and Frigg and Freya, the goddesses of home and the life of women. There was also a host of lesser goddesses. Women played a not unimportant role in the mythology and religion of the Old Norse world. The worship of Balder, "the white *Ás*," is of special interest, since it suggests the influence of Christian ideas. The significant fact of the mythology surrounding his name is his death, brought about by the trickery of Loki, and the expressed hope that after Ragnarok he will return from Niflheim. The numerous place names incorporating his name give proof that the worship of Balder must have been quite widespread.

There was repulsive brutality in the old Norwegian worship, as in that of all primitive warlike societies, and the Æsir were pictured as possessing human frailties, as were the divinities of classical mythology. Yet, especially in the worship of Odin as the god of wisdom, there was evidence of refined ethics. The myths often represent struggles between light and darkness, life and death. The finest picture of the complete view of existence according to the Asa faith is found in the *Vøluspá*. In this magnificent poem the unnamed author, who must have been a man of deep thought and wide knowledge as well as of rare poetic gifts, has welded the stories of the Æsir into a noble sequence of all life from the beginning of things to Ragnarok, the "doom of the gods," and the rise of a new world. Some scholars have thought that the lofty conception of existence with which the poem is permeated could hardly have been obtained without contact with Christianity. "The poet of *Vøluspá* was a brooding and searching spirit, fostered by the Viking Age in its ferment. He sought to solve the problem of the combination of the traditional mythic world with the new Christian ideas. The result was the creation of a work full of beauty, inspiration, profundity."[1] Others hold the opinion that it is an expression purely of the highest development of the old faith. Although there was much break-up of the old, and skepticism was rampant especially among returning vikings, the old worship was vital and vigorous, as is evidenced by the stubborn resistance to the new faith, and by the persistence of some elements of the old religion far into Christian times. It seems reasonable to think that the *Vøluspá* was a great factor in perpetuating the old.

¶ The *Vøluspá* has come down to us from the Viking Age in a group of poems known as *The Poetic Edda*, or *The Elder Edda*, which were written down in Iceland during the great century of saga writing, about 1150 to 1250, after having been preserved orally, some of them for two centuries and more. Most of the poems were composed during the Viking Age, probably in the tenth century, and are the finest expression we have of the thought and life of the pre-Christian North. The names of the authors are not known, but they were from different parts of the far-flung viking world, perhaps some of them much traveled, for in some of the poems scholars detect traces of Irish influence—just how much they do not agree. One of them was composed in Greenland.

The poems are divided into two groups. The first is made up of lays of the gods. The most comprehensive and most sublime is the *Vøluspá*, the Sibyl's Prophecy, in which the *vølva*, or wise woman, rises at the call of Odin and reveals the secrets of the past and the future. The second poem, *Hávamál*, the Sayings of the High One, is a collection of wise sayings attributed to Odin. It reminds one of the Biblical Proverbs and is replete with shrewd wisdom, sometimes with a touch of satire, expressing a high standard of conduct rather than of morals. A third poem that must be noted is the *Rigsthula*. It has a mythological background, but differs from all the others in being mainly a description of the origin of social classes. It was written in praise of royalty.

The second group in *The Poetic Edda* is composed of poems based on the old heroic legends dating back to the Age of Migrations. Some of the heroes in fact are identified with prominent leaders in the folk wanderings of the fifth century. Though the themes were not Norwegian, but foreign or common Germanic in their origin, the legends were more fully preserved and more highly developed among the Scandinavians than among other peoples; in modern times, of course,

[1] Olrik, *Viking Civilization*, 138.

they have become most widely known through the Wagnerian operas.

There was a wealth of verse composed in the general style of the Eddic poetry which is not included in that collection. Though much has been lost, enough remains to show the extent and diversity of pre-Christian poetry in the North. This verse includes riddles, legal formulas, heroic lays, and religious poems. It is northern in origin, heathen in spirit, and "unliterary, that is, unbookish,"[2] in form, although one weird poem, "The Sun Song," pictures the transition from heathen to Christian thought.

Only a part of the heroic tales was given poetic form; many were preserved in prose. Allusions to them are frequent also in skaldic poetry, and themes from the legends, such as Sigurd slaying the dragon Fafnir and Gunnar in the serpent's pit with his hands bound, playing his harp with his toes, were for centuries frequently employed in art, even on the door posts of Christian churches.

The religious background is prominent in the heroic poems. They express not only belief in the gods, but emphasize strongly the Norns, or fates, who ruled the destiny of men and gods alike, and the strange unseen forces that everywhere made themselves felt in life. Yet human beings could control them if the right methods were known. By magic, forces for good or evil could be restrained or unleashed. This power, it was thought, lay in potions concocted out of the strangest things, and also in magic words, incantations, and songs. In their mastery over words, poets were thought to have fearful and wonderful ability to help friends or wreak vengeance on foes. But the most complete supernatural power was believed to be within the reach of the man or woman who knew runes. The runic alphabet was reduced from twenty-four to sixteen letters, and it continued to be used for incantations even as in the Old Iron Age. They were especially potent in warding off evil and harmful magic from the living, and even from the dead.

Quite different from the simple Eddic lays and magic charms is the highly artificial skaldic poetry which appeared full-fledged in the early ninth century in the work of Bragi. The verse form is intricate and the poems abound in symbolism and elaborate, sometimes far-fetched, metaphors, or kennings, which may obscure the meaning for the uninitiated; but they are strong, vivid, and sonorous. Though love, friendship, loyalty to chief, and devotion to the gods were expressed in the skaldic poems, they dealt first and foremost with war, and lavished praise on warriors who "gave drinks of blood" to Odin's

[2] Lee M. Hollander, *Old Norse Poems*, XI, New York, 1936.

ravens and "fed the wolves." Rare indeed was the skald who did not love battle.

Men, and women too, of the highest talent devoted themselves to the difficult art of poetry. Bragi and the other early skalds were all Norwegians, but in the eleventh century the art was practised chiefly by Icelanders. The skalds were often attached to the courts of kings, where the poetic gift was an open sesame to royal favor. Though the court skalds devoted themselves to singing the praises of their king, they were no mere sycophants, but often expressed criticism and advice in tactfully turned verse. Notable in this respect is Saint Olaf's devoted friend, Sigvat Thordarson. Unlike the Eddic poets, the skalds did not conceal their names, but won honor and respect as well as gold in their lifetime and their names have been kept green to a later day. Two hundred and fifty names have been preserved, and they form an unbroken line for five hundred years. Thoroughly northern and heathen in its origin, the skaldic poetry later adapted itself to Christianity. After the eleventh century, however, it lost its vigor and finally gave way before Latin, churchly influences. But the fame and work of the skalds was immortalized, sometimes in sagas bearing their names, more frequently through stories and quotations in other sagas. Snorri Sturlason did more than any other man to preserve the knowledge of the skalds and their poetry. He not only depended on them as his most reliable primary source in writing history, quoting from them extensively, but has given a scholarly discussion of the art in his *Prose Edda.*

¶ Like the literature, the burial customs are evidence of the importance of religion in the life of the Viking Age. The grave finds are by far the most important archaeological remains from this age, and they are richer than those of any other time. The increase in the number of graves may be partly a result of the growing population and wealth, but it seems even more to indicate that religious faith had taken a deeper hold and had spread to more people. The burial customs expressed strong filial piety, deep loyalty to family and clan, coupled with some vanity, of course, as well as faith in the hereafter. The feast was as sumptuous as the wealth and station of the family permitted. The tables were loaded with food, mead flowed freely for days, and sacrifices were offered to the gods. The burial, too, consumed a large portion of the estate left by the dead. The grave was looked upon not only as a resting place for the body, but also as a dwelling. The aim, whether among plain folk or among royalty, was to provide the dead with all they needed to live in the next world in the manner to which they were accustomed on earth. So the common man was buried with his farm tools, his weapons, and sometimes his horse, and even cooking utensils for hunting and fishing trips; in the grave of his wife were placed her personal belongings and all she needed to carry on the many activities of the household; and chieftains were laid to rest with the greater splendor that had belonged to their earthly life.

Burying in a boat was a quite widespread custom among all classes, and it is unique in that no trace of this has been found among any European people outside of Scandinavia. Evidences of the idea of a boat trip to the next world have been found as far back as the Bronze Age, and boat graves have been discovered from the time of the folk wanderings, though they may have existed earlier. In the seventh century they became common in all the Scandinavian countries, but were especially so in Norway in the ninth century. In some cases the finds are meager, for often goods were stolen and sometimes the boat with all its furnishings was consumed in a huge funeral pyre. Fortunately for the student, however, cremation was not a universal custom; but mounds were built over the ship, and efforts made both in construction and in the selection of material to preserve the grave as long as possible. This was especially the case in the royal burials.

The royal boat graves, though naturally few as compared with the many others, are not only examples of the finest and most luxurious form of burial in Norway, but they are the richest archaeological finds in all northern Europe. The first such grave to be discovered was found in 1751, on Rolvsøy, a little island at the mouth of the Glomma River. It is one of a group of graves from a royal family of which we have no other record. Across the Oslo Fjord, at Borre in Vestfold, lies the largest group of royal graves, consisting of nine mounds of tremendous size and fifteen smaller ones. Though these have, with one exception, not been completely excavated, it is certain that they constitute the main burial place of the Yngling family, the most prominent royal dynasty in the Viking Age. South of the Borre group are two other Yngling graves, the Oseberg Mound and the Gokstad Mound. Both have been scientifically excavated and the contents carefully preserved, the Gokstad grave in 1881 and the Oseberg grave in 1904. The only other group of mounds comparable to those of Vestfold is on the island Karmøy off the southwestern coast. As these graves, two of which have been excavated, are of the same type as the Vestfold graves and are close to the place where Harald Fairhair took up his residence after the conquest of Norway, it is natural to associate them too with the Yngling family. One other grave of the Yngling type has been found in the far North on the little island of Leka, quite a distance north of Namsos. The largest mound yet discovered is inland, in Romerike, and naturally not a ship grave. According to tradition it is the burial place of King Rakne, and may date back even to the Age of Migrations.

The royal grave mounds are imposing in size, the largest being more than 150 feet in diameter, containing ships that are sixty feet long or more. Near the center of the boat was erected a funeral chamber in the shape of a ship's tent, constructed of heavy oak planks. There the body was laid to rest in a luxurious bed of down bolsters and surrounded by all manner of articles that belonged to royal living. The Gokstad ship is the most perfectly preserved viking warship that has been excavated. The richest finds, however, are from the Oseberg Mound, which had been very successfully sealed so that things were well preserved. There a queen was buried; she is thought to be Asa, the grandmother of Harald Fairhair, a queen worthy of the honors accorded her. She was buried in her magnificent pleasure yacht with a slave woman, probably sacrificed to be the queen's companion in the next world. The ship was built broad and flat for use in shallow waters, with fifteen pairs of oars and a mast, and ornamented with elaborate carving. The equipment was the most complete imaginable. There were all the things needed for sailing and for life on board, such as anchor, water pails, and gangplank; but provisions were also made for life after the voyage had been completed. There was a richly carved wagon, a most unusual find; four sleds, three of them elaborately ornamented; harness, dog chains, and the remains of an ox, four dogs, and fifteen horses. There were also tools and kitchen utensils, and flour, apples, and nuts, besides beds and chests. Although robbers long ago carried off any precious metals and ornaments, the remaining personal belongings of the women, such as their toilet articles and down coverlets, are most interesting. The queen wore a dress of rich purple woolen cloth, embroidered in wool and trimmed with many-colored silk ribbons. Still more remarkable are numerous remnants of woven tapestries, some of them picture-weaving of unusual intricacy and beauty. The women were well equipped for carrying on their handiwork, having spindle, scissors, winder for yarn, and two looms.

The Oseberg ship is the richest antiquarian find in Northern Europe, and in no other single place is found so complete a picture of the life and civilization of the age of Charlemagne. There are articles procured through trade, such as the silk trimmings, a walnut, and a pail of English manufacture, and other evidences of foreign influence. But most of the things are of native manufacture and give a vivid picture of what Norwegians had achieved at the beginning of the Viking Age.

¶ The royal graves show most dramatically the height which the art of the shipbuilder had reached by the ninth century. The Norwegians had used boats even in the Stone Age, though there is lacking evidence to prove just what the ships were like. But scholars have been able to trace an unbroken evolution in boat building from the Bronze Age to the Viking Age. The Kvalsund boat bears witness to the seamanship and love of the sea of the Norwegians two centuries before the Viking Age, as does the salty tang of the heroic legends.

But only in the ninth century did the experiments in solving building problems, carried on for centuries, reach the most perfect solution. The ships in the burial mounds, built for the personal use of royalty, were among the finest though not the largest boats, and show that the craftsmen could construct vessels adapted to various purposes. The Oseberg ship, from the beginning of the ninth century and built for the pleasure of a woman, was not especially strong, but graceful, light, and richly ornamented. The Gokstad ship, on the other hand, is a fine type of viking ship from the close of the century. It has little ornamentation; its beauty lies in its perfect proportions, its graceful lines, and the noble curves of prow and stern rising high above the water, the brightly colored sail, and the painted shields fastened along the sides of the ship. But though the builders expressed their love for the ship in the beauty they gave it, their main interest was to make it seaworthy. It had to be strong, yet light and elastic, adapted both to rowing and to sailing. The Gokstad ship was equipped with sixteen pairs of oars up to eighteen feet long, and carried a large square sail of wadmel with the simple rigging it required. Solid construction was needed to carry the mast and heavy sail in a strong wind, and yet the body would have to give to every wave. The seaworthiness of the Gokstad ship has been most effectively tested, for in 1893 an exact replica of it was sailed across the Atlantic to the exposition in Chicago. Captain Magnus Andersen and his crew found the vessel easy to handle, and it remained perfectly watertight though the bottom yielded to a heavy sea, rising and sinking as much as three-fourths of an inch. A viking ship was supplied with tools needed on the voyage, a tent that could be raised over the ship, and beds for those of high estate. The men generally slept in sleeping bags of skin, two to a bag. Equipment for camping on land, such as tents and cooking utensils, was also carried. The vikings were well prepared for their voyages over the seas.

¶ While the viking expeditions were the most striking expression of the ferment of the age, the expansive energy of the people gave rise also to occupation of new lands within Norway, and to increase of the coastal trade and travel.

A remarkable account of one man's travels has been preserved in Alfred the Great's translation of the history of the world written by Orosius, a fifth-century presbyter in Spain. Alfred added to Orosius's very meager account a description of Northern Europe which includes information that had been given him by a visitor at his court named Ottar, or Ôhthere, who lived "farthest north of any Norseman." Ottar gave a brief, accurate description of a voyage he had made along the northern coast of Norway around the North Cape and then south into the White Sea, visiting Bjarmeland, the home of the Permians, "who had built their land well." He had sailed three days north from his home in Haalogaland, then four days east, and then five days south. He had gone to explore and to obtain walrus tusks and hides, both valuable articles of trade. Carrying with him goods to be sold in southern markets he then sailed along practically the whole coast of Norway to the harbor of Skiringsal in Vestfold. In favorable weather it took a month's sailing from Haalogaland when one camped during the night and sailed in the day. From Skiringsal Ottar sailed between Sweden and Denmark, south to the busy trading city of Hedeby.

Ottar's story was included among the accounts of famous English voyages published by Richard Hakluyt in the days of Elizabeth, when English sailors reopened the old Norwegian route to Russia. Unmindful of the nationality of his hero, the editor remarks: "Wil it not, in all posteritie, be as great renowne unto our English nation to have bene the first discoverers of a sea beyond the North Cape (never certainly known before) and of a convenient passage into the huge Empire of Russia by the bay S. Nicholas and the river Duina?"

While Ottar probably never reached the Dwina, he had an accurate knowledge of the geography both of Norway and the lands around the northern seas. There is no indication that Ottar's interests were anything but peaceful trade and curiosity about new lands, and there were probably many others like him. Even Bjarmeland was generally known, though visits to it were among the greatest adventures of the age; and trade along Ottar's route was maintained until the thirteenth century.

Although the Norwegians of this age influenced the development of cities in foreign lands, there were no real towns in Norway. Skiringsal was the greatest trade center, but hardly a town; and in the time of Harald Fairhair it gave place to the near-by center which became the city of Tønsberg. Konungahella, another place that figures prominently in the sagas, was probably not much of a town. There were a number of other fixed marketplaces where booths were erected and people came for trade and other intercourse at regular times, but although some became towns later, they had no fixed population in the ninth century. Norway was entirely rural.

The population was growing and wealth was increasing, however, and unless outlets were found, life would be cramped and the standard of living would decline, a disagreeable thought to the self-confident individualist of the Viking Age. On the western and southern shores, the main outlet was, of course, across the sea, but even from this section some people, no doubt, moved inland to find suitable homesteads, for there was close communication between the coast district and the interior. Others went north to Haalogaland and even Finmark, where there was a noticeable increase in population.

Ottar is an example of the men who developed and exploited the Far North. He was an independent chieftain owing no political allegiance to anyone. He held extensive lands worked by dependents. Some cultivation of the soil was carried on, horses being used for plowing, but he depended much more on his herds, especially his tame reindeer. He had only twenty sheep, twenty cows, and twenty swine, but he had six hundred reindeer. Among them were six very expensive decoy animals used for catching wild reindeer. Ottar did more hunting than did the farmers farther south. Fishing, whaling, and walrus hunting furnished both food for his large household and costly wares to sell in southern markets. Ottar had still another source of income: he collected from the Lapps a tax paid in furs, feathers, and ropes from hides. Of another magnate, Thorir Hound, one of the slayers of Saint Olaf, the sagas tell the unsavory story of how he appropriated unto himself extensive lands, drove the peasants off, and worked it with his own slaves.

In the interior farming district of the Eastland and Trøndelag energy found an outlet in clearing and building up new farms, so that in some districts the number increased fourfold. Many of them were situated in higher altitudes than the older settlements and this may be indicative of an improvement in climatic conditions which many scholars believe took place at this time. Sometimes new settlements were formed, but often the old were expanded by clearing and occupying the wastes that had separated communities, and thus the different neighborhoods were brought into closer contact and political consolidation was furthered. The division of the land held by a larger family group into farms for individuals also went on by leaps and bounds. Many a farm of this period bears the name of the man who started it, and even an unmarried woman, a *mær* (pl. *meyjar*), might build a home of her own, as is indicated by the name Møyarstader. Obviously there must have been a sharp increase of population; the standard of living was also rising, as is indicated by the increased stature of the people; and the archaeological finds, in some places ten times as rich as for the Old Iron Age, prove beyond doubt a general increase in wealth. That the individual ownership of a farm became common indicates that it was easier to make a living and that a person did not need the cooperative work of the larger group. It was an age of new opportunities for the individual.

¶ Though we know little about the buildings on a farm in the Viking Age, we can get a rather complete picture of daily life. Even in the interior of the country the influence of the oversea movement was felt. New vegetables, such as turnips and cabbage, were introduced from the British Isles and also new breeds of stock. The Norwegians also learned better methods of agriculture, which the English and Irish had inherited from the Romans. From the Celts they learned to stack their hay, to thrash with flails, and to build ovens for drying the grain. New tools, for example the spade, and new household utensils were also brought in from the British Isles. Life on the farm was enriched and assumed much of the character that it was to retain until the introduction of machinery revolutionized rural methods.

Both archaeology and poetry picture a highly developed rural society interested in the pursuits of peace. The *Hávamál* expresses the principles and ideals of such a society. Thrift, early rising, careful provisioning, not least when on a journey, the care of one's clothes—but not too ostentatiously—the value of independence and of a "house though a hut it be," for "a man is master at home," are all emphasized. The author reiterates the admonition to practice moderation in food and drink, perhaps because he was aware that gluttony and heavy drinking were not the least of the faults of his countrymen. To be judicious in speech, for "All know what is known to three," and self-controlled in act were looked upon as part of that balanced wisdom which alone could form a safe basis for effective living:

> The fairest lives do those men live
> Whose wisdom wide has grown.

The writer has much to say of hospitality, the supreme virtue of the age, and among the greatest blessings in life he counts a good name, which "will never die," and friendship, for "man is man's delight":

> If a friend thou hast whom thou fully wilt trust,
> Then fare to find him oft:
> For brambles grow and waving grass
> On the rarely trodden road.

Although the author of the *Hávamál* cannot refrain from some of the conventional comment on the fickleness of the fair sex, an honorable and dignified place was accorded to women in old Norwegian society. They could control their own property. They associated freely with men and were socially on equality with them, although legally largely under male guardianship. The sagas and legends abound in striking pictures of women, and among the personages of early history are such women as Aud the Deep-minded and the queen of the Oseberg ship.

While the contents of the Oseberg ship embrace practically all that belonged in a wealthy household, other less significant graves and buried treasures show that even the common farm had adequate equipment for the many activities carried on. A great many household articles were made of wood, though only a few have been preserved. Those are ornamented in the style of the striking decorative art of the age, characterized by intricate patterns based on animal and sometimes plant motifs elaborately intertwined. Occasionally a less developed pictorial form was also represented. While, of course, all articles were not so elaborate, many tools of the kind still used in wood carving have been found and indicate that the art was commonly practiced. There was no distinction between the craftsman and the artist in those days. Iron was used very extensively for pots and pans and all manner of utensils and tools, for good iron was plentiful. Though most farms had their smithy, there were professional blacksmiths also. The iron articles were well made, but were generally of simple, purely utilitarian design. Dishes and kettles of native soapstone were also made for home use and for export.

For trinkets metal was, of course, imported, and much of the work done by professionals. Sometimes ornaments looted or bought in foreign lands were worn, such as covers of books and tops of reliquaries brought home by vikings and made into brooches. Most of the jewelry, however, was of native make and pattern—with sometimes a touch of foreign influence—representing the same type of art as the wood carving. It was made of the less costly metals, preferably bronze, and the beauty lay in the gilding, the design, and the skill of the artist best displayed in fine filigree and inlaid work. Men generally wore only one ornament, a large brooch to fasten the cloak on the shoulder. Women sometimes decked themselves in splendor, wearing gaudy necklaces and three brooches, one on either shoulder and one in front, all of barbaric size and showiness.

The women's chief contribution to the arts was weaving. The Oseberg finds bear out the statements in poetry and saga that the walls were hung with handsome woolen tapestries woven in intricate patterns, sometimes in pictures. The long dresses and loose cloaks of the women were often of richly dyed and finely woven wool. Sometimes linen was used for undergarments and occasionally, among the wealthy, for sheets. Down and feather pillows and woven coverlets might also be used, but often the short built-in beds were fitted only with straw and fur coverings.

As in the preceding age, the farm was practically self-sufficient and was well equipped for the many activities that belong to the routine of peaceful everyday life. On the other hand, in even the most peaceful home the danger of violence was ever present. The *Hávamál* warns that:

> Away from his arms in the open field
> A man should fare not a foot;
> For never he knows when the need of a spear
> Shall arise on the distant road.

Every man was buried with his weapons. They were, in the wording of the old laws, spear, sword, axe, bow and arrow, and shield, and often all these are found in the grave. Other warlike remains from the age are the forts which were built large enough to be a refuge for the whole non-combatant population of the neighborhood.

¶ While the whole social organism was much the same as in the Age of Small States, some changes were going on. As a result of the warlike, aristocratic spirit of the age, chieftains were taking over a number of farms. Slaves were more easily obtained and therefore more numerous. Tenantry was also growing. Though the tenants might be economically dependent, they did not become unfree but were under a contract, sometimes only for a year at a time, and there was some legal recognition of their rights. Still, farmer ownership continued to be common, both in the old families which had the odal right and on the newer farms where ownership might be more shifting. The grades in social importance are indicated by the bot collected for a slain person.

Political organization had not reached anything like a modern form. The sense of kinship retained its old strength even when the family became scattered on different farms, justice was still mainly a private matter, and blood revenge a most sacred duty. Yet there was a steady development of the *thing* system which had originated earlier in the needs of the community, and the feeling that "By law must the land be built," as begins the Icelandic law, was deeply rooted in Norwegian consciousness. The law and *thing* provided for honorable agreement between the two parties to a quarrel through the mediation of worthy men, but if a peaceful agreement could not be reached, blood vengeance remained a recognized recourse. There is no better picture of the interplay of the two ideas than the one given in *Njal's Saga.* Only gradually did first public opinion and finally law require that a reasonable offer of settlement be accepted.

Even when judgment had been pronounced there was no public machinery for enforcing the law. This continued to be the duty of the kindred. When there was need of common action to enforce a decree of outlawry, resist violence, or beat off bandits, a hue and cry went out to the community. In the Viking Age there was increased need for this. Norway was no more free from viking attacks than were other countries, as vikings came from over the sea, especially from the Orkneys, to raid and leave again, and others returned to live in Norway, bringing with them habits of plunder and fighting. The homes of the chieftains filled with booty from abroad were special objects of attack. Neighbors became enemies and clan wars started. For two generations the western shore region especially was a "seething witches' cauldron of tense development and ever shifting strife." There was need not only of land defense, but of means to meet attacks from the sea. As a result some small coastal states organized the first systematic coast defense, the *leidang.* The state was divided into districts, each to furnish one ship, while subdivisions were obliged to provide one man with definitely described equipment. This early military system, though as yet neither fully developed nor uniform, came to be of great significance later and was one of the institutions which were to be of value in building a united kingdom.

The problems of the age, however, were not met by organization for defense only. As war and trade were breaking down local isolation, the need of larger units of legal jurisdiction was felt so strongly that groups of shires (*fylkir*) were organized into a *lagthing* with a central *thing*. The word *lag* is used to designate either the law or the district to which the law applied. The origin is obscure, but there were three *lagthings*, one in each of the important sections of Norway, formed perhaps early in the ninth century. The first to be organized was perhaps the Eidsivathing in the Uplands of eastern Norway which meted out justice to the Eidsiva folk about Mjøsa, Norway's largest lake. Snorri says that the law was formed under King Halfdan the Swart, who ruled in the first half of the ninth century, but it may have been older. In the region surrounding the Trondheim Fjord the eight shires inhabited by Trønder formed Trøndelag, with the Eyrathing meeting every June on the sands near the mouth of the Nid River. Every able-bodied man was expected to attend.

The Gulathing with the Gulathinglag has taken its name from the meeting place on the west coast, on the boundary between the three shires—Sogn, Hordaland, and the Fjords—which first united under a common law. It must have been organized some time before 930, when it furnished the model for the law of Iceland. Probably the farmers came together, having with them lawmen who could repeat the old laws from memory. As the assembly listened to the reciting of the local laws the crowd expressed its will by clash of arms, thus selecting what was to be the law for all. Then a *lagret*, or lawcourt, was elected to prepare recommendations for the *thing*, which, however, retained the power to make the final decision.

Though the chieftains—jarls and local kings—may have had some influence on the *lagthings*, they were essentially of, for, and by the people. "We are forbidden to commit any sort of evil deed" is a characteristic beginning of a law. These *things* were lawmaking bodies, but more important were the duties of keeping alive the knowledge of the old legal principles and of acting as courts of law. They were the most striking manifestations both of the respect for law and the insistence upon their rights which from early times were characteristic of the Norwegians.

Though the organization of *lagthings* was a great step forward in forming larger political units, union of the whole country could come only through a forceful chief.

In the midst of ferment and disruption can be detected certain tendencies indicative of the unification which was to be consummated in the following century. Although it is hardly possible to speak of a national sentiment among Norwegians of the ninth century, there was manifest a feeling that the territory which was later comprised within the boundaries of the kingdom of Norway was one country. The earliest description of Norway which we have is Ottar's brief account given to Alfred the Great, at the very time when Harald Fairhair was struggling to make a political unity out of the long narrow land which Ottar measured in days' journeys.

The sense of kinship among all Norwegians was developing in the Viking Age, but it was not strong enough to save the people from attacks and raids even by their own countrymen, and traders especially suffered as they carried their goods along the coast to foreign markets. The people needed, and in some cases would welcome, a power strong enough to protect their farms and their trade. On the other hand, jarls and petty kings were winning strength and wealth and often resisted the development of any power stronger than their own.

Among the many local rulers in the land, two families stand out. In the North, in Haalogaland, a family of jarls had been building up their power over the surrounding land and extending their sway southward into Trøndelag. They hailed from the neighborhood of Tromsø close to the northern limit of Norwegian settlements, but in the ninth century they made their home at Selve, at the mouth of the Trondheim Fjord. Strong as the Haalogaland jarls were, however, unification was coming from another source.

By the ninth century Vestfold, which was a sizable kingdom, had come under the rule of the Yngling family. In the *Ynglinga Saga*, which constitutes the first part of *Heimskringla*, Snorri Sturlason has related the story of the early kings. Much that is mythical has been introduced into the story, but Snorri is perhaps right in tracing the family back to the Swedish rulers at Uppsala, the oldest and most distinguished dynasty in the North. When the last Swedish ruler of the house was killed, his son fled north to Vermland, cleared land there, and married the daughter of a petty Norwegian king in Solør, just across the border. A son of this marriage, Halfdan Whitebone, was brought up in Solør and became king there. He conquered much of the Eastlands and the regions farther south, and is the first king of Vestfold whose name we know. His son married Asa of the Oseberg ship, who killed her husband and ruled in the name of her son, Halfdan the Swart, during his childhood. Halfdan was the father of Harald Fairhair. But more complete than any saga is the history revealed in the grave mounds at Oseberg, Gokstad, and Borre, which picture a rich civilization worthy of the kings whose descendants were to unite Norway.

These kings controlled a large part of the Uplands and much of the Vik, the region about the Folden Fjord, or the Oslo Fjord as it is called today. They combined the position of inland and sea kings. Vestfold furnished the chief access to the sea and became the home and burial place of the kings. It was a rising power at the same time that Norwegian chiefs were conquering land in Scotland and Ireland, and its people took active part in viking activities extending far and wide in foreign lands.

There were ups and downs in the history of the early Vestfold kings, with conflicts whenever a new reign began. In some measure they were under the Danish kings who were exercising control over the lands all around the Straits and the Skager-Rak, but it is impossible to ascertain the extent of this dependence—the sagas are silent about this phase of early history, which does not add to the glory of the Norwegians. Certain it is, however, that even into the eleventh century, Danish claims to lands in Norway were a disturbing factor. Nevertheless, the Yngling dynasty built up a kingdom of considerable size and power, and rulers like Asa and Halfdan the Swart had ambitions far beyond their own realm. It was a strong state and large aims to which Harald Fairhair fell heir.

¶ There is an old tradition that Queen Ragnhild, the wife of Halfdan the Swart, dreamed one night that as she stood in her garden she pulled a thorn out of her dress. She held it in her hand, and it grew and became a large tree. It struck root in the soil and lifted its branches high toward heaven. At the foot, the tree was blood red; farther up, the trunk was a shining green, and the crown was snowy white.[3] Ragnhild became the mother of Harald Fairhair.

Harald has always loomed so large in the history of Norway that stories began to be told about him even in his lifetime and legends have

[3] Similar stories are told among other peoples, notably about the mother of Cyrus, the founder of the Persian Empire.

so encircled his name that it is difficult to ascertain the exact truth, but all that is told of him bears witness to his ambition, his energy, and his power, and emphasizes his youthfulness. He became king at a very early age—when he was ten, the sagas say.

There is no way of telling whether at the beginning of his career he had conceived the idea of bringing all Norway under his sway, or whether the plan grew upon him gradually as he advanced step by step. The conception of Norway as one country existed in his time, and the example of the Swedish and Danish kings, who were uniting their countries, no doubt had a potent influence on Harald. Norwegians, too, among them the far-famed Olaf the White, were ruling large kingdoms in the West, and conquest was in the air. Moreover, most of Norway's warriors were too busy in other lands to oppose Harald's plans.

The somewhat confused story of the conquest can be summarized very briefly. As Gorm, the Danish king, had just completed the unification of Denmark and was pressing his claim to Vestfold, Harald had to move northward to find an outlet for his ambitions. The saga tells that after the death of Harald's father, Halfdan the Swart, the Uplands were in revolt and so the young king's first task was to reconquer this region. He then crossed the Dovre Mountain into Trøndelag. There Haakon, the jarl of the great Haalogaland family, met Harald with an army, but, it seems, the two came to an agreement without a serious conflict. Haakon was allowed to establish himself at Lade, near the present city of Trondheim, and to control the eight shires of Trøndelag in return for recognizing in some way the overlordship of Harald. So the line of jarls who were to be the most serious rivals of the Yngling family and the chief obstacle to the unification of Norway, became more strongly entrenched than before and came to be known as the Jarls of Lade.

After acquiring the necessary naval forces Harald proceeded to the conquest of the Westland, the subjection of which was to the interest of Jarl Haakon as well. First the coastal region directly south of Trøndelag was subdued and the mighty jarl, Ragnvald of Møre, became the king's ally and friend. Then Harald turned to the southwestern districts of Hordaland and the coast still farther south. This was the area of the most violent viking activities, and vikings came even from the western settlements to fight Harald. The struggle culminated in the Battle of Hafrsfjord. This is the only battle of Harald's about which we really know the details. It has been immortalized in a poem by the skald Thorbjørn Hornklovi. Ships came from afar, he says, and:

They carried a host of warriors,
With white shields
And spears from the Westlands
And Welsh wrought swords.
The berserks were roaring
(For this was their battle),
The wolf-coated warriors howling,
And the irons clattering.

In this poem Harald was first hailed as king of all Norwegians. As the date for this decisive battle, 872 has generally been accepted, but later study of the chronology has led some historians to conclude that probably it was not fought much before 900.

Harald lived to be very old, eighty years the sagas say, and ruled with a strong hand for many years after Hafrsfjord. With him the Yngling family moved its residence from Vestfold to Rogaland in the Southwest. The rich court life with which Harald surrounded himself had its center at the royal residence at Avaldsnes. This section, which he had fought hardest to conquer, he kept under his own personal rule. The rest of the country he controlled through the strongest chieftains in the land, who kept their position and wealth in peace as long as they recognized the overlordship of Harald and gave him the military support and financial aid he demanded. So Norway was a conglomeration of small states held together only by the king's army and personal power. Besides jarls Haakon and Ragnvald, petty kings continued to do pretty much as they pleased in eastern Norway for another century. The old local laws and *things* were left undisturbed and were used by the king when it was to his advantage. Though he did little to establish any systematic new government, he furthered the development of *lagthings*, especially of the Gulathing in the district which he controlled personally.

Riches were as dear to the king as power. He captured much viking wealth, confiscated farms, and fined heavily those who opposed him. It is not strictly correct when the sagas say that he destroyed the odal right of the freeholders, but his financial demands, which constituted a somewhat irregular form of taxation, were new to the Norwegians and seemed to them to interfere with their property rights. Another lucrative source of income was the control over the trade along the whole coastal fairway of Norway as well as with foreign lands. The income from the Finmark trade, especially in furs, became an important asset to the king and he took toll on goods brought into the country for sale. While this is mentioned in connection with the Icelandic traders only, it doubtless affected others as well. To collect a "gift" from traders was an old right which Harald took over with many of the estates he confiscated.

Harald's foreign relations indicate that he was a ruler of considerable prestige. As his queen he took the Danish princess Ragnhild, scorning, the skalds say, women of lower birth, and thus establishing his equality with the Danish king. However, Danish claims in Norway were not surrendered. Harald maintained friendly relations with Iceland and he enjoyed a certain prestige there, although he had no political authority on the island, and Icelanders could keep their rights as citizens in Norway. Harald made a military expedition to the Western Islands, mainly to put an end to viking raids on Norway, but politically the venture had no lasting results. He made a treaty with King Aethelstan of England, promising to withdraw any support from vikings in Northumbria. To strengthen the friendship he sent his youngest son to be educated at the English court, and in token of the friendship he gave Aethelstan "a ship with a golden beak and a purple sail, furnished within with a compacted fence of gilded shields."[4]

Harald was the greatest of the warrior chiefs who fought their way to power and wealth in ninth century Norway. He was the first who could in any degree claim to be the king of the whole country and the only such king who was wholly heathen. At his court the old viking civilization of the ninth century reached its climax. He gathered about him a large band of warriors, called the *hird*, and young men eagerly flocked to the service of "the wise dispenser of gold." The king's men, say the skalds, were known by their gold, and "the warriors who cast dice in the king's court" had splendid weapons and lived lavishly. Skalds won royal favor and costly gifts by poems written as eulogies of their master, the two most noted among them being Thjodolv of Hvin and Thorbjørn Hornklovi.

Except for some difficulties with his nine sons during his last years, Harald kept a firm hand on his domain and ruled successfully. While his death brought to a close the last and greatest era of the old civiliza-

[4] William of Malmesbury, the only English chronicler who mentions the friendship of the two kings.

tion in Norway, his career also marks the beginning of a new era, for his idea of a united Norway was never to die. The exact place of his burial is not known, but probably his body rests in one of the great Karmøy mounds which are constructed after the manner of his ancestors in Vestfold.

CHAPTER 5

FORMATION OF A NATIONAL CHRISTIAN STATE

HARALD FAIRHAIR had left as a heritage to the Norwegians the idea of a united country. He had won his kingdom by force of arms and maintained his position by his prowess. Thereby he had, according to generally accepted usage, established his right to rule, and this prerogative was the legal inheritance of his sons. Fundamental, too, in the early Norwegian sense of justice was the duty of every man, be he king or yeoman, to risk his all to win and retain the property and position which lawfully belonged to his family. And so in the struggle for what they considered their rights the men of Harald's blood fulfilled the mission of keeping alive the idea of a united Norway, as one by one they fought and fell to win what they thought legally theirs. This struggle filled the century following the death of Harald, until 1030 when the idea of unity won a signal victory with the death of Saint Olaf.

At the same time another conflict was taking place which led to the establishment of Christianity. Up to the tenth century Norway had experienced an unbroken development, and foreign cultures had never exerted any dominating influence on this indigenous civilization. Christianity was the one great force from without which in the tenth century was becoming an integral part of Norwegian life. All the men of Harald's house who in these years fought for the crown of Norway had spent many years of their youth abroad where they became acquainted with Christianity, and all but Eirik came from across the sea to win their kingdom. By 1030 Christianity had won its duel with the old religion, and, though the country had by no means become thoroughly Christian, any return to the old faith was out of the question. Norway had joined the ranks of Christian countries.

Events within Norway were, of course, less known and of less interest to the outside world than were the adventures of Norwegians in other lands, and references to them by foreign chroniclers and historians are very few. Moreover, as the writing of history, or any writing beyond brief runic inscriptions, had not yet begun in the North, the contemporary material from this age is very meager. But skaldic poems were composed and stories were told and retold and by this means events lived in the memory of the people until they were written down in the sagas and histories in the twelfth and thirteenth centuries. As it is often referred to in these pages, mention must be made of the greatest of them all, *Heimskringla, the Sagas of the Norwegian Kings*, by the renowned Icelandic historian Snorri Sturlason (1178-1241). It is a continuous history of Norway to 1177, the like of which few if any other countries possess. Written in the terse but vivid style of the sagas, it is constructed with consummate skill, the story reaching its climax in the *Saga of Saint Olaf*. Snorri was a careful, critical historian who weighed his sources. He cannot vouch for all the events and details in his writing, he says, but they have been believed by wise and discerning men. Critical scholarship has found that there are many details in *Heimskringla* which are not reliable and, what is more important, that Snorri, like so many historians of all ages, wrote from the point of view of his own times and that this influenced his interpretation of events and the motives back of them. Nevertheless, *Heimskringla* is not only a work of signal literary greatness, but our most important source for the history of Norway in the period it covers, particularly for the events centering upon the kings.

¶ As in other countries, notably the Carolingian Empire, the kingdom was looked upon as personal property, and all the sons of a king claimed equal rights to it and to all royal prerogatives. Harald had recognized this by distributing his wealth among his sons and establishing several of them as petty, subordinate kings in eastern Norway, while to maintain unity he made Eirik his successor and king over the whole country. Although not the oldest son, Eirik was given preference because of his royal mother, Ragnhild, the daughter of the king of Denmark. His half brothers had been brought up in different sections of the land, generally in the home community of their mother, and naturally identified themselves with the feeling of local independence which was as yet stronger than any loyalty to a united Norway. They were therefore unwilling to recognize Eirik's overlordship. Even in Harald's lifetime conflicts broke out, and Eirik's reign of two years was spent in continual fighting. Eirik, who had been a viking for eight years and had harried far and wide, was a mighty warrior and determined to maintain his father's kingdom by force. His contemporaries gave him the nickname "Blood-Axe," and later attempts to whitewash his name by blaming his misdeeds on his queen, the Danish princess Gunhild, have no historical foundation. Although he killed several of his brothers, he was not able to exert any control beyond his own special realm in the Southwest.

While Eirik was fighting his other brothers, the youngest of them, Haakon, was safe. He was growing up in England, probably spending most of his time in the old royal city of Winchester as the foster son of King Aethelstan. Snorri says Aethelstan "had Haakon christened and taught him the right faith and good habits and all kinds of learning and manners. He loved him much, more than he did all his own kin, and so did everyone who knew the boy. He was later called Aethelstan's foster son. He was the greatest in sports, bigger and stronger and more handsome than any other. He was wise, of fair speech, and a good Christian." He was the only Norwegian king of this period who was brought up in a thoroughly Christian environment, where he had also become acquainted with the English form of government and the laws of Alfred the Great. But of his own country he knew very little, and when he returned to claim his heritage he brought with him no memory of the old laws or the Asa worship of his ancestral land.

When Haakon was fifteen, Snorri relates, some Norwegians came to England, told him of the dissatisfaction with Eirik, and no doubt invited him to Norway. Sigurd, Jarl of Lade, the most prominent man among Eirik's opponents, probably originated the plan of getting Haakon to claim the throne, both because he had an affection for the boy and because he thought it a good plan for himself personally and for the country. Haakon accepted the invitation and went directly to Trøndelag to Jarl Sigurd. Eirik could offer no resistance and left the country to seek his fortune in Northumbria.

Haakon's purpose was to win recognition, not by arms but by conciliation and compromise, and if Sigurd first formed the policy, the young king's training and temperament made him ready to fall in with the plan. He conciliated the yeomen by calling them together to meetings of the traditional *things* and asking them to accept him as king. In return he promised to respect the old laws and to lighten the demands made upon them by his father and brother. He refrained from collecting an obnoxious tax on land which, the people felt, interfered with their old property rights. He retained the friendship of

Sigurd and recognized the undiminished authority of the jarl in his large territory. In fact, Sigurd's power grew, for the jarls of Møre disappeared from history at about this time and the northern part of their territory fell to the Jarl of Lade. In the eastern part of the country petty kings, some of them Haakon's own nephews whose fathers had been slain by Eirik, were left in peace on condition that they accept Haakon as overlord. Personally Haakon controlled the southwestern districts that Eirik had held and some of the Møre lands farther north. By diminishing the royal prerogatives that his family had begun to build up Haakon won general recognition as king of the whole country, reigned many years in peace and prosperity, and earned the title "the Good."

When Haakon came to Norway he hoped to establish his own faith in his realm, for, says Snorri, "he was a good Christian." He met with strong opposition and, following the advice of Sigurd, abandoned the whole plan. It was left for a later time to realize Haakon's hope of associating the kingship with the Christianization of the country. Snorri's story of the bold yeoman, Asbjørn of Medalhus, who was the spokesman of the people of Trøndelag in their opposition to the king, illustrates both the tenacity with which the people clung to their old traditions and the stubborn courage with which they time and again successfully resisted the will of the king.

There was probably a growing infiltration of Christianity into the country in Haakon's time. As the warlike activities of the vikings had abated, peaceful contact with Christian countries, notably England, increased. The king's own life indicates that even when he joined in heathen sacrifices he did not desert the ethics of the faith of his youth; and when later rulers took up missionary work in earnest, the ground had to some extent been prepared, though we lack any tangible evidence of Christian influence. On the other hand, there is ample proof that the old faith still had a firm grip on the people. Skaldic poetry of the old heathen type, shot through with religious allusions and metaphors, was flourishing as never before. The skalds still looked upon their art as a gift from Odin, and their references to the gods seem no mere conventional usage but expressions of firm, warm conviction.

Egil Skallagrimsson, the most renowned of the heathen skalds, lived at this time. His father, Skallagrim, had migrated to Iceland in bitter enmity to Harald Fairhair. After avenging a brother whom Harald had slain, Egil made his home in Iceland and died there at a very old age. But his poetry tells little of Iceland. He was a great wanderer. We meet him fighting and making poems in England, and he visited Norway four times. Egil was a poet with a keen mind, rich imagination, and passionate feelings. Most noted, perhaps, is his poem written to express his grief over the death of his favorite son, "my son, the son of my wife." He must have felt that a new, softer age was coming. Faithfulness was rare, he thought, in an age when people "sell the body of their brother for rings," that is, accept a bot in the place of blood revenge.

Though Haakon's policy in a way weakened royal power, his name is associated with two developments which were to further the unification of the country, the *leidang* and the *lagthing*.

The sagas speak of Haakon as the organizer of the *lagthing*. Although the beginnings in reality go farther back, the name of Haakon is definitely associated with the further development of at least the Gulathing. New regions were added to the district until it comprised all the Westland. As the territory increased, it was necessary to change the *thing* from a primary to a representative body, and this in all probability took place in the reign of Haakon. The shires were definitely organized as subdivisions of the *lag*, each having its own *thing* and sending representatives to the larger meeting. Nothing shows more clearly how much the people valued it than their willingness to assume this burden. Four hundred men were sent to the Gulathing every year and they had to be fitted out with food and ships for the journey.

Although the Eyrathing continued to function in Trøndelag, a new *lag* was now formed, including in addition to the eight Trøndelag shires, more territory to the south. It was called Frostathinglag from Frosta, the place of meeting. The old Eidsivalag in the East continued without any change; and when the Borgarthing in the South was organized at the time of Saint Olaf, the arrangement prevailing in the later Middle Ages was completed.

The king was ready to aid and abet the maintenance and strengthening of the *lagthings*, for through them he could get all his agreements with the people legally accepted, and one by one the fundamental laws upon which the Norwegian state was built were established.

The first arrangement for national defense belongs definitely to the reign of Haakon. In the larger new state the king needed more military authority than had been held by the local kings of old, and emphasis had to be placed on coastal defense, as there was practically no danger of any land attack. Haakon therefore made use of the earlier local *leidang* as the basis for the defense system. In parts of the Vik region and along the southeastern coast he could employ the earlier arrangements made by the Danish kings, but in the Gulathinglag the *leidang* was established through detailed agreement between king and people. There was a series of compromises, as the king tried to get as many men and as large ships as he could, while the thingmen held back. Yet king and people had a common interest in defense, and the king obtained more than did the rulers in the other Scandinavian countries. In the Frostathinglag the system was somewhat different but it too may well have been organized under Haakon. Imperfect as it was, the *leidang* fleet successfully defended the country from the Danish attack.

Haakon knew that he would need his fleet. Danger from abroad was hanging over him because of the old Danish claims to Norwegian land. When Eirik Blood-Axe fell in England in 954, his sons made an unsuccessful attempt to win Norway. Gunhild and her sons took refuge with her brother, the king of Denmark, who not only provided richly for his sister, but gladly backed up the claims of his nephews to the throne of Norway. Knowing that the conflict was unavoidable, Haakon took the offensive. He won in battle, raided the Danish coast, and captured much booty, but the victory was not decisive. When the Danish fleet later attacked, the *leidang* did good service and won the battle, but the king was mortally wounded.

Shields and hard skulls
Were both cleft
By the hardy blows
Of the Norsemen's lord,

says Haakon's skald, Eyvind Skaldaspiller, expressing not only love and admiration for the king, but a bit of national pride in the king of Norway, "slayer of Danes." The king, says Eyvind, was welcomed to Valhall, for he "had guarded well the temples"; and he adds,

Unbound
Against all the world
The wolf Fenri will go,
Till in his destroying tracks
Kings of equal worth
Are found.

When Haakon died, the Gunhild-Sons, as they were generally called, had no rival claimants to the throne. There were five of them, but Harald Graypelt was practically sole king, ruling with the advice of his mother, who, in spite of her bad reputation, seems to have had qualities of statesmanship. Departing from Haakon's policy of conciliation, Harald was determined to rule by force as his father and grandfather had done. He increased his resources by robbing the temples, by making an expedition to Bjarmeland, winning wealth from the northern trade and capturing much booty, and by laying heavy fines on Haakon's supporters. He killed the men whom he feared most—his cousin, King Tryggve, and Sigurd, Jarl of Lade, the latter by treacherously setting fire to the house in which Sigurd and his men were gathered. Harald was not popular. His rule was oppressive, and when hunger stalked the land he was blamed even for the poor harvests. He must, however, have been a man of energy and ability. To him belongs the credit of being the first king who established Christian missions in Norway, but little is known about this phase of his rule.

The ambitions of the Danish king both helped Harald to win his throne and caused his fall. In his desire to become a really independent ruler of all Norway, Harald assumed control over the Vik region, the section which the Danish king claimed as his. So the Dane plotted with Haakon, the exiled son of the murdered Jarl Sigurd, and Harald Graypelt was killed in an ambush laid by Haakon with the connivance of the Danish king.

¶ For about twenty-five years no descendant of Harald Fairhair ruled in Norway. When Harald Graypelt had been killed, the Danish king, Harald Bluetooth, accompanied Jarl Haakon to Norway with a powerful fleet and took possession of the country without meeting any resistance. Old Queen Gunhild with her two remaining sons took refuge with her daughter, who was married to the jarl of the Orkneys. A foreign ruler tried to usurp the rights of the family of Harald Fairhair; the work for the unification seemed undone. Harald Bluetooth kept for himself eastern Norway, the Uplands, and the Vik as far as Lindesnes, ruling through Norwegian local chiefs and kings. There was no national resentment against foreign rule, in fact a king who was far away was sometimes preferred because he interfered less with local independence.

The Westland was to be ruled by Haakon as the jarl of the Danish king. For the first time that old title was used, as it often was later, to designate a relationship that resembled vassalage, Haakon owing certain financial obligations as well as military aid to the king. In the land that had belonged to his family Haakon was independent of any outside authority. The Danish king soon found that the jarl was not as subservient as he had hoped. The king had expected Christianity to advance in the whole country, as it continued to do in the eastern section, but Haakon was aggressively heathen both from conviction and from policy. The old faith still had a strong hold on the people, not least in Trøndelag. The skalds praised Haakon for the speed with which he made the groves of Thor once more into real sanctuaries and "let joyous men frequent the sacred ground of the gods." Surely the god of war himself must dwell in a chief who could defeat even a king; and as the old gods returned to their sanctuaries after the fall of Harald Graypelt, the soil gave fruit, there was fish aplenty and good times came once more.

The jarl was too ambitious and independent to satisfy the Danish king, and a break came between the two. Harald Bluetooth died, but under his son Svein Forkbeard, who claimed to be the king of all Norway, a large Danish fleet was sent against Haakon, and with it were the fiercest warriors of the day, the vikings from Jom, a fort on the southern shore of the Baltic. With the *leidang* fleet Haakon won a decisive victory at Hjørungavaag, defeating the Danish attempt to assert authority in western Norway. Wild and heroic stories were told about this great battle, and in them Haakon was honored as the hero in a great fight against foreign rule. The beginning of a national feeling can be detected in western Norway. But success made Haakon arrogant, the people of Trøndelag rose against him, and he was slain by his own men.

Jarl Haakon represented an age that was passing. He was the last chieftain to be an independent ruler without even claiming royal blood; and though he led a purposeful, almost fanatic reaction against Christianity, he was the last genuine heathen to rule in Norway.

¶ The history of the last thirty-five years of the Viking Age (995-1030) is dominated by the names of the first two kings of Norway to bear the name of Olaf. There are several similarities between the two: both went out as vikings in their youth as a matter of course, just as young men of today go to college, and both had notable careers during that revival of viking activities which came late in the tenth century. They were both of the family of Harald Fairhair, and both came from beyond the sea to claim their kingdom. Moreover, both had in their travels become acquainted with the religion of the White Christ; each in his own way embraced the new faith with all the ardor of a strong nature, and each according to his own lights became a missionary.

And so the two great movements, toward a united national kingdom and toward the establishment of Christianity, became definitely connected. It seems that the second Olaf, at least, was conscious that the two developments were inextricably intertwined and would fail or succeed together. The comparison might be carried even farther. Both the Olafs were for a time successful, but finally lost their lives in the struggle for a united Christian Norway. Furthermore, they soon took their place as the most striking heroes in the annals of Norway, and about their names grew up a mass of story and legend that often baffles the historian. In spite of similarities, however, the two are strikingly different in their character, their careers, and their influence.

¶ The first Olaf was the son of that Tryggve who was killed by Harald Graypelt. Tryggve was a grandson of Harald Fairhair and a local king in the Vik region near Folden Fjord. He was killed a little before Olaf's birth. Olaf's mother, Astrid, fled with her child to the viking kingdom of Gardarike, where, it seems, Olaf's childhood was spent. At the age of twelve he began his career as a viking with a ship fitted out in Russia. According to the sagas, his course took him to almost every shore from the Baltic to the Isle of Man and Ireland. Certain it is that in 991 he joined in the viking attacks on England which had been renewed with the succession of the boy king Aethelred the Redeless in 980. Olaf was already so famous that he could collect a fleet of 390 ships for his attack on England. After ravaging the land about the Thames, he inflicted such a smashing defeat on the English that they bought peace with a Danegeld of 10,000 pounds of silver. The peace, as was often the case when the enemy had been bought off, was only a truce, and before long Olaf was harrying and burning cities in Northumbria. Then he joined Svein Forkbeard of Denmark in an attack on London. Though the invaders were repulsed with terrific losses, they still ruled the sea and harassed the shores so badly that the English again bought peace, this time with the payment of 16,000 pounds of silver. To seal the peace, Olaf, who, the sagas say, had earlier received baptism on the Scilly Islands, was now confirmed by the Bishop of Winchester with the English king as sponsor.

Olaf, who had doubtless obtained for himself a large share of the Danegeld, was now rich in gold and silver and probably the most renowned viking of his age. Then word reached him that the people of Trøndelag were rising against Jarl Haakon. Perhaps the men who brought the news invited Olaf to come to Norway; at any rate, he thought the time was opportune and promptly set out to win the kingdom. He had good wind, the saga says, wherever he sailed.

Olaf landed at Moster a little south of Bergen, where he later built the first church in Norway. Thence he sailed north and entered the Trondheim Fjord about the time that Jarl Haakon was murdered by his own people. At the Eyrathing, Olaf was acclaimed king, and Haakon's sons Eirik and Svein fled to England. This is the first time the Eyrathing is mentioned in connection with the recognition of a king. Olaf then turned to the South, where his father had reigned and where his mother was still living, and there he was readily accepted as king. On the western coast he won recognition largely through the support of the powerful chieftain Erling Skjalgson of Sola, who was allowed to retain control over a large number of shires and was married to the king's sister. In the North, Olaf won Haalogaland by force. Thus Olaf gained control over practically the whole coast of Norway, and even the Western Islands to some extent acknowledged his overlordship, but the interior of Norway he never even saw. Furthermore, he was vouchsafed neither time nor opportunity to build up any system of administration that could give his rule permanence and stability. He was in reality a viking sea king—although the most powerful who had yet appeared—whose rule depended on his own personality and presence.

Olaf won great admiration from his own age. He was handsome, skilled above all others in the feats of arms and sports, and Snorri relates many of his deeds. He could play with three swords so that one was always in the air. Brave and quick-witted he was, too, and overflowing with cheer and generous friendliness. But he had an unbending will, was relentlessly harsh in the face of opposition and cruel to his enemies. An ideal viking, he was loved and worshiped by his followers.

It was natural that Olaf should make the Christianization of Norway as much a part of his policy as the political conquest. On his travels he had seen the importance of the church in other countries, in Poland, Denmark, England, and Russia, and he had no doubt been impressed with the art and pageantry connected with Christian worship in places like Kiev, "the city of churches." When he embraced Christianity he certainly gave to the White Christ the complete loyalty that would accord with his intense, untutored nature. There are, however, indications that he clung to some of his old superstitions, and we find no evidence at all that the new faith meant any break with his former life, any inner struggle, or any conflict between ideals. Certain it is that he was filled with a passionate zeal to force Christianity upon his people and that this contributed to his downfall.

He brought several priests with him to Norway, most of them having English training. In his home district he made it clear that acceptance of him as king meant the adoption of his faith, and he met no opposition, for the contact with Christian countries had through many years been very close and earlier missionaries had done preparatory work. A large stretch of western Norway was officially Christianized without violence, through the action of the Gulathing and through the mass baptisms celebrated in the different communities when the leaders came home from the *thing*. In northern Norway, both in Trøndelag and Haalogaland, Olaf met stubborn opposition, which he tried to crush with force, torture, and the destruction of the old sanctuaries. Olaf's influence reached far beyond Norway. When prominent men from the islands visited him, he contrived to detain them until they could be persuaded to accept baptism and to carry Christianity home with them. Thus Olaf was instrumental in introducing the new faith into the Shetland Islands, the Faroes, Iceland, and finally, using Leif the Lucky of Vinland fame as his ambassador, into Greenland.[1]

Though Olaf's work was not without results, it could not achieve any complete or thorough Christianization. As with the government, no institutions were developed and no church organized, but all depended on the personal influence of the king. The establishment of the shrine of Saint Sunniva at Selje can be definitely attributed to Olaf. A strange luminous effect, it is said, led to the discovery of some remains which were believed to be the bones of an Irish princess Sunniva who with her maidens had taken to the sea to escape from a forced marriage to a heathen. Though the story is apocryphal, Saint Sunniva became the most important saint in western Norway and her shrine one of the most remarkable in the land.

As Trøndelag caused him most difficulty, Olaf spent the greater part of the time there. He built a residence at the mouth of the Nid River and attracted to this place the trade which had earlier gone to Lade, thus making a small beginning of what was to become the city of Nidaros, now Trondheim. Because he tried to force his faith on them, the Trønders never loved Olaf; and by centering his efforts upon

[1] *Njal's Saga* contains the story of how the *althing* made Christianity the official religion, but allowed freedom of private worship. The Orkneys and Hebrides had been largely Christianized earlier.

Trøndelag he lost his hold on the rest of the country and when he needed them most the people failed him.

Olaf might, however, have coped with his problems in Norway had it not been for his viking propensities and his enemies abroad. The ambition of the Danish king to control at least a part of southern Norway had not subsided. As Olaf recognized no Danish claims to overlordship, and King Svein of Denmark had large imperialistic ambitions, it was natural that a clash should come. Eirik and Svein, the sons of Jarl Haakon, supported the Danes and persuaded the Swedish king also to join the alliance. He was probably interested in pushing his power toward the sea in the west. This would mean the occupation of the Ranrike region, then Norwegian but today a part of Sweden.

Olaf prepared for the coming fray by building large ships, among them his famous flagship, the *Long Serpent*, the like of which had never been seen in Norwegian waters. He made an alliance with Boleslav, the Polish king, ruler also over the Wends, a powerful Slavic tribe in northern Germany which for years menaced Denmark. Finally Olaf decided to take the offensive and called out the Norwegian *leidang*, but it did not respond. Olaf waited in vain and then, accompanied only by a few ships from the Vik, set sail to join his Slav ally as had been agreed. Boleslav, too, failed to keep his word, and, surrounded at Svold by the superior forces of his enemies, Olaf faced inevitable defeat and death. The Battle of Svold, the most notable battle in the history of Norway since Hafrsfjord, was fought in the year 1000, the first date in Norwegian history which is generally accepted. It is a stirring story, teeming with dramatic incidents, that tells about this first recorded battle in which forces from the three Scandinavian peoples met in combat. After an heroic fight against impossible odds, Olaf and the men who remained with him on the *Long Serpent* leaped into the water, and when about to be captured by his enemies, the king covered himself with his shield and sank. Soon the story went that Olaf had swum to safety and joined his mother's men on a Wendish boat. "But," Snorri adds, "however that may be, he never returned to his kingdom in Norway." His reign had lasted but five brief years, but nothing is more convincing proof that this impetuous young viking possessed traits of real greatness than the exalted place as an ideal national hero that he came to occupy in the hearts and imaginations of his countrymen. He had revived the memory of Harald Fairhair, and one more step had been taken toward the consummation of a united Christian Norway.

During the first fifteen years after Svold, however, it looked as if all efforts to unite Norway had come to naught. The Danish king Svein controlled the Vik, as his predecessors had done off and on in the past. His main efforts, however, were centered upon the conquest of England, where he succeeded in being recognized as king a few weeks before his death in 1014. The only indication that he had any influence in Norway beyond the Vik is that the two jarls of Lade, Eirik and Svein, accorded him a vague personal allegiance. They had returned to their parental estates and were the recognized leaders in Trøndelag. Though they had accepted Christianity, they interfered with no person's religion. Beyond Trøndelag they made no effort to exercise any power which might encroach upon the independence of other chieftains. For the last time the local chiefs, very few of whom bore the title of king, were their own masters, subservient to no higher authority.

¶ Another Olaf, who was six years old at the time of the Battle of Svold and was no doubt stirred by the accounts of that far-famed action, was destined both to make the new faith the religion of the land and to assure the success of plans for a united Norway. Olaf Haraldsson was the son of Harald Grenske, a descendant of Harald Fairhair and king in Vestfold under Danish suzerainty. His mother, Aasta, was the daughter of a prominent man in the Uplands, perhaps in Gudbrandsdal. Harald died early and Aasta then married a local king, Sigurd Syr, who became Olaf's foster father. At an early age Olaf went out as a viking, ravaging the shores of the Baltic, Jutland, and Frisia. Snorri has Olaf tell his men about these adventures in later years when Christian principles were influential in his life. Often, Olaf says, he and his men had nothing but what they took, and many a time they spilt innocent blood and risked their lives and souls for loot. He spent several years in England, most of the time in the service of the English king fighting the Danes. He won wealth, military experience, and acquaintance with the European systems of government. Although he was probably baptized and confirmed in Rouen, most of the Christian influence on him too came from England. When Svein, the victor at Svold, won the upper hand in England, Olaf found it safer to transfer his activities first to Spain and then to France. But the opportunities for a successful viking career were not what they used to be. The age of wars between states had begun, and Olaf won most of his wealth and renown in the service of a king. He was the last great viking chief.

As his chances for the life of a viking were closing, greater opportunities opened for Olaf. Svein died soon after his conquest of England, the English rose once more against Danish rule, and Svein's famous son Canute fitted out a powerful military force by means of which he established his rule in England. Not a few Norwegians joined Canute's expedition, among them Eirik, Jarl of Lade. Olaf could have found no more auspicious time to lay claim to the kingdom of Norway. Canute was busy in England and with him was Norway's mightiest jarl. When Olaf conceived the idea of conquering Norway or how far his vision reached we have no way of knowing. He must have been fully conscious of his royal ancestry and of his rights to the throne according to the law and usage of the age, and he certainly had made enough observations to see the possibilities of building a united Norwegian kingdom.

As we read of how he and his one hundred and twenty followers set out for Norway, not in warships but in two merchant vessels, we sense at once that the Viking Age was passing and that the new claimant to the throne expected to win by the help of forces raised within the country itself. He no doubt intended to sail directly to the Vik, but storms carried his ships west and north so that he first sighted land at Selje. Through a lucky coup Olaf captured Haakon, the son of Jarl Eirik, whose ship happened to lie in the fjord, and gave him his liberty on condition that he leave Norway and never fight against Olaf. Encouraged by this success, he tried a surprise attack on Trøndelag, but had to retreat before the forces of Jarl Svein and his brother-in-law, the famous hero of the sagas, Einar Tambarskjelve. So he sailed south, and late in the autumn arrived among his kinsfolk in the Uplands.

There Olaf met with astonishing success. Before winter set in he controlled a realm which, an old skaldic poem says, had hitherto been held by five kings. Thus the nucleus of Olaf's kingdom was the interior, which had scarcely been touched by the movement toward unification, and which was slower than any other section in responding to the national feeling that was beginning to stir in the land. Although the interior had been less influenced by the expansion in the Viking Age, the social fabric had changed even there. The chiefs and tribal kings—the title "king" was in more general use than in other sections of Norway—had gained much wealth and were able to exercise an arbitrary power which met with deep resentment from the proud yeomen. Even among the farmers themselves the differences in wealth and distinction had been growing, and the democratic features in the old rural society were on the decline. By winning the support of the yeoman Olaf swept away the petty kings, seemingly with little effort.

His ancestry gave him prestige, the wealth he had acquired abroad was lavishly used to win friends, and he promised freedom from the exactions of the local kings and chiefs.

He won so much support that in the spring he had ships and men enough to challenge his foes. All winter Svein and Einar had been arming for a decisive battle, and early in the spring they set sail for the South. On Pentecost Day in 1016 the two fleets met at Nesjar in Folden Fjord, where Olaf won a decisive victory. Svein fled the country and died soon after without having made any effort to regain his power in Norway. Olaf was now virtually sole ruler in the land, and as he sailed along the shore he was hailed as king in one *thing* after another until he reached the Eyrathing and was acclaimed there also.

In the next twelve years, during which Olaf reigned in peace, he established the first national government Norway had ever had. During his first days in the Uplands he already showed keen insight into conditions in the country and inaugurated the policy which he and the kings for a century after him were to follow consistently. As the opportunity for winning wealth abroad was passing and the power of viking chiefs declining, influence and such wealth as there was—far less than at the height of viking activities—came from the ownership of land. Olaf depended for his chief support upon the leading odal freeholders and their followers, and so allied himself with the new yeoman aristocracy. Among the yeomen he selected men whom he raised into prominence in opposition to the old chiefs, new men whose power rested upon their land and the favor of the king, not upon military prowess and viking adventure. Though this was not democracy, it satisfied the rank and file better than earlier conditions.

The people wanted peace and security. Olaf's skald, Sigvat Thordarson, as well as others praised Olaf because he punished great and small with equal severity. The vikings, says Sigvat, often tried to buy safety "with gifts of red gold," but "our chief had no compassion for the thief." Regardless of rank, criminals were punished with death and mutilation, and thereby Olaf won the support of the people. The different *things* continued to hold the place they had of old, and in fact their position was strengthened through their cooperation with the rising power of the monarch. Most of the law continued to be local until the late Middle Ages. Although tradition for centuries to come persisted in speaking of Norway's old law as "King Olaf's Law," it is impossible to prove that any definite legislation outside of the church laws owed its origin to Olaf. But the idea of law enforcement by a national government certainly grew as a result of his work. The king was under the law, however, and only the freeman assembled in *thing* could make legal decisions or add to the law.

At the same time that Olaf was striving to give the country political organization he was working just as hard to make his kingdom Christian. When or how deeply the new faith gripped him we cannot say with certainty, but there seems to have been in him an earnest intensity that is sometimes characteristic of new converts. He was nicknamed Olaf Digre, the Stout, and was not so romantic a figure as the handsome, impulsive Olaf Tryggvason, but he seems more human. The many incidents told of him showing his faults—sometimes petty ones—and his virtues give the impression of a man in whom a struggle was going on between the old heathen and the new Christian ideals. His Christian personality, according to the old accounts, reached its full stature only in the last years before his death when he was an exile on Gotland and in Gardarike. An incident which according to Snorri occurred in Gardarike illustrates well the submission to rule and discipline which the new faith introduced among the untutored Norwegians: Sitting in deep thought, Olaf began to whittle a stick he held in his hand. "Tomorrow is Monday, my lord," said a lad who was waiting on him. Then Olaf, realizing that it was Sunday, gathered the shavings and let them burn in the hollow of his hand.

As soon as he was able, Olaf began systematic efforts to get Christianity established throughout the land. In southern Norway and in the Westland there was little if any difficulty in establishing the church. In the interior and in the North, however, there was strong opposition from leading men who represented both the old system of society and the vigorous vitality of the old faith in its last struggle with the new. In some cases Olaf used harsh methods to force baptism upon unwilling heathen, but such incidents are the exception rather than the rule. On the whole he met with success. Christianity, which had been at work in the country for a hundred years or so, was quite generally accepted. While remnants of heathenism continued to be found for centuries, Norway may be counted among Christian countries from the time when Saint Olaf had done his work. There was no possibility of a return to the old religion.

Not satisfied with mass baptisms, Olaf began the organization of the church as an institution. In this work he had the help of able and earnest missionaries who had come with him from England and who brought English influences to bear upon the new church. Most notable among them is Bishop Grimkell, probably of Norwegian blood, whose name is coupled with that of the king in the church laws that were enacted. In 1024, Olaf called a large meeting at Moster, the place where Olaf Tryggvason first landed in Norway, to make regulations for the church. This was in reality the birth of the Church of Norway. Olaf's laws formulated at this meeting are the first national legal enactments in Norway, yet they were not really laws before they had been approved by the various *lagthings*, each making some alterations in them. In the laws of the Gulathing the new faith was adopted in this form: "The first commandment in our legislation is that we shall bow toward the east and pray to the Holy Christ for peace and a fruitful harvest and that we may keep our country settled and tilled and that our sovereign lord may have strength and health; may he be our friend and we his friends, and may God be a friend of us all."[2]

The bishops had a good deal of authority over the churches; they appointed the priests and provided for services. The people were to build and maintain the churches, pay the clergy, and keep the holy days upon which the king and bishop had agreed at Moster. The church buildings were important as they furnished something concrete that could help keep up the faith. They were built as places for worship, to the glory of God, not for listening to sermons or getting instruction, of which there was as yet very little. Although the church thus organized might well be called a state church, the king had little power. Olaf saw the need of establishing relations with the Catholic church, and as he was not on friendly terms with King Canute of England, it was natural that he sent Grimkell and others of his clergy to Bremen to receive consecration. The whole North was officially within the archbishopric which Saint Ansgar, the Apostle to the North, established at Hamburg and which later moved to Bremen. The archbishop exercised little authority in Norway, however, and the connection with Rome was very loose. A few missionaries from Germany, called in by Saint Olaf, preached in southern Norway; but the clergy trained in England continued to be most numerous and to exert the greatest influence on the Norwegian church. In both countries the vernacular was used in the church side by side with the Latin. Alike, too, were the two peoples in emphasizing Christ as the heroic conqueror of His enemies; Who when He wanted to set mankind free, "Stripped Himself, God Al-

[2] Laurence M. Larson, *The Earliest Norwegian Laws*, 35, New York, 1935.

mighty, when He wanted to mount the cross, courageously in the sight of all men."[3]

Thanks to the connection with Bremen, we have a remarkably full and dependable account of the beginnings of the Norwegian church. It is found in *Gesta Hamburgensis*, the history of the archbishopric by Adam of Bremen, one of the most reliable and scholarly historians of the time, who wrote in the second half of the eleventh century. He gives a vivid and attractive account of English and German missionaries working side by side.

After twelve years of tireless effort for the organization of the kingdom and the establishment of the church, Olaf's peaceful reign came to an abrupt close. It was foreign war that brought his downfall. Olaf's foreign policy seemed at first to be successful, as the Western Islands gave him at least a nominal recognition. Olaf and the king of Sweden were rivals for the possession of the district east of the Folden Fjord, but after long and difficult negotiations in which Olaf used his faithful skald Sigvat as ambassador, the two made peace and Olaf married the Swedish princess Astrid. The king of Sweden was already at war with Denmark, and the two kings recognized, no doubt, that they had a common enemy in the strongest king in the North, Canute, who ruled both England and Denmark and had ambitions to win an even larger North Sea empire. It was natural that Canute should try to reconquer the land in which his father had exercised authority before the coming of Olaf. It may be partly because he recognized this danger and partly because there was still a good deal of the viking left in Olaf, that he took the initiative both in forming an alliance with the Swedish king and in attacking Denmark. Canute could therefore say that his campaign against Norway was an expedition of vengeance.

Canute made his plan well known in Norway and sent men and money to win support, promising the chieftains that he would give back to them the golden freedom of which Olaf had robbed them. Many of them had remained hostile to the new system and many more fell away, hoping to be on the side of the victor and to gain greater independence under a king who dwelt across the sea. Even among the common people there were many who had resented the imperious way in which a new faith had been thrust upon them. And so when Canute in 1028 approached with a large force, only a small number of the Norwegians flocked to the support of the king, and he could do nothing

[3] A runic inscription on the old Ruthwell Cross possibly derived from the "Dream of the Rood," ascribed to Cynewulf.

but withdraw before the superior force. With a few faithful followers he crossed over the mountains to Gudbrandsdal, then passed through Sweden, and took refuge in Kiev, where Jaroslav ruled as the last of the viking kings of Gardarike. Jaroslav was Olaf's brother-in-law, being married to Astrid's sister Ingegerd. She had first been wooed by Olaf, the sagas say, but had been given to Jaroslav who was considered a better match, although she continued to love Olaf, whom she had never seen. The quiet months spent here gave Olaf opportunity for rich spiritual and emotional experiences at the same time that he was pondering upon the ways and means of returning to his kingdom.

Meanwhile Canute had sailed along the coast of Norway, receiving support everywhere; and when he reached Trøndelag he was acclaimed as king at the Eyrathing. He made Haakon Eiriksson his jarl and then returned to England. This was the Haakon whom Olaf had captured upon his arrival in Norway and set free on condition that he would not fight against the king. The jarl did not long enjoy his return to power, as he died in a shipwreck in 1029. He was the last of the great family of jarls of Lade who off and on for over a century had been the rivals of Harald Fairhair and his family. Canute then sent his son Svein with Svein's mother Aelfgifu to rule Norway. They had barely reached the Vik in southern Norway when Olaf was returning in the North.

The news of Haakon's death had determined Olaf to take up the struggle to regain his kingdom. In the spring of 1030 he left Gardarike and came to Sweden with his small band of faithful followers. A few hundred Norwegians from the Uplands joined him, among them his fifteen-year-old half-brother Harald Sigurdsson. Otherwise he had to gather men as best he could on his march. Some were attracted by promises of reward in the form of the lands of their opponents. It was not an imposing force with which he returned to his kingdom. As he rode over the Kjøl and looked westward he was deep in serious thoughts, Snorri tells. "It came into my mind," he said, "that many a day had I been happy in that land."

On July 29, 1030, Olaf met his enemies at Stiklestad, where rich meadows slope gently down toward the shore near the head of the Trondheim Fjord. Olaf faced an army twice the size of his own. There were gathered farmers who feared the loss of their homes and lands and chieftains who had been used to call no man master, among them Haarek of Tjotta and Thorir Hound. In telling of this most important battle in the history of Norway, Snorri reaches the very height of his power. It is a story of heroic fighting and loyalty, but it has a somber hue, and there is in it none of the wildness and joy in battle that is found in the accounts of earlier clashes of arms. Olaf fell and most of his men with him. Today a tiny eleventh century church marks the spot where, according to tradition, the king fell.

At Stiklestad the chieftains had fought to throw off a strong royal power which had already lessened their independence; but the son of the mighty Canute and his mother established a more arbitrary rule than Norway had ever felt, and laid heavy burdens on high and low. It was not long before both farmer and chieftain rued the day when they had killed the king who had been the bitterest opponent of Canute. The day of the old local independence was over, and a return to the old faith was not even thought of. On the contrary, Olaf's death had strengthened the hold of the faith he had established. Almost at once tales of miracles gathered about the name of the slain king, and on August 3, 1041, Bishop Grimkell declared him a saint, placed his body above the high altar of the church in Nidaros, and induced Svein to recognize Olaf's sainthood. It did not take long before Saint Olaf received adoration even to the ends of western Christendom. Churches and shrines were built in his honor in London, many places in Sweden, and as far away as Rome, and he was the last western saint to receive recognition in Constantinople. The center of Saint Olaf worship was naturally at Nidaros. His shrine there attracted so many pilgrims from all lands that the great number, around Saint Olaf's Day in particular, became an economic problem to the community. No holy person must be refused food or shelter, but who could distinguish between the true pilgrim and the tramp who sought hospitality under the holy garb?

First and foremost, however, Olaf was honored in his own country. A wealth of folklore grew up about his name, telling of his prowess, his victories over trolls, his miracles, and his saintly life. Above all, he came to symbolize the achievement of a united Christian country. He holds a preeminent place in both the political and religious development of his country as the saint and "Eternal King" of Norway. The circumstances of his death and the events that immediately followed it caused an exaggerated veneration of Saint Olaf to spring up almost over night, and his name became a banner through coming ages. Probably this could not have happened—certainly not so rapidly—had it not been for a greatness in Olaf which, in spite of all disagreement and controversy about his personality and his life, shines through the fog of legend and has set his stamp on the history of his country throughout the ages.

PART III

The Middle Ages, 1030-1536

CHAPTER 6

FOLK KING AND FOLK CHURCH, 1030-1130

THE VIKING AGE was followed by a period of about three centuries which constitute the high Middle Ages in the history of Norway. This was the time when medieval civilization all through Western Europe was at its height, and the people of Norway now had a much larger share in European civilization than in earlier times. In the Viking Age the Norwegians had entered upon the European scene, exerting an influence the extent of which cannot be accurately estimated. Certain it is that the vigor they infused and the trade they helped to open were among the contributing factors in the rapid development of the later Middle Ages. Yet, as Rome was conquered by Greece and the Teutonic invaders of the fifth century by the church and classical civilization, so the vikings too were conquered by the older Christian civilization. Only in the islands that had been practically uninhabited before the coming of the vikings did there continue to exist Norwegian communities for any length of time, and today Iceland is the only state that is a direct continuation of the Norwegian settlement in the Viking Age. The home country, too, received influence from abroad in art, customs, and ways of life. The most significant importation from abroad, however, was Christianity, and as it spread Norway became for the first time culturally and religiously a part of Europe as a whole. Nevertheless as the North had long stayed outside of the general European development, the characteristically Norwegian civilization had become deeply rooted and, while joining the European stream of development, Norway retained much of the old. This gave individuality to Norwegian history and helped to make the Middle Ages a rich and great age. This period falls naturally into sections of about a century, each with marked characteristics of its own.

It is entirely fitting to call the eleventh century the Century of Folk King and Folk Church, for the royal power and the church were built upon the support of the freehold farmers who constituted the most important element of the population. Although a period of less striking events than the centuries before and after, the accomplishments were no less great. It was an age of stabilizing, of marked internal growth, with the establishment of a national royal power and a well organized church. Merely to assimilate Christianity into the Norwegian mode of life and thought and develop an ecclesiastical order must have taken intense, keen mental activity.

¶ The grumbling against foreign rule, which had begun immediately after Stiklestad, continued to grow. The leader of the opposition to Canute's representatives was one of Norway's strongest chieftains, Einar Tambarskjelve. He had never loved Saint Olaf, but had stayed away from Norway in 1030 when Olaf returned to his kingdom, and had maintained a discreet neutrality. Soon after Stiklestad, however, Einar called Olaf holy and he opposed Svein Aelfgifusson in the midst of the yeomen assembled in *thing*. In 1034, Einar and Kalv Arnesson, the commander of the army that defeated Saint Olaf, went with a large body of Trønder to Gardarike, and returned next summer with Magnus, the eleven-year-old son of Olaf. They were prepared to use force to place the boy on his father's throne, but there was no need of it, for Aelfgifu and Svein fled without making any attempt to retain their power, and, in marked contrast with the preceding age when every king had to fight for his crown, Magnus was acclaimed king with no opposition. Like Magnus, all the later kings of the century also succeeded to the kingdom peacefully. They neither came as viking chiefs from over the seas nor did they—with two exceptions—meet a violent death as had the kings of the tenth century.

Before a man could become king two things were necessary, hereditary right and recognition by the people assembled in *things*. All the sons of a king had an equal right to the inheritance of the estates of their father, consisting chiefly of the many farms which had one by one become royal land and which were considered entirely private property. So the kingdom too came to be looked upon as odal in the family. Yet the old rights of the people also had to be taken into account. Any heir to the throne could present his claims at a *thing* and ask to be accepted as king. If approved, he was acclaimed and led to the royal seat. Recognition by the Eyrathing came to be considered most important, but as the king traveled through the land or sailed along the shore, it became customary that he summoned one local *thing* after another and asked to be accepted as rightful heir and king. It happened several times in the eleventh century that two or more kings ruled jointly. As there was no established way of arranging a joint rule or of dividing the power and income, the kings personally made any kind of arrangements they wished. In no such case were there harmonious relations between the rulers. At times hostilities threatened to break out, but the followers of the kings would not tolerate war and insisted that some kind of peace be patched up. Though there was not enough explosive stuff to cause a real civil war, the unification of the country was not absolutely completed, and two kings had serious trouble in the Uplands, which had not been entirely won over to the national idea of unification. But it was a great advantage that a succession of strong and able men ruled Norway in this century.

Magnus the Good (1035-1047), Snorri says, owed his throne next to God to the loyal help of Queen Astrid, who called together a large *thing* in Sweden and obtained support for her stepson. In reality, however, it was the wish of the thingmen that gave him the kingdom. He was first recognized at the Eyrathing and then, as he traveled southward, by other local assemblies. In spite of promises to the contrary, the boy king yielded to the temptation to punish the enemies of his father and take their lands; but when Olaf's skald Sigvat Thordarson bravely and wisely warned him against any vindictiveness, Magnus heeded the advice and later came to be known as Magnus the Good. When Magnus had ruled seven years, Saint Olaf's half-brother, Harald Sigurdsson, who had fought at Stiklestad, came to Norway and demanded to be recognized as king. He was a somewhat modernized viking who, after innumerable adventures, came from abroad with fame and wealth which he had won chiefly as a member of the Varangian guard of the Byzantine emperor. War seemed imminent, but a peaceful settlement was made, Harald shared his wealth with Magnus and was accepted as joint ruler. Harald the Hard (1042-1066) was so called because he used his hird against his own people when he put down opposition in the Uplands with fire and sword in a veritable reign of terror lasting through three summers. He added much to his estates and thereby to his power through extensive confiscation of the land of those who had joined in the resistance.

The descendants of Harald the Hard ruled for three generations. He was succeeded by his son Olaf Kyrri, or the Peaceful (1066-1093), a brother Magnus being joint king with him until his death in 1069.

Olaf's reign is characterized by works of peace and his name is associated with almost every phase of internal progress.

Quite different was his adventurous, warlike son, Magnus Bareleg (1093-1103), so called because he wore Scottish kilts, who was like his grandfather in his vigorous policy and his viking spirit. Like him, too, he had trouble in the Uplands, where his popular young cousin Haakon was taken as king. To the generous son of Olaf he offered half of Norway; but the well-spoken Magnus would have it all, says the saga. Soon Haakon died; Magnus punished his followers as Harald had done, and the flames of their homesteads leaping to the sky taught them submission, as a skald expressed it.

Magnus was succeeded by his three sons. Olaf, the youngest of the three, was a mere child when his father died and was under the control of his brothers and died in 1115 without taking any active part in the government. The other two, Eystein (1103-1122) and Sigurd Jerusalemfarer (1103-1130), had the longest joint rule in the history of Norway. The brothers were opposites physically and temperamentally and Snorri's account shows how near they came to a clash of arms. Sigurd's long absence on his crusade helped to keep the peace and left Eystein undisturbed to foster internal progress. After his return Sigurd, too, did much to develop the country and strengthen the church, although he did not always personally submit to its discipline. Snorri tells that when Sigurd was arranging in Bergen to marry another woman while his queen was still living, the bishop protested in great anger: "How could you, my lord, think of doing such a thing in my bishopric and thereby scorn God's laws and commandments and the holy church? I am astonished that you, my lord, intend to treat our episcopal office as well as your own royal dignity with such great contempt. And I will do my duty and forbid this wrong act in the name of God, Saint Olaf, the apostle Peter, and all the saints." The king did not use the sword he had in his hand, though the bishop stretched his neck up to make it easy for him, but he went to Stavanger and there married his beloved Cecilia. He was not more satisfied, however, with the bishop of Stavanger, who allowed him to "make amends to God and us" for his sin with gifts, than he was with him who had forbidden the marriage. It seems poetic justice that Cecilia deserted him on his deathbed. When Sigurd died in 1130 he had, according to the sagas, some presentiment that the time of peace would soon be at an end.

¶ In contrast with the preceding period, Norway was now recognized as an independent sovereign nation and made alliances and treaties with other countries as with equals. The kings had a definite foreign policy, and at times it was so aggressive that it was bound to be disastrous. Some of the old viking spirit remained in the kings, and besides they had in their hird a little standing army which, like a war horse straining at the bit, was eager for action.

Most important were the relations with Denmark. In 1035, the year that Magnus Olafsson became king of Norway, Canute the Great died and his North Sea Empire vanished. One of his sons, Harald, became king of England, and another, the young boy Harthacnut, of Denmark. The leading men of both Norway and Denmark were afraid that a revival of Danish claims to the Norwegian throne might lead to war and therefore arranged a meeting between the two boy kings at the Göta River, where the two realms joined. A treaty was signed agreeing that each king was to be the heir of the other, so that when one died the survivor should rule over both kingdoms. Canute's sons were quite unworthy of their great father. When Harald died after a brief inglorious rule, Harthacnut took over the throne of England. When he also died, after a two years' rule even worse than his brother's, the crown returned to the English royal house in the person of Edward the Confessor.

In accordance with the treaty he had made with Harthacnut, Magnus the Good claimed the Danish throne, but he had a rival claimant in Svein, the son of Canute the Great's sister Estrid, who had been left in charge of Denmark when his cousin Harthacnut went to England to rule. Most of the Danes supported Magnus because they needed his help against the Wends who were harassing southern Jutland with great frightfulness. Magnus defeated them decisively in the great Battle of Lyrskog Heath and the danger to Denmark was ended. Then Svein Estridsson, who had become the jarl of Magnus—too powerful a jarl, as Einar Tambarskjelve said—took up arms to win the throne. Magnus was successful in battle, but died suddenly on an expedition to Denmark, having bequeathed his claims to the Danish throne to Svein. Harald the Hard, having no intention of abiding by the bequest of Magnus, continued to claim Denmark. He won some battles, but he received only half-hearted support from the Norwegians, and Svein kept the throne. There was no background for a union between the two countries and no demand for it among the people. The wars were a dreary waste, and the only positive result for Norway was the awakening of what may be termed a real national feeling.

The Norwegian kings also advanced claims to the English throne. Magnus the Good, who looked upon himself as the heir of Harthacnut, wrote to Edward the Confessor that he would attack with both Danish and Norwegian forces and "he will then govern it [England] who wins the victory." But Svein Estridsson kept him occupied in Denmark and he was not able to put force back of his big words. Harald the Hard, however, after he had failed in Denmark, fitted out a large expedition to conquer England. In 1066, when Edward the Confessor died, there were three foreign pretenders to the English throne, all of Northern blood: Svein claimed it as nearest in blood to the house of Canute, Harald the Hard as the heir of Magnus, and finally Duke William of Normandy, a descendant of Rollo the Walker, as cousin and acknowledged heir of Edward the Confessor. The English witan, however, chose Harold, the son of the English Earl Godwine and his Danish wife Gytha. Harold's brother Tostig, who had attempted intrigues with all three pretenders, joined Harald the Hard and his Norwegian forces when they landed in northern England. After a forced march from the south, the English met the invaders on September 25 at Stamford Bridge, in the greatest battle Norwegians ever fought on English soil. Nine-tenths of their forces were cut to pieces and Harald received the "seven feet of English ground—or more since he is taller than other men"—that Harold is said to have promised him. Olaf, the son of the Norwegian king, obtained a truce and departed with the remnant of the army—he could man only twenty-four of the three hundred ships with which the Norwegians had landed—and never again did Norwegians try to claim any part of England. We need not relate how the capable, resourceful English king, after another forced march to the south, met the Norman invader at Hastings. A stray arrow killed Harold, the battle was lost, and as a Northern skald, Thorkill Skallason, sang,

> Cold heart and bloody hand
> Now rule the English land.

In spite of the strength of Norman rule, Svein was slow to realize that any attack on England was futile. In 1075 he sent a fleet to England; it met with no support there, and returned after merely taking some booty. This was the last attack on England from Scandinavian lands, the last viking raid.

Conflicts with Sweden also marred this age. Harald the Hard was almost constantly at war with Sweden, and after the reign of Olaf the Peaceful, who carried out a consistent policy of peace, Magnus Bareleg renewed the wars and harried the enemy's land in good old viking style. But the desire for peace was strong, and in 1101 a peace meeting was arranged at Konungahella of the three Scandinavian kings, Magnus of Norway, Inge of Sweden, and Erik of Denmark. Says Snorri: "It was the tale of men that more lord-like men had never been seen. King Inge was the biggest and most skilful and seemed most venerable; Magnus seemed boldest and most active, but Erik was most handsome of them all."

It was agreed that each was to keep the land he had and punish his own men for any harm to property. Thus Norway retained the land east of the Folden Fjord down to the Göta River, much of which today belongs to Sweden, and the boundary line was definitely established about as it had been from the time of Saint Olaf. To seal the peace, Magnus received in marriage Inge's daughter Margaret, known hereafter as the Peace Maiden, and the disputed lands were designated as her dowry. A modern monument has been erected to commemorate this first peace treaty of three Scandinavian kings.

To the east of Trøndelag is a district with easy communication to the west which, though Swedish today, belonged for centuries to Norway. Jemtland recognized the Norwegian king from the reign of Haakon the Good until it was lost in the time of Saint Olaf. Eystein was able to reunite it with Norway, but ecclesiastically it continued to belong to the diocese of Uppsala. Herjedal was also Norwegian and belonged to the diocese of Nidaros.

The Western Islands offered the only real opportunity for the imperial ambitions of the kings of this age, for there lived people of Norwegian race and culture for whom it was not unnatural to have both political and ecclesiastical ties with Norway. As there was little difficulty in controlling the Shetland Islands and the Faroes, the kings centered their attention upon the Orkneys. Harald the Hard obtained some help there for his ill-fated English expedition, but generally the shifting influence of the Norwegian kings depended on the conflicts between different claimants to the position of jarl, some seeking support from Norway and some from Scotland.

Magnus Bareleg brought a change in the situation. He made two expeditions, strong enough to conquer the Orkneys, the Hebrides, the Isle of Man, and Dublin. Then he was killed in Ireland on a foraging expedition to supply his ships with meat for the return voyage. The control of the Isle of Man and Dublin was not lasting, but the Orkney jarls continued with some interruption to recognize the king of Norway until 1468. The bishops both of the Orkneys and the Hebrides arranged to have their dioceses be a part of the Norwegian church. Good will between Norway and the islands was increased when the Norwegian government recognized the sainthood of Jarl Magnus, who had been treacherously killed by a rival. He came to be regarded as the special patron saint of the islands.

No account of warlike enterprises would be complete without mention of the only crusade led by a Norwegian king. Sigurd Jerusalem-farer's expedition was fitted out with great expense and care, with the help of his brother Eystein. Sigurd spent on the crusade three and a half years packed with bold adventures and picturesque incidents. The first winter he lingered in England, living on the hospitality of King Henry I but giving rich gifts to the churches. Then he sailed to Lisbon, and lent his sword to Spanish crusades against the Moslem. On the voyage through the Mediterranean he stopped first at the Balearic Islands, where he smoked out Moorish pirates from their den, and then visited his kinsmen, the Normans in Sicily, bestowing upon Duke Roger the title of king. In the Holy Land his main achievement was to help capture Sidon, and his most valued reward was a splinter of the cross of Christ which he promised to place in the shrine of Saint Olaf. He returned by way of Constantinople, where he was sumptuously entertained by the emperor. Many of his men remained in the service of the emperor, and Sigurd left all his ships there and traveled home across the continent. In Denmark he was hospitably received by his stepmother, Margaret the Peace Maiden, then married to the Danish king. She gave him a fully equipped ship in which he returned to his kingdom. He brought with him great wealth, much of which he bestowed upon churches, for he had acquired a knowledge of the church as a great institution which he wished to strengthen in his realm. Otherwise Norway gained nothing from the crusade except some intangible mental stimulus and a little closer contact with the outer world.

In spite of valor and victories the kings accomplished little by their aggressive policies. The only exception was that the Western Islands became more closely tied to Norway. Foreign conquests were finally abandoned because the people were reluctant to go on armed expeditions to foreign lands. Any attempt to raise a large army would have met with dubious success; the hird alone was not large enough for extensive undertakings, the king's military power rested solely upon this body of personal followers for he had neither the power nor the legal right to force the *leidang*, which was intended as a coast guard, into foreign service. The people were more intent on farming than on fighting, and far more significant than the wars, the tales of which fill the sagas, were the works of peace at home.

❡ Although the development of anything resembling a modern state was only in its beginnings in eleventh century Norway, government and law were extremely important, and they found expression through two types of institutions, *thing* and king.

The old institution of *things*, which had grown out of the needs of the people even in pre-viking days, reached the highest development in this age. The *thing* of the local community as well as that of the shire continued to be strictly of, for, and by the people. The king's thanes were by law excluded from them and must not even be within hearing distance of the meeting, while all the yeomen were expected to attend. When there was need, a man or even a woman could summon a *thing* by sending out arrows that had to be carried from farm to farm until the whole district was notified. In some parts of the country the local *things* were the highest legal authority, for the four large *lagthings* did not embrace the whole country. In the eleventh century these four were all representative bodies and on account of the long distances this was advantageous, if not necessary. Though the thingmen were chosen and fitted out by the people, with the growing difference between the upper and lower ranks in rural society the *lagthing* came to be controlled by the upper group and became increasingly aristocratic in character. All thanes were expected to attend, but the *lagret*, the smaller body which had the real power, had to be composed of yeomen only.

The *thing* system and the legal practices which had developed in pre-Christian times remained basically the same even when the country became Christian. The complexity of the early legal system is illustrated in Snorri's story of a lawsuit between the brothers Eystein and Sigurd who, though kings, were still under the law. When a case was brought before the *thing*, the facts were generally established not by taking evidence, but by an elaborate system of witnesses and compurgation, or oath-taking, most often by men of the community. The ordeal under supervision of the clergy was sometimes used in Christian times. The function of the *thing* was to declare the old law, but it had no machinery for enforcing it. That was the duty of those in whose favor judgment was pronounced, in the case of murder the duty of the kindred; and only gradually did the power of the king and the impact of Christianity put an end to the old practice of feuds and blood vengeance. Slowly but irresistibly Christian ethics produced changes in the laws of the conservative rural communities, as the church took a strong stand especially against slavery, exposing of infants, dueling (*holmgang*), and the like. It insisted also on the sanctity of marriage. Gradually new principles, humanizing the legal system, were incorporated into the old law. The most important new enactments were connected with the church, and as in the days of Saint Olaf even ecclesiastical laws had to win the approval of the *thing*, which was expressed by clashing of arms against the shields. There was no majority rule, but discussion and compromise preceded the acceptance of new laws.

Late in the century the laws of the *lagthings* began to be compiled and written down, probably with very few changes. Though much has been lost, Norway has an unusually large treasure of old laws extant, which furnish the richest sources we possess for the study of the whole civilization of the age. Of the Eidsivathing and Borgarthing laws only the sections regarding the church have survived, but what seems to be the entire body of Gulathing and Frostathing laws has been preserved. The oldest manuscript of the Gulathing law dates from the middle of the twelfth century and of the Frostathing law from the thirteenth century, but they were copied from older manuscripts.[1] Some city and local laws have also been preserved.

The *things* continued to be local or sectional, and it fell to the king to represent and further the newer national phase of Norway's development. He worked in close cooperation with the *things*, however, and this tended to enhance rather than diminish the influence of the assemblies of the people. Not only did the king have to obtain the approval of the *things* to establish new laws, but the relationship between the two organs of government was also strengthened through his efforts to enforce law and order. He became a real executive and in contrast to the *things*, his power extended over the whole country. To enforce the law he could use the hird as police, but he was far from being an absolute ruler. Nor was his person sacred, for the conception that the king can do no wrong was foreign to old Norwegian ideas. This is well illustrated by a provision in the Frostathing law: "No man shall attack another in

[1] These laws are available in English in Larson, *The Earliest Norwegian Laws.*

his home, neither the king nor any other man. If the king does this, the arrow shall be sent forth through all the shires; and [men shall] go upon him and slay him, if they are able to seize him; and if he escapes he shall never be allowed to return to the land."[2]

Although the king's power was growing, there was no administrative system in the modern sense and no definite law defining the power either of the monarch or of his officials. The king traveled about almost constantly, exerting his royal power in person wherever he happened to be and keeping in touch with his people, thus becoming more and more of a national figure. The most pressing reason for traveling, however, was economic. The king had some little income from fines, but although this became valuable later as the judicial and executive power of the king increased, it was not important as yet. Duties on imports yielded a little revenue, and the tax on the Lapps, Norway's subject people in the North, had become a royal monopoly. By far the most important source of income, however, was from the royal farms, the crown lands. As the king moved from place to place, he generally lived on one of his own big farms with his following of perhaps one hundred and twenty housecarls besides others of his family and household. The supplies that had been collected in preparation for the visit were hardly enough to feed such a company, so it became customary to ask the farmers of the vicinity to make contributions of food and drink. Often they were willing and at any rate it was not easy to say nay to the king, but when he tried to have the gifts legalized, the people were obdurate and their *things* refused to incorporate the practice into law.

Distances were long, roads and travel were difficult, so even a perambulating king found it necessary to have local officials to represent royal power and interests. These were of two classes. The higher in rank were the thanes, or *lendmenn*, who were the leading men of the community, often from the old chieftain families, and generally owned considerable land. Their dignity was enhanced by the royal office and their substance increased by the income from certain parts of the king's land, and as time went on, they became less and less local leaders and more strictly royal officials. Their power varied in different sections of the country, being greatest in the Westland, where the chieftains had been strongest in the Viking Age. In the age with which we are dealing, their authority was not clearly defined and was seldom evoked except when that of the humbler officials was inadequate. These were the bailiffs, or *aarmenn*, who did the real work for the king. They acted as

[2] Larson, *The Earliest Norwegian Laws*, 278.

police when needed and were the managers of all the king's farms except such as had been specially assigned to thanes, and it was their duty to see that adequate supplies were on hand when the king arrived in the course of his progress through the land. Like Saint Olaf, the later monarchs depended mainly on the support of a landowning aristocracy rooted in the soil. This meant the reestablishment of the old close relationship between the king and the yeoman society which had existed in the Age of the Small States, and furnished a stable foundation for royal power.

¶ The change in social classes that had begun in the late tenth century continued in a more marked degree in the eleventh, as the chieftain aristocracy of the viking type, built on war, trade, and plunder, was passing. The doughty Einar Tambarskjelve was the last of the old chieftains who tried to maintain the power and independence that had belonged to his class in bygone days, and kept a strong hird in an age when the king claimed the sole right to have an armed following. While Magnus the Good reigned, Einar practically controlled the government and was loyal to the king. But Harald the Hard, resenting and fearing the headstrong old chieftain, told his men in a verse that he would not be safe on his throne before Einar had "kissed the thin lips of the axe." Forthwith Einar and his son were surrounded and hewn down. While the chief men of the new aristocracy were the thanes whose prominence was based on royal favor and the ownership of land, the yeomen were still important, but there was a tendency for a few to rise and for the majority to sink to a lower economic and social level. As the passing of the Viking Age had brought an end to emigration, the surplus population had to find room at home; since the new land brought under the plough in this period was insufficient, the farms tended to become smaller, tenants became more common, and free laborers grew in number. Thralldom gradually disappeared, as with the end of the viking raids there was no new influx of slaves, and the church took a stand against it. In the old Norwegian laws, slaves were things, not human beings, an idea contrary to the Christian conception of the value of any human being, which slowly asserted itself in favor of emancipation.

Another development was the rise of cities. A very small beginning dates back to the Viking Age. At that time definite marketplaces had been established which were often also centers for worship and *thing* places. A few of these which had especially good geographic conditions might very naturally develop into towns. Booths were often put up and used year after year, and storehouses where goods brought from over the sea during the summer might be kept until market time, which was often in the winter when the farmers could most easily get away from home. When such a trade center, or *kaupang*, first became a little town cannot definitely be determined, but in each of the important centers royal action had something to do with giving the place a definite status of city, though it is clear that no mere royal command could create a town. Later in the century, when the bishoprics became definite territories with the bishop living in the cities, they received a religious and even more an economic stimulus to further growth.

Besides Tønsberg, which is the oldest city in Norway, and Konungahella, situated at the mouth of the Göta River, there were beginnings of other cities: Sarpsborg dating from the time of Saint Olaf; Hamar, which is barely mentioned as a *kaupang* but became a town only when it later became the seat of an episcopal see; and Stavanger, which owed its growth chiefly to the new bishopric established there by Sigurd Jerusalemfarer. But of more significance are three towns, one in each of the important sections of the country. Each became the principal city of the region in which it was situated as well as the center of worship for one of the three popular saints whose sainthood was established by the end of the century.

Oldest is Nidaros on the broad coastal plains of Trøndelag, the beginning of which is associated with Olaf Tryggvason. It became important on account of the dominating place of Trøndelag in the political development of the tenth and eleventh centuries and even more because there was the shrine of Norway's Eternal King, who was preeminently the national saint. In the following century when a Norwegian archbishopric was established with its center at Nidaros, it became even more the spiritual capital of the land. In the reign of Harald the Hard an old marketplace became the city of Oslo. Harald established there the shrine of Saint Hallvard, who, says Adam of Bremen, was a saint from among the common people. He lived a saintly life in everyday obscurity, "but he could not remain entirely unknown. He was killed by his friends when he tried to protect one of his enemies." His martyrdom is pictured on the old seal of Oslo.

Last came the city in the Westland. "King Olaf [the Peaceful]," says Snorri, "set up a market town in Bergen; many rich men soon settled there and thither sailed merchants from other lands." It is not known whether Bergen had been a center of trade earlier, but this "window to the West" soon became the largest, most important, and most cosmopolitan city in Norway and continued to be so until quite recent times. Facing the West, where Norway's main oversea interests lay, it soon attracted trade and owed its growth more definitely to commerce than did any other city. From the eleventh century until far into the thirteenth it was in a sense Norway's capital. There the kings spent more time than in any other place, there the first coronation took place (1163) and gradually the scene of important events shifted from Nidaros to Bergen. Although the center of the bishopric in the Westland was officially at Selje until 1170, when the seat of the bishop and the relics of Saint Sunniva were formally transferred to Bergen, it is probable that the bishop had earlier taken up his residence there.

The towns had their own *thing*, or moot (*mót*) as it was called in the cities, where all householders met to decide the affairs of the town, but royal officials with duties much like the rural bailiffs were present to look after the king's income and to exercise police duties. Guilds were found in the cities quite early but were not as important as were the rural guilds that had existed even in pre-Christian days. The guild festivals were part of both the religious and social life, and guild brethren helped each other in case of illness or death, thus to some extent making up for the weakening of family ties which resulted from moving into a town. The cities were very small, their organization was simple, and their influence in this century very slight, yet these beginnings were a significant part of the organizing work of the eleventh century.

¶ No contribution of the age was more important than the forming of the national church. The Norwegian church continued to be a missionary church until about 1070, that is, the work was carried on by men trained in foreign countries; and these missionaries were chiefly responsible for establishing that close contact with Europe which distinguishes the later Middle Ages from the Viking Age. The church in Norway was to a large extent organized after the general European pattern. Still it retained a great deal of independence at the very time when the powerful Pope Gregory VII was using all his influence to establish the Cluny reform program in the continental churches and was with great success asserting the Gregorian ideal of a universal church submissive to the Roman see. Neither the Gregorian program nor the canon law made itself felt to any large extent in Norway before the twelfth century. There were several reasons for this. The church grew up in close relation to the monarchy, the missionary bishops were attached to the court, and king and priest worked together to Christianize the land. Moreover, although Danish-German influences were felt in the South, most of the missionaries were trained in England. Therefore certain English traits were naturally introduced, and the English church had maintained a greater independence of Rome than was the case on the continent. Furthermore, king and clergy had a keen understanding of local needs, and the arrangements for the church were carefully adapted to Norwegian conditions. Finally, it must be remembered that the early church law was made a part of old Norwegian law through action of the *things* and the thingmen were no blind tools of higher powers. So the Norwegian church became a national and a folk church.

From the time of Saint Olaf the diocese of the archbishop of Bremen extended over the whole North as far as to Greenland and even Vinland. This arrangement continued until 1104 in the reign of Sigurd Jerusalem-farer, when a separate archbishopric for the North was established at Lund in Skaane, which was then a part of Denmark. The archbishop had little power in Norway. He generally ordained the bishops, although they were appointed by the king, who was in reality the head of the church. At first the bishops traveled about, each in his own section of the country. After 1070 they were settled in one place within their diocese, and as the sees gradually were filled by Norwegians, the day of the missionary church was over. At first there were three episcopal sees, one at Nidaros, one at Oslo, and the third at Selje. King Sigurd established a fourth see at Stavanger, gave to it a great deal of his wealth, and called in an English bishop from Winchester. He began the construction of the cathedral, built in the Romanesque style of Winchester Cathedral and dedicated to Saint Swithun, a former bishop of that city, relics of whom were brought from England and placed in the church. Before long the islands, too, received separate bishops: Iceland, the Faroes, and even Greenland. The Orkneys had a bishop earlier. The Icelandic annals tell us that in 1121 Bishop Eirik, who may have been the first bishop of Greenland, went in search of Vinland, but nothing further was heard of him.

At first, when it was difficult to obtain priests, the parishes were large and the priests few, but within a century the parishes took about the shape they continued to have for hundreds of years, and services were conducted regularly with all the impressive ceremonial of the medieval church. To announce services the priest sent out little wooden crosses which it was the duty of the people to pass on to the nearest neighbor, just as they did the arrow calling to a *thing*, until the announcement had spread to the whole parish. The parish priests had a very lowly position. They were to be supported by the people, but often they had no salary except such offerings as were given them in return for masses or other services. Conditions became better when Sigurd Jerusalem-farer established the tithe which gave the church a regular income. The position of the priests was often difficult because they could not conform to heathen usages which were still common, notably that of blood revenge, for according to the old law he who refused to do his duty in this respect was a man without honor and could be treated like a thrall. A rise in the priests' social status is indicated in the Gulathing law which provided that they should atone for any misdemeanor by a fine: "For we have abolished [the custom of] punishing them with blows, since we have entered into marriage relations with them and allow [them] to give our sons instruction. Our priests shall enjoy the same security in their persons as we all enjoy [in our dealings] with all other men in the land."[3]

We notice that celibacy was not expected of the Norwegian clergy at that time. At first the people had a great deal of influence on the selection of their priests, but with the development toward greater ecclesiastical authority the right of election disappeared by the end of the century. There is a provision in the Frostathing law, however, which shows that the rights of the people could not be wholly ignored: "The bishop shall govern the churches and rule in all matters of religion. He shall appoint as priests whomever he will, but he has promised we shall have such priests as are agreeable to us and [who] know the ritual correctly. That is old law."[4]

The building of churches was going on throughout the land and they were often erected where had stood the old temples which had all been torn down. The people were required by law both to construct and maintain them and even the private chapels were not allowed to go to ruin. Olaf the Peaceful, Eystein, and Sigurd Jerusalem-farer were all actively interested in church building. Small churches were often erected by private individuals just as heathen sanctuaries had been, and the priests in such chapels were entirely under the control of the owner.

In addition to their religion, the most valuable contribution the

[3] Larson, *The Earliest Norwegian Laws*, 45.
[4] *Ibid.*, 231.

missionaries brought to Norway was the Latin alphabet. Norwegians had acquired some knowledge of this in their contact with other countries during the viking expeditions, but it had not been taken into general use. The runic alphabet, somewhat improved through the influence of Latin letters, continued to be the only form of writing, but so far as we know was not used for any extensive literary works. Saint Olaf's missionaries, Grimkell and his co-workers, must have taught Norwegians to read and write Latin. Latin writings were produced very early as is proved by a manuscript of a Saint Olaf mass dating from about 1050; and when Magnus the Good corresponded with King Edward the Confessor of England it must have been through men at his court who knew Latin. It was referred to in an old poem as the "book language," and when Snorri says that Olaf the Peaceful could read the holy books, he doubtless meant religious books in Latin.

It did not take long before the alphabet was adapted to the writing of Old Norse. This was achieved in Norway much earlier than in Sweden and Denmark, where continental influences dominated, and is quite in line with the English practice of using Latin and the vernacular side by side. It was no simple task to reduce the language to writing. We do not know exactly when or by whom it was done, but it was completed in the latter half of the eleventh century. By that time Norway had not a few of her own men who had received a higher education abroad—Gregory VII, for example, urged Olaf the Peaceful to send young well-born Norwegians to the papal curia to get Christian learning—and probably such men, familar both with Latin and the native tongue, first wrote Old Norse using the Latin alphabet. Thus began the Old Norse literary language, but while the laws were written down, we have no evidence that written literature was produced before the twelfth century.

In an old graveyard are found two monuments of about the same age: one is a cross and the other a heathen symbol. They bear mute evidence to the way in which the two faiths for a time existed side by side. A heathen monument might be found in the cemetery, but the church had difficulty in breaking the old custom of burying on the homestead. The change, it was felt, weakened the old family solidarity, and the old mounds continued to be revered long after the belief was firmly established that burial in holy ground was a wise precaution to ensure to the deceased a blessed resurrection. Even after it was no longer good form to be a heathen, much of the old faith remained, and even where Christianity had taken a real hold many an old superstition lingered.

Among the unlettered the heathen gods became trolls and evil spirits which carried on a stubborn though losing battle against the powers of light. On the roofs of some of the oldest churches are dragons, which, banished from the interior by the cross, are poised as in flight.

It was not easy to eliminate old practices sanctioned by custom and law which were contrary to Christian ethics. Yet much was achieved. Gradually the moral tone became softened and more humane, although discipline was a new conception among the old Norwegians, who were not naturally meek or gentle. It is no more possible in Norway than in other countries to judge how deeply the new faith gripped the common people, but they were under the constant and not ineffective influence of regular services and of a new rhythm in their lives dominated by Sundays and fast days, saints' days, and Christian festivals. Even the militant spirit of the Crusades reached Norway, inducing several prominent men, chief among them King Sigurd Jerusalemfarer, to join the expeditions against the infidels, and the ecstatic spirit which characterized this age found expression also in the founding of monasteries. Four were erected in the first two decades of the twelfth century, one of them a nunnery, but they played a small part in the church of the time.

The archaeological remains from the eleventh century are few. The great burial mounds equipped with all that was necessary for the continuation of the struggles and the pleasures of this life had given way to the simple Christian grave, which was called a "resting place." With the decrease in wealth, the number of articles produced also declined. Yet a few objects of high artistic value can definitely be assigned to this century and show that the development from viking to later medieval art was in progress. In its poetic and historical productions the period was in a sense a bridge between the Viking Age and the time of saga writing which began late in the twelfth century. The skaldic poems continue to tell of the great deeds of heroes and kings in whose honor they were composed. As most of them deal with events about which the skald had first-hand information, they are our most dependable accounts of the happenings of the day, and the poetic form has helped to preserve the stories unchanged. There were also produced at this time tales in great profusion, some fact and some fiction and many a baffling mixture of both. Religious legends, especially about the Norwegian saints whose adoration was established at this time, were many. No hero caught the imagination of the storytellers quite as did Olaf Tryggvason, who excelled in all manly virtues and whose religion, according to the legends, found expression especially in fighting trolls and all manner of supernatural beings. Similar, in fact sometimes the same, stories were later told about Saint Olaf, who came to be revered even more than the first Olaf. So a mass of material, historical in a sense though uncritical, took shape and prepared the way for the writers of the following centuries.

The age was certainly not lacking in creative energy. The national monarchy was formed, the old folk laws and *thing* system reached their finest development, cities were in their beginnings, the use of the Latin script opened the possibility for written literature, the church became an institution of the people which began to reshape their life, and finally the contact with older Christian civilization gave stimulus to new achievements in culture. Yet the old was not lost. The motto of King Sigurd is expressive of the age:

> Yeomen seem to me best,
> Built land and lasting peace.[5]

[5] Quoted by Absalon Taranger in "Da Norge var misjonsmark," *Bibliotheca Norvegiae Sacra*, 1924, p. 50.

CHAPTER 7

SOCIAL CONFLICT, 1130-1228

THERE WAS A MARKED CONTRAST between the hundred years before 1130 and the century following that date. The eleventh century was characterized by conservative stability and quiet progress, all rooted in Norway's old society of freeholders. The twelfth, on the other hand, was replete with vigorous personalities and striking events. It has been called the Age of Civil Wars. That name, however, gives little conception of the many-sided conflict between ideas and social forces which, though less conspicuous, is more important than the clash of arms between claimants to the throne. Out of this turmoil and ferment there emerged a new order in state, church, and society, new institutions were born in the strife, and, although destructive forces were loose, the twelfth century is counted among the great constructive eras in Norwegian history.

The ever-present cause of civil war was the question of succession to the throne, for there was no definite law determining the legality of the various claims to the crown. As in the past, the right of all male descendants of a king was recognized, and sometimes even the claims of less direct heirs were admitted, as had been the case with Harald the Hard, Saint Olaf's half-brother. The older brother had no stronger claim than the younger, and legitimacy was no prerequisite. Still the church had done something to establish its ideal of marriage, and the son of a rightful queen had a somewhat greater prestige than his half brothers. The civil wars were still further complicated by the fact that the Danish king had not given up his ambition to acquire control of part of Norway, so he was ever ready to fish in troubled waters.

It is told in one of the sagas, *Morkinskinna*, that shortly before his death, Sigurd Jerusalemfarer dreamt that he saw a dark shadow far out in the ocean. It appeared to be a large tree with its roots in the sea, moving toward the shores of Norway. It broke against the land and into every inlet drifted splinters of the shattered tree. The tree was Harald Gilchrist's kin.

At about this time a young man who called himself Gilchrist, "the Servant of Christ," came from Ireland and claimed that he was the son of Magnus Bareleg. He was a worthless young man, addicted to strong drink and women, but possessed of not a little personal charm which won him many friends, and his claim seemed plausible. Magnus has left a skaldic verse saying that his whole heart was in Dublin with the Irish maid who never denied him and whom he loved more than himself.[1] To prove his claim Gilchrist submitted successfully to the ordeal of walking over nine hot ploughshares. Sigurd then accepted the young pretender, thereafter known as Harald Gilchrist, as his brother, and Harald in turn promised that he would not claim the throne during the lifetime of Sigurd or his son.

In 1130, Sigurd Jerusalemfarer died and was buried in the Saint Hallvard Church which he had built in Oslo, and there his son Magnus was at once proclaimed king. In nearby Tønsberg, Harald Gilchrist, in spite of his oath, also took the name of king. The two young monarchs agreed to share the power and managed to keep peace for three years, but then war broke out. At first Magnus was victorious and Harald fled to Denmark. Before long he returned and, with the help of the Danish king, defeated Magnus who, after being blinded and castrated, was confined in the Nidarholm Monastery located on a little island outside of Nidaros. Harald was then sole king for the brief space of a little more than a year; but the cruelty with which he pursued the followers of Magnus, now called the Blind, "grieved the minds of all good men." It seemed just retribution when, in 1136, he was murdered by Sigurd Slembe, a bold, resourceful, and unscrupulous young man, who also claimed to be the son of Magnus Bareleg and so the half-brother of Harald.

Before Sigurd Slembe could obtain recognition of his claim to the throne, Harald Gilchrist's queen Ingerid had hastened to call together the Borgarthing, where her year-old son Ingi was proclaimed king. And in the North the Eyrathing hailed as king another son of Harald Gilchrist, the three-year-old Sigurd, later nicknamed Mouth on account of his ugly mouth.

For three years civil war raged between the supporters of the child kings and Sigurd Slembe. To bolster his none too popular cause Sigurd

[1] Fredrik Paasche, *Kong Sverre*, 5, Kristiania, 1920.

allied himself with Magnus the Blind whom he took out of the monastery. Not a few men rallied to the support of Sigurd Jerusalemfarer's unfortunate son and some Danish help was also secured. Yet the two pretenders were not strong enough to win any decisive victory. In 1139, Magnus fell in battle and Sigurd Slembe was captured and tortured to death in a most cruel manner.

This ended the first phase of the civil wars. So far the fighting had been merely between rival claimants to the throne and their personal followers. The fighting forces were very small and there was no general war. The daily life of the people was little affected and the economic development went on with little interruption. Nor were any issues beyond personal rivalry involved, but in this strife were expressed the old ideas of right of private revenge and loyalty to one's kin and chief. Of the great changes that came later in the century only one was discernible—the growing power and importance of the thanes.

¶ For more than two decades, sons of Harald Gilchrist held the title of king in Norway. When Ingi and Sigurd, the two brothers who had become kings directly after their father's death, had reigned for about six years, an older brother Eystein came from Scotland and was also proclaimed king at the Eyrathing. He had no strong following, and when he went on a viking expedition he became even less popular. There was a fourth brother also, but he died early and is of no importance in our story.

The position of the youngest brother Ingi was by far the strongest and the period might well be called the reign of Ingi. To his support rallied the aristocracy, both lay and ecclesiastical, which was rising into power at this time. Ingi was tractable and gentle and, as the son of Ingerid, Harald Gilchrist's Swedish queen, he alone had the prestige of being a legitimate son, born in wedlock. When he was a baby, he was carried through a battle by one of his faithful men, and received injuries which crippled him for life. He was therefore nicknamed Hunchback. Even this disability served him in good stead. It caused him to lean more heavily upon the strong men about him, and his helplessness seems to have roused in the ambitious thanes a loyalty and warm affection which could rise above mere opportunism. This was especially true of Gregorius Dagsson, a heroic figure, fearless, resolute, and able, who watched over the king with unswerving devotion. More calculating and deliberate was Erling Wryneck. With Ragnvald, jarl of the Orkneys, he had gone on a crusade that was far famed in the North.

He came home with new honors and distinction, but also with a crooked neck, caused by a slash from the saber of an infidel. His prestige was also heightened by his royal marriage to Christina, the daughter of Sigurd Jerusalemfarer.

Though these two were the most important, the thanes were all powerful men. The rise of this class was a result of the shift in land ownership which was going on through the centuries after the Viking Age, and which was the fundamental background for all the great changes of the era of the civil wars. While there is still much uncertainty in our knowledge of these elusive social changes, they seem in the main to conform to the description that follows.

The population continued to grow as rapidly as in the Viking Age, perhaps even more rapidly. As the chance for emigration was almost gone, the surplus population had to find some outlet at home, but even there the opportunities were not great. The age was marked by no great technical advance, such as the development of iron had been in days of yore, and the best land was gone. Land was cleared and many new homes were built, but the homesteads were small and meager, quite different from the opulent new farms of the earlier centuries which had lent dignity to the odal freeholders. Often, too, the old farms were divided into three or four, or even eight or nine, parts in order to give younger sons a chance. The economic pressure was great. Not only was land less plentiful, but church and state made demands on the people unknown in earlier days. The increased needs were met by more intensive and extensive use of the common land (*almenning*), both forest, mountain, rivers, and shores, and a great variety of produce and many articles of handicraft were used to pay tithes, rent, and taxes. Even so it was easy to run into debt and sell or mortgage the farm—it was never redeemed—to a rich neighbor. So tenants became more and more numerous and thanes built up for themselves wealth and power, based on the ownership of many farms. It must be remembered, however, that there still continued to be many freeholders of substance and prestige and that the rural class never lost its freedom. By the thirteenth century the last remnant of slavery disappeared and the descendants of slaves often became crofters who as freedmen occupied outlying sections of a large farm and paid their rent in work. They were, however, not nearly so numerous as in later centuries; in fact, there was a tendency for the farmer class to become rather more homogeneous than it had been in the past.

The king could acquire land in the same ways as his thanes. In addition, as the royal power was developed, it came to be assumed that he had some jurisdiction over the common land. There was no desire—nor would it have been possible or practical—to restrict the use of the commons that had belonged to the people from time immemorial; but probably before the close of the twelfth century it became established by law that the many farmers who built up homesteads on new land which had been a part of the commons were tenants of the king.

Civil war could much more easily break out under these conditions than during the eleventh century with its stable yeoman society. The landless had nothing to lose and much to gain in war, the tenants were dissatisfied, and yeomen both rich and poor resented the growing encroachments of the large landowners. Class consciousness was increasing and there was even material for a lower class party, though it took time for it to develop.

At first all the advantages were with the large landowners. They were wealthy enough to maintain a strong force of housecarls, or personal followers, whose business was fighting and who were used on the slightest provocation. The thanes believed their position could be maintained through the consolidation of royal power in the hands of one man. At this time, therefore, their ambition could best be served by upholding Ingi Hunchback as sole king.

Ingi received support also from another source, as, for the first time in the history of Norway, the clergy entered politics. They backed Ingi because he was the only legitimate son among the brothers. They desired both to maintain the idea of marriage held by the church, and to keep peace which, they believed, would be threatened by recognizing the claims of bastards.

By this time the leading churchmen, having been trained in universities abroad, had been imbued with the ideas which the fiery and powerful Gregory VII (pope from 1073 to 1085) two generations earlier had made the reform program of the church. Conditions in Norway did not call for the emphasis on the abolition of abuses, either financial or others, on which Gregory insisted, and celibacy of the clergy did not begin to be enforced in Norway until a century later and even then the policy was only partially carried out. The reform group centered upon the fundamental exalted Gregorian idea of the universality of the church, as opposed to the national idea. Emphasis was placed upon the centralization of the church under the sole authority of the pope, the vicar of Christ on earth, and this gave direction and character to the development of the Norwegian church at the time when its organization was being completed.

The church was gaining more power and control over the life of the people than it had held earlier. It was not only adopting the general European pattern for its institutions, but the vital emotional and spiritual currents that were sweeping through the whole church reached Norway in a remarkably brief time. Chief among these was the evangelical revival, which received its main impetus from Saint Bernard of Clairvaux. The depth of religious feeling and the emphasis on the passion of Christ are most poignantly expressed in Saint Bernard's hymns, of which the best known is "O sacred head now wounded." Equally important was the warm, sentimental devotion to the Virgin. As early as in the 1140's the Cistercian order, which was the chief bearer of these religious ideals, reached Norway from England, and the first Cistercian monasteries were founded, one on Hovedøy outside of Oslo, another at Lyse near Bergen, and a nunnery of the same order, Nonneseter, also near Bergen. Although the monastic life never filled as large a place in Norway as in countries farther south, the influence that permeated from these points can be detected in the new emotionalism that found expression in the religious poetry and art of the age. As Christianity took a firmer grip on the feelings of the people, it was no doubt easier for the organized church to strengthen its position.

The first and chief aim of the reform party was consummated in 1152, when the archbishopric of Nidaros was created, thus separating Norway from the archbishopric of Lund which had comprised all the Scandinavian countries. Preparation for the event had most certainly been made in 1150 at a great meeting in Bergen which was summoned by Ingi and attended by leading men, both lay and clerical, from all Norwegian lands. Bishop Reidar was sent to Rome where he was consecrated archbishop by the pope, but he died on the way home. The pope then sent to Norway the English-born cardinal, Nicholas Breakspeare, later Pope Adrian IV, and, says Snorri, "no foreigner ever came to Norway whom all men respected so highly and who could so influence people." He consecrated Jon Birgerson archbishop in Christ Church in Nidaros, which held the grave of Norway's eternal saint-king. The veneration which was accorded to this sanctuary is well expressed in Einar Skulesson's poem *Geisli* (The Sunbeam), which was read at a great royal meeting in Christ Church the following year. Saint Olaf is the beam from Christ, the Sun, and the sanctity of his grave is the main theme of the poem.

The leaders succeeded in uniting under the Norwegian prelate all Norwegian lands to which the king could raise any claim. The new archbishop had ten bishoprics under him: the Hebrides and Isle of Man, the Orkneys and Shetland Islands, the Faroes, Greenland, two on Iceland, besides four in Norway where Hamar had been added to the older bishoprics of Bergen, Oslo, and Stavanger. Directly after 1152, chapters of canons, or groups of clergy connected with the cathedrals, made their appearance in some of the bishoprics. When the chapters acquired prebends in the form of sizable landed estates and the cathedral schools became the centers of all book learning in the land, the canons became influential. But that came later.

Snorri says that Nicholas "improved many of the customs of the Norwegians while he was in the country." A letter was drawn up on this occasion which defined the ecclesiastical liberties, but its exact contents are not known nor can it be determined how much it helped strengthen the church. The boundaries of parishes and bishoprics were more definitely drawn and the church was put on a better financial basis. Most important was the legal recognition of the right of the individual to will up to a tenth of his land to the church, thus affording it an opportunity to become a great landholder. This was grudgingly granted and caused much strife, for it made serious inroads into the old odal right of the family. The authority of the clergy was also increased as the legal power the church exercised over its members broadened. The development of canon law and ecclesiastical courts which characterized the twelfth century had an influence on Norway too, though clerical powers were not as wide in scope as in other countries. The church controlled, it seems, all cases involving clergy, but it never attained complete jurisdiction over the laity in cases involving moral or religious issues. In exercising its authority through confession and penance—often in the form of a bot—it nevertheless cooperated with the state in maintaining order and discipline.

The establishment of the Norwegian archbishopric, while agreed to by all three kings, was really a victory for Ingi's party. The whole development in the church would naturally tend to destroy the close relation between the king and the folk church which had characterized the preceding century, and met opposition from conservatives who clung to the old institutions. This later became a serious cause of strife.

Though a peaceful joint rule was maintained for over fifteen years (1139-1155), there was no love lost between the young kings and, as they grew to manhood, relations between them became more and more strained. Snorri tells one story after another of violence committed by their men. Since the thanes gave their allegiance to the mild and tractable Ingi, discordant elements gathered about the two older brothers, but although a few of the aristocrats were among their supporters they were not able to build up any strong party. Sigurd had his following mainly in Trøndelag where he had been brought up, and in the Uplands where the old yeoman society remained intact. In the church, too, among the lower clergy there was an element which felt bound up with the interests of the freeholders and wished to see the church fitted as of old into the national rather than the international system. Eystein was the first king to gather about himself a flock of landless proletarians eager for the plunder of war. No consolidated articulate lower class movement had as yet developed, however, and the young kings themselves seemed to have no policy higher than that of personal ambition. Nor was there anything in their character to make them worthy of great loyalty.

In 1155 Sigurd and Eystein formed a plot to dethrone Ingi Hunchback, for, they said, a cripple was not worthy to be king. Gregorius Dagsson, ever on the alert, discovered the plot and hastened to Bergen with Ingi. A *thing* was called at which Ingi revealed the secret and pleaded for support. Although Sigurd insisted that there was no truth in the accusation, he was attacked soon after by a party of Ingi's men, and so many weapons flew against Sigurd's golden shield that it seemed, says Snorri, as though one were looking into a snowstorm. Calling in vain upon his brother for mercy, Sigurd fell, only twenty-two years old. The two remaining brothers began to gather men and ships for a decisive battle, but in 1157, before war broke out, Eystein was pursued into the woods and killed. The sagas try to exonerate Ingi as far as possible from responsibility for the death of his brothers, but their followers could hope for no mercy from Ingi's men. They were, therefore, determined to keep up the party. Although the best opinion of the day seems to have been that as long as one of the joint kings remained, no other pretender could legally claim the throne, they chose as their candidate for the throne Haakon the Broad-Shouldered, the ten-year-old bastard son of Sigurd Mouth. King Haakon, says Snorri, "was cheerful and friendly in conversation, playful and boyish in his ways and was loved by the people."[2]

For four years (1157-1161) the conflict raged between Ingi and Haakon. This second phase of the civil wars was quite different from the

[2] *Heimskringla, The Saga of Magnus Erlingsson,* Chapter 8.

first, which had been a strife only between kings and chieftains with their personal followers. This was a war of parties which, however, had grown out of the old principles of private revenge and personal loyalty. Haakon had strong support in sections of the Vik, in the Uplands, and in Trøndelag. His party represented the interests of the freeholders in opposition to the thanes. As he was a minor the real leader was a powerful odal yeoman named Sigurd Hallvardsson who assumed the title of jarl. This term had lost its old meaning and was now for the first time used to designate the one man next to the king in power and dignity. The title was to be borne by many strong men in years to come.

At first Haakon's men could not defeat Ingi. In desperation they ravaged the land in a manner unheard of since viking times and roused much indignation. At last the tide turned. As Gregorius Dagsson was leading an attack on the enemy he hesitated to cross a river because the ice was unsafe, but egged on by accusations of cowardice, he rashly rushed forward. He sank through the ice and was slain by Haakon's men. Angered and grieved at the death of the man he loved best, Ingi rushed into battle and was killed. Princess Christina, the wife of Erling Wryneck, cared for the body of Ingi and had it buried in Saint Hallvard's Church in Oslo. Concealed in the church she listened to the counsels of Haakon and his men and sent word to her husband that the king was not to be trusted.

¶ Ingi Hunchback's death left Haakon the Broad-Shouldered sole king of Norway, but his control of the country was precarious and there was no chance that he would be left to enjoy his position in peace. The factional strife had been too bitter, the old law of personal revenge still permeated the social system, and there were others who according to old usage had as great a claim to the throne as he.

Among Ingi's followers no man had greater prestige than Erling Wryneck. He was ambitious and an astute enough politician to grasp the opportunity offered by circumstances. He called together Ingi's men, who agreed to unite and take as king "him who was born to it." The choice fell upon Magnus, the five-year-old son of Erling, who was of royal blood through his mother Christina, the daughter of Sigurd Jerusalemfarer. No doubt the fact that he was Erling's son weighed heavily in the decision: "And here is also a man to be his adviser, and whose duty it is to take care of him and his kingdom; and that man is his father Erling, who is both prudent, brave, experienced in war, and an able man in governing the kingdom."[3] The other leading men did not, it seems, try to share Erling's control over the king and the kingdom. Civil war was felt as a curse upon the land, the desire for peace and security was growing, and the landed aristocrats who made up the Ingi party believed that this could best be obtained through one strong king.

In his fight against Haakon, Erling obtained help from King Valdemar of Denmark, promising him the Vik and perhaps suzerainty over the rest of the land. In 1162, Haakon was defeated and fell in battle, at the age of fifteen. Erling then took his little son to Trøndelag where the Eyrathing hailed him king of all Norway.

Nevertheless the position of the young king was not secure. He was of royal blood, to be sure, but the opposition raised anti-kings with equally good legal claims. That he was descended from a king on his mother's side only might be a disadvantage, but it was not so serious, for the principle had not been established that the right to the kingdom passed to the male line only; and on the other hand, it was an advantage to be born in rightful wedlock. But while the idea that there must be only one king was coming to the fore as offering an escape from civil wars, it was not so generally accepted that rival kings might not get large followings.

To strengthen his son's position, Jarl Erling sought the aid of the archbishop. Eystein Erlendsson, a member of a strong chieftain family in Trøndelag, had upon the death of Jon Birgerson in 1157 been appointed archbishop by Ingi Hunchback. He was an able and upright man, well beloved throughout the land, and he understood the trends of his age, especially in the church. He went to Rome and there received ordination from the pope. He came home perhaps even more imbued with Gregorian ideals than he had been before and impressed with the splendor of the church as he saw it manifested in the capitals of the South. Striving to make his archbishopric powerful, he needed all the economic strength he could obtain, especially as he was engaged in building the greatest monument of the Norwegian medieval church, the Nidaros Cathedral, begun by his predecessor. When Erling suggested that if the archbishop would lend his spiritual prestige to the throne of Magnus, the jarl would back up his efforts to increase the revenues of the church, Eystein was ready to enter into an agreement. It is not fair to say that his motives were only financial, for he was

[3] *The Saga of Magnus Erlingsson,* Chapter 1.

earnestly concerned about the welfare of the church and the peace of the country.

The accord introduced into the political ideas in Norway new elements that may well be called revolutionary. Late in the summer of 1163 the archbishop anointed Magnus and crowned him king in the presence of all the great men of the land. This first coronation in Norway took place in Christ Church in Bergen amid splendor and festive pomp, and Latin forms were used resembling those employed in other countries where coronation had become the usual practice. This introduced a spiritual element into the conception of royal dignity, the idea of the sacredness of the person of the king, which was foreign to old Norwegian law. Magnus called himself "the Lord's Anointed" and "King by the Grace of God," titles formally recognized in the following century in the laws of Magnus the Lawmender. This implied that pretenders not so sanctified were guilty of a crime in rising against the Lord's Anointed.

The two leaders made an arrangement to settle the questions of succession which was approved by the various *lagthings* and thus became the law of the land. It provided that there must be only one king—royal power was indivisible—and he must be "properly born," that is legitimate, although that conception was less rigidly defined than today. He must be the nearest heir unless there were serious reasons for departing from the rule. In such event the choice would rest with the archbishop, the bishops, and the twelve "best men," i.e. thanes, of each diocese selected by the bishops. They were to meet at Nidaros "near the sainted King Olaf," and select the most suitable of near heirs. As in church elections, the majority would decide, but never in opposition to the bishops. Votes must be weighed as well as counted.

The law bears the impress of Eystein's keen mind and of the canon law. If carried out, it would add dignity and stability to the royal office. But it was a breach in the old law, both because the right of inheritance in the royal family was limited and because it disregarded the time-honored power of the *things*. The new law enhanced the importance of the church, yet there is no indication that the archbishop even tried to exercise any authority over the ruler.

The king, as stated in a Latin letter issued by Magnus, felt that he had received his kingdom from God and Saint Olaf, that he was the vicar of Norway's Eternal King: "Undaunted I will go forward, whatever pain, trial, and tribulation call me, to maintain law and justice, to defend the country as Saint Olaf's property, safe in God's and his protection—go forward in battle with him as my chief. As his warrior and in his camp will I fight, and if they raise up forts against me, my heart shall not fear."[4] His fervent confidence, which believed defeat impossible, added to the tragedy of his final failure.

It was no easy life that faced the child king, who would rather "have played with other boys than sit among chieftains."[5] Erling had to fight a twofold war, against the Danish king and against the partisans of Haakon the Broad-Shouldered, who feared Erling's vengeance more than war. Party feeling was growing. First one and then another anti-king was raised and Erling met stubborn resistance. The opposition came to be more and more a proletarian party which attracted unsettled, discontented elements. Often these warriors had to take to the woods and mountains and had nothing but birch bark to bind about their legs. In disdain their enemies gave them the nickname "Birchlegs," which came to be adopted by the party as a name of honor.

Magnus generally accompanied his father on his campaigns and travels about the country. As Erling was bent on the business of defeating his foes, he became increasingly hard and relentless. He had no time for the lighter side of life. He dressed in simple, somber clothes of a bygone style and forced his son to do the same. Magnus felt oppressed by the wars which made his reign a curse to himself and "every person in the country"; he craved gaiety and loved women, and when he became his own master, says Snorri, dressed lavishly.

The war dragged on. Finally in 1177 Magnus, who was then twenty-one, administered a decisive defeat to his enemies, at Re near Tønsberg. *Heimskringla* ends thus: "King Magnus then returned to Tønsberg and won great renown through his victory, for it had been in the mouths of all that Jarl Erling was breastplate and shield for himself and his son. But, after King Magnus had won this victory over so strong and large a force with fewer men, it seemed to every one that he surpassed all others, and that he would become a warrior as much greater than his father Jarl Erling as he was younger."

It looked as though the future might be bright; but then Sverri Sigurdsson came upon the scene.

¶ "God sent here from some outlying skerries a little, low man," King Sverri said of himself. He was born in Bergen, but, shortly after King Sigurd Mouth had been killed, he had been sent to the Faroes, the

[4] Paasche, *Kong Sverre*, 131.
[5] Magnus's last speech to his men, *King Sverri's Saga*, Chapter 89.

colony most closely tied to the mother country. There he was reared by Bishop Hroi, prepared for the church, and, though below the canonical age, ordained as a priest. When he was twenty-four his mother Gunhild came out to the Faroes and disclosed to him that he was the son of Sigurd Mouth and so had a better claim to the throne of Norway than had Magnus Erlingsson. It took about a year, his saga says, before Sverri made up his mind to undertake the hazardous task of claiming the throne. He was not only ambitious, but had the sense of honor and duty of his age that made it mandatory for a man to claim what was rightly his, and he held the belief common in the Middle Ages that a people was bound to suffer if it had the wrong ruler. When he was tempted to give up "the wretched kingdom" which gave him not a moment of peace, the thought of his people, he said, made him continue the struggle.

Much ink and investigation have been spent on the question of whether Sverri had a legal claim to the throne, and the problem can never be solved. "No one knows anything about my parentage," he said, "nothing but what I myself relate." There can be no doubt, however, that he himself believed both in his royal birth and in his mission. Otherwise his personality and career would have been impossible. "A fool would Sverri be," he said, "if he would sacrifice so much to win this wretched kingdom: lose his soul and salvation for it." Moreover the people about him, even his enemies, believed in him with no reservations, and not once was there a suggestion that he might be an impostor. At any rate this "little, low man" had been schooled in the most storm-swept and barren of the Norwegian islands to bear the hardships he was to encounter; he had been trained by the bishop to meet the spiritual and intellectual problems which confronted him; and he was richly endowed with the qualities that could make him one of the most remarkable persons in the history of Norway.

Sverri came to Norway some years before the Battle of Re left the Birchlegs defeated and leaderless. He had traveled about even among Erling's men to find out the conditions in the country, preparing no doubt for the time when he was to advance his claims to the throne. Across the Swedish border in Vermland, he met the remnant of the defeated band of Birchlegs, and, according to his own saga, he somewhat reluctantly accepted the leadership of the ragged little flock. But having taken command he attracted more men to his banner and imbued his followers with his own daring courage and dauntless, even joyous, faith in his own mission. In June 1177 Sverri made a sudden attack upon Trøndelag, defeated a force several times the size of his own, took possession of the city and of Saint Olaf's standard, and succeeded in having the Eyrathing acclaim him king. This recognition no doubt added to his prestige, but with his small force and inadequate equipment he could not maintain himself in Nidaros. There followed two years of uninterrupted guerilla warfare, as the Birchlegs fought their way over seemingly impassable mountains, through trackless forests, and in outposts of population where the scattered people were untouched by Christianity and scarcely knew whether a king was an animal or a man. With rapid marches through snowstorms or spring thaws, this army of the wilderness suddenly dashed out in the most unexpected places from Trøndelag to the Vik and withdrew before superior forces as rapidly as it had advanced, never resting, always fighting, if not against man then against nature. The whole account would seem like a fabulous tale if it were not dominated by Sverri, whose personality grips the modern reader as it did his followers of yore. His resourcefulness, his daring and his strategy, as well as his quiet sense of humor, his kindliness and optimism, his joy in life even in the midst of tragedy, and his faith that his cause was the cause of God, all enabled him to achieve the seemingly impossible.

On June 19, 1179, Sverri won his first major victory and Erling suffered his only great defeat. The battle illustrates Sverri's strategy and shows how the jarl, aged through heavy drinking and twenty years of unbroken conflict, had lost his elasticity and watchfulness, although he could not bear to see this priest, possessed of the devil, occupy his son's throne. Erling was hunting for a Birchleg fleet which had eluded him in the fog. Sending some of his ships to Bergen, he and Magnus with most of the fleet set sail to Nidaros. As they arrived they saw Sverri's ships lying in the fjord apparently ready to leave, and Sverri's standard hastily moving along the road on the other side of the Nid River. The jarl's men pursued and were caught in a trap: Sverri was not with his banner, but was lying in ambush in a near-by vale. Erling's men were driven back into the city, and the Birchlegs were seemingly withdrawing up the valley. A few days later, when in spite of warnings the jarl had grown careless and many of his soldiers had been carousing, the Birchlegs returned. On the hill which gave the first view of the city Sverri knelt in prayer and then addressed his men in one of those speeches which never failed to bring results. In spite of their smaller number he was sure of victory and he promised that each man should be given the rank of the man he slew: he who "slays a thane shall become a thane." The Battle of Kalveskinn (the Calf's Hide), fought near the cathedral, was sharp and short. Erling received a spear wound, but when asked whether it was serious, he replied, "There is nothing the matter with me. Follow the king's standard." Magnus bent over him, and when he saw his death was near, kissed him: "We shall meet on the day of joy, father." The army fled in wild confusion and Magnus barely escaped and sailed to Bergen. Archbishop Eystein, who was in Bergen at the time of the battle, did not return to his see, but went to England where he stayed in exile for three years. "King Sverri's power increased so much that there was no man in Norway who did not call him king except King Magnus and his men," says his saga. While later events showed this to be a gross exaggeration, his real power dates from this battle.

The importance he attached to the event and his plan to concentrate power in his own hands are expressed in his speech at Erling's grave: "Times have greatly changed, as you can see, and events have taken a strange turn, as now one man only stands in the place of three—of king, jarl, and archbishop—and I am that man."[6]

Definite changes resulted from this victory. Trøndelag fully recognized the authority of Sverri and he could depend upon its support. This helped to give the district the preeminent place in Norwegian history which it was to occupy for about a century. Trøndelag was still a stronghold of the old type of yeomen who looked with ill favor on the growth of the landed magnates, whether lay or ecclesiastical. When these substantial farmers joined Sverri, the Birchlegs were no longer a lower class party, as in the past when it was largely made up of discontented elements from the Vik and Telemark. That Sverri had no idea of democratizing the government is clear from his speech before the Battle of Kalveskinn. Humble people who had served him advanced into the upper classes, wore the splendid clothes and carried the weapons of the slain aristocrats, and were so puffed up by their new glory that they wanted to forget their lowly past.

Magnus would not give up. Deprived of the father who had made decisions for him and deserted by the man who had placed the crown on his head, he still felt that as the Lord's Anointed he must be true to his coronation oath. So the war went on, becoming almost a war between two states, Sverri having his stronghold in Trøndelag, while Magnus controlled most of the land farther south, especially the Westland. Though he had more men and greater resources, these advantages

[6] *King Sverri's Saga,* Chapter 38.

were more than outweighed by the personal superiority of Sverri who always outwitted his enemy. Sverri never let his men go into battle without a speech that filled them with confidence: "You spoke as the best of all kings," and "it was never a lie when you promised us victory."

After four years of fighting Sverri won a decisive battle at Bergen, gained control of the Westland, and put his sheriffs in charge throughout the region. The people, however, were still loyal to Magnus. A rising in Sogn against the demands of Christmas entertainment so incensed Sverri that he, who generally restrained his men from violence, let them plunder and ravage the countryside. Scattering far and wide they forgot their usual caution, and for once Sverri was taken by surprise. On June 15, 1184, Magnus, who had returned from Denmark with a superior force, sailed into the fjord to Fimreite, where Sverri's fleet lay. This time their king could not promise the Birchlegs victory, still they would rather fight than flee. Sverri's strategy again won. Magnus Erlingsson with almost his whole army found death in the battle. It was rumored among Sverri's opponents that he had with him a daughter of the devil who caused the sea to open and swallow Magnus's fleet.[7] But to Sverri it seemed an act of God.

At Sverri's command the fallen king received a fitting burial in Christ Church in Bergen where twenty years earlier he had been crowned. Sverri "spoke many fair words, for he did not lack words nor the skill to turn his speech wherever he wished." As he watched Magnus's men pass the casket, many of them weeping, and saw one of them sobbing as he bent to kiss his fallen king, he remarked, "It will be long before such can be trusted." But Sverri's whole policy was conciliatory, and the people submitted readily when their leader was gone, though, the saga intimates, men might kiss the hand they wished were struck off, and many of the aristocrats could not forget their old loyalties.

Sverri sailed on to the south and east, "no man spoke against the will of the king." He further strengthened his position by marrying Margaret, the daughter of the Swedish king Erik the Saint. The policy of seeking friendship in Sweden to counterbalance the constant threat from Danish influence can be traced even at the time of Saint Olaf, and was continued throughout the next century by Sverri's descendants. Sverri was more powerful than any of his predecessors and developed a more effective administration. Although he felt that he was the king

[7] "Habebat enim secum quandam filiam diaboli, potentem in maleficiis," William of Newburgh, *Historia Rerum Anglicarum*, Book 3, Chapter 6.

of the people as a whole, not of a class, he depended on the new men of the aristocracy he was building up. He created few new thanes, but relied mainly on his sheriffs. They were paid not in land but in a share of the income from taxes and fines, and therefore became more dependent upon the king than the old nobility had been. The hird had grown into a large army, so many of the hirdmen no longer stayed at the court, but lived about in the country, acquired land and were in a way a lesser nobility in the king's service. The *leidang* became a regular royal tax. In the legal system, too, the king's power was enhanced. More and more he took the initiative in lawmaking. Sverri made an innovation by appointing lawmen whose duty it was to bring about agreement outside of the *things* and prevent complicated litigation, thus introducing more elasticity into legal methods.

The king welcomed to his court skalds, saga writers, and learned men, and made it a center of cultural and civilizing influences. He laid down strict regulations for his hird and wished the inscription on his seal to be considered their rule as well as his own: "Suerus Rex magnus, ferus ut leo, mitis ut agnus."[8] "Warriors should in time of peace be gentle as the lamb, but in war fierce as the lion," he said after his men had been involved in a brawl caused by the consumption of too much of the wine brought in by German merchants. This is probably the most forceful speech against abuse of strong drink found in old Norwegian literature.

In this speech Sverri gives quite a little picture of Bergen with its hustling cosmopolitan air. There came traders from Iceland and all the Western Isles, and English merchants brought wheat, flour, honey, textiles, wax, and kettles. These were all welcome, but the king censured the Germans who came in large ships and wanted to take away butter and fish, which were needed at home, and gave only wine in return. Sverri often stayed in Bergen, which was the most flourishing town at the time and became almost like a capital. Both there and in Nidaros he built a royal residence and a fort—Sverriborg in Bergen and Zion in Nidaros—of greater dimensions than had ever been constructed before.

In the middle of the twelfth century a period of rapid growth of towns had begun. Foreign trade was reviving, and in contrast to viking times, it was concentrated in the cities. A movement of population from the rural districts had begun, although a mere trickle, and the country people brought their way of living and building to the city. As on a farm, they had different houses for all purposes, but they were strung

[8] "King Sverre Magnus, fierce as a lion, gentle as a lamb." William of Newburgh, Book 3, Chapter 6.

out in one long row back from the street. The towns were uncomfortable, unsanitary and filled with noisome smells to a degree that we can hardly imagine. Yet, though small, they were playing a greater and greater part in the events of the age, and with their growth came a greater diversity in life and more specialized occupations. Merchants and craftsmen made up the bulk of the town population.

Though Sverri was king in fact as well as in name after the fall of Magnus, he was not allowed to reign in peace. In the next decade no less than five young pretenders came forward to claim the throne. The first two were instigated by prominent followers of Magnus who were seeking revenge, and found their chief support in the Vik region, mainly from the well-to-do people in town and country. The three later conflicts, which also occurred in the Vik, were chiefly lower class risings and were put down by the upper classes without any help from the king. In this district the economic changes that were producing a marked class distinction had proceeded farther than in the rest of the country. The distress and discontent were great, and the very elements in society from which Sverri had drawn his first support now rose against him. The social unrest made it easy to stir up a class war. It became a phase of the last and greatest rising against Sverri.

The church magnates were from the beginning in opposition to Sverri, and his conflict with them was part of the current European struggle between the Gregorian ideal and the older, now reviving idea of a national church largely controlled by the king. A truce was called when Archbishop Eystein Erlendsson returned from his exile in England. The king allowed the church its "liberties," which, however, were not clearly defined. Eystein confined himself to his church duties, revised and reformed the Frostathing church law, and edited a work on Saint Olaf's martyr death and miracles. But the greatest monument to Eystein's many-sided activity is found in the Nidaros Cathedral, to the building of which he devoted himself with untiring zeal. Eystein and the king lived in harmony, and before the archbishop's death in 1188 "each forgave the other all things that had come between them."

Eystein's death, however, brought the harmony to an end. He had wished Eirik Ivarsson, the bishop of Stavanger, to be his successor. Sverri was not pleased, but he yielded. Eirik had been trained at Paris in the most extreme theories of the superiority of the church over the state. He was European-Catholic in his outlook, narrow, intense, and uncompromising. There was more than enough inflammable material. The amount of money the archbishop could collect, the extent of the jurisdiction of the church courts, and the election of the clergy, especially of the bishops, all were subjects of controversy. Most important was the last. In this respect Sverri was both conservative and advanced. He maintained the old principle that bishops should be chosen by clergy and people, and that as the head and representative of the people, the king had a right to be consulted and be present at episcopal elections. This was in accord with general European thinking, but Sverri's arguments were better developed than most. Another source of irritation was Sverri's request that the archbishop crown him. Eirik, who was reluctant to crown this bastard who had so often opposed the church, referred the question to the pope, and there the matter rested.

The break came over the question of the number of warriors the archbishop had about him. Sverri, who insisted that the old legal number of thirty was large enough, referred the matter to a *thing*. The people decided in favor of the king, and the archbishop was given five days in which to get rid of his extra men. Instead Eirik gathered all the men and property he could and set sail for Denmark, where he was received with open arms. The pope authorized him to use the ban against enemies of the church, and Eirik was not a man to let this power go unused. The bishops did not follow their chief, but were even persuaded to crown Sverri. For this they were punished with a papal ban, and one by one they deserted the king.

The man who was to turn this controversy into actual war was Bishop Nicholas Arnesson of Oslo. He was of an old aristocratic family close to Magnus Erlingsson, and more of a warrior and politician than an ecclesiastic—crafty, ambitious, and vengeful. Working quietly to strengthen his own position, he helped the risings against Sverri, while outwardly submitting to the king. He joined Archbishop Eirik in Denmark, and with his approval raised the standard of revolt, returning to the Vik in 1196 with a fleet. He brought with him as pretender to the throne Ingi, a son—whether real or pretended is not known—of Magnus Erlingsson. Thus began the bloodiest and most bitter civil war ever waged in Norway, the Bagler, or Crosier, War. Though begun as a struggle between king and church, it was also a social conflict in which Nicholas appealed to proletarian discontent, as well as a rivalry between two kingdoms, as the Vik and Upland regions under the Crosier party practically formed a separate state, while Trøndelag and the Westland were held by Sverri. The war was not only fought on a larger scale than had been the case earlier, but with greater violence especially on the part of the Crosiers.

The battle of words and ideas also became ever more extreme and relentless, and in this Sverri showed an unquestionable superiority. When the mighty Innocent III became pope in 1198, the papacy made its strength felt all over western Christendom and beyond. Innocent issued a more inclusive bull of excommunication against Sverri's partisans than had his predecessor, and every Sunday Eirik pronounced a ban from the altar of Lund Cathedral. Sverri's reply was his "Speech against the Bishops." It is one of many documents in the controversy that raged throughout Christendom. It was written in Norwegian and is couched in Sverri's forceful language. It also shows the legal learning of the Bologna lawyers and employs their arguments, but the principles were more sharply defined than in other documents of so early a date. It must be noted that Sverri never blamed the pope, but implied that he had been misinformed by the bishops. The king's quarrel with the bishops in no way reflects on his personal religious faith.[9] His conflict with the church naturally caused Sverri to develop his theories of royal power, and there too he stood above his contemporaries. His "Speech against the Bishops" contains the most complete statement of his idea of the exalted position of the king who is "placed above all other dignitaries." Bible passages are freely used and the author draws the conclusion: "Such a great number of examples show clearly that the damnation of his soul threatens everybody who does not show complete loyalty and perfect obedience to the kingly dignity; for kingship is ordained by the word of God, not according to human desires."

"Starting from conservatism, King Sverre became a precursor of the great innovators of royal power and its theory in the thirteenth and fourteenth centuries."[10]

In strategy, too, Sverri surpassed his enemy, but was generally fighting against larger and better equipped forces. In moral stature he rose above both his opponents and his followers. Occasionally his anger was so roused that he let his Birchlegs loose upon the countryside, but he was never happy about his own lapses of temper. When a child ran out from the woods and begged him not to burn its father's farm, Sverri called off all burnings; and on another occasion he forcefully told his men that he would have no more cruelty inflicted upon the people. When victory was in sight in his last battle after a long arduous struggle, he asked his men what they should do with the captives. As the

9 "A Defence of the King against the Bishops and Clergy, out of Canon Law," *Sverrissaga*, translated by Sephton, Appendix.

10 Halvdan Koht, "Scandinavian Kingdoms until the End of the Thirteenth Century," in *Cambridge Medieval History*, 6:382, New York, 1936.

men grumbled at the mere idea of being deprived of just revenge, Sverri said, "See here, my good men, who among you feels so great that he is not willing to be compared with me? Can you remember that any one censured you for following my example?" After telling what he had endured he added, "Now I want to forgive them for God's sake, and I expect His forgiveness for what I have done against Him. You have souls just as well as I, and you must remember that no one will call you soft or cowardly on account of this." As the *thing* closed, all agreed that the king should have his way.

Soon after, Sverri died in Bergen, finding great satisfaction in the fact that he could die in his high seat surrounded by friends and not, as Nicholas had predicted, hewn to pieces and cast to the dogs and ravens.

¶ Sverri had made careful preparation for the succession of his only surviving son, Haakon. Nevertheless a quarter of a century was to pass after Sverri's death before Norway attained permanent internal peace and union. It is rather a confused period. Whatever ideals had been back of the wars in Sverri's age were lost sight of, but even so the fundamental constitutional principles advanced in the earlier struggles became firmly established.

Haakon was accepted as king first by the hird and then by the Eyrathing, as was the old usage. There was no thought of any joint rule, for the principle that there should be one king had won out. The new king was attractive and popular and pursued a clear-cut policy of conciliation. He catered to the support of the common people who wished peace and kept his men under strict control. Following the advice of his father, he also made peace with the church leaders, and the bishops all returned to their sees. Even Archbishop Eirik came back and removed the ban from the king and all his followers. The king guaranteed to the higher clergy all the liberties to which Holy Writ and the agreements with earlier kings entitled them, in return for the promise that they would show him the honor due him according to the Scriptures and the laws of the land. Though vague, the compact enabled the bishops to carry on their work in peace and withdraw their support from the opposition which still continued to bear the name of Crosiers.

When Haakon died suddenly in 1204, a four-year-old grandson of Sverri, Guttorm Sigurdsson, was made king, but died within a few months. As far as people knew there was now no heir to the throne in the direct male line. The peace party of the Trøndelag yeomen, backed by the church, forced through the choice of Ingi Baardsson, the son of Sigurd Mouth's daughter Cecilia. Though Sverri in his conflict with Magnus Erlingsson had of necessity maintained that a claim to the throne could descend only through a male line, his theory was not advanced in opposition to his sister's son. During Ingi's reign (1204-1217) the little Crosier kingdom continued to exist and there were clashes between the armies of the two realms until 1208 when peace was made. Throughout the reign strong men vied with each other for the control over the weak king and laid plots for the succession of their favorite candidate.

When Ingi died the most powerful pretender to the throne was his half-brother, Jarl Skule Baardsson. Skule was not of royal blood, however, and the only claim he could advance was as the personal heir of Ingi. His high ambitions were thwarted at the Eyrathing as the Birchleg army forced through the choice of their favorite, Sverri's grandson, Haakon Haakonsson (1217-1263).

Haakon was the posthumous son of King Haakon Sverrisson and Inga of Varteig, a girl from Østfold. The first part of his saga is the story of the last great Birchleg adventure, reminiscent of Sverri's early days. Born in the realm of the opposition, the child was in constant danger of being seized or killed. Faithful Birchlegs guarded him carefully; and finally, after a secret journey across the mountains in the dead of winter, full of hazards and hardships, brought him and his mother to Nidaros to King Ingi, at whose court he was reared. He was only thirteen when he became king, and Jarl Skule continued to control the government as he had done in Ingi's time, receiving a third of the royal income. Haakon placed great confidence in Skule and later married his daughter, Margaret.

In the very year of Haakon's succession the Crosiers lost their king by death, recognized Haakon, and made a formal agreement with him. The following year the Crosier name was discarded and the party, which had been the chief fomenter of civil war for over thirty years, disbanded. Even this did not bring peace, however. The peace was made only by the leading men of the two parties—the old aristocrats from before the time of Sverri and the newer Birchleg group, indicating a growing sense of upper class solidarity. The common people of eastern Norway on whom the Crosier cause had depended for its chief support had no strong personal loyalty to the warrior chieftains, and refused to follow them now. For a decade Haakon was harassed by uprisings. First came a revolt of lower class people against the economic oppressions of his sheriffs and thanes. It was definitely a class war. Later the wealthier freeholders under their yeoman chieftains also rose, as opposition to the growing dominance of the landed aristocrats tended to unite all the other social forces. Various bands with successive leaders and pretenders took up the battle. There were good fighters among them, but their equipment was inadequate, they had no gifted military commander, and found no pretender worthy of great devotion. They were not a match for the brilliant Jarl Skule and his trained army, and the wars only worsened the condition of the people. In 1228 the farmers themselves hanged the last rebel chieftain, and the civil wars were finally over.

In Haakon, Sverri's family in the direct male line was firmly established on the throne and was to continue to rule through a great century in Norway's history. The country came out of the internal conflicts peaceful, unified, and consolidated, as fully a developed national state as was to be found anywhere in Europe. Kingship had been at the center of the development. The conflicts were never between king and nobles, as in feudalized countries, but always between kings and would-be kings. In view of later developments, Sverri's words at Erling Wryneck's bier seem prophetic. The establishment of one strong king gave the land peace and greatness, but this royal power was built upon the support of aristocrats who were both landholders and royal officials. The king thereby lost that close contact with the common people which had characterized the eleventh century. Yet in spite of new methods in administration, the popular will could still be expressed in the *things*, and, even though royal lawmaking had begun, the old folk law was still the basic legal system. The people still made themselves felt as a vital force, while their deep devotion to the king shed a rare luster about royalty in Norway.

¶ During the civil wars ruthless soldiers with fire and sword sporadically brought the misery of war to town and countryside; but on the whole daily life went on much as it had in the past. On the farms, the many activities were carried on fundamentally in much the same way as in prehistoric times. A lively exchange was carried on between different districts, as, for example, the fishermen on the treeless shore procured bast rope from regions where linden trees flourished and lumber and tar from the great pine forests. On the whole, life was richer and more varied than in the preceding period. Not least is this evident in the art and architecture. The general European influence which characterized the whole medieval period was increasing, yet the indigenous Norwegian elements left a strong mark. The art for daily use, weaving, metal work, and wood carving, continued, of course, but the articles that have been preserved are not nearly so numerous as from the age of heathen burial customs. Of secular architecture practically nothing has survived. Pine was the material used, and the fire hazard was great. Even the great halls of the kings were built of wood richly carved, and fortifications were often mere wooden palisades, although stone walls were occasionally erected as in Sverri's forts, Sverriborg and Zion. However, the main effort of the age was not devoted to secular building.

Christianity had brought in new needs and new impulses which dominated the art of the age, and in no period before or since has the development of ecclesiastical architecture been so rich or the number of church buildings so great. The main religious influence emanated from the parish church, which was closely bound up with the daily life of the people. The priest was often one of the community, lived like the rest of the people and obtained much of his livelihood from the parsonage farm. His duties and his rights were regulated by numerous laws. He must not only perform the services with the Latin ritual, but teach and preach in the language of the people. The church buildings were erected and maintained by the people; and from the nearby belfry, the church bells, the importance of which can hardly be overestimated, were pealing over fjord, vale, and hill, calling the people to higher things. It has been estimated that eight or nine hundred wooden parish churches were built throughout the land in the Middle Ages. While some were built in the eleventh century, the greatest number dated from the twelfth century, and not a few from the thirteenth.

The parish timber church (*stavkirke*) is the most intimately Norwegian of all monuments from the Middle Ages. In it the people's mastery of the use of pine in building and art, which had been developing from time immemorial, reached an unparalleled perfection. The complete absence of metal nails and spikes as well as the elasticity of building, which allowed for expansion and contraction, helped to give the structure remarkable endurance. The architecture, however, had to be adapted to the needs of the medieval church services. So the interiors were built on the general plan of the Romanesque basilicas characteristic of the age, with choir, three aisles, and rounded arches. The wood carving, especially of the doorways, was intricate and elaborate, resembling that of the Viking Age. The pine panels of the altars, also ceiling, pillars, and walls, were decorated with strong designs in brilliant primary colors. The bold, restless luxuriance of both carving and painting was reminiscent of pre-Christian times, yet there were also Romanesque and even Byzantine influences to be seen in patterns and themes. There were Christian subjects, southern acanthus leaves, and even a trace of the oriental in the frequent use of the dragon. Yet all was blended into a thoroughly Norwegian whole.

Stone architecture was an importation which was also used by the church, and at first foreign masons were employed. Of Norway's twenty-seven monasteries about half were built in this century, their architecture often influenced by the mother house in foreign lands. Episcopal residences were also erected, but most numerous were the churches. Small stone parish churches of the simple Anglo-Saxon style of one aisle and a small square choir were built as early as the eleventh century and continued to be erected throughout the Middle Ages. But in the twelfth century the richer parishes began to build more pretentious Romanesque basilicas, such as West Aker Church in Oslo. In them ornamental details are few, but the classic poise, the harmonious proportions, and the dignity of massive pillars and round arches lend to these edifices a noble beauty. In the seats of the bishoprics, imposing cathedrals were rising. The oldest is the one in Stavanger, begun by Sigurd Jerusalemfarer, which borrowed much from the Winchester Cathedral. Not so imposing but of equally pure Norman style is the lovely Mary Church in Bergen. To both these churches Gothic choirs and other details were added later. More impressive than either was the Hamar Cathedral of which only a few tragic columns and arches are standing. Mention should also be made of the Magnus Cathedral of the Orkneys, next to the Nidaros the most magnificent Norwegian edifice from the Middle Ages.

No other church is so tied up with the history of Norway, in its periods of greatness and of tragedy, as the Christ Cathedral in Nidaros. In the eleventh century Olaf the Peaceful had built a plain little stone church as a shrine to Saint Olaf. The high altar was directly over the spot where Saint Olaf's body had rested the first night after Stiklestad and where a spring had burst forth. Above the altar was placed the casket of the saint.

Soon after Norway had acquired its own archbishopric, in 1152, plans for a larger church were made and the first archbishop began the building of a magnificent Romanesque transept which was completed by his successor Eystein. Eystein also planned and began a Romanesque nave, but probably did not get much beyond the foundation. Of all his undertakings the cathedral seems to have been nearest to Eystein's heart. When he returned from exile in 1184 he had with him plans for a church more glorious than any Norway had seen. He had stayed near Canterbury where was being built the first Gothic cathedral of England as a shrine to the murdered Saint Thomas. From this must have come Eystein's idea of the beautiful Early English Gothic octagonal shrine, altar, and choir. They occupy the place of the earlier modest church, which had to be torn down. Eystein's energy, enthusiasm, and artistic sense, as well as his intimate knowledge of Gothic architecture were phenomenal, and in conception and workmanship, though not in size, his church has a place among the finest in Europe. Eystein's return from England marked the introduction into Norway of Gothic architecture, which soon exerted an influence on the neighboring parishes. Not before the following century did it come into general use, and even then many rural communities clung to the earlier Romanesque, as employed in the timber churches, which had become completely their own.

¶ The oldest Norwegian manuscripts extant are of religious content. Through the church the intercourse between Norway and lands farther south was growing as learned men of the clergy received their training in the universities of England, France, and Italy and brought to the North ideas and influences from these countries. Works of practically every prominent ecclesiastical writer were translated from Latin into Norwegian. A great number of homilies and legends were written, the contents of which—stories, symbolism, and admonition—are in general European; but the form, the language, and the feelings are Norwegian. The same holds true of the religious poetry, the oldest of which dates from the twelfth century. Even the kennings are new in these lays to the glory of the God "who holds the whole world in His hand," yet they have retained not a little of the typically Norwegian, sometimes consciously employing the style of the Eddic poems.

As writing became more general, it played an increasingly important part in the political as well as in the religious life, and some official documents of great value to the historian have survived. Moreover, the writing of Norwegian history was also begun at this time. It was one of the many manifestations of the seething activities of the age, and a result of the awakening national sense, which quite naturally found one expression in historical writing. In the age of the twelfth century renaissance, an intense interest in history writing pervaded Western Europe, and travelers from the North, both men and women, traders and clerks, men of affairs and the aristocrats who went for pure love of travel, brought home impulses from other lands.

As the church had introduced literary writing and European ideas, it was natural that the first histories should come from the monasteries and be written in Latin. Such a work is *Historia Norvegiae*. It is highly probable that it was written about 1170 in Munkeliv Monastery in Bergen by the earliest Norwegian scholar whose name we know, Master Arnulf.[11] The last part of the work is lost, the extant section covering the period from the early Yngling kings to the arrival of Saint Olaf in Norway. It must be classed with the monastic chronicles which the Middle Ages produced and has little literary merit. Yet it is significant because, as far as we know, it was the first attempt in Norway to write a complete history of the country, and gives older and, in some cases, more reliable information than the sagas.

Further history writing comes from the Nidaros region, the richest and most populous section of Norway, where civilization flourished as in no other place and political development had its center.

About 1180 a monk in Trøndelag who called himself Theodricus wrote another monastic chronicle, *Historia de antiquitate regum Norvagiensium*, dedicated to Archbishop Eystein. He carried his story only to the death of Sigurd Jerusalemfarer for, he says, he did not wish to record the shocking events of the following years of civil strife. To about the same time belongs *Agrip*, a compendium written in Old Norse, in all probability by a Norwegian cleric from the Trøndelag region. These two histories reflect the conflict between Sverri and Eystein, Theodricus favoring the archbishop and *Agrip* the king, indicating that the battle was fought both with sword and with pen.

Theodricus says that his writing was based on information received from Icelanders, who, it was generally agreed, knew more about these things and were more interested in the past than any other people in the North. More than half a century before his time, critical research into the history of Norway had begun in Iceland. The Icelandic monastic schools were not only notable for theological and classical learning, but for putting into writing the traditions and history of the people. The clerics were in close touch with the lay aristocracy, from which they sprang, and, moreover, young men who were to pursue a secular career

[11] *Historia Norvegiae* was discovered in Scotland by P. A. Munch. Scholars have devoted much effort to determine the authorship and date of the book. I am following Halvdan Koht's conclusions. "Den fyrste norske nationalhistoria" in *Innhogg og utsyn i norsk historie*, 199-231.

as chieftains often received clerical training. Among them were the two founders of historical writing in Iceland, Sæmund Frodi and Ari Frodi. It was natural to write about Norway. The ties with the mother country were close, and in an age when the history of Iceland was uneventful, the interest in Norway was intense, and people asked eagerly for news from the many travelers returning from the greater country to the east, be they traders, soldiers, skalds, or scholars. Sæmund, who was versed in all the historical learning of his day, wrote in Latin a chronicle of the Norwegian kings. It was translated into Old Norse in verse form under the title *Noregs Konungatal* and was much used, but has unfortunately been lost.

Sæmund's younger kinsman, Ari Frodi, Snorri says, was the first historian to write in Old Norse. His condensed history of Iceland, *Íslendingabók*, has survived. Another history including a genealogy of the Norwegian kings has been lost, but Snorri probably incorporated it all into *Heimskringla* for he depended much on Ari's scholarship. Ari was a scientific historian who examined carefully his sources—all of them oral—weighed the evidence, and recorded only what could be well established as reliable. He wrote in a terse objective style without the artistry of the saga writers who followed him, but he was the very cornerstone on which they built; he influenced their style and scholarly approach, and furnished much of their material. In the historical sagas the art of the storyteller, developed by narrators who had preserved and passed on the old traditions orally, was combined with the scholarship of Ari.

Although most of the saga writers were Icelanders, the background for the production of early Norwegian historical writings must be largely sought in Norway. Some of the sagas were written in Norway and for a Norwegian public. The authors knew the country and its traditions through travels and visits, and had often served the kings as skalds or warriors. The two countries were really one society culturally and to some extent also politically, for Icelanders retained their Norwegian citizenship even after emigration.

More important than any other work of the century is *The Saga of King Sverri*. Like other rulers of his age, notably Emperor Frederick Barbarossa, Sverri saw to it that the history of his reign should be written. So he engaged an Icelander at his court to write his saga, and, says the introduction, "Abbot Karl Jónsson wrote when King Sverri sat over him and settled what he should write." Only a part of the saga was produced in this way and it was later completed in Iceland and given the form in which it has come down to us. It is in usual saga style with the interest centering upon the story, which is told with remarkable frankness about friend and enemy alike. Outside of Snorri's it is probably the greatest of the sagas. Vivid in style and characterizations, it is close to the events it relates in time and in emotional reactions. The impetus Sverri gave to history writing is of great significance.

Snorri found it unnecessary to continue *Heimskringla* beyond 1177, the year with which Sverri's saga began. Snorri's time—the early decades of the thirteenth century—was the most productive period in the age of saga writing, and authors had rich contemporary material on which to draw for the many-sided history of the twelfth century.

CHAPTER 8

A PERIOD OF GREATNESS, 1228-1319

AFTER THE WARS came a period of peace and stability that may well be compared to the time before the civil conflicts. But much water had flowed under the bridge since 1130, and the fabric of society had changed. In the thirteenth century the state no longer rested upon the old yeoman society, but upon a strong king depending on the support of a consolidated landowning aristocracy, both lay and clerical, whose position of power became more strongly entrenched as the century advanced. Though it was not a period of scintillating personalities or great adventures, there is justification in calling this the Age of Greatness in earlier Norwegian history. It marks the culmination of the development into a united country and people that had been going on since the time of Harald Fairhair. Norway was a better organized state than were most of the European countries of that age, and even more than in the past the growth of the state depended upon the growth of royal power.

¶ The four kings of this period were all direct descendants of Sverri. They all looked back to him as the hero of their dynasty, the precursor of their whole policy and rule, and though lacking his genius they possessed some of the qualities that made Sverri a great ruler. They were genuinely religious and literary in their tastes and interests. They were energetic workers, busy with many undertakings, and looked upon their kingship as a serious responsibility. They lacked, however, Sverri's sense of humor, his elasticity, his joy in life, and his bold originality.

The most famous among them is Haakon IV Haakonsson, the Old (1217-1263). The very length of his reign gave room for many achievements. And his saga is the longest and most detailed of all the sagas of the kings. Writing at the behest of Haakon's son, Sturla Thordarson had access to a mass of material—earlier records of events, official documents, and letters—which he used conscientiously The saga is, however, an apotheosis of kingship in general and of Haakon in particular.

During the early, difficult years, Haakon had the stanch support of his uncle Jarl Skule, an energetic man and more brilliant than the king. The king bestowed upon him the new-fashioned title of duke and the control of a large part of the kingdom and the royal income thereof. Nevertheless, after the civil wars were ended, Skule seems to have grown more and more dissatisfied. Finally he took to arms, assumed the title of king, and won the recognition of the Eyrathing. There was no general war, and Skule was defeated and killed in 1240. No more pretenders arose to dispute the claims to the throne, and the king could give undivided attention to his many undertakings. The last chapter in his saga, containing a somewhat hodge-podge yet impressive list of the building he did, such as forts, farms, churches, and huts for travelers, gives an idea of his many-sided achievements.

In 1247 Haakon was crowned in Bergen by the papal legate, William of Sabina. The festivities were marked by a luxuriance and colorful pageantry hitherto unknown in Norway. The saga takes delight in describing it in great detail, even to the seating at the banquet. The papal legate had been warned, he said, against going to this outlandish country, where the people would behave more like animals than human beings, where bread would be scarce and poor, and the drinks limited to water and diluted milk. But when he came he saw a greater multitude of ships than he had ever seen in one harbor and a large assembly of well-mannered people, and he found an abundance of good things to eat and drink. The coronation festivities were but an example of the splendid court life that made its appearance in this reign.

Haakon made careful provision for a peaceful succession. Quite early his oldest son, Haakon, was given the title of king, while the other son, Magnus, was made duke. The king was hereafter called Haakon the Old to distinguish him from his son. When Haakon the Younger died in 1257, Magnus was recognized as heir to the throne, and was crowned king before his father set out on his last great venture, an expedition to the Western Islands. Magnus acted as regent during his father's absence, and when the news of Haakon's death reached Norway, his son ascended the throne without further ceremony.

Magnus Lawmender (1263-1280) was so called in later times because he had the greatest share in the legal work which was the most eminent achievement of the age. He was a kind, pious, excessively serious and conscientious man on whom the crown rested as a heavy burden. His is the last of the sagas of the kings, and only some fragments of it are extant. The age of thrilling adventure and war, which delighted the saga writers, was also over.

At a meeting of the council in 1273 he issued a law regulating the succession to the throne. Twelve heirs were mentioned in order of succession, and it was provided that if none of these were to be found the nearest male heir according to the general law of inheritance was to succeed. At the same time, his oldest son Eirik, although a mere child, was given the title of king.

As Eirik Magnusson (1280-1299) was not of age when his father died, a regency of leading nobles was established. The queen mother, Ingeborg, an able and strong-willed woman, had great influence with the regents and the young king. Eirik was well-meaning, but weak and sickly, so that even when he came of age in 1282 he could not assert himself. His reign was therefore a rule of the aristocracy with some abuse of power and much wrangling, especially between the lay and ecclesiastical magnates. For this Eirik was blamed and has undeservedly been nicknamed Priesthater, although he wished peace with the church. In this his brother Haakon supported him. Haakon was created duke and was assigned a third of the kingdom, where he performed practically all the functions of a king.

Haakon V Magnusson (1299-1319) succeeded his brother without any difficulties. Almost at once he obtained the recognition of the Eyrathing and was crowned with much magnificence. He took up his permanent residence in Oslo, which from then on became the capital of the country. Among the stone work in Nidaros Cathedral is an unusual fragment of a statue of Haakon, showing the upper part of his face and head. It is the face of a sensitive, serious, intellectual, and worried man. Haakon was perhaps the most gifted of Sverri's descendants and like his mother, strong-willed almost to stubbornness. He had high ideals about the kingship and was conscientious in fulfilling his duties. He believed the office was instituted by God for the good of the whole people, especially those who had little chance to protect themselves. He systematically built up royal power by checking the aristocracy, which had grown powerful during the reign of his brother. Nevertheless, it became more feudalized in character, and there was danger that men who held fortresses might assume the independence of feudal lords. Although Haakon's rule was in many ways beneficent, it was unfortunate that royal power should reach its height at a time when the succession was dubious.

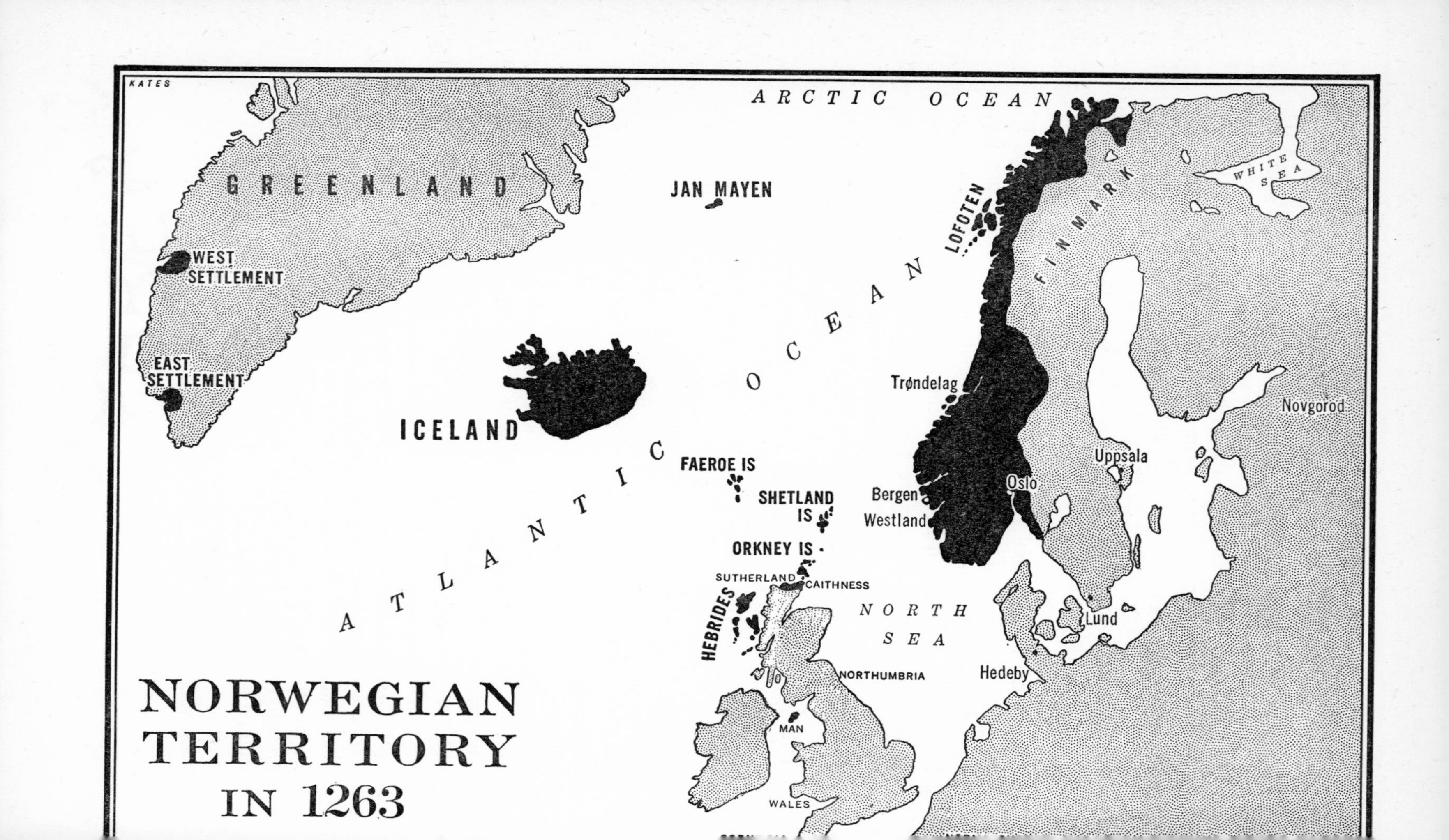
KATES
ARCTIC OCEAN
GREENLAND
JAN MAYEN
WEST SETTLEMENT
EAST SETTLEMENT
ICELAND
ATLANTIC OCEAN
LOFOTEN
FINMARK
WHITE SEA
Trøndelag
Novgorod
FAEROE IS
SHETLAND IS
Bergen
Westland
Oslo
Uppsala
ORKNEY IS
SUTHERLAND
CAITHNESS
HEBRIDES
NORTH SEA
Lund
Hedeby
NORTHUMBRIA
MAN
WALES
NORWEGIAN TERRITORY IN 1263

Haakon's marriage brought him only one child, a daughter, Ingebjørg, born in 1301. The following year a new law of succession was adopted. It provided that if Ingebjørg had a son the throne should pass to him, if not, to Ingebjørg herself. The third in line was to be the son of Agnes, a much older illegitimate daughter of the king. Provisions were made for a regency of twelve men to rule if the heir were a minor upon the death of Haakon. In spite of these precautions he no doubt looked toward the future with serious misgivings. With him the direct male line of the royal family became extinct.

The rulers of this century looked upon themselves as kings by the grace of God. "He is so highly honored and exalted upon earth that all must bend and bow before him as before God" and "he bears God's own name and sits upon the highest judgment seat upon earth."[1] Thus writes the unknown author of *The King's Mirror*. As he probably was a cleric attached to the court of Haakon the Old, his words may be considered almost official. He explains at length the God-given authority of the king, but also the limitations on his power and his responsibility to God and man. He must always pass judgment, with Truth and Justice, Peace and Mercy at his side.

To serve the king as a member of his hird, even of the lowest rank, says *The King's Mirror*, affords a security and honor that even the greatest of men value. "The king owns the entire kingdom as well as all the people in it, so that all the men who are in his kingdom owe him service whenever his needs demand it," and so "why should not every sensible man regard it a greater advantage to be in the king's full protection and friendship?"[2]

We have heard of the king's hird even from the time of Harald Fairhair, and its importance grew with the rising eminence of the kingly office. Therefore it naturally reached its fullest development in the thirteenth century.[3] In the past the hird had first and foremost been the nucleus of the king's army, although even then it constituted the king's court on which he depended for all manner of services. Now the military functions had largely disappeared; but the court duties had been increased and elaborated, and from the hird the king selected most of his numerous officials. The complex rules governing the hird

[1] Laurence M. Larson, trans., *The King's Mirror.* (*Speculum Regale—Konungs Skuggsja*), 246 and 247, New York, 1917.

[2] *Ibid.*, 174 and 175.

[3] Laurence M. Larson, "The Household of the Norwegian Kings in the Thirteenth Century," *American Historical Review*, 13:459-479 (April 1908).

were codified in Magnus Lawmender's Court Law (*Hirdskraa*), probably based upon a code of Sverri's time which has been lost. *The King's Mirror* gives meticulous, somewhat snobbish directions as to how a king's man should comport himself on all occasions. The hird was divided into four grades, each organized as a guild, even to maintaining an old age and illness insurance fund. The king appointed and promoted men, but not without the consent of the guild concerned. The hirdmen were highest in rank and served in the king's council; the gests often looked after the king's interests away from court as spies and soldiers; the candleswains (*kertilsveinar*) were expected to emphasize courtly duties; and the housecarls, who constituted the lowest rank, performed the manual work.

The punctilious etiquette might give the impression of greater refinement than the Norwegian court—or for that matter any court of this age—really attained. Yet there was a new culture in the land, with an extravagant display in dress and festivities hitherto unknown in Norway, and a parvenu delight in it all. Chivalric romances were translated in great number, and the courtiers read them with real or affected pleasure. Queen Euphemia, the wife of Haakon V, especially, had a strong romantic devotion to foreign literature. The ceremonial, too, resembled feudal usages, although Norway was fundamentally not feudal either in its kingship or its aristocracy. Feudal titles took the place of the old Norwegian forms. Thus the man next to the king was created duke, not jarl. Magnus Lawmender established the rule that the thanes (*lendmenn*) were to be called barons, and the candleswains knights, and that all men of the rank of candleswains or above should be addressed as lord. The glory was not to last long, however. In 1308 Haakon V abolished the title of baron, and after his death, when Norway only occasionally had a resident king, the hird declined and finally vanished.

¶ Powerful as he was, the king was not absolute. In fact, he had more difficulty in making himself felt than under the simpler conditions of earlier times. As the complexity of the government had increased, the king was even less able than in the past to handle affairs personally, and more elaborate administrative machinery was therefore developed. Three organs of the central government need to be noted. From the time of the civil wars it had become customary that one of the clergy attached to the court was also chancellor, but in the thirteenth century there developed a chancellery with a number of clerks to take care of the growing volume of documents and correspondence through which the government was carried on. The chancellor needed considerable learning, especially legal, and had to keep record of all important events in the government. Moreover, he was the keeper of the king's seal,[4] a great responsibility in the days when personal signatures were not used, and the seal alone authenticated a document. So quite naturally the chancellor became the king's chief official.

Side by side with the chancellery, the council was developed. Like the chancellery, it functioned regularly from the early years of Haakon the Old's reign. The membership was somewhat shifting, but it was composed of aristocrats both lay and clerical. Magnus's Court Law provided that thanes, or barons, were, next after duke and jarl, to be the king's advisers, and so were entitled to sit in his council. They were not many, perhaps ten or fifteen at this time, and were, except by special appointment, not connected with the local government. But they were the pinnacle of the aristocracy. The council was most powerful during the minority of Eirik. When Haakon V abolished the title of baron, it was largely to make the council more of a royal and less of an aristocratic institution. It became firmly established and continued to exist through various vicissitudes until 1536.

Less fixed in organization was the assembly of magnates (*herremøte*). On occasions, such as coronations, when pomp and circumstance were desired, all the notables of the country as well as representatives of the people were summoned. But the meetings also discussed and acted on matters of general interest. There are indications that smaller meetings were also held which served to keep the king in touch with local conditions. It would seem that out of these meetings a parliament might have developed, as in other countries; but this did not happen. Unlike the council, the assembly of magnates never became an established, regular institution in Norway.

These agencies of the central government show the importance of the aristocracy, which had a strong class feeling and was a nobility of the realm, dissociated from the people and with little of the old local feeling. The dominance of king and nobles in local affairs was almost as marked as in the central government.

Though the king was not as dependent on popular support as he had been, public opinion was still a force, and old laws and usages demanded respect. While there was no legal way of controlling the king, he was

[4] Seals were rather new. About 1280-1290, the lion with crown and axe became the seal of the royal family. When it may be considered the seal of the realm cannot be determined.

bound by his coronation oath to keep the law of the land, and even Haakon V, who did so much to build up royal power, sought the recognition of the Eyrathing before his coronation.

¶ The high respect for law in the whole nation exercised a restraint on arbitrariness on the part of king and upper class. "Our land shall be built up by law, and let it not be laid waste by lawless behavior. And whoever will not allow another his legal right shall not enjoy law."[5] After the lawlessness of the civil war period there was need of a new emphasis on law; moreover, it was necessary to revise the law to bring it into harmony with the development of the state. A far-reaching legal work was perhaps the greatest achievement of this age. It was begun under Haakon the Old, who consulted with the leading men about "all that weighed upon the kingdom and the holy church"; but the task was pursued with greater vigor under his son Magnus Lawmender. The work was largely one of revision and codification with the older laws as the basis: "It seems to us most reasonable, to begin with, that the law of the holy King Olaf should be kept [exactly] as he established it."[6] A most striking change is that the wording of the laws now recognized the king and not the people as possessing supreme law-making power. Even so, the laws were presented to the *lagthings* for approval, which was generally but not invariably obtained.

The work was very extensive. The old laws of the four *lagthings* were collected and codified and continued to be the main law of the districts. Magnus also had a general law compiled for the whole land. This was approved by all the *lagthings* except Borgarthing, but it was not completely carried out, and the main provisions were modified time and again. Most of this code was derived from the Gulathing laws, but much new was added. The form was more modern, and a more generally European legal language was used, showing that men with university training and knowledge of Roman law were employed by the king. The revised laws were more humane than the older. Stealing to avoid starvation, for example, was treated leniently. The most fundamental change, however, was that the state interfered more with daily life and that crimes were now considered offenses against the state, not against the individual or family. At the same time a new city law was also enacted to take the place of the older. The Court Law has already been mentioned. A new church law, not included in the general code, rounded out the legislative work of the reign of Magnus.

[5] Larson, *The Earliest Norwegian Laws*, 224. [6] *Ibid.*, 213.

¶ The increased power of the state was only one phase of the growth of organized society. Though the government was expanding its sphere of activity, its control over the individual was much more limited than in later absolute states. The whole conception of undivided sovereignty, or of the unlimited power of any group or individual, was foreign to the thought of the Middle Ages. It was perfectly natural that the church, as another branch of society, should also increase and define its power. The church was concerned mainly with morals, religion, and church government, matters which had never been under the control of the state. The two institutions could therefore strengthen their power and at the same time work in harmony as they had done in the first century of Christian kings with the difference that had come through the spread of the Gregorian ideas of church independence. That the line of demarcation between the two authorities should cause difficulties was inevitable, but only the economic phase brought serious conflict in the thirteenth century. The difference was neither so dramatic nor so fundamental as in the time of Sverri.

The papal legate who came to the coronation of Haakon the Old expressed great satisfaction with the position of the church in Norway; Haakon's saga boasts, not without justice, that he did more to strengthen Christianity than any other king since Saint Olaf. He gave rich gifts to churches and monasteries and helped spread Christianity among the Lapps by erecting churches in Ofot and Tromsø; he urged the people to pay all church dues, and even induced them to assume a new burden, the donation of a penny for each head of cattle on the farm. This, it seems, was done to finance the building of the nave of the Nidaros Cathedral, which was begun the year after his coronation. During Haakon's reign the mendicant orders, the Franciscans and Dominicans, entered Norway. Unlike earlier orders, they built their houses in the towns and, instead of living cloistered lives, traveled about and performed all the functions of parish priests wherever their services were wanted. This gave rise to abuses and sharp clashes between friars and secular clergy; but the friars were popular with the people, and their preaching helped to increase Christian knowledge and interest.

When Magnus began his legal work, Jon the Red was archbishop. Jon is a striking figure in Norwegian church history, able, energetic, zealous for the church, hierarchical in his views, and learned in both canon and Norwegian law. He protested against any revision of the church law by the king, and the Frostathing upheld Jon. Magnus yielded, for he had established as law the principle that God had given the king power in secular matters and the bishop in spiritual. He seems to have entered into negotiations with the archbishop about formulating a church law that might apply to the whole country and have the support of both church and government.

The result was the famous Concordat of Tønsberg of 1277, formulated in the Franciscan monastery in Tønsberg. In the main this friendly agreement simply defined and established legally the power and position of the church, and so it completed a development that had begun long ago, even as did the other legislation of the time. The bishops formally resigned the power over election of the king which they had claimed in 1164, and in return received freedom from the *leidang* for a larger household than formerly. Jon then completed his church law in which the elements of the national and the canon law were blended into a harmonious whole.[7] It was sanctioned by the king and approved by the bishops. These two documents continued to be valid as long as the Roman Church held sway in Norway.

When Magnus died in 1280 and Eirik became king, there occurred a serious breach in the peace between church and state. The regency, in which there was no clerical representative, began at once to interfere with the rights of the church. After trying in vain to reach an agreement with the government, Jon excommunicated the regents. They paid no attention to the ban, but forthwith drove the archbishop and two of the bishops into exile. The strife grew very bitter. The regents were domineering and acquisitive and abused their power, while the clergy, though probably to a lesser degree, stretched its rights to the limit and beyond. Soon the people became weary of the strife and the consequent disruption in the church. They complained of the unjust financial burdens laid upon them by the church, yet they sided with the church. Jon, who died an exile in Sweden, came to be looked upon as holy, and serious epidemics and a fire in Nidaros that came at this time were looked upon as direct punishments from God for the treatment of the archbishop. King Eirik and Duke Haakon were also eager for peace. Eirik made a pilgrimage to Nidaros and approached the new archbishop, Jørund. Next year, in 1290, an agreement was made at Bergen by which it was decided that the people should not be burdened beyond what had been agreed upon earlier; in other words, the clergy abrogated any tithing or other tax which they had acquired, whether legally or otherwise, after the Tønsberg agreement. This concluded the conflict between state and church.

[7] Bang, *Den norske kirkes historie*, 111.

In the years that followed, however, there was much discord within the church itself. The chapters of canons attached to the cathedrals, which had acquired rich prebends, controlled the bishoprics during a vacancy and the election of bishops. They were powerful and independent and would not submit to episcopal authority. In Nidaros the strife between Jørund and the canons was so tense that it led to scandalous behavior, and Jørund was afraid to show himself on the street. Though both pope and king attempted to intervene, the fight ended only with Jørund's death in 1309. Almost as notorious was the similar conflict in Stavanger. Bishop Arne was brutal and pugnacious and began the trouble by appropriating some of the tithes that belonged to the canons. Finally Arne appealed to the pope, but when the papal representatives gave a verdict against him he refused to yield. King Haakon V laid a fine on Arne and ordered him not to interfere with the rights of the canons, but the obdurate bishop refused to submit and the wrangle continued with increasing violence until his death.

The canons also had trouble with the mendicant friars. In Bergen an old rivalry between the canons and the Dominicans flared up again and again. In Oslo the hostility between the canons and the Franciscans, who were planning to build a monastery there, went so far that some of the canons tore down a little chapel which the friars were erecting. The leader of this destruction was summoned before the pope and, though the outcome is not known, it seems that the friars were permitted to continue their building in peace.

Another source of dispute was the peculiar position of the clergy of the royal chapels. When churches were first built in Norway, many were erected by kings or other individuals on their own land. According to the old Norwegian church law, the right to appoint priests for such chapels belonged to the individual who founded and endowed them. The canon law, on the other hand, did not recognize this right of patronage and stated that the appointments belonged to the bishop, although the pope could make exceptions. He had done so in the case of Haakon the Old. By the Concordat of Tønsberg the king had given up this patronage, but Haakon V won it back with the consent of the pope. The priests appointed by the king were to be outside the jurisdiction of the bishops in most matters. Just where the line should be drawn was not clear and this was naturally a fruitful cause of disagreements. There were by this time fourteen such chapels scattered over the whole country. The clergy attached to them was a group by itself, a court clergy, under the supervision of a master of the royal chapels who had episcopal authority and wore the garb of a bishop. After Haakon's time this institution lost its importance. The royal policy was to hold in check the growing power of the ecclesiastical hierarchy, which nevertheless was consolidating the clergy into a thoroughly unified body under the power of the bishops. The greatest strength of the church was in its organization, and it produced not a few great jurists and statesmen. Rules for the clergy demanded among other things that the priests should live celibate lives, wear no garb but the clerical, and refrain from politics. This tended to separate the clergy from the people. The regulations were never fully enforced, however, and especially in out-of-the-way places the priests continued to share the life of their parishioners and were on the whole popular. They were often guilty of the vices common among the people, notably drunkenness, which was hardly looked upon as a vice at that time. Many priests, too, entered into a sort of civil marriage with the full approval of the community. Their concubines, as the church labeled them, were often loved and respected by the people.

Considerable efforts were made to spread Christian knowledge. Archbishop Jørund, to mention an example, caused to be adopted a rule that all parish priests must preach every Sunday, teach the fundamentals of Christian doctrine to old and young, and examine the people when they came to confession. There is no way of knowing how far these regulations were carried out. The average priests had themselves received a modicum of training at the cathedral schools conducted by the canons, while those who filled the higher positions had generally studied in foreign universities. In spite of all the beneficent influence of the church, there remained much dark ignorance and superstition—some of it fostered by the church itself—and even heathenism. It seems that in this century of its greatest glory, the medieval church in Norway was stronger in institutional development than in its inner life. Yet the age is not lacking in evidences of a deeper religious consciousness. The spiritual beauty of the religious literature and, even more, the glory of the Gothic architecture are the finest achievements of the medieval church. About the turn of the century the nave of Nidaros Cathedral was finished. The cathedral stood complete as this period of greatness was drawing to a close.

¶ The bonds between Norway and the Norwegian settlements to the west had never been broken. The relations between the mother country and the colonies had not been legally defined, however, nor were they the same at all times and in all places. Only in ecclesiastical matters was there a definite union established in 1152, when all Norwegian territory was joined in the then organized archbishopric of Nidaros. The settlements in Ireland, Scotland, and England were, of course, no longer Norwegian. It was to be expected that at a time when the national state was being centralized, the colonial empire should also be consolidated and enlarged. It was in the illustrious reign of Haakon the Old that Norway's empire reached its greatest extent.

The two island groups nearest Norway, the Shetland Islands and the Faroes, had always maintained close contact with the mother country and had never been independent, so there was no change in their status. Before Sverri's day, it is true, the Orkney jarls had from time to time exercised some authority in the Shetland Islands. Both island groups needed to import grain, lumber, iron, and manufactured articles, all of which Norway furnished either from her own products or from her imports.

Equally dependent on Norwegian trade were the Arctic colonies, but there no political control was exercised by Norway. Soon after his coronation, Haakon the Old sent men to the farthest outpost of the Norwegian settlements, asking that Greenland acknowledge the sovereignty of the Norwegian king. In 1261 they finally returned with a satisfactory agreement. The Greenlanders recognized the authority of the king and promised to pay taxes to him in return for a guarantee that he would maintain trade with Greenland. Any material gain to the king was probably negligible, but Greenland profited, as commerce was kept up until far into the fourteenth century when the ships arriving there became dangerously few.

Iceland had close cultural and economic intercourse with Norway, but maintained political independence quite successfully until the middle of the twelfth century. Then conditions began to change and by the thirteenth century they were quite chaotic. In the first place, the balance of power between the chieftains was broken and the rivalry between them led to disorders. Moreover, Icelandic shipping decayed. The great landowners devoted themselves more exclusively to agriculture than before and did not go out and get the goods they needed as they had done in the Viking Age. Again and again Norwegian help was sought and given, and now even political union with the mother country began to seem desirable. Jarl Skule was the first to take definite steps in this direction; but before the union was consummated there was a long period of civil war in Iceland, called the Sturlunga Age because of the prominent part taken by the Sturlunga family, Snorri among them. In 1262 a voluntary agreement was finally made by which Iceland recognized the Norwegian king and promised to pay taxes and fines in return for the guarantee of trade. Icelandic law was to be retained. There was some grumbling when Magnus, contrary to the agreement, promulgated a code for Iceland which, though recognizing peculiar Icelandic conditions, was not unlike the Norwegian. He also appointed Norwegians as sheriffs and lawmen. The island received, however, a stable government instead of the rule by domineering restless chieftains. Gradually there arose in the various settlements a group of men of substance and prominence in the local community who supported the government loyally. But the union did not stem the economic decline of the common people; it rather hastened it, for the expensive bureaucratic government increased the financial burdens of the poor.

In the western seas Norwegian aggressive policy had reached its height in the early eleventh century under Magnus Bareleg. During the civil wars the interest had subsided, although both the Hebrides and the Orkneys continued to recognize the overlordship of Norway's king. This was purely theoretical, however, except when some jarl needed help against a rival. Even the ecclesiastical bonds were weak. Under Sverri a new arrangement was made. The Orkney jarl had supported with considerable forces one of the later risings against Sverri. When a punitive expedition was threatened, the jarl and bishop came to Norway to make a peaceful settlement. Sverri confiscated the land of Orkney men who had fallen in the war against him and arranged that the king was to receive a definite share of the income, particularly from fines, in the islands. Except for one rising in 1209, this agreement continued for over a century of peace. The islands were anxious to maintain connections with Norway because the Scottish kingdom was consolidating its power and pushing northward, threatening to engulf them. Both the Orkney jarls and the petty kings on the Hebrides preferred a master who was farther away and closer in kin.

The conflict between Scottish and Norwegian claims came to a head in the reign of Haakon the Old. The king of Scotland sent repeated urgent demands to Haakon that he sell him the Hebrides. Haakon steadily refused, and then word came that the Scots were attacking the Hebrides. Haakon delayed action, discussing the matter with his council over and over. Finally in 1263 he called out the *leidang* and gathered as many men and ships and as large supplies as the country could furnish. And with a greater fleet than any earlier king had commanded, he set sail to maintain the prestige of his throne. He could easily control the sea about the islands and make successful sallies along the Scottish coast, for the Scots had no fleet to speak of. But the two parties, one having a fleet only and the other a land army, did not meet in any decisive fray. Neither king cared to risk battle. While Haakon's fleet was lying in the Firth of Clyde, negotiations were begun. The Scottish king delayed and played for time until lack of food and October storms forced the Norwegians to set sail for the Orkneys, neither victorious nor defeated. Most of the fleet returned to Norway as soon as possible. Worn out by it all, the king fell ill and about Christmas time he died in the Orkneys. Any permanent victory was impossible and the time for viking adventures was over.

Soon after the old king's death the first piece of his vast empire was cut off. In 1266 Magnus sold the Hebrides and the Isle of Man to Scotland by the Treaty of Perth. Besides a substantial purchase sum the Scots agreed to make a small annual payment, evidently to help Magnus save face and keep up some pretense of Norwegian sovereignty. Soon all payments ceased, however, but the loss of these distant islands was of no real economic significance. The people of the ceded islands did not submit to foreign rule without opposition; in fact, the Isle of Man was never pacified before it came under English rule. The next break in the empire did not come before the fifteenth century.

The strength of Norway's vast empire lay in its national and racial unity and common economic interests. Built by settlement, not conquest, and held together by bonds of race and tradition, it has been compared to the modern British Empire. It was not easily defended, however, when Norway's sovereignty was challenged. The colonies were scattered, distances long, the climate harsh, and the seas rough, but for the time being Norway was mistress of the most far-flung colonial empire and the greatest sea power of the North.

¶ No Norwegian king before our time has been so highly esteemed by his contemporaries abroad as Haakon the Old. And he was anxious to increase his prestige by establishing contacts with as many foreign rulers as possible. He exchanged letters and gifts with Emperor Frederick II, he was invited by Louis IX to join him on a crusade, his daughter Christina was married to the brother of King Alfonso of Castile, and even to the Sultan in Tunis went Haakon's messengers bearing gifts.

Closest were the relations with England. In the year of Haakon's succession Jarl Skule made a trade treaty with Henry III of England, the first commercial treaty in Norway's history, and in the first part of his reign messengers with presents and letters passed between the two courts almost every year. With the other Scandinavian countries the relations were not of the best. Although Sweden had been unfriendly during the last rising against him, Haakon brought about a reconciliation with its ruler. The old enmity with Denmark had been sharpened by commercial rivalry, and finally Haakon set sail for Denmark with a large fleet. A clash was averted, however; a treaty was signed, and Haakon's son Magnus was married to Ingeborg, the daughter of the Danish king. When the marriage had been solemnized in Bergen, Magnus was proclaimed king and he and his bride were crowned with great splendor. The only serious break in Haakon's peace policy was the fatal expedition to the Western Islands.

Under Magnus there was some decline in Norway's prestige, the one definite indication of which was the Treaty of Perth. But on the whole, Magnus followed his father's policy of peace, and Norway continued to hold a high place until his death in 1280.

In the reign of Eirik Magnusson there was disruption and decline in Norway's international position and foreign trade, as in other respects. He was not strong enough to follow a consistent policy, and the regents disported themselves at will, generally not for the good of the country. When he was thirteen, Eirik was married to Margaret, the daughter of King Alexander III of Scotland. Margaret, who was several years older than her husband, exerted a good influence on him and was popular in Norway. She died early, leaving a baby girl who was given her mother's name. When two years old little Margaret became the nearest heir to the Scottish throne and when she was six she was sent to Scotland to be reared there. The passage was stormy and hard, the princess became ill and died in the Orkneys; but the name of the "Maid of Norway," as she was called, lived long in the traditions of the common people of both Scotland and Norway.

Edward I of England had favored the recognition of Margaret as the heir to Scotland, and had hoped to strengthen his own position by arranging the marriage of his son to the Maid of Norway. Upon her death, however, the traditional ties of friendship between Norway and England were weakened. Eirik advanced a claim to the Scottish throne as his daughter's heir, but naturally received no support whatever. Anxious to maintain close relations with Scotland, he then contracted a second Scottish marriage with Isabella Bruce. She was very young when she came to Norway, but lived to be eighty years old. For sixty years after Eirik's death she lived in quiet retirement in Bergen. The marriage did nothing to strengthen relations with Scotland, and soon the contacts between the two kingdoms almost ceased, but as Isabella was of a family famous for its resistance to English domination her marriage to Eirik helped to break off the old friendship between Norway and England.

Another episode occurred which might have brought Norway into more serious trouble with England. Audun Hugleiksson, one of the most unscrupulous of the nobles and a favorite of the king's, went to France to replenish Norway's empty treasury. He received 6,000 marks sterling in cash as an advance payment for a military force of three hundred ships and 50,000 men which Norway promised to furnish the French king in case of a war with England. Fortunately the threatened war did not break out, so Norway was never called upon to fulfill the impossible terms of this nefarious bargain. The money obtained was used to pay the debts to Hanseatic cities with which Norway was becoming more and more involved.

Worst of all were Norway's relations with Denmark. The queen mother Ingeborg had not received her inheritance from her father and repeated requests for a settlement were made, but the Danish king, Erik Klipping, gave no satisfaction. Then one of Ingeborg's favorites, Alv Erlingsson, fitted out privateers and raided the shores of Denmark, and when this drove the Danish king into an alliance with the North German cities, Alv turned against them also. When Ingeborg died, he turned his fighting into a revolt, even burning Oslo, but the rising was promptly put down. Although Alv himself escaped this time, he must have indulged in later adventures, for he finally landed on the scaffold. Meanwhile internal unrest in Denmark seemed to the Norwegian council to offer an opportune time for a war, and they began to prepare vigorously, even hiring mercenaries in England. Erik Klipping did not wish war and made a partial settlement with Ingeborg; but in the midst of the troubles he was murdered and his minor son, Erik Menved, succeeded to the throne. Nine of Denmark's leading men were suspected of the murder and though they insisted that they were innocent and no proof of their guilt could be found, they were banished. In spite of Erik Menved's pleas, these outlaws received a refuge in Norway, and war was declared, for the war fever was strong in the council of the king. In 1289 fighting began in earnest, the Norwegians being the aggressors. Time and again the *leidang* was called out for attacks on Denmark;

but the *leidang* was never effective in aggressive war and the attacks were limited to raids that roused a deep hatred for the Norwegians among the common folk of Denmark. Even worse were the ravages of the Danish outlaws, protected by the Norwegian fleet. In 1295 an armistice was signed. Nothing had been gained from the war, and both countries, especially Denmark, had suffered much. In Norway coarseness and lawlessness ran riot, economic conditions were bad, and the government hopelessly in debt. The war gave the German cities, against which Eirik had also fought, a chance to gobble up much of Norway's trade. The adventures of men like Alv and the Danish outlaws furnished rich material for folk stories and ballads.

When Haakon V succeeded his weaker brother, he tried to inaugurate a stronger, more positive foreign policy, but with no good results for the country. He continued to follow the lines indicated in Eirik's reign. He modernized and improved the defense of the country by building stone and brick forts garrisoned by professional soldiers. One was built at Vardøy as a frontier protection against the Russians, who had occupied Bjarmland, taken over much of the fur trade, and were threatening Finmark. He tried to make Finmark really Norwegian, but distances were great and the people few. Both Russian and Norwegian influences were active there and the poor Lapps paid taxes to both.

More important were Haakon's forts in the southeastern part of the kingdom, Baahus on the Swedish border, Tønsberg, and Akershus in Oslo. The last, which was used as a fortress until 1815, was the most notable. Both the location of the fortresses and the fact that Oslo now became the capital indicate that Norway's foreign policy was definitely oriented toward the East and South as it had begun to be under Eirik. Haakon was married to a North German princess, Euphemia, noted for her love of chivalric romances. Haakon's policy was disastrous for the country. It brought Norway under the dominance, both commercial and political, of the Hanseatic cities, and caused a break in Norway's friendship with England. Haakon was strongly anti-English and made a treaty with Robert Bruce, which was an unfriendly act toward the English king.

While continental influences, particularly German, kept growing, Norway became more involved with her Scandinavian neighbors also. Most of the responsibility for this rested on one man, a brother of King Birger of Sweden, Duke Erik, handsome, debonair, and unscrupulous, an able warrior, and unrivalled diplomat. He had wild ambitions and with his younger brother Valdemar he built up a strong following among the nobility of Sweden augmented by the support of the Danish outlaws. He also made advances to the Norwegian king. He succeeded in making an impression on the upright, unsuspecting Haakon, while the sentimental queen and her ladies-in-waiting were enraptured by the dashing duke. Before long he was betrothed to Haakon's daughter, Princess Ingebjørg, then only a year old. Soon after Erik broke with his brother, King Birger, and fled to Norway. In the following years Erik was the central figure in the maze of intrigue and war that characterized northern international politics of that time, as he was plotting to form a central Scandinavian state under his rule. Haakon endowed him with valuable fiefs bordering on Sweden, supported him with money and men, and even renewed Norway's war against Denmark, with which Erik was also at war. But finally Haakon awoke to the realization that he was being used as a pawn in the game of the reckless adventurer, turned tables on him, and demanded back the fiefs. When this was refused, he attacked Erik, but could not dislodge him. So peace was made, and after some ups and downs in the relations between the two the marriage of Erik and Ingebjørg was celebrated, and from then on Haakon faithfully supported his son-in-law against the kings of Sweden and Denmark. But the year before Haakon died, King Birger captured his brothers Erik and Valdemar, and they perished miserably in prison, left to die of hunger, it is believed. In Sweden this led to a rising of nobles which swept Birger from the throne, and Erik's two-year-old son Magnus became a favored candidate for the crown. The child was also the heir to the throne of Norway. No wonder Haakon looked into the future with deep concern. To make matters worse, Norway's disastrous and unwise foreign politics had been expensive. Her dominance of the sea was gone, and both her purse and her trade had fallen under the control of the Hanseatic cities. There was an intimate connection between international politics and foreign trade, though the relation between cause and effect is far from simple. It took time, however, before the decline was fully realized either at home or abroad.

¶ The greatest period in the development of Norwegian cities was from the middle of the twelfth to the middle of the thirteenth century. Though they never became large, there was a vigorous growth in the old cities, and many a new trading place, or *kaupang*, also sprang up, either to disappear later or to grow into a real town, depending on the location. One of the best evidences of the importance of the cities is the new City Law promulgated by Magnus Lawmender. In addition to the general code it contained special laws which differentiated more between the urban and rural regions than had been the case earlier and provided for more local self-government for the cities. The king's officials also functioned in the towns, but the exact relations between the local and royal authorities is not quite clear. Often royal sanction of local regulations was obtained. The oldest extant document of this sort is from 1282 and has the official approval of the queen mother. But the kings also issued orders that had the force of law, and a somewhat paternalistic control of the cities naturally became a part of the general policy of centralizing the government in the hands of the king.

The council which governed the city was elected by the members of the general guild, which corresponded to the merchant guild in the cities of England and other countries. The members were the full-fledged burghers who either owned a city *gaard*, a large complex of buildings, and had their main income from the rent, or who rented at least half a *gaard*. Political importance was thus tied up with real estate, and the householders constituted a substantial part of what we might call a budding bourgeoisie, or upper middle class. With them must be grouped professional merchants and shipowners engaged in foreign trade, who formed a new and fairly substantial though not especially wealthy class.

The lower class, or petite bourgeoisie—there was really no proletarian element—lived in rented quarters and had practically no opportunity to become wealthy. To this class belonged the retail traders and shopkeepers, and the artisans. The retailers handled mainly imported luxuries, ornaments, cloth, spices, wine, honey, and wheat flour, for which there was a growing demand among the more prosperous part of even the rural population. Cobblers were more numerous than artisans of any other craft, for city-made shoes with genuine heels and soles were in great demand. There were a great many artisans. The laws mention shield makers, comb makers, and many other highly specialized craftsmen, besides tailors, butchers, millers, blacksmiths, and goldsmiths, each craft by order of the government living in its own part of the town. There was no sharp line between classes, and, as in all medieval cities, a bit of rural atmosphere remained in the city, while craftsmanship and trade still flourished in the rural sections. But the policy of the king was to restrict commerce to specified places in the towns, and to establish staples whenever practicable. Retailers liked to set out with a pack and peddle their wares through the countryside, but the king frowned upon this practice of "making a mart at every door." The king also tried to check the natural movement of population to the cities. Haakon the Old complained that nothing harmed Norway so much as the lack of labor in the country, as nobody wanted to work for the farmers and everybody wanted to engage in foreign trade. So men of small means, having goods of less than three marks value, were prohibited from going on any trading expedition between Easter and Michaelmas.[8]

The flow of goods and people into the cities, which was the basic factor in their growth, was stimulated by the increasing wealth of the landed aristocracy and by the growing power of state and church, all making greater demands upon the people than in earlier centuries. Rent, tithes, and taxes were all paid in kind. There must have been a steady trek of draft animals to the town houses of the landlords, to the bishop's residence, and to the king's palace, bringing meat, hides, butter, malt, chickens, furs, and other goods. These payments took most of the farmer's surplus, but he might have a little left to sell so that he could purchase some goods from the city retailer and craftsman.

The chief patrons of the artisans, however, were the dwellers in the city who were not a part of the burgher population. The kings, who were less ambulatory than in the past, built chapels, forts, and residences in the important cities. During the first and more prosperous part of the century, the kings usually lived in Bergen, and in the last reign Oslo became the capital. But even when the king was not in residence, a large number of people attached to his service remained in the town. Not a few great landholders also lived in the cities. Most important, however, were the clergy, especially in the cathedral cities. The greatest building undertakings were those of the church—episcopal residences, monasteries, cathedrals, and other churches. The church was the greatest patron, too, of weavers, workers in wood and metal, and other craftsmen. In fact, Stavanger and Hamar had almost no population beyond people connected with the bishop and the chapter of cathedral canons.

The only opportunity the city offered for acquiring any great wealth was foreign commerce. The requisitioned goods not consumed locally furnished a basis for the development of such trade, and to this was added a considerable supply of goods brought in voluntarily. The wealthier farmers had some surplus produce which flowed into all cities.

[8] *Den norske sjøfarts historie,* 1:188.

The towns of eastern Norway and Nidaros received quite a large supply of masts and hewn boards also, and to Nidaros were brought large quantities of fur from Jemtland. The chief non-requisitioned article of trade, however, was the dried fish from Lofoten and the rest of northern Norway.

Every year vast fleets of boats sailed to Bergen, and when the city was made the fish staple, all the fish trade of western Norway was concentrated there. Thus Bergen became the largest and busiest city in Norway. A Dane who visited Bergen shortly before 1200 has left a vivid picture of the town:

"With keen keel they plowed the crest of the foaming deep and sailed in a swift course between skerries and capes until they reached the city and laid the prows up to the pier in the presence of a great crowd. At once brisk men came running with ropes, towed the ships to a safe place, and made them fast with great skill. The city is the richest and most noted in the country, provided with a royal castle and adorned with relics of holy virgins. There Saint Sunniva, her whole body intact, is entombed in the cathedral. The city is very populous with cloisters for monks and nuns. It is full of supplies; dried codfish is found in such masses that it is beyond measure and number. There you can see a stream of ships and people that come from all quarters: people from Iceland and Greenland, Englishmen, Germans, Danes, Swedes, Gotlanders, and others whom it would take a long time to mention. There is an abundance of honey, wheat, good clothes, and also silver and other goods. You can get enough of everything."[9]

Norway's foreign trade had never been so flourishing as in the early thirteenth century, and from it was derived most of the surplus wealth which formed the basis for the greatness of the age. While the main export was fish, lumber, for which the Netherlands furnished the chief market, also came to be very important before the close of the century. English customs rolls, which are important sources for our knowledge of Norway's trade, list among imports from Norway, timber, herring, dried codfish, hides, fur, falcons, and butter. Similar records in Bruges list as imports from Norway, falcons, barrel staves, butter, tallow, cod-liver oil, tanned hides, and goat skins, "of which Cordovan leather is made." Norway imported largely manufactured articles like fine clothes, and luxuries from southern climes to vary the limited diet that native products could furnish. Most important was wheat, which at first was a luxury for the rich, but before long the importation of grain became a

[9] Quoted by Holmsen, *Norges historie*, 1:236.

necessity. Rye and barley, which could be raised at home, were also imported, for the country could not produce enough grain to supply the growing city population and the increasing number of people who were engaged in fishing and did not raise enough grain for their own needs.

To engage in foreign trade was a highly respected occupation. *The King's Mirror* contains an excellent description of the life of a merchant.[10] It is in the form of a father's advice to a son who wishes to travel, "for I would not venture to seek employment at court before I have observed the customs of other men." Commending his plan, the father impresses on his son that much knowledge is needed to cope with the perils and experiences of the trader. He should know navigation and oceanography; the tides, winds, physical geography; and even astrology and natural wonders, like sea serpents. He must also know the law, customs, and manners of the people among whom he sojourns, and foreign languages, "first of all Latin and French, for these idioms are most widely used; and yet, do not neglect your native tongue or speech." Much of the advice the father gives is quite reminiscent of Polonius. The father was a "kingsman" and advises his son to retire from active participation in trade when he has gained experience and made money. He might still have some of his money in trade, but it was well to invest in land and live the life of a landed gentleman.

Much of the foreign trade was in the hands of aristocrats, who either commanded their own boats or employed others to do it for them. Nobles, king, and bishops all owned ships engaged in foreign commerce, and the greatest capitalist of them all was the archbishop. While these aristocrats had more resources and greater investment in trade, there was also developing a burgher class of professional merchants, who had some share in foreign commerce and controlled most of the colonial and coastal trade. They were not especially wealthy; often a group of them owned a ship jointly.

While Norwegian merchants frequented the towns of the Baltic and North Sea shores and beyond, the English trade was by far the most important, as it had been even from the eleventh century. London, Boston, Yarmouth, Newcastle, Lynn, and other cities, all had a lively trade with Norway. At one time more than half the imports brought into Lynn came in Norwegian ships. England's earliest commercial treaty was with Norway. Sverri had a treaty with John of England, who sent engineers to help him capture Tønsberg in 1201. Some decades

[10] *The King's Mirror*, 79ff.

later Henry III of England wrote to Haakon the Old, "We rejoice greatly and will continue to rejoice, because our realms are so united that merchants from your kingdom may unhindered come to us, and ours likewise to your realm."

In the early thirteenth century the bulk of trade was in the hands of the Norwegians, although foreign traders had begun to visit Norway very early. It has been noticed that they were numerous even in Sverri's reign and that by the time of Haakon the Old, Bergen had acquired quite a cosmopolitan atmosphere; but other regions, too, especially the Vik, were visited by foreign merchants. They often spent the summer in Norway, but rarely wintered there, and did not become an integral part of the city they frequented.

It was natural and normal that foreign merchants should be welcome, but gradually the Norwegians began to lose out in the competition with the foreigners. This was perhaps an inevitable development, but at any rate nothing was done to check it, and the policy of the government was detrimental rather than helpful. It was interested in having the needed goods come into the country, but was not concerned about exports or about developing a strong Norwegian trade. Nor was the king interested in the growth of the burgher class. Quite the contrary. By forbidding people of small means to enter foreign trade, Haakon the Old probably helped the labor situation on the farms, but also checked the growth of the burgher class. More serious was Eirik's abolition of the guilds formed by groups of merchants, notably the England-farers. At the same time the aristocrats were withdrawing from active participation in trade, which later in the century was not considered as honorific as when *The King's Mirror* was written. Thus Norway had no strong professional merchant class with the initiative or wealth to compete with the traders from abroad who were more efficiently organized, and had greater capital and better technique. Moreover the Norwegian ships were out of date. The Norwegians still used the viking type of boats which had once ruled the waves, while others were building larger, safer ships that demanded smaller crews and therefore could carry more freight proportionally. They also had decks and covered storage space, while on ships of the viking type the freight was only strapped on with ropes and covered with canvas. The fleet which might have protected the trade was also on the decline, though the full effect of this was not felt before the following centuries. The very nature of the *leidang*, which had served well in the past, prevented progress in shipbuilding. As the people of the local districts built the ships they were to furnish, they naturally did not keep pace with modern developments, but were conservative and not interested in increasing the size or cost of the vessels.

Merchants came from far and wide, from Gotland, the Netherlands, even France; but most numerous and it seems, most welcome, were the English. In the last part of the thirteenth century, especially after 1290, the trade between England and Norway was more and more falling into English hands, the lead being taken by the merchants of Yarmouth, among whom is mentioned a woman, Sibilla Flathe. There was little danger that the English would monopolize the Norwegian trade, and the relations between the two countries continued fairly good for many years. Nevertheless, there were complaints from English merchants, sometimes justified and sometimes not, that Norwegian officials confiscated their goods and imprisoned their men. During the reign of Haakon V, who pursued a definitely anti-English policy, the clashes between English traders and Norwegian officials became frequent and more than once led to bloodshed. In 1312, to mention one striking instance, some Englishmen, after years of irritation, murdered a king's sheriff and ten other men in the Vik. As reprisal, English ships were confiscated, English merchants arrested and their goods appropriated, and the attempt on the part of the English king to reach a friendly agreement was spurned. For years the English traders almost disappeared from Norway. Haakon seems to have felt that Norway no longer needed them. The chief complaint of the English was that they were not granted the trading privileges accorded to their hated and feared German rivals.

Meanwhile the Hanseatic merchants were gradually, inch by inch, winning the control over Norwegian trade which was to destroy Norway's seafaring completely. The first German merchants in Norway were from western Germany, but in the thirteenth century the Baltic cities grew rapidly to great power and wealth until, through the Hanseatic League, they controlled all the trade of the North from Russia to England. Haakon the Old gave the first trading privileges to Lübeck, the chief Baltic city, probably about 1230, and in 1250 he took the initiative in making a general trade treaty with Lübeck. Norway already felt the need of the grain which the Baltic cities furnished. Haakon saw to it that the foreigners did not exceed their rights, but Magnus was more yielding. The Germans were allowed to rent or buy houses and winter in Norway but their privileges were definitely defined. Step by step, however, the Germans increased their power and when the Norwegians tried to check them, they were brought to terms by a boycott.

Under Eirik the control of the trade was definitely passing to the Germans. In 1294 he granted the Hanseatic cities a charter which gave their merchants extensive trading privileges and explicitly exempted them from many obligations resting on citizens, such as the *leidang* and the night watch. It was couched in general terms and gave opportunity for many abuses. It seems clear that the aristocracy and perhaps also the country people and fishermen liked the German trade because of the security it gave.

During the reign of Haakon V all Norway's foreign commerce was a monopoly in the hands of a group of Germans, but when they also tried to capture the internal trade, Haakon promulgated several acts to hinder it. Thus the basis for the later Hanseatic domination was laid in this period of greatness.

¶ Though cities and trade rose to a new importance in this age, the urban population was a very small fraction of the whole people, smaller than in countries farther south. Also, though the nobility was stronger than at any other time in the history of Norway, it was neither so numerous nor so wealthy nor so dominating as in a more completely feudalized society. The rural population therefore continued to hold its own as perhaps in no other country except Switzerland. Yet that pressure from above which we noticed in the preceding century persisted with growing force. The amount of land owned by the farmers themselves continued to shrink by the same processes as in the past, and the holdings of church, king, and nobility to grow proportionately.

The church land increased most. Although the population was only one-sixth of the present, the rural priests and churches were far more numerous than in modern times, and the twelve hundred churches and six or seven hundred parsonages were maintained largely by the income from land. Some of the priests, especially in the Westland, were as poor as their parishioners; but in richer sections their income was often substantial, though not large enough to burden the people unduly. The greatest landowners were the monasteries, the cathedral canons, the deans of royal chapels, and the bishops. The Oslo bishop, for example, controlled 350 farms or parts of farms. Richest of all was the archbishop, whose landed estates in the fourteenth century included 2,000 farms or parts of farms. Much of the church lands consisted of small pieces. This tended to lessen the control of the church over the people, and it was therefore to their advantage that land was held by the church rather than by the lay nobility.

It has been estimated that the nobles held about a sixth of Norway's land—less than the church controlled. The land of the nobles, however, was more often consolidated into large estates, and the owners had therefore a firmer grip on their tenants and frequently laid illegal burdens upon them. The bailiffs of absent nobles were often petty tyrants bitterly hated by the people. Nobles also managed the land of the king. The king, however, made more effort than most of the nobles to see that justice was done to the people. He had always had much land, and it has been loosely estimated that in the thirteenth century he held about a fifth of all farm lands, but much of it was in small pieces, as it had largely been obtained in payment of fines. The city people also owned some land, though probably not any large amount.

It is evident that the land owned by the tillers of the soil themselves must have been considerably less than half. Some historians estimate it at a scant one-fourth, and much of this was the poorer land. Even a smaller number of farmers than these figures would indicate actually owned their whole farm. Often a farm was worked as a unit even though the farmer had settled a fine or debt by allocating the income of a part of it to his creditor. Thus a large majority of the farmers rented all or part of the land they worked—rented from king, church, nobles, burghers, or other farmers. There continued to be among them odal farmers, men of substance and leaders in the community, but there was also an increasing number of poor cotters. In spite of the diversity within the class, the pressure from above induced a sense of solidarity among the farmers, causing a strong class consciousness and a wider cleavage between the people and the aristocracy.

The new economic and political system rested heavily on the people. The lawful demands on them—taxes, rents, and tithes—increased, and in addition they suffered under the abuses of grasping officials and landlords. It seems that on the whole the people were able to meet their legal obligations, but they were very sensitive with regard to extra-legal demands, and any abuse on the part of officials was met with protest and even violence. In one case the farmers whose duty it was to maintain certain churches complained that the bishops appropriated the tithes intended for that purpose. Repeatedly there were complaints that justice could be obtained by gifts and favoritism, and that bailiffs and their subordinates took advantage of ignorant cotters. Always it was misuse of power, whether directed against freeholder, renter, or cotter, that brought protests.

These complaints had a deeper cause than merely the economic. Through centuries a love of personal freedom, a passion for justice, and a respect for law had become ingrained in the Norwegian people until they were a part of their very being. The old laws guaranteeing and defining the rights of the people were still intact and they were not forgotten. Not only were the people awake to their rights, but the kings, much as they built up royal power, were not tyrants. They took their responsibility seriously and tried to protect the people. In 1273, in the reign of Magnus Lawmender, a meeting of the leading men adopted a form letter, a copy of which every royal bailiff was required to sign and file with the chancellor. He promised to break neither his own oath nor that of the king to the people under him, to administer justice with fairness and equity, to be lenient with the king's renters and exact no extra gifts or entertainment, to bring the king's dues to the designated place and treasurer, to keep correct accounts, and to make annual reports. Haakon V took still further measures to fight abuses in the administrative system. Before he came to the throne he issued a decree applicable to districts under his control that lower officials should be chosen from among the upright freeholders who had homes and family in the community and whose conduct toward the people had been above reproach, not from among the personal followers of aristocrats, who practiced their tricks on unsuspecting cotters. As long as sound legal principles were kept alive and some control was exercised, misuse of power did not become especially disastrous.

The real misfortune of the age lay in the fact that little room remained for the old vigorous institutions of self-government. The king's bailiffs, of whom there were about fifty, had a double function in their districts. They collected taxes and dues for which they were responsible to a treasurer appointed by the king. Their other duty was to enforce the law. In this they had greater freedom, and often examined persons suspected of misdeeds and came to a private agreement about the fine without going to law. The culprit was saved embarrassment and the bailiff made money, for he kept one-third of the fine. The king sanctioned this practice in small matters, and there was no extensive abuse for, as the saying went, "many are the king's ears."

The regular judges in both civil and criminal cases were the royal lawmen, ten in number. In the laws of Magnus Lawmender it was implied that they should perform their judicial functions at the people's *lagthing*. In reality more and more cases were summoned before the lawmen and decided outside the *lagthings*. The four old *lagthings* continued to exist and new ones were created with the intention of having *lagthings* over the whole country with a presiding lawman for each. The system was never fully carried out; the new courts were not important, and before long the Frostathing alone functioned somewhat in the old way as a court of the farmers presided over by the lawman. The courts conducted by lawmen and held in the cities became dominant. The historic Gulathing was moved to Bergen about 1300. Decisions could legally be appealed to the king, who could even set aside a law, "for he is above the law." He sometimes appointed commissions to act as a court of appeal, but seldom acted as judge himself, probably because there was no need of it.

The smaller local *things* were also gradually fading out of the picture, though they did not completely disappear. They continued to function in the eastern part of the country, especially in the more distant, isolated communities where farmer ownership of land was most extensive and the centralizing power of the government least effective.

¶ The return of Archbishop Eystein to his see at Nidaros in 1184 marks the introduction of Gothic art into Norway, for he at once resumed his work on the cathedral, employing the new style. It was due to his genius that Gothic architecture came to Norway remarkably early, while it was still new in England and before it had begun to find entrance into Germany. Moreover, in the octagon which he built about the high altar and the casket of Saint Olaf, the Gothic ideal found an expression that was never surpassed in beauty, richness, and originality.

The development of Gothic art in Norway conformed quite closely to the general European pattern. It must be remembered that Norway had closer contact with the rest of Europe at this time than at any other period of her history before the nineteenth century. Her whole civilization had therefore a cosmopolitan character. The Gothic art did not assimilate with the folk art or become as uniquely Norwegian as did the Romanesque. Yet the Norwegians were no mere imitators. A small and poor country like Norway could not make as large a contribution to Europe's wealth of Gothic art as France or England, and of what was produced much has been lost. Enough remains, however, to show that Norway's best productions can well hold their own with the art of the larger cultural centers.

With 1184 began a period of transition from the Romanesque to the

Gothic. During the first decades the old form predominated, the building of the timber churches being at its height around 1200. Gradually the Early Gothic, showing a marked English influence, won acceptance. This age of transition and Early Gothic, when art forms were fluid, was a highly creative period of much diversity and individuality. Norwegian art blossomed forth. The pointed arch, the upward-striving lines, and all the other typically Gothic features came in, except the flying buttress, which was never generally used in Norway. But the transition was not only one of architectural forms. There was also a change in spirit, until Norwegian art came to express the intense religious feeling of the age which is best represented by Saint Francis.

The High Gothic period may be dated from 1248 when in the reign of Haakon the Old the construction of the nave of the Nidaros Cathedral was begun, and it continued through the first half of the next century. The Gothic art had at this time reached full maturity. The forms had become fixed. It had lost in flexibility, but gained in sureness and elaborate richness.

Though the Nidaros Cathedral holds undisputed preeminence among Norway's Gothic churches, other fine churches were erected, mainly in the cities. Bergen had several Gothic churches that have been destroyed. Noteworthy also is the choir of the Stavanger Cathedral, built by Bishop Arne. It has not the height characteristic of Gothic art, because it had to conform to the Romanesque nave; but it has an unusually harmonious unity of design, due in part to the fact that it was constructed in a short space of time. The ribbed vaulting rising from clusters of low pillars has lines of noble beauty, while the capitals and other details are decorated with the richest Gothic leaf designs. Among smaller churches may be mentioned the latest and smallest of medieval cathedrals, the one in Kirkebø on the Faroes. The ruins that remain show richness of design and delicacy of workmanship.

Besides the churches, the monasteries deserve mention. Several were built in the Romanesque style and later enlarged or rebuilt in Early Gothic, for example Lyse Monastery near Bergen and Hovedøy Monastery outside of Oslo. The only one of which enough remains to give a real idea of the construction and atmosphere of the medieval monasteries is the Gothic Utstein Convent near Stavanger.

Only a few wooden buildings from the Gothic age are found here and there in the country, and these have undergone great changes. Of secular stone buildings only two are noteworthy. The archiepiscopal residence at Nidaros was large and monumental in its effect. More beautiful was the Haakon's Hall in Bergen, built by Haakon the Old in 1250 just as the Early Gothic was merging into the High Gothic. The festal hall with its span of roof forty feet wide was both impressive and satisfying. Haakon V's castles and forts might also be mentioned though not architecturally important. Most imposing was probably Tønsberg Castle, and most pleasing to the eye, Akershus. It is an example of the use of brick which was coming in.

Sculpture and painting, as always in Gothic art, were intimately connected with the architecture and largely used in its service. Even more than the buildings themselves, the painting and carving express the changing spirit of medieval art. Earlier they had been used mainly to produce rich, decorative effects. Pictures of persons were of secondary importance and were represented with unemotional aloofness, but gradually the spiritual ideals of the Gothic found expression. Paintings of Christ and the saints, especially the Virgin, and the representation of sacred stories predominated; and the expression of emotions, first only suggestive, grew in intensity and variety.

In the interior of the cathedrals stone sculpture was lavishly employed, though the exterior was less ornamented and simpler than in countries farther south. The remains in the Nidaros Cathedral range from delicate, intricate Early Gothic patterns to remarkably forceful statues and grotesque figures of brutal strength and sardonic humor. Four unusually fine portrait statues in the Stavanger Cathedral represent Bishop Arne and the last three kings of the Sverri line. Otherwise practically nothing remains except a few statues in Oslo and Bergen, although stone sculpture had been employed also in other churches. While most of the stone sculpture dates from the High Gothic period, wood sculpture had its blossoming period in the Early Gothic age. The rich development of wood sculpture in the reign of Haakon the Old shows both French and English influence. While these statues in wood lack the massive strength of the stone work, many of them are marked by a charming delicacy and emotional restraint.

Painting also developed from the Romanesque until it became quite typically Gothic before the close of the thirteenth century. It was strongly influenced by the illuminations in manuscripts, of which Norway has some fine examples. Among the treasures from this age there are several ceiling paintings, but altar frontals of great variety and interest predominate.

Mention should also be made of the work in precious metals, ivory, and wood, of the reliquaries and crucifixes of gilded bronze, of the silver chalices and crucifixes carved in ivory from walrus tusks. Enough has survived to show that these crafts were not wholly employed in the service of the church. Drinking horns ornamented with metal, sometimes with a coat of arms, and an interesting set of chess men found on the Faroes are good examples of carving done in ivory—as always, from walrus tusks. Of furniture very little remains, but one chest has survived which indicates that also in this field Norway's Gothic art attained distinction.

¶ The kings of the Sverri dynasty made their court the center of learning and literature. They had a scholarly bent, were genuinely interested in knowledge, and were at the same time eager to enhance the glory of the court and keep abreast of the times. Nevertheless the achievements of the age were meager. Important to the historian are the many official documents, laws, and letters, which increase in number as the century advances. Under Haakon V the royal documents became particularly numerous. They were written in Old Norse as in the past; but the language was losing the earlier impress of Trøndelag and the Westland and acquiring the peculiarities of the language as spoken in eastern Norway.

The only original large literary work extant is *The King's Mirror*. The sagas of the kings in the early part of this age were written by Icelanders. *The King's Mirror* is a didactic work in the form of a conversation between father and son, probably written at the instigation of Haakon the Old for the instruction of his son Haakon the Younger. It is important both as a literary production and for the light it throws on the life and thought of the day. It shows wide knowledge of the seas and far-off lands, notably of Greenland, but, as always in the Middle Ages, superstition is mingled with learning. The author must have been a cleric of wide experience and extensive travel, as well as an attractive personality.

The literary taste of the day reflects the close contact with the rest of Europe and the eagerness to appropriate foreign culture which characterized the age. French was fashionable. Few people really knew foreign languages, however, and most of the literature read at court was in translation. Haakon the Old began to import from England and France the chivalric romances of the day and had them turned into Norwegian prose. Shorter poems were translated into verse, notably the work of Marie de France, replete with chivalric sentiment. Haakon was also interested in religious literature, and he knew some

Latin. When he lay ill in the Orkneys he had holy books and lives of saints in Latin read to him, but as he grew weaker and found it difficult to listen to the strange tongue, he called for the sagas of the Norwegian kings.

Magnus Lawmender continued the importations begun by his father, and his son Eirik may have learned both French and English from his Scottish queen, who was much concerned about educating her young husband. Under Haakon V, the last of the line, the court became the center of considerable intellectual life. His German queen Euphemia was enamored of the sentimental, romantic literature of chivalry which was the fashion of the day, and she encouraged the translation of it. The king's interests were more serious. He was quite learned, had read many classics, and could make speeches in Latin. He established schools for the hird clergy at Bergen and Oslo, and ordered the translation of several sagas of chivalry. The volume of translations was considerable, including the stories of Roland, Charlemagne, Thidrik (Theodoric), Tristan and Isolde, and many others. They were called sagas, though far removed from the old sagas in content and style. It was a literature adapted to reading rather than reciting, and it introduced into Norway a flowery style and sentimentality.

No institution in Norway was more universal in character than the church. The higher clergy had studied abroad and owned fairly extensive libraries, both of classics and theological works. And in any effort to raise intellectual and spiritual standards they had the cooperation of the kings. Norway seems to have produced very little church literature in Latin, even making allowance for what may have been lost. Extant are some bits of historical writing, some synodical resolutions and laws, some hymns, and—most important—the rituals used in the festivals of the three national saints. Like every other country, Norway also added something of her own to the liturgy of the church. The Norwegian language was used much more than the Latin. The sermons were in Norwegian and seem to have been short and to the point, popularized by the frequent use of stories from home and abroad. As in the secular literature, translations that brought the church classics to the people were of great significance. Legends of the Virgin and lives of saints were popular. Haakon the Younger sponsored *The Saga of Barlaam and Josafat*, a vigorous and idiomatic translation of the remarkable religious romance believed to have been first written by John of Damascus in the early eighth century. Its emphasis on worship of the saints and its glorification of the life of the anchorite caught the imagination of the age.

No achievement, however, is a finer tribute to the church than the masterly Bible translation, also dating from the reign of Haakon the Old. How much it included is not known, but quite a large part of the Old Testament has survived. It is perhaps the most distinguished translation of the Bible into a vernacular which Europe produced in this age.[11] "It is a real pleasure to read this masterly translation," says a preeminent scholar.[12] About half a century later, a monumental Biblical work planned by Haakon V was begun. Hitherto, the preface states, the king had caused lives of saints to be translated and read to him and the hird on holidays, but now he wanted Holy Writ to be used. The work was a literal, not especially interesting, translation from the Vulgate, interspersed with lengthy commentaries drawn from theologians from Saint Augustine to the scholastics. It never got beyond Exodus 18; it was too ponderous, and is of little interest to moderns except as an evidence of the learning of the Norwegian theologians.

The knowledge of the vision literature so popular in the Middle Ages was also brought to Norway through translation, and an unknown author produced a magnificent vision poem, *Draumkvæe* (*The Ballad of Dreams*). It tells of a young man who slept from Christmas Eve to Twelfth Night and awoke to relate that he had made a grueling journey through the regions of the dead:

> Something I learned of all things,
> Of all that makes men wise.

It has the form of a folk ballad and, like other folk poems, was preserved by being passed on by word of mouth from generation to generation. When the scholar who recorded it first heard the poem chanted with solemn intensity and ecstasy in the trembling voice of an aged woman, he was deeply moved. "It seemed to me that I had been given power to look through turf and stone into a bygone era, an era of vast dimensions, of admirable simplicity and originality."[13]

This ballad may well be classed with the folk literature, which was developing apart from court and clergy, and which is Norway's richest literary heritage from this age. Though it cannot be dated accurately, much of this folk literature belongs to the next century, in the era of decline which followed the height of the Middle Ages.

[11] Bang, *Den norske kirkes historie*, 263.

[12] Finnur Jónsson, *Den oldnorske og oldislandske litteraturs historie*, 2:974, København, 1923.

[13] Moltke Moe. For a translation and analysis of the poem by Sigurd Bernhard Hustvedt see *The American-Scandinavian Review*, 19:713-722 (December 1931).

CHAPTER 9

LAST KINGS OF THE OLD STOCK, 1319-1387

In contrast with the preceding period the fourteenth and fifteenth centuries seem drab. Somehow Norway was sapped of her vigor and had no longer the capacity to handle her own affairs. The causes are many and complicated, some deep-seated and some accidental, and no explanation is quite satisfactory. It was natural that, as in the rest of Europe, these centuries should be marked by a disintegration of medieval institutions and culture; but, unlike the countries to the south, Norway experienced very little of the rejuvenating influence of the Renaissance and seemingly had little new to take the place of what was lost.

Yet the picture is not so drab as a casual glance might lead one to suppose, for the people itself had not lost its vitality and a healthy growth from below held promise for the future. The age demonstrated that a nation can retain its vigor even when its statehood is all but lost, and that continuity in the life of the people can exist through breaks in the political history.

This is an important age, which influenced the history of the country for centuries to come. The story is complicated, as Norway was caught in a mesh of Scandinavian politics which brought her into union first with Sweden, then with Denmark, then—after a brief interlude—with both, and finally with Denmark alone. Having the smallest population and the least wealth of the three countries, Norway had no chance of equality in any such union.

The age falls naturally into two parts: the period before 1387, with which this chapter deals, when kings of the old Sverri line, rightful heirs to the throne, reigned in Norway, and the period after that date, when foreign kings ruled from abroad. Although the old royal house was extinct in the direct male line after the death of Haakon V, his family continued to reign for sixty-eight more years, as three successive descendants of Haakon through his daughter Ingebjørg occupied the throne. They had not inherited the greatness of their forebears and were not wholly Norwegian either in blood or interest. Most of the time the king of Norway either was the elected monarch of one of the neighboring countries or was striving to win another throne, and although the country held its own pretty well as long as there were kings of the old stock, there was a tendency for Norway to sink into a place of secondary importance.

¶ Upon the death of his grandfather, Haakon V, the three-year-old Magnus Eriksson (1319-1350) was the lawful heir to the throne of Norway; there was a movement afoot to make him king of Sweden also. In contrast to Norway the kings of Sweden and Denmark were elected by the nobles, who, however, selected a member of the royal house whenever it was feasible. Seven prominent Swedes met with the royal council at Oslo, and a friendly agreement was reached. It was decided that Magnus should become king of both countries and reside part of the time in each. They should give each other military aid in case it became necessary to defend the child king, but each kingdom was to be governed by its own council and regents. Magnus was elected king of Sweden, and soon after the Norwegians, assembled in the Haugathing near Tønsberg, swore allegiance to him. The following year the Icelanders also paid homage to the child. The union, formed as a result of an unpremeditated dynastic situation, was merely personal and was looked upon as temporary.

One person, however, had influence in both governments. The king's mother, Duchess Ingebjørg, sat in on the meetings of the Swedish council and of the Norwegian regents and, though not legally a part of the system, virtually acted as a regent. Ingebjørg was interested in continuing the plan for a central Scandinavian state which had been inaugurated by her husband, Duke Erik, and retained his fiefs, the Swedish-Danish-Norwegian border provinces. Erik's successor in her affections was Knud Porse, a Danish nobleman from Halland, who was her intimate friend and adviser. He continued Erik's policy and abetted the duchess in her efforts to add Danish Skaane to her Mid-Scandinavian realm. As Ingebjørg had obtained possession of the Norwegian seal and had been allowed a voice in the allocation of the state monies, Knud raised an army and declared war on Denmark largely at the expense of Norway. The people were annoyed by illegal exactions, and the treasury became so depleted that it was impossible to provide decently for the child king.

The leading men in Norway took effective action against these abuses. At a large meeting of hird and bishops, the archbishop was authorized to appoint a head of the government, to whom all promised support as long as he kept the laws and his oath to king and people. A splendid representative of the Norwegian nobility, Erling Vidkunnsson, was selected, and took the title viceroy. With the aid of the council Erling conducted the government with great ability and high sense of duty. Before long Ingebjørg had to resign the seal and lost her influence. She was treated with all due respect, however, until she married Knud Porse. Then her Norwegian fiefs were withdrawn and the government severed all connections with her.

In general Erling followed the policy of Haakon V, but he had a firmer hold on foreign affairs. Like Haakon, Erling made efforts to keep the Hanseatic merchants within bounds, but also gave them some new privileges. He made "eternal peace" with Denmark and concluded a treaty with Russia which ended a three-year state of war and promoted the settlement of the Finmark boundary. His consistent policy of allowing no foreign influence and no foreign officeholders in the government came to an abrupt close when Magnus Eriksson himself took over the government.

Magnus was declared of age in 1332 when he was only sixteen years old. He was a headstrong, self-willed boy, and Norwegian neither in education nor in interest. He developed into a popular national king in Sweden and many progressive reforms are associated with his reign. His main interest, however, inherited from his parents and his stepfather, Knud Porse, was to enlarge the Mid-Scandinavian realm under his personal control.

To Norway he seldom came, yet he was unwilling to relinquish or delegate any of the royal power, and Norway was actually without a government. Twice the nobles revolted, demanding an effective administration. There was nothing for Magnus to do but to negotiate and each time a compromise was reached. When the king was absent, as he was most of the time, the care of the seal and other administrative power was left in the hands of leading men in the council. One of these was the archbishop, who had been chancellor during the regency and was thus well versed in public affairs. The ecclesiastical magnates of this age adhered to the same universal-church principles as their predecessors in the twelfth and thirteenth centuries and consistently defended the prerogatives of the church. Nevertheless, the archbishop became more and more the leader in upholding Norwegian national rights and opposing foreign encroachments.

King Magnus did not keep his part of the bargain, however, for, except when there was a question of obtaining Norwegian funds or lands, his interests were elsewhere. When he married Blanca of Namur, his "morning-gift" to her was several fiefs in southern Norway, among them Vestfold, including Tønsberg, Norway's most redoubtable fortress. He was striving to obtain the Danish territory Skaane and he succeeded temporarily. But he became involved in war with Lübeck and could obtain peace only by renewing the charter of Haakon V and giving some additional privileges. In this charter of 1343 the German cities were for the first time designated as "the German Hansa." While the settlement was a gain for the Germans, it was not without some advantage to the Norwegians also, for the encroachments of the foreigners were never as troublesome as when there were no legal arrangements. Moreover, the king could not renew the charter of the Hanseatic merchants without the consent of the council, and this was obtained only in return for concessions.

The very same year, an agreement was reached to sever the dynastic union with Sweden. The king had two sons, Erik and Haakon. Although the older was the heir to the throne, the king and council could legally set aside the law, and agreed that the younger son Haakon should be king of Norway and begin the rule when he came of age. Swedish leaders promised to choose Erik as successor to the throne, and both parties agreed that neither brother should have any claim to the throne of the other. Meanwhile Magnus was to rule during Haakon's minority and, after retiring from the throne, retain Haalogaland, the island colonies, and the fiefs in southern Norway which were held personally by him or his queen. Next year the Norwegians gave their allegiance to Haakon at a unique meeting in Baahus. For the first time representatives of the cities and from the rural districts appeared as separate classes side by side with the nobles and bishops. It seemed like an incipient estates-general of four estates.

In 1350, at a meeting in Bergen attended by the whole royal family, the ten-year-old Haakon VI (1350-1380) was placed on the royal throne. Thanks to capable, patriotic leaders, an efficient national government was maintained through the first half of the fourteenth century. With the exception of a continued decline in shipping and trade, life went on much as before. Then came the Black Death, which affected every phase of life and added much to the difficulties of the following reign.

¶ Haakon was declared of age and took over the government in 1355 when he was fifteen years old. During most of his twenty-five years' rule he was king of Norway only, the last such king—except for a few months in 1814—before Haakon VII. He had been brought up in Norway and was much more of a Norwegian than his father. He had the good sense to lean heavily on the best men in the land, and as he grew older he called the council together often. In spite of the ravages of the Black Death, Norway still had capable men in the administration, and the government continued to be national and to command the loyal support of leaders and people. Haakon was an able man, respected and loved by high and low. "People called him a good man," says an Icelandic saga (*Flateyjarbók*), while the noted Aeneas Sylvius writes, "He is said to have been a splendid man, wonderfully loved and obeyed by his subjects." He was determined to uphold the interests and honor of his kingdom, but he neglected the internal administration, and the country, impoverished as it was by the Black Death, did not get the attention it needed.

Scandinavian politics and dynastic ambitions absorbed too much of the energy of Haakon, and his close association with his father encouraged him to pursue an unjustifiably aggressive policy. Although he was quite successful, neither he nor his kingdom reaped any real benefit in proportion to his expenditure of men and money. On the contrary, Haakon became involved in a maze of intrigue and war. Through it all he tried to follow a straight course, and he compares favorably with the wily Valdemar, the scheming Mecklenburgers and Holsteiners, the grasping Hansa, his envious brother, or even his simple-minded father, whose ability fell far short of his ambition.

Soon after Haakon's accession, Erik, who felt that his position as successor to the Swedish throne was less honorific than that of his younger brother in Norway, rose in revolt against his father. A strong party of the Swedish nobility supported Erik, and Magnus had to agree to a division of the royal power. Erik was to have the southern and southeastern part of Sweden and thus Magnus's share was contiguous with his and Blanca's Norwegian fiefs. Contrary to the agreement of 1343, Haakon was designated as his brother's successor.

Erik died soon afterwards, and in 1362 Haakon was acclaimed king of Sweden jointly with his father Magnus. Meanwhile King Valdemar of

Denmark had outwitted Magnus and regained full control over Skaane. Angered at this, Swedish magnates, in behalf of the two kings, formed an alliance with the Hanseatic cities against Valdemar. Both kings found this alliance distasteful and pursued the war with indifference. Before long, in 1363, they made peace with the Danish king, and Haakon was married to Valdemar's daughter Margaret. It was a bold stroke by which it was hoped to unite the three countries. Though Magnus was rather popular with the common people, the nobles had been increasingly impatient with his autocratic tendencies as well as with his weak foreign policy. The complete loss of Skaane was the last straw. They broke with Magnus and Haakon in 1364 and put an end to the Norwegian-Swedish union. They chose as king the next in blood, Magnus's nephew Albrecht, the son of the Duke of Mecklenburg. The two kings refused to be deposed and next year invaded Sweden with an army made up chiefly of Norwegians. They were defeated, Magnus was captured and held in prison for six years, and Haakon was forced to retreat.

Haakon, who had quartered his shield, using both the lions of the Norwegian kings and of the Swedish Folkung dynasty, was determined to free his father and to defend his claim to the Swedish crown. Looking for help, he made an alliance with his father-in-law, the king of Denmark. This, however, only brought him another war. Both kings had refused to renew the privileges of the German merchants, and Haakon had even encouraged the commanders of his forts to harass them in revenge for their support of the Mecklenburg cause. The German cities, which had advanced in power and in 1367 formally organized the Hanseatic League, made war on Denmark and Norway, ravaged the shores, and declared a general blockade. Enough English merchants carried on trade with Norway to prevent excessive suffering from the blockade, but it was soon evident that the Hansa was superior on the sea. In 1370 Valdemar was forced to conclude a humiliating treaty, and Haakon, eager for peace, signed a truce for five years.

This left Haakon free to invade Sweden again (1371). In return for a large ransom, Magnus was liberated and allowed to retain his western Swedish provinces. He spent his last years in Norway, where he was generally popular. Upon Magnus's death in 1374, Haakon took over these provinces and thus became involved in new troubles with Sweden which were not settled at the time of his death in 1380. Throughout the conflict the nobles of western Sweden supported Haakon and were therefore often in Oslo; Haakon often chose his chief officials from among them, and encouraged the marriage of Swedes into the depleting Norwegian nobility. Thus Swedish influence was penetrating into Norway and the nobility became more Scandinavian in its interests.

The Norwegians, too, supported their king in all his aggressive foreign ventures, but the country was too poor to provide adequately for his extravagant undertakings. The wars brought great expenses, and the ransom of Magnus was an additional heavy burden. Haakon mortgaged crown property, borrowed from churches, debased the coinage, and tried to maintain its current value by a law which, according to the old custom of the *things*, was approved by the people assembled at Tønsberg by clash of arms. The king was especially embarrassed by the Black Death, as the income of his estates was reduced to a fraction of what it had been.

One of Haakon's chief concerns was a settlement with the Hansa. A meeting in 1372 led only to the extension of the armistice signed two years earlier, for Haakon, though he might personally have gained by a speedy settlement, held out firmly against unreasonable demands on the part of the Germans. The final agreement was not reached before 1376.

Meanwhile the queen, whose dynastic ambitions were even greater than those of her husband, had realized one of her aims. Her father Valdemar died in 1375, and Margaret had hastened to Denmark probably as soon as she heard of his illness. The candidates for the throne were two grandsons of Valdemar. His older daughter, Ingeborg, was married to Heinrich, son of Albrecht, Duke of Mecklenburg and brother of the Swedish king. She had died but had left a young son also named Albrecht. The other grandson was Olaf, the five-year-old son of Haakon and Margaret. The old Duke of Mecklenburg began at once to work for the succession of his grandson, but in politics he was no match for Margaret. The queen, who was then twenty-two years old, displayed political astuteness and driving force, as well as disarming charm. She won the support of enough Danish magnates to carry the election if she could secure the neutrality of the Hanseatic cities. This, too, she achieved, but not without commitments in behalf of both Denmark and Norway. On May 3, 1376, Olaf Haakonsson was elected king of Denmark.

Although Haakon seems to have approved of the queen's policy, he kept out of Danish affairs. In August, Haakon with the aid of his council finally made a treaty of "eternal peace and friendship" with the Hanseatic League, which was the legal basis for the trade relations between the two parties for another century. It renewed all the "freedoms, rights, privileges, and old usages that they [the Germans] had ever enjoyed," but Haakon firmly held his own against any extension of power. The chief gain of the Germans was that all the cities of the League now received the privileges earlier granted to the most favored cities, and its right to wage war was recognized. In the main the agreement was kept for a time.

In 1380 Haakon VI died, only forty years old, loved at home and respected abroad. During his reign Norway, though weakened by war and pestilences, had maintained an honorable place among the nations, largely through the efforts of the king. But times were serious and difficult, and upon the death of this last really Norwegian ruler the country slipped into another unhappy union.

¶ Haakon's heir was his ten-year-old son Olaf (1380-1387). This accession brought about the dynastic union with Denmark which Margaret had planned, and thus began the long union which was to last until 1814. Each country, however, continued for the present to have its separate administration.

On Saint Olaf's day 1381 Olaf was acclaimed king at Nidaros. At the same time a regency consisting of the regent, Ogmund Finnsson, and the council was instituted to rule during Olaf's minority. They kept a firm hold of the government and, having profited by the experiences with Ingebjørg during the minority of Olaf's grandfather, did not allow Margaret any share in the internal affairs of the realm. Some unfortunate episcopal appointments were made during these years and undesirable Swedish and Danish men given office. Margaret has been blamed for this. There is no proof, however, that the fault was hers. In fact it was not unusual for the pope to appoint to sees in any country men of other nationalities, and in the council there were already two men of Swedish birth who had served under Haakon. Margaret had made good friends among the Norwegian nobility in the days when she faithfully stood by Haakon in all his troubles. They were attached both to her and to the young king. The council delegated to her complete control over foreign affairs and formally notified the Hanseatic representatives that she had authority to make arrangements binding on council and king during the latter's minority.

Thus she managed the foreign affairs of both Norway and Denmark and looked after the welfare of both, although she was chiefly interested in Denmark. With great skill she regained complete control over

Skaane, which the Hansa held under a treaty of 1370, and still maintained the friendship of the cities by giving them unhindered passage through the Sound. Of Hanseatic privileges in Norway nothing was said and they were not renewed before 1398. Margaret's next problem was to establish security on the southern border, and that she accomplished easily. The Holstein dukes held Slesvig, the southernmost Danish land, as conquered territory. Margaret offered it to them as a hereditary fief under the Danish crown, and though countless disputes about the matter rose later, for the time being the difficulty was settled. She had gained two victories which won the admiration of her contemporaries and especially the respect of the Danish nobility. She had a firmer position and more power within the country than any Danish king had possessed for many years.

The greatest battle, that of driving the Mecklenburg family from the Swedish throne and placing her son upon it, remained to be won, and when Olaf came of age in 1385, his mother had him assume the title "Rightful Heir to Sweden." Conditions in Sweden were none too happy. Albrecht was hardly more than king in name, the powerful nobles—Swedish and German—held sway, and lawlessness and oppression were rampant. Margaret played upon the general dissatisfaction, which was directed mainly against the German nobles who came in with the Mecklenburgers. When Albrecht saw his chance and tried to assume real power, many of the higher nobles turned to Margaret and victory seemed within her grasp, when Olaf suddenly died. He was buried at Sorø, Denmark, and on his gravestone can still be seen the inscription in Latin: "Here rests Olaf, son of Queen Margaret, whom she bore to Norway's King Haakon."

The loss of her only son was a terrible tragedy for Margaret and it seemed that all her schemes must come to naught. His death was even more tragic for Norway, for he was the last of her old royal house to be born in Norway, the last really national king before our century. "King Olaf Haakonsson disappeared," say the Icelandic annals. "The Danes said he was dead, but the Norwegians would not believe it."

¶ In the first half of the fourteenth century daily life went on much as it had in the past. In a sense the country was still in the Age of Greatness, and there was considerable wealth and well-being in the land. But some unfortunate tendencies noticeable in the thirteenth century were more pronounced in the fourteenth. The cleavage between the classes, social, political, and cultural, became more marked, and the aristocracy held a more dominant place than ever before, both economically and politically.

The nobility was becoming more consolidated and class conscious. Land was the main wealth of the age; it gave pretty good returns and furnished the chief opportunity for investment. So the nobles made every effort to get possession of land by purchase, marriage, or inheritance, or by other means less fair, and also tried to consolidate their scattered possessions. Even more characteristic of the age was the concentration of land in the hands of churches and monasteries. Except for tithes and other dues, the ownership of land was the only way of financing such institutions. There is record of one rural church (Trondenes) which owned sixty-five farms or parts of farms.

This meant that the number of tenant farmers increased greatly. Some of the old patriarchal relation between tenant and owner still remained, but there was less and less of it as the personal contacts decreased and the landlords used hired bailiffs to look after their interests. Though the renters were subject to restrictions, especially as to the use of the forests, they had contracts which sometimes became hereditary, they enjoyed legal protection, and remained free men. Any attempt to encroach upon the rights of the people met with more resistance than in other countries. There were still courts in the land, the old laws were in force, and the people had a highly developed sense of justice.

The pressure from above became heavier, however, as the foreign marriages became more common within the nobility. Swedes and later Danes and even Germans who married Norwegian heiresses thereby became "Norwegians" with all the privileges of their wives' families. These foreigners were far removed from the people. Their contempt for the common man and a sense of their own superiority had been developed in the more completely feudalized countries farther south, not only in the other Scandinavian countries but even more in Germany. Moreover, the whole aristocracy became less national and more class conscious. Changing political conditions also gave it more opportunity than in the past for aggrandizement of power and wealth. Under the well-organized government of the thirteenth century the king had maintained a pretty close supervision over the officials in the interest both of royalty and of the people. The union kings were not able to keep this up. Even as early as the minority of Magnus Eriksson, nobles made use of the situation to further their own advantage at the expense of the state and of the people. When Magnus took over the rule, he had to reprove the nobles for keeping on their farms soldiers who were always ready to join any disorderly element in robbing the subjects of the king.

Although never completely feudalized, the administration became more feudal in character. A larger district was now termed a fief (*len*) and the holder of a fief was called lord (*lensherre*), while the head of a subdivision of the fief (*herred* or *fogderi*) was a sheriff (*foged*). King or landed magnate employed bailiffs (also called *foged*) to supervise his estate and collect all rents and dues. Gradually most fiefs were farmed out, granted, that is, in return for a certain sum of money, and officers became much more severe in collecting fines when they could pocket a goodly share themselves. After 1387, when the castles were no longer occupied by the royal family, the most important lords were the governors of the four chief fortresses, Tønsberghus, Akershus, Baahus, and Bergenhus, to each of which one or more fiefs were attached. They had royal power, subject, however, to Norwegian law at least in theory. The king might grant fiefs for an indefinite period or for any term of years he pleased; but not beyond his own reign. The council maintained—with uneven success—that upon the death of a monarch they, like all royal authority, reverted to it, to be held until a new king was established on the throne.

On the whole, the changes in the local government seem to mark the beginning of a process of disintegration of the old rather than reorganization, and this process went much further in the fifteenth century.

The same holds true of the economic life. It has been noted that even in the Age of Greatness the Norwegians began to lose their hold on foreign trade and that in this century it had become practically a monopoly of the Hanseatic merchants. They were forcing from the kings, who were deeply in debt to them, more and more grants of privileges, and were getting a strangle hold on the whole North so that they could make their influence felt in every important political or international event. The residents of the town suffered under their lawlessness, brutality, and grasping greed. Yet Norway could not do without the imports brought by the foreigners, her traders could not compete with them, and the government was unable to keep them within bounds.

A Norwegian burgher class did exist, however, though neither large nor strong. The retail trade was reserved for the natives, but to prevent the Germans from pushing into this field required repeated efforts from the kings, especially Haakon VI, and they were not wholly successful. The government tried to keep the foreigners within bounds by minute regulations, but trade could not develop within these strict rules and the Germans often evaded them. As early as in 1331 there was complaint that the Germans bought up everything, so the people could hardly get the necessities. The trade with the islands was also to be reserved for Norwegians, but there English merchants found entrance. Until 1350 the annual ship went to Greenland, but later intercourse with that little colony on the edge of the Norwegian empire was neglected and became very irregular.

Though it would seem that the towns offered few attractions, there was so much movement of population to the cities that the government tried to check it. People without fixed occupation and residence were made to take service in the country, and the old law from the time of Haakon the Old, which forbade poorer people to go on any trading expedition between Easter and Michaelmas, was still in force. This policy was dictated mainly by the interests of the landed aristocrats who complained of lack of labor, but it was also the intention to restrict trade to the cities. Thus it helped to emphasize the difference between country and town and to develop a distinct urban class.

¶ No other single event had as much influence on the retrogression in the latter half of the century as the Black Death. This terrific calamity, the worst of all the oriental plagues which scourged Europe in this age, had disastrous effects on the whole life of the country. A ship from England brought the disease to Bergen in the summer of 1349, and through the autumn and winter it spread over the whole country, carrying off about one-third of the population. The Westland and the regions of densest population suffered most severely. Especially exposed were the officials who came into contact with many people. Of the fourteen lawmen only two or three escaped the plague, and of the five bishops only one. Among the clergy the death rate was highest, for their official duties brought them close to the sick and dying, and they showed great courage and devotion to duty. In 1371 the archbishop complained to the pope that in his diocese there were forty priests as against three hundred in the early years of the century, and many of them were old and decrepit.

In other parts of Europe the death rate was just as high, but in Norway the recovery was particularly slow, for even before the plague the population was small and thinly spread out. According to the highest estimates Norway before the Black Death had less than half a million people. She lost a third of them and then came later pestilences in 1359 and 1371 which still further depleted the scant population.

No wonder the Black Death left Norway poor, very poor. The price of land took a sudden drastic fall. Prices in general fell to about half of what they had been before, and all classes suffered, from the king down. All income from land declined, for there were not enough workers to produce as much as earlier. And the way of life in the country, with the laborious gathering of food and fodder, took many hands. Many farms lay unused. Tenants gained security, as they were much in demand, and their social status came to be about the same as that of farmers who owned their land and who were forced to retrench. On the whole, however, the farming class did not advance but suffered from the lower prices as did the whole population.

In no class was the change as devastating as in the nobility. At the beginning of the century there were three hundred noble families, but late in the century at the most sixty. Some had died out and many were too poor to keep up the expenses of their rank and began to live like odal farmers. Only the richest families could keep up their noble status: they intermarried with foreigners and appropriated to themselves immense estates and all the highest offices.

The church, too, suffered from the fall in prices. The monasteries became poor and their well-managed estates fell into decline. The tithes and dues went down to about one-half, and no clerical fulminations could change conditions.

The king's income both from the crown lands and from taxes declined enormously. We have striking evidences of the financial straits into which the royal family fell. As long as there were kings of Norwegian blood, some of the castles from the thirteenth century were improved and enlarged and continued to serve as royal residences. At first Magnus Eriksson lived in a style somewhat befitting his position, but after the Black Death there remained hardly a trace of the regal splendor of the past. When Magnus's queen Blanca died at Tønsberg Castle, where she had been living for several years, an inventory of her possessions was taken. These are listed as "a couple of table cloths which have often been on the table, and a pair of sheets which have often been on the bed; some velvet and other cloth; some pepper, ginger, and cinnamon; a few table knives and four silver spoons." Her son Haakon VI enlarged Akershus, but the meagerness of life in the castle is graphically pictured in a letter which his young queen Margaret wrote to her husband in 1370. "You must know, my lord," she writes, "that I and my servants suffer and are in dire need for lack of food and drink, so that neither they nor I get the necessities. And so I beg you that you will find some way out so that things may improve and that those who are with me shall not leave me on account of hunger." She had borrowed from the master of the mint and from her secretary, and still had no ready money. She asked the king to arrange so that she could charge what she needed with a German merchant and begged him to be patient with officials who were doing what they could to raise money, and to be lenient with tradesmen from whom some aid would come. Margaret's letter shows the growing dependence on the Hanseatic merchants, which increased with the general economic difficulties that were to continue throughout the fifteenth century.

The effect of the Black Death was noticeable in every phase of life. Yet its influence on the spiritual and cultural life of the people was not nearly so tangible as on the social and economic.

¶ The crumbling of the old political and economic institutions had an effect on the whole cultural life of the country. Meagerness and poverty pervaded also the higher sphere of the mind. As the artistic and literary activities within the upper circles declined, however, the very cleavage between the classes gave an opportunity for the common people to carry on independently the old traditions of their rural culture. While firmly rooted in the past, it was enriched by influences from the upper classes and from abroad, most especially from the church.

With regard to art, the Norwegians of the later Middle Ages lived largely on their heritage from the past. During the first half of the fourteenth century High Gothic art retained much of its glory. Yet the creative impulses were even then losing their strength, and after 1350 little remained of the vigor and originality which had characterized Norwegian art from the dawn of history.

The building of churches had in the main ceased by 1300, chiefly because the country was already covered with churches. After the Black Death in 1349 the reduced population neither needed nor could afford new edifices. Of the thousand churches in medieval Norway only a bare two hundred belonged to the later Middle Ages and nearly all of these were wooden buildings of cheap and poor construction. Still the church was the institution that did most to keep up artistic production, not so much of edifices as of the many small articles needed in the services and the furnishing of the churches. There remained enough of these in metal, walrus ivory, and wood, and also some illuminated manuscripts, to show that art objects in good Gothic tradition continued to be produced.

In the upper classes, especially among church men, there remained some interest in learning, literature, and the history of the past, but it was limited and unproductive. As the king seldom resided in Norway, the country lost the stimulus of the royal court, which had been the center of literary activities in the preceding century.

To find the Norwegian literature of the age, composed in the mother tongue, we must turn away from court circles and the church and go to the rich unwritten folk literature which was handed down from father to son and even more from mother to daughter until modern times. There are evidences in the sagas that folklore, sayings, and tales were current among the people from time immemorial, but the richest development of folk literature came in the later Middle Ages with its blossoming period in the thirteenth and fourteenth centuries. Then must have lived the men and women who told the stories and composed the poems that have come down to us, in about the form in which we have them today. But the names of the authors have been lost, and their work was so thoroughly appropriated by the people that it became in every sense a folk literature. It began to blossom forth in the Age of Greatness, when Norway's intercourse with the outside world was most lively. Even in an isolated mountain valley like Setesdal, which has made rich contributions to every phase of folk culture, the repercussions of this intercourse were felt. Obscure cultural currents passed from country to country, and Norway gave as well as received. Tales were told where sailors stopped on the shore; they spread along the trails of inland trade and even more along the pilgrim routes, especially the much-traveled path across the Dovre Mountain to the shrine of Saint Olaf; and the many stories, used in sermons, both preserved and spread tales from all lands. But whatever Norway acquired was completely assimilated and took on a strong Norwegian flavor.

Most exclusively Norwegian are perhaps the nature myths. With a lively imagination, stimulated by the long winter evenings and the many changing moods of nature, the Norwegians peopled their surroundings with all manner of supernatural beings that seemed part and parcel of nature itself: ponderous trolls that appeared to be the very mountains brought to life; the specter (*draug*) in his half-boat, who appeared to sailors about to be lost at sea; the nix (*nøk*) who sang his plaintive song in the brook; the seductive fairy of the mountains (*hulder*) with her cow's tail, and—not to be forgotten—the domesticated little goblin (*nisse*) who loved to play impish tricks on the dairy maid amidst the weird shadows of the cow stables. Some myths clearly date back to the Old Iron Age worship of the forces of fertility.

Norway has a greater wealth of fairy tales than any of the neighboring countries. The hero and the ideal of the fairy tales is not a bold viking, but a country lad called Askelad, the Cinder Lad, a male Cinderella. He overcomes trolls, outwits the king, and wins the princess and half of the kingdom by good-natured kindliness, shrewd wit, and common sense. But the glittering palace east of the sun and west of the moon also has a large place in the fairy tales. It takes little imagination to see it on the snow-covered mountain peaks, sparkling in many colors just as the sun is setting.

Equally important is the folk poetry. The poems cannot be classified perfectly. Some are pure lyrics, personal, intimate love songs and lullabies, simple songs expressing almost every human emotion. Many combine a lyric and an epic element in a ballad form. The ballads clearly had their origin in the Age of Chivalry, that is, the thirteenth and fourteenth centuries. Like the literature of the court, the folk ballads dealt with themes borrowed from all lands and folks, Biblical themes, occasionally classical, oriental, and Russian; but most are West European, especially French, many of which reached Norway via England and reflect the same interests that dominated court circles. Often the poems themselves are common to many lands; especially are many of them found in the different Scandinavian countries. Where they originated cannot always be determined, though in some cases a Norwegian origin can be established. Even the new form showed foreign, mainly French, influence. The alliteration, the elaborate form and intricate kennings of skaldic verse disappeared. Instead came the brief stanza of two or four lines with the rhythmic accent and rhyme of modern poetry. The whole structure shows a highly developed artistic sense.

In this age dancing was also introduced from the south, probably from France, and the passion for it swept over the whole North, from palace to hut, entering even the sacred halls of the cloisters. The people danced to the tunes of the folk songs, the leader singing a stanza and the dancers joining in the refrain. So poetry, song, and dance with a strong national flavor developed together and became a characteristic expression of Norwegian folk life.

The ballads deal with lords and ladies, sometimes historical persons, their loves and hates, adventure and war, wild passion and gruesome revenge. Many of the lyrics, on the other hand, express the less dramatic experiences of common folk or tell of the supernatural beings that were everywhere about them. There is a new spirit in this literature, a wealth of emotions and lyric color foreign to the earlier skaldic verse. Love, family affection, religious feeling, appreciation of nature in her gentler moods, and the beauty in little, simple everyday things, all find expression. Many of the themes as well as the sensitive treatment indicate that women have had as large a part in the authorship of folk literature as in its preservation.[1] The poems lived in the memory of the people until reduced to writing in the nineteenth century. Much was lost, yet vast riches remain. Although something new was added, even the form was essentially unchanged, the language being only gradually modified through the centuries.

The folk literature shows better than anything else that there was in the people a vigor which could not be crushed by the calamities of this age or the greater misfortunes yet to come.

[1] Moltke Moe, *Samlede Skrifter*, 1:169, Oslo, 1925.

CHAPTER 10

SCANDINAVIAN UNION, 1387-1536

WITH THE PASSING of Norway's last native-born king, the country entered upon a long period of rule from abroad. If it had been difficult to maintain Norway's status among nations when the monarchs were at least partly Norwegian in race and interests, it now became practically impossible, and by the close of this period Norway had sunk to the lowest point in her political history. The events that brought about this situation are extremely complicated, involving the history of all the Scandinavian countries.

¶ When Olaf died it seemed as though his mother's ambitious plans for a united North must come to naught. There was no acceptable heir to the throne. The next in line were the Mecklenburgers, first King Albrecht of Sweden—who, however, had no claims to Denmark—and second his nephew Albrecht; but they had legally forfeited their rights to Norway by warring on the country. But the situation was not hopeless and Margaret was not a person to give up. She was popular and respected, and it seemed that she could best save the North from the Mecklenburg house, which through long years had been the enemy both of Norway and Denmark. "Nothing shows more clearly the immense influence that Margaret had attained," says the Danish historian, Kristian Erslev, "than the ease and speed with which she overcame this crisis."

Shortly after Olaf's death Margaret was chosen temporary ruler by the Danish people and took the title "rightful heir and ruler of Denmark." The Norwegians went even farther. On February 2, 1388, a bishop and hird meeting, in reality an enlarged council, elected "the highborn princess, our beloved lady, Lady Margaret, by the grace of God queen of Norway and Sweden and rightful heir and regent of the kingdom of Denmark," as the "mighty lady and rightful ruler" of the kingdom, and decided that she should have full power in the whole kingdom and all its dependencies through "all her living days."[1] On their own behalf and that of the people, those present took the oath of allegiance prescribed by law and she took the usual royal oath. An open letter was sent out with the "request and advice" that the people, assembled in their local *things*, take the same oath of allegiance and thus confirm this action. Margaret is the only woman who has been raised to the position of a "king," with full royal power, in Norway.

Almost at once Margaret assumed the negotiations in Sweden interrupted by Olaf's death. In March the dissatisfied nobles chose her as their own and Sweden's "mighty lady and rightful ruler." They promised never to make peace with Albrecht without her consent and to take as king, either in her lifetime or after her death, the person she designated. She affirmed the old laws and privileges from before Albrecht's time, thus virtually canceling the restrictions of royal power to which he had been forced to submit.

Within the space of six months Margaret had become the recognized ruler of the three countries—we might say four, for Finland was united with Sweden—and she could use the title Norway's and Sweden's queen and Denmark's "rightful heir and ruler."[2] In a general rising Albrecht was defeated, and Margaret controlled most of Sweden. The mighty nobles, usually very highhanded, were remarkably submissive, but Stockholm was held by the Germans, who had settled in the city in large numbers. Supplies were brought to them by privateers called the Victuals Brothers under the protection of the Mecklenburg cities Rostock and Wismar, and their activities degenerated into far-flung piracy harassing the shores of all Scandinavia. In Norway the worst incident was the sack of Bergen, which destroyed the remnant of independent native commercial enterprise. In 1398 Stockholm was finally handed over and Margaret's victory over Albrecht was complete, but the same year she renewed the Hanseatic privileges in her whole realm.

Though Margaret had been elected for life in two of the kingdoms, and in Norway her heir was to be heir to the throne also, it was generally understood that the arrangement would be temporary, and she doubtless felt that her power would be more secure if she found a king for the realms. Passing by her nephew and nearest heir, Albrecht of Mecklenburg, because of opposition from the council, she adopted

[1] *Norges gamle love, anden række, 1388-1604*, Vol. 1:3-5, Ed. Absalon Taranger, Christiania, 1912.

[2] *Norges gamle love*, 1:11.

Erik of Pomerania, a five-year-old grandson of her sister and a nephew of Albrecht. The Norwegian council recognized him as rightful heir and the succession was to be reckoned from him. There must have been dissatisfaction with the placing of a foreigner on the throne. That there was some attempt to secure a native king is indicated by the fact that Sigurd Jonsson, a descendant of Haakon V's illegitimate daughter Agnes, took an oath, probably at the demand of the queen, declaring that he had no right to the throne and no desire for it. On September 14, 1389, the child was brought to Nidaros and acclaimed king at the Eyrathing, and with this date began the reign of Erik of Pomerania (1389-1442) in Norway. Not before 1396, however, did Margaret succeed in having her adopted son chosen also king of Sweden and Denmark.

While the countries now had the same king, the governments of the three were separate. Margaret was working toward a united hereditary state as her ultimate ideal, and to achieve this she called together a large all-Scandinavia meeting in Kalmar in 1397. Although the Norwegian episcopate was not represented, Erik was crowned with impressive pomp as king of all the Scandinavian countries. After the coronation a draft for a closer union was drawn up, but not ratified. The Norwegians especially shied away from any arrangement in which their country would of necessity play a secondary role. At any rate no agreement was reached, and what we speak of as the "Kalmar Union" was really only a dynastic settlement. Nevertheless it brought the North one great blessing—peace. When Margaret could not obtain the kind of agreement she wished she seems to have given up the effort to obtain any documentary basis for further realization of her aim, but worked in other ways toward the same end.

¶ After the Kalmar meeting the queen devoted most of her energy to building up a centralized government and strong royal power, as was the aim of most of the rulers of the age. It was inevitable that Denmark should be the center and principal part of the realm. This country was the richest and most densely settled of the three. In fact the population was more numerous than that of the other two countries together, while location made Denmark more important in international affairs. Margaret very seldom called any joint meeting of the councils of the three countries. Occasionally she summoned a few men from Sweden and even more rarely some from Norway to consult with her and the Danish council. Generally she personally controlled her whole realm with the help of the Danish chancellery. To a certain extent she worked with the Danish nobility, but even in Denmark she more and more concentrated the power in her own hands, employing officials of lower, often of non-noble, even German, birth, who were responsible to her personally. There was much grumbling during her last years.

In Sweden the complaints were more vociferous, and with good reason. Distrusting the Swedish nobility, Margaret gave fiefs to Danes or Germans and brought much land under the crown. She systematically broke down the national government and entrusted the local administration to bailiffs and sheriffs often taken from among the lower officials of the Danish court. The queen could not supervise them properly, nor was she especially interested in doing so, and the abuses were many.

In Norway, too, Margaret followed the policy of weakening the national government and controlling affairs from Denmark. There was no viceroy; the state seal was brought to Denmark; the chancellery lost its important national functions; and the council, of which the queen had made much use while winning her position, was never called together in its entirety. On her rare visits to this inferior part of her realm she gradually shoved into the background the men of the older nobility who opposed her Scandinavian policies, and advanced her own supporters. She strengthened the Scandinavian tendencies by promoting international marriages among the nobles and by occasionally giving fiefs to Danes and Germans.

As a state Norway gained least and lost most in the union, but there was less interference with the daily life of the people. The law courts of Norway retained considerable independence and could check arbitrary actions even of the ruler. In one case when the queen tried to gain possession of an estate, the court decided against her, and nothing further was done. The queen appropriated less land than in the other countries, but she supervised strictly the financial administration. Norway also had to help bear the expenses of a costly government and satisfy the heavy demands of the queen for money, but her generosity, especially to religious institutions in which she was genuinely interested, to some extent counteracted the dissatisfaction.

It had been the understanding that Margaret was to retire when Erik came of age, but she continued to rule all the countries until her death in 1412. She was in the midst of trying to solve the problems of Slesvig so as to regain control of the duchy, and had just made her entry into Flensborg and received the homage of the city, when she was stricken with the pestilence and died on board her ship.

Margaret belongs in the brilliant galaxy of women rulers of the Renaissance Age. She was competent and successful, but she lacked the vision which might perhaps have enabled her to build upon a more enduring foundation. In maintaining the dominance of her own country, Denmark, she ignored the national pride of the other two, and caused strained relations between the countries which might well have led to a rift in the union. She enlarged the royal power at the expense of the church, the nobility, and the common people, without striving to win that loyal support of either the leaders or the people which alone could have given solidity to the throne. In this respect it is interesting to contrast her with Elizabeth and the Tudor policy of strong royal power built upon popular consent. Nevertheless, even at the time of her death Margaret was held in high esteem in Norway, but she had so built that the future depended too much on the personality of the ruler.

¶ Erik had from childhood been trained for his great task by Margaret, who had indoctrinated him with her own political ideas. He was a willing pupil, for he loved and admired his great foster mother and was deeply grateful to her to whom alone he owed his position. She also helped to educate his queen, Philippa, the daughter of Henry IV of England, who came to Denmark at the tender age of thirteen. Philippa was a good and able queen and became Erik's stanchest helper in his days of trouble. When he was fifteen he was declared of age in Denmark and Sweden, but in Norway not before 1405, when he was twenty years old. From now on he had a share in the government, although Margaret kept the final authority in her own hands.

When he came of age he made his last visit to Norway. Margaret sent with him lengthy instructions about how to meet every situation and solemn admonitions to control his hasty temper. But Erik could never acquire his foster mother's cold self-control, and his quick temper and stubborn self-will were to lead him into trouble. He was more open and straightforward than she, but lacked her tact and could not imitate her cunning diplomacy and political methods, however earnest he was about carrying out her policy. Yet he had an attractive personality, and when he took over the government upon the death of Margaret, he was received with general good will.

Norway continued to suffer from the lack of a national government. Even more frequently than before, Danes and Germans were placed in castles and fiefs and given positions in state and church. The bishops were treated as minor officeholders and worst of all, in some cases men of scandalous life filled the episcopal sees. Local conditions were fairly good and law and order were upheld much as usual, but even there foreigners were coming into office who knew little of Norwegian law and cared less. They mulcted the people to satisfy the king's demands for money and their own greed, and were lawless and brutal. Yet legal redress could even then be obtained. There were so many complaints—not only of foreigners—that when the kindly, well-meaning Queen Philippa was ruling for Erik, she tried to get a survey of the situation and bring some redress. No permanent solution of the trouble was reached for there was no adequate organization to supervise conditions throughout the large state Margaret had organized. Had he been ever so willing, the task Erik inherited was too great for him, perhaps impossible, and the union of the North was not so strong as it appeared on the surface.

Erik himself was deceived, and this gave him courage to pursue bold power politics. In an attempt to complete Margaret's plan he entered upon a struggle with the Holstein dukes for the possession of Slesvig. The war dragged out for twenty years and the treaty signed in 1435 was a mere stop-gap, leaving the Slesvig question unsolved.

Meanwhile Erik had become involved in hostilities also with the Baltic cities. With Lübeck in the lead they became the allies of Holstein and declared war in 1426. Erik had secured supremacy over the Baltic by building up the Danish fleet and erecting strong forts, Visby on Gotland and Kronborg on the Sound. The best evidence of his courage and power was the establishment in 1425 of the Sound dues, levied on all passing vessels.

The worst feature of the war had been the activities of the Victuals Brothers, which were revived with greater intensity than ever before. Northern freebooters, too, did their share to make the sea unsafe. Norway suffered most, as the country was practically blockaded. For some time the Hanseatic merchants braved the dangers, but in the spring of 1427 they left Bergen in fifteen ships carrying with them all their wealth and the whole personnel of their office. Soon after, the Victuals Brothers attacked Bergen and after plundering and burning they set sail for Hamburg with immense booty. A *leidang* fleet of about a hundred vessels was gathered. But although the pirates had but seven ships, they were large and equipped for modern warfare, and the small old-fashioned Norwegian boats could do nothing against them. Some of the *leidang* ships were captured, some were sunk, and the rest fled. This was the last appearance of Norway's old fleet; it could no longer fulfill its original purpose of defending the coasts. Not before the close of the century were the seas cleared of pirates, and then only through the repeated efforts of the Hansa.

Erik was not much of a warrior, and soon after his treaty with the dukes of Holstein he also made peace with the cities, renewing all their privileges from before the war and arranging for annual meetings to settle differences. No mention was made of the Sound dues. In the end Erik's energetic foreign policy had brought meager returns.

Before his wars ended there was grumbling and unrest throughout his realm. In Denmark the nobles feared Erik's autocratic ideas and his efforts to make the monarchy hereditary, and resented his high-handed policy toward the church. In Sweden, where abuses had been most rampant, the revolt broke out first and had the most enduring results. The first outbreak occurred in Dalarna, where the free farmers and miners rose against the foreign sheriffs and bailiffs. Their leader was Engelbrekt Engelbrektsson, a man of the lesser nobility who had twice in vain pleaded the cause of the people with Erik. The movement spread, castles were destroyed, and foreigners driven out. The council was forced to renounce its allegiance to Erik; upon Engelbrekt's insistence, a meeting of the four estates was called in 1434, and thus the Swedish diet was instituted through a popular rising. Engelbrekt was chosen regent and he put Swedes into all important positions. However, negotiations with Erik were taken up. The Swedes insisted upon a national government and the appointment of only natives to all posts in the land, and when Erik consented to this, he was anew recognized as king.

But Erik refused to be a "constitutional" king and almost at once broke his promises and left for Denmark. A second time Engelbrekt raised a revolt, and Stockholm was captured. As the country was practically without a king, a dashing young noble, Karl Knutsson Bonde, was chosen regent, while to Engelbrekt was assigned the duty of ridding the land of foreign officials. In the midst of his work he was treacherously slain by a personal enemy, and Sweden lost one of the most remarkable men in her whole history. After his death the control of the movement, which had risen among the common people, passed to the nobility, but the spirit he had roused lived on among the people and finally led to freedom and national greatness.

This spirit was contagious, and even before Engelbrekt's death there was open revolt in Norway, in the districts about Oslo. In this part of the country the influx of Danish officials was greatest and there were complaints enough of them, their bailiffs and servants, and of the general lawlessness in the land. This popular rising was inaugurated by men from among the odal farmers and lesser nobility, who chose as their leader a nobleman, Amund Sigurdsson Bolt, a relative of Archbishop Aslak Bolt. The aim was "out with the foreigners," and the establishment of a national Norwegian government. Amund took possession of the episcopal residence in Oslo, but before long he had to surrender to the commander of Akershus. He was treated with great leniency, for no doubt many of the nobles had sympathized with the revolt and even encouraged it. The rising became a signal for the council to act upon its own initiative, as it had not done for years. Its members wrote to King Erik asking him to yield to the demands of the people. He replied that they should put down the disturbances and come to Kalmar for consultation. Instead the council took matters into its own hands and entered into an armistice with Amund. It was agreed that Danish officials with a few exceptions should be out of the country by July 29, Saint Olaf's day, and that the council with five lawmen designated by the king should meet in October and consider individual complaints and mete out justice to all. Little was done at the October meeting, however.

To Erik the most pressing problem was to reach an amicable settlement with the Swedes. He saw no way out but to appeal to the Hanseatic cities for support, and it was agreed that all differences were to be settled by representatives from the Hansa, the Norwegian council, and the Danish council at a meeting in Kalmar in 1436. Critical conditions at home kept the Norwegians from attending, but the Danes sided with the Swedes and administered to the king a serious reprimand with many admonitions regarding his rule in all three countries: "And then do not forget Norway, but send such officials and sheriffs as is proper, so that there may be a better government than we have heard that the country has now." Erik had to agree that each country should hereafter be ruled by its own government, and a scene of reconciliation and pardon was enacted with much ceremony.

Erik realized, however, that if he yielded permanently, he would repudiate all the ideals of government in which he had been indoctrinated from childhood. "You want me to be your yes-man," he said to the Swedish council, "it was not thus I received the kingdom from the Lady Margaret of blessed memory." Rather than submit to this, he left his kingdom and withdrew to the fort he had built on the island of Gotland.

¶ When Erik deserted, the three kingdoms were virtually without a king, and the government of each country was completely in the hands of its council. In Norway the events of 1436 inaugurated a last period of power for the council, which was to continue for about fifteen years.

In Sweden and Denmark, however, the councils took a much more positive position than that in Norway. In name Erik was still king and was hoping to regain his power; it was an impossible situation with many complications into which we need not enter. In 1439 he was finally deposed, first in Denmark and then in Sweden. Even before the deposition the Danish council had called in Erik's nephew, Christopher of Bavaria, to be regent, and in April 1440 he was chosen king. Thereby the council passed over Erik's other nephew, Burislav of Pomerania, who was of an older line, and thus defeated Margaret's and Erik's plan to convert all the northern countries into hereditary monarchies. Sweden was loath to place another foreigner on the throne and a movement was on foot to elect Karl Knutsson Bonde, who had been serving as regent during the troubles with Erik. Karl, however, was won over to support Christopher and in October 1440 the Swedes also elected him king. In each of the countries Christopher of Bavaria was forced to sign a charter which left the real power in the hands of the nobility acting through the council.

Meanwhile the Norwegians clung with strange tenacity to that recalcitrant king who showed no interest in them whatsoever. In Norway the royal power was hereditary, and this conception of the kingship had taken firm root in the thoughts of the people from the lowest to the highest, developing a deep-seated loyalty to their kings. Moreover, this form of government had given a stability that compared favorably with the brutal conflicts resulting from the elective method in the neighboring countries. The Norwegian system had not produced so powerful and aggressive a nobility as had developed in Denmark and Sweden. The council felt that a repudiation of the hereditary monarchy was both revolutionary and undesirable, and would worsen Norway's position in the union.

When the council came to the fore early in 1436 to deal with the popular rising under Amund Bolt, it acted as arbiter between the rebels and the king's government, and yet it sided with the people and made all their demands its own. The meetings with representatives of Amund's party had achieved only a truce. So it was decided at a provincial church council—the first held in seventy-five years—to call a meeting of the estates, similar to the Swedish diet inaugurated by Engelbrekt. In addition to the council, there met lawmen and representatives of the common people, and thirty-one named men of the people issued an open letter declaring their loyalty to "our gracious lord King Erik," and stating that the council had promised to lay their demands before the king. They asked complete pardon for Amund, the abolition of illegal taxes, removal of all foreign officials, the return of the seal to Norway, and the appointment of a viceroy.[3] Thus a rising to get rid of an obnoxious sheriff had grown into a movement for the reestablishment of a national government.

The council then declared peace in the land and promised to lay all requests before the king and urge that he consider in God's name his own welfare and that of all the people in the realm.[4] But he was as slow in responding to their repeated requests as to the Swedish demands, and discontent continued. There occurred a local rising against some Danish sheriffs who had not been banished as promised and, led by a yeoman, Halvor Graatopp, a poorly organized band made an unsuccessful attack on Akershus. Halvor and several of his followers were killed and the abortive rising was easily put down. The council displayed none of the leniency it had shown toward Amund Bolt.

The unrest finally induced Erik early in 1439 to turn his attention to Norway, but instead of granting any particular requests he called a meeting of the estates with representatives from all classes which was to hear all complaints. The assembly merely repeated the demand for a national government. Erik yielded, appointing Sigurd Jonsson as governor with full authority, and making the dean of St. Mary's Church chancellor, as had been the usage of old. Thus the government by the council gained strength and unity. Nevertheless, the situation in the country went from bad to worse as a Dutch fleet which was supposed to support Erik was harassing the land, cutting off trade, and causing real want.

Finally, when Erik ignored all appeals and Christopher of Bavaria was firmly established in the other countries, there seemed nothing for Norway to do but to fall in line. Christopher was chosen king of Norway in the summer of 1442, at Lødøse, where the councils of the three kingdoms had agreed to meet. Though the election was in reality decided by the council, the right of the people to have a say was recognized, the governor appointing men to represent them, but their participation in the election was a mere formality.[5] Thus the Norwegians

[3] *Norges gamle love*, 1:173-178. [4] *Ibid.*, 1:178.
[5] *Diplomatarium Norwegicum*, vol. 3, no. 771.

departed from their old law by virtually deposing a king and choosing a successor who was not the nearest heir. The country was becoming an elective monarchy.

Soon after his election, Christopher of Bavaria (1442-1448) was crowned in Oslo and took an oath to respect the law and independence of the land as he had done in Denmark and Sweden. The king generally followed the advice of the council, which in Norway had more power than it had held since the days of Haakon VI. Yet the process of administrative disintegration continued, and the lawlessness and abuses by local officials grew worse. There was no unity in the administration; the council lacked energetic leadership and strong personalities, and several members were foreigners who were often called by the king to meet in Denmark. Only toward the Hanseatic merchants and artisans did the council follow an energetic national policy. At first the king sided with the Norwegians, but later his financial dependence on the German cities caused him to grant them more privileges than ever.

In 1448 Christopher died without having won the affection of any of his peoples. Almost at once the Swedes elected Karl Knutsson Bonde, while Christian of Oldenburg was elected in Denmark. In Norway an interregnum of two years followed the death of Christopher. It seems that many Norwegians favored a national king. But the only candidate who could be considered seriously was Sigurd Jonsson, who refused; and when it came to a choice between a Danish or a Swedish union, the people probably leaned toward the latter. The power of deciding, however, rested entirely with the council. While all the leading men thought a union with one of the neighbors expedient, even necessary, they were divided into a Swedish and a Danish party.

On June 3, 1449, the council elected Christian and later issued an open letter to the people announcing the choice. The Swedish party, however, did not submit to this decision. Karl came to Norway in October and was chosen king at Hamar by a meeting of men of all classes. He then proceeded to Trondheim and was crowned by Archbishop Aslak Bolt, the actual head of the government in the North. Aslak died soon afterwards, and at a peace meeting in May 1450 Swedish representatives gave up Norway to Christian without even consulting Karl. Though the Norwegian council had not acted with strength or unity, the election of Christian was more in accordance with law than that of Karl, and there was no further opposition to his succession.

¶ Christian I (1450-1481) was the first king of the Oldenburg family which was to rule Norway as long as the union with Denmark lasted. He had given a charter—the first of the kind in Norway's history—guaranteeing the rights of the people. The king's word meant little, yet the charter emphasized that the kingship was not definitely hereditary and established a precedent for the future. Even when the promises were not kept, such a document was a recognition that the people had rights and a method of asserting them. In the summer of 1450 Christian proceeded to Trondheim with an escort of five Hanseatic ships. He was crowned with much pomp by a German bishop, a pseudo-papal legate with a shady past whom he had in his escort. Afterwards he went to Bergen, where the first union agreement was signed by the councils of the two countries. It provided that the two kingdoms should be "eternally" united in "love and friendship," with a common ruler elected from among the legitimate sons of the former king if there were any. If not, the choice was to be unrestricted. The two countries were to help each other in need, but war should not be declared without the consent of both councils. The right of each country to be governed by its own laws and by native officials, as well as other promises made in the charter issued upon the king's election, was reaffirmed.

The equality of the kingdoms was emphasized, yet the inferiority of Norway's position is obvious—the Danish language was used in both copies of the treaty, and among signers on Norway's behalf were a German bishop and several nobles of Danish birth. The council was not so watchful of the country's independence as it had been, political promises were cheap, and in spite of treaty and charter, Christian I gave Norway as poor an administration as the country has ever suffered.

Christian's whole policy was dictated by dynastic interests and greed for power. He succeeded in bringing under his rule a larger realm than any king in the North had held since the days of Canute the Great. As both Swedes and Norwegians had feared, war broke out almost at once between Christian and Karl Bonde. Norway suffered most. All the eastern border districts were harassed, and even Trondheim was occupied for a short time and the cathedral so defiled that a contemporary account says it looked like a stable. In 1457 peace was made. Karl, who had not been a successful or popular ruler, fled and Christian was recognized also in Sweden. He further increased his realm by winning Gotland from Erik of Pomerania and by pushing the Danish boundary farther south. In 1460 he was elected duke of Slesvig and count of Holstein, on condition that the two duchies should never be separated. Slesvig was part of the Danish kingdom and Holstein was German and held as a fief under the emperor. But Christian's success was short-lived. In winning the duchies he had contracted a huge debt which he never could pay. His attempt to collect extra taxes caused the discontent in Sweden to break into revolt. During the disturbed years that followed Karl was twice called back to be king. After Karl's death Christian suffered a decisive defeat at the hands of Sten Sture and lost Sweden.

Meanwhile Christian had arranged the marriage of his daughter Margaret to the king of Scotland. The extravagant, luxury-loving king had nothing wherewith to pay his daughter's dowry, so in 1468 he surrendered the annual payment that was to be made for the Hebrides and the Isle of Man and also mortgaged the Orkney and Shetland Islands to the Scottish king. They were never redeemed and were thus permanently lost to Norway, and three years later the pope separated them also from the Norwegian church. The nobility and clergy had been Scottish for a century before the transfer, but the common people of the islands were still largely Norwegian in language and had kept their old laws. In the following two centuries they lost their Norwegian nationality, though much in their customs and language is even now reminiscent of their ancestry. An even more disastrous result of Christian's power politics was that in his financial straits and his Swedish war he needed the help of the Hanseatic cities. The cost of this aid was paid by Norway, and finally all opposition to the Hansa dominance came to an end.

The king seldom visited Norway and did nothing to establish a strong government to act in his absence; and the council which alone might have furnished leaders for a national policy, lacked vision and vigor. There was little supervision over officials, and the people groaned under oppressive sheriffs, although the king kept one of the promises in his charter and placed mainly Norwegians in office except in a few of the highest positions. The disposal of fiefs he kept in his own hands and he gave most of them to nobles, often Danish, whose friendship he needed. They became very independent, and the country seemed on the verge of feudal disintegration. Hartvig Krummedige is a notorious example of how a foreign nobleman through marriage and royal office could build up power and wealth in Norway. His account books list 270 farms from which he collected rent, and the complaints of his greed and brutality were many. Christian followed a policy of amalgamation of the two kingdoms, which was never completely successful. Sometimes he settled purely Norwegian matters after consulting the Danish council only, and sometimes members of the Norwegian council were summoned to meet with the Danish. People were becoming accustomed to thinking of the councils of the two, or even the three, kingdoms as a unit, as was in accordance with the policy of the king. There might have been some advantages in this if the Norwegians had been able to assert themselves, but the long journeys to Denmark were a burden, few went to the meetings, and even those who attended often lacked a broad outlook or sense of responsibility for their country, though they did complain of the failure of the king to keep the promises of his charter.

Christian took steps to secure for his family the succession to all three thrones. At a joint meeting of the councils in Skara, Sweden, the Norwegian council, and a little later the Swedish, followed the lead of the Danes and recognized the king's three-year-old son Hans as successor to the throne. Later the resolution was approved by the councillors who had not been present, by burghers of the larger cities, and by representatives of the rural population. The king did not accomplish his purpose without making concessions. To the clergy he guaranteed the old rights as set down in the Concordat of Tønsberg in 1277. He kept this promise, gave up his earlier attempt to turn the church into a virtual state church, and refrained from interfering with ecclesiastical elections. Consequently, before his reign was over most of the higher clergy were Norwegians, recruited mainly from the lower nobility. The lay members of the council the king propitiated by removing the commander of Akershus, Hartvig Krummedige, and depriving him of his fiefs. Although he later received back his command, he never regained his former wealth and influence.

An interregnum of two years followed the death of Christian I in 1481. Fearing that to return to a hereditary monarchy would endanger the freedom of the country, the council repudiated its recognition of Christian's son Hans as his successor and under the leadership of the Norwegian-born archbishop, Gaute Ivarsson, assumed full control of the government. It made a treaty with the Swedes, who since the defeat of Christian I in 1471 had had no king, agreeing that the two countries should act together in the coming election. The Norwegians presented a detailed statement of all the abuses of the preceding reign and asked help against the Danes, declaring that the union had not been to their advantage. As in the days of Aslak Bolt, Norwegians desired a union with Sweden but not with Denmark. The Swedish council answered evasively and gave no assistance, for within its ranks the party that favored an all-Scandinavia union was just then dominant. Norway, having no system of defense even against pirates along the coasts, was not in a position to risk a war with both Denmark and Sweden. There seemed no course open but to join with the Danish council in a common election of Hans, which took place in January 1483. The Swedish regent, Sten Sture, however, prevented the participation of his country in the election, and only when Hans invaded Sweden and won a victory did that country also submit to him.

Hans too, signed a charter as his father had done before him, with the difference that this document applied to both Denmark and Norway and that the two councils agreed if necessary to cooperate in enforcing it. An interesting provision is that no new tax should be levied without the consent of the council, the nobility, and some of the common people "in accordance with law."

¶ Hans (1483-1513) was the ablest ruler of the North since Queen Margaret. He pursued the power politics of Erik of Pomerania, but with more skill and success. He was well aware of the growing power of the rulers and the increasing centralization of the governments that characterized his age. He perceived the new emphasis on the state, whether it were the Italian cities or the rising national states—the Spain of Ferdinand and Isabella, the France of Louis XI, the England of Henry VII—and the Machiavellian principles that dominated them all. Denmark alone was not strong enough to hold its own with these powers, so it became extremely important to retain Norway and, if possible, win a union with Sweden also.

Hans isolated Sweden by forming a cordon of alliances around her. Cooperating with the union party, he invaded the country and forced Sten Sture into submission. In 1497, a hundred years after the Kalmar Union, Hans was elected king of Sweden, and a little later his son Christian was recognized as heir to the throne. Before long, however, Sweden was once more in revolt, with Sten Sture as regent. After his death, the conflict continued under two other men of the same family, first Svante Sture and then Sten Sture the Younger. Twice the Swedes were defeated and promised to elect either Hans or his son as king, but nothing came of it and Sweden continued to be an aristocratic republic.

The Swedes had been encouraged by the news that Hans with an imposing army of arrogant Holstein nobles had suffered a crushing defeat in the swamps of Ditmarsh, as the heroic people opened the dikes and flooded their lands, maintaining their freedom as a little peasant republic. The news of the king's humiliating defeat gave courage to lovers of freedom in Norway also. Hans took his duties more seriously than his father. He paid some attention to Norway's internal administration and did not quite forget all the promises of his charter. He was, moreover, as eager as were the Norwegians to check the power of the Hanseatic cities. He wanted to build up his own power by developing the economy of his realms, and his whole reign was a tug-of-war with the cities, in which both sides used every weapon fair or foul except open war. In diplomacy Hans was more than a match for the cities. He renewed their privileges for only a year at a time, and the right of the Norwegians to carry on the trade at home and with the colonies was fully confirmed. Moreover, he gave the cities of the Netherlands, which were quite able to compete with the Baltic cities, the same privileges as were granted to the Hansa. But he brought in many foreign nobles, and they as well as the bailiffs they employed treated the people with complete disregard of and contempt for their rights, just as nobles farther south, especially in Germany, were in the habit of oppressing the peasantry. So there were constant grumbling and several riots and murders. Hans issued orders to check the abuses, but also to curb the right of the people to complain. But those in authority, including some Norwegians, were too much interested in maintaining the abuses for any great change to be effected.

There was a general rising directed especially against the powerful noble Knut Alfsson, who was half Swedish and half Norwegian. Hans soon after removed him from his position as commander of Akershus, and, because he helped in the Swedish rising, deprived him of all his Norwegian fiefs. Knut retaliated by raising a revolt in Norway against all foreign officials. After initial successes, he was defeated and treacherously murdered by Henrik Krummedige, the son of Hartvig and now the king's most powerful friend in Norway. Hans, suspicious of all Norwegian nobles, adopted the policy of not giving them any positions either in state or church. So the aristocracy added their influence to the seething unrest. By 1506 things had come to such a pass that the king sent his son Christian as viceroy to Norway. The country now had a central government of its own, but it was not Norwegian.

Prince Christian pursued his father's policy with great force and consistency, and accomplished much during his five years as viceroy. He called himself heir to the kingdom, although since 1450 it had been legally elective; and an assembly of notables, largely Danes, declared that disobedience to him was treasonable and punishable with death, although according to Norwegian law disobedience even to a king brought no penalty beyond fines. A revolt led by Herlog Hudfat in eastern Norway was ruthlessly crushed, and all opposition dealt with so summarily that neither noble nor commoner dared raise his voice in complaint. In the church some resistance continued. The aged popular Bishop Karl of Hamar was held prisoner for four years without show of justice and died while in the prince's power. The pope readily pardoned the prince, but old Archbishop Gaute stubbornly refused to crown Christian while his father was living. When Gaute died, however, Christian got his revenge by forcing upon the canons the election of a Dane, Erik Walkendorf. He was a capable, mature man, learned in the Scriptures, experienced in affairs of state and church, and loyal to king and church. But his election did not bode well for the independence of the Norwegian church. The king had become practically absolute in Norway, and the country had become a virtual dependency, so that special Norwegian political ambitions were considered treasonable. Norway was subdued.

The election of Christian II (1513-1524), which took place in Copenhagen five months after his father's death, shows how powerless the Norwegians were. He was chosen by a joint meeting of the councils of the two kingdoms, but there were twenty-nine in the Danish council, while only seven or eight men had come from Norway, and of those four were Danes. The king signed a charter which was common to the two countries, but paid no attention to any special Norwegian rights, giving as his reason that the Norwegian nobility was almost extinct. There was not the slightest pretense of recognizing any equality between the two kingdoms. Christian catered to the Danish nobility, and yet a careful reading of the charter reveals that he did not actually give the Danish council a chance to assert authority in Norway. He wanted no interference with his own power. Soon after the election Christian was crowned in Denmark. Somewhat later, in July 1514, perhaps on Saint Olaf's day, he was crowned in Oslo by Archbishop Walkendorf. This was the last coronation in Norway during the union with Denmark.

Christian II was a typical Renaissance man, attracted to the new ideas of the age, filled with restless energy. He was handsome and gifted, but thoroughly selfish, of unstable temperament and uncontrolled passions that sometimes obscured his judgment. Though he had genuine sympathy with the oppressed, he met all opposition to his own will with cruel ruthlessness.

In the manner of his age, Christian worked to build up a centralized state with the power concentrated in the king supported by a strong burgher class. His policy is most clearly seen in Denmark. He disregarded the council and checked the power of the higher clergy, while he tried to protect the peasants from the landed aristocracy and favored the burghers. In keeping with this were his great schemes for exploring Greenland and opening a northwest passage to India, and for making the Baltic a Danish sea through the organization of a large trading company of the North. While these two schemes came to naught, his policy of furthering the welfare of the middle and even the lower classes against the privileged made him popular with the masses but roused the antagonism of the nobles.

They vented their hatred, however, not on the king, but on an extraordinary woman, Sigbrit Willums, whom they held responsible for his bourgeois policy. She was a Dutch woman who had been running a little bakeshop in Bergen, and she had a daughter named Dyveke who by all accounts was virtuous and wondrously fair. Christian met her when he was viceroy in Norway and with her mother's consent she became his mistress. Wherever he went he took her with him and provided a home for her near his own residence, for he had a lasting, warm affection for his "Little Dove." And with her went Sigbrit, with her coarse features and red face. She was as unlovely as her daughter was beautiful, but she was gifted in many ways. She was skilled in the art of healing and an ardent disciple of the pseudo-science and even of the occult arts of her age. She herself believed that she had supernatural powers, so it is not strange that others thought her a witch. She had a strong influence over people and a firm faith in her ability to control their actions. Over the king she exercised extraordinary power. She used her influence not only to obtain preferments for brothers and friends of questionable merit, but to direct the king's political actions. "She was his other hand; both his nobles and his councillors sought her, hat in hand."[6] And in the eyes of the nobles her influence was evil, for she was stoutly bourgeois.

Before long, in 1517, Dyveke died, probably poisoned. The nobles who had hoped that this would put an end to Sigbrit's influence were bitterly disappointed. She now transferred her motherly affection to the queen. On the day of his coronation Christian had married by proxy Isabella, the thirteen-year-old sister of Charles who was soon to become Emperor Charles V, and the next year she came to Denmark. She became a devoted wife who won the affection of her husband, but in a letter to her sister she expresses the feelings of many a little princess: "It

[6] Huitfeldt, quoted by Sverre Steen, *Det norske folks liv og historie*, 4:52.

is hard enough to marry a man whose face you have never seen, whom you do not know or love, and worse still to be required to leave home and kindred and follow a stranger to the ends of the earth without being able to speak his language."

In Denmark the king's energetic, ambitious policy was causing strained relations between the estates and rousing opposition from the nobles. In Sweden, where Christian was engaged in a serious war to win the throne, the situation was even more difficult.

In contrast to the violent dramatic events in the other two countries, the history of Norway during Christian's reign was uneventful. Norway was outside the stirring events of the day. There was no central government, no national political life, no system of defense, and the country took no military part in the king's war for Sweden. Christian spent several weeks in Norway at the time of his coronation, after which he never returned as reigning king. The government was practically in the hands of the commanders of the chief forts, Akershus, Bergenhus, and Baahus, each controlling a large section of the country. They were men of non-noble birth and therefore despised by the aristocrats, both Danish and Norwegian, both lay and clerical. They were able men, loyal to their king and his absolutist idea, but arrogant and tyrannical toward high and low. Most notorious was Hans Mule of Akershus. He drove out the bishop of Oslo, and in spite of his own scandalous life forced the canons to elect him to the see. The pope, however, refused his sanction. Archbishop Walkendorf, who, though loyal to the king, placed the welfare of the church first and was outspoken in his criticism of the abuses under which church and people suffered, was forced out of his position through the enmity of the anti-clerical Sigbrit. He went to Rome to appeal to the pope but died before his case was taken up.

The common people did not escape injustice. The king needed money, more money than any earlier king, especially to pay the mercenary soldiers he employed in Sweden. That meant heavier taxes than the Norwegians had ever paid, and any money payment was hard under the primitive conditions, when barter economy prevailed. Moreover, contrary to law taxes were imposed without the consent of either council or *thing*. It took hard measures to collect them, and sometimes the ire of the people burst out in petty revolts against the system. But the risings were local and of no political significance, quite different from the days of Amund Bolt and Knut Alfsson. At first the penalty was heavy fines, but later there were a number of executions. One man was executed whose only crime was that he had undertaken to go to Copenhagen and lay the complaints of the people before the king, as was the well established right of even the humblest.

Yet the king had some sympathy for the lowly. He issued comprehensive orders to check abuses and uphold the law. How far they were effective is another matter, but they did gain for the king a certain amount of popularity among the common people. He had also won the loyalty of the burghers through his consistent policy of restricting the liberties of the Hanseatic merchants. The nobility was dying out, and since the council never met, the nobles had no organization through which they could act. So the whole social and political structure—or lack of structure—was not conducive to any united action either of class or nation. In Norway, Christian had succeeded in establishing his system more completely than in the other countries, but his tyranny was felt less grievously.

Meanwhile the opposition to the king in the two other countries was working toward a climax. After the death of the Swedish leader, Sten Sture, his wife Christina held Stockholm for some time, but was finally forced to surrender. Christian was master of the situation, but used his power to perpetrate the Stockholm Blood Bath, a mass execution of his opponents, nobles, bishops, and burghers. Then the common people of Dalarna proclaimed the nobleman Gustaf Vasa leader of Sweden, and all classes rallied to his support. Lübeck joined the Swedes, hoping to regain lost privileges. Before the year was out the Danish nobility, infuriated by the king's tyranny, raised a revolt in Jutland and offered the throne to Christian's uncle, Frederik. Christian had lost confidence in his own cause and let events take their course. On April 13, 1523, he set sail from Copenhagen with his wife, his children, Sigbrit Willums, and his close friends, to seek refuge in the Netherlands with his queen's relatives. As the crowds watched them depart many among the common people wept.

Less than two months later, June 6, 1523, Gustaf Vasa was proclaimed king of Sweden, the first of a family that was to reign for almost three centuries, until 1818. Thereafter no Danish king ever ruled in Sweden: the union between the two countries was over.

¶ Although conditions were not promising, the flight of Christian II offered the Norwegians an opportunity to make one more effort to assert their national rights. Unfortunately the people were less than ever able to have any effective influence on events, and the future of the country seemed to be in the hands of the few nobles, lay and ecclesiastical. Action had to come through the council. Soon after Christian's flight a few of its members met and declared the throne vacant. According to old law they assumed that all fiefs reverted to the council, and so they divided them as they wished. Their leader was Nils Hendricksson, a noble who had greatly enhanced his power and wealth by marrying Inger of Austraat, who had inherited all the land of one of the few remaining old noble families.

Meanwhile Swedes and Danes plotted to gain power and wealth within the borders of the weaker neighbor, and there followed a period of scheming and intriguing, with a confusing array of motives, good and bad, personal and patriotic, the like of which cannot be found in Norwegian history. Gustaf Vasa, renewing old plans for a Swedish-Norwegian union, occupied the Vik regions, and issued a proclamation asking for support and promising to keep the laws of Saint Olaf. He got little help and was forced to withdraw. Before long he made an alliance with Frederik against their common enemy, Christian II.

In Denmark Frederik I was firmly established on the throne by August 1523. To secure the election he had to sign a charter which repudiated Christian's absolutist claims as well as his bourgeois policy, and to some extent strengthened the nobles, both their political power and their hold on the peasantry. The treaty of union of 1450, which provided for a joint election for the two countries, was disregarded. There was no intention of letting Norway go her own way, however. To force his election, Frederik sent to Norway the seasoned old royal stand-by, Henrik Krummedige, and a new man, Dr. Vincens Lunge. Lunge had all the advantages of native ability, noble birth, and influential connections. He was university trained and versed in the learning of the Renaissance. He was also well acquainted with the Reformation, had some leanings toward its doctrines, and was fully awake to the opportunities for financial aggrandizement that it offered. Lunge was a professor at the University in Copenhagen for a short time, but gave up the academic life for the more lucrative pursuit of politics. His dominating passion was greed for power and wealth. Before many months Krummedige was able to win the support of all southern Norway for Frederik. Lunge was just as successful in Bergen and all of the West and North. He had also looked out for his personal interests. He obtained Bergenshus as fief, and married the oldest daughter of Nils Hendricksson and Inger of Austraat, thereby becoming a "Norwegian" noble and a member of the council. The elderly Nils soon died, but Lunge had the backing of the powerful and ambitious Lady Inger.

When it seemed that there remained no obstacle to Frederik's assumption of power over Norway, the new archbishop, Olaf Engelbrektsson, came upon the scene. He had been unanimously elected as soon as the news of Erik Walkendorf's death reached Norway. Although not a few foreigners had occupied sees in Norway, the prelates were on the whole more Norwegian in blood and interests than the lay nobles, being recruited largely from the gentry and odal farmers. Throughout the period the archbishop especially, as the head of the council, had been the leader in upholding the rights of the nation as well as of the church. Olaf was well fitted to follow in the footsteps of his predecessors. He was of a prominent farmer family, a friend of Walkendorf, and trained in foreign universities. He grieved over his country's decline, and was filled with indignation at the decreasing respect for the old church. He knew little about the Reformation except its evils, especially the opportunity it offered for predatory attacks on ecclesiastical property. He deeply loved both his country and his church, and devoted himself to the defense of both with an unflinching courage and a singleness of purpose which has no equal in this age of intrigue. His seeming inconsistencies show changes in circumstances, not in aim, but he lacked political astuteness, and there is something heavy and inelastic about him. Even if he had possessed all talents, however, he probably could not have succeeded, for his national policy was inextricably intertwined with the old church, which was doomed in the North.

In the summer of 1524, Olaf called a meeting of the council to elect a king. Christian II was deposed and Frederik (1524-1533) was elected on condition that he agree to a charter which confirmed and enlarged the power of the council, promised that fiefs and offices would be given only to nobles who were Norwegian by birth or marriage, and guaranteed the church against the Lutheran heresy. Lunge, who was cooperating with Olaf, went to the king as a representative of the council and secured his approval, and the council felt strong enough to take control of the chief fiefs, even depriving Krummedige of his holdings.

Olaf's victory was only temporary, however. As soon as he was strong enough the king began to deprive Norwegians of lands and offices and put in Danes, appropriating even the archbishop's temporal fief of Trøndelag. He tolerated Lutheran preachers and opened the way for the secularization of church property. The Lutheran leanings of both Lunge and the Austraat family were quite marked by this time, and Lunge found it profitable to break with Olaf and remain loyal to the king. Olaf defied the king, built Fort Steinviksholm in the Trondheim Fjord, and procured soldiers and ships. As the king had broken his promises, Olaf declared that he was no longer bound by his oath of loyalty, and in 1529 entered into negotiations with Christian II.

This landless king had busied himself concocting schemes for winning back his kingdoms, roaming about to raise money, and often making himself a nuisance to the friends and the relatives of his wife. Charles V promised help to his brother-in-law on condition that he maintain Catholicism in the kingdoms. Late in the autumn of 1531 Christian set sail for Norway with a large fleet, but most of it was destroyed by storms and he landed in Oslo with only 1,200 men. Though clergy, nobility, burghers, and farmers gave him their support, Christian was not able to take Akershus Fortress, therefore negotiated with Frederik, and went to Denmark on a safe conduct—only to be thrown into prison. The Norwegians had no choice now but to swear allegiance to Frederik anew, but even now all was not lost.

In the spring of 1533 Frederik died. Olaf called a meeting which, contrary to all usage, was to be held at a little place named Bud in Romsdal, far from threatening fortresses. He summoned not only the members of the council but representatives of the people, both burghers and farmers. It was decided that the council, with the archbishop as its head, should rule during the interregnum, and that it should take part in the meeting for a common election which the Danes had summoned for the next summer. This meeting was never held, for when the Norwegian councillors arrived in Copenhagen, Denmark was in the midst of a civil war.

The Count's War, as it was called, received its name from a German count who commanded the forces of Lübeck. It was more than a conflict about the succession to the throne: it was a commercial and a religious war, but above all a war between the social classes. At first there were three parties. Christian, Duke of Holstein, the oldest son of the late king, was supported chiefly by the Holstein nobles who, like the duke, were ardent Lutherans, though not from purely religious motives. The prelates, who naturally wanted to uphold Catholicism, preferred Christian's twelve-year-old brother Hans, and most of the Danish nobility joined them. And finally there was a burgher party under the leadership of Lübeck, which now had turned Lutheran. Lübeck wanted to control the Baltic trade and crush the domination of the nobility in the North. It chose the imprisoned Christian II as its candidate. His tragic fate—though well deserved—had increased his popularity, and the Danish burghers rallied to his support. They were aided by the oppressed peasants, who rose against their lords, harried the land, and burned the castles. As so often, the peasant risings made the nobles forget their differences, and they all joined in supporting Christian, Duke of Holstein. He was then able to conquer district by district, and as he advanced he received the oath of allegiance of the population as Christian III. In July 1536, starving Copenhagen, the last bastion of the burghers, was forced to surrender. In August the council arrested all bishops, abolished the office, and decreed that "the holy gospel and pure word of God must be rightly preached and proclaimed here in the kingdom."

While the civil war was raging in Denmark, Lunge, who in 1534 had sworn allegiance to Christian III, was working in Norway for his own and Christian's cause. Reading the signs of the times, he knew that the day of clerical leadership was over and he felt safe in disregarding the hated archbishop and his national policy. He succeeded in having Christian elected by the council of southern Norway, but in the North Olaf held off, hoping for a national election. When news reached him of Christian's progress, he declared his willingness to support him, but through Lunge's intrigues this statement never reached the king.

Christian, acting as though he already were king of Norway, sent a loyal Danish-Norwegian noble, Claus Bille, to straighten out the affairs in that country. Claus insisted that the councillors of the South go with him to Trondheim to meet with the archbishop, and reluctantly Lunge and the bishops trekked northward on the dark, short December days.

Olaf had suddenly lost interest in the meeting. Christian II's daughter Dorothea had married a good Catholic, Frederick, elector of the Palatine. In November Olaf received a letter from Charles V promising to help Frederick win his father-in-law's kingdom. This seemed to offer a chance to save Norway and the church, and Olaf believed this worth fighting for. Secretly he called together the canons, the city authorities, and many of the citizens, and complained of the illegal acts of the southern council. It was agreed that Lunge must die and the others be imprisoned, and men rushed off to carry out the decision. A few days later the city *thing* approved the coup. Olaf issued letters to the people telling what he had done and urging them to rise for the freedom of their country, and he sent his small military forces against the Danish-held forts. But the people, though in sympathy with Olaf, did not rise, perhaps because they had so long been only spectators while a great drama was being enacted by the aristocrats. Elector Frederick also failed to appear, and no member of the council came to Olaf's support. Alone as he was, the archbishop saw that he could not win, and he declared that he was willing to have Christian elected if it could be done according to law. But the king was in no mood to negotiate and sent Eske Bille to conquer Olaf's fief. News also reached Olaf of the arrest of the Danish bishops. He saw the writing on the wall and prepared for flight or resistance as the case might be. When he heard that the king's men were advancing toward Trondheim, burning, looting, and raping, he was deeply grieved. To spare his people further suffering he set sail in April 1537 with ships sent by Margaret, regent of the Netherlands, to "seek a more friendly neighbor than you are," as he wrote to Eske. Next year he died in Brabant. Olaf Engelbrektsson is a heroic but tragic figure, fighting on for a cause in which he believed but which was doomed to failure, until at last he stood practically alone.

Before Olaf's departure Christian III had affixed his seal to a charter which in reality was an agreement between the king and the Danish nobles regarding the general conduct of the government. Most important for Norway was the clause that the country should cease to be a separate kingdom, and be incorporated into Denmark. At the same time a recess was issued establishing the Lutheran faith in the whole realm. In these events of 1536 Norway lost her national church as well as her status as a nation, and reached the lowest point in her political decline.

¶ In Norway's loss of statehood, not only political, but also social and economic forces were involved. In most of Europe this was an age when the rising power of the bourgeoisie gave character to the whole culture. In Norway this was not so, inasmuch as Hanseatic merchants held sway in trade and city life. Their monopoly prevented the development of a strong city class. That there were Norwegian burghers and that they were not entirely without influence is clear, but they did not gain prominence before the Hansa had lost its sway. The Hanseatic merchants had two stations in Norway, one in Bergen and one for Oslo and Tønsberg. The foreigners were strongly entrenched and well organized and the German artisans were closely allied with them. More and more they disregarded Norwegian law and showed contempt for the authorities, misused their power by selling poor goods and taking exorbitant profits, and dominated the city life with their lawless brutality. As the kings—always in need of money—were financially dependent upon them, the Hansa cities were able to extort increasing privileges; at the same time they were strong enough to play a decisive part in every political crisis in the North. To make matters worse, the government pursued no consistent policy toward other foreigners, Dutch or English, who might have been a counterpoise to the Germans. Moreover, the trade with the Norwegian islands, which had been a royal monopoly since the thirteenth century, was not kept up in an adequate manner. The last boat to Greenland sailed in 1410 and fewer ships than had been promised went to Iceland.

The Hanseatic merchants were especially strong in Bergen. When the Victuals Brothers had left the city in ruins, the population fled, the native merchant and house owner class virtually disappeared from the city, and the English traders stayed away. When the Germans returned with the coming of peace in 1435, they had everything their own way. They became owners of the houses, not renters as they used to be, but did not become citizens and did not pay taxes or otherwise spend their wealth for the general good. Though the country was dependent on the trade with the Hanseatic merchants, their dominance was not accepted without resistance. In the reign of Christopher a protracted struggle went on between the Germans, who wanted their privileges confirmed and enlarged, and the Norwegian council, which tried to confine the foreigners to their old legal rights. The leader was the aggressive commander of Bergen, Olaf Nilsson, who did not hesitate to employ illegal confiscations bordering on piracy to carry through his purpose. At first the king supported him in his imperious policy toward the Germans, but later he removed him and renewed all the privileges of the Hansa merchants. By threats of aiding the Swedes, Olaf got himself reinstated, but the Germans in a riot murdered him, his brother, his good friend the bishop, and about sixty of his supporters. The murderers went scot-free, and all active Norwegian opposition to Hanseatic dominance came to an end.

The kings, however, were becoming more and more aware of the need for checking the intruders, and this became the consistent aim of Hans and his son, Christian II. In a measure they were successful. They gave other foreigners the same privileges as the Germans and upheld the rights of the natives to the retail trade. Both father and son favored the burgher class, but at first the benefits from their policy fell mainly to non-Norwegians.

Like the burghers, the Norwegian nobles furnished no constructive leadership for the people. A decline in the nobility was going on all through the fourteenth and fifteenth centuries. Many of the older families died out, while others had joined the ranks of the well-to-do farmers, and there was no native king to advance new men. The few who remained were generally neither wealthy nor prominent; they had no training in bigger affairs and little education or travel, and their outlook was provincial. Norway lacked the sharp division between classes that characterized Danish society.

Nevertheless clashes were not lacking. Landowners, whether state, church, nobles, or even powerful farmers, oppressed the tenants with arbitrary restrictions, extra dues, and unreasonable fines. The representatives of the crown were of the same class as the landlords, although more of them were Danish than Norwegian. The king was far away, and often the government was run more in the interest of the officials than of state, king, or people. Lawlessness reigned, pirates and robbers were unchecked, and often the sheriffs and bailiffs were worse than robbers. Although the lower nobility was beginning to merge with the common people, the opposition to tyranny came to be both a class and a national conflict.

The three leading revolts show how both the social and national elements entered into the movements. The rising led by Amund Bolt, beginning as a class conflict, ended with a demand for the removal of foreign officials and the organization of a national government. Its significance became mainly political and it received the backing of the council. Halvor Graatopp, who led the next revolt, was a leader—the first, in fact—who came out of the common people. This was a rising against upper-class landed magnates and officials. It was suppressed without having had any support from the council. The third revolt began as resistance to Knut Alfsson's brutal bailiff, but Knut turned it into a nationalistic movement under his own leadership. After his tragic failure there was no general rising.

There continued to be a vigorous, healthy life among the people,[7] but this energy was spent in local affairs and had little opportunity to influence national life. Old organizations, such as the local *things*, where they still existed had become more detached from the state. Most of the courts, subdivisions of the old *lagthings*, had been removed to the cities, and even when thingmen met the decision was in the hands of the king's lawman. It was natural that people should lose interest in the state. Nevertheless, the old political traditions were not lost. Sometimes local *things* assembled to give their oath of allegiance to a king,

[7] In her two great novel cycles, *Kristin Lavransdatter* and *Olav Audunssøn*, Sigrid Undset gives an unsurpassed account of daily life toward the close of the Middle Ages in its many facets.

and sometimes representatives of the people met in assemblies of the realm to have a part in the choice of a new ruler or to approve new taxes.

The people were particularly sensitive about their right to control taxation. They contributed less to the state at the close of the Middle Ages than in saga times, but they also received less. The legal taxes were paid with only the normal amount of grumbling. It was only against illegal demands and brutality in the collectors that opposition rose, and there were enough abuses to develop in the people a tenacious, stubborn spirit of resistance which has lasted even to the present.

Nevertheless, the economic pressure on the people was not especially heavy, not so heavy as in the following centuries. There was not the systematic exploitation of the lower classes which came later with the growth of capitalism. After the country had recovered from the worst effects of the Black Death, the people were fairly well off. Until the very close of the period, about 1500, the prices of land remained on a low level. There was little advance in agriculture and practically no expansion of the cultivated area. But there was no lack of land, for there were plenty of deserted farms that could be occupied again as the population slowly increased. Although, or perhaps because, this was not an age of great economic advance, a simple, modest prosperity and well-being was general in the land.

The most remarkable descriptions we have of daily life in fifteenth-century Norway are accounts by an Italian, Pietro Quirini and two of his companions, who spent several months there in 1432.[8] Quirini was shipwrecked and after many hardships he and ten of his men landed on Røst, one of the outermost islands of the Lofoten group. It was a tiny rocky island with only one hundred and twenty inhabitants. They lived mainly by fishing, going to Bergen every spring with an immense amount of fish to sell. They brought back with them sack cloth, iron goods, spices, rye flour, and other things, and stopped on the way to gather fuel for the winter.

Life was primitive. The people lived in one-room log huts with a fireplace in the center and only an opening in the roof which could be covered with translucent fish skin, or opened to let smoke out and light in. The food was simple, but plentiful and good, and as each family kept several cows, dairy products were important in the diet. The people were rather well off in a simple way. They had high standards of cleanliness and the other decencies of daily living, so their life never became sordid. They seemed to Quirini happy and contented.

[8] In Gjerset's *History of the Norwegian People*, 2:56-64, Quirini's account is quoted at length.

Quirini received a similar impression of the people in other communities, as he and his companions made their long journey home, by boat to Trondheim and from there by land across to Sweden. Everywhere they were met with unlimited hospitality and were astonished at the people's ability and willingness to supply their needs and give costly gifts to boot. Other sources bear out the account of the Italian visitors. Hospitality was so general, says Absalon Pedersson, that a person could travel from Vardøy to Baahus without spending a dollar. Daily life had not changed much from earlier days. There was the same toil to raise and gather food, the same type of food, houses, and clothing. Though everyday clothes were very simple, the influence of foreign styles reached even rural communities, and on special occasions there was a display of rich and splendid attire. The wealthier farmers had better and larger houses than those on Røst, and the number of buildings on a farm depended on the needs and means of the family. Life on the farms, especially the wealthier ones, was not without its festivity. There were large weddings and parties at which mead flowed freely and the tables groaned under loads of food. There were ball games and contests—sometimes fights—and skating and skiing, and gay, wild dancing to the accompaniment of the singing of folk songs. There were festivals of the guilds, which were less economic and more social-religious than in the past, and church festivals on saints' days, especially on Saint John's Eve, June 24th, when there was dancing on the green around a great bonfire throughout the bright summer night.

In social customs and morals there were, it seems, greater extremes than in earlier and later periods. On Røst Quirini found a peaceful community where people lived together in childlike simplicity, innocent of vice. At the other extreme are accounts from Telemark which picture a brutal, coarse community. Brawls were frequent even when people were sober and infinitely worse when they were drunk. The knives "sat loose in the sheath," and blood often flowed. Documents testify that murders were more frequent and gruesome in Telemark than in the rest of the country, though brutality was common in other parts of the country also, and political conditions tended to increase acts of violence. These two extreme pictures are both true, but in most places were found, in different proportions, some characteristics of both. Roughness there was aplenty. On the other hand there are evidences of greater religious earnestness and Christian virtue than in earlier periods.

❡ Though the medieval church was still a strong institution, it was losing power and influence. Nothing shows the change better than the way in which Olaf Engelbrektsson at last stood alone against the forces of a new age. One cause was the interference of the government; the church served best when it was allowed to manage its own affairs. But more important was the new spirit that dominated just before the Reformation. As in other countries, the church was growing worldly, and financial abuses—always present—became more frequent and brazen. Ecclesiastical magnates joined with lay lords in using every means of acquiring landed property. One man was even deprived of his farm as penalty for eating meat in Lent. It became easier than before to obtain absolution through mere purchase of indulgences without any sign of remorse. The church was laying more stress on organization and externals and less on education and personal religion. Yet it maintained its authority with strict discipline and enforcement of law.

Scattered over the country, moreover, often in locations of extraordinary natural beauty, the twenty-five monasteries continued to wield a wide influence. They were surrounded by gardens and orchards where were raised all the fruits and vegetables that could be grown in the northerly climate, and burghers, nobles, and farmers learned from the monks both agriculture and crafts, as well as religion. Most important, however, was the local church, which was the center of community life and close to the people in all the important events of life from baptism to burial. At church they met for services and lingered in the churchyard to meet friends and to discuss practical matters. Quirini's account shows that the influence of the church penetrated even to small, isolated communities. It was the institution that demanded most from the people, but it also gave most. The parish priests came from among the people and were close to them.

Thus even as the old church was moving toward its fall, it seems that the religious life of the people was going forward. Though there were no schools and the general ignorance was great, the people had been drilled in the fundamentals of the faith, and even when the church was negligent, the knowledge was passed on from parents to children. There were strange superstitions and charms from heathen times mingled with the credos and paternosters, and yet the people understood the central teachings of the church and knew the creed and prayers in their own language as well as in Latin. They learned more through pictures and their allegorical interpretation than from sermons, for every ceremony and emblem had its meaning and preaching was sadly neglected.

The whole rhythm of life was regulated by church festivals and saints' days. The priests were supposed to send out crosses to "every house from which smoke rises" to announce services. But as they became negligent, the people had to make their own astronomical observations, however faulty, and old men and wise women kept simple calendars on a long stick (*primstav*), designating the days by the symbolic mark of the church—in the picture language of the church. That also among those who taught the people the evangelical spirit lived on in the midst of decline is indicated in the following words of a fifteenth century bishop: "God give me a true heartfelt repentance, the sanctification of my life, the comfort of the Holy Spirit, and eternal life when I depart this body."

Whatever art the age produced also shows the strong influence of the church. Resources were lacking for large architectural undertakings, and the court and upper class were disintegrating and could not maintain the luxury of earlier days. The only notable church construction was the rebuilding of the Nidaros Cathedral, and even that was not on a par with the achievements of the preceding age. Symbolic of Norway's history in the late Middle Ages is the tragic fate of this finest expression of past greatness. Hardly had it been completed—possibly it was not even quite finished—when in 1328 a fire destroyed much of its glory. Rebuilding was no doubt interrupted by the Black Death, and was probably not completed when a second great fire occurred in 1432, shortly before the suppression of the last peasant rising. The restoration was achieved mainly by the archbishops Aslak Bolt and Erik Walkendorf, but it progressed slowly. Not long after its completion, in 1531, a third fire more devastating than any earlier destroyed both the city and the cathedral. Nothing could be done to save the church, and bit by bit the arches, pillars, and walls crumbled into ruin. Six years after the fire, the casket of Saint Olaf was sent to Denmark.

Though churches were not built, the furnishings within them were becoming richer and more profuse. Most of the art objects of the age were produced to meet the growing demand for images of saints, altars, and other church furnishings. The triptych came to occupy a central place in church ornamentation. When closed it presented a flat, though elaborately painted surface; but when opened it revealed complicated carvings, often figures of saints under canopies showing a tendency toward the perpendicular style. Images and background were gorgeously colored, and the perspective added to the richness of the effect. Most of these articles were either imported, chiefly from the Hanseatic cities, or were the work of craftsmen who were either foreigners or trained abroad. As in all Europe, bourgeois taste dominated in art, and there is about some of the products an air of the complacent smugness often seen in German art of this age. Even rural churches often possessed a remarkable wealth of tapestries, images, chalices, and crucifixes, and the people paid for them and valued them highly.

As they lived with this church art, it was natural that it should exert some influence on them and that thus the secular rural art also should show a trace of the Late Gothic characteristics. The articles of Norwegian workmanship that have survived are not very numerous, most of them coming from the Uplands, where foreign art exerted least influence. There is enough to show that the old crafts were maintained and to some extent improved. The houses were well built and sometimes adorned with wood carving. This was especially lavished upon the *stabbur*, the two-story building which combined storage space and guest room. Locks and keys and other iron work for doors, chests, and the like were beautifully wrought by skilled smiths. Goldsmiths and silversmiths, too, kept up the arts of old, and in weaving also the traditions of the past were maintained.

¶ There is no written Norwegian literature at the close of the Middle Ages. Some learning there was and some interest in the new humanism among the higher clergy, but no literary production. There are, however, thousands of private letters and public documents which are of value to the student of history. As in other countries, a rapid change in the language was taking place. The documents for about a century (1350-1450) were written in a strangely mixed language, Norwegian with a great many Swedish and Danish words. After 1450 the royal communications to Norway were written in Danish, and, although the chancellery in Oslo continued to use Norwegian for some time, Danish gradually became the official language.

The spoken tongue, however, continued to be Norwegian; but it was Middle Norwegian, not Old Norse. After 1350 old forms were gradually dropped, forgotten, and finally no longer understood, and the language took on a more modern shape. Thus inflections were lost, and the use of little words like prepositions increased. The evolution was strongly influenced by the neighboring countries where a similar development was going on. The linguistic boundaries were not so sharply drawn as in modern times, and Norwegian as spoken in the Vik region was not far removed from the language of near-by Danish and Swedish districts. This facilitated the entrance of foreign characteristics into the language, as did also the absence of written literature in Norway. Most striking was the great influx of foreign words, which far exceeded the normal adoption of new words found in many other languages. At first the adoptions from the Swedish were most numerous; then Danish words were used in greater numbers, and toward the close of the period German words also found entrance. Through the Hanseatic merchants a strong Low German influence made itself felt, reaching even the daily speech of the rural people and introducing everyday words that are now hardly recognized as foreign. The same was true in Denmark and Sweden. As the linguistic evolution brought Norwegian closer to the languages of the neighbors to the east and south, a cleavage took place between the language of the mother country and the island colonies, at the same time as the economic and political ties were loosening. It was unfortunate that the changes came in a period of decline, so that they could not produce a strong modern language and literature as in other countries, but rather paved the way for the victory of the Danish in the next century. One little incident from 1488 has been recorded which shows that there was among the people some feeling against the entrance of foreign elements into the mother tongue. A farmer in Telemark who became furious when a neighbor used some Low German words exclaimed: "Let us talk the language of our fathers and mothers. We won't be better than they were."[9]

It was in the rural districts that the language remained purely Norwegian, but there it became more differentiated into local dialects. The only Norwegian literature of the time was the folk literature discussed in the preceding chapter. There was probably not as much produced in the fifteenth as in the fourteenth century. But this, the greatest treasure inherited from the later Middle Ages, continued to flourish and to add poetic beauty to daily living.

[9] Didrik Arup Seip, *Fornorskningen av vårt språk*, 13, Oslo, 1933. *En liten norsk sproghistorie*, 18-21, Oslo, 1933.

PART IV

The Danish Period, 1536-1814

CHAPTER 11

THE AGE OF THE REFORMATION, 1536-1596

ALTHOUGH NORWAY AND DENMARK had been ruled by a common king almost without interruption since 1380, the union had been primarily dynastic, and it is only the centuries following 1536 that may most properly be called the Danish Period. Not before that year did the old national government of Norway finally disappear. The flight of Olaf Engelbrektsson marked the defeat of the long, ever-weakening conflict to maintain Norway's position as a state. After that Norway had for a long time no opportunity to act as a unit in relation to other countries. Margaret's plan for a united Danish-ruled state—without Sweden, however—was almost realized.

Yet in spite of political impotence, the people continued its own folk life; the centuries of the Danish union were a "Danish period" only on the surface, and the history of the people could therefore show a gradual development toward complete national self-assertion. "The country rose from the degradation without any visible gigantic effort, without dramatic crises, but by virtue of an inner strength which was never broken, a strength which increased through the century."[1] All the great movements of the age, the Reformation, the Renaissance, and the Commercial Revolution, surged in from the South, and for Norway too the sixteenth century meant the beginning of modern history.

¶ Christian III (1536-1559) aimed to establish a strong state with as much power as possible concentrated in the hands of the king. By his coup of August 1536 he had played havoc with Denmark's form of government and taken the reins into his own hands, and two months later at a meeting of the estates, nobles and burghers approved two documents, both dated October 30, 1536, which were to determine Denmark's government for many years to come. One was the charter, es-

[1] Sverre Steen, *Det norske folks liv og historie*, 4:170.

tablishing the form of government by king, council, and nobility. The other was a recess, or statute, which legally established the Lutheran Reformation.

Both documents were enacted as Danish laws, but it had become habitual to take for granted that Norway, lacking the power to act independently, would have to accede to any disposition made, and that Danish enactments would apply to the northern kingdom as well. This proved to be the case in this instance. The only mention of Norway is in the clause: "It shall henceforth be and remain under the crown of Denmark the same as any of the other provinces, Jutland, Fyn, Zealand, or Skaane, and it shall henceforth not be called a kingdom, but a province of the kingdom of Denmark, and subject to the Danish crown forever."[2]

This provision, if carried out, would have laid the country wide open to exploitation by the Danish nobility without regard for any troublesome Norwegian laws and privileges. What the king could gain by it is not so clear. He might perhaps think it gave him some legal basis for any course he might choose to pursue. At any rate, he kept the act unknown both in international diplomatic circles and in Norway.

Christian claimed that he was king of Norway from 1534 on and that any opposition to him was rebellion. He addressed open letters to the people urging submission and picturing the misery that would ensue should he be forced to order in his armies. He found no occasion to carry out this threat. Royal commissioners were sent with a small force to obtain control of Norway. Steinvikholm Fortress fell not long after the archbishop had left, and there was no further opposition. All the principal fiefs were in the hands of Danes, and almost unconsciously the country slipped into the new order. No official act or document marked Christian III's assumption of complete control over Norway. There was no royal charter to afford the people even the limited guarantees that such documents had promised in the past. Christian had not been elected, although the Act of Union of 1450 which made the monarchy elective was still the legal basis of the union. Like his predecessors, he had tried to revive the old hereditary conception of the Norwegian crown; but that could not be too much stressed, as his uncle Christian II, the "Old King" as he was called, was of an older line. Nor had he been acclaimed by the people and received their oath of allegiance, as old Norwegian law required. Cognizant of that law, he emphasized the fact that individuals and local groups had sworn allegiance

[2] B. J. Kidd, *Documents of the Continental Protestant Reformation*, 334, Oxford, 1911.

to him, and repeatedly expressed his intention of going to Norway to receive the recognition of the people as a whole and be crowned there. But he never carried out the plan. Many years later he sent his son and heir Frederik to Norway. With much pomp Frederik accepted for his father and himself the homage of a large assembly of men of all classes from all parts of the country. This gave a certain legal basis to the reigns of both. Up to this time Christian, ignoring legal forms, had in reality ruled as a usurper, simply taking advantage of the impotence of the country.

The control of the church by the state was an integral part of Christian's new order. In Norway this seemed especially important, for there the church had often led in the opposition to the kings. As both king and queen were sincerely Lutheran, Christian's religious and political interests happily coincided. Olaf's flight left the archbishopric vacant, and by summer all the Catholic bishops had been removed.

Old Bishop Mogens of Hamar had armed for the purpose of resisting. He had two copper cannon, two serpentines, a few muskets, two barrels of powder, and some food and clothes. When he realized that resistance was futile, he surrendered and was led captive to Denmark, where he died in prison five years later. As he was about to enter the boat which was to carry him into captivity, says the famous old *Chronicle of Hamar*, he knelt on the shore and thanked God for every day he had lived. He bade good night to all, priests and canons, burghers and peasants, asking them to pray for him and expressing the hope that he would soon meet them again. Weeping, he prayed, "O God, Father in heaven, if we do not meet earlier, then God grant that we meet in heaven, vale, vale, vale."

The Lutheran worship and the new church organization were formally established through a Latin Church Ordinance, written by Luther's friend, Bugenhagen, to which the king affixed his signature, September 2, 1537. It was to apply to the whole realm, but a special ordinance for Norway was to be issued when Norwegian conditions had been studied.[3] This promise was not fulfilled, however, before 1607. In June 1539 the ordinance in a Danish translation was accepted for Norway at meetings of the *lagthings* in Oslo and in Bergen, and thus the new order won the approval of the people, formally at least. Even before the ordinance was framed, the king's commissioners had begun to take over the property of the bishoprics, all of which was soon absorbed by the crown; the episcopal residences were destroyed or put to

[3] Kidd, *Documents of the Continental Protestant Reformation*, 328.

secular uses. The church was allowed to retain other property, but even this was really under the control of the government, and valuables in the churches were confiscated, although it had been promised that they were not to be removed.

The political and economic part of the Reformation was carried through with speed and efficiency and was practically completed in 1539. A state church under the direct control of the king had been established. Thus Norway became more dependent on Denmark than ever before and the power of the state was much enhanced. The political changes that came with the reign of Christian III were the final result of the gradual decline in the fifteenth century. Therefore they did not seem revolutionary, and the Norwegians were hardly conscious that anything new was happening. At the same time his reign marks not only the passing of the old, but the beginning of a transition to modern institutions, which continued through the century.

One characteristic of the age, in the North as well as in the rest of Europe, was the new emphasis on the state rather than on the king and his officials as individuals. The king's authority was paramount, however, although Christian followed a conciliatory policy and ruled with wise moderation. Able though not brilliant, he had a keen sense of his great responsibility as ruler and exercised admirable self-control. He was ably assisted by his queen, Dorothea, who may well be classed with the famous ruling queens of the sixteenth century.

The clause in the Danish charter of 1536, which has become so notorious in history as fixing Norway's subordinate position, was unknown to the Norwegians and was never carried out. Norway was never incorporated into Denmark, and it continued both to be and to be called a separate kingdom. It was a shorn kingdom, however, for what remained of dependencies was brought directly under the crown, and finally lost to Norway. It was furthermore a kingdom without leaders and without a central administration of its own. The council simply disappeared without having been formally abolished; the only national office that remained was that of chancellor, and this was sometimes left vacant. The ruling power was in the hands of the king, who used Danish nobles in practically all important posts.

The administration lost much of its feudal character. The governors of the fiefs were the direct representatives of the king and often appeared with considerable splendor, surrounded by a court of young Danish nobles. Lower officials were now better trained and paid only a modest fixed salary. Supervision over them was stricter than in the past in order to protect the people and guard the king's revenue. In both aims the government was fairly successful. The royal income was larger than ever before, and the people suffered fewer arbitrary abuses at the hands of sheriffs and bailiffs than in the past. They had faith that the king had their interest at heart and that he would secure justice for them, and in this they were not entirely deceived.

Christian III recognized the old rights of the people by following the policy of "consulting" them. Often he ordered officials to lay before the people matters of local concern. Especially were *things* called together when new taxes were needed, for the old claim of the people that taxes should not be levied without their consent could not be entirely ignored. Nevertheless, by the close of the reign they had practically ceased opposition to taxes fixed without consulting them, if they were "necessary." What that meant was not defined. Christian repeatedly promised that the people were to be governed according to the old "laws of Saint Olaf," as they were called. It would have been more correct to have said the laws of Magnus Lawmender. As the laws were Norwegian, it was necessary to have Norwegian lawmen at the head of the *lagthings*, or district courts. Justice was still administered by local *things* in town and country, and, although the political system was Danish, the legal system was Norwegian in law and personnel, except for the supreme power of the king. The Norwegians were ultra-conservative in insisting upon their old laws. In many localities thirteenth century parchment copies were preserved and still used. But the language had so changed that even the lawmen had difficulty in understanding the original, while Danish officials could not read it at all. So a semi-official translation into a modern form of both Norwegian and Danish came to be used more and more, but there was no one official text before Christian IV's Danish translation was published in 1604. Although new laws, some of them Danish, crept into use to meet the needs of changing conditions, judgment was in the main passed according to "the laws of Saint Olaf" even in the king's courts.

At times high court sessions were held at which royal commissioners consulted with the lawmen and representatives of the estates. The final decision was in the hands of the commissioners, subject, of course, to the king's approval. People flocked to the meetings from all directions and complaints poured in which could not be ignored. Often it was impossible to satisfy both the king's demand for new taxes and the people's insistence on their old rights. They therefore continued to send committees to lay their grievances before the king, believing that many of them would be righted if brought to the personal attention of the sovereign. Though inadequate as a means of securing redress, these appeals were not without their effect in calling attention to the needs of the country. One notorious case deserves mention. A certain Rolf Halvardsson and some companions were selected to lay the grievances of their community before the king. Frederik instructed his governor at Trondheim, Ludwig Munk, to see that the matter was settled justly. Upon the return of the emissaries, however, they were arrested for some trifling irregularity and executed without legal trial. This caused great indignation and the decision was later reversed, but the incident shows the risk incurred in appealing to the king above the heads of local officials.

Although much of the old remained, Norway had no national government and the king was an absentee ruler. The Danes, moreover, were inclined to look with contempt upon the "backward" folk among the cliffs of the North who without a struggle had slipped into a position of inferiority. This passivity seemed to indicate that the Norwegians were not able to direct their own affairs, and upon occasion they were reminded that they ought to be thankful for the blessings the union brought them. Nevertheless the development from 1536 on shows that the national consciousness, which had never been dead, was growing in strength and could not be ignored. A potent influence was exerted by a tragic war in which Norway was involved against her wishes.

¶ While Christian III was interested in the welfare of Norway, his chief concern was the realm as a whole, with Denmark as the principal part. Denmark alone could not hold the place in international affairs to which Christian aspired, and Norway, though of little strength by itself, was necessary to the Danish king in this age when the Atlantic seaboard was gaining in importance at the expense of the inland seas.

The king followed a consistent policy of peace, but this was not easy when Spanish and Burgundian fleets ruled the waves and privateering was a part of naval warfare; when wars raged all about and Charles V was threatening the balance in Europe; when the claims of Christian II and his daughters to the throne were not entirely abandoned; when Sweden still remembered the Kalmar Union and was not only a rival for supremacy in the Baltic, but also for the control of Norway; and when English ships were following the old Norwegian route to the White Sea. Christian had an alliance with Gustaf Vasa, and Charles V signed a treaty promising to give no support to the claims of Christian II. A few years later the reigning king also made his peace with the "Old King," who, subdued by his years of adversity, was eager to make friends. He spent his last years in comfort, though still a prisoner of state, dying in 1559, a few months after Christian III. Thus Christian succeeded in keeping peace, but he realized that it was an unstable peace and that no treaties could put an end to the privateering and piracy which were endangering commerce and harassing the shores, especially of Norway. There was need of building up the defenses of the state.

Practically nothing was left of Norway's old system of defense. The ancient custom of mustering out the farmers in case of danger had gone into disuse, and even if the people had been willing to respond as of old—which they were not—many of them did not even own firearms. Christian could not do much to develop land forces, but he placed capable Danish nobles in charge of the forts and supplied each with a small band of mercenary soldiers. To defend the coast, a fort was erected on the island of Flekkerøy, near the present Christiansand. To build up a fleet he harked back to the old almost forgotten *leidang*, appealing to Norwegian patriotism and loyalty to the old laws. Each fief bordering on the sea was to supply a ship meeting certain specifications, and if needed, Dutch builders should be employed. A number of ships were furnished and were joined with the Danish, forming the Danish-Norwegian navy, manned largely by Norwegians, which was to play a distinguished part in the years to come.

Upon Christian's death, his son, Frederik II (1559-1588), succeeded to the throne and was crowned in Copenhagen. The only notice taken of Norway was that a few men from that country, some of them Danish nobles, were present at the coronation, and one Norwegian bishop assisted at the anointing. Unlike his father, Frederik was impulsive and ambitious, prone to plunge into great undertakings without counting the cost. Unrest was in the air and, in spite of the warnings of his older advisers, the young king eagerly rushed into war. First he conquered Ditmarsh and added this district to Holstein, thus avenging the humiliating defeat inflicted upon King Hans six decades earlier. Victory stimulated Frederik's warlike ambitions, and it was all too easy to begin a contest with his rival for the dominance of the North. In Sweden, Gustaf Vasa was succeeded in 1560 by his vain and reckless son Erik XIV, who was as willing to fight as was Frederik. The two kings, Frederik especially, were responsible for precipitating their countries into the most disastrous war that had ever been fought in the North, the Northern Seven Years' War, 1563-1570.

The Baltic trade and the interests of the rival kings in Livonia and Estonia, where both countries had possessions, did not concern the Norwegians. Nor did they care especially whether or not the Danish king continued to include the three crowns in his coat of arms, although to Erik this was the chief *casus belli*, as he considered it symbolic of Frederik's claim to the Swedish throne—a claim which had never been given up. It was not Norway's war. Yet that country was the chief stake in the contest and had to pay a disproportionate part of the cost in money and suffering. Erik had hopes of winning Norway, and a lively propaganda was carried on from Sweden to convince the Norwegians that they would be better off in a union with Sweden. There was some pro-Swedish sentiment, but before the war was over it had all but disappeared.

There were a number of naval engagements during the war, with shifting success, but by and large the Danish-Norwegian fleet was the stronger, and Denmark maintained control of the Baltic. Norwegian seamen contributed their share to the naval warfare, but this did little to aid their own country.

The land forces on both sides consisted largely of mercenaries, mostly Germans. The Danes attacked Sweden from their provinces in what is now southern Sweden, while the Swedes directed their offensive against the unprotected borders of Norway. A force of mercenaries under a French commander captured Trondheim with little difficulty, and the people readily took an oath of allegiance to Erik of Sweden. A reaction soon set in, for the conquerors were arrogant and brutal. Help came through Erik Rosenkrantz, the Danish commander at Bergen. With great difficulty he raised a levy among the people of the neighborhood, who had no interest in this far-away war and grumbled at the financial burdens imposed. With this force he liberated Trondheim, and the whole region returned to the Danish allegiance. The foreign soldiers were carried captive to Copenhagen, and many of them were hired by the Danish king to fight their erstwhile employer.

The eastern fortresses of Baahus and Akershus held out, defended by able Danish commanders and mercenary garrisons. The people near the eastern borders were much opposed to the war and inclined to make their own peace with the invaders (*bondefred*), that is, they would promise not to fight if they were left alone; but such terms could not easily be made with mercenaries who seemed unable to refrain from plunder and murder. It was, however, hastily levied troops of the people themselves which drove back the last army that raided the eastern valleys and which freed the soil from the foreigners. The war dragged on until all the countries were exhausted. There were no great battles or victories, but all three countries suffered intensely, as larger regions than ever before in their history were devastated with ruthless fire, plunder, murder, and rape. Perhaps Norway suffered most.

Finally peace had to be made, although there was no real victor. The Kalmar Union was completely dead, but Denmark retained some advantages on the sea and a superiority in Baltic waters. It was not to be expected, however, that Sweden, having failed to get any part of Norway, would permanently submit to being thus shut off from the Atlantic. There were no territorial changes and no results that might from any point of view have justified the war. The peace was so made as to create a desire for revenge, and the depredations of the armies had created a hatred between the peoples such as had never existed before. It had, on the other hand, tended to tie Danes and Norwegians closer together. They had fought side by side and were bound together by the common enmity toward the Swedes. But this did not mean that the Norwegians were satisfied with the union as it was.

¶ As the century progressed national pride was becoming stronger and more articulate in its insistence on national recognition. A notable expression of Norwegian opinion is found in Absalon Pederssøn Beyer's *Om Norgis Rige* (Concerning the Kingdom of Norway), written in 1567.[4] Master Absalon bemoaned the sad state into which his once glorious country had fallen, but he believed that the land was full of untold riches and that the people had the old virility to make Norway rise again if only there were a ruler in the land who could maintain daily contact with his subjects. He urged the king to visit the country in order to know conditions, "especially as a foreign people [Germans] lives here and many strangers sail hither," for "it is not to be wondered at that the people are somewhat unwilling to defend their ruler when they never or very rarely see their king." The author expressed the loyalty to the king and confidence in him which had characterized the Norwegians through the ages. Frederik II did not follow the advice of Master Absalon to visit Norway, but he was no longer the hasty youth who had plunged into a tragic, ill-considered war. He had become more like

[4] See below, page 274.

his father and devoted himself with energy and interest to the rule of his realms.

The war had revealed the need of a reorganization of Norway that should recognize more fully its unity and status as a kingdom, for, although capable, energetic Danish officials kept things going, the war effort was hampered by the lack of a national government. Moreover, the demands of the Norwegians were growing in persistence and volume. Accordingly in 1572 a central administration was again established in Norway. The king then appointed the commander of Akershus, Povel Huitfeldt, statholder "in our whole kingdom of Norway, to do and perform all things during our absence." His duties were many: he was to hear complaints against officials and judge them with the help of the nearest lawmen, see that the bailiffs neither oppressed the people nor cheated the king, and that the bishops performed their duties—in short, act as the king's representative with supervision over all his officials. Constantly traveling over the country, Huitfeldt did an immense amount of work during his five years' administration. But as no one man could possibly act on the mass of complaints that poured in, several high court sessions were held during his administration and later.

Other assemblies also helped to foster a national feeling. When state affairs were to be considered, the king summoned larger meetings; we have just seen that the *lagthings* in Bergen and in Oslo were called upon to approve the Church Ordinance, the most important enactment of the century. The different classes had, moreover, developed sufficiently to form the basis for a political system, and the king might summon any or all the estates—nobles, burghers, or farmers. The others spoke only for their own local community, but the nobility acted as a national class and its humble petitions are evidences of awakening national political ambitions which had to be reckoned with.

In 1582, Frederik called a meeting of the nobles in order to secure their promise to support the succession of his son Christian. They gave the desired pledge in return for new privileges. It was the first time the nobles were not only called upon to speak for their country, but were recognized as a distinct upper class with a legal status different from that of the common people.

When Frederik II died, the Danish council at once elected his eleven-year-old son as King Christian IV (1588-1648), and chose four of its members to serve as a regency during his minority. An able and prominent Danish noble, Axel Gyldenstjerne, was appointed statholder of Norway, and the government was continued in the spirit of Huitfeldt.

Not before 1591 did Christian visit Oslo to receive the oath of allegiance of the Norwegians. The young king came with nine ships, and the occasion was celebrated with a pageantry and splendor such as Norway had seldom, if ever, seen. On a platform covered with scarlet cloth, raised outside of Akershus, sat the king "resplendent in jewels and gold," and round about stood crowds of spectators in colorful array. The representatives of the estates came forward in turn and, kneeling before the king, took the oath of allegiance read by the Danish chancellor—nobles, lawmen, and bishops, then the representatives of the burghers, and last the rural representatives, by far the largest group. It was the first complete estates general, truly national in scope, that had ever met in Norway. The nobility received new privileges, and obtained the two modest political demands, that the position of chancellor, which had been vacant since 1572, be filled by a Norwegian who understood conditions, and that two clerks (*svorne skrivere*) be appointed for each parish "to copy and to instruct the six members of the local court."

The clergy, too, was recognized as the second estate, thus completing the four estates. Though such meetings were held at intervals until the establishment of absolutism put an end to the practice, no genuine estates general grew out of these beginnings.

And so, at the close of the period when Christian IV took over the government, Norway was again organized as a kingdom with a central administration of its own, one which was modern and fairly efficient and with laws enforced better than they had been for a long time. One of the chief reasons why Norway had to be given consideration was its economic development, whereby the country could contribute more to the greatness of the whole realm and not least to the income of the sovereign.

¶ After the stagnation of the preceding age the sixteenth century inaugurated a period of intense economic and social development, as the modern age was dawning with new opportunities. Everybody was searching for precious metals, and it was believed that the hard mountains of Norway contained untold riches of "silver and gold and other precious things." The king claimed the ownership of all minerals, and the exaggerated hope of winning wealth increased his interest in Norway. In the time of Christian II a diligent search for metals was begun, and the first royal license to open a mine was issued to Bishop Mogens of Hamar; he started a copper mine which the king took over after the Reformation. Christian III opened three small silver mines with German engineers and laborers. But the farmers objected to these foreigners who came and took possession at their own price of whatever farms they wanted, who demanded free transportation, and paid for farm produce with money in which the people had no faith. They resented the arrogance of the German mine operators and the extra burdens placed on them, especially that of hauling wood for the smelting. Some disturbances occurred as the farmers tried to defend their rights, armed with axes and bows and arrows. The risings were summarily put down, but operating the mines was very expensive and before long they were closed, thus ending the first attempt to mine precious metals. The iron mines, opened about the same time in the region about Oslo, were more successful and continued to be operated, though on a small scale, some of them by English miners.

Much more important was the wealth of herring and cod. Nor was the salmon fishing in the many streams by any means negligible. The schools of herring came and went in the most unaccountable way, a gift of God in a special sense, it was felt, which might be withdrawn at any time as a punishment for sin. After a period when the sea was "black," a wealth of herring, the "silver of the sea," appeared both outside of Bergen and around the whole southeastern shore, bringing together thousands of boats manned by farmers, burghers, servants of the king, and officials, for a haul of fish the like of which had never been seen. There was ample chance for roistering, cheating, and drinking; the government stepped in with its police while moralists issued dire warnings. For some twenty years this wealth continued, and then suddenly disappeared. The cod fishing was more stable and was the chief occupation of a large part of the people of northern Norway—Finmark and Haalogaland, with the Lofoten Islands as the center of operations. From viking times cod had been the chief source of the wealth of Haalogaland, and fishing had been going on in much the same way from boats not unlike small viking ships. The Hanseatic merchants, who had created a wide European market for the cod, had gradually won a monopoly of the trade, only to lose it again before the close of this century.

A newer enterprise was lumbering. The expansion of European trade, the shifting of commerce from the inland seas to the Atlantic, the growth of seaboard cities, and the international rivalries for the control of the sea, all increased enormously the demand for lumber. There was need of more, larger, and stouter ships. There were houses and wharves to be built; and in the Netherlands the thousands of piles on which the buildings rested and the extensive dikes required a vast amount of lumber, and most of it came from Norway. England, too, bought Norwegian lumber. There was a greater demand for boards and planks than for logs. But boards hewed by axe were slow to make, and Norway could not have met the demand had not a saw operated by water power been introduced just at this time. This saw was a simple, inexpensive thing, and wood was practically to be had for the taking, so it required almost no capital to begin lumbering, and by every stream little sawmills were set up. Such a saw could be operated by one man, who had to work long, lonely hours in the woods. If his water power was seasonal, he would at flood times work around the clock, ceaselessly feeding his saw. The lumber was floated to the sea and sold to any comer. As the seaboard was rapidly stripped of trees large enough to furnish the immense logs needed for the heavy planks produced by these early water saws, lumbering went farther and farther inland until there, too, the giants of the forests were gone.

The government tried without much success to restrict the exportation of lumber, claiming that the country had no timber to spare. Later, however, the king followed the more modern policy of encouraging the industry and thereby increased his income through export duties. Several eastern cities owe their rise to this new business, which more than any other single factor gave opportunity for the growth of national trade, city life, and a native burgher class. The saw was second only to the ship in building up Norway's new economic life.[5]

With increased production came increase in trade, and Norway shared in the commercial expansion of the age. The exported fish products grew both in volume and variety; they included train oil, cod liver oil, and blubber. And the lumber products exported were not only logs, beams, and boards, but many other simple articles of everyday use, such as capstan bars, barrel staves, parts of wagons, and the like. Some farm products, especially meat and hides, were also quite important exports. The main imports continued to be grain and flour, malt, hops, and salt, but there were also manufactured articles, many of them luxuries which added zest to daily living. There were metal wares, tools and weapons, paper and ink, glassware, bedding and household goods, also wines and new foods, such as Dutch biscuits, and raisins and spices—pepper, ginger, mace, and cloves.

Domestic trade also increased as the people had more to sell; the use

[5] Schreiner in Bugge and Steen, ed., *Norsk kulturhistorie,* 3:115.

of money spread into the rural communities and cash was needed to pay the new taxes. While the fairway along the shore, the fjords, the rivers, and the lakes were used when possible, there was much traffic by land. Most routes were precarious footpaths over swampy plateaus and across mountain ranges, along rushing brooks, and down deep ravines. Faint traces of such trails, long disused, may be seen even today. A few roads, rough, steep, and narrow, had been constructed where sleighs could be used in winter. But in summer pack-horses had to carry the goods, for wagons had not come into use. Travelers walked or rode horseback, though occasionally a passenger would be carried in a portechaise with one horse in front and one behind.

Trading, which had been carried on by all manner of people, came more and more to be a distinct occupation, taken over by professional merchants. In their efforts to get all possible trade into their own hands, the burghers had the backing of the government, which desired both to stimulate the growth of cities and to break the foreign control of commerce. In the domestic market the chief competitors of the burghers were at first the officials and especially in Catholic times the clergy, for as long as rents, fines, taxes, and tithes were paid in kind the collectors had to dispose of the goods. Burghers and farmers joined in complaints, and the government stepped in, sharply curtailing the commercial activities of the official class.

Royal orders went out repeatedly that the country people could trade with whomever they wished, their trade increased faster than that of the officials declined, and before long the farmers were the chief competitors of the burghers in their energetic campaign for trade monopoly. Sometimes they became citizens of a town in order to acquire trading privileges, much to the chagrin of the burghers, while city shopkeepers were trading extensively out in the rural communities. The rivalry between the two classes became very sharp and bitter. Government ordinances attempted to draw the line between them. Retailers had to confine their transactions to either town or country, and a citizen had to take up residence in the town and could not be both farmer and trader.

By the close of the century the burghers had control of the trade north of Bergen, and the fishermen had to sell their fish in the town. It was even ordered that if a fisherman was in debt to a merchant he must trade only with his creditor. When, as often happened, his haul was small and he received goods on credit, this order placed him at the mercy of his creditor and thus inaugurated that economic serfdom which in coming years kept the fishermen of the North in dire poverty. In the rest of the country the rural people retained the right to trade with whomever they pleased, but the burghers were gradually winning control of the domestic market.

Foreign trade, however, presented greater opportunities. The country people had entered this field also as they sold lumber directly to foreign ships at any convenient place along the coast. Besides they had innumerable fishing smacks and many little sloops which not only plied the fjords in the inland trade but crossed the straits to Denmark, and even visited the Western Islands. Some of the larger boats also were Norwegian; in the early years of the century only a few, but the number increased toward the close of the period. Most of the foreign trade was still carried in foreign ships; a few came from England, Scotland, the Netherlands, and occasionally from the Orkneys and the Shetland Islands. The Germans continued to hold the lead, however, even into the seventeenth century, especially in Bergen, which was the chief trade center of the country. If the Norwegian burghers were to secure a larger share in overseas commerce, it was most important to loose the Hanseatic stranglehold on the trade of Bergen. The power of the Rostock merchants in eastern Norway was broken early in the century. The Germans in Bergen, on the other hand, were ensconced in the old city north of the inner harbor, Vaagen. This German Wharf (*Tyskebryggen*) was in fact a foreign city, paying no attention to the law of the land; confident of the backing of its powerful parent cities, it refused to read the signs of the times and see that the great day of the Hanseatic League was already past. Norwegians, expelled from the old city, had established themselves on the south side of the harbor. Some foreigners, Danes, English, Scottish, and Dutch who settled among them, strengthened the Norwegian burghers, and by the middle of the sixteenth century they had become an alert, aggressive group. Repeatedly they came into conflict with their rivals across the bay, and in most cases the government sided with the Norwegians, though guardedly.

Christian III followed a cautious policy of restricting the Hanseatic merchants without violating their old rights, for he was not in a position to offend the powerful city of Lübeck, and step by step the Germans receded from their place of dominance. He appointed his secretary, Christopher Walkendorf, governor of Bergen and all the country north of it, with instructions to carry out his policy. Walkendorf was one of the striking personalities of the age, a gifted, distinguished young nobleman, who occupies a prominent place in the history of Norway. He advanced boldly yet warily. He closed the most obnoxious of the German-supported brothels, which made the street behind the Hanseatic Wharf a stench in the nostrils of all decent people. He insisted that the German shoemakers' guild conform to the Church Ordinance, which they had hitherto ignored, and that they return to the Norwegian congregation Saint Hallvard's church, which they had appropriated. Finally, in 1559, Walkendorf put the old Bergenhus Fortress in a state of defense with cannon and guards, and gave the German artisans the ultimatum that they must either swear allegiance to the king and become Norgewian subjects or leave the town. Encouraged by the Hanseatic merchants, the only authority they recognized, the artisans took their time about replying and even threatened that for this reason many a child would become fatherless and weep in its cradle. Not impressed by the "big useless words," Walkendorf prepared to use force, and nailed down the shutters on the shops of the obstreperous shoemakers' guild. Realizing that the two cannons they had placed in the slender steeples of the twelfth century Saint Mary's Church were no match for Walkendorf's weapons, the foreign artisans agreed to leave the city.

This event completely broke the Hanseatic hold on Bergen and thereby on Norway, and the foreigners never again defied the authorities. There was no objection to them when they no longer had a monopoly. On the contrary, they added to the wealth of the city and the income of the king. Gradually some of them moved to the other side of the bay, married Norwegian women, and became citizens. But the Germans continued on as a separate community into the nineteenth century, and have left a marked impress on the picturesque city with its cosmopolitan atmosphere. Walkendorf's last official act was a recess excluding all but the Bergen merchants from trade in the North. Germans and Norwegians joined in efforts to enforce this ruling when they found others poaching on their preserves. Elizabethan sea dogs searching for the Northeast Passage had opened the old Norwegian route to Russia, and both English and Dutch were expanding their traffic in the northern waters.

In 1560 Frederik II recalled Walkendorf and sent in his place Erik Rosenkrantz, who continued the policy of his predecessor and played a distinguished part in the Seven Years' War. When the war was over, Frederik revived the idea of building a separate Norwegian fleet, and quite a few warships were built in Norway and many more came there for repairs. Without again getting involved in wars, Frederik maintained the Danish supremacy in the Baltic, and built the impressive castle of Kronborg near the entrance to the Sound. Moreover, he secured control over all the Norwegian seas as far as Iceland and beyond. He sent ships to capture Dutch merchantmen trading with Russia, and ordered the commander of Norway's most northern fort, Vardøyhus, to stop all foreign ships going to Russia. This order was aimed especially at the English Muscovy Company, and after long negotiations with England the company agreed to pay a yearly sum for permission to pass the North Cape. Other nations made similar agreements, and thus recognized Norway's supremacy in the northern waters. The king planned to reestablish Norway's old claim to Greenland also, but for the present nothing came of it.

Supremacy on the seas implied the duty of clearing them from pirates, who everywhere endangered peaceful trade, and the fleet had to be constantly on the alert. Norway had many redoubtable sea captains, some of them with checkered careers including both piracy and service in the fleet, not unlike the English sea dogs. Most famous among them is Mogens Heinessøn, a Norwegian born in the Faroe Islands. He was a romantic figure, a sort of Robin Hood of the sea, and the stories of his adventures still live in the folklore of the Faroes. At times he was smuggler and freebooter, at other times he pursued pirates and served the king. Finally he was imprisoned and executed without a fair trial, but later the judgment was reversed and his widow given redress.

The Norwegians were again finding their place on the seas. Not only was the Danish-Norwegian navy strong enough to win respect, but this age also marks the beginning of Norway's modern merchant marine. It was chiefly the burgher class which profited by the many opportunities of the new era.

¶ Sixteenth century society shows the disintegrating restlessness of a new age, but also its constructive vigor.

The incipient estates general is an evidence of the importance of social classes and of a growing class consciousness. There is a striking difference between the opening and the close of the period we are studying. In 1536 Norway was a farmer community which had lost the upper-class leadership of the past and acquired no new aristocracy. Before the century ended there was an approach to the system of four estates; yet one hesitates to use that term, for the lines between the classes were not sharply drawn and many persons cannot be placed in any one of them.

The whole social fabric was closely bound up with the spread of money economy. The most striking evidence of this is the growing prestige of the burgher class—the third estate—which drew its sustenance mainly from commerce. The burghers, though not numerous, had a local government and courts of their own, with a burgomaster and council chosen from the leading families. Every city had its rising group of burghers, but the rivalry between towns was stronger than class interest or national feeling. By far the largest and most cosmopolitan city was Bergen. Walkendorf procured native artisans to take the place of the departed Germans and gave to the town a new market place and city hall. His successor, Rosenkrantz, built an imposing tower which bears the name of Walkendorf, and maintained a splendid house which was the scene of many festivities. Both governors stimulated civic and class pride.

With the death of the redoubtable Lady Inger of Austraat in 1555, the old nobility of the first rank had practically died out, as had also the Danish families that had intermarried with them. But there was a rise of new families. The most distinguished were founded by Danes who acquired land in Norway, took up residence there, and became thoroughly Norwegian. Among them were two sons-in-law of Lady Inger. One of them, Jens Bjelke, acquired Austraat and became the ancestor of a notable family. Other Danish nobles, who returned to Denmark and became wholly identified with that country, owned much land in Norway. Erik Rosenkrantz, for example, had vast estates in Norway, but he never enjoyed staying there and never became Norwegian. His landed wealth could be equalled only by that of Lady Gyrvhild, the granddaughter of Knut Alfsson, who owned 600 farms or parts of farms. She transferred all her possessions to the king in return for smaller Danish fiefs, thus vastly increasing the crown lands.

Besides the semi-Danish aristocracy there were also a number of Norwegians who took definite family names, won recognition as nobles, and began to consider themselves leaders of the people. The Norwegian nobility, however, never became so distinguished and prominent as the Danish nor did it produce such outstanding men. The Norwegians lacked the wealth to build fine houses and live as great lords. They were too few to form an exclusive social group, and, as in the past, the gentry were not above the well-to-do farmers in wealth, general outlook, types of homes, or standard of living. From petty officials the nobles might take lessons in exploiting the people, but not infrequently they made common cause with them in opposition to those hated tyrants. Though not especially distinguished, the nobility had risen to be the most powerful class both socially and politically—the first estate.

In Catholic times the leadership had been in the hands of the higher clergy, while the nobles held second place. Now this was reversed. In the first decades after the Reformation there was no sense of class solidarity within the clergy, and when the estates met the clergy was not summoned as a class nor represented as a group. Before the close of the century the clergy had attained a more respected place in the community; it formally took its place as the second estate for the first time at the meeting called to take the oath of allegiance to Christian IV.

The farmers—the fourth estate we may call them—still constituted by far the largest body of the population. It is a mistake to look upon them all as a downtrodden, exploited lower class; they were in fact not inferior to the burghers, but they represented an old social order that was on the defensive. Rural life lagged behind in the development of money economy which dominated business and government, and the country people profited least by the economic advance of the century. There were, it is true, opportunities for earning a little by fishing, working in the mines, and by cutting timber, hewing planks, and the like. Moreover, the growth of cities and trade increased the need for farm products, and the rise in prices, which characterized the sixteenth century all over Europe, insured good pay for whatever the farmers had to sell. But the growing claims upon their earnings by government and landlord deprived the people of most of the added income. The growth in population increased the demand for land, and Christian III encouraged the expansion of farming by making newly broken land tax exempt. Abandoned farms that had been lying idle perhaps since the Black Death were once more occupied, new homesteads were cleared on the common lands, and on the old farms more land was brought under the plough. Moreover, it became a general practice to divide large farms among several heirs, something which had rarely been done since early in the Middle Ages. But to divide a farm and all its appurtenances so that each heir received his fair share of both the poorest and the best land was an involved problem, and the different pieces that fell to one heir were seldom contiguous. Some parts, perhaps pastures, salmon stream, iron bog, or even some building, might continue to be held in common. So a certain amount of communal activity was necessary, and this gave the individualistic Norwegian farmers a lesson in cooperation which stood them in good stead. The village system characteristic of most European countries never existed in Norway.

The greatest landowner was the crown. It is estimated that by the close of the century the crown and church owned 45 per cent of the land, while only 15 per cent belonged to the nobility. Of the remaining 40 per cent some belonged to the burghers and the rest to the farmers. Those who owned their land constituted the most substantial group among the farmers and were the leaders both socially and politically. As they rented out some of their fields, it is estimated that about 70 per cent of the land was worked by tenants, who made up the large majority of the rural population. In a lower category were the crofters (*husmenn*) who were classed with the landless laborers. A crofter had a small holding on a large farm, generally in a poor, outlying section, and paid his rent mainly in labor.

Great as was the divergence within the class, the farmers had a common interest in defending their old rights according to the "laws of Saint Olaf." In this age of high prices and high living the landlords needed more money, and as it was difficult to raise the rent, they found devious ways of adding to their income by demanding new cash payments or increasing customary dues. One of the worst abuses was the collection of a large payment upon the renewal of a lease. The old right of entertainment also offered a means of fleecing the people. One bailiff, for example, who according to custom was entitled to entertainment for himself and two companions, traveled about with a company of twelve men who ate up the farmer's reserve of food, drank up his ale, and abused the women of the household to boot. The royal sheriffs had the double duty of collecting dues from the crown lands and of representing the state as administrative officers and tax gatherers. When extra payments were levied to meet some emergency, the people objected more because they were new than because they were exorbitant.

Thus the struggle to keep up the old social order took the form of a conflict with the officials. There was a good deal of unrest and violence, as oppression was met with force and even murder, but more often legal methods were used. The people still had a considerable share in the administration through the local *things*, but as the sixteenth century advanced the officials interfered more and more with the freedom of the *things*. As legal cases became more complicated, the people willingly let the burden of decision slip from their hands and be transferred to the king's lawmen, but they continued to lay their complaints and requests before the king or his representatives. The protocols and other documents of the day are so replete with complaints that they sound like a tale of unmitigated woe. It must be remembered, however, that they give the dark side only and, like the *cahiers* of the French Revolution, cannot be interpreted as a complete picture of the age.

On the whole, the burdens of the people were not so heavy as in countries farther south, and taxes were lower than in Denmark. In fact it has been estimated that if there had been an independent government taxes must have been heavier. Nevertheless, there was sufficient justification for the struggle of the people to protect their rights. Most of the sheriffs were from the Danish lower nobility, with an increasing number from the burgher class. As supervision at the best could not be strict, the temptation to feather their own nest was too strong for many of them. In telling of one sheriff who was hanged for his misdemeanors, Absalon Pederssøn writes that the sheriffs in the North "have lived like lords and dressed in velvet and damask and practiced great arrogance and injustice, tormented and taxed the people, driven them from property and money, and the poor people have called upon God in heaven and their prayers have been answered. I hope it will strike those who have deserved it most. It has begun at Vardøy. Perhaps it will extend even to Baahus. God save the pious."[6]

It is clear that the whole development of the age tended to sharpen class distinction and deepen the gulf between noble and commoner, country and town, and even, though to a lesser extent, between the parishioner and the clergyman.

¶ To picture the general social conditions of any time is a most elusive problem which baffles historians. This is especially true of an age like the sixteenth century, which abounds in striking contrasts, rapid transitions, disintegration of the old and rise of the new.

Even in the cities life was monotonous and hard. There was no thought of sanitation; pigs wallowed in the streets and the stench and filth baffle description. The growing concentration of population as well as the increased contact with the outside world brought to the cities several severe pestilences, which spread also to the rural districts with terrifying rapidity. The only effective checks on the epidemics were the devastating fires which time and again swept through the crowded cities and reduced to ashes the thatched wooden houses.

There were, on the other hand, diversions and times of gaiety. Generally festivities were crowded into the days when some great meeting was held in town, a district court or, even better, a national as-

[6] Quoted by Yngvar Nielsen, *Norges historie*, vol. 4, part 1, p. 309.

sembly which brought to the city many prominent people, farmers, burghers, clergy, officials, and especially many of the nobility. Theatrical performances by the boys of the Cathedral School were given in the churchyard or outside the city hall, sometimes Latin and sometimes Norwegian plays with local color. Weddings were celebrated with much pomp and often nobles and burghers rubbed elbows in the throng of guests. At one such wedding eight courses were served and plenty of wine and ale. We are told how "the bride was dressed in brown velvet, magnificently arrayed in a crown and many gold chains about her throat, shoulders, and elbows; she had gold chains hanging down toward the ground and her hair hanging loose."[7] The Spanish court dominated fashions as well as international politics. The styles are an example of the many foreign influences that reached Norway from beyond the seas, especially by way of the Netherlands. The Norwegian seamen who took service on Dutch ships brought home all manner of wares.

As to the physical well-being in the rural districts, it must be remembered that nature was chary in Norway and to make a living meant unending toil. Life centered upon the problem of providing sufficient food for man and beast through the long winter. With the unscientific use of the land, crop failures and years of famine, when the people had to resort to bark bread, were unavoidable. A few, we are told, had flatbread to carry them through a year of crop failure, but such foresight must have been rare. Among the fishermen of the North one visitor found such misery that "it would make a person weep unless he have a heart of stone." Yet the best authorities of the time describe Norway as a good land to live in, where there was little wealth but also little actual want. The chief reason was the diversity of livelihood. If the food from flock and field was short, it could be eked out from the vast hunting grounds of the highlands and the streams teeming with salmon.

There was little change in the daily living. The houses were about as they had been since viking days. In most places, however, the old hearth in the middle of the floor with the hole in the roof for the smoke to escape had given way to a corner fireplace with a chimney, and lamps filled with train oil supplemented the sticks of pitch pine as illumination. Stoves and glass windows, which were just coming into use, had not reached the home of the average farmers. Yet they had a little more cash than in the past and a little closer contact with the cities, and began

[7] *Liber Capituli Bergensis: Absalon Pederssøns Dagbog . . . 1552-1572*, p. 107, Christiania, 1860.

to purchase hitherto unknown articles which brought a little variety into their lives. Some of the fashions which the townspeople had imported from abroad, for example, were copied in the rural districts, adding richness to the gala dress and becoming part of the national costume. The passing of the old church, on the other hand, tended to make life more drab, as religious pageantry and festivity under the auspices of the church were discontinued. But the young people in country and town continued to gather for play. There were folk dances and songs and rhymes and all manner of games and matching of wits. Men wrestled and vied with each other in physical prowess, and when ale or stronger drinks had flowed freely, knives might be drawn.

The new age had a disintegrating effect on morals and manners, and life was often raw and wild. Nevertheless Absalon Pederssøn gives an attractive picture of the people, whom he describes as refined, lively, and generous. He particularly praises their hospitality. A traveler could journey from Baahus to Vardøy without spending above a dollar. Peder Claussøn Friis[8] also found the people near the coast "well off" and "pious"; but generally he is not flattering in his accounts of his countrymen: "The inhabitants of this country have their origin and descent from a hard race, for they have always been hard, obstinate, disobedient, wilful, extravagant, restless, rebellious, and murderous, which I cannot deny that they still are, especially in places and spots where they still hold to their old customs and habits (that is up in the mountains, far from the coast there still live wild and evil people)." Even Master Peder himself used his knife in a quarrel with a friend, but that did not destroy their good relations.

There were many reasons for this growing lawlessness and brutality. Not least was the introduction of distilled liquor, which had a devastating effect on people accustomed to nothing more potent than ale. The frequent clashes between government representatives and the people fostered a hatred, if not more bitter, at least more vocal, than in any other age before or after. The inhuman trials and punishments had no counterpart in olden times, and human rights and life were no longer sacred. Cruelty sanctioned by law produced hardness in the people.

Superstition and fear were also demoralizing influences. Early in the century gypsies began to appear in the North, seeping in from the South. These mysterious strangers, sneaking noiselessly through the forests, appearing unexpectedly and then vanishing in the wilderness, were accused of many crimes besides those of which they were really

[8] See below, page 275.

guilty—chiefly petty pilfering—and it was believed that through their magic arts they were in league with the devil. Church and state joined in persecuting the wretched folk. The clergy were ordered to have nothing to do with them and to "neither bury their dead nor baptize their children." In 1536 they were outlawed and ordered to leave the country, but as other countries gave them no better welcome they had nowhere to go and scattered in small bands, prowling in the dark, chased from place to place. How ineffectual the measures against them were is shown by the repetition of the order in a more stringent form in the code of Christian V promulgated a century and a half later. Long after that, almost into present times, the gypsies constituted a problem. Under a somewhat more humane treatment they finally lost their language and their racial isolation, attracted to themselves many people not of their race, and gave their name to the whole motley vagabond element of the population.

The fear of the gypsies was only one of the manifestations of the fantastic superstition that dominated the minds of both ignorant and learned and furnished a somber contrast to the intellectual progress of the Renaissance.

Most terrible was the witchcraft craze which for two centuries cast a dark shadow over all Western Christendom. During the Middle Ages it was believed that the devil often appeared in human form to practice his arts among men. But he was not greatly feared, for, though he might be wily at times, he was thought to be rather stupid, so that any bright boy might get the better of him. The "poor devil" was a comic rather than a terrifying creature, and as such he appears in the Norwegian fairy tales. Later he became a much more sinister figure. Probably the persecution of heresy, which was closely associated with witchcraft, helped to produce the changed conception. The belief in witchcraft spread with terrific speed; the papal bull of 1484 is proof that it was accepted even by the highest authority in the church and had taken firm hold before the Reformation.

To Norway, however, the witchcraft craze came with all the other new things, both good and bad, from the South, rather late in the sixteenth century. It was not directly connected with the Reformation, though the new faith tended to increase the fear of the devil, inasmuch as the security of the old ecclesiastical system was removed, leaving the individual to face the problem of his salvation without much help from the church ceremonial. The practice of the magic arts became common and the belief in them even more general. Lurid tales were spread of how people had sealed with blood their compacts with the Evil One whereby they obtained certain magic powers in return for paying the final price of Faust. There was white magic practiced for the good of one's fellowmen and black magic used for purposes of evil. Magic formulas were compiled, and the possessor of a "Black Book" was looked upon with fear and suspicion. These collections, the very mention of which made people shudder, today look innocent and even ridiculous.

At first local authorities were very moderate in their treatment of those accused of witchcraft. But as the practice, especially of white magic, spread, the king issued a stringent prohibition of all magic arts, and with that the persecution was in full swing. Not only did the accusers believe that their victims were in league with the devil, but the victims themselves often believed in and confessed their own supernatural powers. Some men were brought to trial, but most of the accused were, of course, women. The sex element was believed to enter into the witch's compact, and women were thought to be more susceptible than men. Besides, in an age when disease was looked upon as a manifestation of evil powers it was difficult to draw the line between the legitimate practice of healing by the "wise women," and the sorcery of those who had supposedly joined the throng of witches who rode their broomsticks to Dovre Mountain on Saint John's Eve. Anyhow, a woman who knew a little too much was always under suspicion. Rank and social position gave no guarantee of safety. Thus Anna Pedersdatter, the widow of Absalon Pederssøn and herself of a distinguished family, was burnt as a witch in spite of the indignation of the clergy in Bergen. There were about five hundred witchcraft trials in Norway before the craze died down toward the close of the seventeenth century. Yet the whole episode was not so gruesome as in many other countries. Torture in the trials was not used so intensively and the excesses committed were less extreme.

Among the many disintegrating influences must also be mentioned the Lutheran Reformation. It was inevitable that this should at first contribute to the disruption of the age before its constructive influence could fully make itself felt.

¶ Though the political and economic change to a Lutheran state church was accomplished quickly and thoroughly, it took a long time and many unhappy experiences before it eventually became a genuine folk church. When the new faith was foisted upon Norway, the country had in no way been prepared for the change. The new doctrine had been preached to a very limited extent in Bergen, and Lutheran practices had found entrance into a few of the noble households along the western seaboard, notably at Austraat, but otherwise only vague rumors of the new faith had reached the people. The old church was crumbling, and yet the people clung to their old habits and beliefs.

Realizing this, Christian III followed a policy of prudent moderation in the reorganization of the church. The parish priests were left undisturbed on condition that they submit to the new order. It was impossible to supply at once a clergy with even a minimum of Lutheran training, and in most parishes the last Roman Catholic priest became the first Lutheran minister. Occasionally he might be a thorough Lutheran, but often he conducted services in the way to which he was accustomed, and there was a strange mixture of the two systems in the church. Many of the country preachers were woefully ignorant and not a few led disreputable lives, becoming involved in drunken brawls, open immorality, and even murders. They were not unlike the communities from which they sprang. Their position was not enviable. In medieval society the place of the parish priest was humble and lowly, but he had back of him an impressive organization which gave him both dignity and security. Now that was gone. When celibacy was abandoned there was nothing in the daily life of the clergy to set them apart. Like others, they raised large families and struggled hard on a meager income to keep the wolf from the door.

Their greatest difficulties came from the hostility of their parishioners, who in some cases offered to pay the government a neat sum of money to be left without a pastor. The removal of the salutary discipline that had been exerted by the old church was one of the causes of the coarseness and violence which characterized the age and added fierceness to the conflict between people and clergy. One man, it is told, boasted that his father had killed three preachers, and when he was drunk he prayed that he might make as good a record.

The most serious clashes were about the tithe. The Danish Church Ordinance decreed that the tithe should be divided in three parts, one for the local minister, one for the church, and one for the king. Its authors did not know about the old Norwegian custom of dividing the tithe in four, reserving one-fourth for local poor aid. Bitter clashes ended sometimes in defeat for the people, sometimes in a compromise, allowing some of the tithe to be kept in the local congregation. The people also resented deeply the desecration of things they looked upon as holy, the removal from the churches of images, decorations, and secondary altars, and the discontinuance of old practices of the ritual and the worship of saints. While there was real concern about the change, the religious indifference and fanatical hatred of the clergy were more conspicuous during the decades following the Reformation.

The frequent complaints and the many government orders attempting to curb the evils indicate a deplorable condition, but show also that there was a constant and conscientious effort on the part of the authorities to mend matters. A gradual improvement was achieved, mainly through the tireless efforts of the higher clergy. The king assumed the authority of the archbishop and practically appointed Lutheran successors to the Catholic bishops, thus depriving the cathedral chapters of their right of election. At first they were called superintendents, but before long the old term of bishop again came into general use. The earliest superintendents were all Norwegian, but most of their successors were Danish, for it was difficult to find suitable men in Norway. They were almost without exception strong personalities, imperious, but able and diligent. They had little assistance in carrying out their numerous duties, for the Reformation had made a clean sweep of many clerical positions. The cathedral chapters continued to exist, but although the king had promised that their property should remain intact, the prebends were secularized one by one, and finally the chapters themselves disappeared. The monasteries were secularized even more rapidly.

The most distinguished among the first superintendents was Geble Pederssøn at Bergen, who represents the best in the early Reformation. He had been a friend of the last archbishop until his flight. Then Geble accepted the new situation. It is useless to speculate upon how deeply he had entered into the spirit of the new faith. He lacked the ardor of a Luther, but had during his studies abroad been influenced by the humanism of Erasmus and was, his contemporaries said, a "fine, learned, honest man." He did good work in his diocese, enlarged the cathedral, built a number of school buildings, and gave extensive aid to the poor. Through many journeys of visitation he furthered the instruction of clergy and laity, and before his death he had secured Lutheran pastors for almost all the parishes. To accomplish this he built up the Bergen Latin School. He gave to the instruction a certain humanistic character, and sent a number of the students to foreign universities at his own expense. His salary was modest, but he controlled the income from the estates of Munkeliv Monastery and used it for the good of the church.

The cathedral schools, or Latin schools as they were now called, continued to exist throughout the century,[9] but they had suffered grievously in the general decline during the first days of the Reformation. The bishop of Trondheim complained to the king that if the school were not kept up, "it is to be feared that this whole diocese will be completely heathen in a few years, for which it will be difficult for his Royal Majesty to answer before God." The government was largely responsible for the disintegration of the schools, for ruthless secularization of church property had deprived them of most of their income.

All the early bishops made it their first task to build up the cathedral schools in order to train pastors. Boys of all classes attended them, though in later years the sons of clergymen were most numerous. It was fortunate that several capable teachers were available, the most distinguished being Absalon Pederssøn Beyer of Bergen. The roughness of the age was seen also in the schools, in the severe discipline, the occasional fights between teachers and students, and the misconduct of the boys. As there was little money to support students, it was customary to hire out groups of them to sing at festive occasions. In vacations the boys toured the country districts, sang, preached, told stories, and—begged. Generally they were well received, were treated to much food and more drink, and often collected a tidy sum of money. The effect on the manners and morals of the boys, however, was far from good. Yet, in spite of all shortcomings considerable honest work was done in the Latin schools, and ministers were sent out zealous for the new church. In the towns there were also a numer of mediocre lower schools, among them one for girls in Bergen.

In the country, education was left to the minister and the parish clerk (*klokker*). This office was created in 1552, but in many congregations it was not filled for a long time as the people were slow about paying out money for the pittance of a salary he was to receive. To instruct the people was not an easy task. Books were woefully scarce. According to the Church Ordinance the ministers were to own seven books, but few had so extensive a library. No Norwegian Bibles were available. Danish Bibles were sent to Norway, but twenty years after the introduction of the Reformation there were only ninety-six copies in the country, not nearly enough to supply all the churches. Books were too expensive for ordinary people to own, and moreover they could not read. Most of the instruction was in the catechism, which was explained at the Sunday services. The minister or the parish clerk would read a section and the listeners would repeat it until they knew it by heart. When the bishops

[9] In 1602 the school in Hamar was removed to Oslo and combined with the older school there.

came on their visitations—and they were tireless travelers—they examined the young people, and sometimes the older ones, too, in the catechism. Before long the new church was giving the people more and better instruction, meager though it was, than the medieval church had furnished even at its best.

In 1569 the first hymn book was introduced, containing Danish and Latin hymns with the music. The hymns were taught in the same way as the catechism and came to be loved by the people, many of whom sang well, and in some places choirs were organized. The congregational singing was the most appealing feature in the new order.

It was unfortunate, though inevitable, that the Reformation did not come to the people in their own language. The ordinances and regulations had originated in Denmark and were not always adapted to Norwegian conditions. The books on which the movement was dependent came from Denmark and were in the Danish language. There was not even a printing press in the country before the middle of the next century (1643). After the first few years many of the clergy were Danes, and the people had great difficulty in understanding them. While the Norwegian clergymen also read from Danish books, their pronunciation was Norwegian and therefore they were much more easily understood. It is probable, too, that many of them preached in the dialect of their community.

In spite of this handicap of language the people gradually became indoctrinated into the new faith, and by the close of the century the Lutheran church was fully established. The Reformation had come as a gradual transition, not as a revolution. In accordance with Luther's principle it had retained the old when not incompatible with the doctrines and usages of the new church. Especially in the more isolated communities it was natural that the people should cling with tenacity to deeply rooted practices and beliefs which were frowned upon by the authorities.

Gradually the church services became simplified, even bare. The ritual was shorn of the elaborate ceremonial of the old, Latin disappeared, and the vestments were plainer. Even before the Reformation the churches had been robbed of many of their art treasures in precious metals and jewels, chiefly by rapacious Danish nobles. Articles of gold and silver were carried to Denmark at the command of the king also, some to be preserved there but many to be smelted into money to meet the growing expenses of the government. Of what still remained much was looted in the Seven Years' War. Sometimes old altar paintings and other decorations were even removed by over-zealous pastors when it seemed that the worship of an image could be stopped only by consigning it to the flames. There were irreparable losses in church art. The Reformation century, however, contributed something to a new ecclesiastical art, for the church interiors had to be adapted to the new services. As these were much longer than the old masses, pews had to be introduced, and as the sermon was a much more important part of the worship, pulpits were erected. More light was needed in order that the ministers at least could see to read, so new chandeliers or windows were required. New windows made some of the old wooden churches more usable but spoiled them architecturally.

The church had been imposed upon the people by the government and therefore the power of the state over them increased. And the clergymen were the servants of the state. Backed by the government, their authority increased and their social and economic position improved as time went on. As their moral and intellectual standards were also raised, they acquired greater influence with the people. Yet they probably never obtained the hold on their parishioners that the medieval clergy had.

The Reformation brought to Norway almost nothing of the intellectual stimulus of theological writing and discussion which it produced in some places. Nor was it accompanied by any general spiritual revival. Conditions were not favorable for either. It is impossible to estimate how far the new church influenced the life of individuals but at least the first steps had been taken toward making the state church a folk church. And though the clergy made little contribution to religious literature, they did yeoman's work in establishing the church and, in addition, as humanists they advanced also the culture and national consciousness of their people.

¶ In Norway, as in all countries of Western Europe, there were men who belonged to the great brotherhood of humanists and who kept in touch with the intellectual currents through travel and visits to universities abroad, through study and reading, and through correspondence with fellow humanists. All were bound together by a common language, and all were intent upon delving into the past and using their knowledge to enrich the present, turning learning into life. This was especially true of the humanists north of the Alps, to whom the Norwegians were most closely akin in spirit.

In Norway Renaissance tendencies antedated the Reformation, but the humanistic movement developed only in the sixteenth century. There were circles of humanists in the cities in which the bishops generally were the leaders, but also individual humanists scattered about, generally in the country parsonages. There was close intercourse among them. Books were few and very precious and were passed around, everyone lending and borrowing whenever he could. Many of the humanists never lived to see their own writings printed, but their works were circulated in manuscript form and in spite of the limited number of readers had a remarkably far-reaching influence. Most of the humanists were clergymen or teachers at the Latin schools, but there were among them some lawmen and a few other nobles and officials.

Next to the interest in education, the most significant phase of the Renaissance in Norway was the national awakening. The humanists had a deep love for their country and for their people. A number of historic topographical works were produced which show some scientific spirit and interest in folkways as well as a love of nature. Unique among these is the *Hamar Chronicle*, a moving picture of Hamar before the Reformation by an unknown writer gently nostalgic for the past. Maps of different parts of the country were also drawn by disciples of Tycho Brahe and in accuracy and detail these excelled any maps produced before the nineteenth century.

The humanists were keenly conscious of the decline into which their country had fallen, in fact so conscious of it that they failed to realize how in their own age an upward movement had already begun. They sought consolation as well as a ray of hope for the future in dwelling upon the greatness of the past. As southern scholars brought to light the Greek and Roman classics, so the Norwegians delved into their own past. *Heimskringla* and other sagas which for two hundred years had been practically forgotten were once more brought into notice. New copies of the old manuscripts were transcribed, translations made of the old sagas, the history of the country was retold in rhyme and prose, and the old laws studied and translated. The scholar's first task was to master the Old Norse. Among the comparatively few who knew the language the lawmen held a conspicuous place, sometimes teaching others and serving as pioneers in the recovery of the old classics. When the humanists did not use Latin they wrote in Danish, although Norwegian was spoken both in country and city. But it was not a pure Danish. The two languages were so closely related that it was quite possible to introduce many Norwegian words, phrases, and even grammatical forms.

Of the humanist groups, the one in Oslo used Latin most extensively, and some poetry and prose were produced, most of which seems a weak imitation of Latin writings in foreign countries and has very little if any literary value. Of some importance is the prolific writer Hallvard Gunnarsson, among whose works is a chronicle of the kings of Norway written in Latin verse. It was printed in 1606 and was the first connected history of Norway to be made available to scholars abroad. The greatest of the Oslo group was Bishop Jens Nilssøn, whose knowledge and interest covered a wide field, medicine and theology, pedagogy and astronomy. He wrote books of instruction in theology and many sermons of distinction, composed Latin verse of some individuality, and made copies of sagas. When he had to flee from Oslo during the Seven Years' War he took with him a precious manuscript of *Heimskringla* and spent the days of evacuation making a copy of it. Most interesting, however, are his visitation books. He tells of the people and of nature, of weather and roads and strange geologic formations, writing with keen but kindly shrewdness and a love of nature that at times rises to lyrical beauty.

The Bergen circle was most strongly nationalistic. The conflict with the Hanseatic Germans roused a new sense of patriotism which found expression in polemics against the intruders. The movement had begun even in Catholic times, and Geble Pederssøn was the first leader. The most gifted and cultured among the Bergen humanists was Absalon Pederssøn Beyer. As a six-year-old orphan he was taken into the house of Geble Pederssøn. Geble kept the boy in school at home and at his own expense sent him to study in Copenhagen and Wittenberg, where he was strongly influenced by Melanchthon. When he returned he became a teacher in the Bergen Latin School, following in the footsteps of Master Geble. For twenty years he kept a diary written "that our descendants may know."[10] It gives an intimate and inclusive picture of daily life in Bergen. The general ignorance which his account reveals was abysmal, and superstition held sway over the minds even of sensible people like Absalon himself. Yet against this dark background can be detected the eager search for knowledge, the scientific interest, the advanced thought, and religious earnestness of humanists like the author.

Of wider scope was Absalon's great historical work, *Om Norgis Rige.*

[10] *Absalon Pederssøns Dagbog*, 10.

It was his contribution to the fight against the "crowd of coarse, impudent fellows who come here to this kingdom, criticize Norway and say that here there has been neither king nor noble." With grief and indignation he described the humiliating oppression that Norway had suffered at the hands of the Germans and the injustice the country had endured because of its absentee government. On the other hand he wanted to demonstrate "that the kingdom of Norway is not yet so old but that there still remains some strength, wisdom, and vigor in it." And with touching enthusiasm he praised the beauty, the humble resources, and the sturdy virtues of his country. Absalon's work is the strongest expression found in his age of the urge for national self-assertion which was to be realized in 1814.

The man who did most to keep this national consciousness awake through the intervening centuries was Peder Claussøn Friis, the dean of Lista. He was a vigorous, full-blooded man of wide interests and broad scholarship. In contrast to most of the humanists, he had scarcely traveled outside his own district and never outside of his country. Yet he had a wide acquaintance with all manner of people from viceroys to farmers, learning something from them all. He obtained a remarkable number of books and made the fullest possible use of them. Though he had the upper-class viewpoint in many ways, he understood the people and had a certain respect for the doughty sons of the vikings, even when they balked at paying tithes. He was ardent and tireless in his professional duties, and many of his writings deal with his pastoral experiences. He worked in close harmony with his superior, Jørgen Erickssøn, the bishop of Stavanger, whose sermons have been characterized as "unquestionably the most beautiful spiritual monuments of the Reformation in our country."[11]

Peder Claussøn was constantly traveling about his district; he came to know it intimately and he put his knowledge on paper. He then gathered from others information about the rest of the country for his comprehensive description of Norway, *Norrigis Bescrifuelse.* This work, as well as his shorter descriptions of the fauna and flora of the country, is strictly factual without any of the political import of Geble's writings. There are mistakes, of course, in the sections on which the author had only indirect information, and he shared some of the current superstitions of his day. He tells, for instance, that the lemmings, which sometimes came in devastating hordes, rained down from heaven. But it is most significant that the descriptions are all from the point of view of the

[11] Bang, *Den norske kirkes historie,* 339.

people and the manner in which they adapted themselves to the resources of the country, for "no one can give any country greater riches or more excellent gifts than God has bestowed and graciously given to each region." The most important of Peder Claussøn's many writings was his translation of Snorri's *Heimskringla* and some of the later sagas of the kings. His knowledge of languages, including English and German, his thorough mastery of the Old Norse, as well as the vigor of his style enabled him to produce a translation that lived among the people for over two hundred years. Peder Claussøn gave back to the people their old sagas.

The humanistic literature of Norway was neither rich nor great, but it stands out as superior both to the preceding and to the following century. The whole intellectual life was more Norwegian than later, and the country experienced a genuine though short-lived national renaissance. Though the reading public was very small, something seeped down by word of mouth and some books were even written to be read and told to the people. Later, when printing and reading became more common, the influence of this age was felt anew, and particularly was Peder Claussøn's Snorri then found in many a country home.

CHAPTER 12

NORTHERN WARS AND ECONOMIC EXPANSION, 1596-1720

In the seventeenth century the developments whereby the whole character of society was being transformed from medieval to modern gained momentum. It was an age teeming with striking events and vivid personalities, and the wealth of documentary material has made the history of the period vivid and alive. At no time, however, did the Norwegian people have less to say about the affairs of their kingdom. More and more they came to be subjects of an authoritarian state which could intrude into their daily life at will, and this government was Danish, as were also the upper classes. Norway was dependent on Denmark in its political, economic, and cultural life. On the surface this seems a gloomy picture, but the Danish-Norwegian government was far more beneficent than most and the common people in Norway suffered less from arbitrary oppression than in most countries. Moreover, the military situation gave an opportunity for some small advance in national self-assertion, and the economic developments opened opportunities for the people to become eventually masters in their own house. The age needed a strong government to direct the many-sided economic advance, to control the rivalry between classes, and to hold its own in the ruthless competition, both economic and political, between states. As in other countries, the king was in the best position to form such a government.

Christian IV was the most striking of the many vivid personalities, both men and women, in which the age abounded and was thoroughly representative of his time, both in its vices and its virtues. He had an intense love of life, was eager to taste all its pleasures and experiences, and had a genuine, though superficial, interest in languages, literature, art, and music. Big-hearted as he was, he could enter into the joys and sufferings of others and was ready to help provided it did not interfere with his own pleasures. For he was really selfish, passionate, and quick-tempered, and would brook no thwarting of his will.

Christian IV was the first king of the Oldenburg family to receive a thoroughly Danish education and had from childhood been trained for the kingship to which he fell heir in 1588 when only eleven years old. His personal rule lasted for over half a century (1596-1648) and he attained publicity as did no other king of his dynasty. He employed more and more men of the middle class, and the nobles, who held all the fiefs and continued to fill many offices, were made more effective servants of the king, who kept a firm hold on local as well as central government. "He wanted to encompass everything within his great brain and his much greater heart, all the knowledge of the age, all its passions, all the weal and woe of the people; he wanted to find a remedy for everything and help everyone."[1]

People loved him for his friendly ways, his regal bearing, his paternal interest in them all, and his boundless energy. In Denmark he was especially popular on account of his love of the sea and his love of building. Under his protection there developed an architectural style which still bears his name. The charming red brick edifices with their graceful spires and steep copper roofs in Christian IV style have lent individuality to the beauty of Copenhagen. People readily forgave his outbursts of anger, and were hardly aware of the sordidness of his family life and the coarseness of the court. His contemporaries did not clearly see that the restless activity they admired led the king to make hasty decisions which were often mere whims, that he undertook more than he could carry out, and that perhaps his ability was not commensurate with his ambition. In several ways his policy brought harm to his countries. True, there were forces at work beyond any one man's control, and besides, there was a dearth of great men among his advisers, but the king must bear much of the blame, for he set himself a program that was beyond human power. He wanted to attend to every detail personally as though he headed a tiny principality, and yet play a big part in international politics as the ruler of a vast domain extending from the Elbe to Vardøy. This far-flung territory Christian IV tried to weld into one strong state under his own personal control.

Norway occupied a large place in his plans and his affections. Within a year of his coronation the king was in Norway. Then followed one visit after another. In all he made about thirty trips to this northern kingdom, more than all the other union kings together. He shunned

[1] Sverre Steen, *Det norske folks liv og historie*, 4:292.

no hardships, was eager for new experiences and adventures, and loved to be on the sea, however stormy. He was concerned about the welfare of the people, mingled with all classes, investigated everything, visited new mines, inspected fortresses, and often presided in person at sessions of the high court.

Christian IV tried to modernize the whole administration of the country. He reorganized the fief system so that the royal income increased and the governors were under stricter control, and, though the old terms remained, the last vestige of a feudal character disappeared. Many of the new special officials appointed were Norwegians. Notable among them was the able and patriotic Jens Bjelke of Austraat, who, in addition to being chancellor for a quarter of a century, served in many other capacities.

The whole legal system, in which the people had hitherto retained some power, was now brought directly under the control of the king. This was done partly to increase his power but chiefly to bring order into a chaotic condition and to make the laws and the courts more adequate to meet the demands of the day. Norway's old law was translated into Danish, and some new laws were added. The king laid the result before the assembled nobles and lawmen for criticism, and after some revision he promulgated it in 1604 as Christian IV's Norwegian Law. It was not a distinguished work, for Norway lacked competent jurists. In keeping with the conservatism of the people, much that was obsolete in the old law was retained and errors in translation crept in. Nevertheless, it was a great improvement to have a printed law book which was the same for the whole country.

In the rural *things* the royal clerk (*svoren skriver*) now became the judge (*sorenskriver*) and the presence of the people's delegates a mere matter of form. In the cities, too, the judicial power of the king's representative increased. In the courts of appeal the lawmen were professional judges, but the other members were still from the common people in town and country. In the high courts the king often presided in person and sessions were held regularly. People of all classes flocked to the meetings, and complaints and petitions poured in. The king was anxious to protect the people, and several important men were brought to trial, the most notorious being Ludvig Munk, governor at Trondheim, who had failed to heed warnings to mend his ways. He was convicted and punished, and more trials followed.

Christian brought the church also more completely under royal control through the Norwegian Church Ordinance which in accordance with a promise made eighty years earlier was promulgated in 1607. With his flair for showmanship the king proclaimed the law personally at a great ecclesiastical meeting in Stavanger cathedral and presented each clergyman with a copy of the new law.

Christian had a passion for building cities. In 1624, when a fire had destroyed Oslo, this "builder king" laid out a new city a little to the west of the old and called it Christiania. Thus he was the founder of Norway's capital, which continued to bear his name until after the First World War, when the old name was restored. In its plan and general appearance, however, Oslo still bears the impress of the founder's ideas. He founded Christiansand near the little island of Flekkerøy, which was a port of call for hundreds of vessels. He rehabilitated the fort, which had fallen into neglect after the Seven Years' War, and then decided to build a city on the mainland inside of the harbor. The streets were laid out wide and straight, and people were ordered to move in from the neighborhood. But in spite of paternalistic care and special privileges the town did not grow as its founder desired. Christian devoted so much energy to the interests of the cities and so won the loyalty of the city people that he has been called the burgher king. In Norway he constructed cities and fortresses, but in Denmark his energy found an outlet in erecting palaces. To a certain extent it is true, as has been said, that Denmark was the land of his pleasures, Norway of his work. And who is to say which he enjoyed more?

The king wanted to utilize the growing wealth of the country to further his ambitious foreign policy. His demand for money led to a calling together of the estates. These meetings gave the estates an opportunity to assert themselves and to obtain some little concession from the crown in return for their consent to new taxes. But they did not present a united front against the growing power of the king, and the meetings served more to strengthen royal power than to further the rights of the people. The loyalty to the king was strong, and his whole policy tended, albeit not strongly, to develop among the people the sense of being citizens of a larger state. One factor which helped to rouse national feeling was Christian IV's aggressive foreign policy.

¶ Denmark-Norway was deeply involved in the maze of ruthless rivalries between states—religious, political, and commercial—which fill the history of the seventeenth century. Standing alone, either of the countries might have been crushed between the larger powers, but together they were in a strong though exposed military and economic position. The foreign policy of Christian IV, as well as of the other Oldenburg rulers of the age, was to strengthen the unitary state and assure it a prominent place among the powers. The special interests of Norway were not considered and the country had no political agencies through which it could take direct part in the conduct of foreign affairs. Nevertheless, it carried heavy burdens and sustained territorial losses in the interests of a policy which in the end brought disaster to the whole realm, Denmark as well as Norway.

Christian IV realized more fully than had earlier kings the importance of Norway, not only on account of its resources but also because of its position and extent. With his love of the sea, he devoted himself to the building of a strong Norwegian-Danish fleet, employing Scottish shipbuilders. He also wanted to share in the colonial ventures of the age. First he tried, as his father had done, to reopen connections with the old Norwegian colony of Greenland. He sent three expeditions thither, the first employing an English pilot. The land was formally taken possession of, but no trace was found of the old colony, and the project was abandoned. The restless king next turned his interests to a search for the Northwest Passage, sending an expedition under Jens Munk into Hudson Bay.[2] When this heroic but tragic venture also came to naught, the king sought an outlet for his colonial ambitions in more friendly climes, on the Nicobar Islands and the Coromandel Coast, where Tranquebar became the center of Danish activities.[3] These colonies had practically no influence on the history of Norway, although Norwegians no doubt helped to man every expedition that went out.

Much more important were the Norwegian claims in the Northeast both as to territory and control of the sea. In 1596 when Christian's personal rule commenced, the situation in the North was especially critical. That year the Dutch discovered Spitzbergen, now Svalbard, and this stimulated their trading and whaling in northern waters. When a treaty between England and Frederik II expired with Frederik's death, Dutch and English traders as well as Germans and others carried on a lively traffic with the Murmansk coast and Russia via the Finmark shore, sometimes paying a small toll, more often ignoring that Norwegian sovereignty over the sea which Christian wished to maintain.

Norwegian territory was also threatened. From early times the Norwegian kings had claimed all of Finmark and beyond—in fact Mur-

[2] Bering Liisberg, "Christian IV and the Northwest Passage" in the *American-Scandinavian Review*, 9:35-38 (January 1921).

[3] Later, in 1671, the Virgin Islands were acquired.

mansk coast means the Northman's coast—and had collected taxes from the Lapps dwelling there. Later the Swedes extended their interests northward and the Russians likewise, and the poor Lapps, who made seasonal migrations to find pasturage for their reindeer, had to pay taxes to two or sometimes three governments. In the sixteenth century territorial claims also were pushed by both Swedes and Russians. Russians founded the famous Petschenga Convent, just beyond the present boundary of Norway, and this became a center of both missionary efforts and trade. By a treaty of 1595 the Russians gave up any right to collect taxes west of an indefinite line from the Varanger Fjord to the Swedish border, but as the treaty made no mention of Norwegian rights, the Swedish king advanced a vague claim to most of Finmark.

Christian IV sensed the situation. He appointed a governor for northern Norway who was to live at Vardøy—not rule from Bergen, as in the past—protect Norwegian interests, and report to the king on conditions in this outpost of his realm. No sooner did this report reach Christian than he decided to visit Vardøy in person, and in April 1599 he set out with a fleet of eight ships on his longest voyage, which kept him away from his capital for three months. On the way he captured some English and Dutch ships which were trading or fishing without his royal license. This first royal visit to the North strengthened the king's hold on the people and at the same time demonstrated to foreign powers that he would stand up for his rights. Some of his courtiers were dismayed at the whole "wild idea" of the trip, resented the hardships, and were appalled at the wretched fort at Vardøy, the little wooden church, and the sod huts of the fishermen. When they came back to "this blessed Bergen for which we have been longing" they celebrated their return from "the ends of the earth" with ten days and nights of feasting and carousing. But the king and his advisers realized the importance of the far-away humble outpost. The situation there was one of the causes of the first of his unhappy wars with Sweden.

Christian IV and Karl IX of Sweden were both aggressive rulers, eager for war. Christian was determined to maintain his sovereignty in northern Norway and his leadership in the Baltic, where his fleet was the stronger. Karl felt hampered by Denmark-Norway's strong position and wanted outlets to the sea. Besides claiming parts of Finmark he built the town and fort of Göteborg on the only spot where Sweden touched the western seas. He allowed the Dutch, who resented the Sound dues charged by Denmark, to reload in Göteborg for the Baltic trade and thus make use of the Swedish freedom from the restricting tolls. Both kings felt they had cause for war. The burghers of Copenhagen supported the king, but the nobility held back, and not before 1611 did he overcome the opposition of the council.

Christian declared war, the so-called Kalmar War (1611-1613), and attacked southern Sweden with foreign mercenaries. He also commanded Danish officers to conscript soldiers in Norway and attack Sweden. But the men deserted when they had consumed the food they had brought with them from home, for they saw no object in ravaging the farms of their Swedish neighbors. In Trøndelag foreign mercenaries hired by the Swedish king were even allowed to pass through the country unmolested. A different fate met a smaller Scottish band which tried to march through Gudbrandsdal to the Swedish border. At Kringen the farmers gathered with resolute courage and killed most of the intruders with guns or by rolling down stones from the mountains. This Sinclair episode, as it has been called from the name of one of the officers, had no influence on the outcome of the war, yet it has been immortalized through song, legend, and a monument at Kringen. And justly so. The incident awakened national pride and a patriotism that looked beyond the immediate neighborhood. The decisive victories were won in the south by the king's mercenaries and the fleet. Sweden gave up any claim to Finmark, and Denmark-Norway maintained its position both in the North and in the Baltic. The war resulted, however, in a serious set-back in the freedom of the common people in Norway; they were made to feel that they were subjects in a powerful state.

The Kalmar War marked a revolution in military technique caused by improvements in small arms and cannon and vast increase in production. Fortifications had to be enlarged and rebuilt; there was need of stronger and larger ships and more of them; the strategy had changed from emphasis on tactics of defense to offensive warfare. The cost of seventeenth-century wars was a staggering burden on the people. By comparison the wars of the preceding century seemed mere trifles. The foreign mercenaries were expensive and moreover were at hand only while a war was in progress. The king therefore wished to build up a large militia. There were repeated royal orders regarding a Norwegian army; a definite outline was drawn up, and, though it continued to be mainly an army on paper, the plan was available for later use. Recruiting for the fleet was also kept up. Enormous taxes and severe penalties—mainly fines on individuals or whole communities—crushed the people's resistance.

Norway happily lay outside the battlefields of the Thirty Years' War, the most destructive conflict of the age. Even when Christian IV recklessly allowed himself to become enmeshed in it (1625-1629) Norway was not directly touched by the conflict. But a large number of Jutlanders, fleeing before the army of Wallenstein, took refuge there and had to be provided for, and the king used Norwegian money and men, especially sailors. The fleet alone fought with any success. Christian had to withdraw from the war, beaten and humiliated.

It was hoped that now Sweden and Denmark would bury the hatchet so that Protestantism could present a united front in the Thirty Years' War; but Christian was unwilling. With growing jealousy he had watched Gustaf Adolf build up an empire on the eastern shore of the Baltic, and when the Swedish king became the leader of the Protestants and his armies went from victory to victory in Germany, the Danish king became apprehensive. As the war was drawing to a close, Christian, ignoring the common religious interests of the North, used every diplomatic means to thwart and irritate the Swedes until he had reason to expect war. Nevertheless, he carried on a policy that antagonized the Netherlands, who might have been friendly, and drove them instead into a Swedish alliance. So Denmark-Norway had to stand alone in the next war with Sweden, which was to decide the leadership in the North. In this war Norway took a more honorable and effective part than in any earlier conflict, owing largely to the new statholder, Hannibal Sehested.

Sehested was the most notable person connected with the government of Norway for many a year. He was gifted, striking in appearance, an able administrator, and endowed with indomitable energy. Moreover, he stood high in the favor and confidence of the king and was married to Christiane, one of the many daughters of Christian IV's morganatic wife Christine Munk. When he came to Norway with his bride he appeared with regal splendor and acted with almost royal authority. Ambitious and self-seeking, he used every opportunity to fill his purse and add to his enormous estates, but he was also determined to develop a separate, national administration in the country.

When Sweden attacked Denmark, he was forced to devote his energy to military affairs. With justice the Norwegians called the ensuing conflict the Hannibal War (1643-1645). Though Sehested was not a military man, the full responsibility for conducting the war fell on him. With a speed and efficiency Norway had never experienced before, preparations were rushed to completion. Ships were procured from the cities or rented from Dutch owners, the garrisons of the fortresses were strengthened with new contingents of mercenaries, the old beacons on the mountain tops were renewed with wood and barrels of tar, every mountain pass was guarded, a levy en masse was made along the eastern frontier where danger was imminent, and the militia was trained under Danish, German, and Dutch officers. The Norwegian farmers could easily be turned into good soldiers, for, as hunting was part of their livelihood, they were skilled marksmen. Though there were complaints of desertions in this war too, the armies fought as they had not done for centuries and were victorious all along the border. Yet peace was bought with old Norwegian land; Jemtland and Herjedal, which had belonged to Norway ever since national boundaries were first drawn, were given up to Sweden. The state had for the first time surrendered land to a victorious foe, and Sweden was now the leading power in the North.

Peace brought rejoicing in both countries. Norway had not suffered nearly so much as Denmark, for Sehested had contrived to keep the fighting largely on Swedish soil. Yet military service had been a heavy burden, and the taxes were beyond anything the country had experienced. On the other hand, the constant need of money caused a repeated calling together of the estates, and they spoke with greater boldness than in the past. The military successes increased the prestige both of the kingdom and of Sehested. He could now devote his whole energy to making Norway an active partner in the union with a strong national government of its own, its own army, fleet, and financial system; and for a time his efforts were crowned with success. He was active in all fields, among other things organizing a Norwegian postal system. But the main problem was military, and with the backing of the nobility, a militia and a fleet were maintained. When the old king made his last visit to Norway in 1646 he was well satisfied with the achievements of his son-in-law. He was not confronted with the usual complaints, because Sehested had handled them competently and fairly before the king's arrival, and, moreover, taxes had been lowered. The nobles were granted new privileges which put them more nearly on the same footing as the Danish. Next year the king agreed to Sehested's proposal that all the royal income from Norway be paid in to a commission at Akershus, which also had the supervision over military affairs. So Norway obtained its own treasury and department of war, both controlled by the statholder. He also had the whole civil administration in his hands and was commander of the army and fleet, responsible to the king only. The gain was short-lived, however.

Christian IV was old and weary now, and unable to hold his own against the council, which feared that Sehested's power would destroy the unity of the state and the influence of the Danish nobility in Norwegian affairs. The council was led by another son-in-law of the king, the ambitious young noble, Korfits Ulfeldt. He was married to Leonora Christine, Christine Munk's most famous and gifted daughter—one of the few people, we are told, whose conversation Descartes found stimulating. In the summer of 1647 the death of the king's oldest son, who had been elected to succeed him, played into the hands of Ulfeldt and the council, for in order to secure the election of his second son, Frederik, the king was forced to yield to all their demands. Before the year was over orders were sent to Norway that all state money except that designated for the army and the payment of the debt should be sent to Copenhagen and that Norway should "without separation or particularly special government remain under Denmark." Sehested's absolute power was at an end. Both he and the king had lost out.

Soon after, in February 1648, Christian IV died, worn out and disappointed, before a successor had been chosen. In April the Danish estates met and elected Duke Frederik king of Denmark and Norway as Frederik III (1648-1670). In order to secure the election he had to sign a charter restricting his authority more severely than had been the case in any charter since the Reformation and making him dependent on the council both in foreign and domestic affairs. No mention was made of Norway, as it was taken for granted that the whole charter applied to both countries, but Norway could not be as completely disregarded as the Danish nobility would have liked.

In August 1648 a full meeting of the four estates was held in Christiania, and the new king received the oath of allegiance of each estate in turn amidst even more ceremonial than had been the case on similar occasions in the past. As in Denmark, the clergy and burghers recognized the king as the rightful heir to the throne, while the nobles refused to do so. Frederik III spent some busy weeks in Norway, receiving and weighing petitions and appeals from all estates. He confirmed the rights of the cities, enlarged the privileges of the nobility, and issued royal letters concerning a great many matters. More numerous and insistent than ever before, the complaints give a dark, though naturally one-sided, picture of conditions. Wherever possible without cutting the king's necessary income, the king and statholder tried to remedy the evils. It seemed as though Hannibal Sehested and his policy had the favor of the king. Frederik, however, was quietly planning to enhance his own power, and rivalries within the nobility could be used to serve his ends. He gave ready ear to the complaints of the council against Sehested, and an investigation was instituted. In the conduct of finances the grasping governor was not without reproach. To avoid prosecution, he declared himself "guilty" without specifying of what, gave his vast estates over to the king, and resigned his position. But though the attempt to give Norway a strong administration of its own was ended, the lesson taught was never forgotten. Sehested's enemies did not profit by their victory. Before long their leader, Korfits Ulfeldt, also fell from royal favor. Less prudent than Sehested, he fled the country, never to return, while his wife Leonora Christine spent eighteen years as prisoner in the Blue Tower in Copenhagen.

The power of the council was declining more and more, and the influence of the whole nobility was dwindling. The king continued the development in both countries of a bureaucratic administration with officials drawn largely from the bourgeoisie. The finances particularly were administered by middle-class men who, as creditors of the crown, became important in this age of rising state debts. In Norway a number of the new officials were Norwegians. Although the military administration was weakened, Norway was expected to take a large part in the war with Sweden which broke out in 1657.

Eager for revenge, Frederik III used the chance when Karl X Gustaf was involved with Poland and declared war. Preparations had to be made with feverish haste. In Norway Jørgen Bjelke, the son of Chancellor Jens Bjelke, was in command. With speed and efficiency he fitted out a coastal fleet, strengthened fortifications, and called out the militia to defend the borders. The Norwegians won several victories and reconquered Jemtland and Herjedal. Meanwhile the Danes were defeated in the South, and Norwegian victories once more counted little in the treaty. By the Peace of Roskilde in 1658, not only were Jemtland and Herjedal returned to Sweden, but she acquired also the Norwegian districts of Trøndelag and Baahus as well as all the Danish territory east of the Sound. Sweden was now at the very height of her power.

Yet Karl Gustaf was not content, for he felt that the interference of the powers had prevented him from obtaining all to which his victories had entitled him. The Norwegians in the conquered provinces had accepted his rule, and he believed he might be able to widen his gains, even acquire all of Norway and perhaps Denmark too. He attacked without even the ceremonial of a declaration of war, invading Denmark from the south, crossing the Great Belt to Zealand and laying siege to Copenhagen. Realizing that the fall of the capital would mean practically the conquest of the kingdom, the Danes fought for their very life, led by the king, who became the hero of the siege. After heavy losses the Swedes had to retreat.[4] They then directed their attack on Norway. The Norwegians under Jørgen Bjelke had driven the enemy out of Trondheim, but only after a small, poorly equipped Swedish force had held out for three months in the unfortified city. Bjelke then rushed to the assistance of Fredrikshald on the southern extremity of the eastern frontier, upon which the Swedes centered their main attack. There the Norwegians performed a real feat of arms, defending the town against repeated violent assaults. As a result of Norwegian victories Trøndelag was returned to Norway by the Peace of Copenhagen in May 1660, and the boundary of the country was fixed as it since has remained. The powers refused to sanction any other territorial change.

The attempt at power politics of Frederik III, as of his father, had brought humiliation and disappointment. Both kingdoms had lost their adjoining territories, which are now part of Sweden, and instead of being neighbors were now several days' journey apart. But as Denmark's loss was by far the more serious, Norway became a larger proportionate part of the realm than earlier.

¶ The three years of war (1657-1660) had made the king a hero and lowered the prestige of the nobility, which was blamed for the defeat. When the Danish estates were called together to appropriate money, the third estate with the backing of the clergy forced the nobles to relinquish their tax exemptions; and sensing that the most fundamental prerogative of the nobility was its right to elect the king, they demanded that the monarchy be made hereditary. Under duress the council consented, and on October 18, 1660, Frederik III was acclaimed hereditary king. The estates, which had expected to retain a large share in the government, authorized him to formulate a recess embodying the changes. But then came Frederik's coup. In January 1661 he sent around an "instrument" asking the signature of leading men of all estates, and most of them complied. Thereby they not only declared that of their own free will they had granted the king hereditary right to the kingdoms of Denmark and Norway, but they also signed the additional

[4] The doughty burgomaster of Copenhagen in this crisis was Hans Nansen, an ancestor of Fridtjof Nansen. Jon Sørensen, *The Saga of Fridtjof Nansen.*

provision—of which they had never dreamed—that the royal power should be absolute.

During the following years the king worked to give absolutism permanent form. His secretary, Peder Schumacher (Griffenfeld), embodied the principles of the absolute monarchy in the King's Law, *Lex Regia*, to which the king affixed his signature in 1665. Though not published before 1709, this was the constitution of the two countries and continued to be so until the termination of the union in 1814. In theory the Danish-Norwegian absolutism was the most logically developed and complete divine-right absolutism in all Europe. Even Hobbes could not have done better.

Norwegians had nothing to do with the events in Denmark, but, on August 15, 1661, the estates meeting in Christiania gave their oath of allegiance to the hereditary king represented by his son Christian. Afterwards the autocratic character of the king's power was announced, and in Norway the estates were even less able than in Denmark to offer any resistance when asked to sign the "instrument" of January by which absolutism was established. Most of the people had no conception of what the change implied. It would seem that the assembled estates might have furthered the development of popular government, but instead they accepted absolutism and were never again convened. The country thereby lost the institution which, with all its limitations, had been a link between the people and the government. In fact the whole social system based on estates was changing, as the higher offices were more and more filled with commoners, and the king began to surround himself with a newly-created nobility of the robe recruited from the middle-class officials. As royal favor and wealth rather than birth determined a person's social position, we hereafter speak of classes rather than estates.

It was long, however, before Norway felt any difference in the social system, and even the administrative changes had no sudden effect. Frederik's policy was to amalgamate the two kingdoms along the lines begun earlier, but the blending could never be complete because of the fundamental differences between the countries. As far as possible the Norwegian government was controlled by bureaucratic, purely Danish colleges organized as the chief administrative departments for both countries; but some separate Norwegian offices had to be maintained. The local government, too, became more bureaucratic, fell more under the direct control of the king, continuing the change begun a decade earlier. The German terms for the districts and the governors, *amt* and *amtmand*, took the place of the earlier *len* and *lensherre*. While there was no lack of opportunity for embezzlement and oppression, the official class of Denmark-Norway was doubtless better than in most countries, and the supervision stricter. The absolute kings up to 1746, though not great rulers, were able and conscientious and willingly listened to the many deputations from Norway and tried to give to every man his just due.

In 1664, Frederik III sent his natural son Ulrik Frederik Gyldenløve to Norway as statholder. Gyldenløve was a handsome, gay young man of twenty-six, a lover of art, of fine clothes, and of women, a much-traveled man of the world and an aristocrat. He had an unusual capacity for winning people and became beloved and popular as no other Danish governor. He saw the poverty of Norway; better than the colleges in Copenhagen he understood the needs of the country and repeatedly sent requests to the king for revision of the laws, for military reform, and, above all, for measures to lighten the taxes of the people and protect them from illegal exactions of officials and landlords. "The prosperity of the farmer," he wrote, "is the basis, root, and fundamental in the preservation of the whole kingdom of Norway. If the farmers are ruined, then they will be unable to pay any taxes to your Royal Majesty, especially in time of war, and soldiers can get no supplies from them." No doubt he was influenced by Sehested, who was again prominent in Danish politics. Little was done, however. Gyldenløve lacked the inclination and capacity for persistent effort and longed to get away from drab Christiania to gay Copenhagen where he spent most of his time. Moreover, the king was growing indifferent for he was occupied with the intricacies of foreign relations.

Frederik III was trying to form an alliance with England to check the commercial supremacy of the Netherlands. He seemed on the point of succeeding when, in 1665, war broke out between the Netherlands and England. In this war Bergen became the scene of an extraordinary episode. A Dutch merchant fleet, laden with gold, jewels, spices, fine cloth, and all manner of riches of the Indies, fearing to enter the English Channel, set its course north of Scotland and took refuge in the neutral harbor of Bergen, there to await a convoy. Seldom had so great wealth, estimated at thirty million dollars, been concentrated in one harbor. Soon English men-of-war came in pursuit and took up battle formation, closing all avenues of escape. When they opened fire, Claus Ahlefeldt, the commander-in-chief of the Norwegian army, came to the assistance of the Dutch, and the English had to withdraw with heavy losses. This is the only battle in modern times fought in the harbor of Bergen. Too late Ahlefeldt received orders from the king to protest against any unneutral act on the part of the English with words only, not with guns. On condition of receiving half of the spoils, Frederik had made a secret agreement with Charles II that he would not interfere with the English. The news of the sordid bargain was noised abroad. The intrigues of the "Fox," as Frederik was called, had ended in disgrace and failure, and he became involved in war with England. His forces took little active part in the conflict and peace was concluded in 1667. Three years later Frederik III died and was succeeded by his son.

The reign of Christian V (1670-1699) afforded Gyldenløve an opportunity to carry out some of his reforms. The new king was a well-meaning, industrious man with average ability and a high sense of his calling. On his travels he became thoroughly imbued with the ideas of Louis XIV, whom he took as his ideal. Realizing his own limitations, he leaned heavily upon his chief advisers in whose hands the real power rested, yet he was suspicious of any man who became too strong. His policy therefore lacked stability. At first Gyldenløve stood closer to his royal half-brother than anyone else, and used the opportunity to put through reforms in the Norwegian army and navy. He also reduced taxes by eliminating unnecessary offices and decreasing the salaries of higher officials. On the other hand, lower officials received a reasonable raise, which eliminated some of the temptation to seek illegal profit.

Though Gyldenløve never lost the favor of the king, his influence soon waned before that of the more sagacious, industrious, and ambitious Peder Schumacher. Schumacher was of the middle class, but, created Count Griffenfeld by the king, he was the foremost of the new nobility of the robe. Following the French pattern, he proceeded to strengthen absolutism and at the same time concentrated offices and power in his own hands, virtually becoming prime minister. He was soon to experience the fickleness of royal favor. In 1676 he was suddenly arrested and after a pro forma trial condemned to death. When he was kneeling to await the executioner's axe, the sentence was commuted to life imprisonment. For twenty-three years he was imprisoned, most of the time in the dreary fortress on Munkholm, a tiny island just outside of Trondheim, and died in Trondheim a few months after his release. Griffenfeld's power and arrogance had given him jealous enemies who constantly fanned the suspicions of the king. But the chief cause of the powerful minister's dramatic fall was his opposition to war with

Sweden, in which he persisted through devious diplomacy even after his country was at war.

Ever since the Battle of Bergen in 1665 the Danish government had been involved in a maze of diplomatic negotiations and treaty making. It was difficult to remain at peace while Louis XIV dominated international affairs; and after he attacked Holland in 1672 and the whole continent was divided into two great alliances, neutrality was well-nigh impossible. Besides, many Danes, especially the generals, were not averse to getting another blow at their old rival Sweden, an ally of France. In 1675 a war broke out which in Danish history is called the Skaane War, because the Danes, although they also had a German front with which to cope, fought largely for and in that province.

In Norway it was called the Gyldenløve War. Though Norwegians had no share in the diplomatic happenings leading to the conflict, they did at least their share in the fighting. As soon as war threatened, Gyldenløve rushed preparations, and when it came the forts were ready to resist attacks and the army to win victories unaided by outside forces. Though they had no enthusiasm for the war, the Norwegians won the praise of their officers, and the king was so pleased with Gyldenløve that he offered him another more important command. But Gyldenløve refused: "I have fortunately never had presumptions about my own capacity. . . . My sphere does not extend beyond the Norwegian cliffs . . . on the wide, broad plains I may easily be lost." During the last months of the war the land fighting on both sides degenerated into ravaging expeditions—"a new French fashion" Gyldenløve called it, though it was not entirely new nor wholly French. The Danish-Norwegian fleet played a very important part, and acquitted itself well under two renowned commanders, the Norwegian Curt Adeler and, after his death, the Dane Niels Juel. Besides contributing their share to the common navy, the Norwegians had their own fleet of defense created by Gyldenløve.

Valor and victories, however, counted for naught in the peace. Louis XIV was at the height of his power, and, as Griffenfeld had feared, the French king dictated a treaty with no territorial changes. Resentment against Louis tended to draw the northern states closer together. At the peace meeting in Lund, June 1679, the ideal of Scandinavianism, which Griffenfeld and Sehested had favored, came to the fore, advocated especially by the Swede Johan Gyllenstierna, who believed that a united North would have a strong place in European politics. An alliance was made, but there was too much mutual distrust to allow the idea of cooperation to bear lasting fruit. In 1680 Gyllenstierna, its chief exponent, died, and before long each state went its own way. For both sides the war had been one of utter, useless waste. All that the Norwegians had gained by their victories was a greater self-esteem which sometimes took the exaggerated form of contempt for the Danes, who, it was thought, had won fewer laurels in the war. The differences between the two peoples were more keenly felt at the very time when the government was trying to draw them closer together.

Christian V used the years of peace to strengthen his absolutism. Like his model, Louis XIV, he was his own prime minister, industriously supervising a mass of governmental detail, allowing no adviser, be he Dane or German, to acquire too great influence. While he continued his efforts to amalgamate the two countries, he had a special concern for Norway, because he was afraid of losing it to Sweden. He was therefore willing to do much for the defense of the country, and mainly to study this problem made an extensive trip through Norway in 1685. He came into close touch with the people and won their good will in spite of the heavy expense involved in providing for his large entourage. In the eyes of the people all reforms were his work.

Christian had the typical absolute monarch's passion for regulating every phase of life. He issued minute paternalistic directions about the rank and duties of officials, about debts and debtors, guardianships, restrictions on begging, dress, food and drink at weddings and funerals, days of prayer, and the like. Economic reforms were especially emphasized, regulations of coinage, of trade, of industry, weight and measures; there was a forest ordinance, and trade regulations for Finmark and even Greenland. In Norway many of the orders remained mere paper regulations because, while intended for both countries, they did not fit Norwegian conditions.

Yet significant reforms were introduced, and for them Gyldenløve deserves chief credit. Among the achievements of his long career were a number of regulations for the protection of the rural population against officials. Though the outbreaks of violence had ceased, there was constant friction between officials and the people, who had no interest in the growing sphere of state activities and resented the many new demands upon them. If they did not promptly pay their contribution to the support of the army, soldiers were quartered upon them who, Gyldenløve said, ate up many times the amount due. Moreover, the number of officials had increased, and they showed great ingenuity in inventing all manner of fees and extra exactions. Gyldenløve was aware of the danger these abuses were to the state as well as to the people. He tried to put an end to exploitation by new regulations defining sharply what fees officials might legally demand, fixing the right of the people to complain, and making it the duty of clergymen to read new orders from the pulpit.

The most significant reform was the promulgation in 1688 of King Christian the Fifth's Norwegian Law. Christian IV's law, never complete or satisfactory, had on many points become antiquated, and Danish laws and legal practices had more and more found entrance into Norway. Often it was difficult to know just what the law was, and the Norwegians suffered under this uncertainty. The need for a thorough revision was glaring, and Chancellor Jens Bjelke and Gyldenløve were especially zealous advocates of the reform. When the Gyldenløve War was over, the king appointed a commission to codify the laws, but the first draft, though excellent, did not satisfy him and was revised to bring it into closer harmony with Danish law. Though more Danish was introduced than desirable, much that was purely Norwegian remained. In his introduction—an excellent expression of the ideals of a paternalistic divine-right ruler—the king declared that he wished "one and all to know and perceive that we have an equal royal solicitude for our beloved and faithful subjects in all our kingdoms and lands."[5] Only once before—in the thirteenth century—and never since has the codification of the laws of the land been undertaken. On the whole it was a good piece of work. Penalties were brutal according to modern standards and much more severe than in the old Norwegian laws, corporal punishments for many offenses being substituted for the earlier fines. Yet the code was more humane than legal practices in other countries; it emphasized the equality of all citizens before the law and protected personal liberty more than was customary in those days. Although the new code was far from perfect, and was disregarded when it came into too sharp conflict with old usages, it did bring order out of chaos and met with general satisfaction.

But in spite of numerous laws and improvements, the king's fear of entrusting too much power to the hands of one man led to divided responsibility, a weak rule, and lack of supervision over lower officials. Good laws helped little when not enforced. In 1699, when Christian V died and Gyldenløve retired, people looked hopefully to the new king for further reforms.

When Frederik IV (1699-1730) ascended the throne, he was over-

[5] *Kong Christian den Femtes Lov*, 5, Copenhagen, 1800.

whelmed with petitions, requests, and advice, much of it expressed with remarkable candor. The king was energetic and kindly, and willingly lent an ear to them all. He was suspicious not only of the old nobility but of officials from the middle class and put many new men, often Germans, into office. To acquaint himself with conditions he made a long tour of the country and was cordially received. It is interesting to notice that so much road-building had been done that in many places where Christian V twenty years earlier had traveled on horseback Frederik IV used carriages. The king formally installed a permanent Commission of Akershus which was to extend the activities of the administration in the country and decrease the amount of business referred to Copenhagen. However, it did not become an effective organ, and once more internal developments were postponed in the interest of foreign affairs and war.

¶ In the twenty years of peace at the close of the century the diplomacy of Christian V had centered upon the stabilization of Denmark's southern boundary, but, in spite of a brief period of rapprochement between the two states, a future war with Sweden was looked upon as inevitable. When it would come depended on the European situation. Toward the close of his reign Christian V made an alliance with Poland, Saxony, and Peter the Great of Russia against the dashing young Karl XII, who had ascended the Swedish throne in 1697. Thus when Frederik IV succeeded the stage was set for war. It broke out in 1700, but at the command of the powers was concluded the same year without solving any problems or averting future hostilities.

While Frederik was preparing for another war, the brilliant but reckless Karl XII was leading his army from victory to victory, defeating Saxony, Russia, and Poland, until his successes were halted in 1709 at Poltava, where Peter the Great inflicted a smashing defeat upon the Swedes. Believing this an opportune time, Frederik renewed his alliance with Peter and launched an unprovoked attack on Sweden. After three minor expeditions against Baahus the king decided that there was to be no offensive from Norway, the army was returned to a peace footing, and the country enjoyed a period of quiet. However, Norwegians continued to be recruited for the fleet and over five thousand of their best soldiers—"exceptionally handsome fellows" said the Danish commander-in-chief—were sent south to join the Danish army, which won a brilliant victory.

Sweden was in a serious plight; the people complained because ever since Poltava Karl XII had lingered in Turkey, and the estates threatened to make peace even without his consent. Then suddenly he came home, the people once more rallied about their hero king, and the war was resumed with new vigor. Early in 1716 Karl threw all his forces against Norway, directing his main attack against Christiania. When it was clear that the city could not be held, the garrison of Akershus was reinforced and the rest of the Norwegian army withdrew to Lier, northeast of the capital. Karl occupied the city, but could not take the fortress or strike at the undefeated army. He concentrated his efforts on breaking through to the west, but every road was stoutly held, the people rising en masse to defend their country and cautiously taking the offensive in several small actions. Finally the Swedes had to withdraw and turned to the equally important task of capturing Fredriksten. This fortress, guarding the southeastern border, was a constant threat to any invader of Norway, and, besides, the neighboring city Fredrikshald (now Halden) had a splendid harbor. After violent fighting Karl captured the city by a surprise attack, but had to retreat because the people evacuated it, burning their homes, while the fortress opened fire on the city. He had a slight hope that he might still capture the fortress if his transport fleet lying in Dynekilen, a little inlet a few miles to the south, could reach him with supplies.

Meanwhile a Danish-Norwegian fleet under the command of a young Norwegian captain, Peder Wessel Tordenskjold, was sailing northward toward Christiania. Tordenskjold was already admired and feared for his brilliant seamanship, his dashing courage, and his resourcefulness. This was the first time he commanded a squadron, and he had been ordered to keep an eye out for the Swedish fleet. When he learned that this fleet was in Dynekilen, he sailed in through the narrows without awaiting further orders, and before evening he had destroyed or captured the whole fleet. When the news reached Karl, he broke camp and two days after the Battle of Dynekilen the last Swedish soldier left Norwegian soil.

Both states spent the next year mainly in diplomatic and military preparations, and with almost superhuman efforts Karl XII raised in his impoverished country a force twice as large as the Norwegian. In 1718 he again attacked Norway. He sent one army under Karl Gustaf Armfeldt against Trondheim, and personally led another against Fredriksten. Early in December the siege was in full swing, the Swedes had blocked every approach to the fortress and had captured some outer fortifications. On Sunday evening, December 11, Karl was standing, only partially protected by the breastwork, watching the work on the trenches. Suddenly he fell to the ground shot through the temple. Whether the bullet came from the fort or from a sniper in the king's own army is still a question. The death of the hero king was felt as a relief even among his own men, and the siege was raised at once. As soon as the news reached Armfeldt, who had not succeeded in taking Trondheim, he began to withdraw. Terrible snowstorms overwhelmed his army, already weakened by disease and food shortage, and the homeward march, though on a smaller scale, may well be compared to Napoleon's retreat from Russia.

Both sides were longing for peace and yet could not come to terms. The following summer Frederik IV personally led the combined Danish and Norwegian armies in an attack on Baahus. At the same time Tordenskjold performed the most brilliant feat of his brief career in the capture of Marstrand. He was the most illustrious and beloved among Norway's many naval heroes of the Danish Period, and his early death—he fell in a duel a few months after peace was made—has only added to the glamor of his name. Not daring to venture far into Sweden, Frederik withdrew; the war stopped, and peace negotiations were begun through the mediation of England.

On July 3, 1720, the Peace of Frederiksborg was signed, thus ending the longest, bloodiest, and—fortunately—the last of the wars between the northern countries which had cursed the preceding century. Frederik relinquished the Swedish territory he had occupied, but his southern frontier was strengthened. Sweden had to give up the earlier freedom from the Sound dues and pay a sizable indemnity, and also suffered a much more serious defeat at the hands of Peter the Great, who acquired most of the Baltic Provinces. Sweden's dominance in the Baltic was ended and the position of the two northern states was more nearly balanced than it had been for about two centuries.

In its last phase the conflict had become a folk war which aroused the Norwegians and united them in a struggle to free their soil of the enemy. Yet it did not awaken a desire for national independence, but on the contrary bound Norway closer to Denmark. The joy and pride in the outcome found expression in legend and song. In many of them Tordenskjold is the hero, but others tell of less distinguished men and women. One humorous ballad relates how Karl XII came to Norway to woo by force a fair maiden named Halden, who repulsed him with a slap in the face, for her troth was plighted to King Frederik.

For the common people the economic progress was more important than political events, although there was an intimate relation between the two. Rivalries and wars tended to draw the boundaries more sharply and to make each state more national, although with the power centering in the king. Every statesman was striving to make his state as self-contained as possible and this, it was believed, could best be achieved by following the mercantilistic policy of which Colbert was the foremost exponent.

Even before the time of Colbert this policy was strikingly manifested in the many-sided economic activities of Christian IV, and his successors followed in his footsteps, developing his ideas still further under the tutelage of the great French mercantilist. As in the political fields so in the economic, the Oldenburgers strove to weld their whole domain into a self-sufficient unit by encouraging home production, particularly of war supplies, and by striving for a favorable balance of trade. Every phase and every step of the economic development was subject to governmental regulations, but, though increased power and wealth were the chief aim of the economic policy, the Oldenburgers were humane and paternalistic, and their avowed policy was to protect the weak and guarantee justice to all. Nevertheless, their love of order led them to promote the concentration of trade and industries in the cities, and to give privileges and monopolies to individuals or small groups and protect them by favorable tariff regulations, thus favoring the bourgeoisie.

The economic development begun in the sixteenth century continued with accelerated speed in the seventeenth, sometimes in spite of, often with the aid of government regulation. The earlier pessimism had given way to a confident optimism which was inclined to overvalue the resources of the country.

In order to make Norway self-supporting, the kings from Christian IV on made persistent efforts to develop manufacturing there, both by investing state funds and by offering substantial privileges to any person, native or foreign, who would establish new factories.

One man, Director of Commerce Jørgen thor Møhlen, was given the use of a part of the Bergen commons and there erected factories for producing ropes, soap, train oil, woolen cloth, nails, salt, gunpowder, and other things, planning to make this a great manufacturing center after the French fashion. But one by one his factories were closed until his vast property looked like a deserted mining town. Other undertakings, too, failed, and only a few plants remained to form the beginning of the next century's industrial system. The needs of the people continued to be supplied by importation and by native craftsmen in small shops. There was no market for manufactured articles. Most people could buy very little beyond the necessities and the few wealthy preferred imported goods. An industrial system was an exotic plant that could not thrive in Norway's meager soil. The country had to win wealth through the utilization of its natural resources.

Mining attracted much of the interest of the kings. In the 1620's a renewed search for precious metals spread over Europe, and Christian IV had a feverish eagerness to utilize Norway's supposedly fabulous mineral wealth, all of which, according to the theory of the age, was the property of the crown. He gave mining a great impetus, the effect of which was not lost throughout this period. The ironworks of the preceding century were continued and enlarged and new ones opened. They were financed by the king, who appointed a superintendent of mines with authority over them all. The skilled miners were Germans, while the farmers in the neighborhood did hauling and other unskilled labor for little or no pay. In 1624 two Danish capitalists and any partners they might wish to include were given a monopoly of all iron mines and works. In addition to paying a substantial tax the company was obliged to manufacture articles that would otherwise have to be imported. Any works that were not kept in operation reverted to the crown. This was, as far as we know, the first purely capitalistic undertaking in Norway, and the capitalists were foreigners who did not take up residence in the country. They made good money, but they soon declared that one company was unable to utilize the many new discoveries of ore. Thereby the monopoly was broken and many small works sprang up. In spite of some crises the industry held its own through the years, and gradually the owners became residents and the capital Norwegian.

Much more thrilling than the iron industry was the pursuit of precious metals. In 1623 country people discovered silver in the mountains west of Oslo. Christian IV became highly excited, and next year the Kongsberg silver mine was opened on a grand scale with a large number of German miners. The king inspected the place in person, laid out and named the town, planned a royal residence there, and ordered the building of a wagon road, the first in the country. The mine was a success, though the results were not commensurate with the plans, and before long this mine also was handed over to a private company. Twice later in the century the king again took possession, the second time in 1683. Then the mine was for a while operated at a great loss because the private owners had underpaid the laborers and failed to make new installations.

Not long after the discovery of silver, Christian IV and the men about him were once more aroused, for in the region just north of the Dovre Mountain some herdboys had found copper. In 1633 the first copper mine, named "God's Gift," was opened at Kvikne as a state project, and two years later the king himself made the arduous journey over the mountains to visit the mine. He stimulated an extensive search for copper, and a great many small mines were opened which were soon exhausted and abandoned. Later came a few larger undertakings, the most important being started at Røros in 1644. This was a private enterprise. With ups and downs it continued to grow and in 1700 entered upon a period of great prosperity. The Røros and Kongsberg works were the only mining operations from which the king gained any sizable revenue. In both, labor and capital continued to be foreign longer than in the iron industry. The crown, however, was still the chief capitalist and retained the right to take over any plants. To guard the interests of the king and to afford the laborers some protection, a growing number of officials, none of them Norwegian, was appointed to supervise and inspect mines. In disputes between labor and operators they generally sided with the former.

Of more importance to the whole country was lumbering. In fact it was so significant that its place has been compared to that of the steel industry today. Lumbering had developed in the sixteenth century without government stimulus and without capitalists, but now conditions had changed. As the forests near the coast were thinned out, lumber was sought farther inland along larger streams in Trøndelag and in the South, but most especially in the broad forests in the East. It had to be hauled or floated from the woods to the mills and then the long way to the sea, and sawing was more and more concentrated in fewer large mills by the great waterfalls of the main rivers. As this required more money than the average farmer could get together, lumbering fell into the hands of well-to-do burghers and officials and the foundations were laid for great fortunes.

This group of lumbermen strove to get complete control over the industry by forcing the small sawmills out of existence. Not content to accomplish this by competition and by forbidding sawmills on their own land, they appealed for government regulation in their favor and obtained most of what they asked. On the whole the interests of the state coincided with those of the lumber magnates. It had long been the king's policy to restrict the farmers' participation in trade and industry and keep them at their work on the farm, and he feared that unchecked lumbering would strip the country of its forests. He was especially concerned about the conservation of the oak, which was important in shipbuilding and of which the country had only a limited supply. It was also in accordance with mercantilist principles to forbid exportation of logs in order to have all lumber sawed at home, and to have the industry so concentrated and organized that it could best be controlled and would yield the largest revenue.

Extensive regulations curtailed the number of small sawmills which produced lumber for local use. In places it was complained that there was not a saw in the whole parish, that homes were falling into ruin because lumber for repairs could not be obtained, and that the old wasteful method of cutting planks with an axe had to be revived in order to get caskets for burying the dead. Exportation of unsawed logs was also restricted. In the southern seaboard districts people had been selling logs to Dutchmen who visited every convenient inlet, and they depended on this resource for their ready cash. In spite of protests and defiance the whole traffic was prohibited in 1733, making the lumber industry virtually a monopoly of wealthy magnates. Most of the forests, however, belonged to the well-to-do freeholders from whom the lumbermen had to buy part of their logs. Though no lowly group, the farmers had difficulty in holding their own against the capitalists in spite of the government's attempt to protect their interests by ordering prompt cash payments. To prevent encroachment on private and public timber land, a definite hinterland was assigned to the lumbermen of each city to which they must confine their operations. The amount of lumber that might be exported from each city was also designated. Drammen led and next came Christiania. Many similar seaport towns, however, owed their rise to the lumber export in spite of the efforts to let the older cities dominate.

As in lumbering so also in fishing, the seventeenth century brought new methods which were to become of tremendous importance to all western Norway. The new methods, as in so many other fields, came from abroad. While Norwegians along the shore were continuing to make their haul from small boats with a single line and hook—even the seine fishing known in saga times having gone out of use—foreigners, Dutch and English, were beginning to fish in the deep sea outside of the Norwegian coast using net, seine, and lines with hundreds of hooks attached to each. Many English and even more Dutch skippers who had been coming to Norway to buy fish settled there and engaged in fishing. Wealthy burghers among the Norwegians also took up the new methods, but it required larger boats and more costly equipment than the common fisherman could buy.

Conservative and unable to compete with the large-scale operations, the fishermen complained that their livelihood was destroyed and the fish frightened away. In vain the government prohibited the new methods, both to protect the poor fishermen and to restrain the lawlessness that accompanied the immense crowds gathering from far and near. There came not only fishers, rich and poor, but traders from Bergen with barrels and salt who bought the catch from the boat, salted and packed it. The fishermen had difficulty in procuring salt and had to sell their haul for whatever was offered, and, as the price of fish was declining while that of grain was rising, their lot was not enviable. They became more and more involved in debt to the merchants, and the economic pressure upon them was heavy. They could not stem the tide and gradually adapted themselves to it; not before the eighteenth century was far advanced, however, were the new methods in general use in the North. As the trade in fish and even some of the fishing became capitalistic, there were built up, particularly in Bergen, many substantial fortunes—more numerous but not so large as those made in lumber in the East.

Whaling, which was revived at this time, was even more completely controlled by city people than fishing, for this hazardous venture required greater capital. Again the English and the Dutch took the lead, and whaling in Norwegian waters came to be the monopoly of companies wholly controlled by foreigners. But as Norwegians were more and more sailing the seven seas, many of them were no doubt employed on the whalers, though the skilled harpooners were generally Basques.

Foreign trade was the life-line of Norway's economic growth. The demand for fish and lumber was so great that as a source of revenue the Norwegian trade was more important to the government than the Danish. After 1640 there was a marked increase in the volume of exports, especially lumber. When England and the Netherlands were at war, lumber was piled up in Norwegian seaports, but when peace came all the surplus was disposed of. The great London fire in 1666 stimulated Norway's lumber trade and it has been remarked that Norwegians warmed themselves by the fire of London. Only a small part of the heat, however, reached the Norwegians, for the trade was largely in the hands of foreigners.

When the Hanseatic merchants lost their grip on Norwegian trade, their place was mainly taken by the Dutch, who in the 1640's had secured favorable treaties that gave them virtual control of the lumber export, and in those years about three hundred Dutch ships made two or three trips every year to get Norwegian lumber. They could dictate the price, and when the volume of trade went up, the price went down. They never obtained the strangle hold on trade, however, that the Germans enjoyed. In the 'fifties the English also entered the Norwegian trade and later outdistanced the Dutch in the eastern ports. Norwegian burghers complained and petitioned the government for help, and they found a ready hearing.

The government realized that to bring money into the country it must encourage the development of a Norwegian merchant fleet. This was done by offering special advantages to home-owned ships, but as long as the citizens could not take over the whole trade, care had to be taken not to offend foreign powers. Increased privileges were given to defense ships, which were to carry on trade in time of peace and defend the coast in war, and home-owned vessels carrying lumber were to pay export duty on only five-sixths of the cargo, while the measure of their tonnage was falsified to the disadvantage of foreigners. Repeated efforts were made to get Norwegian ships to engage in traffic with Greenland, but all attempts failed. On the other hand, some trade with Portugal and a lively commerce with France were developed, although the authorities had their scruples about the importation of lace and silk and wine which would encourage extravagant French fashions in food and dress. Bergen merchants also traded with Archangel and took some part in the colonial traffic, though most of that was in the hands of companies in Copenhagen.

In 1680 began an unprecedented growth in seafaring and shipbuilding which in the early 'nineties reached proportions not again equaled before the last of the eighteenth century. The Norwegians had always done some shipbuilding. From the Southland simple little homemade boats had long been plying the Skager-Rak to Jutland. And Bergen had early begun to build a merchant fleet. But now new shipyards sprang up along the whole southern shore; in two decades the tonnage almost trebled, and five hundred Norwegian merchantmen sailed the seas. During the great European wars of the 'nineties Norwegians competed successfully with the great sea powers, even in the carrying trade. An armed neutrality pact was made with Sweden, and four times a year large merchant fleets set out, convoyed by Swedish and Danish-

Norwegian men-of-war. Losses were heavy but did not prevent Norwegian boats from carrying lumber and tar, fish and hides, meat, butter, and other products to nearly all the shores of Europe—to the White Sea, England, France, the Netherlands, Portugal, and the Mediterranean. The modern age in Norway's seafaring had begun.

How modern the age was is shown by a glance at all the new ways by which business was facilitated. Much was achieved by private enterprise: insurance companies in Copenhagen and Hamburg, the exchange in Bergen, new banking methods with notes, credits, and bills of exchange, and business connections with banks in London, Cadiz, and Lisbon. The government did even more. A Danish-Norwegian bank brought order in a confusion of moneys, often poor, and the first paper currency was issued. Paths began to be transformed into wagon roads and the first lighthouses were erected. Navigation schools were established in Christiania and Bergen, where embryo skippers and merchants could get some knowledge of modern bookkeeping, business correspondence, foreign languages, cartography, and navigation. And when they came into the chief ports in Western Europe, they could seek the aid of Danish-Norwegian consuls.

Norway had attained a well-developed economic system and was much richer than ever before. Wealth had been produced within the country and capital attracted from abroad. To what extent the new prosperity benefited the Norwegian people is another matter.

¶ The whole social fabric became more complex in the seventeenth century than it had been earlier. It is evident that the population increased considerably. Though exact figures are lacking, it is estimated that in 1665 the population was about 440,000 and by the end of the century 500,000. More striking and better known is the increased mobility of the population, the immigration and emigration.

Not since the Viking Age had Norway lost so many of her young people by emigration as in this century. Dutch skippers, who visited every seaport in Norway, liked Norwegian seamen, for they were capable, frugal, and brave, and thousands of young men from the Southland shipped on Dutch vessels. A few came home, but many more stayed in Amsterdam, and others moved to the Netherlands with their families because of better opportunities to get work. London, too, had a sizable settlement of Norwegians, and Norwegians helped to man the fleet of Peter the Great. Some went to America, probably most to the Dutch colonies.[6] It is interesting that many of the old Knickerbockers have among their ancestors a Norwegian midwife, Trina Jonas, and her daughter, Anneke Jans. The exodus from Norway was so extensive that the government feared a dearth of soldiers and sailors and therefore forbade emigration. The prohibition had little effect, and the movement continued until the boom of the 1780's offered greater opportunities at home. Meanwhile Amsterdam was the center for recruiting Norwegian sailors for the warships and merchant fleets of Western Europe. Even the Danish-Norwegian king had to send thither to induce the men he needed to return to the service of their own country.

The Norwegian emigrants exerted little influence in the countries where they settled. Moneyless and unschooled, they came to older, more highly developed communities, which afforded them little opportunity to rise. Nor did the movement exert any appreciable influence on the mother country, though many individual Norwegians—sailors and soldiers, craftsmen and students, young noblemen and inveterate wanderers—traveled abroad and returned home bringing with them new things and ideas.

More significant was the immigration into Norway. No foreigners played a larger part than the royal officials, who increased in number with the expansion of the functions of the state. Except for the clergymen, many of whom were Norwegians, they were generally Danes, though sometimes Germans from Holstein. Some stayed for life, and their families became Norwegians; others, chiefly in the higher positions, returned to their homeland. Of another type were the refugees from war-ravaged sections of the continent, especially from South Jutland. Many were poor people who had lost their all and hoped for a new start in a peaceful land. A few were political refugees, some were businessmen who had traded in Norway or invested capital there and who, when war destroyed their livelihood at home, moved to Norway.

The chief inducements to immigration were the opportunities offered by an undeveloped country with resources which were not being utilized, and the special privileges offered by a government which sought to attract foreign enterprise. Though mining brought capital and skilled labor, the influx into the towns was even more important.

[6] John O. Evjen, *Scandinavian Immigrants in New York, 1630-1674*, Minneapolis, 1916. Torstein Jahr, "Normenn I Ny Nederland, Anneke Jans fra Marstrand, hennes farm og hennes slegt," *Symra*, 9:9-34 (1913). Halvdan Koht, "First Scandinavian Settlers in America," *American-Scandinavian Review*, 32:136-142 (June 1944).

There came laborers and sailors, adventurers and social climbers, but most of the newcomers were substantial burghers who brought with them business experience and money. As they belonged to the upper strata of society, their influence was out of proportion to their number; and as they became citizens and eventually Norwegian in interest, their talent and money stayed in the country. Not before the next century, however, was the full significance of their leadership felt, for at first their efforts were concentrated upon economic affairs. But even so, the most distinguished Norwegians of the time had foreign blood in their veins. The ancestors of the beloved hero Tordenskjold, for example, were from Holstein and Holland.

Connection with the old homeland was not broken. Boys were sent back to England, Germany, the Netherlands, and Denmark for their schooling, and travel and trade continued. In the southern coastal districts the constant seafaring created a milieu all its own. Characteristic were the homes of retired skippers which, though built in Norwegian style, were furnished with articles from across the sea. Dutch influence predominated, with English coming in more toward the close of the century. In the towns foreign influence was especially marked, coloring every phase of daily life. In Bergen the children used the same games and songs as the children in Hamburg and the Netherlands and of course had Dutch skates, and their elders built their houses in Dutch or English style and dressed in French fashions at least for state occasions. In the East the Danish and German elements were stronger, the wealthy in Christiania, for example, coming largely from South Jutland.

There was a growing cleavage between the wealthier burghers—merchants, shipowners, and lumbermen—mostly of foreign descent, and the class of small shopkeepers, artisans, and the like, of Norwegian blood. Craftsmen played an important part in the development of the cities. The royal regulations of Christian IV in 1621 gave their guilds, formed in the sixteenth century, the status of legal corporations and laid down rules for their organization. Although many crafts were unorganized, the seventeenth century was a flourishing age for the guilds, especially in Bergen. Each had its own rules and government, its guild hall, banner, and seal. Handsome goblets and jugs used on festive occasions indicate the wealth of the guilds, as well as the high standard of workmanship they maintained. The rules governing apprenticeship were stringent, and many journeymen traveled abroad before becoming masters, the international connections of their guild insuring them a ready welcome and needed aid wherever they came. There seems to have been no nationalistic basis for the class feeling; but, though they made money especially in the flush times of the 'eighties, the craftsmen chafed under the limited opportunities open to them, and during the crisis following the European peace in 1697 the resentment became especially vocal.

During the fire of 1702, the worst of many conflagrations that Bergen suffered, the people watched the flames consume the houses of the wealthy without lifting a finger. Vice Statholder Frederik von Gabel, who happened to be present, pleaded in vain with the people. Upon looking into the causes of the obvious class hatred, however, his sympathy was with the small burghers, and he berated the leading men for taking unto themselves illegal privileges and changing the town government into a narrow oligarchy, contrary to the king's wishes. He wrote eloquent letters to the king advising reforms to help the poorer burghers, but said nothing of the proletarians, who by this time constituted quite a group and whose condition was wretched. They were tolerated, as they supplied servants and unskilled labor, but were not admitted to citizenship. Although the king was in sympathy with von Gabel's proposals, little was done and before long the Great Northern War consumed the energy of the government.

There were sharp rivalries also between the cities. The chartered cities which had royal privileges were few. They were the old towns, Trondheim, Bergen, Stavanger, Skien, Tønsberg, and Christiania, the newer Fredrikstad, and the artificially created Christiansand, besides three in Baahus which in 1660 was ceded to Sweden. There had grown up, however, a great many small seaport towns, eighty-two in number, of which all but eight were on the southern seaboard, nearly all the product of the lumber industry. The chartered cities appealed to the king to reinforce their privileges, and were assigned the monopoly of trade in definite districts. Some of the smaller towns were to be abandoned and the others were to buy goods only for home use, not for resale. But there were hundreds of violations of these orders; little by little the rigorous restrictions were abandoned, and the new towns granted special privileges. While some small towns vanished with the decline of the lumber trade, others grew into prosperous little cities.

The population cannot be so simply divided into city people and country people as in earlier days, for communities arose that were neither rural nor urban. About the larger mines there grew up mining towns with a character all their own, the most important being Kongsberg and Røros. In both places towns were laid out with straight streets and rows of company-built houses for the laborers. There were also barracks near the entrance to the mines, a church, administration buildings, and stately homes for the higher officials, a little jail, and perhaps a tavern. In the outskirts some of the laborers made a clearing in the woods, built a home, and kept a cow or two.

The mine owners depended on the country people for their transportation. The farmers hauled the ore to the smelting furnace and the metal to the nearest city, bringing back supplies for the community. And they brought to the mines charcoal and wood in such masses that mining became more destructive of the forests than lumbering. Young men from the farms also worked in the mines during the slack season, others drifted in from here and there or moved in from the farms, but most of the skilled workmen were brought from Germany. The mining communities, therefore, became different and distinct from the rural surroundings, especially at Røros, where the countryside was thinly populated. Both city and foreign influences were felt in the daily life of the miners, in their dress, their food, and their speech. They were united in a common effort to assert their human rights against the company which controlled their life and owned the town.

At Røros, particularly, disputes between laborers and management were numerous. The men complained that they had to work longer hours than their contract called for and make up time lost by holidays, that they were paid in poor goods, or that some of them had not received their wages for two years. They appealed to local government officials, and if this brought no results they sent a representative to lay their cause before the king, just as the farmers did. Once the popular "Fiddle-Ola" was chosen as an emissary. When the management did not care to have Ola go, and found a pretext for arresting him, it caused a near-riot. Not daring to break the king's seal on the lock, the miners lifted up the whole building, freed Ola, and sent him on his way. As a rule the men acted with restraint, and the disputes led to reforms and regulations which gave greater security and better working conditions. By the close of the century the mining communities had taken shape and the miners had developed class consciousness and even a certain class pride.

The lumber industry, like mining, developed a new labor class of its own. Around the large sawmills in eastern Norway there gathered a large group of poor workers who owned nothing but their labor, and lived in the utmost poverty in little huts or barracks crowded about the mills. Among them were drivers who guided the long caravans of perhaps fifty sleighs that hauled lumber to the wharves. The horses knew the way, so one man could take care of from three to five sleighs. When such a train returned empty, it was a terror to all travelers. The drivers shouted and yelled and the horses galloped wildly, turning in of their own accord at some tavern where their master was in the habit of stopping for whiskey. Not before the next century were the lumber workers able to improve their conditions by acting as a group.

The vast majority of the people—probably nine-tenths—were still farmers. As the new age brought no changes in agricultural methods, the daily life on the farm went on much as of old, and in many ways the country people clung to their traditional idea of self-sufficiency and subsistence farming. Nevertheless, they became more and more involved in money economy. The general rise of prices, which continued until about 1670, worked to the disadvantage of the farmers, but through consistent efforts they held their own until better times came.

The most persistent and bitter struggle of the country people was against the trade monopoly of the cities. In Nordland the fishermen-farmers became practically economic serfs of the Bergen merchants, as they had to sell their fish and buy grain, and in Finmark conditions were even worse. Although the rest of the country was much more prosperous, it also depended more on the importation of grain than in the past. Stock farming had increased at the expense of grain raising, so that only the East produced enough grain for its own use. Every one of the many regulations for the monopoly of trade by the cities was secretly evaded or openly defied. It is interesting that the German merchants in Bergen often sided with the country people. When the government decreed that grain should be imported from Denmark only, protests came from town and country alike, as the supply of Danish grain was inadequate and inferior. Every crop failure and famine in Norway caused the bars to be let down for the time being. In spite of opposition the cities attracted most of the trade, and burghers established stores and taverns in rural communities. Yet the country people were not absolutely at the mercy of the burghers, for when the big markets were held there was freedom of trade and all laws slept. Some old markets had been discontinued or moved to a city, but others were held as from pre-viking days at a crossroad or the head of a fjord. There people gathered from far and wide, from city and farm, coming by boat or sled, and there was selling and buying, fighting and drinking, frolic and fun. These markets served as a general clearinghouse for the internal trade.

More dramatic and more successful than the struggle about trade was the conflict between tenant farmers and landlords. The rise of prices and standard of living tempted the proprietors to increase their income by fair means and foul, and so exorbitant were their demands that had these exactions become permanent the tenants would have been reduced to a position akin to that of the peasants farther south. In 1660 the financial strain on the government was so severe that much of the crown land was sold. It was bought in large lots by wealthy nobles or burghers. Tenants who under a lenient king had enjoyed almost the security of owners were now transferred to private proprietors and felt the change keenly. Some even asked the king to buy the land back and offered to pay half of the re-purchase price. This was not possible, but thanks chiefly to Gyldenløve, the king inaugurated a policy friendly to the country people. Gyldenløve urged on the king the necessity of protecting the tenants. A commission appointed to investigate the situation sided entirely with them, and in 1685 regulations were made to prevent abuses on the part of the proprietors. The restrictions were radical beyond anything else in the age. Two years later they were incorporated into the law of Christian V, though somewhat moderated, and stand as a notable achievement of the popular statholder. While they could not always be enforced, it meant much to the tenants to have the law on their side.

The farmers had awakened to an appreciation of the importance of owning their land, and the remarkable vigor of the whole rural population is seen in its readiness and ability to utilize the opportunities that were opened to it. In the late 'eighties crown lands were again offered for sale. This time smaller, individual farms were sold and prices had declined. And now the buyers were the earlier tenants, who often became owners of land they had worked for years. This shows that the farmers had money in their chests which now was brought out—money made perhaps by selling timber or working in the mines or sawmills. Before long private proprietors also began to sell one farm after another. The new laws tended to make landowning less profitable, and the new economic conditions turned investments into commercial or industrial ventures. And again the tenants were the buyers. A little later, in 1723, a law required anyone who sold a farm to give the tenant the first chance to buy.

This transfer of both crown and private lands into the hands of the farmers continued into the eighteenth century. Often land was sold cheap, for it was difficult to get renters, as the expanding economic life offered other openings than farming—in the woods, in the mines, on the sea, or even in foreign lands. In the middle of the seventeenth century only a fourth of the farmers owned their own land, while three-fourths were tenants. A century later the figures had been reversed so that three-fourths of the farmers were owners and perhaps two-thirds of the land was owned by the tillers.

Ownership of land gave dignity and social prestige. The number of substantial odal farmers, who as in the past were the leaders in their community, became much larger, forming a rural aristocracy. This raised the whole level of the rural population at the very time when the nobility was declining. The full effect of this was to be felt in the next century.

¶ Only weak reflections of the great art of the Renaissance had reached Norway in the Age of the Reformation. The church, which in the Middle Ages had been the center of artistic production, now destroyed more than it contributed, and fires added to the ruins. The beautiful monasteries, episcopal residences, and even churches, which had been demolished by royal command, served as quarries for constructing forts and dwelling houses. The most important buildings of the sixteenth century were the massive tower and handsome mansion erected in Bergen by Erik Rosenkrantz, who employed Scottish stonemasons. Dignified residences in the formal yet simple style of the Renaissance began to make their appearance. Characteristic is a resolution concerning country parsonages adopted by a meeting of the clergy in 1589: "The buildings must not be too countrified or modest or placed without any order, but rather (where the terrain permits it) form a square facing the sun (as is customary in Denmark) and have an appearance worthy of the ministers. The houses should be few and spacious, divided conveniently into rooms, rather than many small cottages." General use of chimneys and stoves made several stories possible, and more glass windows, letting in light, encouraged the rich, colorful interior decoration expressive of the exuberant joy of living of the Renaissance. The assertive individualism of the age is seen in the new emphasis on privacy for the individual and the family. The formal gardens were quite in harmony with the buildings.

Imposing manor houses, common in the other Scandinavian countries, were scarce because the native nobility lacked the necessary means. Among the few built in the seventeenth century the most famous was that of the Bjelke family at Austraat, which was destroyed by fire in

1916. Through the parsonages and other official residences the new influence were gradually making themselves felt in the rural districts, and in the homes of the well-to-do farmers the old smoke-blackened walls were beginning to give way to rich tapestry, bright painting, and carving. In Christiania, where building regulations limited the use of wood, brick in warm tones of red and yellow in a style suggestive of Christian IV's came into use in the seventeenth century. At this time church building, which had been almost at a standstill, was resumed, the finest survivals being cruciform churches with a tall, slender spire. In the midst of new trends, conservatism remained strong. The Hanseatic quarter of Bergen, for example, which was one of the historic survivals from a by-gone age—long before the German influx—was rebuilt in the old Gothic style even after the fire of 1702. There was no distinctive line between the creative artists and the skilled craftsmen, and, as in the humbler trades, the artists were associated in guilds with close international connections. Many of them were of foreign birth, but generally they became thoroughly acclimated in their adopted land and their work underwent a subtle change, adapting itself to the northern traditions, tastes, and temperament. Often it is impossible to know whether an artist is a native or a foreigner; and while Norway was enriched from abroad, the country also lost some talented men who went to other lands never to return. Impulses from abroad reached even isolated mountain communities, but the people were not mere imitators. They made the new so thoroughly their own that, as a critic has remarked, even the exotic acanthus leaf became as Norwegian as though it had grown on a mountainside in Gudbrandsdal.

The age excelled in wood carving, which was used even more than painting to decorate the interior of the churches. Altar, pulpit, and font were richly decorated. Before long the earlier Renaissance restraint gave way to restless rococo luxuriance. Scrolls, intertwining vines, and flowers in buoyant profusion surrounding figures of spirited angels and strong apostles or whole biblical scenes produced a festive effect even though a bit excessive and heavy. Almost as rich was the wood carving that decorated the homes of burghers and officials. Much of the finest work was done by foreign masters, but the Norwegians, who had excelled in this art from pre-viking times, had not lost their old talent and skill. The most famous Norwegian sculptor in wood and ivory was Magnus Berg, a country lad from Hedmark. He was discovered by Gyldenløve, who sent him abroad to study. He never returned home, and his work is found in foreign museums, mostly in Denmark.

In other crafts Norway also ranked high. The goldsmiths and silversmiths were on a par with any in Europe. Tin and brass were also used with good effect, and the craftsmen employed by the iron works produced designs of high artistic quality. Tapestry weaving was also revived, especially in the rural districts. Gobelin influences seem apparent, but in the designs straight strong lines took the place of soft curves as the motifs took on a northern character.

The only paintings from the sixteenth century which deserve any attention are a limited number of vigorous and individual portraits, chiefly of the leading clergymen of the day. In the following century this form of art showed a marked development, as it met the demands of the times. The interest in secular painting was still largely confined to portraits. The age abounds in pictures of dignified prelates and ample burghers and their wives, often surrounded by their large families. They were done after the Dutch manner, often by mere skilled workmen, but sometimes by artists of marked talent. They have left us a few delicate sensitive pictures of youth and of women, but more portraits of the domineering, vigorous men characteristic of the age. Altar paintings were also much in demand, as there was a revived interest in expressing religious truths pictorially and in adding life and richness to the church interiors. Patterns from the South were followed, but the execution was original in color, detail, and expression, and sometimes the result had considerable real merit. Thus foundations had been laid for a rich unfolding of art in the next century.

¶ The nationalistic humanism of the Reformation period ebbed out in the early seventeenth century, leaving Norway poor indeed in learning and literary production. Though wealth was increasing, the country lacked the surplus necessary for sustained scholarly or literary achievements. Even the well-to-do burghers, except a few lumber magnates, worked hard by the side of their hired help and had little thought for anything beyond amassing a modest competence and adding some distinction to their homes, leaving bookish interests to the clergy and a few others. The intellectual poverty was not due to isolation. European influences were more dominant than in the Reformation period and cultural impulses were received from all countries of Western Europe. Norwegians had to go to Copenhagen for a higher education, as they had no university at home, and had to have their writings published in Denmark. In 1643 the first printing press was at last established in Norway through the efforts of a Danish clergyman.

Among the few scholarly works of importance is *Historia Rerum Norvegicarum*, a history of Norway from mythical times to 1387, written in Latin by the Icelander Thormod Torfæus. Although uncritical, he possessed wide knowledge, and his book includes summaries of many manuscripts that have since disappeared. An excellent source for the economic conditions of the time is a large topographical-statistical work, *Danmarkis oc Norgis Fructbar Herlighed* (Denmark's and Norway's Fruitful Splendor). The author was Arent Berntssønn, a Norwegian who lived in Denmark and used the Danish language, but wrote about the land of his birth with warm affection.

The poets continued to write Danish with a strong Norwegian coloring, but the influence of the High Renaissance introduced a new emphasis on form and a taste for the sonnet, Alexandrine verse, high-sounding adjectives and allusions to classical mythology, much of which seemed out of harmony with northern thought and expression. Though the conscious striving for artistry was a first step toward the development of modern poetry, the many rhymesters of the age produced little of artistic value. Occasional verses abounded, wordy, lugubrious, and pompous, written for funerals, weddings, fires, natural catastrophes, or events in the royal family. The religious poetry was of somewhat greater worth and made the widest appeal in its own age. The most popular of the many hymn writers was Dorothea Engelbretsdatter, a minister's wife in Bergen. Her "mournful numbers" and pedestrian style satisfied the taste of her time, and her simplicity and warm, somewhat sentimental sincerity made her generally loved. A few of her many hymns have been retained in modern hymnaries. She and her poetry won the high esteem even of Petter Dass, Norway's one and only seventeenth century poet of real greatness.

Petter Dass towers above his contemporaries like a gigantic mountain dwarfing all its surroundings. He was the son of a Scotsman, Peter Dundass, who with his sister Maria fled to Bergen during the difficulties with Charles I. The newcomer married the daughter of a sheriff of Haalogaland and settled there as a merchant on a little island. Here Petter Dass was born and in that vicinity he spent most of his life. He went to school in Bergen and was fortunate in that the Latin school was still conducted according to the ideas of Geble Pederssøn. He then spent two years as a student in Copenhagen, when lack of funds forced him to return home. For some years he tried all the toil and hardship of farming in the far North to eke out the meager salary of a curate which, he said, gave him bread but no butter. He then became pastor at Alstahaug where he remained until his death. There he lived a full, rich, and happy life. He worked ceaselessly, traveling about his extensive parish, going by boat from island to island, shunning no hardships, dauntless in the face of danger. He lived with and for his people, and his ample income and frugal life enabled him to obey his generous impulses and help those in distress. The hardy and dictatorial, yet gentle, pastor won the love and respect of his parishioners.

It was his poetry, however, that made his name a household word throughout Nordland both among the people of his own time and in later generations. It became the property of the people before it received general recognition among his own class, and was kept fresh in their memory when the educated neglected it. Dass himself felt that there was in his poetry something for all classes. He was fortunate in having a circle of congenial friends and relatives, both men and women, among whom he circulated hand-written copies of his poems and to whom he dedicated his catechism songs. These poems, explaining Luther's *Little Catechism* and written, as the author says, to teach first the grown-ups and then the children, were probably the most popular of his works. His other religious poems were also dearly loved. Just at this time reading was spreading to the common people, and their chief interest beyond the daily grind was religious. Dass had the mastery of form that his times demanded, and his contemporaries did not mind that he occasionally fell into the stilted wordiness characteristic of his age. His sincerity and strength, his warmth unmarred by even a touch of sentimental emotionalism, his optimism, and his simple—to us naïve—directness struck a responsive chord in the hearts of the people. Even his religious poetry breathes the atmosphere of the region in which it was produced, but his deep love for his own land and people is best expressed in his chief secular poem. *Nordlands Trompet* (The Trumpet of Nordland) is a detailed description in verse of Nordland, its geography, its nature and climate, its resources, its people and their struggles to wrest a livelihood from a stormy sea and meager land. There is a salty tang and smell of fish about the poem, and the feeling of short, stormy winter days and long, dark nights, as well as the spell of the northern summers. And Dass writes of the struggle of the people during the most difficult period in the history of Nordland, not as an outsider filled with pity, but as one of themselves, one who has shared their poverty and hardships as well as their courage and acceptance of the life imposed upon them by the nature of the land in which they live.

But with it all, Dass and his poetry were a product of the upper-class sphere.

The folk literature continued an unbroken development from the Middle Ages. The old songs lived in the memory of the people and a few new were added, and many of the fairy tales, too, took on new form. New literary impulses reached the people through Danish translations from English, French, and German. There were romances about kings and knights, and tales of thrilling adventure, heroic deeds, and fierce passions. These were retold in the language of the people and before long became thoroughly Norwegian. Some of the folk literature was written down and a few poems have been preserved in copies from the late sixteenth century. Soon after the printing press was introduced, a few items were published in the dialects, enough to show that the speech of the people has changed very little from that time to the present. There were even plans afoot for a large Norwegian dictionary, and a few clergymen had begun to collect words in their parishes, but nothing came of it. Not a few educated men had an interest in the language and literature of the people, sometimes patriotic, more often purely academic, but fully in harmony with the taste of the age which foreshadowed the romanticism of the future.

Thus two literary streams, both mere insignificant trickles except for Petter Dass, flowed side by side yet apart. Any contact between them came through the church.

¶ After the upheaval of the Reformation, the church settled down to a period of peace and slipped into the Age of Orthodoxy. Only faint repercussions of the Counter Reformation and religious wars reached Norway. Early in the period some Calvinistic tendencies were detected in the church, but Christian IV was inclined to ignore them as not dangerous. He even wished to give Calvinists a certain religious freedom, for he was anxious to make Dutch businessmen feel welcome in the country; but public opinion was against him and he abandoned the idea. Toward any manifestations of Romanism the policy was more uncompromising. Rather active Jesuit propaganda was carried on, using Sweden as a base. The most striking figure in the movement was an able young Norwegian named Lauritz Nilssøn (*Klosterlasse*) who had studied in foreign Jesuit schools. Not a few other young men who had also attended Jesuit institutions in Prussia, which offered them an inexpensive education supposedly neutral in religious matters, returned with Roman predilections. When Romanism was detected in the church, clergy and government joined to take prompt action. Four clergymen lost their positions and were banished, and it was decreed that no appointments in church or school were open to men who had studied in Prussia. In 1624 all Jesuits were banished and the death penalty imposed for returning to the country. With Gustaf Adolf's victories in Germany, fear of the Roman church became less acute, and Christian IV even allowed Catholic worship to be conducted in a few specified places in the country. But these services were for foreigners only, not for his subjects. Jesuits and monks were still forbidden the country, as were also Jews.

Orthodox Lutheranism was the only legal religion for all subjects of the king, and it had come to be generally accepted by the people without any questions or doubts either as to the truth of the doctrines or the power of the king to impose them on his realm. The government also tried by one regulation after another to check the wild, coarse manners and morals of the day; but such legislation proved ineffective, and there continued to be more orthodox profession than holy living, even among the clergy. Yet there was a noticeable improvement throughout the century, and to this advance the work of the clergy contributed more than any other factor.

The clergy itself improved. The rescript of 1629, requiring that all clergymen take a theological examination in Copenhagen, was a step toward higher standards, although the test was far from exacting. Some of the ministers, however, sought greater learning in the universities of Scotland, England, France, the Netherlands, or Germany. Royal appointment probably gave the country rather better men than the earlier, supposedly popular election had done. Though not a few scandal stories about preachers have been preserved from that day, closer study has revealed that most of them were, according to the standards of the age, upright, earnest men who filled their positions adequately. At any rate much of the disrespect for the church which had come with the Reformation gave way to reverence.

The sermons had little to do with producing this change. A few ministers preached simply and directly in the dialect of the people, and some spoke with warm persuasiveness, but most of the sermons were interminably long, dry, formal, and filled with far-fetched allusions and learned obscurities. Any departure from the accepted form or orthodox content was dangerous. Much more effective was the instruction in the catechism, on which great emphasis was placed. Books of questions and answers were written as an aid in this instruction. Most of the teaching was done by word of mouth, but those who wanted to learn to read and write could get private instruction from the parish clerk or the preacher. Not a few availed themselves of the opportunity, and occasionally a wealthy farmer even employed a tutor in the family as did the officials. Family prayers, week-day meetings, and the writing and reading of devotional literature show a reviving interest in things religious.

Hymns were almost as important as the catechism. Late in this century Norwegian writers produced many hymns that satisfied the demand of the age both in form and emotional expression. Besides Petter Dass and Dorothea Engelbretsdatter, perhaps Samuel Bruun deserves mention. But the greatest contribution came from Denmark. In 1699 a new authorized hymnary was published under the title *Kingos Psalmebog*. The best part of the book was the eighty-five of Thomas Kingo's own hymns. They cover as wide a scope as Christianity itself, and he writes out of a deep personal experience, expressing himself sometimes with majestic grandeur and at other times through simple imagery. He took, as he says, "gay, worldly tunes" and with true musicianship transformed them into new chorales. The fresh melodies helped to find for his hymns a ready entrance into the hearts of the people. Though some of his religious poems may well be discarded as of another age, he has given his church a wealth of hymns of ageless depth and beauty.

Thus in the midst of the Age of Orthodoxy there were in the church, too, some manifestations pointing toward richer growth in the future. To many, however, a Black Book of occult arts seemed as powerful as the Good Book, and religion mainly a useful weapon against all the evil forces that threatened on every hand. Later influences were to develop more marked individualism, and the dark cloud of superstition was to be penetrated in part by the enlightenment of a new age.

CHAPTER 13

A HALF CENTURY OF QUIET GROWTH, 1720-1770

A NEW ERA DAWNED with the close of the Great Northern War. The whole North was rejoicing at the return of peace and facing the future with optimism, while it grappled with post-war problems. As the two states were now quite evenly balanced, neither Sweden nor Denmark-Norway could attempt to play the part of a great power, and both felt apprehensive about the Russian Bear which had suddenly grown very large and come alarmingly near. Their general international position had not improved, but the peace which all three countries sorely needed had been attained, and with it the opportunity for concentration on internal development.

For Denmark-Norway the early eighteenth century was a period of few striking, epic events, and Norway played a less important part in political and international affairs than in the seventeenth century. The new equilibrium in the North had removed the danger of conquest by Sweden; Denmark's position on her southern boundary line, which had been the chief issue in the country's foreign policy, had been strengthened, and this orientation toward the south was even more marked after 1720. Thus it was found necessary to maintain the army at about war strength, while the fleet, in which Norway was strongly represented, was neglected. Still another reason for Norway's humbler place in the union was the decrease in trade—and thereby in revenue—which came early in the period and took many years to overcome. Nevertheless, Norway had a share in the full, many-colored life of the Enlightenment, and experienced a far richer cultural life than in the century which had just passed.

¶ Frederik IV was the last ruler to retain personal control of the government. To prevent the growth of national separatism he filled most posts in Denmark with Holsteiners or other Germans and sent Danes to govern Norway. To prevent any one man from gaining too much power he kept so many details in his own hands that the administration was weakened; and corruption was increased, as often happens, under post-war conditions. Lower officials complained that they could obtain appointment only by bribery, and burghers evaded their duties as citizens and criticized the magistrates. One rural sheriff was so tyrannical that the people wrote to the king, "We beg most humbly that Your Majesty make us your own slaves, but not the thralls of another." Frederik succeeded, however, in greatly improving the money affairs of the state during the first years of peace. He practiced stringent economy in the government, although he was very lavish in his court. His success was all the more remarkable because the tax system was extremely complicated and the revision which was planned could not be carried through. Moreover, the king was careful not to add to the taxes of the Norwegian rural population, toward which he felt especially friendly. And indeed their burdens were heavy enough as it was. But even before his death the control was beginning to slip out of the king's hands.

The Oldenburg family, which in the two preceding centuries had produced strong, handsome men and able rulers, suffered a period of decline in the eighteenth century. Christian VI (1730-1746), though kindly and well-intentioned, was regal neither in looks nor in character. He was small and insignificant in outward appearance, weak, hesitant, and of mediocre intellect. Morally he was above the average and lived a quiet, model family life. Both he and the queen were deeply, sincerely religious, but their piety was of the gloomiest pietistical type. It was natural for Christian VI to withdraw from the public, and the fact that he used the German language almost exclusively isolated him still further from the people. Quite different was Frederik V (1746-1766), who learned Danish in the public houses as he caroused with his wild companions. All pietistical bars were now down, and the gay king was popular in the capital, though mentally quite incapable of ruling. Even worse was Christian VII (1766-1808), who became actually insane. Inevitably the government fell into the hands of the officials. Christian VI had placed a great many of his own personal friends, most of them Germans, in office. On the whole they were competent, reliable, though unimaginative bureaucrats. The machinery of administration was complicated and slow and the volume of business great, so many a proposal was lost in transit as it made its devious way from department to department. As the kings, conscious of their own weaknesses, distrusted others, no minister was given sufficient authority to lend unity, direction, or force to the government.

In theory the king was absolute, and practically no one desired to change this. To the common people he was still the paternal ruler by the grace of God, and the popular devotion to royalty was little influenced by the personal character of the king. This was especially true of the Norwegians, who were far removed from contact with court life. Christian VI made a long tour through Norway with a party of 177 persons; and a brief trip was made by Frederik V, the last of the absolute monarchs to visit the kingdom. Both kings were received with extravagant expressions of abject flattery in atrocious verse. Although these professions ring rather hollow and lack personal warmth, no doubt the old loyalty to the sovereign was still strong.

The officials, though somewhat more critical, were also loyal to the king, regardless of his personal qualities. But among them the new "enlightened" conception of monarchy was becoming increasingly prevalent. They paid respect to the king not as an individual, but as an expression or symbol—almost an incarnation—of that higher something, the state. To them the welfare of the state was of primary importance, and to this all personal, group, or class interests must be subordinated. The officials, whether from the landed aristocracy or the merchant class, became professional bureaucrats who made the service of the state their life work. Their power was great, their confidence that they alone knew what was to the advantage of the state was unbounded, and their conviction that the people existed for the good of the state was unshaken. Most of them were Germans and brought no sense of nationality into the administration, but as a Danish national sense awakened, they were inclined to think and speak of the double monarchy as Danish.

In spite of this policy, Norway, while practically shorn of its dependencies, continued to exist as a separate kingdom both legally and in the conception of the people, although they had little control over their own affairs. The greater political currents of the day, especially in foreign affairs, were less felt in Norway than in the preceding period. It was of importance to the country that the Danish diplomats succeeded in maintaining neutrality in the midst of European wars. The chief credit for this belongs to Johan Hartvig Ernst Bernstorff, the minister of foreign affairs under Frederik V and the ablest member of his government. While this devious diplomacy of neutrality did not secure for Denmark-Norway a prominent place on the international scene, it was profitable and no doubt popular.

In the local government of the cities the people still retained some influence, as the officials appointed by the king seldom took any important action in opposition to the representatives elected by the burghers. Even in the country leading men met for the court sessions, or *thing*, and the local bailiffs were chosen from the common people, who also controlled poor relief and, after 1741, the elementary schools. The majority of the sheriffs, judges, local governors, and clergymen were also Norwegians though not of the common people. But the higher the rank the fewer were Norwegians, and most bishops and governors were Danish, as was every statholder. Even officials of Danish birth, however, identified themselves more than before with the country in which they served and joined with Norwegians in demands that the government give due consideration to Norway's special interests. As the century advanced, the issue became more nationalistic and began to grow into a protest against both the unitary state idea and Danish supremacy. While the officials were the chief champions of Norway's rights, the only mass protest against the government came from the peasant class upon which the burdens weighed most heavily.

The cost of the government was constantly mounting and during the latter years of the reign of Frederik V the state debt grew enormously. The king was extravagant, and large sums were recklessly poured out as subsidies to private companies; and both the collection of taxes and the administration of state funds was often casual, inefficient, and even dishonest. The largest item in the budget was for military expenses; and when the Seven Years' War (1756-1763) broke out, Denmark-Norway found even neutrality expensive. An army including 13,500 Norwegians was kept in Holstein to guard the southern frontier. This added greatly to the debt, until finally something had to be done.

A German financial expert employed by the king conceived a scheme for laying an extra poll-tax on both kingdoms, exclusive of Finmark and the islands, to be used for paying the debt. The plan, which seemed very simple, was put into operation in 1762. An equal tax of one rixdollar a year was laid on every man, woman, and child above twelve years of age, even paupers and lepers, and upon the local officials devolved the duty of assessing on others the payment for those who were too poor to meet this extra demand. Taxes were already high, times were hard, and many of the poor never possessed a dollar. The only redeeming feature was that the tax was believed to be temporary.

So accustomed were the people to shoulder the loads placed upon them that in the first year the tax was paid in full, and the following year, too, collections were good. Complaints began to pour in, however, and in several localities collection was resisted. Most notable was the so-called Stril War. *Stril* (pl. *striler*) is a name applied to the peasants on the seaboard near Bergen. This was the poorest and most densely populated place in the country. The farms were small, the soil lean, and rents high—most of the land was owned by citizens of Bergen—and only by endless toil on land and sea could the people eke out a wretched living even without the extra tax. Remarkably successful agitation was carried on for a strike against the payment of the tax. Notes were distributed—no one could learn how or by whom—urging all men to meet in Bergen on March 1, 1765. Several hundred assembled, demanded to see the governor and presented to him a letter of complaint written for them by their judge. The governor promised to send their petition to the king and bade them return for an answer in six or seven weeks. But local troubles continued, and the reply from the king was slow in coming. On April 18 a crowd of several thousand peasants, augmented by many of the city people, thronged the streets of Bergen. Some of them broke into the governor's residence and manhandled both him and the sheriff, but on the whole the mob showed remarkable restraint and little damage was done to persons or property. The governor was thoroughly frightened, however, and shouted that he would refund the tax, which was more than anyone had thought of asking, and he was as good as his word. The *striler* returned to their homes victorious.

As the news of the events in Bergen spread, the refusal to pay the tax became more widespread. The authorities were thoroughly alarmed. A commission sent to study the Bergen uprising expressed sympathy for the common people, and upon its advice no penalties were meted out except to the leaders, who were punished more severely than the commission had recommended. It was realized that the tax was a mistake, that its collection had been bungled, and that it detracted from the dignity of the state to have a law that was not enforced; and in 1772 the extra tax was finally removed.

The whole rising was almost nationwide in its scope, although not national in its purpose. Earlier there had been only local incidents, generally directed against abuses by individual officials, while now a law and thereby the government itself was defied. The traditional loyalty to the king weakened as it became clear that the monarch no longer was in control of the government. The risings are evidence of a new sense of solidarity within the whole rural population, strengthened by increased communication and the spread of reading and the use of printed material. The people acquired a new self-confidence as they learned that if they all refused to pay a tax the government was powerless to enforce collection. They had achieved their end mainly through passive resistance. And, strangest of all, the greatest victory had been won, not by substantial leaders in the rural communities, but by a poverty-stricken, exploited group of peasants. "The people," said a sheriff who could hardly collect a penny of the tax, "want to prescribe the laws. Their word is brief: the common people say so, think so, want it that way; and with this we have to be content."

The background for this new spirit is to be found largely in the economic and social development that had taken place within the last four or five decades.

The economic progress of the people was of as great concern to the government as it had been earlier. Although there was less emphasis on the care of a paternalistic monarch for the well-being of his subjects, advance was made along the lines of poor relief and organized education, while the policy of protecting the people from undue exploitation was continued. The government had a pious wish to abolish poverty. The dominating idea, however, was that the welfare of the individual was important chiefly in so far as it would profit the state. Though the lower classes must not be abused, maintaining class distinction between master and servant was necessary for the increased production in all lines which the government desired. That economic prosperity was the very foundation of the strength and honor of the state was the opinion not only of bureaucrats, but of the intellectuals; and science, learning, literary talent, and even art were devoted to the service and glorification of the state.

Mercantilism was still the policy by which the government hoped to attain its ends, and Denmark-Norway was as strictly mercantilistic as perhaps any state in Europe. This meant the regulation and stimulation of the whole economic life so as to make the state as self-sufficient as possible. Only slowly did the newer idea of freedom of enterprise begin to find entrance into government circles. In the 'forties a member of the chancellery, Henrik Stampe, diplomatically and cautiously induced the authorities to adapt its policy to existing conditions and break down a few old restrictions. This beginning of *laissez-faire*, however, affected internal conditions only. In all relations to the outside world the mercantilistic theory was still applied.

In spite of the emphasis on the unitary state, the whole realm was not treated as a unit, some regulations applying to Denmark only and some exclusively to Norway. At times Denmark was given special advantages, and at other times Norway suffered because the bureaucrats did not understand conditions in the northern kingdom. Copenhagen was avowedly favored in order that Denmark-Norway, like Sweden and France, might have a great capital to reflect the glory of the absolutist state. The purpose was achieved. Copenhagen was an impressive city—cosmopolitan in character, though with a charm and personality all its own. Every monarch strove to build a palace and add to the city's magnificence and beauty. The wealth and culture of the age was centered there. But the whole realm had to bear the expense.

With this policy of economic centralization, Norway's interests were naturally not given the same consideration as in the past. This was especially evident in two ventures of the 'twenties. From its geographic position Finmark was considered politically important. Economically it had been more of a liability than an asset, but the government was interested in its development and had even been sending criminals up there in order to increase the white population. Now serious efforts were made to strengthen the political hold on the region and improve the general situation. But the economic conditions, not least among the Danish-Norwegian population, continued to be exceedingly bad, and the merchants from Trondheim and Bergen failed to bring in the goods needed. Bergen tried to secure a monopoly of the trade, but could not guarantee the payment the state demanded. It was then offered to the highest bidder, and in 1729 a group of Copenhagen merchants, headed by Jacob Severin, was granted the monopoly. The center of the Finmark commerce was thus moved from Bergen to Copenhagen.

The same fate met the trade with Greenland, which was also resumed upon the initiative of a clergyman named Hans Egede. He conceived the plan of combining colonization of Greenland and the development of trade with missionary work. He went to Bergen to interest merchants there in forming a company to carry on whaling and trade with Greenland and at the same time support his mission. In 1720 the Greenland Company was organized after the pattern of the day, with forty-seven stockholders. The government granted it exemption from duties, but did not dare to give it a monopoly for fear of offending the Netherlands. The following year an expedition of three ships set sail for Greenland, where a little group of forty-seven people formed a settlement on the western coast which they called Godthaab (Good Hope). Thus the second colonization of Greenland was begun.

But the men sent out by the company were unable to compete either with the skilled Eskimo hunters and fishermen or the more experienced Dutch whalers and traders. Before long the Bergen merchants ceased their activities and the government took over, and all Greenland traffic went out from Copenhagen. The same year an expedition of five ships was sent out to establish a second colony on a larger scale. A fort was built, but the settlement suffered from all the ills that generally afflicted early colonization—improvidence, dissension, mutiny, lack of wood and of fresh food, and finally scurvy. When Christian VI became king, he decided to abandon the whole project, and in 1731 all the colonists left except Hans Egede with his family and ten sailors. Yielding to the pleas of Egede and the persuasions of Copenhagen merchants, the king continued to equip a Greenland ship every year until 1734, when Jacob Severin was granted the monopoly of the Greenland trade also. In 1742 a new settlement called Frederikshaab was made, but though the Norwegians were valued as colonists, they had no share in the management.

Before long Severin was forced to withdraw both from the Finmark and Greenland trade. The government believed that in order to hold these outlying regions politically it was necessary to keep up commercial connection and supply them with food, and that this could best be done through monopolistic companies, the state taking over only when private enterprise failed. When a "general commercial company" which had obtained control of the Greenland, Iceland, and Finmark trade also had to give up, the government was, in 1774, forced to assume control.

The year 1729 marks an important retrogression, as Bergen and the kingdom of Norway lost both the Finmark and the Greenland trade. The immediate financial loss was not great, but it meant a weakening of Norwegian influence on the government. This is indicative of a general decline in shipping and industry, as the 'twenties, which had opened in gay optimism, came to a close in a far-reaching depression, the effect of which extended through the next decade and beyond.

Nevertheless, the age was permeated with the over-optimistic confidence characteristic of the eighteenth century that with relative ease hitherto undreamt-of material improvement could be achieved which would bring strength to the state and happiness to mankind. The need of increased production was keenly felt. New wants created in the flush years of the preceding century were continuing to grow, and the demands upon the people were also increasing. Furthermore, there was a growing population to feed and clothe. It has been estimated that in 1720 the people in Norway numbered about 530,000. In spite of emigration, epidemics of smallpox, and years of famine, there was a continuous, though uneven, increase during the next half century. This is indicated by the vital statistics which were begun in 1735. From then on the minister in every parish kept records of births and deaths, which were reported to Copenhagen through the bishop. In 1769 the first census of the realm was taken, and it shows the population to have been about 700,000.

Great effort was centered upon the struggle to meet the rising demands for food and the rural districts prospered. New land was cleared on the old farms and this entailed great labor. To supply this, thousands of crofters were settled on the outlying parts of the larger farms, and they with their families cleared large stretches of land. Generally they had the use of a small plot for which they paid rent in work, but much of their income came from day labor for farmers and lumbermen. Their lot was poverty and endless toil, often for hard masters and without economic security. However, in 1750 a law was promulgated to guarantee them legal protection by requiring that they be given a lease to the land they used, while the proprietor was assured that the tax on his farm would not be increased because of new crofts. Thus the crofters, of whom there had always been a few, became a legally recognized class of tenant peasants and their number increased rapidly, until by the close of the eighteenth century they composed one fourth of the rural population.

While the labor of the humble crofters was expanding the arable land, burghers and officials were striving to introduce new crops and better methods of agriculture. Many of them lived on their newly acquired land and managed it themselves instead of letting it out to tenants. They had capital and knowledge and made their estates into model farms. They read the works of French physiocrats and encyclopedists, and were—in theory if not in practice—enamored with Rousseau's ideas of the return to nature. Better plows and seeding machines were imported, the ground was better fertilized, new crops like clover, turnips, and, most important of all, the potato, were introduced. Vegetable gardens with rhubarb, beans, peas, herbs, and tobacco, berry patches and orchards were emphasized. Nor were parks and flower gardens neglected. Something was done to improve the breeds of animals. Besides setting an example, public-spirited men gave prizes for ditching and building of fences, and the clergy especially tried to spread the new methods among the people. They came to be known as "potato priests." And the farmers were learning. Although suspicion of everything new lingered long, there were many intelligent leaders among them. Hardanger and Sogn became especially famous for their orchards. Although there was a steady progress through these years and money economy was becoming more common, life on the farm continued much as of yore. The farmers still engaged in hunting and fishing, felled timber, burned charcoal, hauled for the mines. Home industry, too, was flourishing, and while there were specialists in the different crafts, most of the things needed were made at home and the surplus was sold in the towns.

In spite of progress Norway continued to be dependent upon importation of grain, and a most serious cause of complaint was the Danish monopoly of this trade. Nothing short of a famine could procure a change. Four successive crop failures from 1739 through 1742, the "black years" as they are called, brought upon Norway the greatest calamity of this age. The grain trade was temporarily freed and measures of relief were taken, but the bureaucracy moved slowly, and the food needed was not obtainable. The governor at Christiania wrote: "This year [1742] I have with deep sorrow seen hundreds of people from the Uplands here in the city looking for work; but we have had nothing for them to do. So they have walked homewards, and some have perished on the way." The effect of this famine, authorities claim, can be seen in the vital statistics for a century.

That Norway's general recovery from the depression was slower than that of Sweden and Denmark was partly due to the absence of a capital city and consequently of an economic and cultural center. This lack was especially serious in an age when government support was considered the very backbone of production and commerce, and most of the state funds which could be used to further enterprises of various kinds were invested in concerns with headquarters in Copenhagen. This contributed to the lack of capital which was a serious handicap for Norway throughout the era. The country also suffered from lack of currency and means of exchange, and, as money economy was winning its way into the far corners of the land, this was felt as a hardship by all the people. There was sore need of a bank, but lengthy negotiations with the authorities in Copenhagen were of no avail.

In spite of these hindrances, however, the period after 1740 was one of general progress along all lines.

Fishing was good through most of this time. Herring and cod were the chief catch, as always, and lobsters were more important than either earlier or later. The sea was open to all, and, as most of the fishermen now owned their boats and tools individually or in small groups, they were more independent than in the days of Petter Dass. Regulations of 1753 gave the fishermen the right to sell to whomever they pleased. Yet, as they often lived on credit, most of them continued to be economically dependent on merchants in Bergen or Trondheim, who strove to keep the price of fish low and that of goods they gave in return high.

After a period of decline, the prosperous decades of the 'forties and 'fifties brought renewed activity also in the lumber industry. New mills were built, improved saws introduced, smaller mills sawing only for home consumption sprang up in many places, and lumbering spread northward into new districts. The government made complicated plans for regulating lumbering. The results were not commensurate with the effort or expense, largely because the theorists in Copenhagen failed to take actual conditions into account; nevertheless something was accomplished. Rules about the size and amount of timber that could be cut, both on private and public land, were made and measures taken—but not always carried out—to prevent illegal practices. Efforts were also made to seed new forests, to utilize wood that had hitherto been wasted in the mines or in the production of tar and charcoal; and new methods and materials were tried whereby a saving of wood might be made. The government was well aware of the importance of the forests to the whole economic life of the country. For the mines they were absolutely indispensable.

During the depression all branches of mining suffered. While the two large copper mines of Røros and Kvikne continued to prosper, smaller works had to be closed, and, as the price of silver declined, the Kongsberg mine operated with an increasing deficit. Labor conditions became intolerable, and, when urgent petitions brought slow results, serious riots followed in which the wives and mothers of miners took an active part. Two women who went to Christiania to complain to the authorities were immediately arrested. Twenty-seven rioters, among them two women, were found guilty of "revolt," and in accordance with law, twenty-five were sentenced to forfeit "life, property, and honor." The investigating commission, however, recommended leniency, and before long the king pardoned them all.

After 1740 mining flourished. Most prosperous was the copper mine at Røros; and eleven ironworks operated without interruption, while Kongsberg, which had come into existence with the silver mine, was the second largest city in the kingdom. In 1769 there were 4,000 workers at the mine and the city had a population of 8,000. As the town grew, private trade was given increasing freedom The city was also becoming more Norwegian. As the employment of Germans for all technical work was not satisfactory, Norwegians were sent to Germany to study, and in 1757 a complete school of mines was established at Kongsberg, and next year the first Norwegian director of the mine was appointed.

Most of the mines were owned by private companies, the control generally in the hands of a few men; but they expected—and received—government aid in the form of subsidy, or tax-exemption in time of special stress, or help in securing fuel. It happened that a mine was closed several years because the owners of the forests went on strike. In 1752 the government issued a general order defining the relations between the mine owners and the farmers who owned the timberland. The farmers within a fixed district must furnish fuel for the mines, but only such wood as could not be used by the sawmills. The price was to be fixed by contract and the authorities were to dictate it only when no agreement could be reached. The order was liberal and clear, and remained in force until after 1814.

A favorite project of the government was industrial development. In 1739 the so-called Norwegian Company was chartered. The capital was Danish, the king and several members of his family being among the participants. The company, which received large concessions, was to utilize all the resources of the country and form subsidiary companies for all conceivable purposes, such as trapping, raising wild animals for sale, making dyes both mineral and vegetable, salt, soap, nails, glass, furniture, and many more things. The capital was inadequate and scattered on many ventures, the people distrusted the company and failed to cooperate, and the whole scheme was too fantastic to succeed. Later the company was reorganized with Norwegian capital and directors, for the one purpose of manufacturing glass. Though it was not particularly successful financially, it made glass windows common all over eastern Norway and introduced glassware and chandeliers into many homes, besides producing articles of great artistic value.

Quite a number of factories were established from the late 'forties and on: flour mills, saltworks, ironworks, and the like. Noteworthy are two faïence factories, which like the glass works were more successful artistically than financially. In spite of the strict protection given industry, however, its place in the economic life of the country was very insignificant. The government did not give to Norwegian enterprise the support it gave to the Danish. Moreover, Norway could not compete with the larger industrial countries and was compelled to take manufactured articles in return for raw material if trade was to prosper.

Commerce and shipping suffered even more than industry in the period of depression, and ships were lying idle in every port. In the 'thirties the whole country had a merchant marine of only four hundred ships, with a tonnage only half that of the Bergen fleet alone in the prosperous years before the Great Northern War. But with the return of general prosperity foreign commerce and shipping also flourished, far exceeding that of Denmark, and Norway's trade again came in for much consideration in the many favorable trade treaties concluded during these years.

The imports were more varied than in the past and there was a greater demand for silk and cotton cloth, tea, coffee, sugar, spices, and the like. People had begun to sense the economic unity of the world, and articles from far-away lands, especially from China, were the height of fashion as they were all over Western Europe and in the United States. "Commerce makes the Chinaman, the Indian, the Frenchman, and the Englishman work and think for me. If I am thirsty, I refresh myself with Chinese tea; . . . if grief oppresses my heart, the nectar from Champagne drives it away, . . . Spanish sheep are shorn that I may be clothed, . . . the whole world serves me without knowing me."[1]

It is impossible to estimate the volume of exports and imports because, in addition to the controlled commerce of the larger seaports, illicit trade was carried on with Sweden and Russia along the whole eastern border to such an extent that officials warned the government that interference with it might upset the whole economic balance. There was also smuggling to the west and south with Iceland, Scotland, Ireland, and southern Sweden. Though strict mercantilistic principles still dominated colonial and foreign trade and any evasion of the regulations was illegal, it was hardly looked upon as unethical.

In the internal trade a more realistic policy was followed. The im-

[1] The historian, Peter Frederik Suhm, quoted by Sverre Steen, *Det norske folks liv og historie,* 6:174.

portance of the burghers, that is the townspeople who had all the rights of citizenship, is indicated by the fact that in the eighteenth century the word for burgher (*borger*) came to have also the broader meaning of citizen which it has today. This class continued its efforts to concentrate in its own hands even the domestic trade, but this was growing more and more impossible. The exchange within the country increased rapidly as the demand for a variety of goods advanced and as the growing diversity in occupations resulted in a larger number of people who had to supply practically all their needs through purchase. The common use of money facilitated exchange; and in order to accommodate the growing traffic a systematic improvement of the roads was begun, and private capital was invested in toll bridges. There was lively travel in little coastal boats and over the mountains between the East and the West. On several routes there was postal and passenger service twice a week.

Most of the exchange was concentrated in the cities and at the markets, which were growing in number; but there was also all manner of petty trade carried on throughout the country to the outermost islet and innermost valley. There were peddlers and cattle traders, innkeepers who also had little shops, and country storekeepers, most of them operating without any license. More and more unprivileged persons were also settling in the cities as hucksters. They generally came from the country and this gave them an advantage in attracting the rural trade. They even furnished lodgings for their country patrons, people with whom the burghers did not care to have personal intercourse. As most of the people who in all these various ways entered the field of trade were from the farms, the struggle of the burghers against these "intruders" assumed a social as well as an economic character. The merchants objected to having common people enter their preserves, and they expressed the fear that the widening distribution of "luxury" goods would corrupt the simple people by creating new wants and encouraging habits of sloth. The old privileges could be maintained by no method except government regulation, and the appeals for such aid were not lacking.

But the domestic trade had reached such proportions that it could not be forced into any strait-jacket and this was understood by those in authority. Besides, the idea that the whole country would benefit by removal of restrictions was finding entrance. As Henrik Stampe expressed it, "The more the taste for monopoly and restraint in trade among us who rule can be abolished, and freedom, which is the life blood of trade, introduced the better it will be." In 1742 Molde and Christiansund were raised to the status of chartered cities without being assigned any definite district in which they could trade, and later Holmestrand and Tvedestrand followed. The monopoly of the older cities within their special district was gradually broken down. An attempt was made to restrict hucksters and peddlers, but step by step they gained freedom of trade until by 1768 the principle of Stampe was accepted that "Every citizen shall support himself as he best can and knows how."

There is something incongruous in the development of eighteenth century society in Norway, but it was the natural outcome of historical evolution. As throughout Western Europe, this was a bourgeois age, but rural society with its culture (*bondekultur*) deeply rooted in the past also reached a high development in the same period. While the difference between town and country was more marked than earlier, much of the rural mode of life was continued in the cities. The contrast between rich and poor was glaring, but wealth was not the chief basis of social distinction. By 1730 there had developed a sharp cleavage of society which was to continue far into the nineteenth century. Birth and tradition counted for much, but fundamentally it was two different modes of living that divided the aristocracy from the mass of the people, or *de konditionerte* from the *bønder* or *bondestand.*

The former, consisting of less than fifty thousand people, may be called the bourgeoisie, but it must be noted that in Norway the bourgeoisie was the upper class. To this belonged professional men, officials, clergymen, nobles, and burghers, including industrialists and wealthier merchants. Among the latter there was a real aristocracy of wealth consisting of a few families which were closely connected by blood and marriage. Within the whole class a consciousness of solidarity not found earlier had developed as a result of a common way of life described by the word *konditionert,* that is cosmopolitan European, modified by Norwegian conditions.

Most members of this group were descendants of immigrants of the seventeenth century, and they had largely intermarried among themselves, because there had been few Norwegians of their class. They read foreign books, followed French fashions, furnished their homes largely with articles from abroad, and the wealthier among them built spacious dwellings planned for ample living. Culturally they were closely tied to Denmark. Those who were born in Denmark or had spent a long time there spoke Danish. Among the others the Norwegian-Danish, or Dano-Norwegian, which had been the "book language" since the Reformation, had finally become also the accepted spoken tongue, though pronounced as spelled, not according to Danish usage.[2] Most of them had come to be Norwegian in interests and sentiment, and from this class came the champions of Norway's rights and the bearers of the awakening national feeling. Just as strong as their national feeling was the upper-class instinct retained by officials even in the outlying rural districts, whose life was inevitably influenced by the communities in which they lived.

Nevertheless it was quite fashionable to exalt the Norwegian *bonde*. Not only was the Rousseauan theoretical romantic admiration for the "simple," rustic life strong, but it was understood that the freeholder in Norway had attained a dignity seldom reached in other countries, and that this was based on the ownership of land. "The Norwegians appear to me to be the most free community I have ever observed,"[3] wrote one visitor, who rightly laid it to the fact that no landlord could drive them from home and livelihood.

In spite of the great economic and social differences between wealthy farmers and lowly crofters, there was a sense of class solidarity, based on common interests and traditions, and a growing sense of the importance of their occupation. But the common people as opposed to the aristocracy included not only the country population but also workers in mines and mills, sailors, and many townspeople. Among the latter were not only proletarians but craftsmen, hucksters, and the like, many of them in comfortable circumstances. In speech and mode of living they had much in common with the surrounding countryside from which they had come. It was the wealthy odal freeholders, however, who gave tone to the life of the common people as a whole. They had won not only economic strength but a sense of self-reliance and dignity which made them recognized leaders of their communities, not least in the age-old resistance to officials or burghers who encroached on their rights. Many stories were told among the people of how farmers matched wit and strength with aristocrats and got the best of it. Still they had no desire to seize control either of state or church affairs. They accepted the "book language" as the only speech suited to sacred things, and a clergyman who tried to come closer to the people by preaching in

[2] Halvdan Koht, "Bokmaal og bymaal," in *Syn og Segn*, 12:102-127 (1907-1908).

[3] Mary Wollstonecraft, *Letters Written during a Short Residence in Sweden, Norway and Denmark*, 63, London, 1889.

their dialect was told to give up such nonsense.[4] A farmer would be very proud to see a son of his in the pulpit, but this rarely happened. The education required was expensive and the obstacles to a career serious. Above all, a man—and even more a woman—found it very difficult to break through the barriers between the two social groups, and if he did succeed he was rarely fully accepted by his new associates. So the two remained separate, and the aloofness was not all on one side.

The farmers could meet upper-class arrogance with pride in their own station and family. Many of them had noble or even royal blood in their veins, and it happened that in the funeral sermon for a freeholder sixteen generations of ancestors were recited. Yellowed family records were hidden in the bottom of old chests. The people had a strong historic sense, and, even when there were no written sagas, stories were handed down by word of mouth and new ones added, many of which enhanced both class and family self-assurance. Though there were exceptions, in general the treasures of rural culture were little known and less valued among the upper class. Much of the folklore had not been put into writing, partly because of the great difference between the spoken dialects of the people and the book language. For the same reason the people's reading was generally confined to devotional books with the addition perhaps of Petter Dass and less frequently Snorri. Though a few farmers read Holberg, on the whole the intellectual currents from abroad had little effect upon them and even the new tendency in the church known as pietism did not produce a genuine folk movement.

❡ Pietism, which came to the North from Germany about the turn of the century, was a reaction against formal orthodoxy as well as a manifestation of the individualism that dominated the eighteenth century. Among the first Norwegians to be influenced by pietism were a number of clergymen, notably Thomas von Westen and six associates known as the Pleiades. They strove valiantly and with some success to realize pietistical ideals, to awaken a more personal, evangelical religious consciousness, and to raise the moral standards of people and clergy. They appealed to the government to come to their aid, and painted a dark picture of unrestrained coarseness and vice, which doubtless was true in detail though one-sided. The results were more extreme than the Pleiades had desired.

The depression of the late 'twenties helped to produce a more somber

[4] Koht, "Bokmaal og bymaal," 116.

outlook on life. Frederik IV was in his last years strongly gripped by the darkest aspect of pietism and tried to put an end to all gay frivolity in his own life and that of his people. Shortly before his death he issued the notorious Sabbath Ordinance which made failure to attend church punishable by fine or pillory. This inaugurated a fanaticism continued through the reign of Christian VI, which has been called the Age of Pietism. All manner of extravagant blue laws were enacted against smoking and dancing, comedies and operas, "funambulists, jugglers, or operators of games of hazard," and any frivolities, even unrestrained laughter. Though the laws were never fully enforced and were repealed upon the death of Christian VI, they left their impress on the morals and manners of future times.

As the pietistic spirit found entrance into court and government circles an interest in foreign missions was awakened, though economic and political motives were inextricably intertwined with the religious. The most striking figure in the church of the age was Thomas von Westen, who in 1716 was appointed missionary to the Lapps with wide authority. Except for purposes of exploitation, the Lapps had received little attention. They might come to church, but little was done to draw them into the fold. Von Westen devoted himself to his large task with a joyous, tireless zeal. He was a man of violent emotions, vigorous faith, and aggressive energy, who gave his health, his property and that of his wife, and finally his life to his battle against evil. As was characteristic of the movement to which he belonged, he placed the emphasis not on the mass Christianity which had satisfied many orthodox pastors, but on personal religion. He traveled about among the Lapps, slept with them and ate with them, spoke to them in their own language, and prayed with them. They had never before seen such a man who shared his all and never looked down on them. They loved him, and came to believe that his religion was more powerful than the many evil forces they in their superstition had feared.

Yet von Westen was doomed to many disappointments. In his fight against the worst devil of all, the liquor with which traders freely supplied the Lapps, he received little support from the authorities. Nor was he able to retain the favor of the government. He was impervious to suggestions or even orders and too busy saving souls to furnish the statistics or reports that bureaucratic officials demanded. Worn out by his exertions, von Westen died in 1727 at the age of forty-five, and with his death vanished the zeal of the "Apostle to the Lapps."

When Hans Egede asked support for a mission to Greenland, the authorities were favorably disposed toward the plan, but believed the commercial companies should bear the expense. Egede did, however, receive an official appointment as royal missionary with a salary of 300 rix-dollars. He was pastor of a small parish on one of the Lofoten Islands. He felt oppressed by a sense of the restricted sphere to which his work was confined. Then he read about Greenland and the heathen people who lived there. Whether he believed that these people, so different from the Norwegians of his day, were descendants of the old Norse colonists is not clear. At any rate he became possessed with the idea of going as a missionary among them.

Egede labored there for fifteen years under conditions that would have crushed a less determined spirit. Though he had not like von Westen been touched by the pietist movement, he was not behind the "Apostle to the Lapps" in zeal and devotion. In nature and method of approach, however, the two men were entirely different. Egede acquired the Eskimo language very slowly, mainly through his children, and always retained an attitude of aloofness. As he taught in the staid and heavy manner of the church of his age, he had difficulty in reaching the untutored minds of the Eskimos. The results of his efforts were discouragingly meager. Yet the influence of this stranger who won the love of the people by giving them food when they were starving and fishhooks to help them in their livelihood, extended beyond the small group of the baptized and helped dispel superstition at least in some measure. In 1733, a devastating epidemic of smallpox struck Greenland and carried away about two thousand of the inhabitants. This took a heavy toll of Egede's strength; three years later, after his wife's death, he left the work in charge of his son and departed for Denmark. There he remained the rest of his life, assisting in the plans of the government for the expansion of missions and in training men to continue the work on Greenland.

The city milieu was most favorable to pietism and the movement caused considerable stir, especially among the lower middle class, in Bergen and the cities along the southeastern seaboard and Oslo Fjord with the surrounding communities. It took a radical form, and sects led by lay preachers began to arise. In order to prevent any break in the state church and to keep all religious activities under the supervision of the clergy, a Conventicle Act (*Konventikkelplakaten*) prohibiting unauthorized, non-churchly religious meetings was enacted in 1741, and Christian VI signed it reluctantly. Although it remained law for a century, its enforcement was irregular, depending largely on the local pastor.

Pietism never gripped the Norwegian people as a whole or caused any sensational revival or marked any new age. It did, however, bring to the country a better class of clergymen who took their duties seriously and improved conditions in their congregations in an unobtrusive way. Most notable among them were Peder Hersleb, bishop in Christiania, and Erik Pontoppidan, bishop in Bergen, men of tireless enthusiasm and energy. They possessed the good qualities of pietism without its extremes, and were imbued with the devotion to learning characteristic of the Enlightenment. Like many of their contemporaries, they believed therefore in popular education in both temporal and spiritual matters, with emphasis on the latter. Hersleb sent men about his diocese to inspect the instruction of the children and to distribute religious books. One year he ordered ten thousand copies of one devotional book. In order to control the preparation of young people for their first communion, he introduced confirmation into his diocese. Largely through his influence, it was, in 1736, legally established in both kingdoms. The same year Erik Pontoppidan published his *Sandhed til Gudfrygtighed* (Truth unto Godliness), an explanation of Luther's *Little Catechism* in the form of questions and answers which was adopted as the basis for the instruction of those about to be confirmed.

By 1730 knowledge of reading was quite general and schools with both men and women teachers were scattered about the country. The clergy were not satisfied, however, and through the School Law of 1739 the state undertook to establish a system of elementary schools, to be financed by a general tax. The law could not be fully carried out because of popular opposition to the expense involved. This subsided when a supplementary law gave the local parishes the right to arrange for their own schools. Thus Norway's elementary school system was organized and until 1827 these laws were the fundamental regulations of the system. By 1750 most communities had at least an itinerant school. Unfortunately the teaching was necessarily from Danish books, foreign to the rural people. The ministers appointed the teachers, who were selected from among the young men of the parish and given some little training. It was forbidden, however, to take men who would make good soldiers. Teachers were difficult to get and poorly trained, and their pay and social status were about that of a farm hand.

To improve conditions it was planned to establish normal schools, but only a slight beginning was made in this age. There was, however, a widespread interest in education and many private endowments were given for scholarships and schools. Private and public schools sprang up in the cities. Professional schools were established such as a military academy and a school of mines. There was also a demand for broader and more modern courses than the old Latin schools furnished. Pontoppidan tried to meet this by opening a secondary school in Bergen for the newer courses, but little was done after his removal to Denmark. It is worth emphasizing, however, that not only the organization of popular education but the early attempts to broaden and liberalize higher education came through the efforts of clergymen who were influenced by pietism. In spite of their religious viewpoint, they had not a little in common with the rationalistic thinkers of the Enlightenment. Chief among the latter was Ludvig Holberg.

In 1720, the very year that peace was made, Ludvig Holberg (1684-1754) published a revised complete edition of his mock heroic epic, *Peder Paars: Poëma Heroico-comicum*. With biting irony he satirized the pedantry, the pettiness, the snobbishness, and the stuffiness he saw in the society of his day. Men in high places accused him of rousing the populace against culture and religion, but more people joined in Holberg's hearty laugh, and among them was Frederik IV. "We talked as in a free country," said Holberg, paying tribute to the king, "we jested, we bantered, and we quarrelled among ourselves with merry whims without fear, for he never took offense at an outspoken or unguarded word." Holberg was typical of his age and at the same time had a great share in creating the milieu in which he lived. He looms even larger because he was the only great literary figure of his time in Denmark-Norway. Upon Norway his influence was more indirect than in Denmark, strong only toward the close of his life, and increasing after his death.

Holberg has been given the credit for "making Danish intellectual life European."[5] His father, a Norwegian farmer's son who had risen to the rank of lieutenant colonel, had traveled far. Ludvig, who resembled his father in many ways, was cosmopolitan in his interests, made many long tours through Western Europe and spent not a little time at Oxford University. He brought home a strong English influence as a counterpoise to the all too powerful German element which many Danes were anxious to throw off. Practically every idea of the Enlightenment, including feminism, found an advocate in Holberg; and every

[5] Steen, *Det norske folks liv og historie*, 6:357.

class and institution of his age was subjected to his keen criticism, the power of the king alone excepted. Like his contemporaries, he was a stanch upholder of absolutism, but instead of believing in kings by divine right he held the rationalistic theory of Hobbes and others.

While never an imitator, Holberg had the powers to utilize his wide knowledge in creative works of genius. All he wrote had a didactic purpose. He wanted to liberate people's minds through the new spirit of the Enlightenment. Literature was secularized and freed from theological or clerical influences, but it was non-religious rather than anti-religious. Typical of his age, Holberg's philosophy was thoroughly bourgeois. He was born in Bergen, and his mother, the daughter of an official there, was a thrifty housewife. Her son extolled the homely virtues of sobriety, frugality, and industry which he associated with his home and native town. He ridiculed the old nobility in the style of good burghers, but, like them, he had a weakness for high-sounding titles and was pleased when he was elevated to the nobility. He was not a democrat.

While cosmopolitan in his outlook, Holberg was also the creator of a Danish-Norwegian literature. Probably to protect his anonymity he wrote one important work in Latin, *Nils Klim*, a satire on society of his day in the manner of *Gulliver's Travels.* Otherwise he wrote in Danish and was a strong force in the movement of his day to nationalize the language by ridding it of many of the foreign elements that were almost destroying its character. The purity and finish that he added to the language helped to win for the Danish tongue acceptance also in Norway.

He introduced the modern drama into Denmark, and within five years after the publication of his early epic he wrote more than twenty comedies in the spirit of *Peder Paars.* As crowds flocked to the theater, his plays were a step toward democratizing and popularizing culture, and roused the people of Copenhagen out of their rut by satire, humor, and laughter.[6] Though the plays of his early years have been the chief reason for Holberg's enduring fame, they were little known in the Norway of his day, largely because the country had no stage. When the pietistical blue laws closed the theater in Copenhagen, Holberg turned to scholarly economic and historical works, among them *Danmarks og Norges Beskrivelse* (The Description of Denmark and Norway) and

[6] For an English version of some of his best known plays, see: *Comedies by Holberg: Jeppe of the Hill, The Political Tinker, Erasmus Montanus* (1914), published by The American-Scandinavian Foundation; and *Four Plays by Holberg*, tr. Henry Alexander (1946), published by Princeton University Press for The American-Scandinavian Foundation.

Danmarks Riges Historie (The History of the Kingdom of Denmark). These works were epoch-making in history writing, shifting the emphasis from political and military events to social and economic developments, and they were widely read in both kingdoms.

Though no ardent nationalist, either Danish or Norwegian, Holberg was keenly aware of the differences between the two peoples. He had lived in Norway until he was eighteen and returned later for a brief period. He described his native country with warm appreciation and took pleasure in emphasizing the good, sturdy qualities of the people. They "differ much from the Danes both in temperament and in customs. Still this dissimilarity does not prevent complete unity and accord between the two nations, and, ever since the renowned union [of 1380] was formed between Denmark and Norway, they have been regarded as one people."[7] He looked upon the two peoples as one state, and was scarcely aware of any conflict between the two. Nevertheless, his name became a rallying point for the new generation of Norwegians who raised the banner of nationality.

About 1750 there began among Norwegians a conscious effort to assert themselves as a nation. Norwegian soldiers and students in Copenhagen formed their own national groups; but of more importance was the movement in upper-class circles at home in Norway. They felt that Holberg was one of them and were proud of him, but emphasized more than he did the difference between Danes and Norwegians. They knew the sagas and their country's history and took great pride in its glorious past. Though the leaders in this national movement were intensely patriotic, they were not parochial. Not a few of them, especially among the clergy, owned extensive collections of books and showed their public spirit by lending them freely and bequeathing them to public libraries. Many of the books were foreign—French philosophy and poetry, German science and literature, or Swedish scientific works—and the readers felt themselves part of the larger European cultured elite. They were cosmopolitan in interests, and they had no desire to sever either political or cultural ties with Denmark. But they wished their country to take the place in the economic and cultural life of the age to which its latent resources and distinguished history entitled it.

The center of the movement was at Trondheim, where leading patriots in 1760 formed The Scientific Society of Trondheim (Det Trondhjemske Videnskabs-Selskab), which in 1767 became The Royal Norwegian Scientific Society. The publication of a scholarly magazine,

[7] Quoted by Steen, *Det norske folks liv og historie*, 6:359.

Trondhjemske Samlinger, was begun at once. The founders of the society were gifted, scholarly men whose interest was centered upon the study of their country past and present. The pioneer in making Trondheim a cultural center was Benjamin Dass, a great-nephew of the poet, but the initiative in founding the society was taken by a younger man, Bishop Johan Ernst Gunnerus. "He had a burning zeal for Norway's honor"[8] and was the first to express the desire for a Norwegian university. Associated with him was Gerhard Schøning, born in Nordland. His chief work was *Norges Riges Historie* (The History of the Kingdom of Norway), in which he aimed to show that Norway always had been and still was a separate kingdom. Peter Frederik Suhm, a Dane by birth who had settled in Trondheim, showed as much enthusiasm for the society as his Norwegian friends. Until the university was founded in 1811, the society was the only center of learning in the country, and later it was to fill an important place in Norway's intellectual development. These men helped to arouse among prominent Norwegians self-esteem and love of country. It was an age of much intellectual curiosity especially along scientific lines. It produced no great scientists but many able students of broad interests. The publication of an agricultural magazine was initiated and many competent topographical works appeared. First among these was Erik Pontoppidan's *Forsøg til Norges naturlige Historie*.[9] This work was based on a wide range of information which the bishop gathered as he traveled about his diocese, and especially gives valuable information about the life of the people. The first newspaper began to appear in 1763 and more followed. They were uninteresting little sheets containing no discussion of the issues of the day, for censorship was strict. The organs of expression were at hand, however, when the opportunity to use them arrived, and a program for action was in the making. Holberg's dispassionate affection for the land of his birth had been succeeded by a patriotism which was ready to assert itself and to spread from the narrow confines of the intellectuals to the people at large.

[8] P. F. Suhm, quoted by Ludvig Daae, *Throndhjems Stifts geistelige Historie fra Reformationen til 1814*, p. 174, Trondhjem, 1863.

[9] This work was translated both into German and English. Pontoppidan, *The Natural History of Norway*, trans. from the Danish original, London, A. Linde, 1775.

CHAPTER 14

PREPARATION FOR INDEPENDENCE, 1770-1814

During the last forty-four years of the Danish union the Norwegian people were passing through a period of intensive preparation for the time when they were to take control of their own affairs. It was an age of rapidly moving events, characterized by striking changes in the government and unexpected diplomatic developments, by ups and downs in the economic life and intensified social differences, and by marked progress in every line. Every phase of European life and thought was reflected or, to be more accurate, was appropriated and adapted, in Norway. Through it all can be traced a constant, though somewhat uneven, growth of national assertiveness which tended to unite the divergent elements of the population into one patriotic people.

¶ The discontent with the old bureaucracy was not confined to Norway. In Copenhagen, even in court circles, there were men bitterly hostile to the clique of prominent nobles who controlled the government. Especially violent was the opposition to the powerful foreign minister, J. H. E. Bernstorff. The changes in personnel at the time of Christian VII's accession in 1766 had brought little if any improvement in the government. The highest law of the land was the will of an insane monarch whose mind was day by day becoming more befogged, and in order to control the government it was necessary to dominate the king. The opposition therefore sought the support of the man closest to him, Johann Friederich Struensee.

Struensee was a handsome young German doctor who through friends at court had been appointed physician to the king. He was a man of strong emotions, sensuous, ambitious, and eager for all the pleasures that life could afford. With disarming complaisance he secured the good will of those about him and unobtrusively won the confidence of the poor king, who needed a friend. He also became the physician and confidant of the ailing young queen. Caroline Mathilde, the sister of George III of England, was only fifteen when she became the wife of Christian VII. Unhappy in her new home, bored, neglected, and friendless, she sat alone in the palace while her husband indulged in riotous debauches. At first Struensee was the paternal friend who sincerely tried—and with some success—to bring about better relations between the king and queen. Before long, however, intimate friendship turned into love, a love which the queen was too happy to conceal, while Struensee, proud of his conquest, seemingly failed to see or was unwilling to see that it might be a hindrance rather than a help in his pursuit of power.

When palace intrigue, in September 1770, brought about the fall of Bernstorff, neither the king nor the courtiers were aware of how great a part Struensee had in the event. Before long, however, his position received official recognition and finally, on July 14, 1771, he obtained authority to issue orders in the name of the king without the royal signature. Thereby his power was absolute.

Struensee held the political ideas that were the fashion of his day and tried to put them into practice. Possessed also of the optimism of the eighteenth century philosophers who believed that the transformation of a political and social system was a rather simple matter, he inaugurated in rapid succession reforms which it would normally have required years to establish. Fundamental was his belief in an enlightened, benevolent despotism. To make absolutism more efficient he concentrated the power in a small cabinet with himself in control, abolishing the council, dismissing prominent officials who might endanger his power, and reducing the colleges to mere administrative bureaus with a minimum of authority. Among the officials precedence was to be given to age and service, not to birth or title. The dominance of the nobility and snobbish love of titles should have no place in the government of this bourgeois age, though they might still hold sway at court.

The people—this was a basic principle of benevolent absolutism—were entitled to an efficient, honest, and economical administration, and to all the benefits the government could bestow, and this Struensee strove to give them. He carried out an extensive program of reforms in the spirit of the Enlightenment, applicable, of course, to the whole realm. He was especially interested in economic development, and as a physiocrat, believed this could best be attained by freedom from restriction. Following to its logical conclusion the liberal policy begun under Stampe, he removed many restrictions on trade, reduced the privileges of the guilds, discontinued the practice of subsidizing industry, and emphasized the policy of economic equality for all sections of the realm as well as for all individual citizens. His liberalism also extended into the religious and moral spheres. He showed tolerance toward nonconformists, abolished superfluous holidays—a measure planned before his day—liberalized some of the regulations of the church, for example with regard to marriage of relatives, and removed the penalty for certain moral offences. The criminal law was made more humane and the use of the death penalty restricted. Most expressive of his belief in individual freedom was his order, issued in the earliest days of his power, removing all censorship of the press. This act, however, helped to prepare the way for his ruin, as it afforded his enemies—and they were many—the opportunity to launch attacks upon him without restriction.

Struensee lacked the arts of the diplomat and the tact of the politician. Arrogant and filled with a false sense of security, he thought it superfluous to win supporters. He could expect no friendship from the nobility and high officials whom he had offended by both his manner and his policy. Copenhagen, especially the bourgeoisie, feared the loss of all economic privileges, the church interpreted his radical ideas as atheism, and the people were offended by his relations with the queen and by the rumor that the king was treated with cruelty. Moreover, Danish national opposition was roused against Struensee, who had no national feeling and did not even try to learn Danish. There had in the past been kings and statesmen as German as Struensee, but a new age was dawning, and furthermore the Danes resented a policy that would reduce their country to an equal footing with the duchies of Slesvig and Holstein and with Norway.

The Norwegians, on the other hand, appreciated the new policy, which it seemed must benefit their country. As the new freedom of the press gave their national feeling untrammeled opportunity for expression, it grew by leaps and bounds. A flood of pamphlets, papers, and periodicals appeared which pictured Norway as a stepchild, possessing rich possibilities for development, but impoverished and a martyr to the selfishness of Denmark, "that envious sister." Norwegians felt entitled to equality and seemed to find pleasure in saying unpleasant things about Denmark, which had seldom been the case in the past.

The Norwegians had no authoritative means of expression for their special demands. Struensee abolished the position of statholder; the governors were not Norwegian in sentiment, and there was no national organization for political actions. The agitation was led by individuals from among the bourgeoisie. They expressed no desire for severance of the union or for a separate political system, but they made concrete demands for their own cultural and economic institutions. A Norwegian university, a commercial department, and a bank were measures strongly urged, and the insistent request that the poll tax of 1762 be abolished was again brought to the fore, supported by all classes. The big businessmen of Christiania took the lead in the agitation for economic reforms, especially for a bank, while the demand for a university came from the Scientific Society of Trondheim, Bishop Gunnerus going to Copenhagen to lay the matter before Struensee. While the petitions found favor with a few Danes, more of them feared Norwegian economic and cultural independence, and Struensee, who had not the courage to ignore the Danish opposition, made only minor concessions. This turned the tide of opinion against him.

Norwegians in Copenhagen took an active part in political discussions, and were more important in the life of the capital than earlier. They formed an aggressively patriotic group, which complained of the injustice their homeland had suffered, sang its praises vociferously, and expressed indignation when Norwegian demands were ignored. When the time was ripe for demonstrations against Struensee, Norwegians took the lead. Two hundred Norwegian sailors who had not received their pay marched to the palace and thoroughly frightened Struensee. Later, when he ordered a guard of infantry, also composed chiefly of Norwegians, disbanded, they mutinied, supported by the townspeople, and the command was rescinded. Then a young Norwegian poet, Johan Nordahl Brun, burst out in a triumphantly patriotic-revolutionary song, "*For Norge, Kjæmpers Fødeland*" (To Norway, Home of Heroes). In spite of police prohibitions it was sung widely in both countries. It looked to Brun as though his compatriots were to take the lead in overthrowing the man who had come to be looked upon as a tyrant.

It was, however, a palace revolution which in January 1772 brought about the fall of the overbearing minister. The conspiracy was organized by prominent nobles and former officials with the connivance of the dowager queen, Juliane Marie, the king's stepmother, and her son Prince Frederik. Struensee was arrested at a palace ball, and, after a perfunctory trial, was found guilty of lese majesty, condemned to death, and executed with repulsive brutality in the presence of a large crowd. The queen was divorced from the king and imprisoned in Kronborg, but upon the demand of her brother George III she was released to him and taken to Hannover, where she died a few years later.

Thus ended the attempt to establish an enlightened despotism in Denmark-Norway. Though brief, the experiment had not been without effect. Some of the reforms introduced were not undone, and the liberal ideas which had been advanced were not forgotten. Struensee's rule was more important for Norway than for Denmark. Though the definite results were meager compared with the expectations, the national consciousness had been strengthened, and the program for reform was not abandoned. "The policy which was carried through to victory in 1814 was created in that remarkable year 1771."[1]

With the fall of Struensee a reactionary government came into power which was to last for twelve years (1772-1784). The clique in control employed skillful propaganda to win support and persuade the people that the king had been "saved." The news of Struensee's arrest was greeted with illuminations, festivals, and wild enthusiasm in both countries, but soon this gave way to a tide of sympathy for the fallen minister, and his execution brought no expression of joy. Norway was suffering under a financial crisis and a famine as bad as that of the early 'forties; the promised reforms were not forthcoming, and complaints were as loud as ever. The one concession made to the people was the abolition in 1772 of the hated poll tax. Although the tax had been practically invalidated because the people refused to pay it, the legal withdrawal removed what might have caused a popular demonstration.

In name, the head of the government was Prince Frederik, a commonplace young man, but the real head was Ove Høegh Guldberg, the very embodiment of reactionary ideas, who attempted to undo the work of Struensee. The centralized administration of Struensee, however, was too convenient to be dropped, and the humanitarian reforms of 1771 were also in the main retained and even broadened. In contrast to his predecessor, Guldberg appealed to the nationalism of the Danes, and he recognized no other nationality, saying, "There are no Norwegians." He returned to the old mercantilist policy, favoring the Danish landed aristocracy. The reintroduction of the grain monopoly was deeply resented, the subsidies to industries had little effect, and the new high tariffs caused clashes between merchants and revenue collectors in many Norwegian towns. In Bergen the merchants took possession of the harbor by force and unloaded their goods. Again, as in the Stril War,

[1] Steen, *Det norske folks liv og historie*, 7:30.

the Norwegians resisted a tax they considered unfair, and did so with impunity, but this time it was the well-to-do burghers who took the lead. This did not discourage the authorities from restoring mercantilistic principles even in the domestic trade through a futile war on unlicensed tradesmen and through an insistence on the old, almost dead, city privileges. Only the North escaped. There the grain monopoly did not apply, and trade had been entirely in the hands of the innkeeper-merchants who were virtually little kings each in his harbor or fishing center.

Before long an upward trend in business was noticeable, and when the American Revolution developed into almost a world war, Norwegian shipping experienced a period of extraordinary prosperity. The demand for tonnage was enormous; the Norwegian carrying trade reached proportions hitherto undreamt-of, and the country's own exports also grew in volume. The merchant marine was increased from 546 ships to 844, while the tonnage was almost doubled. It was a home-built and home-owned fleet, which held its own even after peace had returned.

The foreign minister, Andreas Peter Bernstorff, carried on the policy of neutrality with the same tireless skill as his uncle, the older Bernstorff, had done in the Seven Years' War. He was especially opposed to war with England, and in 1780 obtained a treaty which he thought would protect the trade of Denmark-Norway. A few days later he signed the Armed Neutrality of the North, an agreement among Russia, Sweden, Holland, and Denmark-Norway. When Catherine II discovered the supposedly secret treaty with England, she was greatly incensed at Bernstorff's duplicity, and Guldberg used it as an excuse to dismiss the foreign minister, who was the most powerful and the most liberal member of the government. The treaty remained, however, and served Norwegian trade well.

The war period brought prosperity to the cities, as merchants, shipbuilders, manufacturers, all made money and gained in influence and self-assurance. Those of foreign descent had become thoroughly rooted in Norway, and, especially in the cities of the South, burghers who had sprung from the Norwegian rural population played an increasingly important part. The burghers were individualists who did not want any of the government's paternalism, but desired freedom such as the Americans enjoyed. They were nationalists also and resented the economic regulations which gave to Copenhagen most of the profits of the good times. The agitation led to some relaxation in the mercantilist policy, but the great subsidized companies were still in Copenhagen.

The war years were very difficult for the rural population, and the hardships were increased by crop failures from 1781 to 1783. The misery was not as intense as in earlier famine years, both because of greater cooperation among the people themselves and because the government acted with promptness to bring help. Though the men in power felt it their duty to relieve distress, they were nevertheless loath to abandon their old policy, but finally even the most reactionary realized that the grain monopoly profited neither country. Yet it was not before 1788 after much dilatoriness that this most harmful and hated of trade restrictions was finally abolished. The protracted irritation had left a residue of ill will toward the Danes especially in southern Norway, the section in which the distress was greatest. Even when not actually starving, the people were impoverished through the necessity of buying grain at high prices, and they felt that the Danes had profited by their misfortunes. Resentment was also directed against the Norwegian burghers, who had not been above making money on the people's plight.

It was, however, the conditions in Denmark which caused Guldberg's fall. The peace which followed the American Revolution brought much more upheaval in the economic life there than in the northern kingdom. The year 1783 was one of financial crisis, and the public finances were in a wretched state. When new issues of currency did not help, Guldberg resorted to an attempt to limit imports by sumptuary laws, especially restricting the luxuries allowed to the common people. The confidence was expressed that "our dear and faithful subjects," realizing that it was for their own good, would appreciate this enforced simplicity; but the laws cured no evils, and complaints were loud. A thoroughgoing reform was needed, and that demanded new men.

The Guldberg government ended as it had begun with a coup which, after long planning, was executed in 1784. The opposition, in which the dismissed foreign minister A. P. Bernstorff was the leader, gathered about Frederik, the sixteen-year-old crown prince, afterwards Frederik VI. He had silently nursed his hatred of his grandmother and uncle who had usurped the place that he felt should be his. When for the first time he attended a meeting of the ministers, he suddenly rose and read a document abolishing the cabinet and appointing the opposition leaders as ministers. He then presented it to his father for his signature. The frightened insane king signed the paper and fled from the room. His signature was sacred, and no one disputed the legality of the coup. The change in the government was accomplished quickly and quietly with no executions or even arrests and without publicity or festivity. In fact, although the change was important, most of the people were unaware of the event.

The new government was composed of able, liberal men, and the crown prince, though well intentioned, was in reality their tool. Among them were, besides A. P. Bernstorff, Henrik Stampe, who years before had been a pioneer in liberalism, and Christian Colbjørnsen, a Norwegian whose name came to be associated with the final abolition of serfdom in Denmark. Like other intellectuals in their countries, these men read Adam Smith, Montesquieu, Voltaire, and Rousseau and held all the advanced ideas of the Enlightenment. While they believed in absolutism, they had abandoned the older conception of the state and held that it existed for the good of the people, and was, in fact, the servant of the individual. Freedom was their slogan—not political, but social, economic, intellectual, and religious freedom—and in keeping with these principles an era of liberal reform (1784-1797) was inaugurated.

Order was introduced into government finances by returning to Struensee's system of organization, and the economic policy of *laissez-faire* was carried even farther than in his time. The colonial commerce was freed from most restrictions. The grain monopoly was removed, though in fact Denmark continued to control the trade. The monopoly of the Iceland and Finmark trade was abolished, giving Finmark greater economic freedom than any other part of Norway, and as a result it grew in population and prosperity. In 1797 the most liberal tariff law in all Europe was enacted. The rates were reduced, most export duties abolished, and 750 items removed from the list of articles the importation of which was prohibited. Nevertheless, the income from the tariff did not decline, for times were better and smuggling decreased. Lumbering was freed from restrictions and fishing regulated so that the new methods should be used in the night only, leaving the day for the old ways. Copenhagen's position as the trade center was weakened by rights given to other cities, and a credit institute in Norway, though not a bank, also helped the business of the country.

The humanitarian spirit of the age found expression in further measures to make the criminal law less brutal. The death penalty was in many cases changed to imprisonment, torture was abolished in executions, law suits were speeded up, and means for arbitration provided. There was a growing demand for improvement in the ghastly prison conditions. Practical reforms were also part of the policy. Roads were built and improved, new postal routes were opened, and a parcel post service was inaugurated. Furthermore, freedom of speech and the press was perhaps more untrammeled in Denmark-Norway than in any other country. It seems as though "Struensee's glorious failure"[2] was turned to success.

The economic reforms were in the interest of the burghers. There was much prosperity in Norway during this age, much more than in Denmark, but most of the gain was concentrated in the hands of a small burgher class. It was therefore natural that the agitation and indeed the whole nationalistic movement was allowed to subside in the upper class. Not so with the mass of the people. Without any intentional injustice, the whole new system of economic freedom for the individual meant that in free competition the strong would win. The government was abandoning the earlier paternalistic attempt to protect the economic welfare of all classes, and the laws enhanced the tendency of the age for the rich to get richer and the poor poorer.

There was widespread resentment among the masses, who felt their economic dependence on the burgher class. There were strikes among miners and lumberjacks and mass protests from the farmers who, even when they owned their homesteads, were largely in debt to the burghers and felt that an unjust pressure was being exerted upon them. Just as vigorous were the complaints against bureaucracy. Though there had been a general improvement in the character of the officials, and there were many conscientious, honorable men among them, especially in the clergy, there continued to be abuses, such as overcharging for services, and even at best the numerous taxes—thirty-six in all—could not be collected without irritation. Often undue severity was employed.

The general unrest reached a climax in the Lofthus Rising of 1786 and 1787. Christian Jensen Lofthus was an unusually gifted leader who carried on propaganda through an extensive section of southeastern Norway and won a larger and more loyal following than any popular leader before him. As of old, spokesmen of the farmers—at one time as many as thirty men—were repeatedly sent to Copenhagen, and Lofthus personally appealed to the crown prince, who received them all kindly. The results might have been greater had not officials and burghers been frightened by the popular demonstrations into united action. They, too, appealed to the prince and obtained an order for the arrest of Lofthus. He and his followers ran afoul of the stringent law against illegal assemblage which had been enacted after the Stril War, but

[2] Mary Wollstonecraft.

soldiers who were called out refused to fire on the people, and time and again Lofthus eluded the police. Finally he was arrested, and the men who captured him were liberally rewarded. He was placed in a wretched dark cell in Akershus fortress, where he spent the remaining ten years of his life chained to a block. Two years after his death his case was finally settled, as the highest court confirmed earlier decisions condemning him to life imprisonment. By that time the unrest had subsided, and the judgment caused little stir. Yet the name of Lofthus was not forgotten, and he may well be considered a precursor of the great farmer leaders of the nineteenth century.

The rising brought some results. A commission was appointed to investigate the complaints of the people and a few reforms were obtained. Detailed rules for extra fees were adopted, many smaller local evils corrected, and some of the worst officials were dismissed or transferred. More important, the people had learned that united action could bring results and they had found a leader in their own ranks. While the movement had been mainly a social-economic rising against the upper class, the demand for Norwegian officials shows that national consciousness had begun to spread also among the common people. But, although the Lofthus Rising had extended far beyond one local community, the people were yet to experience a common movement of truly national scope.

¶ In trying to compare society at the close of the eighteenth century with the time before 1770, we find that while no revolutionary change separated the two periods, there were marked differences. As the century was drawing to a close, life took on a more rapid tempo. The whole picture is complex, but details stand out etched in clear-cut lines with deep shadows and bright highlights. It was a stirring period abounding in strong, colorful men and women. As society was more fluid, more individuals crossed the barriers that divided social groups, but on the other hand the contrasts were more marked and class consciousness more acute. At the same time a growing national feeling began to unite the divergent elements around a common cause.

Opinions became more vocal, as the ideas that reached their climax in the French Revolution had taken hold on the rank and file of the townspeople. Clubs, which were the order of the day, were forums for discussion, and the newspapers, small and few though they were, enjoyed quite unusual freedom of expression and increased the interest in the outside world. Never before had there been so much discussion of national and world affairs, both political and religious. There was much talking and writing about liberty and equality, but, it was added, Norway already had liberty and the demand for equality was largely theoretical. Sometimes the papers contained rabid revolutionary ideas and one man even suggested that the country would never be free before all officials were abolished, as in France.

The sympathy for France and interest in French ideas were strong in western Norway, particularly in Bergen and Trondheim, partly because during the Revolutionary wars English men-of-war intercepted merchant ships more often than the French did. The main interest of the burghers was centered upon civil and economic freedom within the local city government. There was no desire for broader political action, and the old loyalty to the royal house continued to the very end of the union. Fulminations against the "aristocrats" were common, and that meant the highest officials and very wealthy merchants, but there were few such aristocrats in the smaller towns, even in Bergen.

The merchants of Bergen were well-to-do but not exceptionally rich. Because of the many races that met there, Holberg had compared his native town to a Noah's ark, but by this time these elements had become pretty well amalgamated into a distinctive type, a group rich in eccentrics. Among them a severe, though sometimes benevolent, patriarchal system ruled in shop and home. Both men and women were sturdy, thrifty, hard working, and individualistic. The women could well assert themselves, for often the family business and estate were originally theirs. Life was frugal except on festive occasions when merriment ran high, and display in clothes and luxury in food were rampant. No characteristic of the Bergen merchants, however, was more important than the stanch patriotism reminiscent of Absalon Pederssøn, as strong in those who were only a generation or two removed from a foreign country as in people of old Norwegian stock.

The wealthiest among them may be classed with the small, very distinct aristocracy of wealth which reached its greatest glory in the golden years at the opening of the nineteenth century. Then new fortunes were built up and old ones multiplied through the boom in industry and even more in trade. In the small coastal towns of the South and East there might be a few families, or even one family, which assumed a patriarchal position and dominated the economic and social life of the town and surrounding district. Notable among them was Jacob Aall of Nes Ironworks near Arendal. He was at the head of this great establishment when the iron industry was at its height in Norway and represents the finest type of industrialist of the age. He not only built up the works to a hitherto unknown efficiency, and took great pride both in the high quality and fine artistry of the articles produced, but he took seriously his responsibility for the welfare of his workers and their families. Decent housing, schools, church, doctors, gardens, care for the disabled—all that belonged to a well-ordered community was provided for. Still Jacob Aall found time to build up a library and spend time among his books.

The chief center of aristocratic life, however, was Christiania, which was the capital of the country in a more real sense than earlier. The small group of wealthy families, closely intertwined through business relations and repeated intermarriage, formed a closed circle. The lumber industry was in their hands and they had invested in mines and ships. Trade had brought a close contact with England which was kept up so assiduously that Christiania society was accused of being a bit of England. Prominent among the aristocracy was the Collett family, which was of English descent and maintained close relations with its ancestral home. A most striking figure was Christiania's foremost merchant, Bernt Anker, of whom it is told that he had his laundry done in London.

With the sudden wealth, the simplicity of only a generation or two ago gave way to a brilliant and luxurious social life the like of which Norway never experienced either earlier or later. The stately mansions were decorated by the best artists of the day and adorned with art objects from the ends of the earth. To satisfy the fashion for rustic life, the social elite also had extensive country estates with romantic grottoes, classic pavilions and statues, bowery retreats and formal gardens. Bernt Anker kept ten carriages and twenty horses, and thirty servants were employed in his household. Social functions had all the elegance of the late eighteenth century. Poets furnished drinking songs, the conversation was often in French or English, and part of the entertainment would be theatrical performances with host, hostess, and guests as actors and sometimes authors. These aristocrats, though not radicals, were responsive to the literary and intellectual currents of their day. They were public-spirited and in hard times gave freely of their money to relieve distress. They were, moreover, vigorously patriotic, active in promoting progressive measures, and ardent supporters of all Norwegian causes. Not a few among them won the confidence of the people and stepped into positions of responsibility.

In the years of crisis, however, it was chiefly the officials who assumed leadership. They were the best educated group in the country, the young men generally being trained to follow the career of their fathers, and they had reached a higher level of efficiency than in the early days of absolutism. Practically all the scientists and poets of the age came from their class. Even conservatives among them were students of the philosophy of the age, though they would never pursue these ideas to the logical conclusion of complete democracy. Their national feeling was growing and the interest in the country and the people, which earlier had been exceptional, was now quite general. From them came the agitation for a university. The advances made in education, health conditions, care of unfortunates, prisons, and the like came through their initiative, often in the face of opposition from frugal burghers and individualistic farmers. They lived more with the people than did the business magnates, understood them better, and could give more practical aid, even in the improvement of farming. It was inevitable that when the crisis came Norway should look to this class for leadership, and the country was exceptionally fortunate in having men of excellent training, broad outlook, and lofty ideals.

Government officials were more numerous than earlier, and more of them lived in the capital. It has been estimated that they and their dependents constituted 20 per cent of Christiania's population. The city proper, however, was only part of the densely settled urban area.

The suburbs had a population at least as large as that within the city limits. It was composed mainly of people who were not wanted in the city, could not acquire citizenship, and had not the means to comply with building regulations. Nor would they have cared to live in the city; they seldom went there except when employed as laborers. Bernt Anker looked with contempt upon these proletarians and the few intellectuals who sympathized with the masses, and, as he watched the spread of revolution, thought it not impossible that his country, too, might some day come under mob rule. His fears were unfounded, for the suburbs had no political program, but when in distress the people were ready for united action against the city merchants. Twice they unloaded cargoes of grain in defiance of all the authorities, paid the market price, but refused to pay the duty. The suburbs developed a life of their own, and it was neither as lawless nor as drab as it looked from Anker's side of the pale. The people there had close contact with the rural population and felt that the two groups had a common cause in opposition to the burghers. The excess population from the country moved into the suburbs and the farmers from far and wide came there for trade. Especially on market days a picturesque and motley crowd thronged the busy streets, the shops, and the taverns. Perhaps even there patriotic and revolutionary songs might be heard.

The new ideas penetrated even to the country people, although their life was less changed by the advances of the late eighteenth century than life in the cities. Perhaps the dignity and self-esteem of the freeholder was strengthened by the recognition the *bonde* received from poets and other intellectuals as a distinctive Norwegian type of which to be proud. The conservatives were trying, in the face of increasing money economy, to maintain the old self-sufficient subsistence farming, opposing the expense of such newfangled things as schools and road building and the like. The more radical accepted the new economy, but insisted that all opportunities be opened to the farmers. There was no conscious cleavage between the two trends and both stood united against burgher privileges and official encroachments on their legal rights. In the country, too, knowledge was increasing, economic conditions improving, and life becoming richer and more varied. There also a new love of country was developing side by side with the old attachment to the soil. Like other groups within the nation, the rural people were moving toward the time when they should be able to take a part in building a free nation. The Lofthus Rising had indicated what was stirring among them, but the first country-wide movement among the people came through a religious folk leader.

¶ The religious development of the age was characterized by two currents diametrically opposed to each other. The Enlightenment brought a widespread secularization of life and thought. In the cities there was little religious interest, church attendance fell off, and holidays were ignored, although most people kept up a perfunctory connection with the church and accepted what was preached there. Only a few adhered to the ideas of the French and English philosophers, who by applying the test of reason to the tenets of Christianity had become deists or atheists. The clergy met the danger from this extreme philosophy with rationalism. This was an attempt to harmonize reason and religion and thereby preserve what was considered essential in Christianity and free it from all so-called superstition. Rationalism, which came to Norway from Germany via Denmark, was so influential in the last quarter of the eighteenth century that those years are often called the Age of Rationalism. It reached its climax in the 'nineties. Then there came from Copenhagen young ministers thoroughly indoctrinated with rationalism in its most extreme form, who not only discarded the miraculous and supernatural elements in Christianity, but also wished to banish from the church the long-used devotional books and all symbolism reminiscent of old "superstitions." Few went to such extremes, however. The older men had a broader outlook. In fact, rationalism never completely dominated the Norwegian church although most clergymen were more or less influenced by it, some of them only for a certain period of their career. Not a few preached the gospel in the old way and tried to stem the new tide. Greatest among them was the poet-bishop of Bergen, Johan Nordahl Brun, a man of rare eloquence, fearless courage, and warm piety, who waged a life-long battle for the old faith.

The country ministers of this age, whether rationalists or pietists, were leaders in their community as no one else. Often they were scholarly men who found added interest in their professional travels by gathering scientific data. Noted among them was Hans Strøm, mineralogist, zoologist, and oceanographer of note, who believed it was a pastor's duty to study nature, for God was revealed in it as well as in His Word. Moreover he could thereby better assist his parishioners. Like many others he believed the farmers should be given all possible help to advance economically and educationally. Another clergyman, Niels Hertzberg, who for over half a century, even after he lost his sight, was like a father to his large parish, was not only scientist, electrician, gardener, lawyer, and carpenter, but also skilled in medicine, and often the parsonage was filled with poor patients who stayed for weeks. The services of such men in advancing rural life can hardly be overestimated, and the country parsonages were the main connecting link between the urban and rural mode of living.

Rationalists joined with pietists in emphasizing education and placed even greater faith in knowledge as a means of dispelling superstition. At times they made use of the Sunday sermons to talk about potato culture, better feeding of the cattle, or even vaccination. Yet they were not irreligious, but preached about God, virtue, and immortality with a warmth that had often been lacking in more orthodox sermons. This did not satisfy the people, however, and much of it they failed to understand. They clung with conservatism to the old faith which had been nurtured among them through the ages of orthodoxy and pietism. There was more vital religious sense among the people than has generally been realized; and, if the sermons gave them little, they had their old hymn books and other devotional literature which was diligently used to keep alive the religious heritage of the past.

Then there arose from among the people a man of genius who was to make this heritage a stronger force in the soul of the nation than it had ever been before. Hans Nielsen Hauge was a farmer boy from Østfold, but as a younger son he had to seek his fortune away from home, and tried various kinds of work. He had a deeply religious nature and in 1796 he went through a conversion which gave him an irresistible urge to share his experience. He began to hold meetings and for eight years traveled the length and breadth of the land even as far north as Tromsø stirring up a nationwide revival unique in Norway's history. Like all great revivalists he sought to reach the individual through preaching sin and redemption, and his success was phenomenal. His fiery eloquence imbued his listeners with some of his own deep earnestness, and with keen psychological insight he looked into the very depths of the individual human soul and sensed its needs. His writings, too, while somewhat unpolished in form, were works of genius and had a wide circulation. From the Age of Orthodoxy Hauge inherited his deep respect for the Bible and his insistence upon the importance of doctrine. In his emphasis upon individual religious experience and holy living he was a pietist. In fact, his puritanism was so strong that it cast deep shadows over the somewhat exuberant rural life of his times. Many a peasant musician burned his precious fiddle, and dance-songs went out of use, causing irreparable losses to the country's rich cultural traditions.

Though Hauge had no separatist plans and wished to do his work within the fold of the established church, his movement became to some extent a class conflict. He never forgot that he was the son of a farmer and appealed—often in opposition to the aristocrats—to his own class, which included the unprivileged part of the town population as well as the country people. His speeches were filled with bitter invective against the clergymen who in their love of filthy lucre, he claimed, laid heavy burdens on their parishioners, and in their vain learning deprived them of the pure Word.

To strengthen his cause Hauge endeavored to bind all his followers together into one brotherhood. He accomplished this not only through his own travels and writings, but by using his friends as itinerant lay preachers or inducing them to make their home in some strategic place in order to keep the movement alive there. Not a few of the revivalists were women. They sometimes preached publicly and took part in discussion meetings as freely as the men.

Hauge believed that the "brethren" should both support the cause and help each other financially, and in his emphasis upon the nobility of work he did not fall behind the rationalists. Understanding that mental and spiritual self-reliance was to some extent dependent on economic independence, he censured the godly for neglecting useful work for "thereby the worldly-minded have become rich and have gained power in this world, who by the wisdom of their wickedness have made the good their slaves and have themselves lived in luxury, splendor, and pleasure."[3] Hauge was almost as great an economic organizer as religious revivalist. He established his followers round about the country in various ventures, such as paper mills, grist mills, printing establishments, salt factories, and the like. He himself became a citizen of Bergen and engaged in trade there. His success was so great that his movement soon had plentiful funds at its disposal, and he was accused of an overemphasis on the material. Besides gaining economic stability, his followers received valuable lessons in discipline and organization.

Hauge was not left unmolested, but the measures taken against him and his followers were efforts to maintain time-honored authority and privileges rather than religious persecution. The business enterprises sometimes ran counter to old special rights to which the burghers still clung, while the lay preaching interfered with what was considered the monopoly of the clergy. An old law against vagrancy, which had been reenacted in 1754, and the Conventicle Act of 1741 from the Age of Pietism were invoked against itinerant lay preachers. Both Hauge and his followers were frequently arrested by the bailiffs, but just as often they slipped away. Finally, in 1804, the central government, which Hauge with old-time confidence in the king had believed would be on his side, took action, and Hauge was taken into custody. He remained in prison for six years except for a few months in 1809 when he was released in order to help relieve the country's distress by starting salt factories. During the last years his arrest was very mild, allowing him to spend much time away from prison, and in 1811 he was released. When his case was finally decided in 1814, he was found guilty of breach of the Conventicle Act, but his penalty was commuted to a very moderate fine.

Times had changed during the ten years since Hauge's arrest. As years of war and famine had brought cooperation between different classes, the officials had learned that common folk, too, could give wise counsel, fight for their country, and meet suffering with dignity. The mutual helpfulness of the "brethren" had been a benefit, not a danger,

[3] Koht, *Norsk bondereising*, 343.

to the country, and Hauge himself was looked upon as an exemplary man who, though his zeal in the past had carried him too far, would now live a quiet industrious life. And so it was. Hauge lived very quietly until his death in 1824, for he too had changed. His piety was as deep and warm as ever, but he had become gentler and more tolerant in his judgment of others. His fanaticism had vanished and he had become reconciled to society. The same was true of his followers.

But the leaven of Hauge's preaching was still a living force, exerting its power in ever widening circles. He had not only awakened among the people a deep Christian consciousness, but he had taught them to act and think independently in religious matters, which led to greater freedom of thought in politics also. More than any one other influence, Hauge helped to unite the common people and prepare them to take their proper place in the life of the nation.

¶ In the last half-century of the Danish period conditions were conducive to a rich artistic production. Businessmen and officials had both wealth and a cultured taste, and the arts were employed mainly to make their private life rich and pleasant, with little emphasis on public interests either ecclesiastical or secular. The roomy country manor houses and palatial city mansions which appeared throughout the land were generally built in the dignified classic style of the age with high ceilings and large windows. All the crafts and industrial arts served in giving splendor and beauty to the interiors, the ornate rococo gradually giving way to the severe Empire style. Furniture of the Louis XVI and Empire periods, Sheraton, Hepplewhite, and Chippendale, were imported from France and England, and skillfully imitated by Norwegian cabinet makers. To meet the great demand, faïence and glass factories furnished objects of art as fine as Norway has ever produced, glittering chandeliers, delicate goblets, and all kinds of ornaments and tableware in gay, bright rococo style. Nor must the products of the ironworks be forgotten. The large, flat stove fronts furnished inviting opportunities for artistic expression and they were so fully utilized that the story of stove manufacturing is an important chapter in the history of Norway's industrial arts.

The fine art of this age, on the other hand, had no great significance and was not distinctively Norwegian. But there was an awakened appreciation of Norway's natural beauty, and a new romanticism made itself felt in art. Norway had earlier roused the interest of students of social philosophy as the home of a hardy, unspoiled race and a bulwark of liberty, and foreigners had come in great numbers to study the people and write about them. Now Norway became the fashion also among artists, especially in Denmark. Log huts were erected on Danish estates and Danes traveled about Norway painting even the more rugged aspects of nature; and still artists and tourists hardly touched the fringe of Norway's mountain wilds. Though this admiration of the country might swell Norwegian pride, it produced no genuinely national art. That was found only among the country people.

Folk art reached its height in this age. It was but one phase of the richer rural life. The increased opulence and self-esteem of the freeholders found expression in more pretentious dwelling houses influenced in architecture by the city style. The old-time low log houses, heated and lighted only from an open hearth, were still prevalent in out-of-the-way valleys and among the poor everywhere, but it was the large light houses which furnished opportunity for the development of the decorative arts. As in the past, the folk art, too, was receiving new impulses from the outside, but there was an unconscious eclecticism among the people as they incorporated into their art only those foreign elements which harmonized with their heritage. The new, however strong the influence, never superseded the old motifs. Hence there was unity in the midst of endless diversity. While this art had its roots in the Middle Ages when local differences were slight, the common origin was discernible even in the eighteenth century when each district had developed an art with a marked local color, excelling perhaps in one phase, carving, weaving, or floral painting.

Weaving was an important industry of the home. After Christmas the loom was set up and until spring one of the women of the household was always busy with it. The many signed tapestries indicate that some women of unusual skill produced articles for sale. While they wove all the cloth needed on the farm, it was in the tapestries and pillowcovers that the art of weaving was at its best. Both the technique and design often went back to the Middle Ages, even to the days of the Oseberg ship. Geometric figures and conventionalized flower and foliage motifs constituted most of the patterns, but picture weaving was not uncommon. Biblical or folk literature themes were used, perhaps copies from an illustration in a book, and mottoes or a whole stanza from a hymn were at times woven into the design. Even when oriental motifs, such as the pomegranate, or heraldic devices were employed, the whole effect was characteristically Norwegian.

Wood carving even more than weaving was built on medieval traditions. The heritage was rich and the artists conservative. Even so, new motifs from each successive period in art from the Renaissance on dominated the eighteenth century carving. Houses and furniture retained the same simple lines as of old, but they were more lavishly decorated than ever before. As every girl learned to handle the loom, every boy was taught to use his knife as an amateur artist. Besides, each community had its professional wood carvers or was visited by itinerant artists. Many of them are known today for their distinctive work. They seem to have disliked unadorned surfaces. Doorways, benches, chests, bedsteads, tools, implements and cupboards were carved, often in intricate patterns of unrestrained luxuriance executed with a bold, sure touch. Often the effect was enhanced by painting the design in different colors, as had been the usage ever since the days of the Oseberg ship.

Much newer was the decorative painting on plain surfaces. Though used earlier, at any rate in the churches, it did not come into general use in the homes before the eighteenth century and reached its full development only in the latter part of the period. This *rosemaling* (flower painting), as it was called because of the predominance of floral motifs, was the most characteristic expression of the rural life of the age. At first strong primary colors were used, but around 1800 rococo influences introduced a more sophisticated coloration, with greater delicacy and variety of shades. The larger flat surfaces afforded the artist wide latitude, and though purely decorative designs dominated, the pictorial phase was not neglected. The pictures were stylized, but strong in composition and execution. More significant, however, are the richness of color, the wealth and luxuriance of design, the joyous abandon and fancy coupled with artistic discipline, which characterized this floral painting. Though some of the numerous painters had gone to the cities for further training, their work was in harmony with folk-art traditions.

It should be mentioned that in this age the so-called national costumes took the forms we know today, and on them artistic skill was lavished. The poets and the fiddlers who added gaiety to rural life must also be remembered. Music and song took on new life. The violin took the place of the simple dulcimer (*langeleik*) and suited the new violent dances which were common Sunday amusement. There was a vigorous development of dances, marches, and songs, and poetic production kept pace with the new spirited tunes, greatly enriching the wealth of folk songs. Norwegian folk art, richer and more varied than that of most peoples, continued to flourish without much change through half of the next century.

¶ Norwegians remembered with pride that one of their countrymen, Ludvig Holberg, was the father of the modern Danish-Norwegian literature, and that after his death the leading poet of the common literature was Christian Tullin, who not only was Norwegian by birth, but spent most of his life in his native land. Then arose a far greater poet, the Dane, Johannes Ewald. But as Ewald was an admirer of the German poet Friedrich Klopstock, his style was somewhat turgid in marked contrast to the prosaic simplicity of Tullin, who like Holberg was influenced by French and English schools. An animated literary feud ensued in Copenhagen, which became nationalistic, as most of Ewald's admirers were Danes and his critics Norwegians. The latter had even earlier begun to gather at definite haunts, and, as the dispute waxed violent, they withdrew to a retreat of their own, and in 1774 formally organized Det norske Selskab (The Norwegian Society) with a definite literary program. This separation into two camps may be considered the beginning of a new national Norwegian literature, or rather a continuation of the literature of which Petter Dass was the last representative. There was an aggressive, earnest group of young men, many of them students, in the Norwegian Society during its early years. They had an exuberant zest for living and too often paid homage to Bacchus as well as to the muses.

Tradition had such a strong hold upon them that much of their writing was in the classic style learned from England and France. Most imitative were the tragedies, which, following French models slavishly, were stilted and artificial. Even the sturdy, individualistic Johan Nordahl Brun wrote in this style a drama entitled *Zarine*, which was a stage success. Soon after appeared a play, *Kierlighed uden Strømper* (Love without Stockings), perhaps the greatest literary product of the age, which satirized *Zarine* and its like so effectively that the alien trend before long disappeared from Danish as well as Norwegian literature. The author, Johan Herman Wessel, was the greatest, perhaps the only, poetic genius among the members of the society. He had a gift for succinct expression, a feeling for language, an incisive critical sense, and a genius for satire bubbling with humor but free of malice. Though he drifted through life aimlessly and produced little, his influence was immeasurable both on contemporary and later literature. He was not strongly nationalistic but found "evil and good in all lands, roses and thorns intermingled," and he thought it rather foolish for people of Norway to think that human beings were born only there or in England. Wessel was gently ridiculing the fervent, militant patriotism which was the dominating passion of his companions. This love of Norway found expression in bombastic patriotic songs—of which Brun's "To Norway Land of Heroes" was the prototype—ballads on themes from history, nature idyls, and poems in praise of the sturdy *bonde*. There was much talent in the society, much warmth and earnestness, and many poets who contributed something that their countrymen have found worth remembering.

As the early members died or were scattered to the various fields of their life work, the Norwegian Society lost much of its vigor and all its pugnacity. Among the members of a later date was Lyder Sagen, one of Norway's most famous pedagogues, who as a teacher in Bergen exerted wide influence through the first half of the nineteenth century. When a university was established in Christiania the need for a Norwegian club in Copenhagen was past, and in 1812 the Norwegian Society was disbanded. But even later it happened that Norwegians sought the old haunts that in the 'seventies had been ringing with song.

As the literary activities in Copenhagen declined they were carried forward in Norway, especially in the country parsonages. Brun, for example, wrote not only hymns of dignity and power, but numerous songs which he hoped would drive out of use the popular drinking songs that he, though no prude, found offensive. He also wrote a play which inspired the organization of a dramatic society in Bergen. It was the heyday of private theatricals, which were cultivated in various clubs. Most noted was the dramatic society organized among the elite of Christiania, which even gave public performances. Bernt Anker, who was one of its founders, both wrote plays and appeared on the stage, while his wife, Mathia Collett, was the director. Another amateur author and actor was Enevold Falsen, a gifted young lawyer and one of the leading public men of the day. His wife was among the most talented actresses in the group.

The interest in scientific and historical investigation and in the study of Norwegian dialects was also growing more general. The program of the scientific society in Trondheim was becoming nationwide, and the increasing number of periodicals gave more opportunity for publication. Of greatest importance was the study of political and social problems, which developed an appreciation of constitutional government as well as ideas of liberty and democracy. The whole literary and intellectual life was permeated with a deep love of country which was to find expression in action in 1814.

Although Norway was becoming prepared to take charge of its own affairs, the final break in the union was forced upon the double monarchy through external events on that larger stage of European politics where Norwegians had practically no influence. From the turn of the century a rapid succession of events led on to a crisis. Neutrality, which since 1720 had been the central idea of Danish-Norwegian foreign policy, was continued through the first part of the wars of the French Revolution. After the death of A. P. Bernstorff in 1797, less experienced hands were at the helm. When the Second Armed Neutrality was formed among Russia, Sweden, Prussia, and Denmark-Norway, England considered it a threat to her control of the sea and sent a fleet under Parker and Nelson which bombarded Copenhagen and destroyed a great part of the Danish-Norwegian navy. The Battle of Copenhagen, April 1, 1801, was the last great combat in which Danes and Norwegians fought side by side.

Although forced to sever its connection with the Second Armed Neutrality, the government continued its traditional policy. The first seven years of the century were a "golden age" for Norwegian shipping and exports. The merchant marine increased to 1,500 ships, chiefly home built, while lumber, iron, and copper were in great demand and brought high prices. There was great advance in wealth, mainly in the South and East, but the chief gainers were the merchant aristocracy while the common people suffered from hard times and, in the first three years, from famine. As the British Orders in Council were becoming more restrictive and Napoleon was expanding his continental system, the plight of neutrals was becoming ever more serious. Should neutrality become impossible, Crown Prince Frederik was inclined to favor England as the Norwegians wished, while most Danish statesmen were afraid of opposing Napoleon. Frederik's course quite naturally became irresolute, and European events determined the outcome.

In 1807, after Napoleon and Russia had concluded the Treaty of Tilsit, the British government demanded that the Danish-Norwegian fleet be delivered to it for safe-keeping. A secret clause in the treaty—known in England, but probably not in Denmark—provided for forcing Denmark-Norway to submit to Napoleon's continental system, and the British had reasons to think that the crown prince would yield. When their demand was refused, the British again bombarded Copenhagen, and sailed away with the whole Danish-Norwegian fleet. A few weeks later, October 31, 1807, the Danish-Norwegian government concluded an alliance with Napoleon and Russia, and almost at once, November 4, Great Britain declared war on Denmark-Norway. The war with England was extremely disastrous for Norway. During the preceding boom the country had become more dependent on trade with England than ever and that was now stopped by the blockade. Worst of all, the importation of grain, which had been in the control of Danish merchants, was discontinued, while frost and crop failure were forcing the people to mix their bread with bark and lichens imported from Iceland. And there was no money in the land. Even the men who had built up fortunes in the earlier years could raise no cash.

Norway had been forced into a foreign policy that was ruinous for the country, and the union government was not equal to the tasks that these critical years placed upon it. The bureaucracy moved with ponderous slowness, and when the crown prince, who had more self-assurance than statesmanship, in 1808 ascended the throne as Frederik VI, he revived as far as possible the personal absolutism of almost a century before. Never had the disadvantages of the union been so glaringly evident.

Nevertheless the war brought Norway some benefit. As the intercourse between the two countries was interrupted, it was found necessary to establish a Governmental Commission, which for three years gave Norway a more independent administration than the country had enjoyed for centuries. Prince Christian August of Augustenborg, who was commander of the army and had already won a well deserved popularity among all classes of people in Norway, was appointed president of the new commission. The other members were competent, resourceful patriots who attacked the many difficult problems of defense and provisioning with vigor. They were hampered and irritated by the dilatory bureaucrats in Copenhagen, and this helped to awaken ideas of separation from Denmark. The most difficult task, that of obtaining grain for the starving people, was undertaken by Count Herman Wedel Jarlsberg. Count Wedel was a man of broad cosmopolitan training and outlook who was to take a leading part in the events of the critical years that followed. He became the moving spirit in the small group which believed that Norway's welfare could best be insured by a separation from Denmark and a union with Sweden.

Meanwhile the powerful allies of Frederik VI drove him to declare war on Sweden in February 1808. "In the whole seven years of war there was hardly any event which in Norway caused such anxiety and dissatisfaction as this untimely and rash declaration of war."[4] The chief burden would have to fall on Norway, which was faced by war on all sides with no prospect of aid from Denmark. The dire need seemed to unite the people as never before, and high and low joined in sacrificing to meet the ravages of hunger and disease and at the same time equip the sorely neglected army. Before long they were rewarded by news of victories won under the able generalship of Prince Christian August. And then in 1809 the prince most unexpectedly agreed upon an armistice. The war engendered no hatred between the two peoples and was no more popular in Sweden than in Norway. Russia had declared war on Sweden and was conquering Finland, while the incompetent Gustaf IV Adolf was unable to cope with the situation. Then Swedish liberal leaders easily obtained the promise from the Prince of Augustenborg that he would not attack without direct orders from the king, and not without giving a ten days' warning. By a coup Gustaf was deposed and Karl XIII placed on the throne. As the new king was childless, old, and sickly, a successor had to be chosen at once. Fear of Russia had again awakened Pan-Scandinavian plans in Sweden. The selection of Frederik VI was therefore considered and when this failed Christian August was chosen crown prince. In Norway efforts were made to have him head a revolution there, assume the crown, and thus unite the two countries. The prince, however, refused to be a traitor to his sovereign Frederik VI, but hoped eventually to bring about a liberal union of all the three countries, and then withdraw. "It shows him as a man of truly great dimensions that he did not for a moment pursue selfish aims, that he never even in the most difficult times compromised with his ideal. On the contrary, he was always willing to sacrifice himself and his happiness in the service of a great idea."[5]

At this time the agitation for a national "rebirth" had become very strong and vocal in Norway, chiefly among the officials, but also among businessmen—men like Count Wedel, Jacob Aall, Enevold Falsen, and Bernt Anker. But even in the rank and file of the people repercussions were felt. In 1809 the Society for Norway's Welfare was organized to work for economic and educational progress. The old idea of a unitary state was dead, the Norwegians wanted all the institutions of a self-governing people, and a few desired complete separation from Denmark.

[4] Jacob Aall, *Erindringer som Bidrag til Norges Historie fra 1811-1815*, p. 136, Christiania, 1859.

[5] Jacob S. Worm-Müller, *Norge gjennem nødsaarene*, 412, Kristiania, 1918.

"Norway, our old proud land of cliffs shall again arise with new glory. Norway's honor and weal shall be the first thought and highest aim of all her sons."[6]

Realizing that the union was in danger and Norway in great distress, Frederik VI finally called in able assistance and did all in his power to relieve the need in his northern kingdom. Nevertheless, true to his promise, he upheld the continental system longer than any other ally of Napoleon, until finally the desire to save Norway from hunger induced him in 1810 to relax the system. England was ready to sell licenses to Norwegians allowing them to run the blockade, and once more the country had a taste of the "golden years." Commerce flowed freely, all manner of people became merchants. Fortunes were made overnight by fair means or foul, wild speculation was rampant, inflation followed and with it confusion in government finance.

A tangible, permanent benefit that Norway derived from the fortunes made in the license trade was the realization of the old hopes for a university of its own. The Society for Norway's Welfare had made this one of its main aims and sponsored an essay contest which was won by the clergyman Nicolai Wergeland, father of the poet. A subscription was taken up to finance the institution, and Wedel laid the matter before the king, declaring that the people would proceed with their plans regardless of royal approval. Frederik yielded and in 1811 issued a decree ordering the establishment of a Norwegian university, and two years later it began its work under the direction of the philosopher Niels Treschow. It received the name the "Royal Frederik's University," which it bore until 1939 when it was legally named the University in Oslo. But even before the new university had opened its doors the flush times had ended in distress greater than that of 1807.

The untimely death of Christian August in 1810 forced the Swedes once more to select a crown prince. The choice fell upon the ablest of Napoleon's marshals, the Gascon, Jean Baptiste Bernadotte, or Karl Johan, as he was called in his adopted country. It was hoped that he would reconquer Finland, but the new crown prince had other plans. He aimed to appease Russia and, in compensation for Finland, bring Norway under the Swedish crown. He broke with Napoleon,[7] made approaches to the allies, and in 1813 a coalition was formed among England, Russia, and Sweden. Sweden was, to put it bluntly, guaranteed the acquisition of Norway in return for helping the allies defeat Na-

[6] Quoted by Worm-Müller, 474.

[7] Franklin D. Scott, *Bernadotte and the Fall of Napoleon*, New York, 1939.

poleon. Once more the blockade on Norway was put into effect with full force. Importation of grain ceased, the public storehouses were empty, and in 1812 the crops failed. The suffering in 1813 was intense. Moreover, the inflation made an increase in taxes inevitable. The resentment against the government was bitter, and it was more widespread among the common people than at any earlier time.

In a last attempt to save the union, Frederik VI sent to Norway the crown prince, his cousin Christian Frederik. The man who had been statholder after the abolition of the Government Commission in 1810 had never been popular. It was hoped that the prince might preserve the union or, if that proved impossible, keep the crown of Norway in the Oldenburg house. With youthful ardor and romantic enthusiasm for Norway, he dreamed of great deeds. And he was to render the country important services though not in the way he had hoped. The handsome young prince, though lacking in strength and endurance, was impulsive, warmhearted, and emotional, and could not but win the affections of the people about him. He traveled through the country, feted and feasted in all the wealthy houses with a splendor and gaiety which to the sober-minded seemed hardly compatible with the suffering of the country.[8] Still he found time to discuss with leading Norwegians important matters, such as the establishment of a bank, the need of which was felt more keenly than ever. Most absorbing, however, was the European development which was to decide the fate of the country.

After Napoleon's defeat at Leipzig in October 1813, Bernadotte hastily marched his army northward to invade Denmark. He met weak opposition, and very soon peace negotiations were begun. On January 14, 1814, the Treaty of Kiel was signed between Denmark and Sweden, whereby Frederik VI relinquished all his claims to Norway in favor of the Swedish king. Thus Norway, shorn of all the old island possessions, which were retained by the Danish king, was separated from Denmark and the union begun in 1380 came to an end.

[8] *Claus Pavels's Biografi og Dagbøger*, Bergen, 1864.

PART V

Modern Norway

CHAPTER 15

1814 AND INDEPENDENCE

"It is a glorious age in which we are living"[1] wrote a Norwegian barely six weeks after the fateful Treaty of Kiel had been signed, and as he looked back on the last day of the year, he remarked, "Without decisive battles, without bloody and violent revolutions, I do not believe the history of any nation can show anything equal to this year." There were good reasons why Norwegians should feel a sense of satisfaction in the achievement of this most remarkable year of their history which had begun so ominously.

The growth within Norway during the preceding decades or even centuries was such that the eventual severance of the union with Denmark seemed inevitable. As yet, however, only a small minority of the people desired a breach, for the old loyalty to the royal family was still a matter of pride. It was no empty praise when Frederik VI in his farewell to Norway wrote, "Never can we, never will we forget the faithfulness and devotion to us and our family of which the noble Norwegian people have at all times and under all circumstances given such evidence. As long as loyalty among peoples is regarded as a virtue the Norwegians will be remembered as equal or superior to every other race in the practice of this virtue." Officials were closely tied to Denmark, where they had spent happy student days and made many good friends. Besides, Norway had not been conquered by Denmark but only united with the sister kingdom under a common ruler. The union had not been created by arms, nor could it have been maintained by force. The Norwegians looked upon their country as the very stronghold of liberty, and resented infringements upon their rights and the inequalities in the union rather than the union itself. They may have realized that because the central government was far away it had been easier to maintain local and individual freedom and to develop a society in which in-

[1] *Claus Pavels's Biografi og Dagbøger.* Entry for February 22, 1814.

equalities were less glaring than in most countries. This was to be a great advantage in the events of 1814.

Though the crisis was forced upon the Norwegians from the outside, events were to show that they had reached sufficient political maturity to turn the humiliating Treaty of Kiel into an opportunity for national progress.

Wild rumors ran riot in the land during the first days of the year, as people with mingled hopes and fears eagerly watched for every fragment of news that reached them. They knew something of Bernadotte's designs on Norway and the promises the allies had given him. On the strength of these he had invaded Holstein, contrary to the wishes of the powers, and forced through the Treaty of Kiel. It provided for an exchange of territory. The Swedish possessions in Germany passed to Denmark, while Frederik VI, on behalf of himself and his heirs, resigned all rights to Norway to the king of Sweden "to constitute a kingdom united with the Swedish." The Norwegians were to retain local self-government, their own laws, and the rights they already possessed. Bernadotte was delighted with the treaty and believed the Norwegians would cause no difficulty at all, but two letters written on the same day lend ambiguity to his own interpretation of the treaty. To his son he wrote: "Norway is united with Sweden, and forms a separate and independent kingdom," but to Sweden he sent orders that Norwegian fortresses be occupied by a troop of 6,000 men: "I believe a larger force will not be needed, as Norway is to be taken possession of, not as a province, but only to be united with Sweden in such a way as to form with it a single kingdom."[2]

Bernadotte would have liked to secure Norway before he joined the allies in the campaign against Napoleon. He well knew that the promise to him was a purely opportunist bargain violating every principle of historic and international rights, and he had little confidence in the pledge of the powers. The statesmen of the allies in turn neither liked nor trusted Bernadotte, who was as much of an upstart as his erstwhile master. In fact it was later intimated by one English diplomat that they would not have been averse to placing him on Bornholm as they did Napoleon on Elba. Bernadotte received peremptory orders from Castlereagh to march west against Napoleon. He complied, though halfheartedly, and could only send a representative with the news to Sweden. To the future governor-general of Norway, Count H. H. von

[2] Gjerset, *History of the Norwegian People*, 2:416.

Essen, he wrote that when the country was occupied the Norwegians must be treated with the utmost consideration. He had chosen the role of liberator, not conqueror. On January 25 the Swedish government formally, on paper, took possession of Norway.

The following day a Christiania paper, *Tiden*, issued an extra, announcing in a bold headline, "Peace, peace in the North," and expressing the pious wish that the peace would be neither harmful nor too humiliating for Norway. The people read it with skepticism, for the news had already leaked out that on January 24 Prince Christian Frederik had received formal announcement from Frederik VI of the transfer of Norway, with orders to hand over the kingdom to Sweden and then return to Denmark. Soon after, the king's letter of farewell to the Norwegians was published. He released them from their oath of allegiance to him and his house and urged that they submit quietly to the new government, "which has promised in a most binding way to allow the inhabitants of Norway to retain and enjoy their laws, exemptions, rights, liberties, and privileges as they are at the present time." There followed an address in which he explained the conditions which necessitated the transfer, emphasizing that it was the only way to save Norway from continued war and famine.

"Frederik VI's last words of farewell to the Norwegian people were touching and did not fail to have an effect on a people which as a whole rejoiced neither in the separation from Denmark nor in the union with Sweden."[3] The first reaction of many Norwegians was one of grief rather than anger, and the separation seemed "like the loss of an old beloved friend."[4] But as time passed and the facts became fully known, the feeling against the king who had handed over the country without consulting the people and, as they thought—the news of the fighting in Holstein not having reached Norway—without striking a blow, grew increasingly bitter. Resentment was felt also against the people of Denmark, although many of them sympathized with the Norwegians in their indignation at the humiliating treaty.

Ever since 1807 there had been a small group who believed that a union with Sweden was the most desirable solution of Norway's troubles. Count Wedel, the chief among them, expressed this opinion freely to leaders in all three Scandinavian countries, but he also made it clear that if Norway found it possible to insist on complete independence he would stand by his country. Others, among them Jacob Aall, looked upon the union as inevitable; but among the people, who,

[3] Jacob Aall, *Erindringer*, 330. [4] *Ibid.*, 745.

as some expressed it, did not want to "become Swedes," the prospect roused a new dislike for the neighbor country and especially for its aristocratic form of government.

The campaign against Napoleon which occupied the powers and the Swedish crown prince gave Norway a respite, but it was evident it would not be long. There was need for resolute decision and prompt action. Within a remarkably short time the nation was united in a heroic determination that, come what might, it would not recognize the Treaty of Kiel. No one did more to weld the people into one and to lift them into a mood of high enthusiasm than Christian Frederik.

¶ "My duty is first and foremost not to desert the cause of the people which the king has entrusted to me and which is attached to me, not on account of my personal merit, but because I am the only member of the ruling royal house who is among them and can hold the rudder of this ship as it is tossed about on the billows of coming events."[5] Thus wrote Christian Frederik in his diary only three days after the treaty had been signed. His romantic love for the country and the people had grown in strength and warmth. He felt ordained to be their leader, and, when the orders to surrender Norway's fortresses arrived from Frederik VI, the prince, "confident that the Norwegian nation will defend itself," skillfully fended for time. He closed the Swedish border and put it in a state of defense, and then set out on a trip through the country to Trondheim in order to gain time and to stir up the people to action. Everywhere he and his plea for resistance to Sweden were greeted with enthusiasm. He had hoped to have himself proclaimed king at the shrine of Saint Olaf, but refrained when he sensed that such a course would meet with disfavor.

Christian Frederik held that in surrendering Norway the king could act for himself only, not for his family, and that the crown devolved upon the next in line. The prince therefore believed that he had the sovereign right to declare himself king and to rule according to the absolutist King's Law of 1665, and that with his succession to the Danish throne the old union would be reestablished. It seemed not improbable that this might happen soon if the present dissatisfaction in Denmark should force the king to abdicate. And in Sweden the crown prince was none too popular, so it was within the realm of the possible that the dreams of a united Scandinavia which had flitted in and out through the years might become a reality under his leadership.

[5] *Kong Christian VIII's Dagbog fra Regenttiden i Norge*, 4 (Kjøbenhavn, 1883).

Even when he felt rising disapproval, he clung to the idea of assuming the crown. In this view he was upheld by a few leading men, most strongly by his closest friend, Carsten Anker, who was an ardent patriot, but certainly not a democrat. When the prince came back from Trondheim to Eidsvoll, Anker had ready for him a proclamation embodying this plan. The prince thought it "a masterpiece," but he added the assurance that the old law would be in force only until it became possible to draw up a constitution in consultation with the representatives of the people. He believed this compromise would satisfy public opinion. Nevertheless, hesitating to act alone, he summoned twenty-one prominent men to meet with him at Eidsvoll for consultation on February 16.

The prince explained his plan to these notables both individually and in a group. Though he was prepared for differences of opinion, he had not realized what clarity and strength the opposition had attained within the space of a few weeks and that the assembled leaders could speak with full confidence that they had the people behind them.

They believed the theory of the sovereignty of an absolute king to be an unsound principle on which to build the future of their country. Even if the people, out of personal affection for the prince, were willing to accept him as their king regardless of his theory, his right to the throne could never serve as a basis for dealing with Sweden or the powers, as it would never be recognized by them. Besides, the theory was both false and out of harmony with the history of Norway. In olden times no man could legally be king without the consent of the people assembled in *thing*, and even in the days of absolutism the idea that there was a law superior to the king had not died out. When, therefore, the leaders, who had made the ideas of Rousseau and the French Revolution their own, advanced the principle of the sovereign rights of the people, it did not seem entirely new or strange.

One by one the assembled men explained this to the prince, but it was left for Professor Georg Sverdrup to win him over to the people's view. The summons to the meeting reached Sverdrup in the middle of the night. About the same time came an urgent appeal from the local governor that he must dissuade the prince from his plan, for trouble was brewing in the country. On one lap of his journey to Eidsvoll, Sverdrup had as driver an old farmer who wondered why so many men were coming to see the prince that day. He feared the worst and warned Sverdrup that he must never vote for handing Norway over to Sweden. He would give his life and his all "not to see the day when Norway is subjected to Sweden." "But," he added, "whatever you say or do, remember that God stands by." This incident made a deep impression on Sverdrup.[6]

He was one of the last to arrive and was met at the door with the statement, "The prince wants to be an absolute king." He was at once summoned to the prince to state his views. Sverdrup explained and argued at great length that when Frederik VI had resigned his rights to Norway, these had reverted to the people, which thus was once more in full possession of its natural incontestable right to determine its own government. He had no doubt that "the Norwegians in a free election will choose the prince who in the hour of danger and distress has with such noble devotion linked his fate to that of the people," and persuaded Christian Frederik that he could acquire the ancient crown of Harald Fairhair and Sverri in no more honorable way than as a gift from a free people. "Now you are becoming poetic," said the prince with a smile. Sverdrup assured him that he spoke only from love of truth and his country. Then the impulsive prince embraced him, saying, "You are right, I have been convinced."

Christian Frederik announced his decision to the assembly of notables, and it was agreed that he should assume the title of regent with full power to carry on temporarily, to pursue the policy of national independence as a mandate from the people, and to call a Constituent Assembly. The prince was buoyed up by the turn events had taken. "I have won more than a crown," he wrote, "I have won the heart of every Norwegian." His proclamation of independence and of his assumption of the regency in the name of the people was received with expressions of enthusiasm for the cause and affection for the regent. "People were as if half-intoxicated with joy," wrote a diarist of the day.

This was an epochal meeting, for regent and leaders had recognized popular sovereignty as the guiding principle for their course. To give their acts legal sanction an expression of the will of the people was needed. Friday, February 25, was therefore proclaimed a general day of prayer, and, on that day or as soon after as practicable, the question was put to every congregation, "Do you swear to maintain Norway's independence and to risk life and blood for the beloved fatherland?" With raised hands and as with one voice the people took the oath—"so help us God and His holy Word." Most impressive were the services in Christiania, where the regent addressed the people and took the oath with them. "There surely was no Norwegian with a love for his

[6] This and the following are from Sverdrup's account recorded in Jacob Aall's *Erindringer*, 343-346.

country, to whatever political faction he belongs, who did not leave this solemn occasion with stirred emotions and the warmest wishes for Norway."[7] Although weeks went by before the most distant congregations in Finmark could take the oath, February 25 was the people's day. The oath was an informal plebiscite, whereby the cause of independence was approved and the sovereign rights of the people declared for all time. On the same day election was held for members of the Constituent Assembly, which was summoned to meet at Eidsvoll on April 10.

With his position sanctioned by popular approval, the regent proceeded to organize his government. There were a closeness to the people and a simplicity about the administrative offices which contrasted favorably with the elaborate red tape of the Copenhagen bureaucracy, and which have characterized the Norwegian government ever since. There was no time for non-essentials in those critical days when all efforts must be devoted to maintaining the rights of the country.

The situation was desperate, but the Norwegians refused to give up hope. The question most frequently asked was what England would do, for without British sanction it seemed impossible for Norway to maintain its freedom. The regent sent his closest friend, Carsten Anker, to England to plead the cause of Norway. Alone he worked with indomitable skill, courage, and patience to dissuade the English statesmen from aiding Sweden. But the British insisted that they were bound by their promises. The prime minister, Lord Liverpool, declared that if the Norwegians would let Christian Frederik return to Denmark, the English would help them to obtain good terms from Sweden. But otherwise they would have to help Sweden conquer Norway.

"Is that your Lordship's ultimatum?" asked Anker.

"Yes, it is, Sir."

"Then this is our death sentence, for Norway will not become Swedish, whatever happens," and Anker slowly withdrew.

It seemed as though Anker's mission had been a complete failure, and yet it was not without significant results. Anker, who had abandoned the absolutist idea even more reluctantly than Christian Frederik, now exerted all his efforts to convince the British statesmen that the rising in Norway was not a scheme on the part of the regent or the Danish king, but a truly popular movement. In this he succeeded. He also did much to create a public opinion in favor of Norway. Thus he

[7] Jacob Aall, *Erindringer*, 363.

prepared the way for the policy that was to win out before the year was ended.

Meanwhile the regent had written to kings and emperors to lay the cause of Norway before them, and, while he was not able to change the policy of the powers, he did succeed in making them a little more favorably disposed toward the Norwegians.

Most important were the negotiations with Sweden carried on by the regent and Count Henrik von Schmettow, one of the few men in Norway who could speak French. The Swedish government believed that the submission of Norway could be won through pressure on Denmark. Sincerely concerned about Norway, the Danish king urged his cousin there to exert all his power to obtain the best possible terms in the union with Sweden and then return home to Denmark. As long as he could, he resisted the Swedish demand that he sever commercial connections with Norway, thereby cutting off her grain supply, but he was finally forced to comply. When the Swedes realized that pressure on Denmark was not sufficient, they addressed themselves to Christian Frederik, believing that if he would yield Norway would do likewise. In a letter to the Swedish king, which—after being duly read—was returned "unopened," the prince tried to show that this was not so.

The conservative Schmettow, who like Carsten Anker had adhered to the absolutist theory, now became an earnest and effective champion of the rights of the people. He assured Essen that the Norwegians were determined to uphold their independence, and refused to recognize the right of the Swedish king to call himself master of an unconquered people. "Has a people come to be a flock of sheep, an article of trade and barter? That is not the will of God, and, in truth, such a thought is as repulsive to you as to me and to every enlightened human being." When the Swedes pointed to their military superiority and the support of the powers which had been promised them, Schmettow was not intimidated. Norway would be a difficult country to conquer, he said, and if attempts were made to starve out the people, they would subsist on what they had, eating bark and moss, and at last descend upon Sweden to take what they needed.[8]

The Norwegian statesmen realized nevertheless that the fate of the country depended largely on the will of the powers, and both Carsten Anker, in an interview with the Swedish representative in England, and Schmettow, in a letter to Essen, intimated that the Norwegians might be willing to enter into a union with Sweden, if it could be

[8] Halvdan Koht, *1814: norsk dagbog hundre aar efterpaa*, 143.

formed as between two equal sovereign nations. The regent declared that he would accept the crown even if offered him on the brink of a precipice and that he would never desert Norway if she was determined to fight, but he thought—perhaps it was wishful thinking—that the Bernadotte dynasty would not last long. Still if the problems of the country could best be solved by his withdrawal, he said, he would not let his personal ambition stand in the way of its welfare. But only the representatives of the people could decide whether they would enter a union peaceably. On one thing only did all these men insist: the defense of Norway's rights as a sovereign nation.

By the end of March it was generally recognized in Sweden that the movement in Norway was a folk rising. The military men planned the campaign of conquest, and Essen reported to Karl Johan that he had attempted to win the Norwegians by gentle means but they had shown no gratitude for Swedish magnanimity. Such a people had to be conquered to learn to obey, and he hoped the crown prince would soon come home with his army.

On March 31 the allies entered Paris, and Karl Johan was free to turn his attention to the North. The burning question in Norway was, would he invade the country? Whatever the outcome, there was still a brief period of respite, but not a moment to lose. It was important that before the arrival of Karl Johan the will of the people should be definitely formulated in a constitution.

¶ On Easter Day, April 10, the representatives of the people met in the little church at Eidsvoll for a dedicatory service before the formal open ing of the Constituent Assembly on the following day. There was an unusual spring thaw, and the delegates had driven through deep mud and slush. They were lodged in the neighboring farmhouses, often with primitive accommodations, some of them several miles from the meeting place. They were supposed to be furnished conveyance back and forth, but to save the farmers' horses they generally walked, arriving spattered with mud. The convention met in the main building of the Eidsvoll ironworks, which the owner, Carsten Anker, had placed at its disposal. It was a new spacious frame edifice in the severe classic style of the day, but quite inadequate for such a large gathering. The meetings were held in a long narrow upstairs room intended for a picture gallery. The walls were decorated with ropes of evergreen, and uncomfortable wooden benches had been erected on either wall along the length of the room and covered with red cloth. Only the chairs and tables on the rostrum gave a slight air of distinction to the bare hall. On state occasions when the prince regent was present, a gilded chair and a damask bedspread on the table were pressed into service.

Seldom if ever has a national meeting been held in the midst of such poverty and such distressing circumstances, but the spirits of the delegates seemed unquenchable. They all had dinner together, and the frugal meal was enlivened with jovial talk, rousing song, and roisterous hurrahs. They found keen delight in the unaccustomed contact with men of different classes. They were young and full of hope for the future. A few, who had been in close contact with the sufferings of the people, felt that it might have been more important to take measures to relieve distress than to make a constitution; but the majority knew that they could best serve the people by concentrating upon the task for which they had been elected.

It had been left to the regent and his advisers to plan the election. Wishing to have all classes represented, he ordered that in every rural parish at least one of the electors who were to choose the delegates must be a farmer, as must also one delegate from each district. The country people, who had little political experience and were accustomed to following the leadership of the officials, did not choose as many of their own number as they were entitled to. Of the one hundred and twelve delegates, only thirty-seven were farmers, sixteen were businessmen, and fifty-nine officials. Twelve of the latter were special representatives of the army and navy, but they had little influence on the proceedings.

The officials naturally took the lead. Not only were they in the majority, but they were less local, more national in their outlook than the others, and were better prepared by education and experience. The assembly was not a democratic group, as it did not include representatives of the lower economic strata either in country or city. The delegates were chosen without regard to opinions or "party affiliations," but on account of their personal worth and standing in their communities. While many were not known beyond their own local district, others were prominent leaders. It was a truly national body, representing not classes but the Norwegian people. The claim is no doubt true that there never was an assembly of men more unanimously and sincerely devoted to the welfare of their country.[9] All agreed that in order to weather the storms of that critical time Norway needed a constitution based on the sovereign will of the people. Yet there were in the convention two parties which repeatedly clashed violently and bitterly.

[9] Jacob Aall, *Erindringer*, 382.

The majority favored absolute independence, and the keynote to the views of the Independence Party was struck in Christian Frederik's opening address: "With a lofty sense of its own worth, the whole people has in the temples of the Lord taken a solemn oath to uphold the independence of Norway. And you, trusty Norsemen, are to seal that oath by organizing the form of government under which you are to live." It was assumed that the oath of February 25 had settled the question of independence once and for all, that it should not even be discussed.

Count Wedel was the leader of the smaller Union Party. He had been absent during the preceding weeks of agitation and upon his return found the sentiment for independence so strong that he deferred any action until the meeting of the Constituent Assembly. Several of the keenest minds in the convention, while not, like Wedel, having any fondness for a Swedish union, believed it the only possible practical solution of Norway's problems, and that the country was unable to maintain its absolute independence. Among them were Jacob Aall from the southern coastal region, which was more dependent on England than any other part of the country; Peder Anker, whose lumbering interests had kept him in close touch with the borderland in the southeast where Swedes and Norwegians mingled with little sense of national differences; and also Nicolai Wergeland, the clergyman who some years earlier in a prize essay on the need of a national university had shown warm patriotism and unusual ability as an analytical debater. In a masterly speech Wergeland stated the opinion that the whole sovereign right of the people had been transferred to the assembly, and that it had unlimited authority to take any action it saw fit. Georg Sverdrup, on the other hand, expressed the view of the Independence Party that the delegates had power only to carry out the expressed will of the people; they could not overthrow the sovereignty of the people and thus make it unfree.

On one important occasion the party lines were blurred. On April 18 Christian Magnus Falsen, the acknowledged majority leader, made a motion that the Constituent Assembly should consider its work completed and adjourn when it had made and adopted a constitution and elected a king. The vote was 55 to 55 and the motion was carried by the vote of the chair. This resolution embodied the opinion of the Independence Party that the convention's authority was limited to the definite purpose for which it was elected, and its adoption meant that neither administrative matters nor foreign affairs were to be considered.

There was one exception, however, caused by dire need: a committee on finance was elected and a new issue of paper money authorized. The party favoring complete independence had won a decisive victory, and the advocates of union accepted defeat. Before many months their policy was to be forced upon the country, but for the present the independence group was in control. Happily for Norway's future, they were able to show the statesmen of Europe that there was in Norway a stubborn, fearless will to be free which could not be ignored.

In contrast to the acrimony displayed in the above-mentioned debates, the drafting of the constitution itself was accomplished with speed and remarkable general unanimity. The differences in opinion did not lead to the formation of parties, and though class interests were manifest, there was no planned consolidated action in the interest of any one group. The constitution was drawn up by a committee of fifteen, who, Wergeland wrote, had one thing in common: they were permeated with liberal ideas and a high sense of citizenship. Important among the members were Falsen, Sverdrup, Aall, Wedel, and Wergeland. Mention should also be made of Captain Peter Motzfeldt, who was a specialist on English law, and Judge Christian A. Diriks, who was a great student of the constitutions of the day.

First the committee submitted to the assembly eleven fundamental principles.[10] The first read: "Norway is to be a limited, hereditary monarchy; it shall be a free, independent, and indivisible kingdom, and the regent shall have the title of king." This was opposed by the Union Party, and its adoption was another victory for the Independence Party. The eleventh, that all male citizens should be under equal obligation to do military service, was a too drastic interference with established privileges to be approved. The rest were general statements, as liberal as any of that day, and were adopted after comparatively little discussion.

Falsen was chosen chairman of the committee and had so much influence on its work that he has been called the "Father of the Constitution." A preliminary draft prepared by Falsen and a teacher named Johan G. Adler was taken as the basis for the work, but sketches by other members were also used. While all these plans show that the authors were well versed in the constitutions of the age, Falsen's draft resembled most the French Constitution of 1791. The committee worked under intense strain and pressure and, members have reported, amid stormy altercations even on the smallest point. Yet after only ten days it had completed its work and drafted a constitution which had the unani-

[10] Listed in Gjerset, *History of the Norwegian People*, 2:425.

mous support of all members. It was a composite product, differing from all the plans, more radical than any of them, and only half as long as the Falsen draft.

In the brief space of seven days of actual discussion the assembly adopted the Constitution, paragraph by paragraph. The most serious debate was on matters involving the question of union or independence. The Union Party failed in its attempt to word the document so that a union with Sweden would not necessitate changes. As the election of Christian Frederik might eventually lead to a renewed dynastic union with Denmark, a clause was adopted which would make it possible for the king to accept the throne of another country also and, with the consent of the Storthing, to carry on the administration from outside of the kingdom.[11] The statement is negative in form. This provision proved valuable in 1940, as it furnished an incontestable legal basis for the government in exile.

Another question that caused much discussion was that of suffrage. It was limited to men of the official class, burghers who owned a house or three hundred dollars, and to farmers who either owned their land or had rented a farm for at least five years. A suggestion that the qualifications for voting should be still further raised by specifying the size of the farm failed of approval. Teis Lundegaard, one of the few yeomen who spoke freely in the assembly, remarked that he thought it was the man not the farm that was to vote, and he had not noticed that a big farm and good sense always went together. The so-called "*bonde* paragraph" provided that two-thirds of the representatives should be from the country districts. It was pushed through by the official class which, as was expected, for many years furnished a large number of the rural members of the Storthing. Thus, while the cities had a disproportionately large representation, the rural districts were given a dominating position, and the common people could assume power in proportion to their political maturity.[12]

The pressure for time made it imperative to settle differences in the briefest space possible, and when the various provisions had been approved the whole document was polished into final form by a committee and adopted without debate. On the following day, May 17, the Constitution was signed, thus becoming the law of the land.

[11] Paragraph 11.

[12] Halvdan Koht, in "Trongen til demokrati i 1814," in *Historisk Tidsskrift*, 34:133-151 (1947), argues that this liberal provision was dictated by the necessity of winning the support of the farmers, who, in case of war, would constitute the body of the army.

The reaction which was already winning control on the continent had not reached Norway. The Norwegian was the last liberal constitution in Europe that grew out of the Revolutionary Era, and the only one that survived the ascendancy of Metternich's system. Of present-day constitutions it can therefore best be compared to the American, both national and state. It is based on the same fundamental principles, notably Montesquieu's idea of the division of power among three departments, and, of course, the theory of popular sovereignty.

While a product of eighteenth century thought, the document was also Norwegian. In its final form it was stripped of all general statements—declaration of rights or the like—and reduced to a hundred and twelve paragraphs, most of them very brief. The language in its brevity and directness is not unlike that of the ancient Norwegian laws. The delegates were consciously connecting the present with the past. Thus the legislative body was, on the suggestion of Wergeland, given the name Storthing (great *thing*) and the two houses were called Lagthing and Odelsthing. The organization of the Storthing is a unique compromise between a bicameral and a unicameral legislature, with the features of the latter dominating. All members are elected to the Storthing, and that body selects one-fourth of its members to constitute a Lagthing. This smaller group is not really an upper house, and much action is taken by the full Storthing meeting as one body.

On the whole, the form of the government has been found workable and has needed only minor changes to adapt it to modern times. The establishment of a liberal constitutional monarchy in place of absolutism, giving Norway a more democratic government than that of any other country in Europe, was a great achievement. Fundamental human rights were guaranteed by clauses resembling the American Bill of Rights, but this involved no revolutionary change, as the people had not suffered under any tyranny. Socially the Constitution was conservative. It was made by the propertied classes, and they continued in control. There was no thought of establishing a perfect democracy, and old privileges were not abolished, but on the other hand there was no concerted action on the part of any group to enhance its rights or gain new advantages. The Constitution opened a way for the continued growth of economic freedom and for the development of political democracy without revolutionary methods, and it laid down principles that spurred on to progress. The immediate need was the assertion of national rights, which the Constitution effectively supplied. It was, both for that time and the future, as Christian Frederik expressed it, "a palladium of the freedom of the people, which injustice and violence shall not assail with impunity."

When the Constitution had been signed, the Constituent Assembly proceeded to its one remaining duty, that of electing a king. The Union Party, in a last attempt to further its policy, wished to postpone the election and thus simplify any future union with Sweden, but when that could not be done they joined with the majority, and Christian Frederik was unanimously elected. Two days later he made his speech of acceptance and dissolved the historic meeting. Before the delegates parted on May 20, they formed a chain of brotherhood and took the pledge, "United and true until Dovre falls." It was a sincere promise to forget differences in loyal service to the country.

Two days later the king made his entry into Christiania amid great rejoicing and enthusiasm. "How happy I am," he writes in his diary, "to wear a crown bestowed on me through the unanimous wish of the people, and not won by bloodshed and intrigue." Optimism and high hope prevailed among the people during those fair, light May days, as they failed to realize that the Constitution could in no way secure their country a place among the nations.

¶ The very day that Christian Frederik accepted election as king, his old Norwegian friend and teacher, Christian Colbjørnsen, was writing to him from Copenhagen warning him that the powers were in dead earnest. He therefore urged the prince to try to win for Norway the best possible terms in a union with Sweden and then withdraw. He would thus do the country the greatest service that it had ever been rendered. Even before this letter reached him, while he was preparing to accept the crown, the newly elected king was assailed by doubts of his ability to carry through the program he had begun, and he walked his room in anguish. But though the situation had been growing steadily more critical, he was not yet ready to follow the policy advised by his teacher.

While the Eidsvoll meeting was in progress, the absolutist powers, Russia, Austria, and Prussia, sent emissaries to Copenhagen to see that the Treaty of Kiel was carried out. The English representative did not reach Denmark before the middle of June, when the others had already, or so it seemed, accomplished their purpose. They had forced the king once more to send peremptory orders to Norway that Christian Frederik and all Danish officials should return at once to Denmark, after handing over the forts to Sweden. He also ordered all communication with Norway to cease. There was, however, much sympathy for the Norwegians among the Danes, and, as the king probably expected, many a Danish vessel laden with grain slipped unnoticed into Norwegian ports. The foreign commissioners had learned in Copenhagen that Norwegian resistance was not a result of Danish intrigue, but a genuine popular movement. It was also clear that England's position would be the decisive factor.

In England there was a great deal of popular sympathy for the Norwegians, and through the influence of Carsten Anker their cause was even pleaded in Parliament. A large majority, however, upheld the government, which insisted upon a Swedish-Norwegian union. The British statesmen were opposed to a renewed Danish-Norwegian union, which had been troublesome during the Napoleonic wars, but they were no more willing to see Sweden become dominant in the North, and therefore wished Norway to retain all possible freedom in the union. Besides, the English were not absolutists, and public opinion was felt in official circles. The government sent John Morier to Norway on a special mission to explain England's position and to sound public opinion. Morier was friendly and sympathetic toward the Norwegians, and recognized that the people, who had clung to the hope for English help, were disappointed, though willing to yield to England in everything except in the matter of the union with Sweden. He had hoped to meet with the Eidsvoll assembly, but as it had adjourned before his arrival, he advised Christian Frederik—whom he did not recognize as king—to summon a special Storthing to decide between union with Sweden or war with the powers.

The king, who had been conducting foreign affairs alone and had done it well, expressed his willingness to accept the mediation of England. Submission to Sweden, he held, would violate that freedom and happiness of the Norwegian people which England had promised to uphold. He hoped, however, for an alliance with Sweden which would safeguard the Constitution, and promised to lay the results of the negotiations before the Storthing. On June 9 he decided in meeting with his cabinet to prepare for the election of a special Storthing to deal with the union question. It shows that he was entering upon the policy advised by Colbjørnsen, and also that he was becoming more fully aware of the implications of his position as a constitutional monarch.

On the same day he issued a call to arms, and the people, eager to fight, responded with enthusiasm. A surge of patriotism swept through all classes, and rich gifts to the country poured in; even treasured household silver was sacrificed. Nevertheless, among the upper strata of society the conviction was growing that a union was inevitable, but that every effort must be bent upon the preservation of the Constitution and the nation's control of its own internal affairs. Even men of the Independence Party at Eidsvoll were adopting the policy of their former opponents.

This was the situation when on the last day of June the commissioners of the powers arrived in Christiania. On their way from Copenhagen they had stopped for lengthy consultation with Swedish statesmen. While their purpose was to force Norway into a Swedish union, they were not much concerned about its exact nature. The English representative would have preferred to have had nothing to do with the matter. The Norwegian king gave them all audience together and then continued the discussion with them individually. He conducted the negotiations as a skillful diplomat. Although he had clung, longer perhaps than served the best interests of the country, to the hope of retaining the crown of Norway, he knew by this time that his own cause was lost and he was only hoping, as he said in a letter to the Danish king, that by sacrificing his personal ambitions he might help Norway to "become less unhappy than the mighty of this earth had planned."[13] He insisted that he was bound by the Constitution and would be committing treason against the people if he gave up his crown except to their representatives. He was willing, however, to convene a special Storthing and resign his power into its hands. Meanwhile the country must have an armistice, and Sweden must raise the blockade which had been put into operation and allow sorely needed importation of grain. The commissioners, to whom the idea of popular sovereignty had seemed dangerous or at the best nonsensical, found Christian Frederik's stand reasonable. When on July 15 he laid before them his peace proposal, they declared themselves willing to present it to the Swedish king with an appeal to his magnanimity. The mediators were really on the side of Norway, recognizing the country's right to be treated as a state that could negotiate with others. Agreement was reached on all but one point. Christian Frederik was to resign his power into the hands of the people, and the blockade was to be lifted. Karl Johan had begun to recede from his insistence upon the Treaty of Kiel, but, it seems, felt it necessary to show in some way that the Swedish king had a right to Norway. He demanded that the two border fortresses of Fredrikstad and Fredriksten be occupied by Swedish troops. Christian Frederik

[13] Koht, *1814*, p. 308.

insisted that to yield Norwegian soil to a foreign country was a violation of Norway's rights as a nation. Both were obdurate, and on July 29 hostilities broke out. The powers had failed in their efforts to prevent war, but they had negotiated with Norwegians as with representatives of any other independent nation, and so the country had taken the first little step toward regaining the place among states which had been completely lost in 1536.

¶ While there was a principle involved on both sides, neither leader desired war. It was really a demonstration—a costly one—demanded by both peoples. In both countries feelings of hostility had been roused. "The Swedes had to have war," said Karl Johan, for there was a growing indignation against Norway. And the Norwegian soldiers were eager to try their strength, sure that as they were fighting for their freedom they could defeat the Swedes as they had in the past. The officers were not so confident. They knew that the ragged little Norwegian army was no match for Karl Johan's seasoned, well-equipped troops, however bravely it might fight. In the northern field the Norwegians did well, but in the main battles farther south they were defeated. There was much criticism of the generals and of the king. The generals knew that victory was impossible, and Christian Frederik, deeply distressed by the war, wished to avoid a decisive defeat which might be a handicap in the peace negotiations begun on August 4.

Karl Johan was more favorably disposed than he had been earlier. The time for the opening of the Congress of Vienna was fast approaching, and he wanted the Norwegian question settled before that. He was afraid to have the matter brought before that aggregation of statesmen, for as an ex-Jacobin he was none too popular among them, while sympathy for Norway had been growing. He had really no desire to conquer Norway, in spite of the strong words he had used. Besides, he had learned to understand the Norwegian position, for Carsten Tank, a former member of the Norwegian government, had explained the whole movement in his country. The crown prince discovered that the newly-made Constitution was similar to the French document of 1791 of which he himself had been a defender. He had intended to call an estates' meeting to make the constitution under his own benevolent supervision, but he now saw that in a country almost devoid of a nobility such a meeting was not practical, and that a constitution like the Swedish could not be adapted to Norwegian conditions. So why not accept the constitution already in operation, save time, and win the approval of the people? As he had himself had a part in the French Revolution, he was not lacking in sympathy for a people willing to fight for freedom.

An armistice was concluded on August 14 by the signing of the Convention of Moss. The credit for the successful outcome of the difficult negotiations belongs chiefly to Minister Niels Aall, who served his country with the same selfless devotion and keen insight as his brother Jacob Aall. "His Royal Highness Prince Christian" was to summon a Storthing to meet in about six weeks, and the Swedish king was to negotiate with it through special commissioners. Karl Johan promised to recognize the Constitution and ask no changes except those necessitated by the union. No mention was made of the Treaty of Kiel. Christian Frederik was to resign his power into the hands of the representatives of the people and leave the country. By a secret agreement he promised to withdraw at once from active participation in the government and transfer the executive power into the hands of his cabinet, consisting of Marcus Rosenkrantz, M. O. L. Sommerhjelm, Jonas Collett, and Niels Aall. The Norwegian cabinet, not Swedish commissioners as had been Karl Johan's intention, were to conduct the government until the Storthing could make a permanent arrangement, and it was to issue its orders "in the name of the highest authority," a conveniently ambiguous phrase. Swedish forces were to occupy the Norwegian district of Østfold to within a few miles of the capital, a concession which Norwegians felt as a deep humiliation.

During the weeks that followed, national morale was at a low ebb. Economic difficulties, unrest among the people, and bitter indignation against Christian Frederik and other leaders were rife, and outbreaks were threatening in several localities. "Almost every one now denounces the king. The transition from exaggerated expectations to condemnation when these are not fulfilled is not uncommon and not to be praised. But if there ever was a human being on earth from whom we were justified in expecting everything it was Christian Frederik; and if the sorrow at seeing these expectations so completely disappointed is mingled with indignation and anger, it is excusable, although undeniably he is more to be pitied than blamed."[14]

There was little understanding of how much Norway had won or of the situation that forced the retreat from the heroic stand of the spring. With patience and tact the cabinet pursued the task of keeping order and winning for the government the confidence of the people. It must

[14] *Claus Pavels's Biografi og Dagbøger*, September 11, 1814, p. 256.

also enforce the Convention of Moss in the face of complaints from the military on both sides and incidents that even threatened the peace. It was careful not to be led into any act which might imply that a union already existed. In its interpretation, the "highest authority" in whose name it acted was still the Norwegian king, and it would assume no authority that would bind the Storthing for which elections were in progress. The king's last official act was the rescript of August 16 which summoned a Storthing to meet on October 7.

The task with which this first Storthing was confronted was much more difficult than that which had faced the Constituent Assembly. There was no enthusiasm or romance as at Eidsvoll, but the Storthing worked soberly, reason holding sway over emotions and realism over dreams. In spite of differences, there were not such violent clashes of parties as at the May meeting. Fifty of the seventy-nine members belonged to the professional class, and the average age was only forty-two. Neither the Constituent Assembly nor any subsequent Storthing has had as large a proportion of young men or of officials. Among the leaders were men who had been at Eidsvoll. Wedel, the only representative of the earlier Union Party, made a notable contribution in shaping the union he had long advocated; but the events of the independence movement had exerted influence on him, and more than earlier he emphasized the need of guarding Norway's rights. Another striking leader from among the Eidsvoll men was Captain Peter Motzfeldt. The chief credit for the success of the Storthing belongs, however, to Wilhelm K. Christie from Bergen. He was a good friend and supporter of Christian Frederik and had acted as secretary at Eidsvoll. In the intervening months he had followed events closely and was probably the best informed man politically in Norway. He still had—as had also the other leaders—an optimistic faith in his people and the future of his country. As chairman of the Storthing he guided events with a clear mind, sure instinct, and consummate skill in such a way as to preserve as far as possible the freedom of the country.

The first problem arose over the formal opening of the Storthing which, according to the Constitution, was the duty of the king. Bound by his secret promise at Moss, Christian Frederik sent a message pleading illness as a reason for not appearing in person, and he certainly was not well, being broken by the strain of the last months. To preserve legal forms Christie proposed that the ministers, who alone could act for the king, should open the Storthing, and this was promptly done. One of them, Rosenkrantz, read the king's speech. It was a frank report on his whole reign and on the conditions that necessitated his withdrawal, and at the same time an appeal to be remembered as a friend who had resigned his happy position in Norway in order to save the country from destruction. Two days later, October 10, Christian Frederik presented his formal abdication to a delegation of the Storthing. "A more tragic scene cannot be imagined," writes Niels Aall, "all eyes were filled with tears; speech died on our lips." The same evening, a dark autumnal night, accompanied by a few friends he boarded a little lugger which carried him the first lap of his voyage back to Denmark. He was deeply hurt at the unjust contempt and coolness which had met him during the last months in Norway, yet not without hope that events there might still take a turn more to his liking: "My heart is still warmly attached to this brave people."[15] When he landed in Denmark after a voyage of many delays and dangers, the Danes greeted their future king warmly.[16]

The question arose in the Storthing as to what measures were to be taken in reply to the king's abdication. Again Christie's view prevailed, that action should be deferred, for until the Storthing accepted the surrender of the crown Christian Frederik was still king. But the ministry called attention to the fact that, as the king could no longer rule actively, it became the constitutional duty of the Storthing to establish a regency. This was done by electing the four former ministers plus two new members to serve in that capacity. While these decisions may seem mere matters of form, they were significant as emphasizing that Norway was governed under the Constitution and that no union with Sweden existed.

The chief duty of the Storthing was to decide whether such a union should be formed. There was still much opposition in the country to any connection with Sweden. There was little understanding of European politics, and the hope that England would support Norway's independence died slowly. Some believed that if the whole country were united—as it was not—resistance might be successful, and a few fanatical patriots were ready to fight to the last mountain top. But any members of the Storthing who had come to Christiania with such ideas changed their opinion before long, especially after hearing a distressing committee report by Motzfeldt on the economic and military state of the nation. Although the outcome was inevitable, a heated discussion

[15] His correspondence with Carsten Anker shows how he clung to the idea that he or at least his son might still succeed Ponte-Corvo, as he continued to call Karl Johan. *Christian Frederik og Carsten Ankers Brevveksling 1814, samt Uddrag af deres Breve fra 1801-13 og fra 1815-17*, Ed. C. J. Anker, Christiania, 1904.

[16] Christian VIII, 1839-1848.

continued for days, the strongest appeal in favor of the union being made by Count Wedel. On October 20, the very last day before the expiration of the armistice signed at Moss, it was voted that Norway should be united with Sweden under a common monarch, but as an independent kingdom. There were only five negative votes, and four of these were cast by delegates from Bergen, who had a mandate from their electorate to vote against union. When they realized the situation, they wrote home asking to be released from this obligation. The request was refused, and the author of the instructions, Bishop Johan Nordahl Brun, remarked: "Though all others become perjurers, I will not."

There was a general sense of relief when the decision had been made. The Swedish commissioners, who had been repeatedly urged by their impatient crown prince to hurry matters, were jubilant. It took two more weeks, however, to make the necessary alterations in the Constitution. Each change was agreed upon in consultation with the Swedish representatives. Karl Johan had selected men of liberal views for this task, and they had been convinced by the debate in the Storthing that, the union having been secured, it would be wise to be conciliatory in smaller matters. They kept in constant touch with Karl Johan who, in spite of some outbursts of his volatile temper, generally agreed to their decisions. Under Christie's guidance the Storthing followed the principle that it had the authority only to make the changes necessitated by the union, but interpreted this to include provisions essential for the protection of Norway's rights as a state. It refused to make any of the changes suggested by the Swedes which would tend to amalgamate the two peoples or increase royal power. By November 3 the necessary alterations had been agreed upon, and some time later the modified Constitution was promulgated by the Storthing. Royal approval was not considered necessary any more than it had been on May 17.

On November 3 the Storthing also formally accepted the abdication of Christian Frederik, thus recognizing that he had been king until then, and on the following day proceeded to choose a new king. As at Eidsvoll, each man dictated his vote, and the choice of Karl XIII of Sweden was unanimous, but again the question of the character of the union came to the fore. Eight men voted to "recognize" Karl as king, twenty-four employed the form "elect and recognize," but the majority, forty-six members, used only the word "elect." Thus it was emphasized that Norway had the freedom of choice and entered into the union as an independent national state.

The election on November 4 of the king of Sweden as king of Norway also, marks the beginning of the union. When the ceremony was over Christie folded his hands and prayed with deep emotion: "God Almighty grant that this union may long endure and be happy for both kingdoms." On November 9, Karl Johan came to Christiania with his son Oscar, submitted the king's oath, and thereupon personally took an oath to uphold the Constitution of Norway. He was received with the proper illumination and ceremonial, but silent crowds watched his entry into the city.

In Stockholm the event was celebrated with gala opera and social functions at which the Norwegian representatives were much feted. There was, however, dissatisfaction with the form of the union, for the acquisition of Norway had been considered a compensation for the loss of Finland, which had been much more closely bound to Sweden. Nevertheless, there was no serious opposition, and the terms of the agreement were incorporated into an "Act of Union," which was later ratified by the Norwegian Storthing also. Officially the Swedish government abandoned the idea that Norway had been acquired through the Treaty of Kiel. In his greeting to the Storthing on November 10 Karl Johan emphasized not only the common interests that naturally bound the two people together, but also the freedom of each nation and the honor they had conferred upon the king by freely offering him the crown. "More than solemn treaty rights, he treasured the dearer and more precious rights which your love bestowed upon him."[17]

In Norway there was no enthusiasm and some apprehension, which proved unfounded, lest Norway might be absorbed into Sweden; but though there were a few expressions of bitter disappointment, most people felt a sense of relief, and, as the days passed, satisfaction and even thankfulness. Caught in a whirl of international affairs, the country had passed through serious dangers and had weathered the storms better than might have been expected. Though Norway had by no means attained equality with Sweden, the union had been formed not as a result of conquest or of the Treaty of Kiel, but on the basis of popular sovereignty and the decision of the representatives of the people. The right of the nation to control its internal affairs had been vindicated, and the absolutism under which the people lived at the opening of the year had been changed to a constitutional monarchy. Furthermore, a sound basis had been laid for steady progress both in national feeling and in democracy. A new age had dawned.

[17] Koht, *1814*, p. 479.

CHAPTER 16

KARL JOHAN AND YOUNG NORWAY, 1814-1844

THE GREAT FORWARD STRIDE that Norway had taken in the eventful year of 1814 gave an impetus to continued advance, slow at first, but exceptionally rapid in the last half of the century, when the nation took a place in the history of the age more striking, perhaps, than that of any other country of its population. The people had no militaristic ambitions and, after the first few years, a feeling of security; and they were so confident that in their position on the edge of the continent they would be left to pursue their own course without being drawn into European politics that the whole emphasis was placed on peaceful pursuits. This seemed justified as Sweden and Norway entered upon a period of uninterrupted peace which was to last until 1940. There was an intensity and fervor about the Norwegian nationalism of this age which can scarcely be found except in a small country, and certain features peculiar to the history of Norway gave its patriotism not only warmth but at times something of a braggadocian air of self-assertion. One reason for this was the Swedish union.

This union was not really satisfactory to either country, and the difference in interpretation of its character was in itself a fruitful source of friction. The position of Norway was entirely different from what it had been in the Danish period. The country retained the statehood won in 1814 and had its own government both national and local. Consequently there was no influx of Swedish officials, nor was there cultural infiltration of any significance from the neighbor kingdom. In fact, the interaction of the two countries upon each other was no more marked during the ninety years of union than in other periods of their history. The union was not a hindrance to the unfolding of a rich civilization; perhaps it was even a stimulus.

Yet there was a decided disparity between the partners. The struggle of the Norwegians to gain complete control of their own affairs and to win recognition among the family of nations not only gave vigor to their love of country, but strengthened that sense of national solidarity which had come to the fore in 1814. No local or class feeling, however bitter or rabid, could crush this sense of unity. It no doubt gave a stimulus to that rapid and far-reaching development of democracy, political and social, which is one of the striking features of nineteenth century history.

After the separation from Denmark and the adoption of the Constitution much remained as of old. The same classes controlled the political and economic life of the country and the old laws were still in force. There was continuity with the past, and only gradually were the principles of the Constitution carried out to their logical conclusion and the country changed into a democracy. Though the political ties with Denmark had been cut, the intellectual, literary, and linguistic bonds had not been severed, and the effects of the long union were not lost. But Norway had her own traditions as well, and her many-sided culture became more and more thoroughly Norwegian in character, as well as more broadly national and democratic.

¶ In the first thirty years of the Swedish union the national growth was only in its beginnings; but those were the years of awakening, we might almost say renaissance, of a new Norway. This was not an easy or a happy time for the country. The problems of creating institutions for the new state, which "stood there like a skeleton without life or blood,"[1] were many and complex, and they had to be met in the midst of a period of acute economic distress, when the people were suffering from a feeling of disillusionment which naturally follows a tense, critical period like 1814. It seemed that if a constitution could be written in a month, other lawmaking should not be too difficult; and when all tangles were not rapidly straightened out, there was irritation and a too impatient eagerness to find a scapegoat. It was easy to blame the union for all ills, and the tendency to fix responsibility for unfortunate or unpopular acts on men in high places is shown by a reckless, ill-considered use of impeachment. The people distrusted the bureaucracy, and even the Constitution itself did not escape attack. The upper classes, in turn, found the common people incompetent to shoulder even the rights and responsibility that should be theirs according to the Constitution.

The men who guided Norway through the critical years are spoken

[1] Jacob Aall, *Erindringer*, 587.

of as the "generation of 1814." The farmers played an even less important part than at Eidsvoll, although their chief spokesman in the Constitutional Convention, Teis Lundegaard, sat in the Storthing until 1845. The influence of the businessmen, who had given lavishly of their time and means in 1814 but were now caught in the depression, was also on the decline. The members of this group who remained in public life were now closely allied with the professional class, which was rising in importance, as the expanding government activities that came with the separation from Denmark opened new opportunities in public service. Retaining its upper-class viewpoint, officialdom guarded its own favored position, while the honeymoon enthusiasm for the plain people of which there was evidence at Eidsvoll faded. Although there was less supervision over local officials than in the last days of absolutism and greater opportunity for abuses and display of arrogance, the services of the class as a whole far outweigh the disservice of some individuals. It controlled the central as well as the local government and set its stamp on the age. It alone had the training and experience to map the direction in which the country should go and to create the institutions necessary for its future success. "With full awareness it took upon itself all burdens—both economic and idealistic—in order to make conditions as liveable as possible for the coming generations, and this is its greatness and shows a truly heroic trait."[2] These men had their background in the bright, optimistic late eighteenth century and carried the ideas of that age over into the lean years after the union, but they had been tempered and hardened by the distress of the war years after 1807 and the crisis of 1814. Above all, their patriotism had been intensified, and their preoccupation with public affairs had grown so all-consuming that other matters, such as personal and private affairs and cultural interests, were relegated to the background. They were convinced that they alone had the qualifications for conducting the affairs of state, and their sense of *noblesse oblige* had on the whole grown with their responsibility. They had a certain feeling for the solidarity of the whole nation, and had inherited from the eighteenth century a faith in the common people. They realized in a measure that the new Norway must draw its strength from the people as a whole, untutored though it might be.

¶ The most pressing problem that faced the Storthing of 1815 was the inflation. As in other European countries, the Napoleonic wars had

[2] Carl W. Schnitler, *Slegten fra 1814*, p. 4.

brought confusion into the monetary system of the Danish-Norwegian state. The Eidsvoll assembly had authorized an additional issue of paper money and in a vain hope of checking inflation had passed the so-called "Eidsvoll Guarantee," promising government redemption of all paper currency at a set rate of exchange. The question of whether to uphold this resolution caused a bitter debate in the Storthing. Christie and others, with an idealistic belief that the national honor must be upheld at any cost, fought for the Guarantee; but it was abandoned as hard, unsentimental business necessity carried the day. Then the country was able to build its new monetary system. The minister of finance, Count Wedel, attacked the problem with energy and wisdom, but, though he had the support of able men, a cautious, conservative opposition in the Storthing retarded action.

The *specie daler* of the eighteenth century, of approximately the same value as the American dollar ($1.08), was adopted as the monetary unit and divided into a hundred and twenty *skilling*.[3] The Bank of Norway was established at Trondheim, and it was to issue paper currency redeemable in silver. Both the paper money and the silver coins were to be legal tender. To obtain the necessary silver reserve, bank shares payable in silver were offered for sale, but the result was meager. It was therefore found necessary to force the purchase by imposing a silver tax on the wealthy. This caused a real artistic loss to the country, and many a tear was shed as heirlooms and table silver went into the melting pot. Nor did the sacrifice bring the desired result; the arrears continued to be great, for the country was very poor. Fearful that the silver reserve was inadequate to meet a possible run on the bank, the Storthing, in 1818, forbade redemption. The silver remained in the bank, the dollar continued to fluctuate and became an object of foreign speculation. The country suffered a period of deflation from 1825 to 1842. There was much monetary regulation; but opposition defeated the two boldest propositions: Wedel proposed the introduction of the bar or ingot standard, which, however, was not put into practice before England's gold standard law of 1925,[4] and Anton Martin Schweigaard, a brilliant economist and professor of law, advised a devaluation. The Storthing decided that the bank-notes should be redeemed at a definite ratio close to the current rate of exchange. Later the ratio was changed to comply with shifting conditions. The mone-

[3] In 1875 these units were changed to the *krone*, equal to about a fourth of a dollar, and the *øre*, a hundred of which make a *krone*.

[4] Keilhau, *Det norske folks liv og historie*, 8:304.

tary situation became more stable, and in 1842 silver parity was finally reached and legally established as the policy of the bank. Thanks to the Bank of Norway, the country's monetary system was in perfect order until 1914.[5]

The government finances were also in a deplorable state. Public servants were kept waiting for their meager salaries, and the payments due the king were far in arrears. The impoverished people were taxed to the limit, there was no chance to borrow money at home, there was nothing to attract foreign capital to the country, and even the meager funds of Norwegians were invested abroad. Norway's position in the international money market was distressing, and twice she suffered severe losses through foreign bankruptcies. In spite of a sharp protest from Jacob Aall, Wedel's enemies managed to have him impeached for this. He was acquitted, but only after having the accusations hanging over him for three years. As it was almost impossible to borrow money abroad, Wedel made use of his own credit and that of his father-in-law, Peder Anker. When a loan needed to meet obligations to Denmark was finally negotiated, the terms were harsh and humiliating.

But the public finances were guided by firm, able hands. The policy was to reduce the indebtedness of the country, and within a quarter of a century the debt which had seemed so terrifying was reduced to a negligible sum. That the state had become free of debt and that the country had—though all too slowly—obtained a stable currency were not the least of the services of the "generation of 1814."

¶ The severe economic depression through which the country was passing gave a somber tone to the first decades of the union. While the causes lay partly in the preceding years, the monetary confusion had a serious effect on the whole economic life. The delay in stabilizing the currency helped to retard recovery, and the timid policy of the Bank of Norway contributed to the severity of the crisis. In spite of remonstrances from experts, the bank issued chiefly only mortgage loans, and business houses could not obtain the credit which might possibly have helped them weather the storm. All in all, the many obstacles in the way of recovery seemed insurmountable, but there was a dogged courage and persistence in the people, and gradually, though very slowly, progress was made toward the more settled conditions of the 'forties.

The lumber trade, which had practically kept up the country's economic life in the decades before 1814 and had furnished many of the

[5] Keilhau, *Norway in World History*, 157.

leaders of the national rising, was hit the hardest. The lack of capital at home and commercial crises in England contributed to the disaster. Moreover, Great Britain, which had earlier been Norway's best customer, imposed a protective tariff on lumber in favor of Canada. It was so worded that Norway became the chief sufferer, and not before 1842 was the inequality removed and the duty lowered. Still more serious was the enormous export duty levied by the Norwegian government, which in 1818 furnished about a third of the national income. When the fiscal situation made it possible, the duty was gradually reduced until finally in 1841 it was brought down to a somewhat reasonable level.

In 1816 the bankruptcies began, and the catastrophe was increased by great fires in the lumber yards of Drammen and Christiania where large stocks of uninsured lumber were concentrated. As this industry was fundamental, other firms were also dragged down into the abyss. First went the fortunes of the "new rich," then the old established firms of the Colletts and Ankers and others. The great estates went under the hammer and sold for a song or found no purchaser at all. Severe losses were suffered by men like Tank, Rosenkrantz, and Niels Aall—the men of 1814, who had been leaders not only in business but in the national movement, in public affairs, in social consciousness, and in cultural life.

Shipping, which was largely dependent on the lumber industry, also suffered under heavy taxes at home and abroad, and ships rode idly at anchor. But slowly it began to develop independently of the lumber export; shipbuilding increased, the profit from foreign carrying trade advanced, and by the close of the 'thirties shipping had entered a new period of prosperity.

Not so with industry, which showed no progress. Many of the factories from the eighteenth century were closed, and no new ones were established. The state-owned glass factories were sold at a wretched price, and that industry, like others, declined. Only the distilleries flourished. The mining and metal industry, which also suffered a set-back, had more than recovered by 1840. In the copper industry the crisis was of short duration, after which production was much increased, technical improvements introduced, and steady progress made. After a period of private management the Kongsberg silver mine was again taken over by the state in 1815. At first it was run at a loss, but later a fair profit was realized, and the prosperity of Kongsberg and the surrounding district was a great gain to the country.

The iron industry went through an extremely difficult period. Norwegian iron now had to compete in the Danish market, where it had earlier had special privileges, and with Sweden and England, which were farther advanced in technical development. Moreover, in accordance with the liberalism of the day, Swedish iron was admitted to Norway free of duty, and the obligation of the Norwegian farmers to furnish wood, charcoal, and hauling to the works was abolished. Among the advocates of these changes were Wedel and Jacob Aall, who as owners of great ironworks would be among the chief sufferers. But though the times were difficult, the iron magnates would not give up. They improved both their technique and the quality of their products, strove to win new outlets, and were by 1840 better prepared than ever before to compete in the world markets.

The fishing industry also had its difficulties, but they were soon overcome. The markets lost during the wars were recaptured in a few years, and after a brief depression caused by a temporary decreased foreign demand, the fish exports doubled in volume. In spite of the monetary situation, import duty on salt, export duty on fish, and other dues, the fisheries on the whole prospered during this age. Farming alone felt practically no ill effects from the economic crisis, for money economy did not even now dominate rural life, and good harvests were more important than high prices. As there was less opportunity to make money at the mines or lumber camps, efforts were concentrated on the farm, and, while there was little change in the daily life or the methods of farming, new land was cleared and the flocks enlarged.

Though the prosperity achieved during these difficult decades may not seem striking measured by modern standards, significant progress was made in many fields. The establishment of savings banks through private initiative is an evidence of the vigor of the people. The first was opened in 1810, and forty years later fifty such institutions were scattered over the country. Not all was left to private enterprise, however, for government played a strong hand. In spite of the gradual breakdown of old restrictions which had been begun in the eighteenth century, mercantilism still had a hold on economic life, and as late as 1818 the last law embodying mercantilistic ideas was passed. It regulated mining in great detail, including rules for maximum hours of work and pensions for the laborers.

Even before this, however, work had begun on legislation to free the economic life. First to go were the special privileges of the owners of the ironworks and of the sawmills. About the same time, 1816, the restrictions on the manufacture of distilled liquor were removed, which, while hailed as a forward step in freedom, brought untold evils upon the country. The lawmakers moved cautiously and slowly so that the changes would cause the least possible injustice or instability. A law abolishing the craft guilds was passed, then restrictions on mining were removed, but provisions protecting the laborers were retained, and finally the regulations controlling the lumber industry were removed in 1860. Free trade had been established in 1842, mainly through the efforts of Schweigaard, who headed a royal commission appointed for the purpose. The central figure in the entire work to abolish restrictions was the industrialist Jacob Aall. It is significant that the men who might have profited most by retaining the old privileges made no protest against their abolition and no demand for compensation, and changes which in other countries caused disturbances were achieved peaceably.

Although the mercantilistic principle was abandoned, no *laissez-faire* theory was adopted in its stead. The authorities continued to hold that the government had some responsibility for the welfare of the people and the progress of the country. In the midst of their hesitancy and timidity in the monetary crisis the authorities gave evidence of confidence in the future of the country. New cities were chartered: Bodø in Nordland, Lillehammer in the Uplands, Vadsø in Finmark; and the old city of Sarpsborg, which had been abandoned in 1570 after being burned by the Swedes, was revived. Several steps were also taken to improve communication. The irritating centuries-old regulation that the farmers had to furnish free transportation for officials was abolished, but the expense of their travel was still borne by the people in the form of taxation. The need for new roads was great. Considerable advance was made in their maintenance, but although the king urged extensive new construction few new roads were built and they were laid at a grade that made driving very difficult. More was done for seafaring, by charting the coast of northern Norway, by building new lighthouses of the most modern type along the southern shore, and by organizing a special bureau for their inspection. More sensational was the purchase by the government of two steamboats for mail and passenger service, which were completed in 1827. The smaller, the *Constitution*, plied between Christiania and Christiansand, the larger, *Prince Carl*, furnished weekly service through the open season to Göteborg and Copenhagen. They were a source of great pride to the people, and their arrival in the little capital attracted great crowds and was a welcome break in the everyday humdrum.

In the 'thirties the economic outlook was beginning to brighten and by the close of the period the improvement was marked. Fundamental as this was, the chief interest of most public men centered upon maintaining the political achievements of 1814 and building further upon the foundations laid.

¶ There was no way in which either one of the two countries could legally interfere in the affairs of the other except through the king, who had considerable authority in both. From 1814 and on, the royal power in Norway was exercised by Karl Johan, who thus virtually ruled thirty years although he was king only twenty-six years, from 1818 to 1844. His journey to Trondheim for his coronation was a triumphal progress, and he was popular among the common people, who had an instinctive liking for the warm-hearted, hot-tempered king from the South. Even a small peasant rising instigated by the wealthy freeholder, Halvor Hoel, which disturbed the peace soon after the coronation, was directed not against the king but against the Constitution and the Storthing, which were held responsible for the increased taxes. It was a demonstration in favor of a return to the accustomed absolute monarchy. Karl Johan won friends because he was ready to forget injuries, loved to reward services, and took pleasure in dispensing generous gifts. Only slowly, however, did he win the confidence of the upper class, especially the officials. They had difficulty in comprehending this strange, exotic person whose language they could not understand and whose erratic emotional outbursts left them with a sense of insecurity. There are indications that not a few of them lived under a constant fear that the imperious king might by a sudden coup try to subvert their hard-won Constitution.

On the other hand, it was not easy for Karl Johan to understand Norway, especially as he spoke only French, which few Norwegians took the trouble to learn. He relied mainly on his statholder, who was generally a Swede, unused to Norwegian conditions. In first organizing the government he chose ministers from among the ablest men in the 1814 group, without regard for personal friendship and party. The Union Party was represented only by Wedel and Peder Anker, who was ranking minister in the group of three residing in Stockholm. But the influence of the ministry was not commensurate with its ability. Norway came to occupy a less important place than the arrangements of 1814 had intended. As the king lived in Sweden, it was easy to fall into the habit of depending on Swedish officials, and for some time there was no protest from Norway.

Although the king did not actually break the oath he had taken in 1814 to uphold the Norwegian Constitution, he was far from satisfied with it, and when he found that it did not serve his plans, he was anxious to have it changed. Such a situation arose in 1821, when it had taken useless wrangling and delay before the Storthing had finally voted the appropriations necessary to carry out a treaty legally entered into with Denmark. He felt that this must be the result of flaws in the Constitution, and tried to correct these by proposing a number of amendments. The trend of them all was to increase the royal power. He wished, to mention only one thing, to give the king the absolute veto instead of the suspensive veto provided by the Constitution. The "Father of the Constitution" was also disappointed in the way the instrument had operated. The opposition in the Storthing had been vitiated by private enmities and personal attacks, by unreasoning outbursts of hostility to Sweden and Denmark, and by appeals to the element among the people which had least political experience. Falsen was disillusioned, and lost his faith in the common people. He therefore proposed amendments which would strengthen upper-class control of the Storthing.

Both Karl Johan's and Falsen's plans were taken up by the Storthing of 1824. The Constitution committee, under the chairmanship of Christian Krohg, presented a report which was a learned treatise as well as an eloquent defense of the Constitution, and every proposed amendment was unanimously rejected. Regardless of all his earlier services to his country, the opposition press subjected Falsen to the most bitter persecution which any man of the period had to suffer. Karl Johan's popularity, on the other hand, does not seem to have been affected in the least, although his plan was laid before the Storthing time and again without ever gaining more than one favorable vote.

These events strengthened the devotion to the Constitution, as the people were proud of having one of the freest governments in the world, and looked upon the Constitution as the sacred symbol of their nationalism.

This feeling found a natural expression in the commemoration of May 17, "the birthday of our Constitution." The first celebration in Christiania occurred in 1824, the Students' Union (*Studentersamfundet*) taking the initiative. Royal disapproval, however, kept the festivities from reaching any great proportions before 1827. In that year there was a gala celebration, but before long the statholder, who had intimated that the king would make no objection, was summarily dismissed. Two years later, after the formal festivities had been concluded, great crowds gathered in the marketplace just to see what would happen. When the police had in vain asked the crowd to disperse, the authorities became jittery and the statholder authorized the use of military force. The riot act was read, and a troop of infantry charged through the crowd, though without firing a shot. Again and again they charged, for the people would not scatter—this was too exciting. The whole city was indignant as well as amused, and both these emotions found their best expression in a cartoon and a satirical farce by a young student who had been in the midst of events. His name was Henrik Wergeland. Official investigation led to no action, and the king was enraged at the statholder, for the use of soldiers against civilians was abhorrent to him. When the luckless man died soon after, Karl Johan left the post vacant, letting the ranking minister in Norway, Jonas Collett, head the government. There was no more interference with the celebration of Constitution day. The people had won the "battle of the marketplace," and the conflict added zest to later anniversaries and deepened the loyalty to the Constitution.

The devotion to the Constitution naturally found expression in laws which in some measure put its ideals into practice. In this category are the economic laws already mentioned. Many other legislative needs had suggested themselves to the men at Eidsvoll, but there was no time to consider them nor did a mass of details properly belong in a constitution. Many tasks were therefore left to the Storthing, some mandatory and others merely implied by the spirit of the Constitution.

The greatest task definitely prescribed was that of compiling a general code of laws to replace Christian V's Norwegian Law, and a committee was even appointed to begin this work. Although there were able jurists among them, the undertaking was too stupendous to be completed in the midst of the many immediate problems of the day, and, indeed, this mandate of the Constitution has not yet been carried out. Efforts were concentrated upon the criminal laws, which the committee found in most glaring conflict with the principles of the Constitution. In 1815 all penalties involving torture or mutilation were abolished, thus completing a modernization begun in the eighteenth century, and after years of thorough work a code known as the Criminal Law of 1842 was completed and received royal sanction.

The constitutional provision for a suspensive veto was successfully tested when the Storthing, defying royal opposition, passed three times a bill to abolish the nobility. Though the Norwegians were proud of now belonging to the only European state which had no feudal aristocracy, the spirit back of this law was not strong enough to equalize the obligation to do military service, and that burden continued to rest almost exclusively on the rural population, especially in the lower economic strata. An advance in personal freedom which must also be mentioned was the repeal in 1842 of the century-old Conventicle Act.

When the Constitution was adopted it was taken for granted that a new school law must follow. The brave efforts of both pietists and rationalists of the eighteenth century to advance education had brought meager results, for a law of 1741 left the control of the schools to each parish. The people, resenting "unnecessary" expenses, defied both bishops and officials and made as scant provisions for school and teacher as possible. Some little improvement was made through a law of 1827, but even moderate reforms were difficult to carry out, and many parishes continued to have only perambulatory schools. The establishment of a normal school was important and eventually meant substantial progress in folk education. But more was necessary to produce a politically intelligent nation.

"The people must not be more backward than its constitution," Wedel remarked. It was the consensus in the Storthing that the voters could best acquire a political maturity commensurate with their privileges under the Constitution through training in local self-government. Certain influential officials, however, feared such a democratic move and the loss of power it would mean for them. At any rate the movement gained little momentum before 1833 when the common people obtained a majority in the Storthing. On January 14, 1837, royal sanction was given to the two Communal Government Acts, one for the cities and one for the rural districts, which placed the control of local affairs in the hands of representatives elected by the voters.

The corporate towns had from the eighteenth century exercised some self-government, but now the local control was made practically complete. Although the old tradition of the rights of the people had not completely disappeared in the rural areas, local self-government there was practically new. The smallest unit of government, the commune or township, which generally coincides with the parish, has since 1863 been called *herred*. It elects a group of selectmen who choose from their number a smaller administrative council, or *formannskap*. Once a year the chairmen of all the local councils within the larger district, or shire, meet to consider matters of common interest. Before 1919 the shire continued to be called *amt*, as in the days of absolutism, but then the name was legally changed to the old Norwegian *fylke*, while the title of the governor became *fylkesmann* instead of the earlier *amtmand*. The governor is appointed by the king, and great prestige is attached to his position as he is the highest representative of the central authority as well as the chief executive in the local government of his district. Except for the expansion of the franchise, there were few changes in the local government until well into the twentieth century, and 1837 is second in importance only to 1814 in the history of Norway's political growth.

¶ The most striking inequality in the union was the fact that Norway had no share in the control of foreign affairs. The Norwegians were at a disadvantage because for the past four centuries they had had no independent international position and were therefore totally inexperienced. Moreover, Christian Frederik, who had had his own ambitions as well as the country's welfare in mind, had kept personal control over foreign affairs and failed to organize a foreign office. It was therefore easy for Karl Johan to take matters into his own hands and make use of the already established Swedish department.

Karl Johan insisted that it was necessary for the two kingdoms to present a strong united front in the face of Europe. He alone of the rulers who had risen as a result of the French Revolution survived the fall of Napoleon and the establishment of the system of Metternich. He knew that his position was none too secure, and that it behooved him to be strong and to walk warily lest he cause offense to the legitimist rulers of the day. Nor could the liberal institutions of Norway be expected to win favor in a time of reaction, and, as Karl Johan saw the concert of powers suppress liberal movements in other countries, he could not feel certain that his kingdoms would escape interference.

Most Norwegians did not understand this background for their king's foreign policy, nor did they fully appreciate that in his whole course he was defending the integrity of his realm. Filled with a strong, pugnacious patriotism, they were keenly sensitive to any real or imagined slight to their national dignity and confident that they were able to defend their country's rights. At first they accepted the king's control over foreign affairs as convenient and economical, but before long they began to resent the preponderance of Swedish influence, which emphasized Norway's humiliating inferior position in the union and prevented Norwegian interests from receiving fair consideration. It was natural—perhaps inevitable—that the demands of Norway for a dignified position as a nation among nations should lead to controversies with the king and later with Sweden, and the issue, first raised in the reign of Karl Johan, continued to reappear until it finally resulted in the severance of the union.

The problem first arose in connection with Denmark's demand for the fulfillment of a clause of the Treaty of Kiel which stipulated that she should be reimbursed for a fair share of the Danish-Norwegian state debt. A few days after the union had been formed, the Storthing, oppressed by the thought of the burden the country would have to shoulder, expressed the opinion that "the adjustment might best be left to His Majesty alone." Karl Johan argued that, as Denmark had not been able to carry out the promise to hand over Norway, the other clauses of the treaty were also void; but he nevertheless found it prudent to take up negotiations with Denmark. The powers backed the Danish claim and as the matter dragged, the members of the Quintuple Alliance assembled in 1818 at Aix-la-Chapelle each sent a sharp warning to Karl Johan. It was even implied that if Norway's obligations were evaded the old Danish-Norwegian union might be reestablished. Karl Johan was furious. He sent an outspoken reply to the five rulers in a tone to which those mighty sovereigns were not accustomed and which offended them all. He attacked sharply the policy of the powers as contrary to the principles which had united the nations against Napoleon, adding that if international differences were to be decided arbitrarily by force instead of by international law, the smaller peoples would be plunged into "an abyss of disasters." There was a claim advanced for the return to Norway of Iceland, Greenland, and the Faroes, which in the Treaty of Kiel had been retained by Denmark. The matter was not pressed with any vigor, however, and the opportunity—if it existed—was lost. With the British minister at Stockholm acting as mediator, an agreement on the debt question which was very favorable to Norway was finally reached in 1819. It remained for the Storthing to appropriate the funds necessary to fulfill the treaty obligations.

From the first there had been strong opposition to paying anything to Denmark. The Storthing of 1821 had been elected mainly on this issue and the leader of the opposition, Jacob Hoel, declared that he would rather have war than pay. Most members realized that the agreement had to be fulfilled to prevent possible war with the powers, but as peace was just as important to Sweden as to Norway many thought she should share the burden. Karl Johan, however, maintained that Norway must carry the debt alone in order to uphold her financial independence and integrity. The Storthing was won over to the king's view mainly through an impassioned plea by Christian Magnus Falsen, who had been on the committee which reported in favor of asking Swedish help but had the courage to change his opinion. The Storthing finally upheld the treaty in full, but only after its delay had caused the government considerable embarrassment.

While the discussion was going on, the king gathered 6,000 Swedish and Norwegian troops near Christiania and Swedish warships entered the harbor. At first there was irritation in Norway, but it soon vanished, as the king visited the troops and praised the Norwegian soldiers. The encampment ended with a grand ball, and directly afterwards warm ovations greeted the king on his visit to Christiania. Probably he wished to impress the Norwegians with this military demonstration, and it is possible that it had some connection with his fear of war, for even now he did not feel sure that the powers might not interfere in Northern Europe as they were doing in the South. A consistent friend of peace for his own kingdoms and for Europe, he maintained close relations with England and France, while the keynote to his foreign policy was friendship with Russia, as it had been since he became crown prince of Sweden in 1809.

While the negotiations with Denmark were going on an incident occurred which had many repercussions later. English smugglers had been busy at Bodø, and the customs authorities finally arrested some of them and confiscated their goods. After their release, the smugglers in turn held some officials prisoner, recaptured their goods, and sailed for England. Through an unscrupulous lawyer with good connections, documents were daringly falsified, and the case was presented to the British foreign office as if Englishmen had suffered maltreatment. Demands for reparation were made in Stockholm, and the government, having inadequate information and being worried about the larger problem of the debt, found it wise to yield—and rightly so. When several years later more details came to light, the matter was presented in a manner that naturally roused righteous indignation in Norway. Though Norwegian ministers shared the responsibility for not having pursued the investigation farther, the Swedish government was blamed, and this Bodø Case, while in itself not significant, was the cause of Norwegian demands for a just share in the conduct of foreign affairs and equality with Sweden in the union.

In 1827 the Storthing adopted an address to the king asking that the minister of state residing in Stockholm be given an opportunity to take part in the discussion of the kingdom's foreign affairs. In the following Storthing in 1830 the able liberal lawyer Jonas Anton Hjelm proposed that the king's attention be called to the fact that, according to the Norwegian Constitution and the Act of Union, the Norwegian ministry should be summoned when diplomatic matters of common interest were to be considered, and that consuls, even though they might be Swedes, had to be appointed also by the government of Norway in order to look after the interests of that country. All he asked was that the agreements of 1814 should be carried into effect, as they had not been; and still neither this Storthing nor the next had the courage to pursue the matter. Soon after, a royal resolution opened the opportunity for one Norwegian to be present when Norwegian matters were discussed, but, while intended to meet Norwegian demands, this was really a retrogression from the union agreement. Later the king decreed that consuls should be appointed in a joint meeting of the ministry of the two countries, and ordered them to take an oath also as Norwegian officials.

While this in part complied with the wishes of the Norwegians, the agitation begun by Hjelm was continued in the Storthing of 1836. But while it was working on the problem, the king summarily dissolved the Storthing. There was great excitement at what seemed a curt rebuff, but before a month had passed a special session was convened. The king had made a demonstration. He thought the time was especially inopportune for any agitation that might indicate a real or apparent weakening of the solidarity of his two kingdoms, for he was nervous about the international situation. The Revolution of 1830 had left Europe divided into a liberal West and a reactionary East, and he feared a clash of arms between the two. Should this happen, his realm would be in an exposed position, and he might have difficulty in maintaining peace and neutrality.

In the reconvened Storthing demands were brought forward to accord Norway greater dignity in the handling of her foreign interests. Special emphasis was placed upon the use of the national flag. The Danish flag with the Norwegian lion in one corner continued to be used until 1821 when the present flag was adopted. But, in spite of remonstrance, the navy used until the end of the reign the so-called union flag, which was really the Swedish flag with a red and white cross in one corner. The chief protest, however, was against the rule which prohibited the merchant marine from using the Norwegian flag south of Cape Finisterre. The Swedish flag had secured Norwegian ships from attacks by Barbary pirates to whom Sweden had paid tribute, but after the French conquest of Algiers this humiliating protection no longer seemed necessary. In 1838 the king permitted every shipowner to use the Norwegian flag in all waters, but at his own risk, and Hjelm, the most ardent advocate of the change, was feted as the "liberator of the flag."

A more important result of the agitation of 1836 was the reestablishment of the office of statholder, and the appointment of Wedel to that position. The selection of a Norwegian caused general satisfaction, and Wedel filled the place with great distinction during the remaining four years of his life. As the king, who had earlier made most decisions himself, left more and more matters to Wedel, Christiania became the center of the administration to a much greater degree than earlier, and harmonious relations were established which continued throughout the last years of Karl Johan's reign.

¶ In the first decades after 1814 life was dominated by the aristocracy of professional men who filled most of the important posts in the central government and the positions of governors, judges, sheriffs, and clergymen throughout the land as well as holding the majority in the Storthing. It is among them and in their homes that we have to seek the life and culture peculiar to the age.

In the rural communities there was little change, and though there was some indication of a growing tendency to adopt the ways of the officials and city folks, the old aloofness was maintained. In the western towns, notably Bergen, which were dependent largely on the fish trade, conditions had also been relatively undisturbed by the depression. Bourgeois life went on as before, the women gossiped and the men talked about the price of fish, and they rather resented the Quodlibet, the little intellectual circle of which Christie was the central figure. In the far North prosperous merchants continued to dominate like petty kings, each in his small community, but they had little influence in the country as a whole. In the towns of the South and East, however, the financial crisis had been keenly felt. The collapse of the great business houses had left in its wake misery for the poor and, even for the more fortunate, the passing of the gay social life which had emanated from the great houses in Christiania made the undeveloped little capital seem even more drab than before.

The confidence and prosperity from the flush times had furnished a momentum which carried the country through the hard war period from 1807 to 1814 as well as the crisis of that year. But now as the old luxurious patrician life had passed, in its place had come a sober, restrained, academic culture of a generation steeled by years of hardship. An intense patriotism dominated the age, as well as an overwhelming sense of the new dignity and responsibility which had come with the Constitution. "Our forefathers had only a home; we have a country. They were only inhabitants, we are citizens," says Camilla Collett. But the cosmopolitan atmosphere which pervaded the Copenhagen of their youth also helped to shape the life and culture in the homes of officialdom.

There were many more of these in the rural districts then than in recent times, and they played a much more important part in the whole life of the community. The spacious houses were designed for ample living, for the innumerable activities of a group that to a large degree was self-sustaining, and for the generous hospitality which, though often a burden, gave welcome variety and outside contact. The architecture was in harmony with the Empire style of the day, though it took a more severe classical form than in most countries, the excessive simplicity being relieved by occasional beauty of detail, especially in the doorways. In the interior also the adaptation of the Empire style was very close to the classic. The furniture, generally the work of Norwegian artisans, showed excellent craftsmanship and sure taste, many a sofa and console table looking as if it were copied from a Greek vase, while porcelain and silver of rare beauty graced the table. There was an air of dignified solidity and beauty in the sparsely furnished rooms.

It took many-sided ability and unstinted effort on the part of the women to maintain the standard of gracious living, expansive hospitality, and patriarchal atmosphere which was considered in harmony with their station. For the income was meager indeed and daily living had to be extremely simple, even though mush and skimmed milk might get monotonous if served twice a day. But the classic spirit came to their rescue by exalting frugality as a cardinal virtue, even as among the early Romans. In the 'thirties, when general economic conditions improved, life in the homes became a little easier and gained in richness; but even then the poet Welhaven while a student had to feign a hardy contempt for overcoats as he saw no way of providing himself with such a luxury.

The exacting academic training through which professional men passed was a narrow classical course. This developed the sturdy virtues they needed and the capacity for organization of law and institutions, which was the main task of this generation. As public affairs were an all-consuming interest among them, the study of law attracted a disproportionately large number of young men. This was not the sole higher interest, however. In 1825 Christie founded the Bergen museum for the collection of scientific, archaeological, and historical material, with the emphasis on the country's early history. Moreover, the Storthing gave grants for scientific research to two university professors, Balthazar Mathias Keilhau, who made geological researches in Norway and Spitzbergen, and Christopher Hansteen, who was the first to publish a complete presentation of the theory of the magnetism of the earth. In this age, Norway also produced one of the greatest mathematicians of all times, Niels Henrik Abel, whose early death was an irreparable loss.

Conditions were not favorable for the production of a rich art or literature immediately after 1814. The country was too poor and too much engrossed in the problems of the moment. It was even difficult to keep abreast of the times, as newspapers, though waging a brave struggle to maintain themselves, gave but inadequate news. The student of today, however, has access to the numerous memoirs and diaries which constitute the most notable writing of the day, as well as to a wealth of letters and documents. Of poetry there was practically nothing before Henrik Wergeland of sufficient merit to deserve immortality. Of interest to the student is Mauritz Hansen's delightful description in Homeric hexameter of life in a home of the professional class.

In architecture something was achieved. Norway was very much in need of public buildings and fortunate enough to have two Danish-born architects of note, Hans Ditlev Frants Linstow and Christian Henrik Grosch. To Linstow was given the task of designing the royal palace, the first great building project of the new Norway. Lack of appropriations forced him to simplify his original plan, and the result was a modest palace of classic design. Linstow also gave much thought to the setting, and laid out along true classic lines Karl Johan Street leading to the palace and the adjoining blocks as a suitable hub of the capital. Though his plan was only partially executed, he did more than anyone else to determine the character of the city and to give direction to the work of the next generation of architects, who were all his disciples. Most important among them was Grosch, who designed a number of public edifices, notably the University buildings. He followed Linstow's idea of three structures about a quadrangle, but employed an even more severe style.

The spirit of the classic age remained strong even beyond the middle of the century. Humble craftsmen and famous architects alike had adapted the art forms of the age to the needs of their own country, and had helped to produce the characteristically Norwegian upper-class style of the period. Of sculpture there was very little. The most talented men were so lost in the admiration of the neo-classicism of the famous Thorvaldsen that they became mere imitators of his style, while they failed to attain to their master's greatness. The work of all these was cosmopolitan rather than national, and painting alone developed along unquestionably Norwegian lines.

Some of the portrait painters, although not especially great, deserve mention. Jacob Munch's strong portraits of elderly Eidsvoll men and other aristocrats are expressive of the dignity and devotion to form of the age. More informal are the works of Mathias Stoltenberg. He traveled about the country painting small portraits suitable for the living room wall, of men and women among the ordinary official class. There is individuality and charm in his simplicity and honest directness of treatment and in the rich coloring used in reproducing the brave finery of his subjects. While portrait painters might make a frugal living at home, landscape painters were forced to seek both their training and livelihood abroad, but it was these artists, who did most of their work away from home, who attained prominence. Among them Johan Flintoe, with his cold detachment, his emphasis on drawing, his faithfulness in depicting details, and his restrained use of color, is close to the classic age. His discovery of the bleak mountain wilds as a field for the artist points toward a new age, and his amusing cartoons of travel difficulties are enlightening to the student. A greater artist was Thomas Fearnley. He had a more romantic approach to nature, a more magnificent conception, and greater strength in his draftsmanship. A restless wanderer, he was cosmopolitan in his themes and in his treatment. He owed much to his teacher Johan Christian Dahl, who is considered the greatest painter of Norway's nature whom the country has ever produced.

Dahl was the son of a poor ferryman in Bergen. He was discovered by the famous teacher, Lyder Sagen, always on the alert for talent among the common people, and was sent to Copenhagen to study. He spent most of his life in Dresden, returning to Norway only for summer visits. But his affection for his country and its nature grew deeper with the passing years. And he expressed this love on his canvases, as he pictured Norway's nature in its many facets with a virile realism—fresh, vital, colorful scenes, free both from the formalism of the classicist and the emotionalism of the romanticist. He loved panoramic views, dramatic effects of the wildest nature and weather, as well as moonlit scenes with sensitive nuances of light and color. Yet he executed details with affectionate care, and painted scenes from his native city and its surroundings with a tenderness best expressed in the silky, soft atmospheric effects of the seaside. Best known, perhaps, is his picture of a magnificent birch rooted in a mountain crevice, which is wrenched and bent by the storm while upon its branches play rays of sunlight from a rift in the clouds. "It is only a birch, yet a poem whose theme is meager soil and ready growth."[6]

Dahl revealed to the Norwegians the nature of their country as they had never seen it before, but he did more. He worked to rouse among them a greater appreciation of art, and was instrumental in getting the Storthing to establish the National Gallery in 1836, to which he gave his own collection of old masters. He also waged a gallant battle against inertia and indifference for the preservation of art treasures from the Middle Ages until in 1844 a society was formed for this purpose. Dahl has been called the father of Norwegian painting and Norway's 1814 in art. In a sense he holds the place in painting which his contemporary Henrik Wergeland has in literature. The work of both is indicative of the decline of the classic and the dawn of the national romantic phase of cultural growth; but, unlike the poet, Johan Christian Dahl had no share in the movement which was eventually to break upper-class social and political control.

¶ There was a new ferment in Norwegian life as the "generation of 1830" came upon the scene. The improvement in economic conditions, though not marked, gave an impetus toward ampler living, but more important was the stimulus that came from the July Revolution in France and the other risings of 1830. These revolutions seemed to vindicate the ideals of 1814 and—even more important—gave the country a new sense of security, for as Western Europe broke the shackles of the system of Metternich, all danger of intervention by foreign reactionary powers was past, and the ideas of 1814 could be pursued with new boldness. An important step on the road to a complete democracy was taken with the entrance of the *bønder* into a more active political life. This brought to the fore a new group of men, known as the "generation of 1830," which realized more fully than the men of 1814 that a truly Norwegian state must be built through the

[6] Jens Thiis in *Scandinavian Art*, 445.

participation of the people at large, the country people—that the national movement must become democratic.

The provision in the Constitution that two-thirds of the members of the Storthing must come from the rural districts offered to the common people a chance to dominate that body. But whether from inertia, lack of leaders, or from a shrewd sense of their own inadequacy and inexperience, they had failed to avail themselves of this opportunity and often elected officials to the Storthing—ministers or judges. The farmers in the Storthing had complained of arrogant sheriffs, grumbled about taxes, and joined the opposition in obstructive tactics; but they had not formed any class policy.

But by 1830 there was a strong feeling in certain elements, both of the common people and the professional class, that the rural population must take the place in public life to which it was entitled. Among the better-educated farmers of the Uplands agitation was carried on through a newspaper, *Statsborgeren* (The Citizen), filled with attacks on public men. More widespread was the influence of Jon Neergaard's little tract known as *Olaboka* (Ole's Book) which the author distributed as he traveled about the country speaking. It emphasized the need of electing more of the common people in order to ease their burdens by cutting down taxes and decreasing the income of officialdom. It was a simple program and won ready hearing.

After the election of 1832, forty-five of the ninety-six members of the Storthing were farmers, and they could easily obtain the few extra votes necessary to put through any measure they desired. Jonas Anton Hjelm, who had probably helped Neergaard prepare *Olaboka*, had conceived the idea of forming a liberal party through the union of the farmers and the liberals from the towns. But his plans came to naught, for he and his fellows did not win the confidence of the rural representatives. These were by tradition more inclined to favor the king than the opposition, and did not stay in power long enough to form any broader national or even class program. In the later elections fewer representatives were chosen from among the common people and before the end of the decade the professional class had once more a complete—though less secure—control of the Storthing, which was to last for another generation. Yet the *bonde* movement of the 'thirties was not without tangible results. The local government act, passed during these years, opened an opportunity for training in politics which prepared the people to take a more significant part later in the larger affairs of the nation. Moreover, among the new members of the Storthing in 1833 was a notable popular leader, Ole Gabriel Ueland. He was of the small, dark type common in his home district in the Westland, far from imposing in outward appearance, and his awkward "book language" might cause a smile among the listeners. Before long, however, he attracted attention by his keenness in debate and his uncanny skill in finding flaws in the arguments of his opponent. He was close to the soil and close to the people, and won their confidence. More than anyone else he was to be instrumental in winning for his class its proper place in the political life of the nation.

But more was needed to awaken the people to their opportunities, and the man who gave direction and richness to an age that seemed halting and barren was the greatest genius that had yet risen in young Norway, Henrik Wergeland. His childlike simplicity, sensitive gentleness, deep tumultuous emotions, and rough strength, together with his broad vision, optimistic courage, and rare poetic gifts, enabled him to exert a far-reaching influence on the growth of his country. Reared by his father, the noted Eidsvoll man, Nicolai Wergeland, in the best of eighteenth century thought, he was cosmopolitan in his outlook, filled with deep pity for the oppressed, and with sympathy for patriots fighting for freedom, be they Greeks or Poles or Spaniards. To all these he paid warm tribute in poetry, regretting that his voice could reach so few because he belonged to a small people. It was he who roused in Norway that sympathy for the Jews which led to their free admission to the country a few years after his death. And the Cliffs of Dover are the theme of one of his loveliest patriotic lyrics, for to no foreign culture did Wergeland feel so closely akin as to the English; he loved Byron, and Shakespeare had a greater influence on him than any other poet.

But above all, Wergeland had a passionate love for his own country and people, not because they were perfect—or even better than others—but because they were his. He had great confidence in the heights to which they might rise, and made it his mission in life to help realize the high ideals he had set for Norway.

Though he was but a child of six during the stirring days of 1814, his most impressionable years were lived at Eidsvoll, where his father was pastor. From childhood he revered the cradle of the Constitution and largely through his efforts, the Eidsvoll Building and quite a little of the surrounding property was in 1837 purchased with money raised by a popular, nation-wide subscription, and turned over to the state. And the spot where, as Wergeland put it, the new Norway dwells "with all its happy promises,"[7] became a national shrine. Through his father, he learned to understand and value the achievements of 1814 as perhaps no one else of his generation except his sister Camilla. In all his agitation for Norway's rights as a nation he drew his inspiration from a return to the ideals of 1814, and there too was the source of his faith in democracy. His father, who was of a yeoman family, had in spite of his own successful career retained some instinctive prejudice against the professional class, and this found ready response in Henrik's impressionable mind.

In 1825 Wergeland came to the University of Christiania, which was the center of the political and cultural life of the country. He entered with abandon into all the pleasures and diversions the city offered. They were few, however, and unfortunately for a student of theology, to be found chiefly in roisterous taverns of questionable reputation, and hindered him from getting the appointment as a clergyman which he desired. With boundless energy and irrepressible ardor Wergeland took up the cudgels in every good cause. Though he did not enter public life and never joined any group or party, he was heart and soul with the opposition which resisted any encroachments on the national freedom of Norway. Best known is his championship of the right of the people to celebrate the Seventeenth of May. He held no personal resentment against Karl Johan, however, but was attracted by the fiery Gascon and in his later years even accepted a poet's stipend from the king.

He felt that the country needed to make the best possible use of all its human resources. He therefore looked upon emigration as near treason, and wrote a drama—of indifferent artistic merit—to combat the "America fever" which was even then beginning to show itself. More often he wrote against the oppressors of the lowly, and even in ballads for children the wicked sheriff appears as the rascal. Every movement to advance the cause of the people found its most valiant advocate in Wergeland. He wrote a great deal for the common people, to teach them not only love of their country but a sorely needed appreciation of decent living, thrift, temperance, cleanliness, and godliness. Most of these writings were in prose, sometimes in the form of highly moral little stories, which can hardly qualify as literature. But lyrics, too, could teach lessons, such as the little poem of the babbling brook tirelessly washing the faces of the stones along its banks, and the cleanly wagtail dipping its wings in the shallows. Nothing was too trivial, nothing too great, to find a response in his rich nature and sound philosophy of life. He poured out his ideas in a wealth of writings on every conceivable

[7] *Henrik Wergelands samlede Skrifter*, Hartvig Lassen, ed., 7:523, Christiania, 1853.

subject, reaching his greatest heights in lyrics of exquisite beauty or of passionate turbulence. Above all, Wergeland was thoroughly Norwegian, and his people have instinctively recognized his life and work as an expression of its best and most vital characteristics. He wanted for his country a culture purely its own, freed from the hated Danish influence with its reminders of centuries of dependence, and built upon the traditions of a great past which still lived among the common people.

Wergeland's ideas found a ready ear among some of his more talented contemporaries. Among them was the violinist, Ole Bull, who, as Wergeland said, brought Norway home to the Norwegians. "Most people knew the folk songs and dances, but were ashamed to admire them. Lifted by him into their confidence and love, these homely melodies suddenly began to gleam like stars, and the people came to feel that they too had jewels of their own."[8] Bull listened eagerly to Wergeland and derived inspiration from him.

Norway had a remarkably great number of gifted young people who, like Wergeland and Bull, are of the generation born in the years of stress immediately before 1814. Most of them, however, belong primarily to the next period and will be mentioned there. The majority of this young intelligentsia were the followers not of Wergeland, but of the other great poet of the age, Johan Sebastian Welhaven.

Wergeland's sister Camilla Collett speaks of Welhaven as storming like a tempest through the turgid society of his day. One can hardly get an idea of his tempestuous vigor from his poetry. There one finds a delightful perfection in form and smoothly flowing rhythm in keeping with his fastidious tastes and artistic ideals. He came from Bergen, where he had been a disciple of Lyder Sagen and had come to share his high regard for aesthetics in every field. When he came to the university, Welhaven was impatient with the uncouth, provincial society, the meager intellectual life, and undeveloped institution, which had only twenty professors and five hundred students, and a very limited equipment. He failed to realize that during these first decades after 1814 the leaders must of necessity focus their attention upon political affairs. His criticism has been compared to "scolding because one could not feel quite at home in an unfinished house."[9] He was especially critical of

[8] Mortimer Smith, *The Life of Ole Bull*, 36, published by Princeton University Press for The American-Scandinavian Foundation, 1943.

[9] Grøndahl and Raknes, *Chapters in Norwegian Literature*, 76.

Wergeland, whose poetry seemed to him grating and whose expressions of patriotism seemed brash and uncouth.

With his intimate friends Welhaven withdrew into a life of aloofness—partly necessitated by poverty—quite different from the convivial democracy of his opponent. He gave vent to his feelings in a long poem, *Norges Dæmring* (The Dawn of Norway), in which he described the low estate into which the country had sunk with a force and bitterness that made him for a while the most unpopular man in the country. Yet he, too, was warmly patriotic and expressed the conviction that:

> What Norway was she shall become once more,
> On land, on sea, and in the rank of nations.[10]

But he had no sympathy with Wergeland's wish to sever the hated cultural bonds with Denmark. The extreme anti-Danish agitation seemed to Welhaven like scorning luscious fruit when one has only potatoes and herring:

> What art brings to us from foreign shores
> Norway's sons must wisely use,
> And gently shield the noble seed
> Until it sprouts among our rocky cliffs.[11]

The antagonistic views of the two poets and their friends brought on the most violent conflict that has ever occurred in Norwegian literary circles. The battle was waged with an intensity found only in a small country, with a virulence impossible in any but a crude, youthful society, and with the earnestness of ardent youth filled with a deep sense of responsibility. In later, mellower years, Welhaven warned his reader: "Should the polemic tone now seem offensive in many ways, it must be remembered that an age of transition, a renaissance, is always an age also of clashes and invective."[12] He believed—and rightly so—that the controversy had a far-reaching, stimulating influence on the cultural life of the whole country. And later history was to show a blending of the two opposing currents of thought, although of the two Wergeland has had the more vital influence upon his countrymen.

Wergeland was not, however, to live to see the effect of his labor upon the coming generation, for he was stricken with a fatal illness

[10] J. S. Welhaven, *Samlede Skrifter*, 1:191, Kjøbenhavn, 1867.
[11] Gerhard Gran, *Norges dæmring*, 98, Bergen, 1899.
[12] *Samlede Skrifter*, "*Forord*," vol. 1.

when only thirty-seven; but even today his "name rings through our saga like a song of patriotism and of battle."[13] Wergeland died on July 12, 1845, Karl Johan in April 1844. These two deaths marked the passing of the generation that knew 1814.

While many of the leaders of the generation of 1830 were disappearing from public life, Ole Gabriel Ueland was to continue for another quarter of a century to champion ideals not far removed from those of Wergeland. Ueland's outlook was narrower, however, and his work concentrated upon the more limited, but also more tangible field of politics. His aim was both to win for his class its proper place in the life of the nation and to rouse it out of its parochialism, and the credit for the progress made along these lines belongs largely to him. His first years in the Storthing seemed to him one continuous martyrdom,[14] so bitter was upper-class opposition to the *bonde* politics he was launching, and the cleavage between classes continued to be sharp. Still Ueland did not pursue a consistent class program, for most progressive proposals of the age—those that became law as well as the many more which were only heralds of reforms to come—had supporters from all classes. Moreover, while the majority of the upper class were not ready to accept political democracy, the intellectuals were not void of the romantic sentiment expressed by P. A. Munch that the *bønder* constituted "the noblest part of the nation."[15]

It may be said that Ueland more than any one else was the bond between the *bonde* movement of the 'thirties and the more mature rising which was to come after the last period of the dominance of officialdom.

[13] Halvdan Koht, *Henrik Wergeland, et folkeskrift,* 1, Kristiania, 1908.
[14] Arne Bergsgaard, *Ole Gabriel Ueland og bondepolitikken,* 1:176, Oslo, 1932.
[15] Quoted by Bergsgaard, 1:514.

CHAPTER 17

THE AGE OF NATIONAL ROMANTICISM, 1844-1872

IN THE FIRST DECADES AFTER 1814 the development of Norway had inevitably been slow; the country was backward economically and intellectually, more isolated than ever before or later. But after 1840 the nation experienced a rapid change which brought the people into the European currents of development, and by 1875 it had an up-to-date social system, economic structure, and cultural life, a transformation which affected not only the upper strata but the masses. The new generation was rich in vivid personalities, and there was much more diversity than in the "generation of 1814," for example. Yet there was a unity in this diversified generation. A buoyant, aggressive national patriotism and a youthful, optimistic confidence dominated country and people. Purely political matters seemed of less pressing importance and received only secondary attention, and few changes were made either in the system of internal government or in that of the union.

¶ The appointment of Wedel as statholder in 1836 had inaugurated some years of peace in the union question which continued until the death of Karl Johan in 1844. When his son Oscar I (1844-1859) succeeded, there were some apprehensions in Norway lest the quiet, retiring new king might be more pro-Swedish than his father. This fear was heightened by the well-founded suspicion that Severin Løvenskjold, who had succeeded Wedel as statholder, was, in contrast to his predecessor, pursuing a pro-royal rather than a pro-Norwegian policy. Moreover, with the succession of a less aggressive king the Norwegians had to deal with Swedish officials rather than with the monarch personally. Oscar quieted somewhat the suspicions by his "morning gift," some minor concession to the Norwegian desire for equality in the union. The name of Norway was to precede that of Sweden in Norwegian documents, the seal of Norway was changed to its present form and given a place equal to that of Sweden in the union seal, the union jack was placed in the flag of both countries, and—most important—Norway received for the first time its own naval flag.

Soon after Oscar ascended the throne, a union committee, appointed in 1839 upon the initiative of Wedel, presented its report to both governments. It was an elaborate plan designed to place the two countries as far as possible on terms of equality and to clarify relationships not mentioned in the Act of Union in 1814. But this document was not published, the Swedish government took no action on the report, Oscar's reign was allowed to pass without conflict about the union, and no one desired to disturb the peace.

Meanwhile Oscar was carrying on a foreign policy which would ultimately make a revision of the union desirable. He responded with enthusiasm to the Pan-Scandinavian movement which had been launched in Denmark. He even hoped to add Denmark to the realm of the Bernadotte family by inducing the Danish king Frederik VII, who had no children, to designate the Swedish-Norwegian crown prince Karl as his heir. When, in 1848, the Prussian army came to the aid of the revolting German element in Holstein and southern Slesvig, and the defeated Danish troops had to withdraw from the duchies, Oscar promised aid if Denmark proper were attacked. He mobilized a small force, although there was little enthusiasm in either of his countries for any military interference or a permanent alliance with Denmark. Fortunately there was no need of using the soldiers except as a temporary force of occupation in the duchies. The protests of the powers caused Prussia to withdraw from the duchies, and this victory for Denmark was also looked upon as one for Scandinavianism. Oscar could not, however, refrain from a military demonstration, which, however, led to no action.

Oscar's reign marks the end of the friendship with Russia which had been an important part of Karl Johan's policy. In 1853, when the Crimean War was threatening, Copenhagen and Stockholm issued identical declarations of neutrality, which Nicholas protested as really favoring the western powers. Oscar in fact leaned more and more to the West, and had England and France attacked Russia through the Baltic as he expected, he would have been ready to help them. Moreover, the hope of regaining Finland made war seem not wholly undesirable. One factor in the foreign policy during the Crimean War was a Nor-wegian problem. The Finmark boundary between Russia and Norway had never been completely drawn, and some districts were held jointly by the two. Mutual dissatisfaction had now brought the question to the fore. England was anxious to make an agreement that would prevent any Russian expansion in Finmark, and when Palmerston became prime minister he pushed for a settlement. Oscar saw a chance to obtain more advantages. The result was the so-called November Treaty of 1855 by which England and France guaranteed against Russian aggression not only Norway's Finmark, but all Swedish lands as well. Whatever advantage there might be in this closer alliance with the western powers, the break in the friendship with Russia left the Scandinavian peninsula more exposed than before, and as Oscar's dreams for a united North were not realized a closer union between Norway and Sweden seemed imperative. Most Norwegians, however, were too nationalistic to be interested.

Hardly had Karl XV (1859-1872) succeeded his father before his two countries were plunged into the most serious conflict about the union that they had ever experienced. Karl, who resembled his emotional, impulsive grandfather—though he lacked Karl Johan's greatness—was well and favorably known in Norway, where he had served as viceroy. When he became regent during Oscar's illness the post of statholder in Norway was left vacant, and Karl intimated his willingness to sanction abolition of the office as his "morning gift" to the Norwegian people. The proposal roused violent opposition in Sweden, and, caught between the conflicting demands of his two realms, Karl lacked the courage to keep his promise to Norway.

The Norwegians found the conservative, aristocratic Swedes who then dominated the policy of their country much more difficult to deal with than the Bernadotte kings. The Swedes maintained that not only the Act of Union of 1814, but also the changes in Norway's Constitution which the union had necessitated were of common interest, and could therefore be amended only with the consent of the joint ministry of the two countries. They also revived the old criticism of Karl Johan, who, it was claimed, by catering to Norway had robbed Sweden of the privileged position that the Treaty of Kiel had stipulated. They demanded a revision of the Act of Union, but not on the principle of equality between the two peoples, which had been the basis of work for the committee of 1839.

The Norwegians, on the other hand, held that, as the statholder was not mentioned in the Act of Union, any question regarding that office was a strictly Norwegian matter. In 1860 the Storthing sent an address to the king stating that Norway alone had authority over its own Constitution and could not consent to a revision of the union based on tl theories expressed in Sweden. Nevertheless, but three years later tl Storthing approved the appointment of a Committee on Revision, an for this the chief credit goes to the king.

Like his father, Karl XV was an ardent Pan-Scandinavian who wishe to make the North a force in European affairs. As a first step he wante to knit more closely the union between his two kingdoms and as crow prince he had already begun to work for closer cooperation in militaı affairs, the field of his special interest. Undaunted by opposition, l continued to press for revision. To achieve a united front in foreig affairs and gain a strengthened position in Europe he was quite willin to allow to each country complete independence in internal matter Dismissing the ministers who had upheld the address of 1860, he place at the head of the government Frederik Stang, who was willing to wor for revision when the Swedish government, under pressure from tl king, had retreated from its extreme claim to supremacy.

In Norway, too, a more conciliatory attitude was gaining ascendanc Stang had the confidence of his countrymen; the farmers, with Uelan as their leader, were traditionally royalist; many of the profession class were strongly for the union, and not a few felt that a closer def nition of the terms of union would strengthen Norway's positio Moreover, the growing fear of Bismarck's ruthless power politics and encroachments by the Russian Bear strengthened the sense of the in portance of Scandinavian solidarity.

While the Committee on Revision was at work, questions of foreig policy reached a crisis. Prussia and Austria in January 1864 declared w on Denmark. Karl XV had steadily advocated a pro-Danish policy an even drafted a strong treaty for a defensive alliance with Denmark. Tl Swedish-Norwegian cabinet, more cautious than the king, refused i approval and, when hostilities broke out and the king desired militar intervention, set so many conditions that the help never materialize This failure of Norway and Sweden to send military aid to Denmar was the death-blow to Pan-Scandinavianism.

The Danish crisis strongly influenced the union question also. Tl committee report, completed in 1867 and approved by both goverı ments, was in 1871 laid before the Storthing for ratification. Althoug the report departed from the basic principles of the address of 1860, seemed as good a settlement as could be gained at this time. It recog nized the supremacy of Sweden in foreign affairs, and stipulated th the foreign minister be a Swede. A keen, vitriolic attack on the repo was launched by Ketil Motzfeldt, one of the ministers who had upheld the address of 1860. More influential probably was the speech of Johan Sverdrup, who was rallying all the opposition forces. Sverdrup, the very incarnation of impassioned nationalism, was a vigorous opponent of Pan-Scandinavianism. After three days of violent debate the report of the committee was defeated by a vote of 92 to 17.

And so the two movements that might have helped to unite the North went down to defeat, and Norway was launched upon an aggressive policy of self-assertion, which eventually led to the termination of the union.

¶ The chief interest of the government was centered upon the economic development. While earlier its policy had of necessity been one of economy, the reform of the monetary system which had been achieved by 1842 opened the way for a much needed active economic program comparable to that of the English liberalism of the same era. A. M. Schweigaard was the moving spirit in the Storthing in its economic legislation, but equal credit should go to Frederik Stang, the minister of the newly established department of the interior, for inaugurating the most rapid economic development the country had yet experienced.

As a first great step in this advance Schweigaard still further developed the policy of free trade, which he had inaugurated in 1842, for, he argued, not only would this be an aid to seafaring, but "infant industries" could be helped more by the duty-free admission of raw material than by a tariff on the finished product.

It took the cooperation of the state and private enterprise to achieve economic transformation. As the country lacked private capital, it was natural that the state took the lead in the modernization of communication. In 1848 the first modern road was begun, running out from Christiania. It was an excellent road and made such an impression that the engineer, Christian Vilhelm Bergh, was put in charge of all further road building. Determined to correct the chief fault of older roads, the steep hills, he established reasonable grades—never greater than 1:20. This was the beginning of the modern roads that we now see winding up the mountains in sharp corkscrew curves. They were expensive, slow to build, and often narrow. While other engineers favored wider roads and more of them, even at the expense of some severe grades, Bergh's system became the basis for the fine roads built throughout the nineteenth century. Bridging the many mountain streams gave the engineers difficult problems, but veritable wonders were performed. About the same time private enterprise established steamboat traffic on Mjøsa, which, despite dire prophecies, was very successful. Building of canals also was discussed, but found unsuited to the Norwegian terrain. Already in the 'thirties agitation for railroads was begun, and slowly the men in authority were persuaded of the feasibility of building them in Norway. In 1851 construction of the first railroad was begun, and three years later it was officially opened. The venture was financed jointly by the state and by British capital, and the supervising engineer was Robert Stephenson, the son of the inventor of the locomotive. The road covered only the few miles from the capital to Eidsvoll, and to many seemed unimportant. But these miles carried the heaviest traffic in the country, and it was not long before the iron horse demonstrated its usefulness, though further railroad building came slowly. The telegraph was introduced in 1855 and the system was developed rapidly. More important to the people at large, however, was the postal reform, following the example of England. The rates, which had been prohibitive to any but the wealthy, were reduced, the postage stamp adopted, and eleven post boats gave regular service along the coast. Passengers found them far from comfortable, but safe. Not one of them was lost.

Also inspired by England was the beginning of modern industry. The authorities and other conservatives believed that Norway could never develop factories, and, seeing the dire social results in England, they feared the effects that new industries might produce. It took scarcely a decade, however, to convert even the most skeptical. Eager young men visited England, studied the methods there, and returned home to put the ideas into practice, sometimes bringing with them English capital and workers. The most important factories were in the textile industry, but others were also established, such as a match factory and several breweries—while happily distilleries were reduced to a small fraction of the former appalling number.

Not a few plants were built by waterfalls away from cities and became the centers of little communities with the owner as patriarchal boss, in keeping with the tradition of the eighteenth century works. Others were on the outskirts of the cities, notably Christiania, and the laborers swelled the city proletariat. The factory was the center of their whole existence and they took a certain pride in it, looking down upon the more wretched, fortunately not large, slum population from earlier times. At first the laborers lived in hovels that sprang up helter-skelter around the factory. In the 'sixties an awakened sense of social responsibility prompted the government to build apartments for laborers, and before long private capital also found housing projects profitable.

While new industries were growing up, the old Norwegian means of livelihood were also receiving new impetus. The lumber industry experienced a moderate boom. New methods in fishing were introduced, the Norwegians, strange as it may seem, learning from the Swedes. Whaling was developed and the number of Lofoten fishermen was doubled between 1840 and 1880. Shipping had held its own better than other occupations through the crisis from 1815 to 1840. Frugality and superb seamanship had kept up the merchant marine even though it was necessary to keep afloat vessels long overage. After 1840 the carrying trade grew rapidly, longer trips were taken, and larger and many more boats were in use. At first they were built at home, but later many were bought abroad. By 1870 only Great Britain and the United States had a merchant marine of greater tonnage than the Norwegian. Though steamboats had come in, sailboats still predominated. The increased seafaring brought home goods from all lands, gave variety and romance to daily life, and developed a justifiable sense of national pride.

No change affected the people as much as the reform in farming, for nine-tenths of the population were still rural. The 'fifties mark an unprecedented advance in agriculture. The government took the initiative and made an appropriation for county agricultural schools, which by 1850 had become quite general. There was a growing interest in agricultural improvements among the farmers also. With the establishment of local self-government in 1837 a new community life had developed with political meetings which furnished opportunity for discussion. Temperance meetings also became common, and agricultural societies were founded, and trained men from among their own ranks became advisers of the farmers, supplanting the clergy.

¶ In the midst of the economic changes a disintegration of the old rural society was beginning. While the valleys untouched by the modern means of communication were more isolated than before, in other places the new roads stimulated the tourist traffic, which was for the first time becoming extensive, and beckoned the young to the unknown. The urban population had always been recruited from the country, but now the greater opportunity for work opened by industry increased the number who moved to the city. Most of these joined the labor class, but not a few entered the middle and upper strata of society, quite a group even attending the university. The drift to the city was not sufficient to relieve the tension of rural life, however, and a wider outlet was found in America.

The chief cause of emigration was economic pressure. At home the new land available was inadequate for the growing population, and the old homesteads were broken up into smaller farms, sometimes too small to support a family. In spite of improvements in methods, it was difficult for the poor, especially in larger families, to find opportunities in farming. But the economic was not the only cause. All the discontent of the age—economic, religious, social, and political—sought release in emigration.[1] It was but a phase of the revolt of the age against the old social system, and the restlessness and spirit of adventure natural in an age of transition developed into a veritable "America fever." It was stimulated by emigration agents, "America letters," and "America books," of which Ole Rynning's was perhaps the most influential.[2] A fascinating picture of the emotions of the emigrants, not least their idealization of America, is found in the emigrant songs of the day.[3]

The majority of the emigrants were from the rural districts, but professional men also joined the stream. It was difficult to get positions at home. The upper class was increasing more rapidly than was the population as a whole. Large families were much more common in the professional class than among the poor, and as a result a greater number of young men were trained for the professions than were needed in Norway. Not a few of them were attracted by the larger opportunities that America seemed to offer. Most numerous among the upper-class emigrants were the clergymen, who were filled with a zeal to keep alive in the New World the spiritual heritage from the mother church, and who were to have an influence on the settlements far out of proportion to their number. They met with little sympathy from their friends at home. The whole emigration movement came upon the country as a surprise, and met with very bitter opposition among the upper class. Especially in the 'forties, a vigorous even passionate campaign was carried on against a desertion of the homeland, which seemed bordering on the treasonable. Preachers, poets, and public men warned against the dangers of the New World and admonished against draining the mother country of its strength, but nothing could stop the irresistible

[1] Theodore C. Blegen, *Norwegian Migration to America*, especially vol. 1, ch. 7, Northfield, 1931 and 1940. Ingrid Semmingsen, *Veien mot vest: Utvandringen fra Norge til Amerika, 1825-1865*, Oslo, 1941.

[2] Theodore C. Blegen, tr. and ed., *Ole Rynning's True Account of America*, Minneapolis, 1926.

[3] Theodore C. Blegen and Martin B. Ruud, eds., *Norwegian Emigrant Songs and Ballads*, Minneapolis, 1936.

flow of people. It is significant that it was in this period the Norwegian immigrants built up homes and communities, schools and churches in the Middle West, which came to bear the impress of the age in which their founders left the mother country.

The first group of emigrants left in 1825 on the famous sloop *Restoration*. After that there was almost no further emigration before 1836, when two hundred persons left for America. From then on there was a small but steady stream, which became quite large in the 'fifties, until in 1861 the number was not far from 9,000. The American Civil War brought a slump, but was followed by a sudden increase, the years from 1866 to 1870 constituting the first great period in nineteenth century emigration. At home the influence of the movement was felt almost at once. Not only did the "America letters" bring welcome financial aid to innumerable families in straitened circumstances, but they supplied an intellectual and emotional stimulus. Moreover, the news from the Land of the Free aroused a keener desire for a wider freedom at home, both economic and political.

¶ Norway was far from democratic in the middle of the century. Not only was voting limited to officials, property owners or leaseholders, and burghers of incorporated towns, but society was permeated with class distinction. Therefore a struggle for democracy of necessity involved class conflict.

As the democratic wave of the 'thirties ebbed out, the professional class was again in full control of the political life. The mid-century was the brilliant era of this old aristocracy, as the improved economic conditions made possible a richer, more varied, and less rigorous life in the homes of the upper class. Public service, however, still occupied the chief place in their thought, but as the more strictly political problems made fewer demands upon them than in the preceding decades, attention was focused upon the economic development which has been mentioned, and upon the many social evils that needed correction. The national feeling and religious currents of the day increased sympathy for the suffering, faith in the common people, and a sense of unity of the whole nation. The result was a number of movements in the 'forties which constituted the beginning of the many social reforms of the nineteenth century. One of the greatest evils of the day was drunkenness, which had increased alarmingly since all restrictions on distilling had been removed in 1816. Public opinion was roused, temperance societies were formed on the pattern of those in the United States, and after a bitter struggle a law was passed in 1845 which limited the production of liquor, and which almost at once showed beneficent results. The increase in crime and the unspeakable conditions in the prisons were also worrying the authorities. As crown prince, Oscar I had used his influence to bring about a study of American and English prisons, and in 1857 a sorely-needed enlightened prison law was passed. Just as great was the need for better treatment of the insane. Not only was there no provision for their care, but superstition and ignorance on the part of the public added much to the misery of the poor sufferers. Thanks to the devoted efforts of Herman Wedel Major, a "Law concerning the treatment and care of the insane" was passed in 1848, which was the most humane and scientific that had yet been adopted in any country.

The growing social consciousness was further expressed in a new concern about other unfortunate elements of society. The Storthing voted a stipend to Eilert Sundt for the study of social conditions in the country. He first made a survey of the gypsies, and then extended his investigation to include other poorer and more backward groups. Accompanied by his able, well-educated wife, he traveled about collecting masses of material which he embodied in a comprehensive report. This is still the greatest source of information on social conditions for the period from 1800 to 1870. The Sundts were romanticists. They found conditions far from idyllic—though certainly not worse than in other countries—but they retained an optimistic, almost naïve faith that but a few helpful suggestions were necessary to raise the standards of cleanliness and of decent living.

Another step in the establishment of social justice was made when in 1854 a law was enacted giving women equal right of inheritance with men. In 1863 the last trace of keeping unmarried women in the status of minors was removed, and one by one different occupations were opened to women, notably that of teaching in the common schools.

As time went on many elements in the upper class took less part in public affairs, and after about 1860 active politics was left pretty much to jurists. This tended to develop a more formal, hidebound, bureaucratic spirit. There was a certain social freemasonry among the members of the aristocracy, and they retained a strong class consciousness which was sometimes even accentuated when they felt that the supremacy of the class was waning; but they presented no united front or class politics. On the other hand, in spite of their active solicitude for the welfare of the masses, most of them were not especially interested in democracy.

The agitation for democracy had to come from other sources, and leaders had to be found who could channel the ferment and discontent among the common people. The cities were not yet ready to take the lead in any such movement. The economic changes had caused the growth of a larger middle class in the cities, a typical petite bourgeoisie with all its conventional ideas of propriety, but with little political interest. In the new urban labor class there was also little conscious mass activity before the 'sixties or even 'seventies. There were successful organizations among them, singing societies and others with beneficent social and educational purposes, but they were philanthropic, begun by outsiders, and political discussions were not on the program. The bulk of the labor population still consisted of farm laborers and crofters, who felt closer akin to the rest of the country people than to the city proletariat.

The only aggressive class politics was carried on by the farmer group in the Storthing. Gabriel Ueland, with his remarkable power of persuasion, welded the group into a unit in support of his policy. He was a stanch democrat, favoring every possible expansion of the people's control of their own affairs in local administration, law courts, and the church. Eager for the rural communities to retain their old character, he consistently opposed the central administration. He was against the expansion of government authority as an interference with liberty, and against placing new financial burdens on the people for any purpose however admirable. National questions were of secondary interest to him. He was a strong royalist and unionist, but favored strengthening the power of the Storthing as opposed to the executive.

The repercussions of the mid-century revolutions that swept over Europe were felt in Norway, chiefly through the influence of one man who became the first modern proletarian leader in the country. Marcus Thrane in his unhappy youth saturated his mind with all the revolutionary ideas of the age. He was a Utopian socialist in his views, believing that to bring about a new social structure he must appeal to the labor class and work "from below upwards." In 1848 he organized a labor society in Drammen which in a few months attained to a membership of five hundred, and began to publish a labor paper in which he attacked violently both the official class and the farmer opposition. Within two years he had organized almost three hundred societies with a membership of over twenty thousand drawn from the lower classes in town and country, who for the first time were made to feel that they had a common cause. His plan was to center his efforts upon certain practical reforms that would improve the condition of the masses: the sale of land to crofters on easy terms, the removal of old restrictions on labor, the abolition of all protective tariffs, better common schools, more stringent restrictions on the sale of liquor, general suffrage, and military service for all classes. These aims he embodied in a petition to the king, to which he obtained almost thirteen thousand signatures. When this brought no response, he presented his program to the Storthing, confident of a favorable hearing from at least a few men.

Meanwhile the whole movement had roused grave apprehensions among the authorities, and Thrane and a large number of labor leaders were arrested. A hundred and thirty-three men were found guilty of crimes against the safety of the state, and were condemned for their opinions rather than for their actions. Thrane himself was given four years in prison. Upon his release, finding his movement completely disintegrated, he made no attempt to resuscitate it but before long left for America. But Thrane's effort had not been in vain; it had revealed a cleavage within rural society, and had given a glimpse of the possibility of labor organization and labor solidarity. Moreover, through the backing of the Thrane group a new man had entered the Storthing in 1850, and he was to be the central figure in the democratic movement for a quarter of a century.

Johan Sverdrup belonged to an old distinguished family which had come from Slesvig in the seventeenth century and has given Norway a long line of able professional men.[4] From early childhood his ideas had been formed under the influence of his aunt and teacher, Elisabeth Sverdrup. This gifted, widely-read woman imbued his mind with liberal ideals, devotion to country, and love of liberty. Sverdrup's aim was to break upper-class control and make Norway a true democracy. This, he thought, could be achieved through a liberal party—as yet the country had no political parties—which could embrace within its ranks liberals of all social strata. He realized, however, that in an agricultural country such a party must first and foremost be built upon the support of the farmers. More than any earlier leader from the upper class he was able to enter into the viewpoint of the people, feel at one with them, and sense their needs. His keen political instinct, his fiery eloquence, his indomitable vigor, and his tireless, passionate devotion to the task he set for himself made him for years the most powerful man in the country.

He worked in close harmony with Ueland, whose objectives in part

[4] Koht, *Johan Sverdrup.*

paralleled those of Sverdrup's program. The older man acquired a broader viewpoint in his later years, and supported the new leader in his wider national aims, though the two differed somewhat in their union policy.

As the time seemed ripe, Sverdrup took up one reform measure after the other. He backed the people in their demands that the obligation to do military service be uniform for all classes, and stopped Crown Prince Karl's plans for a military reorganization which would incorporate the Norwegian regiments into a union army. He also united the opposition forces behind a demand for expansion of the suffrage. Sverdrup did not win a substantial victory before 1884. Then the right to vote was extended to men with an annual income of 800 crowns in the cities and 500 in the country. Class was no longer a criterion for voting, and the efforts of these earlier years laid the basis for one of Sverdrup's greatest achievements.

In his greatest battle of the 'fifties, however, Sverdrup suffered defeat. He introduced a bill for the establishment of the jury system, which would give the common people a share in the administration of justice. After much opposition, the bill passed the Storthing only to be vetoed. Later, when he was assured of royal sanction and confident of victory, he presented a new bill only to have it also defeated. Søren Jaabæk, who was gradually taking the place of the aging Ueland as the leader of the farmer group, had withdrawn his support and carried with him enough votes to defeat the bill. He had been convinced that the jury system would be very expensive.

Søren Jaabæk was self-taught but well taught, and could from the first make himself felt in the Storthing. He was of and for the common people and a veritable apostle of economy. It must be remembered that the tax system had not been reformed, and the burden of the poor was disproportionately heavy. Jaabæk opposed any expansion of government functions, whether cultural, military, or political. He attacked the fee system which constituted an important part of an official's income and could easily be abused, and he carried on a keen, merciless, sometimes petty fight against all privileges and pensions, however reasonable. This made him hated and feared by officialdom. But he also had a positive program favoring the democratic ideas of Ueland and even Thrane, and at least in one instance went farther: he favored suffrage for all, including women.

In 1865 Jaabæk began to found clubs among the farmers. The movement spread rapidly and furnished the best opportunities for political discussion the people had ever had. Jaabæk was an able agitator and had for a time even more influence than Ueland had attained. Modest by nature, he yielded in national affairs more and more to the leadership of Sverdrup. In January 1869 the two men agreed to join forces, and from this event we can date the beginning of the Liberal Party for which Sverdrup had been striving. The first achievement of their united effort was that Sverdrup's long-cherished plan for annual meetings of the Storthing went into effect in 1871. Hitherto the Storthing had met only for a few months every three years. This chief political advance of the period introduced an age of increased interest in politics, and gave the Storthing a far greater power in the affairs of the country.

But while Sverdrup and the farmer leaders were battling for democracy and Schweigaard, Stang, and the businessmen were striving for a richer economic life for the nation, the majority of the educated people, especially the young, were neither politically nor economically minded. Their heart was set on a cultural and spiritual regeneration of their country.

¶ Although the spirit of national romanticism pervaded even the economic and political life, it was the cultural renaissance which really gave character to the age. Norway was developing a rich many-sided culture of its own, cosmopolitan-European and yet markedly Norwegian in character. The Norwegian movement was much indebted to influences from countries farther south—Denmark, Germany, and to a lesser degree England—where romanticism had made its appearance at a somewhat earlier date. In Norway the 'forties and the 'fifties most properly constituted the Age of National Romanticism, though many of the characteristics of those decades pervaded also the 'thirties and the 'sixties. The chief bearers of the movement were the members of the Intelligence Party, formed in the 'thirties in opposition to Wergeland. They dominated the intellectual life of the capital for many years, even when a new generation began to make itself heard.

A unity of purpose pervades the whole age, as the motive force was a conscious effort to build a national culture based upon the half-forgotten, long-neglected past, and the treasures preserved in the traditions of the people. The romanticists carried over into the new age the eighteenth-century admiration for the odal freeholder, but added a new warmth and fervor to the sentiment. Equally important was their romantic glorification of the past, the Viking Age and the Middle Ages, the time before the country came under "deadening" foreign domination.

Most of the leaders in the romantic movement could not completely enter into the life and thought of the people, but pictured them mainly in Sunday dress and holiday spirit, while nature appeared only in her friendlier moods and the vikings as idealized heroes. Yet it is a grave error to think that the romanticists blindly followed the dictates of emotions and ideals. There was a strong element of realism in their thought and work. Although the scholars of the day—historians, archaeologists, philologists, and scientists, even students of medicine—were of the romantic school and accepted its fundamental tenets, they were withal tireless seekers after truth and thorough, penetrating scholars who exerted a marked influence on many lines of thought of their age. Artists and poets, too, were in a sense realists. Welhaven, for instance, believed that the best artistic work was based on personal experience and on sound knowledge acquired through slow, painstaking effort. Thus even at its height, the national romantic movement, so to speak, kept its feet on the ground.

In the rediscovery of the past, so fundamental in romanticism, historical scholarship played a vital part. There had been some attention paid to the history of the country even earlier. Wergeland had, in addition to shorter biographies and other articles, written an extensive history of the Constitutional Assembly, for, he thought, "No nation has ever experienced a more marvelous year than Norway in 1814."[5] A more important book is Jacob Aall's memoirs, a balanced, scholarly work remarkably free from prejudices. When a new edition was published in 1859, the editor remarked that it was "still the only continuous presentation which our literature possesses of the memorable events in the North in the years from 1800 to 1815."

The historians of the romantic movement did not particularly concern themselves about that epoch, and in fact, their whole generation seems to have had little appreciation of the achievements of 1814. They turned to the time of vikings and sagas. In contrast to the opinion then commonly held, especially in Denmark, that the North had of old been one people with one language, they advanced the theory that Norway had been settled by an immigration by way of the North, quite distinct from Sweden and Denmark. This theory was valiantly defended by Peter Andreas Munch, although in his late years he began to doubt that it was tenable, and it was, indeed, later repudiated. Munch was, on

[5] *Henrik Wergelands samlede Skrifter*, 7:75.

the other hand, successful in combating the then current belief that Old Norse literature was an expression of common northern tradition. He demonstrated that "Old Norse" (*Norrøn*) was a term used to designate not the language and literature of the whole North, but of Norway and its settlements to the west. Thus it was established that in cultural traditions Norway was not the poorest but the richest of the Scandinavian countries. Munch's greatest work was *Det norske Folks Historie*, a history of Norway to the Kalmar Union, in eight weighty tomes. But he also wrote innumerable shorter brochures and articles. He had an unlimited capacity for work, a keen critical sense, and an uncanny instinct for rooting out hitherto unknown material abroad, particularly in the Vatican Library. He was a pioneer in research in many lines, and ranks even today as Norway's greatest historian. He influenced the whole intellectual life of his time as perhaps no one else, many sought his help and advice, and to them all he gave freely of his vast store of knowledge and experience. Like the other romanticists, Munch tended to look upon the Danish period as a mere "spurious soldering," as Wergeland said, between Norway's past and present. To establish the continuity in the history of the country was left to a group of historians twenty years younger than Munch, who had just begun their work in 1869 when the Norwegian Historical Society was organized.

Nevertheless the Danish period had not been entirely neglected by the romantic school. In spite of his famous saying, Wergeland himself came to see that there was a development going on even during the Danish period, and scholars recognized the truth in Schweigaard's contention that a people could not neglect four hundred years of its growth. The first two great undertakings in the publication of historical sources in the exact original form began at this time, and much of the material was from the Danish period. In 1847 appeared the first part of *Diplomatarium Norvegicum*, a collection of letters and other documents from the earliest time to 1570, and the publication has continued into recent years. From 1846 to 1849 three volumes of old laws were published, *Norges gamle love indtil 1387*, edited by Munch and Rudolf Keyser. Later two supplementary volumes edited by Gustav Storm and Ebbe Hertzberg were added. The University made it part of its program to publish other manuscripts, and in 1857 a fund was established by the Storthing for that purpose. Gathering archaeological material begun in the eighteenth century, also received new impetus when Keyser became director of the University collection in 1828. Loca history also deserves mention, and genealogy, in which virgin field Wilhelmine Brandt was the pioneer.

It was not enough for scholars to rediscover the past, but the result of their work must be made the property of the common people. Old literature was translated into modern Norwegian, and poet and scholar helped to put the old stories into new form, either prose or verse, attractive even to children. As this work progressed, it revealed a close relation between the history of the past and the folk culture, which, though a living force among the people, had its roots in the dim past.

To recapture the folk culture, to reveal the "hidden Norway," and to make the treasures concealed among the people the common property of all was one of the great achievements of national romanticism. Earlier there had been some rather academic interest on the part of a few, but in the 'thirties there awoke a real love for folklore, and this grew in depth and strength through the following decades. Tireless enthusiasts—writers, scholars, musicians, and painters—wandered over the countryside collecting, recording, writing, and publishing. "It was as though a dam had burst; the whole Norwegian folk culture, the rich heritage of all manner of folklore gushed forth with a force which carried everyone along."[6]

It is impossible in a few paragraphs to give any adequate idea of the wealth and variety of material that was brought out, or to mention more than a few of the many who had a share in the great work. An impetus to the collection of folk song was Jørgen Moe's introduction to a thin volume published in 1840. He urged that the "gold mines" in the people's language be searched for treasures: "these mines contain metals with a clear, strong ring, tones which express exactly what a Norwegian has to say or sing." His suggestion stimulated Olea Crøger to begin to collect and record folk songs. She was a clergyman's daughter who had a farm of her own and lived close to the people. She placed her material at the disposal of her pastor, Magnus Brostrup Landstad, who was engaged in the same pursuit. Upon her suggestion he decided to publish his collection, and the appearance of his imposing volume of folk songs, *Norske Folkeviser*, was an epoch-making event. P. A. Munch called it "a direct bridge from our past to our present." Even after the great scholar Sophus Bugge a few years later published a more scientifically edited volume, Landstad's continued to be the work into which artist and poet delved for inspiration and which the farmer purchased or borrowed from his neighbor.

[6] Halvdan Koht in *Norsk historisk videnskap i femti aar, 1869-1919*, p. 228, Kristiania, 1920.

Landstad's work included an appendix of folk melodies contributed by Ludvig Matthias Lindeman, for forty-seven years the organist in Our Saviour's Church in Christiania. He too owed much to Olea Crøger. With her guitar on her back, she wandered to out-of-the-way places where lived old people who, she had heard, knew a good song. In her gently persuasive manner she induced them to sing and jotted down the melody. Lindeman, too, had the ability to coax half-forgotten tunes from timid old men and women with cracked voices. With sure musicianship and reverence for the old, he caught the beauty of the melody and preserved it in a simple, pure form. *Eldre og nyere norske Fjeldmelodier* (Old and New Norwegian Mountain Melodies) he called his three-volume publication. All who wished to compose truly Norwegian music had to draw upon this most important collection of musical source material. Two decades earlier an infant prodigy violinist had begun to arouse appreciation of the folk songs and dances which he heard near his home in Bergen. Ole Bull not only played for his own people, but introduced the Norwegian folk music to large parts of Western Europe and America, and everywhere he was received with wild enthusiasm.

Other folk arts, too, were attracting attention. Folk dances were displayed, pictures of costumes were published, and the folk crafts were revived. Much of value had already been lost; especially tragic was the decreasing number of medieval timber churches, and when a society was organized in 1844 for the preservation of the artistic heritage from the past, it was in the nick of time.

Legends and folk tales were much more alive among the people than were the songs. An astonishing number of tales of great variety in content, form, age, and origin, had been told and retold for centuries, changing with the age and the individuality of the teller. Often many variants of the same story existed. A large number of the folk tales picture people and conditions of the late Danish period, although many are older. This wealth of tales, as rich as that of any country, was in this age given its final written form and made the possession of the whole people. Norway was exceptionally fortunate in having two men who worked together on this important task with such harmonious effect that it is difficult to distinguish the contribution of each. Jørgen Moe and Peter Christen Asbjørnsen, though opposites in temperament, had been friends since their student days. Each had begun the collection of folklore independently, but they soon agreed to cooperate.

Their problem was not so much to find the tales, for they were everywhere, as to decide in what form to re-create them. The use of the dialect in which the story had been told would limit the audience, but on the other hand the literary language of the day, with its marked Danish influence, would rob the folklore of its characteristically national tang. Moe's sure judgment and sound scholarship combined with Asbjørnsen's sense of humor and closeness to the people did not go wrong. The two writers used a language nearer the vernacular than usual among literary men—but not a dialect—and retold the story in the spirit, though not in the exact language of the narrator. By choice of words and idioms, and by little turns of speech, they gave their language a Norwegian flavor. The folk tales as told by Asbjørnsen and Moe are as thoroughly Norwegian in character as anything can be, and the language became increasingly Norwegian with every edition—even more so later, when Moltke Moe took over the task of editing.

While Jørgen Moe quite soon left this work to devote himself to his duties as a pastor, Asbjørnsen continued to collect and publish not only fairy tales but a wealth of legends which embody the superstitious beliefs of the people. In his later years his many-sided interests led him away from folklore. He devoted his writing and his wide scientific knowledge to agronomy in order to introduce into the farming communities some of the many sorely needed improvements. On his wanderings he also noticed that, especially among the poor, much food value was lost through poor preparation. Asbjørnsen, whose jovial zest for living also included the pleasures of the table, tried to help remedy the evil by writing a cook book, published under a pseudonym. In spite of such deviations, Asbjørnsen's contributions to the preservation of folklore and the development of the modern Norwegian language were second to none.

The idea of making the language more national was not new with Asbjørnsen. Back in the 'twenties—and earlier too—men like Jacob Aall had consciously tried to introduce more words from the dialects. Practically every one of the intellectuals of this age was sympathetic toward efforts to Norwegianize the language. The chief reason was the strong national feeling, but on the part of many there was also a desire to come closer to the common people. Landstad, for example, regretted that the clergy stood too far apart from their parishioners, and the chief barrier was the language. While the changes seem very conservative to us, they were not accomplished without criticism, and were often delayed by public opinion. Yet a development had begun that was to continue with increasing momentum even to the present.

But to many people mere changes in the current Danish-Norwegian appeared no solution of the language problem. The possibility of combining the dialects into a "completely Norwegian language" had been suggested even before the separation from Denmark, and continued to occupy liberal thinkers. The dialects, it was felt, furnished historic continuity with the Old Norse, and constituted unused linguistic treasures. Their use might, at least to some degree, wipe out the memory of national humiliation and add to the dignity of the nation. It might also give rise to a language which could be understood by all and thus bind the people more closely together.

It was left to Ivar Aasen to put these ideas into action. Aasen was a peasant and proud of it. He came from an unusually advanced, well educated community, Sunnmøre in the Westland, and represented the best in his class. He was mainly self-taught, and, when offered assistance to obtain a formal higher education, refused it. He did not want to take time from his main studies and was anxious to demonstrate what a man of the common people could achieve, and moreover, he sensed that he would not feel quite at home in university circles where a man of his background was a rarity.

Aasen was a highly gifted linguist and philologist. Being versed in Latin, Greek, German, French, and English, he began to ask himself why the native dialects were not as worthy of study as other languages. In 1836, he wrote that the dialects of all the main districts ought to be studied and a vocabulary collected, and from this material scholars should build a common language and write a grammar and dictionary. Believing that this enormous task had to be done by a man of his class, he decided to undertake it, and the next year he began with a grammar of his own dialect. After years of study of other dialects, he published first a grammar and then a dictionary of what he called the Norwegian folk language. *Landsmaal*, he called it later—and that name has been retained—the speech of the country as opposed to the official language largely an import from Denmark. Then he began to write in *landsmaal*. It is a semi-artificial language in which are normalized the forms from leading dialects. Aasen leaned strongly toward the words that were close to the Old Norse, and in this he was encouraged by Munch, who found in Aasen's work evidence that almost the whole Old Norse vocabulary had been preserved in the speech of the people.

Aasen's work was met with much enthusiasm, especially from educated people, and his advice was sought even by those who desired only moderate changes. As time went on and the influence of his work was growing, he met more opposition, and many a battle was waged over the language.

Ivar Aasen continued to work with a persistent tenacity and systematic orderliness that made him especially fitted for his task. From his dreary bachelor quarters in Christiania he set out each summer to gather new words; and publication after publication came from his pen. When he could not find the words he wanted, he made them. His aim was a Norwegian language adequate for learned books without dependence on a single foreign word. In him national feeling and class feeling were inseparable. He looked upon everything and everybody not of Norwegian peasant stock as foreign, not genuinely Norwegian. Thus, while trying to form an all-Norwegian language he helped to widen the cleavage between the two cultural tendencies in Norway which other forces were trying to unite. Aasen lived to see his pioneer work continued by others, and his influence grew as the language controversy colored the whole cultural and nationalistic life in modern Norway.

The romanticists, however, were not only scholars and collectors, but creative artists as well. They had a strong sense of the close bonds among all the arts, poetry, music, and painting, and were all pervaded by the same emotional, even sentimental—always subjective, never abstract—love of Norwegian nature, and found inspiration there. When asked who taught him to play, Ole Bull answered, "The mountains of Norway." At no other time in the history of Norway have artists and poets alike been so inspired by the one great emotion of romantic love of country, its nature, people, and cultural heritage.

Painting was dominated in technique and coloration by Düsseldorf, where the Norwegian artists did most of their work; this was a break with—certainly not an improvement on—Johan Christian Dahl and his school. The spirit of the art was romantic, with its striking light effects and the emphasis on the moods of nature, whether it be idyllic peace or brooding melancholy. It was also patriotic, as the artists pictured their own country with nostalgic fervor and the joy of personal experience. The most typical landscape painter of the period was Hans Gude, whose canvases—wide panoramic views with every detail executed with loving care—are generally idyllic. He painted several pictures together with Adolph Tidemand, who is the most important representative of the other trend in the art of the day, the interest in folk life. The sketches Tidemand made while traveling about the country reveal a careful study of interiors of houses and types of people. He painted the peasants in their local dress and in Sunday mood, generally with an atmosphere of gentle sadness. Only occasionally did he indulge in a bit of humor. But as he gained deeper insight into the life of the people, a note of realism appeared in some of his later works—a lurid picture of religious fanatics, for example, and a stark painting entitled *Nød* (Want).

Among the musicians of the age, Ole Bull is perhaps most widely known. Although he was himself a romantic fairy tale, he needed the stimulus of an audience in order to compose; and as his improvisations were seldom recorded, he transmitted few works to posterity. Three other composers of this age who must not be omitted are Halfdan Kjerulf, Ludvig Lindeman, and Rikard Nordraak. Lindeman, inspired by the songs he found among the people, gave his country a wealth of hymn melodies, some of them adaptations of folk songs. Kjerulf, also inspired by folk music and folk life, was the creator of the Norwegian romance and furnished music for some of the finest poems of the age. Nordraak won immortal fame by setting to music Bjørnstjerne Bjørnson's *Ja vi elsker dette landet*, which became Norway's national anthem.

The poetry of Welhaven, Jørgen Moe, the highly romantic Andreas Munch, and others is shot through and through with nature descriptions of the same tone as the melodies of the composers and the colors of the painters. As Welhaven says:

> In my dream on the mountain
> Below the rushing waterfall,
> A fairy gave me her harp.

The interrelation of the arts is well expressed in the poem of Munch, set to music by Kjerulf, describing a bridal party gliding across the Hardanger Fjord as pictured in the famous painting by Gude and Tidemand. Believing with Jørgen Moe that poetry should "mirror the life of the people in clear, pure tones," the poets also took their themes from folklore, sagas, and early history. Welhaven's ballads are a good example, whether the subject be a legend of Saint Olaf or of a doughty peasant. Jørgen Moe, who was the son of a wealthy farmer, had an even more intimate feeling for the Norwegian nature and people, especially of his own Ringerike.

Another poet who expressed the spirit of the age was Landstad. Most of his secular poetry is not distinguished, but it shows a strong influence of the folk songs to which the author devoted so much love and labor, and breathes a warm sympathy for the people, especially the poor and unfortunate who were most in need of the help of the pastor. More important was Landstad's hymnary, which was completed in 1869, meeting the deep-felt need for a modern hymn book. The language of old hymns was revised to make it more Norwegian, and several excellent new translations by Landstad were added. He also included a number of his own hymns, some of which hold a high rank in Lutheran hymnology, and are at the same time peculiarly Norwegian, filled with the mood of the countryside on a Sunday with the rural church and the pealing bell. Gradually the book was widely adopted by the congregations and came to exert a marked influence both on the poetic sense and spiritual life of the people. But Landstad did not succeed in making the language of the hymnary as popular as he had wished. He introduced so many forms and words from the dialects that the authorities insisted on a partial revision along old, conservative lines before approving the work.

At the same time, the *landsmaal* took its place as a literary language. That is was a suitable medium for poetic expression was proved by the lyrics of Ivar Aasen and Aasmund Vinje, both poets from among the common people. Like Aasen, Vinje was self-taught and one of the keenest minds in the country. He lacked Aasen's persistence and orderliness of thought and work, but possessed far greater poetic gifts. In his poems Aasen "gave the truest and most pregnant expression to folk life in Norway and to the peculiar wisdom and courageous common sense of the peasants."[7] Vinje was more lyrical and more deeply imbued with the love of nature. His chief work, however, was as critic and journalist, especially as the editor of *Dølen*, the first *landsmaal* journal. As a strong champion of freedom of thought and expression he had far-reaching influence.

The central figure in the literary development of the 'forties and 'fifties was Asbjørnsen. In the field of creative literature perhaps his most notable contribution was in providing the frames for the local legends he collected. He wove together bits of such stories and gave them a setting, sketching the background against which they were told. The settings are "the first genuine genre pictures of Norwegian literature." In later editions "the genre picture has become the principal thing, the legends are secondary. One of the best examples of this is a story called 'Plankekjørerne,' a vivid account of the lumberjacks of Romerike

[7] C. J. Hambro in introduction to *Anthology of Norwegian Lyrics*, Charles Wharton Stork, tr., XXII, published by Princeton University Press for the American-Scandinavian Foundation, 1942.

gathered in a wayside inn for a drink and a game of cards. The technique, utterly realistic, borders on naturalism."[8]

As the 'forties were drawing to a close, the element of realism was becoming more prevalent. The Thrane movement had called attention to the social ferment abroad in the land as well as to the lamentable conditions back of the unrest. Eilert Sundt's investigations had still further revealed a far from ideal life among the less fortunate elements of the population, and the experiences of tourists, scholars, and artists who had traveled about the country confirmed the findings of Sundt. This lent a more somber hue to their work, and introduced a realism which shocked conservative tastes.

Even the peasant stories of Bjørnstjerne Bjørnson, which may be called the climax of romanticism, contained an element of realism which met violent criticism. These were the most widely read books of the 'fifties, for Bjørnson was close to the people as no poet had been since Wergeland. They are in the mood of the age—Bjørnson said they would never have been written but for the paintings of Tidemand—and yet indicative of Bjørnson, the realist and champion of the people in the coming decades. In the 'fifties his most spectacular contribution to the movement for an independent Norwegian culture was his fight for a national theater free from Danish actors and language. At the same time Henrik Ibsen's first historical dramas appeared, and these in subject, and to some extent in manner of treatment, fit into the romantic age.

The romanticists had been interested only in the distant past and in the country folk. Asbjørnsen alone had pictured city life but mainly among people who had lately moved in from the country. In 1855, however, appeared a novel dealing with the professional class, *Amtmandens Døtre* (The Governor's Daughters), the first full-fledged modern realistic novel in Norwegian literature. The author was an attractive ethereal little woman, Camilla Collett. She was the sister of Henrik Wergeland, but largely estranged from him because she adhered to the Intelligence Party. That she loved Welhaven did not improve the situation. Although he did not return her love, he was greatly attracted to her and, he confessed in later years, could neither let her go nor hold her fast. A complete break came, however, and she married Jonas Collett, with whom she enjoyed an almost perfect companionship. With unstinting love and infinite patience, he helped to direct her

[8] Henning Larsen, "Glossaries to Asbjørnsen's *Huldreeventyr*," *Illinois Studies in Language and Literature*, vol. 29, no. 1, Urbana, 1942.

talents into literary channels. He died, however, before her epoch-making novel was completed.

Amtmandens Døtre inaugurated the whole movement for women's rights in Norway. Somewhere along the road from saga times, women had lost the independence which used to be theirs. In the middle of the nineteenth century the disparity between the sexes was becoming more glaring, especially in the upper class. The conscious effort to make social life more refined resulted in more exacting conventions which, as usual, put the greatest demands on women. Moreover, there was practically no "ladylike" occupation outside of marriage to which a woman could resort. Fru Collett championed women's rights as individuals—to love, to express their love without waiting for the male to take the initiative, to win for themselves a happy life, to be free from the bonds of the unjust conventions of a masculine-dominated society, and to work for a remuneration equal to that of men. She rebelled against relegating to women alone the Christian virtues of long-suffering and patience, and failed to be moved by the feminine ideal represented by Solveig in *Peer Gynt*, raising "the iconoclastic question whether the saving of a few paltry remnants of a man's life at the expense of a woman's whole being was really worth while."[9]

Camilla Collett wrote with a bitterness and burning indignation wrought out of her own experiences, and imparted some of her own spirit to the feminist movement of later times. Although she wrote only the one novel, she continued for many years her impassioned battle and had a wide influence, notably on Jonas Lie, who was a feminist in his own gentle way, and on Ibsen, in whom Fru Collett saw the magician who was to liberate the soul of woman. Perhaps her greatest disappointment was the lack of response from her own sex, and this was not entirely due to inertia.

Among the lesser women writers of the age was Hanna Winsnes, a clergyman's wife who probably represents a larger number of the women of her class than her greater contemporary. Using a masculine pseudonym, she wrote a number of stories which, though now forgotten, were widely read. Though she opposed any crass "realism," she believed that a writer must experience the life he pictures and deign even "to sit down at the loom of the peasant girl or bring in the porridge." She praised the freedom of the Norwegian *bonde*, believed in the *landsmaal*, and was interested in Ueland. She spoke with humorous irony of "the less esteemed sex," but was not a crusader.

[9] Hanna Astrup Larsen, *Camilla Collett and Ibsen: Two Norwegian Feminists*, Ms.

She was happily married and found that her work, if "less esteemed" than that of her husband, required just as much resourcefulness and brains. Her letters give a charming picture of the rich, strenuous life of one who must be "mother" to the whole parish and manager of a large household where guests came and went "as at a hotel."[10] It is quite fitting that the most famous and influential of her writings is her cook book, which Arne Garborg has called "a sketch from the old parsonages and magistrates' residences. . . . There is peace, calm, and idyl; good food and a good conscience. There is Christmas spirit and Sunday mood."[11]

Side by side with the national awakening, Pan-Scandinavianism was part and parcel of the romantic movement of the mid-century. There was neither any sense of incongruity between the two nor any clear conception as to how the unity of the North was to be obtained without sacrificing national individuality. The effects of German romanticism reached Norway—the influence of the Grimm brothers on Asbjørnsen and Moe is a well-known example—but partly as a result of Denmark's precarious political position, it took little general hold in the North, while an old sense of northern solidarity became once more vital. Most of the cultured Norwegians felt closely tied to Denmark. While they were aggressively asserting the apartness of Norway's cultural heritage, they were influenced by the Danish romanticists. Even some of Ibsen's early poetic utterances have the lilt of Danish ballads. The feeling toward the Swedish union was also friendly, and in 1854 the Union Day, November 4, was celebrated with much flow of eloquence.

There had been several meetings of Scandinavian scientists during the 'thirties, but when the Norwegians were invited to a students' convention to be held in Copenhagen in 1845, the majority held back, fearing that Norway's less developed culture might be lost in competition with the others. An enthusiastic group of about a hundred Norwegian students attended, however, and, carried away by the emotions of the moment, vowed to stand by the sister countries even in war. Three years later, when war broke out between Danes and Germans, only a few Norwegian and Swedish students kept their vow and fought as volunteers for Denmark, and a feeling of disappointment pervaded friends of Pan-Scandinavianism.

Before long, however, the movement gained new strength, and in 1851 and 1852 students from Denmark and Sweden were entertained

[10] Barbra Ring, ed., *Fra Hanna Winsnes' Prestegaard*, Kristiania, 1911.

[11] Fredrik Paasche, *Norges litteraturhistorie fra 1814 til 1850-aarene*, 376.

in Christiania. The most feted guest was Nikolai F. S. Grundtvig, Danish poet-pastor, who was a strong nationalist and an idealistic Pan-Scandinavian. There were toasts and songs innumerable with texts by Welhaven, Moe, A. Munch, Ibsen, and others. The Norwegians were proud to show the beauty of their country and to meet their comrades from other lands as equals. But all the warm talk of brotherhood ebbed out in expressions about the racial and cultural unity of the North and the need of closer cooperation. There was no program of action, and the emotions of the students struck no responsive chord among the people as a whole and had no political consequences. As the position of Denmark was becoming more critical, there was a resurgence of a demand for action. When in the war of 1864 Bismarck robbed Denmark of Slesvig and Holstein, with no interference from the Swedish-Norwegian government, and only a few volunteers from Sweden and Norway went to the aid of their southern brethren, ardent "Scandinavians" felt that their movement had gone down to ignominious defeat. Bjørnson uttered scathing criticism of his countrymen who had failed "a brother in need." And in his two great dramas, *Brand* and *Peer Gynt*, Ibsen flayed the Norwegians for their evasions, for their fair words that led to no action.

These two dramas, while prophetic of a new age, may well be considered the last great works of the romantic age. The youthful, vigorous, optimistic period of the mid-century had passed.

¶ Like all the other phases of life, the religious and the educational also bore the impress of the age. The influence of the Hauge revival had both deepened and broadened as, during the years of distress early in the century, many people from all strata of society turned to a serious personal religion. The effects of this revival entered the University with its first two theological professors, Svend Brochman Hersleb and Stener Johannes Stenersen. The new professors emphasized old-fashioned evangelical doctrines in harmony with the traditional tenets of the Lutheran church in contrast to the rationalism which had earlier dominated theological circles. As pastors trained by these men gradually replaced the older clergy, rationalism went into slow retreat.

Foreign influences also helped to revitalize religious life in Norway. From Denmark came Grundtvig's joyous, emotional Christianity. Chief among Norwegian exponents of Grundtvigianism was the Christiania pastor Wilhelm Andreas Wexels, who exerted wide influence through his hymns and his devotional books, and whose elo-

quent sermons attracted ever-increasing crowds, not least from amo
the students. Following the British example a Norwegian Bible Socie
was organized in 1814, made possible through a generous gift fro
Karl Johan. Through its efficient work, thousands upon thousands
Bibles were distributed, and the Bible became the reading of the peop
as never before; indeed for many it was, till about the middle of t
century, practically their only reading matter, greatly enriching n
only the religious but the whole intellectual life of the people. It was
oft-quoted saying that the "Bible and the Constitution" expressed t
spirit of the peasant homes.

An evidence of the religious awakening is the missionary work beg
in this age, which has ever since been continued on a scale large in p
portion to the economic resources of the people. Most of it was und
the auspices of the Norwegian Missionary Society, founded in 18
with its center at Stavanger, where a school for missionaries was esta
lished in 1859. Seceding from the society, and often in opposition to
a gifted theologian, Hans Paludan Schreuder, carried on a mission
South Africa, which of late has been taken over by a daughter chur
in America.

The new spirit tended to bring the clergy into closer touch with t
people and to democratize the church, and religious freedom was e
panded by removing the legal restrictions on dissenters. This refor
was pushed through the Storthing by the clerical members. Co
servatives feared that the new freedom and the unrestricted reading
the Bible might unleash harmful, dangerous forces, and it seeme
especially in the 'forties, that their apprehensions were not entirely u
founded. Those years were characterized by a number of extrem
fanatical religious movements, resulting in the formation of spec
groups which hurled invectives against one another. Some of them r
mained within the state church, while others formed dissenting sec
with a varying degree of zealotry. There occurred a few instances
extreme fanaticism. One sensuous young leader, for example, ma
religion an excuse for gross sexual abuses; and in the Finmark town
Kautokeino, a group of Lapps attacked their Norwegian neighbors a
tortured two of them to death. When the emotional wave had abate
there remained remarkably few dissenters, the divergent elements bei
absorbed in the fundamentally united state church, which is really
folk church.

The authorities, aware of the need of reforms in the church, to some ineffectual steps in that direction. But afraid to yield to the demand for a general synod, they lost a great opportunity to democratize the church.

The man who more than anyone else was to direct the future of the church was Gisle Johnson, who became a member of the theological faculty in 1847. He was a bold thinker, an aggressive personality, and an uncompromising champion of traditional Lutheranism—not the more modern German form—and all orthodox forces rallied about him. Cooperating with Johnson was Carl Paul Caspari, a brilliant German Jew of extraordinary Old Testament scholarship. Caspari was even more popular among the students, many of whom were out of sympathy with Johnson's sternly puritanical view in peripheral matters, which was not traditionally Lutheran. These two zealous men had a decisive influence on generations of theological students, who were to shape the development not only of the church in Norway, but also of daughter churches in the New World.

In spite of an intense interest in popular education, there was for years little tangible improvement in the schools, because there were two sharply conflicting views. A plan for integrating all the schools into one unified system was presented to the Storthing, but failed to pass, because it was dominated by the idea that the classics were the only true basis for a higher education. Schweigaard, himself an adept in the classics, took a lead in attacking this old educational theory. Others joined him in demanding that a place be made in the schools for studies more directly related to daily life, such as modern languages, sciences, gymnastics, and singing, and more practical subjects, even housekeeping. There was also a demand for a thorough study of the mother tongue and the history of Norway.

In 1848 a law was passed requiring every town to maintain a common school, and making attendance compulsory from the age of seven to confirmation. The course, which had in the past contained little beyond reading and Christianity, was broadened. This law was not applied to the rural districts because of opposition to the expense. The ambulatory school, Jaabæk said, was suited to rural conditions and quite adequate. These exceedingly primitive schools had one redeeming feature, their intimate cooperation with the home. This may be one reason why the intelligence and knowledge among the people were often much greater than might have been expected from their schooling. The ability to read was quite general and interest in books not rare. Concern about adult education was never wholly lacking, although no one else had shown such tireless enthusiasm for it as Henrik Wergeland.

The opportunities for schooling were meager for children of the professional class also. They did not attend the common schools but were entrusted to tutors of very limited qualifications, to say the least. The boys were then sent to Latin schools and given a severe but narrow classical preparation for the University. The more advanced schooling of the girls was limited to a year or two at one of the few girls' schools in the cities. It is a mystery how so many of them became well informed, well read, and able to use several languages. Some credit no doubt goes to the lively social intercourse, as a guest who spent weeks at a parsonage, for example, was expected to give some stimulating return for the hospitality he enjoyed.

In the 'fifties, Hartvig Nissen continued Wergeland's work by forming a "Society to further popular education," which made a large contribution through the publication of a popular periodical. Nissen became the central figure in the movement for educational reform. He established two advanced schools, one for boys and one for girls, in which he experimented with the newer educational ideas. Through his efforts, the secondary schools, which had been badly neglected, were so organized that the classics had a less dominating place and that a choice was possible between a classical course leading to the University or a more practical one. Even the University requirements were slightly modernized.

More important was Nissen's plan for reform of the common school in the country, which formed the basis for a new law of 1860. While religion was still the central subject, writing and arithmetic were given increased emphasis. The law also provided that the school readers should contain selections on history, geography, and general science. Moreover, permanent schools had to be established except where the population was very scattered. The day of the ambulatory school was largely over, and the modernizing of Norway's system of elementary education had begun. Gradually the teachers attained a more secure and respected position, and often succeeded the pastors as leaders in the community. Nissen's plans for advanced rural schools met with little success and were not realized before thirty years later, when another group of laws further modernized the schools.

More successful were the special folk high schools, the first of which was established in 1864. Although they were greatly influenced by Grundtvig and the Danish folk high schools, Christopher Bruun was the real father of these schools in Norway. They were built not so much on the conventional plan of imparting knowledge as on the idea of awakening higher aspirations in the student by inspired emotional appeal through word of mouth. While it is impossible to estimate their effect on the youth, it is certain that these schools had a great influence during the next decades.

CHAPTER 18

LAST DECADES OF THE SWEDISH UNION, 1872-1905

AN INTENSE NATIONAL PATRIOTISM was a strong motivating force in this age, and it was accompanied by a more persistent democratic aim than in the past. These ideas found effective expression in the new Liberal, or, as it was more commonly called, Left Party, which dominated the political development and caused a new system to break through. The Left attracted to itself a great many elements: the new middle class in the cities, the labor class, and the farmers. Low-church elements, the opposition group in the Storthing of whatever class, and not a few lawyers were also drawn to the new party. Above all it was a party of youth, rural youth inspired by the folk schools, and the students and other young men of the intelligentsia, who chafed under the restraint, as their elders tried to set up a norm of what they were to believe and think. Ardent young nationalists, they resented any leanings toward Pan-Scandinavianism, and friendliness toward the Swedish union was even more objectionable.

Foremost among those who shaped the ideas of the young Left were an historian, a poet, and a statesman. Johan Ernst Sars has been called the "ideological creator of the Norwegian national democracy."[1] He developed an historical philosophy which the Left made its own and which was to have a decisive influence on history writing for at least half a century. He emphasized the continuity in historical evolution: that during the Danish period the main threads in Norwegian development had remained unbroken, and that the Danish union had come as a stage in Norway's growth toward democracy and in no sense showed any inferiority in the people. Ardently nationalistic, Sars was against a strong union with Sweden. That his viewpoint was narrowly political in no wise detracted from his popularity, for few among the young cared to be reminded of Norway's grim poverty before 1840. More im-

[1] Keilhau, *Det norske folks liv og historie*, 10:64.

portant in rousing the youth to an excessively patriotic anti-unionism, and even republicanism, was Bjørnstjerne Bjørnson. He looked upon himself as the successor of Wergeland, and expressed this in his enthusiasm for the "pure" flag, his initiative in establishing the children's parade which became a part of every Seventeenth of May celebration, and his dedication of a Wergeland statue. On every patriotic occasion his facile pen was ready with a contribution, his poetry and even his dramas having greater significance as propaganda than as literature. He was the hero of the common people and a veritable chieftain among them. To carry out its program, however, the Left had to depend on Johan Sverdrup, with his long parliamentary experience, his faith in democratic principles, and his ability to put measures through the Storthing.

The new Left met no organized opposition in the 'seventies. It became customary to speak of the conservative elements as the Right, but they can hardly be called a party before 1884. The officials retained the old prejudice against parties, or at least they believed that officeholders should be the servants of the whole people and that this could best be accomplished if they were outside of parties. This was the view of Frederik Stang, who was at the head of the government from 1861 to 1880, a man far to the left of the ultra-conservatives. Yet as it became evident that a conflict with the new forces was inevitable, a Right Party began to take shape. It was not officials, however, but landed proprietors who took the initiative. For the first time the press now became a real means of propaganda, and the conservatives began to use effectively folk mass meetings, with an influence not unlike that of Jaabæk's Friends of the Farmers. Even so, the conservatives did not put forth any well-organized efforts against the overwhelming leftist wave of the 'seventies and early 'eighties, which saw the bitterest, most involved political battle in which the Norwegians had ever been engaged.

The king seems at times to have been caught between the bark and the wood. Oscar II (1872-1905), who succeeded his brother Karl XV, possessed the artistic talents of his family, had a highly romantic view of his royal office, and was eager to win the good will of the people. Anxious to heal the discord in the union, he decided that his "morning gift" to the Norwegian people should be the abolition of the hated office of statholder. To Frederik Stang belongs much of the credit for putting this measure through. He was naturally appointed to the new post of minister of state to head the government in Christiania, holding the same rank as the minister of state who resided in Stockholm. He became the center of attack in the coming conflict.

From the early days of the Constitution the idea had frequently been advanced that the ministers ought to be admitted to the Storthing, though of course without a vote. Men like Falsen, Hjelm, and Wedel had favored it, and Stang and his colleagues also believed that open discussion between the legislative and executive departments would result in greater harmony and cooperation. But the farmer group in the Storthing, fearing domination by the ministry, had opposed the move.

Now a change occurred. Johan Sverdrup expressed the opinion that if all governmental power were concentrated in the Storthing a real awakening would sweep over the country, and that this could be furthered by seating the ministers in the Storthing. Gradually he won the rural members over to his view, chief among them Jaabæk. It is not clear whether Sverdrup saw that this would lead to ministerial responsibility, or whether he found it unwise to advocate a parliamentary system, upon which the moderates even among the Left looked with suspicion. Stang and the conservatives saw that Sverdrup's plan would lead to a parliamentary system and were afraid of it. They believed that conservatism in the ministry would produce a sound balance in the government, and that only by separation of power could liberty be maintained.

Three successive Storthings passed a constitutional amendment providing for seating the ministers in the Storthing, and each time the king, upon the advice of his government, vetoed the measure. Feeling ran high, and the bitterness was augmented both by the unnecessarily provocative form the ministry gave to the veto messages and by the fact that other leftist measures were also denied sanction. The Storthing had, for example, voted an appropriation to support rifle clubs which were formed throughout the country and which, it was intimated, might be useful in case of trouble with Sweden or even in a domestic revolution. Naturally the ministry opposed the measure. The election of 1879 was especially critical. As the moves to expand suffrage had not yet succeeded, the old property qualifications for voting were still in force. The Left increased its strength by helping men to obtain title to marshy wastes and thus acquire the right to vote. But even without these "marsh men," or "fagot men," as they say in England, Sverdrup's party would probably have won, for its victory was overwhelming.

When Sverdrup's measure was passed for the third time, on March 17,

1880, it was hoped that the king would yield, but again came a veto, accompanied by a clear-cut statement that in constitutional matters the king had an absolute veto. This challenge raised a perplexing constitutional issue. As the Constitution made no mention of the veto in connection with amendments, it had been assumed that the king had the same power as in ordinary legislation, and so far the Storthing had acted on this principle. Now the conservatives advanced the theory that the nature of monarchy implied an absolute veto. Jaabæk, on the other hand, claimed that the king had nothing to say about constitutional amendments, basing his argument on the wording of the Constitution, on the precedent from 1814 when the Constitution had been changed without royal sanction, and on the principle of popular sovereignty. This view was adopted by the Left Party, and the more impatient element, among whom Bjørnson was the chief fire-eater, urged quick, decisive action. Sverdrup, who had been advancing cautiously, welcomed this prodding. On June 9, 1880, he presented in the Storthing a resolution stating that the amendment seating the ministers was now a part of the Constitution and asking the government to promulgate it. The resolution was passed by an overwhelming majority and was greeted with enthusiasm by the people. "It was the happiest day of my life," said Bjørnson. Sverdrup was the man of the hour.

What could the government do? Frederik Stang resigned without taking official cognizance of the action. Stang was an eminent jurist and had been one of the chief promoters of mid-century liberalism, serving his country with tireless devotion. He suffered, it was said, from an unhappy love for the Norwegian people, and now it repudiated him because he opposed any one-sided, uncontrolled power, placing more emphasis on how well the people should be served than by whom.[2]

The king then appointed Christian August Selmer to head the new ministry. He and his colleagues, though upright men, as were most officials of the age, were narrow bureaucrats of small caliber, who lacked the political imagination which might have helped them to find a satisfactory way out of the dilemma. Holding to the theory of the king's absolute veto, Selmer consistently refused to recognize the act of June 9 or to yield to the Storthing.

The only constitutional method, it seemed, by which the Storthing could now enforce its will was impeachment. Sverdrup was loath to go to such extremes, and in spite of pressure action was postponed until a

[2] Nils Vogt, "Fredrik Stang," in Gerhard Gran, ed., *Nordmænd i det 19de aarhundrede*, 1:452, Kristiania, 1914.

new election in 1882 had given the majority a more direct mandate from the electorate. Then the Odelsthing proceeded to impeach the ministers, who were tried individually by a high court consisting of the members of the Supreme Court and the Lagthing. Excitement ran so high that there was fear of violence. Scores of arguments were advanced on both sides. The most learned legal opinion, including the law faculty of the university, supported the king and the ministry, but the decision was political rather than juridical. On February 27, 1884, Selmer was found guilty and condemned to loss of office and to payment of costs. Similar judgment was passed on seven other ministers, while three escaped with a fine only.

Selmer had tried to persuade the king to disregard the decision, but Oscar II, finding it unwise to force the issue, dismissed the Selmer ministry with the added statement that this in no sense altered his prerogative. Failing to obtain another government of the Right, he asked the majority leader to form a ministry, and on July 2, 1884, Johan Sverdrup and his colleagues took their seats in the Storthing midst the plaudits of the assembly. This event marks the establishment of parliamentary government, on the same principle as the English, and, as Sverdrup said, all power was gathered "in this hall," i.e., the Storthing. The control was in the hands of the Left; the power of the old officialdom was broken.

Sverdrup's ministry carried through important liberal reforms which had been promised: the extension of suffrage, the new school law, the introduction of the jury system, and the reorganization of the army, as well as the establishment of a labor commission. But Sverdrup was not primarily an administrator, and there was complaint that the new folk rule brought inefficiency. Moreover the radical wing was disappointed, feeling that Sverdrup had no eye for the need of reforms beyond those for which he had spent himself. Occupied with his own interests, he had failed to keep pace with the new spirit of the youth of the 'eighties. Nevertheless, the prestige of the old leader was still sufficient to carry the election of 1885, in which loyalty to Sverdrup was the rallying point. But next year the schism became definite and clear-cut. The government presented a bill for the establishment of local self-government in the congregations. It was defeated by conservatives who favored centralized control and radicals of the Left who, influenced by the intellectual currents of the 'eighties, feared the pietistical element especially in the rural churches. Defeated at the polls in 1888, the government after some months of delay yielded to the parliamentary principle and resigned. Sverdrup, who still had a loyal following, was returned to the Storthing in the next election, but died early in 1892 before he had a chance to take his seat, and the man who "first created politics in the land"[3] had passed off the scene.

The crushing defeat the conservatives had suffered when Sverdrup took over the government made them realize, though with some reluctance on the part of older men, that they could exert influence only through party organization. This was effected under the leadership of Emil Stang, a worthy successor of his father, Frederik Stang. With sure judgment and consummate skill he drew the divergent conservative elements together into a party. He accepted the new order resulting from the parliamentary system and recognized the social changes which made the bourgeois industrialists and businessmen the main conservative element rather than the old officialdom. When Sverdrup resigned in 1889, Stang took the helm. Although his party never had a majority, Stang was a dominating personality in politics, whether as leader of the opposition or head of the government, until 1900, when he refused reelection. Lacking a majority in his own party, Stang had to depend on the support of Sverdrup's followers of the Moderate Left. In two years he was succeeded by a government of the Pure Left, the section of the Liberal Party which had repudiated Sverdrup. From then on there was a shifting of ministries and political groupings, until 1905 produced a temporary unity.

The distinction between the objectives of the parties was not always clearly drawn, and there was wavering in accepting fully the parliamentary principle. This seemed to increase the vituperative bitterness of the factional and personal strife. Yet, as Stang said, "That which divides us is as nothing compared with that which binds all Norwegians together: the love for our common country." The credit for initiating the economic and social laws of the period belongs to the Right. "The Conservative Party is a liberal party," said Stang, and he pursued a consistent policy of social betterment and development of the country's resources. Yet the Right believed in great care in public finances while the Left abandoned the earlier policy of stringent economy in favor of greater government spending financed by new taxes falling chiefly on the higher income groups. The Liberals centered their efforts upon the development of democracy.

While not a little was accomplished, more internal reforms would doubtless have been achieved but for the fact that the main political

[3] Koht, *Johan Sverdrup*, 3:580.

interest of the day was centered upon the relations to Sweden. It was first and foremost the problems of the union that caused the rise and fall of governments, as the logic of events was relentlessly moving on to the crisis of 1905.

¶ While political democracy was developing, the economic changes begun in the 'fifties continued with accelerated speed after 1870, causing a disruption of much in the time-worn social system and the rise of new conditions involving new problems.

As foreign commerce was fundamental in Norway's economic growth, it was important that hindrances to trade be removed. Norwegians were therefore interested in the attempts of the late 'sixties to decrease the multiplicity of monetary systems in the world. As no broader international agreement could be reached, a Scandinavian Monetary Union was formed. At first Sverdrup and others who felt that this harked back to Scandinavianism held back, but by 1875 Norway joined the others in adopting as the standard monetary unit the crown, which is about equivalent to a quarter in American money. Two years earlier, in 1873, Norway had adopted a gold standard in conformity with the developments abroad.

Little consideration was given to the possible effects of this monetary change on the general economic life. It doubtless was an important cause of the downward trend of prices which prevailed in the whole period from 1873 to 1896. In the shorter economic cycles of this age Norway conformed to the pattern of world conditions, with its ups and downs; but except for a crisis in shipping in the early 'eighties and a boom and crash in Christiania in the late 'nineties, with chiefly local repercussions, Norway escaped serious crises. Although lower prices brought a long period of financial stringency, this did not mean a general decline. In fact more fundamental was a gradual advance without sudden leaps, based on a sound development of national resources, largely with Norwegian capital.

The effect of the protracted hard times in the 'seventies was mitigated by extensive railroad building. As in the 'fifties, this was a government venture financed by loans in England. While this increased the national debt, it provided credit abroad, stimulated shipping, reduced unemployment, and opened new districts to trade. Unfortunately no over-all plan was followed, and especially did it prove to be a great mistake that a number of roads were narrow gauge. The 'eighties brought a pause in railroad building, as in so many lines, but in the 'nineties came a new period of activity. The greatest undertaking and most impressive engineering feat of the age was the railroad from Christiania to Bergen, uniting the East and the West, which was completed in 1909.

The merchant marine continued to flourish through the 'seventies. All along the shore small shipyards boomed and Norwegian vessels active in the carrying trade sailed the seven seas. It was the heyday of the sailers. Many were old and small, not seldom unseaworthy hulks, but the crews were expert seamen from boyhood who knew their vessel from stem to stern. Often the skipper owned his ship, at least in part, and the members of the firm of shipowners received their training not in the office but on shipboard. While this organization of the business suited conditions, there was neither the capital nor foresight needed to keep abreast of the times and modernize the merchant fleet. The depression of the early 'eighties took a heavy toll from the shipping business as one by one the firms, which had been clinging to the past, failed. But by 1887 shipping was winning back what had been lost, and by the 'nineties the merchant marine was well on the way to its new preeminence. The old sailers were rapidly edged aside by steamboats, and the business was organized on a larger scale along more purely capitalistic lines.

Fishing was a basic occupation, little affected by the economic cycles. Gradually new methods were introduced and new markets opened. The greatest single advance was Svend Foyn's invention of the harpoon gun, which was to revolutionize whaling and make it one of the country's most profitable occupations. The export of klipfish and stockfish increased from 27,000 tons annually around 1850 to 72,900 tons in the early 'nineties. More emphasis was placed on quantity than on quality, however, so the chief markets had to be sought where the standard of living was low. But before long new methods were to place Norwegian fish products in the forefront also in quality. In 1879 Norwegian sardines appeared on the market; a decade later Bjelland's fish cannery opened in Stavanger, and the following year there were nine canneries in the city.

This is only one phase of the industrial undertakings of the age. Margarine also was produced for export in the 'eighties; and in the manufacture of wood pulp, which had begun in 1863, new methods brought a rapid increase. Stone quarrying was resumed, often in the very same places as in the Stone Age, and the export of granite reached considerable dimensions even in the 'seventies. In 1885 electricity was used for the first time in a factory. There was a healthy growth in industry chiefly on a small scale and financed by capital accumulated through many small savings. The number of factory workers, which in 1870 was 30,000, doubled in the next three decades. At the same time there was a rise in the average standard of living as is indicated by the increased importation of luxuries, especially sugar and coffee. Among the reasons for the industrial advance were technical development, easier credit, and improved means of communication. Significant, also, were the growth of population, better educational facilities, and free trade, which was maintained in spite of protectionist agitation by smaller industrial as well as agrarian interests.

Agriculture more than any other occupation felt the steady pressure of the declining prices in the whole period from 1873 to 1896. The general shift from subsistence farming to production for the market caused a dependence on the current price level, which the farmers had not earlier experienced and for which they were not prepared, and they complained loudly. Those who had bought land when prices were high often became hopelessly involved in debt, and it grew increasingly difficult for one son to purchase the family farm. An old law required that he pay the current price, the law of 1854 gave all the children (daughters as well as sons) an equal right of inheritance, and with improved health conditions more of the children grew up to share in the estate. The result was a marked tendency to divide the land into smaller farms. At the same time much more of the land became the property of the tillers, as proprietors sold off their estates in small farms, the state disposed of the old church lands it still held, setting the money aside for the schools, and old commons were being divided up. By 1880 only 4½ per cent of the land was worked by tenants.

No occupation received as careful study as agriculture. Officials and leaders among the farmers themselves were working to overcome conservatism and lethargy and win general acceptance for improvements that had been inaugurated earlier. They found strong allies in prevailing conditions. As the price of grain fell more than other prices, new emphasis was placed on stock raising. Moreover, since the smaller farms could be profitable only with intense cultivation, all available fertilizer had to be utilized. As the farmers learned that it paid to keep one good cow rather than two poor ones, better feeding, cleanliness, and sunshine in the barns became prevalent, and the old custom of keeping many half-starved cows through the winter became a disgrace. The increase in the scale of wages hastened the introduction of labor-saving devices which made the farmers less dependent on hired help, while the expanding markets created by the growing city population stimulated production.

With the economic development came also social changes tantamount to a revolution, as the old order passed and a new took its place. While the old rural culture held its own through the first half of the nineteenth century, it had lost its creative vigor, as it now retreated before the new. Time-honored handicrafts fell into disrepute, as the new roads and railroads brought the city close to the country, and all manner of fine new things could be bought from the peddlers and country storekeepers —clothing, household furnishings, even curtains and pictures—so that the homes assumed a new citified appearance. But this cost money and intensified the economic pressure, adding to the social unrest.

The poor, especially the crofters, felt the social stigma of their position as they had not before, and, even though wages increased, resented the customary obligatory labor. Economic necessity no longer forced them to stay in their former position, for new outlets were found in the demand for labor on roads and in factories and, even more, in the El Dorado across the seas. The farm owners also found the crofter system unprofitable, and the most striking change in the rural communities was the decrease in the number of crofters and the improved condition of those who remained. Among the comparatively well-to-do, also, there was a similar movement away from the farm. The highest ambition of a farmer was to have a son enter a profession, preferably the ministry. So extensive was the migration from the rural communities that in spite of the increased population there was often a distressing shortage of labor.

The *bonde* movement, which dominated the politics of the 'eighties, was an outgrowth of the rural unrest; and the financial pressure explains the policy of stringent economy associated with the name of Jaabæk. In joining Sverdrup's Liberal Party the farmers set aside their own special interests in favor of national policies. Their feeling against the upper class was expressed with a bitter boldness born of the new age, not least when officials took a public stand against Sverdrup. The story is told that when a general read the riot act to a company of soldiers and accused them of treason for supporting Sverdrup, they closed in on him with charged bayonets till he begged for mercy.

The farmers were not content only to give the Liberal Party their support, but sought to further their own interests with organizations outside of political parties. Most important were the many cooperative ventures both for production and trade. By 1896 the three main sections of the country, the East, the Westland, and Trøndelag, each had one organization for cooperative buying. Moreover, the Norwegian Farmers' Union was formed, which has become perhaps the greatest force in advancing the interests of the whole rural population and developing a general nationwide agricultural program. Gradually the government also developed a scientific modern policy toward forestry and agriculture, until an agricultural department with a constantly growing budget was organized in 1900.

The changes in rural society of necessity brought in their wake some emotional chaos and cultural losses for the new generation and heartaches for the old, until a reawakened appreciation of the past eventually exerted a healing influence. The folk high schools fostered among the people a wholesome respect for their own personal worth, the *landsmaal* created pride in the speech of their own locality, and the interest of the intellectuals in preserving folklore and folk art after a time reacted also on the people themselves. The rural organizations became not only economic cooperatives, but educational clubs as well; and youth groups took up sports and folk dances. The new viewpoint is indicated by the fact that the law of 1889 which improved the common schools and broadened the curriculum, met none of the opposition which had greeted a similar law of 1860. Progress was made toward a high standard of intellectual as well as physical life, thoroughly modern but with roots in the past.

There was a marked growth of the cities during these years. In 1875 the urban population constituted a little over 18 per cent of all the people and in 1900 it was 28 per cent. Norway ceased to be chiefly agricultural, and the census of 1890 is the last that shows a majority of the people engaged in agriculture and forestry. But many people of other occupations, chiefly fishermen and sailors, lived in the country, and smaller industrial plants were also often located in rural districts, so the line between the city and country workman was not sharp. There was, nevertheless, a growing class of industrial laborers living in the cities, many of them in slums. While conditions did not become as bad as in England, for example, the factory system grew up without restrictions and the usual grave abuses followed—long hours, unnecessary danger, and inadequate pay. While the regulations passed in mercantilist days and in the 'forties were still in force, they applied only to specific occupations, and did not include the new factories.

The evil which first attracted attention was child labor, noticed by the school authorities. The Frederik Stang ministry took the first action, and in 1875 an extensive study of the situation was made by Jacob Neumann Mohn. An inclusive law was proposed, but no action taken, the excuse being that Oscar II had initiated a general study of labor conditions. In 1885 a labor commission was appointed, which three years later published its report, but nothing further was done in the 'eighties.

A change was already on the way, however. The Society for Political Economy organized by specialists did much to arouse interest in reform, especially among public men of the Conservative Party. Among the people at large several social currents had a powerful influence. The temperance movement, originating in England, developed a vigorous club life and grew to such proportions that in 1913 there were 250,000 members of the different societies. Fully as important were the cooperatives. The first had been started in the 'sixties, both in country and in town, and had by 1875 reached a membership of 30,000. After a period of decline they took on new life in the 'nineties when Ole Dehli began a work of extensive organization, making the cooperatives a power in the national economy. In 1906 the National Cooperative Society of Norway was organized with a membership of 32,000. Branching out into numerous activities, the society grew enormously, embracing in 1920 four hundred societies with a membership of 80,000. While about 50 per cent of the membership were laborers, it included individuals from all occupations, not excluding the farmers, who also had their own organization.

Even more significant was the labor movement. In the 'seventies trade unions sprang up, some of them new and some survivals of the old craft guilds, and they became quite general in the 'eighties. These unions formed a national organization, the United Norwegian Labor Union, with a broad program, and gave loyal support to the Liberal Party in its rise. But after 1884 the laborers were bitterly disappointed in the Sverdrup ministry, and many of them had socialistic leanings. There followed a struggle between the Liberal Party and the socialists for control of the labor vote. In 1887 the Norwegian Labor Party was formed upon the instigation of the socialists Holtermann Knudsen and Carl Jeppesen, and two years later it adopted a socialist platform. Under a number of capable leaders the party gained strength through the 'nineties, but not before 1903 was it strong enough to elect a member to the Storthing. The party did not pursue a consistent socialistic policy, however, because, like the rest of the country, it was strongly nationalistic, and because the chief interest of the rural element was to acquire land.

A combination of the above-mentioned influences brought about social legislation in the 'nineties which was largely based on Mohn's plan of 1875 and the report of the commission of 1885. In 1892, an inclusive factory law, proposed by the Emil Stang ministry, was passed. It forbade the employment of children under twelve years of age, and limited the labor of children from twelve to fourteen to six hours and that of "young persons" from fourteen to eighteen, to ten hours. It provided, moreover, for special protection of women and for some precautions against accidents. Factory inspection was also initiated and a beginning made to regulate labor-employer relations. Two years later an accident insurance law sponsored by Gunnar Knudsen was passed. Sickness insurance and old-age insurance were proposed, but not acted upon as yet. Mention should be made also of the abolition of public prostitution in 1887, the modern criminal law which in 1902 replaced that of 1842, and the law of 1896 "concerning the treatment of neglected children." The two latter were largely drawn up by Bernhard Getz, the most prominent among jurists in the work for humane laws.

Emigration was part and parcel of that transformation which Norwegian society was undergoing. A new epidemic of the "America fever" spread over the country, and this could be stilled neither by the disillusionment of earlier emigrants, by warnings from officials, nor by tales of wretchedness of the passage and suffering in the new home. The hardship had begun to abate, however, as the emigrant traffic was transferred from the Norwegian sailing ships to foreign, especially English, steamboats, and as the first harrowing days of pioneering were passing. The emigrants were not so predominantly rural as in the past, but even later when the majority came from the cities, they had often moved to town but a short time before. While most were still of the poorer classes, crofters and laborers from the country, industrial workers, servants, and the like from the urban population, there were among them a larger number of sons of well-to-do farmers and young professional men who found their opportunities at home narrowly circumscribed. Besides clergymen there were doctors who brought healing to their countrymen on the frontier or later won a place in the larger American society; and engineers who in large measure contributed their technical training to the development of the United States and other new lands.[4]

[4] Kenneth Bjork, *Saga in Steel and Concrete*, Northfield, 1947.

The chief economic reason for emigration must now be sought in the fact that the industrial development did not keep pace with the sharp increase in population and that there were not other openings adequate to the needs. It was stimulated also by the greater mobility and instability of society, and by the new courage to break with the past. The waves of migration do not correspond to the economic cycles through which Norway was passing, but were probably influenced more by good or bad times in America. Directly after the Civil War, from 1866 to 1873, came a brief period of unprecedented emigration, as 110,896 persons left for America compared with 77,874 in the preceding forty-five years. After a brief slump, 1879 brought another rise reaching the peak in 1882, when there were 26,000 emigrants to America. In the late 'nineties the number went down, but the first decade of the twentieth century comprised the third and last great wave of emigration, with its highest point in 1903, when 25,000 emigrated.[5] By 1910 more than 695,000 people had left Norway for the Land of Promise in the West. There were smaller movements of population to other lands as well, taking Norwegians to the ends of the earth, but these were almost counterbalanced by the immigration into Norway, consisting mainly of returning Norwegian-Americans and of Swedes.

The exodus furthered the growth of the merchant marine and relieved the pressure of a growing population on the means of subsistence at home, but, on the other hand, the outpouring of youth robbed the country of energy and talent and might thus tend to retard its development. However, the losses and gains from emigration were probably pretty well balanced. Earlier efforts to stem emigration by branding it as unpatriotic now gave way to a desire so to improve conditions at home that there should be no reason to leave. Thus emigration became one of the many factors in the demand for economic and social legislation to raise the general standard of living.[6] But no extensive study of the influence of emigration on Norway was made, and only sporadic efforts to check the exodus.

¶ Even while interest had been centered upon the political conflict to such an extent that other issues were shoved into the background, a ferment had been at work which broke out in full force in the 'eighties, letting loose intense intellectual activity. For the first time in modern

[5] Blegen, *Norwegian Migration to America*, vol. 2, ch. 15, gives a brief summary of emigration in its relation to the mother country.

[6] Brynjolf J. Hovde, "Notes on the Effect of Emigration on Scandinavia," *Journal of Modern History*, 6:253-279 (September 1934).

history Norway's cultural achievement was of sufficient cosmopolitan import to receive general European recognition. Currents and cross-currents of thought created conflicts as personal, petty, and bitter as is possible only in a small society, and yet produced much that was high-minded and significant.

The tragic element of the age was the break between the older and younger generation. The old could not understand this break, as they had received their knowledge of the past from their fathers and had experienced nothing of the kind. Many parents worried—often with good reason—about the effect that the whirl of new ideas would have upon their sons and even their daughters. The older generation had been indoctrinated in the authoritarian orthodoxy of the Gisle Johnson school, which was suspicious of religious discussion. This tended to drive the young to the other extreme. The new evolutionary scientific theories, while known to the earlier generation, were making themselves strongly felt in the 'seventies, when great interest was centered upon the biological sciences. Norway was plunged into long debates between the old orthodox viewpoint and the new scientific, a controversy in which there was no approach to reconciliation before the twentieth century. The most striking incident in this conflict was Bjørnson's repudiation, in 1879, of historic Christianity, an event which caused bitter disappointment in orthodox circles and stirred up an acrid discussion in all the Scandinavian countries.

One cause of the cleavage between the generations was the ignorance of the youth about the immediate past. The better educational facilities gave them access to knowledge their elders lacked and newspapers kept them abreast of the events of the day, but they had very little conception of the economic and cultural achievements that had transformed the backward country of 1840 into the more modern state of 1870. They believed that their fathers had been out of touch with modern thought, while they were themselves guilty of the provincialism of which they accused their elders, provincialism in time if not in space. The theory was advanced that conflict between young and old is inevitable and that youth is always right.

The viewpoint of the age was not pessimistic. The right of the individual to develop his personality hampered neither by inner inhibitions nor outer restraints was paramount. Fundamental in attaining this was truth, which must not be veiled by discreet concealment or roseate romanticism, but laid bare for all to see, be it ever so ugly. Then only, it was felt, could evils be remedied. The 'seventies, and even more the 'eighties, therefore, brought a free discussion of all problems, social and religious, such as Norway had never before experienced.

The interest was confined chiefly to the intellectuals, the city people or people of the official class with a city background. Of the great writers only Arne Garborg, who clung to the soil of his home with undying love and longing, drew chiefly upon the rural people for his themes. He alone of the great writers generally used the *landsmaal.* He waged a wordy warfare with Bjørnson, who asserted that the *landsmaal* was a repudiation of cultural development and, anyhow, there had been too much glorification of the *bonde.* Yet at this very time, 1885, a law was passed putting the "folk language" on a par with the city speech in the school system. Though this had little immediate educational effect, the language question was thereby introduced into politics, and was no longer a purely cultural issue.

As in earlier periods, many intellectual impulses came to Norway from abroad, especially from Denmark. The brilliant religious philosopher, Søren Kierkegaard, exerted a strange influence on persons of the most divergent views, who often understood or accepted only certain phases of his philosophy without pursuing the ideas of the Danish thinker to their ultimate conclusion. Later the more radical thinker, Georg Brandes, became almost an intellectual dictator in the North. As Norway had no great philosophers of her own at this time, the leadership in thought fell almost wholly to the literary writers, of whom the country had a brilliant galaxy.

While these writers cannot, either in time or in the scope of their genius, be confined to any one literary period or tendency, they were at the height of their power in what is called the Age of Realism of the 'seventies and early 'eighties. Overshadowing all the others is, of course, Henrik Ibsen.[7] After breaking with romanticism, he developed into a writer of incomparable "social" drama which gave him a place of influence in the literature of all western civilization. Second to Ibsen in his international reputation was Bjørnson, the incarnation of national patriotism, the violent protagonist of causes. His chief medium at this time was also the drama, though his plays never approached in depth or in artistry those of his greater contemporary.

The first great novels, with the exception of Camilla Collett's *Amtmandens Døtre*, also appeared in this period. As no other writer of the

[7] Hanna Astrup Larsen, "Norwegian Literature," in *Columbia Dictionary of Modern European Literature*, New York, 1947. As the literature from Ibsen on is generally known and accessible to English-speaking readers, it seems permissible to treat it with a brevity out of proportion to its importance.

time, Alexander Kielland had a sense of historical continuity, acquired through the knowledge of his own ancestors, a wealthy merchant family in Stavanger. He pictured his family in the novels *Garman & Worse* and *Skipper Worse*. The books teem with delightful descriptions of life in the old town for which, with all his cosmopolitanism, he retained a warm affection. A patrician himself, he was keenly aware of the glaring inequalities in society, a sympathetic champion of the underprivileged, and a merciless critic of the evils in the established order. Jonas Lie was gentler and more subtle in his criticism. There was a romantic, mystic strain in Lie which found expression both in his earlier and in his later works. During this period, however, he confined himself to realistic novels, inimitable pictures of the life of seafaring folk or of people of the professional class. The books about the latter group, of which *The Family at Gilje* is the best known, were influenced by Camilla Collett, although Lie was the more finished artist and the more objective observer. While he showed how sham, injustice, conventionalities, and economic pressure stunted and thwarted the development of individuals, he never lost his optimism or his faith in the established social and religious institutions. He alone among the great realists was untouched by the naturalism of the 'eighties.

Nearly all the literary works of the age were dominated by some social or moral purpose, and society was conveniently blamed for the ills that befell individuals. Throughout the 'seventies it was the social evils, not the fundamental institutions, that were attacked. But for a short time in the 'eighties naturalism had a strong influence. It emanated chiefly from the more radical, rootless group of students who liked to call themselves "Bohemians." The movement found expression in *Fra Kristiania-Bohemen* (From the Christiania Bohème) by Hans Jæger. It is a dreary, negative book of little literary value, presenting an anarchistic view of all society. The naturalists condemned not only weaknesses but society itself, and, holding fast to nothing but rational scientific conclusions, they threw into the discard religion and social institutions in a search for absolute freedom. Among their tenets free love became the center of discussion. The naturalist movement was confined to certain circles in Christiania, but within these it brought moral and intellectual ruin to alarmingly many youths. The only great writer who was a consistent naturalist was Amalie Skram. A frank discussion of the ugliest phases of life and an utter hopelessness pervade her stories. Arne Garborg, a genius among Norwegian authors who seems to fit into no classification, was for a time an apostle of naturalism. But he had reached this position only after a long, tragic inward struggle, and even in his most drab and earthy pictures of the life of the people he did not quite lose sight of the fact that there is a bright heaven above. In his last works, notably *Den burtkomne faderen* (The Lost Father), are indications that he had fought his way back to an undogmatic religion which, together with his love for the soil, gave meaning to life.

In no other age has literature exerted such far-reaching influence on all problems of society. It is therefore natural that the question of women's rights should break through and become a national issue. While some improvements in the legal status of women had been made in the preceding period, other developments had increased the difficulty of their position. Not only had the social code tightened, but the submission of women had been emphasized to a degree that Hanna Winsnes and her like had never thought of. Even more powerful was the economic change, felt especially in the professional class. The solidarity of the family as an economic and social unit was dwindling. The women especially—circumscribed though their earlier life had been—lost the sense of economic and social security and importance that the old family life had afforded, and went through a difficult transition period before they won for themselves a place in the new age in which the individual is the unit. As many activities were removed from the home and suitable outside employment was almost nonexistent, the unmarried state became harder than in the past, and unhappy marriages of the kind described by Camilla Collett and Jonas Lie were all too common.

The literary battle, begun with Camilla Collett's novel and continued by her, Jonas Lie, Ibsen, and others, caused lively discussion. In 1879 Ibsen, who, however, disclaimed any feminist leanings, for the first time made woman's place in society the central theme of one of his dramas. *A Doll's House* became a most significant piece of propaganda and won world-wide recognition within a few years. Before this, early in the 'seventies, Aasta Hansteen had entered the fray. She had the courage to be associated with the small group of "emancipated" women, some of whom, so the papers said, even cut their hair and wore trousers. Her personal peculiarities, the illogical confusion of many of her utterances, and even her indomitable zeal made her the butt of much ridicule. Yet she dared to be a martyr, and in the midst of her hazy ideas there were gleams of light and prophetic vision.

Among the women who made a definite contribution to the cause was Cecilie Thoresen. As a result of her request, the Storthing in 1882 opened to women the entrance examination to the University leading to the bachelor's degree, as well as the more advanced "second examination." As it was feared that women could not master higher mathematics, it was proposed that they be allowed to substitute German, but no action was taken. Cecilie passed her mathematics with distinction and became the first woman matriculated at the University. Two years later, in 1884, all University degrees and all professional examinations were opened to women, but not before the 'nineties did any woman complete the requirements in law, medicine, philology, or theology.

Organized agitation for women's rights really began in 1884 with the formation of the Norwegian Society for Women's Rights (*Norsk Kvindesagsforening*) through the initiative of the journalist Hagbard Berner, who became the first president. Before long, however, he was succeeded by Gina Krog, who continued to work for the cause with untiring devotion until her death in 1925. Her well-poised personality and her unswerving confidence helped to disarm criticism and win respect. The society won a large membership of both men and women. Its purpose was "to strive to obtain for woman the rights and the place in society to which she is entitled." It was largely educational, continuing by lectures, publications, and branch societies the work begun in literature and reading circles. The first concession obtained from the government was the appointment of a woman, Hedevig Sophie Rossing, on a new commission for the folk schools. By the close of the 'eighties most positions had been opened to women, legally if not actually, and measures had been taken to give married women the legal and economic rights which had earlier been accorded to their unmarried sisters. These advances had met little opposition and brought no revolutionary changes, but the struggle for political rights was to be a harder battle. Under Gina Krog's leadership a separate society to work for women's suffrage was formed in 1885, but at first it had only ten members. While persistent efforts were carried on through the 'nineties, victories were not won before the twentieth century.

One phase of the social injustice to women was brought to the attention of the public through a unique book of the 'eighties, *Albertine* by Christian Krohg. Albertine is a sewing girl who, caught in the meshes of Christiania conditions, becomes a woman of the streets. The story was a contribution to the war on legalized prostitution which was being successfully fought, but even more an attack on the methods used by the police to enforce moral regulations. But *Albertine* is more noteworthy for its illustrations than for the text, as Krohg was the most powerful painter of the day; and if naturalism had a dubious influence on literature, it gave new vigor to painting.

Young Norwegian artists had discovered Paris and there acquired the new ideas of impressionism and of painting in the open. They did not stay long in Paris, however, for Christiania was by this time large enough to attract artists, and painters of nature found a greater wealth of subjects in their own country than abroad. Norway had for the first time a group of artists living at home, but they had to fight a hard battle of words before they won recognition.

Truth was the slogan of painters as well as of writers, and Christian Krohg was as much a champion of truth as Ibsen. He believed that society demanded a picture of itself as it really was, and that art had a social function. His paintings abound in strong, vigorous types, and are generally typically Norwegian, although the naturalists disclaimed any nationalism in art. Fritz Thaulow felt no mission in his art except to reproduce nature as he saw it, but a discriminating taste guided his choice of themes. Shimmering water and snow in subtle nuances of color furnished most of his subjects. His impressionistic treatment, his emphasis on color rather than composition and drawing, and his use of light, cheerful tints instead of rich, somber brown shades mark a definite break with the past. Erik Werenskiold produced as sensitive portraits as have ever been painted in Norway, as well as landscapes of marked Norwegian character. He was an avowed nationalist in his art. With keen insight he pictured the life of common people shorn of the romanticism of Tidemand, stark at times, but imbued with greater depth of feeling. He is most widely known for his delightfully humorous illustrations, especially of the fairy tales, which have given children of all later generations their visual idea of the tales. While these three were the early leaders in the school of the 'eighties, many other distinguished painters arose who were to show the influence of naturalism through the succeeding decades. Among them Harriet Backer holds a unique place. Though modern in treatment, her interiors, painted with infinite care, are reminiscent of Vermeer, showing the same delicacy in detail, mastery of color, and exquisite, studied light effects.

As in the past, sculpture was less important than painting, and it was less influenced by naturalism. Among sculptors, Stephan Sinding is the chief, noted for his modeling of the nude and for expressing in marble warmth and intensity of emotion.

In music the 'eighties became notable mainly through the work of Edvard Grieg, who more than anyone else won for Norwegian music recognition both at home and abroad. In the most unromantic decade of the century he was a thorough national romanticist, more Norwegian, it has been claimed, than the folk music from which he drew his inspiration. He continued to be the central figure in Norwegian music until his death in 1907, and remained always the romanticist. On the whole, it was easy for Norwegian art to glide into the neo-romanticism of the 'nineties.

¶ A wealth of creative energy burst forth in the 'nineties. The lines of thought and achievement were so varied that they do not easily lend themselves to classification. Yet in the midst of the diversity there are certain tendencies in art and literature which fully justify describing the decade as the Age of Neo-Romanticism. The year 1890 forms an unusually sharp dividing line between the past and the future in literature. There was a reaction against the literature of the 'eighties dealing with society as a whole and its influence upon the individual, and a turn to more personal problems with an attempt to probe into the innermost recesses of the soul. The general outlook was less cosmopolitan and less urban, and the writers were little concerned with the political and social movements of the day. This departure from the earlier utilitarian purpose brought a renewed emphasis on form and beauty of expression.

Like the earlier romanticists, the writers of the 'nineties were inspired by a strong national feeling; but they tried to delve more deeply into that undying, intangible something, the national soul, and its manifestations in the life of every individual. Many believed, as did Moltke Moe, that the national culture was a combination of the old rural traditions with the heritage from the cities and the elements that had more recently been added to the population. Others held with Ivar Aasen that only he was a genuine Norwegian whose ancestors had tilled the soil of Norway from time immemorial, and it was quite in keeping with this view that the use of the *landsmaal* was greatly increased.

Many of the neo-romanticists, whether they came of poor peasant stock or descended from rich farmers or landed proprietors, had an intimate "feel" for the land that the earlier romanticists had not attained. They often drew inspiration from the people, traditions, and nature of their own district and produced literature with marked regional characteristics, sometimes having as its theme the mysterious, indissoluble bond between the family and the farm. There is at times an element of symbolism introduced, occasionally religious though rarely of a confessional type. While the immediate surroundings furnished material for literature, poets found inspiration also in the distant, lofty mountain wilds. Scarcely known hitherto, these wilds now became familiar as scientists penetrated them, tourists sought ever more thrilling adventures, and sportsmen more daring exploits. There is, however, a marked element of realism in the neo-romantic literature, and it was strongly influenced by the contemporary French decadent school.

It strengthened the neo-romantic movement that the great men of the older generation had a part in it: Ibsen, whose *The Wild Duck* and all succeeding plays contain a romantic element, Jonas Lie, who as early as 1890 published *Troll*, in which he used the tradition-bound form of the fairy tale, and Garborg, whose later works were also in the spirit of the 'nineties. The dramatist Gunnar Heiberg, who had attained prominence in the 'eighties, retained the outlook of that decade, although in form and method of handling his work belongs to the later period. Bjørnson was the one of the older writers who refused to yield at all to the influences of the new romanticism.

It was, however, the "rebirth," as it has been called, of lyric poetry that really inaugurated the new age. There was a strong lyric current in modern Norwegian literature from the time of Wergeland until the utilitarianism of the 'eighties seemed to dry it up. Ibsen himself declared that lyric poetry was a dying form of art, and even Bjørnson's vivid poetic outbursts were somewhat dimmed. One young lad, Nils Collett Vogt, who has been called the "last follower of Wergeland," persisted in producing lyrics in the 'eighties in spite of advice to turn to other forms. He became a virile poet of protest and of forthright honesty and idealism, and although he won recognition rather slowly, he exerted great influence on younger poets.

It was Vilhelm Krag, however, who in 1890 burst upon the literary horizon with poetry which departed so far from the strict traditional forms that it constituted a revolution. The captivating beauty of his verse, the direct simplicity of his emotions, and the romantic local color in his treatment of the region about his home city of Christiansand won for him almost instantaneous popularity. He was a propagandist of the new movement and gained a hearing also for other poets of his group. Greatest among these, and with more depth than Krag, was Sigbjørn Obstfelder, whose work was also a revolt against naturalism. There is something mystical—symbolic and vaguely incomplete—about his unrhymed verse and lyrical prose writings. A protest against the unconventionality in poetic forms which became a studied vogue, is found in the more conservative lyrics of Theodor Caspari. He, too, was a romanticist, and has described the rugged mountain nature with intimate knowledge and warm love. The increased use of the *landsmaal* is represented by Per Sivle, whose forceful lyrics on themes drawn from the sagas are reminiscent of the skalds of old.

Among the prose writers Knut Hamsun, probably the greatest genius of the age, was the father of neo-romanticism. His first novel, *Hunger*, appeared in 1888, and the 'nineties constitute the most markedly lyric-romantic period of his career. While rooted to the soil, he expressed the two-fold urge so marked among Norwegians, attachment to the soil, and love of the sea and longing for distant lands. Nowhere is this duality stronger than in the North, which is the background for Hamsun's work. His most magnificent description of northern nature is found in *Pan*, and nowhere are the sensitive nuances of Hamsun's language more marked or the depth and breadth of his feeling for nature better expressed. The influence of Nietzsche—introduced into the North by Brandes—is clearly evident in Hamsun's contempt for the average man and the masses.[8]

The decade brought to the fore such a wealth of prose writers that it is well-nigh impossible to select any of them for special mention. They give a richer and more varied picture of Norway than any earlier literature had produced. Most of them have a distinct local color in their works, and deal with folk in the humbler walks of life. Not a few go back to the traditions and history of their community, and in treatment they range from idealistic romanticism to the starkest realism. The following may be mentioned to illustrate the wide scope of themes and forms: Hans E. Kinck's philosophical stories of the conflict between the two old cultural traditions in Norway; Hans Aanrud's delightful idyls of simple rural life; and Trygve Andersen's stories from the decades immediately preceding 1814, which throw into sharp relief the contrast between the solid farmers and the official families deteriorating in their isolation.

Next to literature, painting continued to be the chief art of Norway; but in painting, the naturalism of the 'eighties merged gradually, almost imperceptibly, into the neo-romanticism of the 'nineties. Impressionism, the new technique developed to catch and fix on the canvas the impression of a moment, influenced most artists of the 'eighties and 'nineties, but their clear-eyed naturalism kept them from yielding too

[8] Hanna Astrup Larsen, *Knut Hamsun*, New York, 1922.

much to this tendency. A far more important departure from the older naturalism was the desire to express the mood of a landscape, which was a dominating passion of the neo-romantic painters. While it affected the older artists, it found its full expression only in the younger men and women, of whom there were a great number. Only a few can be mentioned, all masters of mood and color: Thorolf Holmboe pictured the dreamy beauty of the fjords and skerries of the North; Nikolai Astrup painted the romantic nature about his home on the Westland, with unsurpassed use of nuances of greens and blues; Christian Skredsvig caught the spirit and even the weird atmospheric effects of the landscapes about his home in Hallingdal; Harald Sohlberg's most famous picture from Rondane Mountains, north in the Uplands, is a unique marvel in hard, glittering blues and whites. Among other landscape painters who rank with these is Gerhard Munthe, but he won even greater distinction for his contribution to historical art, which was also an important part of the neo-romantic movement. With the cooperation of other artists, especially Halfdan Egedius and Werenskiold, he created the classic illustrations for Snorri's *Heimskringla*. By conventionalizing his themes he produced an art modern in technique yet closely akin to that of viking and saga times. Later he employed the same style in easel paintings and in mural decorations, notably of the Haakon's Hall in Bergen.

No Norwegian artist has been so highly acclaimed or has roused such heated controversy as Edvard Munch, whom critics have pronounced the greatest genius of all times among the country's painters. He defies classification. Although traces of every tendency and current in the development of painting from the 'eighties until far into the present century can be seen in his work, he was mastered by none of them. There is soul-searching back of his paintings; and with uncanny power he transferred to the canvas man's most baffling problems and deepest emotions. Conservatives, who may find Munch's later works obscure in their symbolism and not appealing to the eye, will probably feel that some of the canvases of the 'nineties, which combine depth of feeling with an ethereal, lyric beauty, are the finest of Munch's paintings.

By the close of the century Norway had an unbelievably large number of artists of superior rank. Painting reached the highest plane the country ever attained before or since, and it is probably safe to say that it was unsurpassed except by the French.

In sculpture Norway's achievements were not numerous. While others might deserve mention, the one supreme genius is Gustav Vigeland, unquestionably the greatest sculptor the country has produced. He might be compared to Edvard Munch, but in his field he towers in more solitary grandeur. Vigeland combines an uncompromising naturalism and sure sense of form with a wealth of imagination. Like Munch's, his art is deeply personal, yet universal in its appeal.

More national in spirit was the development of wooden architecture. It was inspired largely by old buildings on the farms and medieval timber churches. Much emphasis was placed on the locality and the suitability of the terrain. National in background also was the development of craftsmanship. Before the close of the century, the folk art had inspired a new generation of artists, and a veritable revival had been achieved. While motifs might be as old as the Oseberg ship, the products were original and modern. Notable was the work in enamel and precious metals, but more striking was the rich production of art weaving which appeared suddenly in the 'nineties and attracted international attention. Gerhard Munthe was the leader in creating the style for this as well as other handicrafts, and the chief pioneers in art weaving were his wife Sigrun Munthe, Augusta Christensen, and Frida Hansen.

In music Grieg's genius continued to set its stamp on the age. Second to him among composers was Christian Sinding, upon whom, in a sense, Grieg's mantle was later to fall, and whose heroic, thoroughly Norwegian music won international acclaim. Norway had at this time also a number of distinguished performing artists, the most famous being the pianist, Erika Nissen. Some of them, as for example Agathe Backer Grøndahl, won recognition as composers as well.

Only a slight indication has been given of the large number of great and near-great men and women who contributed to the richness of Norway's literary and artistic life in the Age of Neo-Romanticism. To a great extent this age gave direction and character to the following decades.

¶ The vigor of the decades after 1870 found expression not only in the creative arts but in every phase of intellectual activity which characterized western civilization in the late nineteenth century. In some lines Norway made contributions of general importance, while others were mainly of national significance.

The 'nineties constitute the first great period in Norwegian criticism, as the many-sided literary and artistic production of the neo-romantic period inspired a wealth of objective criticism of marked originality and insight. Not only was the current production of literature, the arts, and the theater given a more competent evaluation than in the past, but more comprehensive works of criticism were written. Most of them, but by no means all, were devoted to the Norwegian field. While both the 'eighties and 'nineties were lamentably lacking in general historical scholarship, considerable research was done in different phases of cultural history, and not a little was achieved in philosophy and jurisprudence.

Theology was a center of conflict for many decades. When a great controversy about Christianity filled the air in the 'eighties, the man who did most to soften the differences arising between theological schools was Professor Fredrik Petersen. As he attempted to restate the Christian view, he accepted everything in the intellectual life of his day which he did not find in direct conflict with the Bible, instead of looking upon the newer scientific scholarship as anti-Christian. Upon the death of this peaceable, liberal-minded scholar in 1903, the question of filling his chair caused a renewed outbreak of controversy. When Johannes Ording, a representative of modern liberal theology, won the appointment, Sigurd Vilhelm Odland, of the opposition, resigned his professorship. In 1908 the conservatives under Odland's leadership established a privately supported seminary (*Menighetsfakultetet*), which five years later was authorized to examine candidates for pastorates in the established church, which thereby recognized both schools of thought.

Like theology, philology and folklore also became involved in sharp debates—this time nationalistic. In these fields two illustrious names stand out, linking national romanticism with the scholarship of the present century. In the late 'fifties Sophus Bugge, then a young man in his twenties, began to gather folk songs and published a very scholarly collection. But, while not abandoning this work, he soon turned his main attention to philology, which had fascinated him from boyhood. His fabulous learning covered a multitude of ancient languages and dialects from Sanskrit on, his unfailing memory kept his knowledge ever fresh, and his creative imagination enabled him to synthesize the results of his research and to advance theories that opened new fields of investigation. His many-sided interests turned more and more to the North, and concentrated upon the origins of northern myths and legends. He stirred up heated argumentation with fanatic nationalists when he advanced the theory that while thoroughly Norwegian, the Eddic poems showed influences from many lands and peoples, even from the Orient, and most markedly from Christianity as found among the Celts of the British Isles. In the language controversy he took a definite stand for the traditional literary form, to which he gave the name *riksmaal*, the language of the realm. It was, he emphasized, the historic tongue of the nation, the language of the Constitution and of all subsequent documents through which the national development was expressed.

Like Bugge, his younger co-worker, Moltke Moe, must have sympathized with Grieg and the many others who resented the implication that they were lacking in patriotism because they were not *landsmaal* enthusiasts. While accepting the *riksmaal* as basic, Moe believed that by adding words from the dialects an enriched language would finally evolve through an amalgamation of the two forms. It was fitting that he should receive as a legacy from Asbjørnsen the task of adapting the language of his fairy tales to changing usage. From close association with his father, Jørgen Moe, Moltke Moe early acquired an enthusiasm for his country's folk culture and lived himself into the thoughts and traditions of the people. With a learning comparable to Bugge's, he made a study of folklore a profession. He gave a lifetime of selfless devotion to the task of deepening the culture of his people through an understanding of all the traditions of the past and blending them into one harmonious whole. Unlike many of his generation, he saw no inevitable conflict between the old and the young, and age-old traditions of town and country, nor even between national and foreign cultural values.

Except for Bugge's philological researches, the influence of these humanistic studies reached but little beyond the Scandinavian North. To the advance in natural science, on the other hand, Norwegians made contributions of far more than national significance.

Most important was Armauer Hansen's discovery of the leprosy bacillus in 1873. Earlier, great efforts had been made to combat the disease and to care for those afflicted with it, but no striking advance appeared before Hansen was placed in charge. In the light of his discovery he obtained effective legislation and supervised its enforcement, with the result that between 1875 and 1910 the number of cases of leprosy declined from 2,100 to about three hundred. Since then the disease has almost disappeared. But even as leprosy was being conquered, other diseases were on the increase. In the 'nineties beriberi was becoming alarmingly prevalent among seamen. The reason became obvious when the Hollander Christian Eikman discovered that the illness was caused by the absence in the diet of an element which later became known as vitamin B. Just at this time the use of canned goods and white bread, which lacked this essential element, had become general on Norwegian ships. This discovery led Norwegian scientists to search for a similar explanation of scurvy, which through the centuries had afflicted seamen, especially whalers. As a result of the research of Axel Holst and Theodor Frølich it was established in 1907 that scurvy was caused by a dietary deficiency in what we now call vitamin C.

Among other nineteenth century scientists, mention must be made of the distinguished mathematician Sophus Lie—a worthy successor of Niels Abel—and of the zoologist-pastor, Michael Sars. During twenty-five years spent on lonely parsonages of the Westland, Sars studied the lower forms of ocean life, laying foundations in the science of marine biology. His work was continued by his son Ossian Sars and his son-in-law Fridtjof Nansen, who also began his career as a zoologist. Nansen soon took up the geographic aspects of the study of the ocean, and later became professor of oceanography. It is very fitting that this distinguished son of Norway should make his most important scientific contributions in this field. It was his polar expedition, however, which first won for him world fame.

The Norwegians had never quite lost the viking instinct for exploring, and not a few of them took a noteworthy part in the great nineteenth century exploration of tropical regions. It was to be expected, however, that Norway's chief contribution would be in the Arctic field, where Norwegians had been pioneers in olden days. In the nineteenth century they added considerably to the knowledge of the North. In 1863, for example, Svalbard was circumnavigated. As whalers kept pushing farther afield, many a skipper recorded valuable meteorological observations and charted hitherto unknown regions. Norwegian ships carried exploring expeditions from other lands, notably those of the Swede, Baron Nils Nordenskjöld, who discovered the Northeast Passage; but it was the general opinion that great ventures must be left to countries with larger economic resources. Nansen was to change this idea.

Nansen's polar expeditions would have been impossible without skis. Achievement in sports had been the pride of Norwegians from Olaf Tryggvason's day far into the nineteenth century. Then came a decided slump—whether because the change in daily living made marksmanship and skiing less important or because the rural youth was trying to be citified. Yet when a new interest in sports emanated from the cities, there were still skiers in the rural districts who could show the way. As tireless efforts on the part of enthusiasts overcame the general inertia, all kinds of athletics were cultivated, but winter sports naturally predominated, first skating and later skiing. Before the close of the century Norwegians had set world records in both sports, and even more significant was the widespread participation by people of both sexes and of all ages. The movement was to gain enormous proportions, reaching out also into the countryside, which had lagged behind, until the Norwegians again became a nation of sportsmen.

As young men and women sought pleasure and adventure in the out-of-doors, they penetrated mountain wilds and climbed hitherto unscaled peaks. So when the call came for volunteers to share in perilous adventures in the Far North, there were hundreds of applicants who had the needed physical fitness and sportsmanship, as well as some little inkling of the lure of the Arctic, and no one better represented their ideal than Fridtjof Nansen.

Preliminary to his more famous achievements was Nansen's Greenland expedition of 1888. With five companions, two Lapps and three Norwegians, of whom Otto Sverdrup is the most famous, he made a hazardous trip on skis across the island from east to west. The equipment was simple, much of it the work of Nansen's own hands, and the expense relatively small; but it had significant scientific results and roused much interest. Not long after his return Nansen began to prepare for a venture based on the theory that it would be possible for a ship frozen into the ice to drift with it across the Arctic regions. In the face of skepticism, his difficult preparations were completed with uncanny foresight, and on July 21, 1893, the *Fram,* with Otto Sverdrup as captain, set sail from Vardøy. All went as planned. The sturdy vessel, built to withstand the terrific pressure, entered the ice north of the New Siberian Islands and was lifted up and carried along with the ice current until open sea was reached west of Svalbard. On August 20, 1896, the *Fram* returned to Norway, just a week after Nansen and his one companion, Hjalmar Johansen, had landed. These two had left the *Fram* in the spring of 1895 to trek farther north by dog sleds. Turning south again, they had wintered on Franz Josef Land, and next summer had the good fortune to meet an English expedition under Frederick Jackson, which brought them home.

The progress of the *Fram* along the coast was one long triumphal procession—the most stirring event of the decade. The expedition was epoch-making. Not only had valuable scientific results been reached, but for the first time it had been demonstrated that by foresight and scientific planning it was possible to avoid the harrowing fate of many an earlier venture. The *Fram* had met practically no mishap, and the men had come out of the Arctic as strong, if not stronger, in body and spirit as they had entered. Norway was now in the forefront in polar exploration.

CHAPTER 19

1905 AND THE END OF THE UNION

AFTER LASTING NINETY YEARS, the union between the two countries of the Scandinavian Peninsula came to a close in 1905 with an abruptness that astonished even many an ardent advocate of separation. During the last half of the union period, it became more and more clear that the men who guided the affairs of the two peoples were unable—or possibly unwilling—to find a basis for settlement of differences that might be satisfactory to both, and each clash of opinions added new irritation. It was also evident that the political union had not strengthened the cultural or spiritual bonds between the two peoples as a whole. There were not a few Norwegians, it is true, who had close ties in Sweden and embraced the union with real affection; more believed that it provided advantages Norway could ill afford to do without; and in general people hardly thought of severing the connection with Sweden, however annoying certain aspects of the union might be.

The basic cause of the repeated conflicts, it must be remembered, was the different conception of the union that prevailed in the two countries. In some circles in Sweden, Norway had been looked upon ever since 1814 as a dependency received as compensation for the loss of Finland. And those who did not have this extreme view could point to many facts in the relations between the two countries which showed beyond a doubt the inferior position of Norway. But Norwegians could reply that by the removal of inequalities in the union through their own action without consultation with Sweden, they had demonstrated that Norway actually possessed the rights of a sovereign state, as she had maintained in 1814. Norway's position had been boldly stated in 1860, and the failure to follow up the statement caused bitter disappointment, but did not weaken the adherence to the fundamental fact. Through the 'seventies and early 'eighties the differences with Sweden had been allowed to rest. Even the controversy over the veto was a conflict with the king, not with the nation.

The chief remaining source of dissatisfaction was the administration of foreign affairs. The foreign minister was Swedish, as was his whole department. While consular and diplomatic posts might be filled by representatives of either nation, most of the incumbents were, as a matter of fact, Swedes, and all were responsible to the Swedish foreign minister. This naturally resulted in a lack of recognition of Norway abroad which was often humiliating. It was embarrassing, for example, for Norwegian delegates to the Inter-Parliamentary Conference to have to insist on Norway's position as a separate state, or to find their country's flag omitted from the decorations. On the whole, it was felt that the union hampered all the work for peace in which Norway was taking an enthusiastic part.[1]

The situation became more objectionable when a change was made in the Swedish government whereby the control of external matters to some extent passed from the king to the parliament. In the early days of the union foreign affairs had been in the hands of the king, who, however, had worked through the Swedish foreign department and the foreign service. Since 1835 the foreign minister had reported to the king in the presence of one member of the Swedish ministry and one of the Norwegian. Though satisfactory to neither party, this remained unchanged until 1885, when it was decided in Sweden that the ministry for discussion of foreign affairs should consist of three members of the cabinet. This increased the inequality between the two countries and, as the Swedish ministers were now responsible to the diet, brought Norwegian foreign affairs more definitely under the dominance of Sweden.

The Sverdrup government hoped to rectify the injustice, and for this purpose Johan Sverdrup himself went to Stockholm. In a joint meeting of the ministries of the two countries, he obtained with little difficulty the agreement that both parliaments should be asked to amend the Act of Union to the effect that three members of the ministry of each country should constitute a cabinet council for foreign affairs. All seemed well, but when the Swedish protocol was formulated it was worded "the minister of foreign affairs . . . two other members of the Swedish and three of the Norwegian ministry." Sverdrup and the Norwegian ministry in Stockholm let it pass unchallenged.

When this became known in Norway it roused violent criticism. In

[1] Oscar J. Falnes, *Norway and the Nobel Peace Prize*, 117-131, New York, 1938.

spite of the actual situation, it had been a source of comfort to Norwegians that hitherto no law or other document had stipulated that the foreign minister must be Swedish. In the efforts to attain equality a backward step had been taken, and never, it seemed, had Norway's interests been so poorly guarded. This failure on the part of Sverdrup was one of the causes of his fall and of the alienation of the Radical Left from their old leader. No immediate steps were taken to undo the fiasco or to continue negotiations. There was a general consensus that the irritating features of the union had to be removed, but there was no unanimity as to how it should be done. Party feeling ran high; it was, in fact, just as bitter as the sentiment toward Sweden.

There were individuals—perhaps in all parties—who already looked upon separation as the only satisfactory solution, and the youth of the Radical Left, who were admirers of Bjørnson, were dreaming of a completely independent Norway. But the majority of the Left still clung to the union, as Johan Sverdrup had always done. The idea of a foreign department completely separate from the Swedish was advanced within the party, but the leaders were not willing to make this their platform as they feared it might endanger the union. They seem to have lacked the statesmanship to form a clear-cut policy or carry a plan through to success. Nevertheless, the Left, no doubt, owed its popularity largely to the fact that it was more anti-Swedish and more critical of the union than was the Right.

The Right had fallen heir to the old conservative position, and even after the romanticism of the days of Pan-Scandinavianism had faded, the party retained a strong conviction that the union was advantageous to both countries, and favored a policy of caution and moderation. Emil Stang made the unequivocal statement that separate foreign ministers would create an impossible situation, and the leaders of the Right were therefore working for one department that would really represent both countries. Even a separate consular service seemed inconsistent with their policy. It was on this issue that the conflict was to be carried forward.

The agitation for a national consular service was of old standing, and when the Norwegian merchant marine had become the third largest in the world while the Swedish was far down in the line, it seemed especially humiliating to have to resort to Swedish consuls in every port. Moreover, the interests of the two countries were different, and it was felt that in the location of consulates the needs of Sweden had been given first consideration. No wonder that shipowners, skippers, and seamen were most vocal in their demand for Norwegian consuls and that in no place was the feeling stronger than in Bergen. Other businessmen also joined in the agitation, for they believed that when Norwegian exports had not grown in proportion to those of Sweden it was because Norway's interests had not been advanced properly. Moreover, when Sweden adopted a protectionist policy and the agreement establishing a great measure of free trade between the countries was first weakened and then abandoned in 1895, the business ties with Sweden were much loosened.

The Conservative ministry of Emil Stang failed to reach any agreement that was satisfactory to the parliament of either country. Stang thereupon resigned in 1891, and was succeeded by the Pure, or Radical, Left ministry of Johannes Steen. The Storthing now proceeded to formulate a bill establishing a separate consular service. It was taken for granted that as this matter was not mentioned in the Act of Union, it could be handled as a purely Norwegian concern. The Right, while agreeing that the course of the Left was within Norway's legal rights, believed it to be unwise and unnecessarily provocative, especially considering that the present arrangement had been entered into with the full consent of both parties. The general opinion in Sweden was that the consular service was so intimately connected with the department for foreign affairs that Norway had no right to act independently. The king, as was to be expected, refused to sanction the bill, and the Steen ministry retired in April, 1893. For a second time the policy of the Left had failed.

As the king was unable to form a ministry of the Left which would comply with his wishes, Emil Stang agreed to save the situation by heading the government. Lacking a majority in the Storthing, he could do little, and became the center of abusive attacks. The Pure Left secured a narrow majority in the election of 1894. Nevertheless, on June 7, 1895, the Storthing adopted a resolution, supported by men of all parties except a few radicals, declaring the willingness of Norway to negotiate with Sweden about the whole state of the union. To implement this, a coalition government under Francis Hagerup of the Right succeeded Stang in October. It was a retreat from the bold course the Left had pursued—a retreat, most people felt, humiliating to the party and the nation—and the adoption of the program of the Right.

A committee of the two peoples promptly began its work. But early in 1898 it ended in utter failure as Swedes and Norwegians could reach no agreement either with each other or among themselves. Meanwhile

Norway was hastening to put her defenses into shape, and the most radical supporters of the military program were extreme Leftists who had earlier had pacifist leanings. Norway's retreat had been unavoidable because the country was not ready for war; Sweden's attitude was threatening, and at the same time the whole North was fearful of Russia and her aggressive course in Finland. Directing Norway's military preparations was Georg Stang, a man of militaristic leanings but of unusual ability and selfless patriotism, and it was estimated that by 1903 the country would be prepared to defend its rights should it be necessary.

This prospect gave new courage to aggressive opinion and contributed to a decisive Leftist victory at the polls. Steen again headed the government, but he allowed the question of the relations with Sweden to rest. Meanwhile Sigurd Ibsen, who was in the government, had made a study of how a separate consular service and a joint foreign department could operate successfully. On the basis of Ibsen's report negotiations were resumed in 1902, this time on the initiative of the liberal Swedish foreign minister, Alfred Lagerheim. By this time Otto Blehr, also of the Left, had succeeded Steen, who had retired weary of the strife and strain; but in 1903 the government was defeated in the election. There was general dissatisfaction with the manner in which the negotiations were conducted and a lack of confidence in the sincerity of the government; and the Right had made the settlement of the consular issue through negotiation with Sweden the chief plank of its platform. For the second time Francis Hagerup headed a coalition ministry. The outlook for a settlement seemed bright; in December it was reported that a general agreement had been reached on a separate consular service for each country, the details to be specified in identical laws passed by the two countries which could be changed only by mutual consent. Then a change came.

In Sweden the conciliatory Lagerheim was forced out, and the future policy was dictated by the uncompromising prime minister, Erik Gustaf Boström. When, after long delay, the Swedish draft for the "identical laws" was presented, it contained six provisions which the Norwegians found contrary to their Constitution and dubbed "the dependency clauses."[2] Boström refused to yield to the Norwegian protest, and on February 7, 1905, a joint meeting of the ministry of the two countries declared the negotiations officially closed.

In the next four months events moved forward with a speed and

[2] These are listed in Gjerset, *History of the Norwegian People*, 2:573.

precision that no one could have foreseen. Boström had succeeded in uniting the Norwegian people in a demand for action. The timidity of the 'nineties was gone. Norway was prepared to defend herself, and the defeat of Russia in 1904 at the hands of the Japanese stilled the fear of the Russian Bear. There was a general feeling that this time Norway must not retreat, but must insist on her rights, come what might. Just what form the action should take was a matter for the statesmen.

Most of them believed that the time for decisive action had come, but there was much diversity of opinion as to the exact course to pursue. Fearful for the fate of his country, Hagerup had the moral courage to stand practically alone in favor of continuing a conciliatory policy of negotiation.[3] The fall of his ministry was inevitable, and on March 11, 1905, the helm was entrusted to Christian Michelsen.

¶ From that day on, the guiding of events was in the hands of one man. Michelsen's position in 1905 may well be compared to that of his fellow townsman from Bergen, W. F. K. Christie, in 1814. While of the Left, he included representatives of all groups except the socialists in his ministry; and he had a remarkable ability to weld all elements together in united loyalty to himself and his program. Before long an unbounded confidence in him had permeated the whole people from high to low, and he held all the threads in his own hands, never shrinking from responsibility. He was a keen thinker, but above all a man of action who had an unfailing instinct for seizing the opportune moment. It must be admitted, however, that events played into his hands and helped to bring about a climax in a shorter time than even he had hoped.

It was felt that the issue should be pushed to a head that very spring, while a unanimity which could not stand the strain of delay still pervaded the country. Michelsen succeeded in getting almost unanimous support for his plan. Last-minute military preparations were rushed secretly and steps were taken to win friends and sympathy through the press abroad. Most influential was a series of articles by Nansen published in London. Nor were efforts to keep the public at home at a white heat of patriotism neglected, and never had May 17 been celebrated as in 1905.

Meanwhile a bill was prepared for the establishment of a separate Norwegian consular service to go into effect at a specified date in the

[3] E. Hagerup Bull, *Fra 1905, erindringer og betragtninger*, 38-49, Oslo, 1927.

near future. On May 27 the Norwegian ministry in Stockholm headed by Jørgen Løvland presented the bill to King Oscar. Sensing the importance of the event, the elderly king, who had suffered a long illness, assumed his personal rule just in time to act on this bill. As he believed it to be unworkable and detrimental to both countries, he refused his sanction, although he foresaw that this might lead to the end of the union. Thereupon Løvland and his two colleagues refused to protocol the king's veto, and tendered their resignation. The king refused to accept their retirement on the grounds that he would be unable to form any other government, but he consented to their temporary return to Christiania, bidding them a hearty, friendly farewell.

Upon their return home the ministers were met with an enthusiastic ovation. But there was great diversity of opinion as to what should be the next step. Michelsen saw in the situation an opportunity to terminate the union without delay, and, forming his plan with consummate skill, he persuaded the Storthing to follow him. In the morning session of June 7, after a serious debate through the night, he and his colleagues resigned from office and presented two resolutions, as terse as the old Norse laws, which were adopted without debate. The first stated that whereas a primary duty of a constitutional monarch was to supply the country with a responsible government and the king was unable to do this, the royal power had ceased to function. Oscar II had therefore ceased to be king of Norway, and thereby the union, which had existed by virtue of a common monarch, had come to an end. The Storthing thereupon requested the ministry to continue to serve as the government, and authorized it to perform the functions of the king. The second document was an address to the king repeating the general statement of the first and asking his consent to elect a Bernadotte prince to the throne of Norway. Thus, at least theoretically, the king was not deposed nor were the bonds with Sweden broken. The Storthing was simply stating the situation—the union had ceased to exist and Norway had no king. The legality of Michelsen's logic might be questioned and later the wisdom of his course was challenged in some quarters. But psychologically and politically he had executed a stroke of genius. The termination of the ninety-year-old union with Sweden was greeted with an outburst of patriotic enthusiasm in which there was scarcely a note of discord, as parties and classes were forgotten in a great national cause. The long, light summer day added to the optimism with which the great throngs that crowded the streets and squares of Christiania looked toward a future of untrammeled freedom.

For about six months after June 7 Norway was occupied with three problems that were inextricably intertwined: filling the place that had been left vacant when Oscar II ceased to be king, winning recognition abroad, and obtaining a settlement with Sweden. In meeting these difficulties it was important to make it clear to the world that the people were back of the resolution of June 7. It was expected, as proved to be the case, that Sweden would ask a plebiscite in Norway as a condition for negotiations. But even before the Swedish stipulations were known Michelsen recommended a referendum. The Storthing unanimously decided that on August 13 the voters should be given an opportunity to "answer the question whether or not they approved of the dissolution of the union which had taken place." The response of the people was unequivocal. Over 84 per cent of the voters turned out, and the events of June 7 were approved by a vote of 368,208 against 184. The women also gave their support. Through the initiative of their leader, Fru Frederikke Marie Quam, 244,765 women signed an address to the government expressing approbation. The unsurpassed unanimity of public opinion greatly strengthened the position of the government in dealing with the outside world.

The problem of the relations with Sweden pressed for solution without delay. A wave of consternation and indignation had spread over that country on June 7, as the news of Norway's action was noised abroad. The next day there was a huge demonstration of sympathy for the old king, who, it was felt, had been treated shabbily in Norway. If Oscar, as he thanked the crowds that had gathered outside the palace for their love and loyalty, had spoken one word of politics or expressed the slightest personal complaint, he might have stirred up hostility and even a demand for war. His restraint was a potent influence for peace. Among liberals and friends of peace there had been, to be sure, in the past months much criticism of the government's policy toward Norway and expressions of sympathy for that country. On the First of May, for example, a mass meeting of laborers sang Norway's national song and adopted resolutions demanding "justice for Norway, peace for Norway." During the critical days after June 7 Hjalmar Branting, the leader of the Swedish socialists, kept this feeling alive, reiterating in speeches and newspaper articles that democratic Norway was fighting the battle of the common man also in

Sweden, against king and aristocrats, and that Norway had a perfect right to abrogate the union. He probably did more than any other man in Sweden to prevent war.

In response to the Storthing's address of June 7, Oscar II sent a telegram of vigorous protest. In its reply of June 19 the Storthing made an appeal for Swedish "cooperation in carrying through the termination of the union and in securing friendship and concord between the two peoples of the peninsula." Next day the diet met in special session. The members had not yet recovered from the surprise of June 7. Chauvinists advocated the use of force, while others, among them Crown Prince Gustaf, supported the motion that the union should be declared dissolved without placing any qualifications whatsoever. The middle course won, however, and a statement of the conditions on which the Act of Union would be repealed was adopted. This roused a storm of protest in Norway, especially against the demand for a neutral zone along the border and the razing of fortresses, several of which had just been built. But through informal private discussions the differences between the two countries were somewhat smoothed out, and on August 31 representatives of the two nations opened negotiations at Karlstad. Michelsen with Løvland, who headed Norway's newly organized department of foreign affairs, led the Norwegian delegation.

The days of the meeting were tense in both countries. On the question of the frontier forts neither party would yield, negotiations were interrupted and seemed about to fail, and troops were mobilized on the border—in Norway without the consent of Michelsen, who was absent from the capital. Finally the Swedish delegation offered a generous compromise which the Norwegians found acceptable. A neutral zone was agreed upon, but the historic fort of Fredriksten was not to be demolished, only demilitarized, and Kongsvinger was to be outside of the neutral zone. Other matters, including a general arbitration treaty, were quite easily settled, and on September 23 the delegates signed the Karlstad Agreement. After violent attacks from the radical leaders, the Storthing ratified the document on October 9 by a vote of 101 against 16. A few days later the Swedish diet also approved the agreement and on October 16 repealed the Act of Union. On October 27 Oscar II announced his abdication of the throne of Norway, which had caused him "so much bitter grief."

To Michelsen belongs much of the credit for keeping the two countries out of war. It would have been a great calamity for Norway to have become involved in war before she had won the recognition of the powers. Within a week after June 7 a foreign department was organized under Jørgen Løvland, who had distinguished himself as Norway's last minister of state in Stockholm and who had loyally stood by Michelsen through the crisis. It was hoped that the new government might obtain formal recognition in other capitals even before it had been secured in Stockholm, but that, quite naturally, proved impossible. Some contacts, more or less official, between other governments and that of Norway were, of course, necessary, and Norwegian representatives, notably Fridtjof Nansen and Fritz Wedel Jarlsberg, were performing distinguished service to win understanding and support abroad. Their efforts produced an effect both on public opinion and in government circles which was highly favorable to Norway. There was, moreover, a strong desire among diplomats to maintain peace in the North, especially as the Morocco crisis of that year supplied plenty of inflammable material.

While the offer of the throne to a Bernadotte prince did not win the good will in Sweden that had been hoped, it was otherwise effective in allaying the apprehensions of conservatives both at home and abroad. No doubt it helped create a friendly attitude toward Norway on the part of both the German and Russian ministers to Sweden. Even the more liberal governments of Western Europe felt reassured by the Bernadotte offer, and moreover, the plebiscite of August 13 was a positive expression of the will of the people which could not be ignored. Foreign pressure in Stockholm therefore helped to hasten the settlement between Sweden and Norway; and the Karlstad Agreement was followed almost immediately by complete recognition of Norway's new government and of the full sovereignty of the country. Norway's most outspoken friends were Denmark and England, the latter even suggesting that unless events were speeded up, Downing Street might recognize Norway without waiting for Stockholm. An added reason for this friendship was that both the British and the Danish governments were favorably disposed toward the candidacy of the Danish Prince Carl for the throne of Norway.[4]

It had been assumed on June 7 that the Constitution of 1814 remained in force, that the form of government was not changed, and that Norway was therefore still a constitutional monarchy. This view found definite expression in the Bernadotte offer, which upon Michelsen's insistence was included in the address to Oscar II without any

[4] Halvdan Koht, "Kongs-vale i 1905," in *Syn og segn* (January and February, 1947). F. Wedel Jarlsberg, *1905, Kongevalget,* Oslo, 1946, gives a most important account of his difficult negotiations.

dissenting vote. There was, however, considerable republican sentiment in the land, some even in the Storthing, enough to cause not a little apprehension abroad. Many of the public men of Norway believed that it would be an advantage during the negotiations with Sweden to have a king who could, like Christian Frederik in 1814, help to unify patriotic endeavor and at the same time win good will abroad. Among the princes mentioned as possible candidates the only one who seemed acceptable was Prince Carl, who was the second grandson of King Christian IX of Denmark, and married to Princess Maud, the daughter of Edward VII. Carl was approached with inquiries as to whether he would accept the throne should it be offered. He intimated that his reply would be favorable if the king of Denmark gave his consent. The Danish king and government, however, though favorably disposed, had close ties also in Sweden and cautiously refused to give their approval before the Bernadotte offer, which Sweden had ignored, had been disposed of. The British government, on the other hand, followed an aggressive policy in favor of Carl, both in Stockholm and Copenhagen. Edward VII repeatedly urged his son-in-law to proceed to Norway without a formal election, but Carl firmly refused to act contrary to the wishes of his grandfather.[5]

The matter was dropped during the Karlstad conference and resumed after the relations with Sweden had been settled. It was generally expected that the Storthing would at once proceed to elect Carl as king, in accordance with the Constitution. The prince, however, expressed a strong desire for a referendum to the people before he accepted the throne, and his will became decisive. A majority in the Storthing was opposed to a plebiscite: the republicans believed it would be a farce, and many others thought it would be contrary to the parliamentary principle of government. Michelsen, on the other hand, was not only anxious to comply with the wishes of Carl, but believed that an expression of popular approval would strengthen the position of the future king and of the country. With the support of most of his cabinet, he proposed to the Storthing that it authorize the government to resume negotiations with Carl about accepting election to the throne, their authority to be conditioned on the popular will expressed in a plebiscite; and that it order a referendum similar to that of August 13 to be held on November 12 and 13. The situation involved the question as to whether June 7 meant any revolutionary change in the Constitution. The government party argued that it did not; the ques-

[5] Sir Sidney Lee, *King Edward VII: A Biography*, 2:315-326, New York, 1927. Sir Sidney quotes the correspondence on the matter in full.

tion was not whether a republic or monarchy were better, for either could give an opportunity for the development of a progressive democracy. But with Norway's historical background and present conditions, a monarchy would be surer of immediate stability and of friendship abroad.[6] After a sharp debate of three days, during which Gunnar Knudsen, the one consistent republican in the cabinet, resigned, Michelsen's proposal was approved.

Much discussion was concentrated in the two brief weeks before the plebiscite, as the republicans fought a last passionate, acrimonious, but losing battle. Their uncompromising, chauvinistic stand during the negotiations with Sweden had weakened their position, and they were disappointed to have lost the support of Bjørnson. He had reached the conclusion that there remained no course for old republicans but to follow the example of Garibaldi: "After serving the republic for a lifetime he chose to serve the king."[7] The desire for a speedy settlement and for security at home and in foreign relations were decisive factors in the vote. Moreover, there was a sense of loyalty to the interim government which had guided the country through the last months and which was under some moral, though not legal, obligation to Prince Carl. The participation in the election was not quite so large as in August, nor was the unanimity so great. Yet, by a vote of 259,563 against 69,264, the people approved the election of the Danish prince as king.

On November 18, 1905, the Storthing unanimously elected Prince Carl of Denmark king of Norway. Before the Storthing adjourned that day it received from Carl a telegram of acceptance. He took the name Haakon VII, gave his little son Alexander the name Olav, and chose as his motto, *"Alt for Norge."* The words of Wergeland to the old castle of Akershus had been brought to his attention: *"O hvad fryd for dine taarne, saa du Haakons tid igjen"* (Oh, what joy for your spires to see once more the age of Haakon). On November 25 the new royal family made its entry into Christiania, and even the cold drizzle could not dampen the enthusiasm of the vast throng that had gathered to greet them. Two days later the king took his oath to the Constitution. Within the short space of exactly six months after the epoch-making day when the ministers in Sweden handed their resignation to Oscar II, the stirring acts and events had been completed whereby Norway had passed from a union with Sweden to a state of absolute independence with a king of her own choice.

[6] Løvland, *Menn og minner fra 1905*, p. 240-253, Oslo, 1929.
[7] *Ibid.*, 237.

CHAPTER 20

NEW NORWAY, 1905-1940

FORTUNE HAD SMILED UPON NORWAY, and the events of 1905 had been guided with such success that the people hardly realized through what a serious crisis their country had passed. When the ties with Sweden had been severed, a new sense of freedom and good cheer pervaded Norway, which strengthened the courage and self-assurance of the nation. While some ill will remained, on the whole the unpleasant memories from the union and the bitterness roused in 1905 happily very soon slipped into the background of the people's consciousness. The settlement of the union question had also removed the main cause of strife between the political parties at home. Unlike those of 1814, the events of 1905 caused little disruption in Norway's affairs, for except in the field of foreign relations she had all the institutions and machinery of government that belong to a sovereign state, and the routine of public affairs went on much as of old. The country had never had a chance to develop a foreign policy, and consequently its statesmen were neither especially skillful in diplomacy nor interested in it. After they had secured recognition for their country and a guarantee of its integrity in case of war, there seemed no need of any further active foreign policy, and the great international crises made little impression in Norway. She was untouched by the militarism which after 1905 began to engulf the powers, and unaffected by economic crises in other lands.

There was every indication that Norway was entering upon a period of good will in her relations to the outside world and tranquillity at home, affording an opportunity to concentrate on purely domestic problems as never before.

The sense of national solidarity which was stimulated by the events of 1905 found new expression in the desire to strengthen the bonds between Norwegians everywhere. This led to the organization in 1907 of Normannsforbundet, a society with branches all over the world. Among the emigrants, too, more was done to maintain the ties with the homeland. With the better means of communication there was not the sense of finality in setting out for a new land that there had been in the past. Moreover, a smaller per cent of the emigrants took homesteads in the interior of America, while many remained on the more accessible seaboards. Among earlier emigrants also, and even among their children and children's children, there began to appear evidences of a growing appreciation of their cultural heritage, and a new pride in the land of their ancestors.

The fact that the differences between country and city people were diminishing no doubt increased the unity within the nation. This tendency, strong in the late nineteenth century, was accelerated in the twentieth. The movement of population to the cities was no longer so marked as in the 'nineties, as more of the advantages of city life reached out into the country. On the other hand, city people felt drawn to the country as never before. Not only were outdoor sports and vacation trips—Easter outings becoming as popular as summer holidays—attracting more and more people, but city folk, even of moderate means, were building homes in a rural atmosphere, until there grew up a belt of suburban districts about the cities, notably Christiania.

Nationalism could not have attained the needed momentum in 1905 if it had not been imbued with a strong democratic feeling. It was therefore natural that the democratization of Norwegian society, which had already advanced far, should be emphasized after that year. In the political field the constitutional amendments necessary to complete the achievements of 1905 were enacted, and both in the local and central governments changes were made to insure a more effective operation of the democratic principle. The introduction of direct election for members of the Storthing is an important example. For the protection of minorities, proportional representation, which had been introduced into the local government in 1896, was in 1919 extended also to national elections.[1] The criticism has been raised that in the effort to achieve as perfect a democracy as possible, decentralization has been carried so far as to introduce an element of weakness into the government.

The greatest single change was the establishment of woman's suffrage on the same basis as that of men. This was accomplished within

1 Ben A. Arneson, *The Democratic Monarchies of Scandinavia*, New York, 1939, contains a convenient description of the government and its operation.

the brief space of twelve years with comparative ease, as the more laborious preparatory work had already been done in the preceding century. In 1898 the leadership fell to Fru Frederikke Marie Quam, a woman of rare judgment and political insight. Through a nationwide organization she carried on a persistent campaign conducted with intuitive tact. The first victory was won in 1901 when women of a certain income group obtained the right to vote in the local elections, and in 1907 this was extended to the national elections. Three years later equal suffrage for men and women was introduced into the local government, and in 1913 this was extended to the national elections as well. Thus Norway became the first country to establish political equality between the sexes.

But at the same time as the growth of political democracy and the partial obliteration of the differences between rural and urban life were strengthening the sense of national unity, the cleavage between industrial classes was widening, and especially among the youth there was a tendency for class loyalty to become stronger than national patriotism.

¶ When the crisis of 1905 was over and Michelsen was asked what of the future, he replied "a new work day." Norway was, in fact, entering upon a decade of a growing prosperity which by 1913 reached an unprecedented height. It was an age of large, bold ventures, characterized not so much by new scientific discoveries as by a wider application to daily life of the results of earlier research. Through private initiative, organization, and cooperation, and through more or less active assistance on the part of the government, new enterprises were begun, and all the age-old occupations were taking on a twentieth century character. While capitalism became more dominant in the newer economic undertakings, in the two basic occupations of farming and fishing, time-honored individualism more than held its own.

In agriculture the changes begun in the last century were still further developed. Vigorous educational work to produce higher standards and a greater sense of solidarity and occupational pride was carried on by a new national agricultural school, which was opened in 1900, as well as by the press, both through specialized publications and the general newspapers, and by the organizations of the farmers themselves. In the decade after 1905 there was an astonishing growth in the number of small farms, and by 1914 there remained only 370 farms as large as 125 acres. The little farms average less than ten acres of tilled land, but with them go outlying pastures and woods, hunting and fishing preserves, which, as from time immemorial, add materially to the income. Though the homestead be ever so small, ownership of land has given to the farmers a satisfaction far beyond the purely economic, and many a tenant, though poor, purchased the land he tilled to give his family security for the future and a more dignified place in the community.

To meet the demand of the small farmers another agricultural school was later established for the special purpose of solving their problems. A new emphasis on diversified farming was essential in order to win a reasonably good living from the small holdings, and near the cities the rising demand for fruit and vegetables gave new opportunities in this line. Other new sources of income, such as fur farming, were also found, while hunting, now regulated by modern legislation, and lumbering were still important. Extensive efforts to conserve the forests marked the early twentieth century. In 1898 the Norwegian Forestry Society was organized by Axel Heiberg, and during the twenty-five years of his presidency vast stretches of forest land were given scientific care, seven tons of seed were planted, and one hundred and seventy million saplings set out.

The fishing industry was modernized as the age of the motor boat arrived. When steamboats began to be used in fishing, late in the nineteenth century, it looked as if the occupation were to become completely capitalistic, as the new vessels were large and expensive. But a variety of small engines which could be installed in the old craft came into general use and thus saved the old ways. The modernized boats as well as the investigations of the oceanographers reduced the hardships and hazards of the fishermen. While the new purse net increased their haul, there was still much to be desired in the care and marketing of their catch. This problem remained to be solved in a later day through the aid of both the state and private capital.

Perhaps nothing did more to transform the country than the vast expansion of modern means of communication. New state-owned telephone lines were erected, and in 1908 extensive railroad building was authorized, including a road to Trondheim besides many lines to smaller towns in the South, every mile of which involved a costly, difficult feat of engineering. The greatest problem of coastal traffic was solved through the establishment of a steamship route from Trondheim as far north as to Kirkenes. Although it was undertaken by a private company, it was heavily subsidized by the state. While flying was still in its infancy, a young skier from Bergen named Tryggve Gran flew across the North Sea from Scotland to Norway on July 30, 1914, thus performing the greatest feat in flying before the outbreak of the First World War.

The shipping business went through important developments in the decade before the war. The change from sailers to steamboats, begun in the nineteenth century, was greatly accelerated. Of the 5,853 sailers afloat in 1905, only 947 remained in 1914, while the number of steamers had increased from 1,734 to 2,107. New was the tanker traffic, which was developed by Halfdan Wilhelmsen, who headed the greatest shipowning firm in Norway. New also were the great Norwegian steamship lines which were added to the tramp ships of the past. Most interesting to us is the Norwegian America Line, inaugurated in 1910 through the support of Norwegians on both sides of the Atlantic.[2]

Even more characteristic of the age was the industrial expansion, the like of which Norway had never experienced. The number of industrial laborers rose from 86,500 in 1905 to 144,000 in 1914, and the increase in production was proportionately even greater, because the technical equipment was better and mechanical power used more extensively. A larger amount of raw material was imported than before, but those industries which utilized native products, such as the paper mills and cellulose and wood pulp factories, were the most prosperous. As in the past, industry was decentralized and scattered over the country. Plants were most often located by waterfalls, and around them grew up towns wholly dependent upon the one industry. The factories were much larger than earlier—the day of big business had come—and electricity played a dominant part.

Norway had kept well abreast of all the new advances which electricity had brought in the preceding decades. Now her scientists, engineers, and public men were filled with an optimistic, really exaggerated, confidence that electricity was to be the power of the future; and with her wealth of easily accessible waterfalls Norway had an unlimited supply of this "white coal."

No one was more impressed by this than the engineer Sam Eyde, who bought several waterfalls in southeastern Norway. He had not decided just how to make the best use of the power before he met Professor Kristian Birkeland, who had discovered a method for ex-

[2] S. Stephensen and E. O. J. Svanøe, *Den norske Amerikalinjes Oprettelse*, Oslo, 1939. C. J. Hambro, *Amerikaferd*, Oslo, 1935. Birger Osland, *A Long Pull from Stavanger*, 70-111, Northfield, 1945.

tracting nitrogen from the air by the use of electricity. In 1905 Eyde organized a stock company, popularly known as "Norsk Hydro," which took over the Birkeland process. Eyde secured capital abroad and established close connections with German chemical companies which might otherwise have become his rivals. In 1911 the great works at Rjukan was completed, an imposing example of the best in modern functional architecture as well as the greatest industrial undertaking in Norway.

The social and political problems resulting from the industrial expansion were the immediate and most potent reason for the disruption of the political harmony which it had been hoped would prevail after the separation from Sweden. The spirit of June 7 and Michelsen's popularity were so strong that the continuation of the coalition government seemed probable, but even this hope was soon to be shattered.

The first indication of the coming break was an interpellation in 1906 by Johan Castberg: "What does the government intend to do to prevent more of the waterpower of our country from falling into the hands of foreigners?" There was a strong national feeling against the growing investment of foreign capital in the country's resources and a fear—which proved unfounded—that it might lead to economic and even political dependence. Moreover, people objected to the wholesale buying up of waterfalls, even by Norwegians, for purely speculative purposes. Government control was quite in harmony with the country's historical traditions, and there was general agreement that some regulation was needed. But the question of just how this was to be accomplished caused the most acrimonious political conflict of the decade, and the discussion was unfortunately not confined to fundamental principles.

In reply to Castberg, the Michelsen ministry could state that work on this problem was already in progress. The same year the government introduced a bill prohibiting any stock company from acquiring a waterfall without government franchise. It was passed promptly and became the first modern concession law, known as the "panic law." It was looked upon as a temporary expedient only, and the following year a draft for a more complete, permanent law was prepared. Although Michelsen had expressed the opinion that it would be well to apply brakes to the general industrialization of the country, the draft was based almost entirely on the nationalistic desire to check the power of foreign capital.

The radicals were not satisfied with the bill. Michelsen, probably weary of the fray, resigned, but in the midst of ovations that showed him to be a popular hero still. He was succeeded by Jørgen Løvland; but the next year, in 1908, the coalition ministry from 1905 was overthrown by a reorganized consolidated Left supported by the Socialists. The new government was headed by Gunnar Knudsen, who had risen into prominence in the 'eighties. He had been a leader of the opposition in the autumn of 1905, and, though the king's tact had disarmed republican sentiment, there still remained an aura about Knudsen's name. During his brief ministry the complete concession laws took shape. They were mainly the work of Johan Castberg and were passed in 1909 by a very narrow majority in the Storthing. They differed from the plan of the coalition government not only in tightening the restrictions on acquiring waterfalls and mines but in applying them to home-owned companies as well as to those controlled by foreign capitalists. And in addition the law strictly limited the right of people outside of the local community to buy up forests. The most severe attacks were launched against the provision that after a certain lapse of time concessions should revert to the government. The constitutionality of this clause as applied to citizens was contested, and accusations that the laws violated the Constitution were flung about in the election of 1909. The Knudsen ministry failed to get a majority in this election, and for the next three years there was a coalition ministry of the Right and the Independent Left, which was neither harmonious nor productive. The concession laws were not taken up for a general revision, and the additions to the laws which were made were in harmony with Castberg's principles.

Desirable as regulation was, the concession laws were a hindrance to the industrial development, which did not reach the proportions that had been expected. Foreigners were discouraged from investing in Norway, Norwegian bankers were timid, and home-owned capital inadequate. When money became abundant during the war boom and a new law gave citizens practically the sole right to develop the resources of the country, they could not fully utilize the opportunity as they had difficulty in establishing business relations abroad. While proponents of the law expected it to check private enterprise, they had faith that the state would enter industry, but in this they were doomed to disappointment.

¶ Meanwhile emphasis was shifting to the more purely social problems, which were gaining new prominence through the growing industrialization. There was a great deal of animated discussion of social problems and a diversity of opinions, ranging from a mere suggestion of pink to an out-and-out red. But while there were many capable men in the radical groups there was no one leader strong enough to unite the different elements and no clear-cut program for action. The Labor Party carried over from the 'nineties its declaration of principles drawn up by Carl Jeppesen. It was socialistic, but lacked definiteness and failed to attract any large following. More radical were the organizations of the "red youth." They were filled with romantic, revolutionary enthusiasm and spoke brave words about the abolition of militarism, of sabotage, and of direct action; but there was among them more individualism than unity. The chief agitator for syndicalism was Martin Tranmæl, who had acquired these ideas in I.W.W. circles in America.

The principal result of the many-sided labor agitation of these years was that in 1911 the craft unions, which for some years had been less active, were reorganized along more radical lines and for more effective action. Yet labor and other leftist elements were not in a position to carry through the legislation which all classes recognized that the country needed.

It was the Liberal, or Left, Party which took the lead in making the years from 1909 to 1915 a great era in Norwegian social legislation. In the past, conservatives had taken the initiative in lawmaking for social betterment, while the Left had leaned toward the *laissez-faire* ideas of traditional liberalism. Now the tables were turned; social legislation became the platform of the Left. This was due mainly to two men: Gunnar Knudsen wanted to extend to the whole country the humane patriarchal method he had employed in his own many economic ventures, and Johan Castberg wished to place Norway in the forefront in social reform. Castberg had been a leader in all enterprises for the common good in his home region of the Uplands, and he now became more than any other individual the creator of modern social politics in Norway and inaugurated the new period in social legislation. He sponsored a number of laws which introduced such reforms as a bank to assist laborers in the purchase of homes and gardens, public contribution to unemployment relief, and sickness insurance for fishermen and sailors. While there was little opposition to these measures from any group or party, it was the election of 1912 which gave Castberg his greatest opportunity. Powerful organizations then rallied en masse to the banner of the Left—temperance societies, youth organizations, the *landsmaal* advocates, and the like—and helped to procure for the party a sweeping victory, giving it seventy seats in the Storthing, while the combined Right and Independent Left went down to twenty-four. The Labor Democrats elected six and the Socialists twenty-three representatives. This election brought in the second ministry of Gunnar Knudsen, which was to remain in power until 1920.

The year after the people had thus so strongly expressed their approval of Castberg's policy, he secured the establishment of a department for social affairs, of which he became the first head. In 1915 a number of laws were enacted which proved to be the consummation of his work. A new extensive factory law superseded that of 1892, accident insurance for all industrial workers was established, and health insurance was broadened. Laws to improve the social and economic position of mothers and of illegitimate children, which had been prepared by Katti Anker Møller, were also put through the Storthing through Castberg's efforts.

These far-reaching measures encountered little opposition from any class or party, but when the government strove to regulate labor disputes, it was a different matter. The labor unions had strong, centralized, national organizations, which emphasized the common interest of laborers throughout the land. The members were well disciplined, and the lot of the strikebreakers was unhappy indeed. Although labor conflicts in Norway were conducted with restraint and moderation, even a minor local dispute might—and in some cases did—develop into a strike of nationwide import, seriously interfering with the economic life of the country. There was, therefore, among the general public a strong sentiment in favor of government control, as strikes had become a danger to society as a whole. Also, Castberg desired industrial peace in order to further the rest of his program. Efforts to introduce compulsory mediation or arbitration met with opposition from both employers and employees, the latter even threatening a general strike. The industrialists, who were nationally organized, feared government interference, and labor looked upon the right to strike as fundamental in the efforts to better its position. It had become strong enough to feel that it could force its will through, and moreover, under the leadership of Martin Tranmæl syndicalistic ideas had won entrance, which placed social revolution, not minor settlements of labor disputes, as the ultimate aim. Although the Left could have put through a law complying with Castberg's ideas, it was considered unwise to do so in the face of opposition from both parties concerned. When a more limited measure was enacted in 1915, it was based on a draft which had been drawn up earlier by Fredrik Stang and bore the stamp of his keen, legal thinking. It made provision for public mediation of differences in interests and established a labor court to deal with disputes about the interpretation of contracts between employers and laborers. This law accomplished its purpose and stood the test of time.

Much was achieved in 1915, but after that the immediacy of the problems connected with the war caused the further realization of Castberg's ideals to be postponed to a later time.

¶ The spring of 1914 was particularly cheerful in Norway. On May 15 there was opened in Frogner Park a delightful exposition which seemed to express the very soul of the country. It was to commemorate 1814 and the achievements of the century of peace which had passed. Few had any premonition that those festive days were but the close of an era, and even in government circles there was a general sense of security. The country was inexperienced in foreign affairs and the conception was not uncommon that a small country might just as well have no foreign policy at all. The program of the Gunnar Knudsen ministry was contingent upon peace, and even as late as in 1913 Knudsen dismissed warnings of impending danger as sheer nonsense.[3] Diplomats and others who had sojourned in foreign capitals were apprehensive, and military men warned that Norway was ill prepared to defend its neutrality should the need arise. The situation had seemed especially critical in 1911 when the German fleet was in Norwegian waters during the Morocco crisis. Had war broken out then, as might well have happened, Norway might easily have become involved. There was sufficient anxiety to induce the Storthing to make a special appropriation for defense, but it came too late to be of much use when the storm broke, and the prevailing calm was not disturbed before the latter part of July.

As the fearful events at the end of July and the beginning of August 1914 came blow upon blow, the people looked on with a terror akin to that with which one faces unknown horrors in the dark. Daily life was disrupted. Tourists—of whom there were an unusually great number—rushed home, some perhaps to meet later as enemies at the front, many to seek safety in their homes beyond the Atlantic, and the Norwegians themselves to take what precautions they could to meet the exigencies of the moment. It was generally realized that lack of food was the most immediate danger; people bought up provisions without rhyme or reason, and innumerable tragi-comic incidents occurred as

[3] F. Wedel Jarlsberg, *Reisen gjennem livet,* 286, Oslo, 1932.

panic seized the public. Although the merchants established some private rationing, supplies were soon sold out, prices soared, tradesmen refused to accept any foreign currency, even that of Denmark and Sweden, gold was hoarded, and there were runs on the banks. The queues were longest at the Bank of Norway, but, as the amount paid out to each depositor was limited to a hundred crowns, gold payments could be kept up. When, against the advice of the director of the bank, the government later ordered the suspension of gold payment, silver also was hoarded, causing much inconvenience. More deep-seated than the fear which gripped the people was the emotional and mental strain that resulted as time-honored ideas and ideals were scattered to the winds. The panic did not last long, however. It began on July 31, reached its climax on August 3, and was subsiding within a week, as the normal sound sense of the people reasserted itself. Moreover, the authorities took prompt action to meet the crisis and quiet apprehensions.

The government was faced with two grave problems: to maintain the economic life in order to secure an adequate food supply, and to uphold the country's historic policy of neutrality. The two were closely intertwined throughout the four years of war, and Norway was repeatedly in a precarious position, more exposed to danger than any of the other small countries which did not become directly involved in the war.[4]

The government immediately took effective action to conserve the food supply. A Food Commission was appointed, the export of certain essentials, as coal and grain, was forbidden, maximum prices were fixed, the right of the government to requisition goods was established, the production of food was stimulated, the use of grain and potatoes for the manufacture of alcoholic beverages was prohibited, and the sale of liquor temporarily forbidden. In order to maintain shipping in the face of increasing danger, compulsory insurance for ships was established, the owners bearing the cost, and a little later a company to cover the insurance of the cargoes was organized, the government assuming 40 per cent of the risk.

A great many new functions were forced upon a government which, except for social legislation, had hitherto followed the policy of interfering as little as possible with the daily life of the people. The weak spot in the government was in the field of finance. There was a failure to coordinate the new agencies, and as great expenses were inevitable,

[4] Keilhau, *Norway and the World War*, is the chief account available in English of Norway's part in the war.

spending became alarmingly reckless. The national debt increased enormously, and no provision was made for new taxes at a time when they would have met practically no opposition. Otherwise, the government acquitted itself well of its many duties, and continued to have the support of the whole people.

During the first two years of the war no great change in daily life was noticed, there was no abnormal unemployment, business was good, and the flow of goods was fairly adequate. Shipping suffered somewhat through floating mines and German submarines, but more than enough new vessels were acquired to compensate for the losses, and in the autumn of 1916 the merchant marine had reached a greater tonnage than ever before. Seamen and merchants were, however, hampered and annoyed by a multiplicity of humiliating restrictions laid down by the warring powers, and the foreign office was constantly dickering with the belligerents concerning some infringement on the rights of neutrals. Most of the disputes were connected with questions of contraband of war. The list of contraband articles grew until it comprised all manner of goods, and often it was impossible for merchants to keep up with the overnight changes.

Meanwhile the coast guard was performing its unspectacular yeoman's service. All through the war little vessels plied along the shore, and the faithfulness of seamen and the tact and good judgment of officers were significant factors in maintaining Norway's neutrality. Fortunately the army did not have to be mobilized, thanks chiefly to the friendliness of Sweden.

Hardly had war broken out when steps were taken to make some arrangement so that Swedes and Norwegians would not "be shooting at each other." On August 8, 1914, the two governments agreed that under no circumstances would they allow the state of war in Europe to lead to hostilities between their countries. Thus a neutrality entente of the North was formed, and before long Denmark was also included. It was quite in keeping with the Bernadotte policy that Sweden took the initiative in this move to maintain peace in the North. It was all the more noteworthy because the memory of 1905 still rankled and Swedish economic interests and sympathy were inclined toward Germany, while to Norway friendship with England was paramount. This entente was dramatized by a meeting at Malmö of the three Scandinavian monarchs on December 18, 1914, and still further emphasized by another such meeting in Christiania in 1917. Throughout the war there was constant cooperation among the three countries. The intercourse between Norway and Sweden was free from the irritation that had marred any common action in union days, and the way was paved for better relations in the future. Several common notes of protest were issued in the course of the years, and generally the initiative was taken and the notes drafted by Hjalmar Hammarskjöld, the Swedish prime minister, who was an expert in international law. And the Norwegian minister of foreign affairs, Nils Claus Ihlen, was, it seems, willing to have it so. He was a practical businessman who did not much concern himself with general principles of law. He based his policy on the supposition that the war would be of short duration, and therefore made no long-view plans, but met with efficiency the many individual problems as they arose. As Norway was in the most precarious position of the Scandinavian countries, she benefited most from their common action. This was especially true after the serious turn of events in the autumn of 1916, which inaugurated for Norway the second, more critical period of the war.

It was in connection with the fishing industry that the crisis came. In the autumn of 1915, as food shortage was being felt in Germany, little German boats plied Norwegian waters, eluding the otherwise effective British blockade, and bought up fish directly from the fishermen. Becoming aware of this, the British threatened that if this traffic did not cease the importation of coal and oil would be cut off. As this might destroy the livelihood of the fishermen, the Norwegian director of fishing, Johan Hjort, began negotiations. As a result, Parliament appropriated the huge sum of £14,000,000 with which to buy fish through a Norwegian firm, and thus defeat the Germans in the open market. Later a more permanent Fish Agreement of August 5, 1916, was made. The British were to continue to buy fish at maximum prices to be fixed for the rest of the war, with the stipulation that credits be extended to them in Norway. Britain retained the right to cancel the agreement after giving a four weeks' warning, and Norway was to limit the uncontrolled export of fish to 15 per cent of the total catch.

The Fish Agreement was to have serious consequences which had not been foreseen. The manner in which the British loans were arranged helped to bring on an inflationary rise in prices in Norway, which so increased living expenses that government aid had to be extended to the poor. The fishing industry was especially hard hit, for, while the price of fish was fixed, that of equipment, oil, and coal soared. To save the fishermen from ruin the government stepped in with subsidies which meant an enormous—though probably unavoidable—expense. But there were even more serious consequences. When the Germans found their buying operations restricted and obtained at least some inkling of the British-Norwegian arrangement, they became furious, and, no doubt in retaliation, let their submarines loose on Norwegian shipping in Arctic waters. Within nine days eleven ships were sunk and ten sailors perished from cold and hunger in open lifeboats. Hot indignation was expressed in Norway, and the government issued a proclamation prohibiting the submarines of belligerents from staying in Norwegian waters. Berlin replied with a note that had all the earmarks of an ultimatum except that no time limit for a reply was set. The situation was serious. While neither France nor England wished Norway to be involved in the war, Downing Street intimated that help would be forthcoming should Norway need military supplies. Denmark and—to Germany's disappointment—Sweden backed Norway vigorously. Sweden's stand had considerable influence in causing the Germans to retreat from their belligerent attitude. More important, however, was the German need of securing by a trade agreement with Norway the importation of at least some fish and other goods. This was obtained, and after Norway had made a slight formal change in the wording of the submarine proclamation Berlin declared the incident closed.

Meanwhile troubles had arisen with England regarding the interpretation of an earlier trade agreement, the British intimating that unless Norway complied with their view the importation of bunker coal would be cut off. Foreign Minister Ihlen played for time until the settlement with Germany had been concluded, and then yielded as he had all the time intended to do. By a Copper Agreement, Norway promised to stop the export of copper pyrites to Germany, and in return the British prohibition on the export of coal to Norway was removed on February 17, 1917.

But more serious difficulties had already begun. On February 1 the Germans opened unrestricted U-boat warfare on all shipping in waters around France, England, and Italy. Neutrals continued to sail the seas, but the casualties were terrifying. Norwegian losses were especially heavy, reaching in March alone—the worst month—106,111 tons, as compared with the American losses of 20,886 tons. As shipping was an absolute necessity for Norway, her greatest problem was to protect the traffic without abandoning her neutrality. The government did what it could through negotiations with Great Britain, to whom the Norwegian tramp boats were of great importance, especially for carrying coal to France. The most satisfactory accord reached, however, was the

Tonnage Agreement made between the British government and the private Norwegian Shipowners' Association. It was agreed that the British should requisition Norwegian ships, not as property, but for use during the war. Thus Norwegian vessels would fly the British flag and could therefore be armed, which was impossible when sailing under neutral colors. Moreover, the British took over the coal trade with Norway, while Norwegian boats were employed in less perilous waters. As a result, losses decreased, but most effective in checking sinkings was the British convoy system adopted in April 1917, which protected the trade between Norway and Great Britain. Norway's own fleet furnished convoys for the coastal traffic. While the total losses were gradually declining, the percentage continued to be high, as the merchant fleet was becoming smaller. In all, Norway lost 49.3 per cent—the largest per cent of any country—of its tonnage during the war, the total loss being exceeded by Great Britain alone. The Norwegian merchant marine fell in tonnage from the fourth to the sixth place, more than two thousand sailors lost their lives as a result of the war, and the number of maimed and wounded was very large.

Another serious peril was added to that from the submarines. The mysterious disappearance of a number of ships seemed to indicate that explosives had been placed on board while the vessels lay in harbor. In the few cases about which it was possible to get any information, the evidence seemed convincing. A skillfully handled investigation by Christiania detectives brought sensational disclosures. Eight hundred kilograms of all manner of explosive devices, from large time bombs to little "cigarettes," were found. All had been brought in as German diplomatic baggage, exempt from custom inspection, and the purpose was, of course, self-evident. Some of the material was, it seems, intended to be sent on for use against American shipping. No doubt just as flagrant abuses of diplomatic privileges were carried on in other neutral ports, but they were not uncovered.

In spite of it all, Norwegians continued to sail the seven seas. The old adage that "men may die, but the seas must be sailed" was more or less consciously the motto of the sailors, long accustomed to face perils; and the inflationary profits from high prices and freight rates were a strong inducement to shipowners to take gambling chances. Thus, while there were many shortages, the country was never completely isolated commercially. This was accomplished only through continuous efforts on the part of both private business and the government, and through repeated agreements with Great Britain. Fortunately it was to the interest of the Allies to have Norway remain neutral, and while there was fear of provoking war with Germany the danger was no longer so great, for by 1916 the Central Powers were not in a position to take on more enemies.

Even when shortages began to be seriously felt, people in Norway retained a faith that, if other sources of supply failed, there was always America to fall back on. This changed when the United States entered the war, especially after July 15, 1917, when the neutral countries were informed that they would have to make general trade agreements with the United States. Almost at once a large commission headed by Fridtjof Nansen with Wilhelm Morgenstierne as secretary was sent over to negotiate with Washington. At no time was the need in Norway so acute as during the long months before an accord with the United States was reached. Not before April 30, 1918, was Nansen able to sign the voluminous agreement which secured for Norway the most essential imports.

During the last part of the war Norway was geared to a planned war economy. From the beginning of 1918 it became necessary to ration grain, flour, sugar, and coffee, later also tea, and the rations were small. In other respects, too, as state activities reached proportions hitherto undreamt of, government interference with daily life assumed as great dimensions as in countries at war. The changes in everyday living were much the same as among belligerent peoples: inflationary prices brought hardships to those who did not share in the higher earnings, while easy money and speculation helped others make fortunes rapidly—often unscrupulously. But shortages and regulations limited the pleasure that could be derived from merely monetary wealth, and the newly won riches did little to stimulate the economic development of the country. And peace, when it finally came, failed to bring the hoped-for return to normalcy. Indeed, Norway was to experience practically all the effects of the war—except the devastations, of course—which the belligerent countries suffered.

¶ Norway came out of the war in a strengthened position and not unprepared to take a more active place among the nations. She had been rudely shaken out of the semi-isolation of the past. The war had been a strenuous lesson in diplomacy, and after it was over, the country continued to be involved in international affairs as never before. Even before the coming of peace, the growing interest in world problems found expression in the organization of the Norwegian Society for a League of

Nations. A list of principles for such a league was drawn up, and early in 1919 published in French, English, and Norwegian. They were, as far as I know, the most democratic and most adequate of the plans formulated during these days of high hopes. Fridtjof Nansen, who was a leader in the Norwegian society, went to London to rouse public opinion in favor of the principles. He then proceeded to Paris and agitated persistently for his ideals. He found all doors open to him, and, although he soon saw that only a small part of his hopes would be realized, there are indications that the wishes of the small neutrals had some influence on the form of the League of Nations.

When the question of Norway's adherence to the League was brought before the Storthing, the opposition gave eloquent expression to the bitter disillusionment that Norwegians shared with idealists of all lands, and there were sharp attacks both on the League and on the Treaty of Versailles. Radicals who sympathized with the Russian Revolution joined the more conservative opponents. The large majority believed, however, that in spite of its shortcomings the League might furnish a measure of security for the small countries and be a medium through which they might exert some influence on the affairs of the world. The Storthing, therefore, on March 4, 1920, voted 100 to 20, to join the League of Nations. In close cooperation with the other Scandinavian delegates, Norway's representatives exerted every effort to make the League what its advocates had hoped it might be, and to make it truly a world League by admitting as soon as practicable both Germany and Russia. "The Scandinavian contribution . . . has been to serve as an ever-alert conscience to the Great Powers."[5] Norway sent to Geneva delegates chosen from her best qualified men and women, selected without regard for party affiliation. The greatest contribution she made to the world was through her first delegate, Fridtjof Nansen, unquestionably the most towering personality of the post-war world.

The achievement of no other one person can even be compared to what Nansen in his capacity of High Commissioner of the League of Nations did to relieve the untold suffering during the 'twenties.[6] Through him, almost half a million war prisoners who had languished in Russian and Siberian detention camps were repatriated, at the incredibly low cost of $8.60 per person; an even larger number of displaced persons who had fled from Russia and were scattered through

[5] Jones, *The Scandinavian States and the League of Nations*, 274.

[6] Clarence Arthur Clausen, *Dr. Fridtjof Nansen's Work as High Commissioner of the League of Nations*, Urbana, 1932.

Western Europe were given help toward a new start in life; and estimated six or seven million lives were saved during the Russian famine of 1922; and in the Near East, between Greece and Turkey, the greatest exchange of population in the history of the world was carried through. So great was the confidence in Nansen that he generally received perfect cooperation from the governments concerned and from the great charitable organizations of the world, and unstinted aid when he appealed to private generosity. The League also gave him some backing and authorized a "Nansen passport" to facilitate repatriation. Yet the men at Geneva were so fearful of revolutionary Russia that Nansen pleaded in vain for aid to relieve the suffering there, and before he could secure funds elsewhere, people had died by the thousands. Even before the League had been formed Nansen had vainly argued against armed intervention in Russia, which he feared would cause a cleavage between the East and the West. He now believed that aid to Russia was not only a humanitarian obligation but a wise political precaution for the future.

The most spectacular incident in Nansen's activities at Geneva occurred in 1923, when Mussolini had occupied Corfu and the League feared to intervene. Nansen made a violent speech against Italy, rallied the small countries about him, and practically forced the powers reluctantly to insist on Italy's evacuation of Corfu. Nansen's last great undertaking was to help the Armenians, the most harassed people of the time, to attain security in a national home; but again the League failed him, and this problem, unsolved at the time of his death in 1930, remained one of the most tragic failures of the League.

Nansen always had the backing of his own country, where the sense of world responsibility had been growing. An instance of the far-reaching relief work sponsored by public and private effort is the care given ten thousand undernourished German and Austrian children by Norwegian foster parents. The closer relations with the other Scandinavian countries which arose out of the war and their united efforts in the League were strengthened by continued cooperation during the following years. In 1919, for example, the society Norden was organized in the three Scandinavian countries, Iceland and Finland joining later. Its aim has been to cultivate a more intimate understanding between the peoples, which might lead also to closer political and economic relations.

There was a strong feeling that especially in a time of conflict between the powers, the small nations had an important mission to fulfill in bridging the cultural breach that resulted from the war.[7] But there might also be times when the small countries needed to unite to protect their own interests.

Such an occasion arose when the nations attempted to mitigate the evils of the depression by erecting tariff walls. This illogical course was especially harmful to Norway. Upon the initative of one of her leading men, Johan Ludwig Mowinckel, a convention for "economic rapprochement" was formed in Oslo, on December 22, 1930. The contracting parties were Norway, Sweden, Denmark, Holland, and the Belgium-Luxemburg Economic Union, and in 1933 Finland joined. The purpose was a closer cooperation along liberal lines, especially in commercial matters, and the maintenance of the ideals of the League. But for all its good intentions, through the opposition of the United Kingdom on the one side and Hitler on the other, the effort proved abortive.

Although the "Oslo States," as they have come to be called, formed an economic bloc, this did not mean any decline in their activities in the League. Among Norwegian delegates who did notable work were Mowinckel, who for many years guarded Norway's special interests; Christian Lange, for twenty-two years the general secretary of the Inter-parliamentary Union, who devoted his life to the cause of peace; Kristine Bonnevie, who served on the Committee of Intellectual Co-operation; and Carl J. Hambro, who won influence and recognition not only through his remarkable eloquence, but also through his work for reform in the organization. As the last president of the Assembly, it became his duty to contribute largely to the international work of committees of the League even during the Second World War, and to preside at the closing session of the League of Nations.

The hopes which especially the small countries had pinned to the League began to wane in the 'thirties. Economic isolationism was growing, the League failed to take action in the Manchurian crisis, and even more serious, the sanctions against Italy at the time of the Ethiopian invasion were not put into operation. Once more Norway was thrown back upon her faith in neutrality.

One phase of Norway's foreign relations remains to be mentioned: the diplomatic problems growing out of the importance of the Arctic and Antarctic to twentieth century Norway.

The interest in polar exploration which Nansen's achievements had

[7] Fridtjof Nansen, "The Mission of the Small States," in *The American-Scandinavian Review*, 6:9-13 (January-February 1918).

aroused continued into the present century. Only two years after the return of the *Fram*, Otto Sverdrup once more set out for the North to circumnavigate Greenland. While weather conditions forced him to abandon this plan, his expedition spent four years in the Arctic, discovering and mapping more land than any earlier explorer. The outstanding explorer, however, was Roald Amundsen. In June 1903 he sailed from Norway in his swift, sturdy ship *Gjøa*, and on August 21, 1905, he completed the Northwest Passage, realizing the dream of explorers for centuries. En route he had also made valuable, though less sensational, scientific observations, especially about the magnetic pole. Five years later he set out in Nansen's ship *Fram*, planning to reach the South Pole. He established his winter quarters at "a Norwegian point" where the Norwegian explorer Carsten Borchgrevink had scaled the Ross Barrier a decade earlier. On December 15, 1911, Amundsen, after a perilous trip over a mountainous continent, reached the South Pole and planted the Norwegian flag there. He had won in a race with the Britisher Robert Falcon Scott for the honor of discovering the pole.

Not content with this great exploit, Amundsen began his efforts to reach the North Pole also as soon as the First World War was over, and pursued his aim with dogged persistence and courage. When expeditions on the motor boat *Maud* did not succeed, he tried a plane, and then seaplanes, without reaching his goal. Unwilling to give up, he once more obtained from his American friend, Lincoln Ellsworth, the necessary financial support to secure a zeppelin built by the Italian Umberto Nobile, who captained the craft. Amundsen named the zeppelin *Norge*, and in it he passed over the North Pole on May 12, 1926. Two years later, Amundsen again set out for the North, this time in a heavily loaded French seaplane. He was going to the rescue of Nobile and his party who, on a poorly planned expedition, were wrecked north of Spitzbergen. Amundsen failed to reach his goal and was never heard from again.

While his achievements expanded our knowledge of the polar regions and were a source of national pride to all Norwegians, Amundsen appealed to the youth of his day even more as the finest kind of sportsman. Sports—especially winter sports—were in the limelight in the late 'twenties and 'thirties. Norwegians were making an increasing number of world records, and the delegations sent to international meets were unexcelled in discipline and precision. Of greater importance, however, was a more general participation in sports than ever before. This was giving a training which was to prove useful in the crisis of 1940.

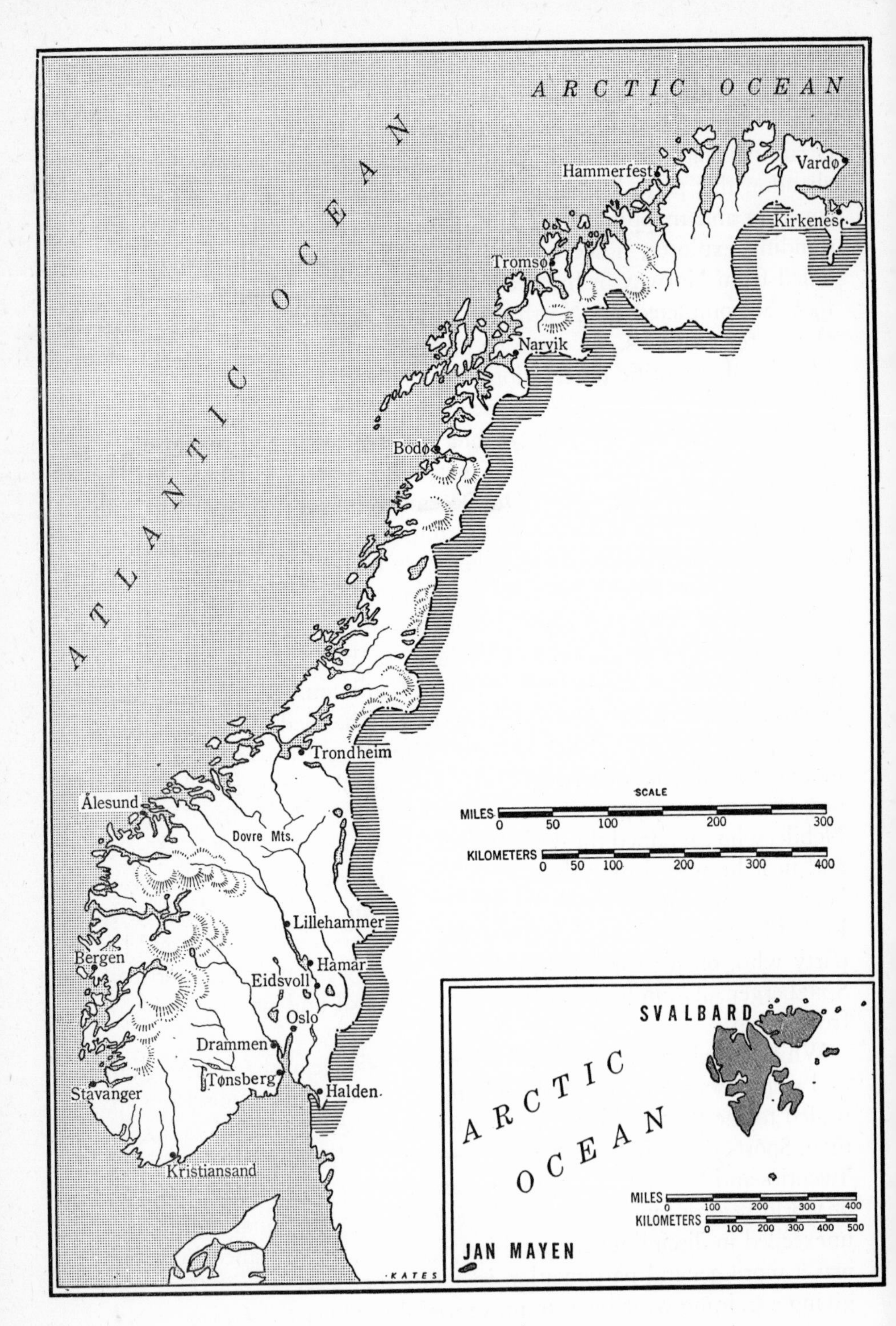

Norway Today

More important, however, were the economic interests in the Arctic and Antarctic, as the whalers were reaching out for new hunting grounds. At the turn of the century the main field of operation was still the northern shore of Norway. But the fishermen were complaining bitterly that their livelihood was threatened by the reckless destruction of the whales, which aided the fishers by driving schools of fish toward the shore. The vociferous demands for government action resulted in a law of 1904, which forbade whaling along the coast of Norway for ten years. In the end this proved a benefit to the whaling industry itself. For some time operations along the Finmark coast had become less and less profitable and new fields had been sought around Spitzbergen and the Western Islands, but without much success. Then, in 1905, an expedition set out from the little Vestfold town of Sandefjord for the far-off seas of the Antarctic. The distance made operations extremely costly, and they could probably not have brought great returns but for an idea of Christen Christensen's. He inaugurated the plan of having whaling expeditions accompanied by vessels equipped for rendering the blubber and extracting the oil on the spot. Before many years the income from whaling was multiplied many times, and hundreds, even thousands, of Norwegian seamen were plying their trade in the Far South. When the close of the war brought more normal conditions, the industry entered upon a new period of tremendous expansion. This helped to create imperialistic ambitions—albeit modest and peaceful.

During the peace negotiations in Paris, Norway was well represented by her most distinguished career diplomat, Wedel Jarlsberg.[8] He impressed upon English and French statesmen that Norway's losses in the war and the contribution of her merchant marine to the victory of the Allies entitled her to some compensation, and took up informal negotiations with the British, solely upon his own initiative. To his disappointment, his hopes for a greater Norway with a "rectified" Finmark boundary and a tropical colony, perhaps in Africa, met with no response from the more realistic authorities at home. But through his efforts alone, Norway won the recognition of her sovereignty over the Spitzbergen island group, which naturally came within her sphere of interest and could supply the country with coal, the importance of which the war had emphasized. On February 9, 1920, a treaty to that effect was signed at Paris by Norway, the United States, the United Kingdom, Denmark, France, Italy, Japan, the Netherlands, Spain, and the Dominions of Canada, South Africa, Australia, and New Zealand.

[8] Wedel Jarlsberg, *Reisen gjennem livet*, 365-396.

Later other nations signed the treaty. Most important among them is the U.S.S.R., which recognized the sovereignty of Norway in 1924 and formally adhered to the treaty in 1933, when it had been recognized by all the signatory powers—the last being the United States. Any change in the arrangements about the islands is subject to the consent of all the signatories, a significant fact in recent developments. Norway was to maintain the general principles of the "open door policy," but this did not otherwise limit her sovereignty. The islands were incorporated into the kingdom by law, and on August 14, 1925, Norway formally took possession of them. They had been given the Old Norse name of Svalbard.

Svalbard was the first land that had been added to Norway since medieval times, but it was followed by other acquisitions. In 1929 Norway occupied Jan Mayen Island in the Arctic, and in 1927 Bouvet Island in the Far South. Jan Mayen was incorporated into the kingdom, like Svalbard, while Bouvet and another Antarctic island, Peter I's Island, were declared dependencies. In addition, Norway also claims a part of the Antarctic continent, but as yet the boundaries have not been absolutely defined.

But Norway's Arctic interests centered upon Greenland. The colonies in West Greenland had remained under Denmark after the severance of the Danish-Norwegian union in 1814, and Norway raised no protest when Danish sovereignty in 1921 was formally asserted over East Greenland also. But when Denmark, in order to protect the native Eskimos, closed the Greenland waters to foreign whalers, Norway protested, and national indignation ran high. Negotiations were taken up, and in 1924 an agreement was made which gave Norwegians the same rights as Danes in the waters about Greenland but made no mention of sovereignty over the island. There was much ill will against the Danes, and, hoping to force a settlement of the question of sovereignty, Norwegians in 1931 and 1932 occupied two points of special importance to the whalers. Denmark appealed to the Hague Tribunal, which in 1933 decided against Norway and confirmed Denmark's sovereignty over all of Greenland. Norway accepted the decision in spite of the nationalistic feeling roused during the discussion, and has shown no inclination to reopen her claims. In fact, the close friendship developed during the Second World War seems to extend even to cooperation in the Arctic. As the war brought the importance of the Far North to the forefront, Arctic interests will no doubt have an even greater influence on Norway in the future than they have had in the past.

The post-war depression in Norway was really a series of crises, and in spite of some upward trends, the 'twenties are characterized by a disruption which threatened the economic position of the country. Norway emerged from the war a creditor nation, rich in money but poor in commodities. The paper currency in circulation was multiplied, prices rose, wages followed suit, and inflation was upon the country. The high purchasing value of the crown abroad stimulated excessive buying, and, as the government failed to repeal the wartime restrictions on exports, the merchants were caught with large stocks of luxury goods that later were sold for a song. Although not a little capital was employed in buying up shares in Norwegian companies which had been held abroad, speculation was rampant. The effect of unhealthy economic conditions soon became evident, and early in the 'twenties the more unsound business ventures failed, prices went down, and the whole outlook was gloomy. Believing that the fluctuating value of the crown was one of the chief reasons for this, economists demanded that it be stabilized at a value in keeping with current conditions, but the authorities failed to heed the warning. Instead, the government tried to stem the crash that seemed imminent by depositing public funds in banks that were on the verge of failure, but this only had the effect of dragging out the depression. During the last half of the 'twenties bankruptcies ran into the thousands. Government finances, both local and national, were in a deplorable state and taxes burdensome. When, on May 1, 1928, gold redemption at the old par had to be resumed, serious deflation set in. During these years unemployment rose to 100,000, in 1927 amounting to 25 per cent; the number of farm mortgages foreclosed reached fantastic figures; and attempts to reduce wages in proportion to the falling prices caused serious labor disturbances, particularly in 1931. It must be noted, however, that technological development was also a strong factor in producing unemployment. No one made money except foreigners who had speculated in the Norwegian crown.

Before long, however, the country was on the road to recovery. The deflation forced the adoption of a more cautious policy; Norway was ready to win some profit from the international boom of 1928 and 1929, and suffered less than most countries from the world depression of the early 'thirties. In fact, in Norway the whole decade of the 'thirties was one of economic progress, the full effect of which was felt only in the last years. One factor in the situation was that when England in the autumn of 1931 went off the gold standard, Norway promptly followed her example, and, until the Second World War broke out, the crown was for all practical purposes stabilized on a par with the British shilling.

The most significant advance was in shipping and whaling. In the First World War, Norway's shipping had suffered sorely, and in 1923 she had sunk to eighth place among seafaring nations, but before war again engulfed the world she had regained fourth place. The percentage of tramp boats decreased as more and more ships plied a regular route. Moreover, the merchant marine, which before the war had consisted largely of old ships and had paid low wages and offered poor working and living conditions, became the best equipped and most up-to-date fleet on the seas, two-thirds of the vessels being driven by Diesel engines. Depending for capital on credit abroad and on reinvested earnings, Norwegian shipping became "the most international business in the world."[9] It was therefore hardly influenced by the crisis in the late 'twenties, and indeed did much to help pay the debt incurred abroad during those difficult years. Whaling also expanded enormously, Norway retaining her lead among the nations. Thus at the outbreak of the last war Norway was a power on the sea, but also was dependent on the sea as never before.

In other lines, too, there was a healthy growth, especially in small industry and farming furthered by technological advances and improvements in agricultural methods. Moreover, the government continued its policy of advancing economic development in every possible way. During the keen competition of the post-war years one of its important duties was the difficult task of guarding Norway's commercial interests, especially its markets in foreign lands, and it succeeded in opening new opportunity for trade. While the expanding cooperatives and other private enterprises were encouraged, state control of utilities was constantly growing. During prohibition days a state wine monopoly was established, and in 1928 a state-controlled grain monopoly was organized, which meant both price regulation and subsidies to farmers. An expropriation law, also of 1928, made it possible to bring under cultivation land earlier left unused by the proprietors; and in the late 'thirties the number of new farms increased from five hundred to two thousand annually. Loans on easy terms were made available to farmers, and small industry too was given government aid. Thus a combination of private and public efforts helped produce that material prosperity which aided Norway in attaining a remarkably high standard of living. Although the per capita wealth was smaller than in the

[9] Keilhau, *Det norske folks liv og historie i vår egen tid,* 443.

United States, its wider distribution enabled Norway to excel richer countries in the average well-being of her people.

The social and economic instability of the period between the wars afforded the Labor Party an opportunity to come into its own such as it had not previously experienced. The two old bourgeois parties, which were in power alternately during the critical years, were not especially successful in solving the problems and came in for much criticism. One reason was the preoccupation with the prohibition question, which had a paralyzing effect on the political life of the day. In 1917 the use of distilled liquor and strong wines was prohibited as a war measure to conserve food. Temperance forces believed that an opportune time had come for making prohibition permanent, and upon their demand a plebiscite on the question was held in 1919. Idealism ran high among the common people, and the temperance cause won a more complete victory than anyone had dared to hope. Feeling the plebiscite to be mandatory, an unenthusiastic Storthing established prohibition in 1921. But the story of the "noble experiment" is rather a sorry tale. The result was complications even greater than had been anticipated with the southern wine lands, on which Norway depended for a market for her fish. Neither Left nor Right could form any consistent policy, and the law was blatantly evaded by illicit distillers, smugglers, and unprincipled doctors. When a second popular vote was taken in 1926, opinion had changed, and the following year prohibition was abandoned. It had proved a failure as a means of decreasing drunkenness, and, moreover, the pressure of hard times was pushing idealism into the background as serious economic interests were coming more and more to the fore. It was dissatisfaction with the old parties during these depressing years which gave the Farmer Party an opportunity to win seats in the Storthing, and also acted as a stimulus on the development of the Labor Party. In the long run it was the farmers and laborers who suffered most from the economic distress.

At the very time when the negotiations with America were being dragged out in 1917 and the pinch of shortages sorely felt among the poor, the Russian Revolution occurred. It struck a responsive chord in Norway, especially among the young. Many of the new generation were far less affected by the nationalism of the post-war years than by the sense of disillusionment and cynicisms toward old ideals which swept over the world. The failure of the Allies, as they felt, to "win the peace" resulted in a strong sense of the futility of war, and made internationalists and pacifists of the young. Radicals in the Labor Party began to organize soviets of workmen and of soldiers, and early in 1918 they won control of the Labor Party. Before long, however, the enthusiasm was waning. There were several reasons for this. A gloom pervaded the country that spring, caused by the influenza epidemic, the "Spanish sickness" as it was called, which struck Norway with devastating effect. Undernourishment weakened the resistance of the people, and the plague continued into the next year and in spots even into 1920. It diverted attention from purely economic problems. Moreover, the conclusion of the American agreement brought more food into the country, and Gunnar Knudsen's conciliatory attitude toward radical leaders, as well as his promise of some concessions and moderate reforms, toned down the agitation. And Knudsen's promises were kept, the most important being the establishment in 1919 of the eight-hour day and the forty-eight-hour week.

Labor was in a stronger position at the close of the war than it had been earlier, but at the same time there was a marked sharpening of social contrasts. The discrepancies were more glaringly in evidence because of the senseless spending, not least among the newly rich, and the frivolous abandon of the pleasure-seekers, unlike anything these cool northern climes had ever experienced. The election of 1918 shows the tendency of the age for the parties at the two extremes to gain and those in the center to decline. The Right gained, as did also the radical groups, though the Labor Party did not win a number of seats in the Storthing comparable to its voting strength. The Left lost the dominant position it had long held, but as no party received a majority, Gunnar Knudsen continued to head the government for another two years.

The most extreme wing continued to hold sway in the Labor Party. When in 1920 the party joined the Comintern, organized in 1919, there was much anxiety and dissatisfaction among the more conservative labor leaders, but they remained in the party in order to present a united front against the bourgeoisie. The next year the Labor Party even acquiesced in the Moscow program. This was a crassly materialistic, uncompromising plan of action to carry through a world revolution, and demanded absolute obedience to the central committee in Moscow. The document was a disappointment to idealistic revolutionaries in many lands, not least in Norway, where a large number of members withdrew from the Labor Party and formed the Socialist Party. The Labor Party's adherence to the Comintern, however, was not of long duration. Moscow was too domineering to win obedience from Norwegian individualists, the idea of a proletarian dictatorship made no strong appeal to people unaccustomed to any dictatorship whatsoever, and the whole tone of the Moscow revolution was foreign to a labor class most of whose members were hardly proletarian. What little interest there had been in world revolution was fading. Accordingly, in 1923 the Labor Party severed its connection with Moscow. But a minority group now formed a small Communist Party with continued membership in the Comintern. Thus there were really three labor groups until 1927, when the Socialist and Labor Parties again joined. New groups—fishermen, small farmers, and city people of the less wealthy bourgeoisie—gave numerical strength to the party thus formed, and emphasized the more conservative trend that came to dominate it.

In the election of 1928 the reorganized Labor Party won an overwhelming victory, capturing a larger number of seats in the Storthing than any other group, and in spite of some bourgeois alarm Norway's first Labor government was organized upon the insistence of the king that the party be given a chance. Its program was frankly socialistic, but it was also made clear that it would employ parliamentary, not revolutionary, tactics to carry out its plans. The Labor government remained in power only eleven days. During the following years no one party was in control, nor was there any stable coalition between groups. In 1935, however, the Labor Party, with the support of the Farmer's Party, won a decisive victory, and the Labor government was organized which was to remain in power until the close of the Second World War. It was headed by Johan Nygaardsvold, the first of a number of statesmen who have risen from the ranks of labor to take a lead in the affairs of their country.

¶ The years between the two wars—in Norway as in other countries—constitute a period of baffling complexity, with many seemingly incongruous trends of development.

The war brought a resurgence of patriotism, which found expression in a renewed emphasis on every national heritage. This resulted in an effort to rid the country of as many as possible of the numerous reminders of Danish times. The terms used in connection with the local government were abandoned in favor of Old Norse designations, and an extensive change in place names throughout the country was enacted. Thus, in 1924, the name of the capital was changed from Christiania to Oslo. While the war was still in progress, in 1917, the Storthing adopted an extensive language reform prepared by a committee of which Professor Didrik Arup Seip was probably the most influential member. Few alterations were made in the *landsmaal*, but radical changes in the *riksmaal* brought the written language closer to the daily speech of the people and introduced a spelling as nearly phonetic as possible. The same year *landsmaal* was made an entrance requirement to the University. The regulations of 1917 remained unchanged until 1938, when some further adaptations to current usage were made. The "New Norwegian" has been put to admirable use by the younger writers, both in verse and prose, but while much is new in the written forms the spoken language remains essentially the same, changing only through the gradual evolution which had been going on throughout the preceding century. The reform achieved its main purpose of bringing the two forms of the language closer together, and thereby the conflict between the proponents of each, which had raged since the times of Ivar Aasen, was somewhat allayed. That the linguistic isolationism desired by Aasen is neither possible nor desirable is evinced by the rapid adoption of new foreign words, especially from the English. The reform of 1917 seems, however, to have brought nearer the time when all Norwegians will unite in the use of one form of the national language.

A deep love of country was a strong factor in the whole social fabric of the age, while the sense of the country's international responsibilities was also growing. In fact, the confidence in international cooperation was so strong that many sober-minded, stanch patriots—notably the leaders of the Labor Party—believed that military preparedness was needless and certainly futile for a small country. Quite different was the element, especially strong among the young, which had very little love of country and which was pacifist largely because it had been swept along by the wave of cynicism that followed the war. While defeatism was strong in youthful circles, there was also not a little genuine faith in the social philosophy that came out of Russia. After the German invasion, however, the "red youth" made a notable contribution to the resistance movement, although some of the more extreme Communists seem to have held back until the break between Russia and Germany removed their last inhibitions.

In spite of sharp differences and bitter disputes between parties, classes, and schools of thought, there was remarkable unanimity back of the efforts for social betterment. The whole modern tendency for the individual to depend upon the state to a greater degree than ever before was more marked in Norway than in most countries. And the small, highly intelligent, homogeneous population made it comparatively easy to carry through a far-reaching program for general welfare. While there were sound earlier traditions to build upon, the war had accustomed people to greater interference with daily life, the depression increased the demand for government assistance, and the better economic conditions in the 'thirties supplied a financial basis for still broader activities in the field of public welfare.

It is impossible even to mention the many steps taken to ensure a greater equality of opportunity for all citizens, and no one party deserves all the credit for carrying out the many-sided program for building a better society. It included a broad public health program and an inclusive system of adult education. As a part of this plan, the state took over broadcasting in 1933. It was left to the Labor government of 1935 to take up again the program of social legislation which Castberg had been forced to leave unfinished in the early days of the First World War. Three important laws were passed: the Labor Protection Act, the Old Age Pension Act, providing pensions for all persons above seventy, and the Unemployment Insurance Act. These laws placed Norway in the forefront among nations in social legislation. An inevitable result of this far-reaching care for the individual by the state has been extremely heavy taxes. But efforts have been made to distribute the burden among individuals in proportion to their capacity to pay, and also to devise a system whereby the richer communities come to the aid of the poorer.

The expansion of public responsibility for the individual first and foremost affects the children. From birth on—in fact even earlier, for ample provision has been made for the care of expectant mothers—the child is under the surveillance of the state. A law, for example, prohibits burdening a child with a name which will be a source of unhappiness to him later, while it also forbids the use of family names as baptismal names. Norway's provisions for child hygiene include dental care for all school children as well as a complete system of physical check-ups, instruction in hygiene, and school lunches. The famous Oslo breakfast, based on the most scientific dietetic principles, is not for the poor only, but for all the children.

During the late 'thirties comprehensive reforms, continuing the development of a century, were introduced into the elementary schools. They are thoroughly democratic, and every effort is made to equalize educational opportunities by free transportation for children in outlying regions, state aid for poorer districts, and free school supplies. The country has an adequate number of trade schools, and theoretically the University is open to everyone with the requisite ability. In reality admission to some professional courses, especially medicine, has been restricted. The success of the elementary schools is evinced by the part the children took in the resistance movement and by the non-existence of juvenile delinquency. General social conditions, notably the relative absence of slums, must be given much credit; and the schools are close to the people, as the teachers are represented on every school board and committee. Important also is the religious instruction which is required in the elementary and intermediate schools.

Through the schools and the age-old place of the church in the community, the influence of the church has become a part of the warp and woof of Norwegian society, albeit there is a strong element, especially in the cities, which is indifferent or even hostile to the church. Ninety-eight per cent of the population belong nominally to the state church, but positive Christianity is expressed more through vigorous organizations and extensive missionary work, carried on outside of the state church, yet in close cooperation with its clergy. While not discarding any essential heritage, the church has within the last decades adapted itself to modern needs, through revising the liturgy, the hymnary, and the translation of the Bible, and through new methods of approach in the sermons. Perhaps no single man deserves more credit for the harmonious blending of the old and new than Gustav Jensen. In the church edifices also the new in art and architecture is employed to enhance the real values in Lutheran traditions.[10]

Even the briefest history of Norway between the two wars should perhaps include a picture of that transformation of society which came with the cinema, the automobile, the radio, the airplane, and innumerable less spectacular mechanical changes; also a sketch of the new social attitudes, manners, and morals. But all this, while familiar to us all, is too much a part of the present to be seen in any historic perspective.[11]

¶ The productivity of Norwegian literature in the present century is overwhelming, but although Norwegians are voracious readers, even the greatest of the authors have not shaped the thought of their time as the literary leaders of the nineteenth century did, whether it be Wergeland, the mid-century romanticists, or Ibsen and Bjørnson. In

[10] Else Margrete Rød, "Modern Norwegian Church Art," in *The American-Scandinavian Review*, 32:151-158 (Summer 1944).

[11] Chr. A. R. Christensen, *Det hendte igår*, Oslo, 1933.

the field of literature the first years of the present century were a continuation of the preceding, with the same great names and the same forms of expression dominating the scene. Yet neo-romanticism was already retreating before a new realism. The preoccupation with economic ventures and the faith in Norway's future as a great industrial country fostered a utilitarian outlook; and in an age when class conflict and social problems engrossed the thoughts, the individualism of the 'nineties seemed out of date, as the individual tended to be lost in the mass. Moreover, the materialistic philosophy of the day, which reached Norway from abroad, tended to subvert old values. The social conditions are reflected in realistic novels by a large number of able new writers, both men and women. The greatest among them is Sigrid Undset. In her novels and short stories we meet mostly young Oslo women, shopgirls and office girls or young wives and mothers, who, filled with pent-up longings, live empty lives in ugly, sordid quarters. Sigrid Undset's heroines retain, however, not only the courage to face life, but a conviction that life is worth while and that woman finds her ultimate happiness in wifehood and motherhood. But the great interpreter of labor is Kristofer Uppdal. In a monumental series of novels, he has pictured the development of the labor movement probing deeply into the complex psychology of a class rooted in the soil, seeking to assert itself in a new industrialized society.

After the First World War, in the midst of the disillusionment that came in its wake, there was a reemphasis on spiritual and moral values. Moreover, writers turned once more for inspiration to the history and traditions of their own country. Rural life of the fourteenth century was the theme of Sigrid Undset's monumental novels *Kristin Lavransdatter* and *Olav Audunssøn* (*The Master of Hestviken*). Unsurpassed in scholarly mastery of her material and unequaled in her ability to penetrate into the daily life and thought of medieval people—above all, their relationship to the church—Sigrid Undset produced the greatest historical novels in Norwegian literature.

Olav Duun represents both the historical trend and the equally marked regionalism of the age. His greatest work, *The People of Juvik*, is a cycle of six short novels tracing the story of a prosperous peasant family from the eighteenth century to the present. The scene is laid in Namdal, north of Trondheim, Duun's own home district. No greater artist has used the *landsmaal* as his vehicle of expression, and no modern writer is so close to the sagas in terseness of style. Saga-like, too, are the men and women who move through the story of the grim struggle of a self-contained family to rise and hold its own against the community. Like Duun, Johan Falkberget also writes with deep understanding of the milieu in which he grew up, in his case the mining community at Røros. Unlike the newer industrial towns, Røros has behind it centuries of tradition which Falkberget has utilized in his great historical trilogy *Christianus Sextus.* While his treatment is frankly that of naturalism, Falkberget's characters, like Sigrid Undset's, find a redemptive force in Christian faith.

Among the many regional writers are Peter Egge, who produced strong novels of his native city, Trondheim, and Gabriel Scott, the author of idyllic stories of the gentler Southland. Perhaps Oskar Braaten's sympathetic sketches from proletarian Oslo may also be classed as regional literature. More widely known than any of these is Johan Bojer's vivid description of the life of the Lofoten fishermen before the day of the motor boat. Among his many books *The Last of the Vikings* first won for Bojer the acclaim of his own countrymen. Not to be classed with localized literature is Hamsun's *Growth of the Soil,* which is a glorification of the age-old struggle to subdue the land and win from it a livelihood. Appearing in 1917, when the war placed new emphasis on the importance of the farmer, it immediately won world fame.

Norway's twentieth century is rich also in lyric poetry of great variety and scope. Most prolific and most popular of the many new writers is Herman Wildenvey, a poet of beauty and young love. He developed an easy flowing rhythm and a charming lightness, rare in the literature of Norway. More somber and more penetrating was Olaf Bull, who delved deeply into the problems of the universe. In 1918 he attacked German militarism with passionate vigor. Norway's most distinguished living poet is Arnulf Øverland, who with passionate anger attacked evils and injustice, entering into the social conflicts of the day as one who himself was sharing the sufferings of the oppressed. A younger equally gifted poet, Nordahl Grieg, also attracted attention by his intensely patriotic verse as well as by his expressions of sympathy for proletarians everywhere. Among the lyricists who have used the *landsmaal,* the great philosopher-poet Olav Aukrust ranks supreme. While Aukrust has his roots in Gudbrandsdal, the very center of old rural culture, the new industrialized age produced also poets who found their inspiration in the city. A pioneer among them was Rudolf Nilsen, whose heart was "without song" when he was away from the din of the crowded thoroughfares.

Ever since the great day of the drama in the 'eighties, the theater has occupied a large place in Norway's cultural life. The fine tradition of superb acting established by artists like Johanne Dybwad, Ingolf Schanche, and others has been maintained both in Bergen and Oslo by a number of actors of unquestioned greatness. They have done inestimable service in interpreting the older Norwegian dramas, especially Ibsen's, and in presenting to the Norwegian public numerous notable foreign plays, ranging from Shakespeare to *Tobacco Road*. With the help of able directors and designers, these artists have, moreover, afforded newer playwrights an admirable opportunity to be interpreted with daring and yet with taste.

During the first two decades of this century, Gunnar Heiberg was the most productive and most prominent dramatist in Norway, and only a few plays of distinction by other authors appeared. But from the early 'thirties the drama has been perhaps the most vital literary form in all the three Scandinavian countries. In this contemporary drama, the tragedy and brutality as well as the courage and hope of these chaotic years have found artistic expression of a high order. In Norway the two most distinguished representatives of this art are Helge Krog and Nordahl Grieg. Krog's works are sparse, clear-cut, classic structures in which the dialogue is handled with admirable skill. A Grieg play, on the other hand, seems like a vast, complex Renaissance canvas come to life, and the interest is focused upon the problems not of the individual, but of the group.

In the concert halls the standards have been as high as in the theater. Music has had the support of a large, enthusiastic, and alert public. This has made possible the appearance, also in Norway, of the complex modern symphony orchestras, and of music composed especially for them. The real creator of the Norwegian symphony was Johan Severin Svendsen, who carried over the influence of Edvard Grieg into the new music of the early years of this century. Svendsen was also a director of note, and appeared as guest conductor in many musical centers of Europe. The visit to Norway of a very large number of foreign artists gave concert life an international character. The composers, too, show in their work a strong foreign influence, not only of the classic German but of the radically modern music, notably that of Stravinsky. But equally marked has been the national trend drawing inspiration from the past. One of the foremost composers in the period between the wars was David Monrad-Johansen. While his debt to German music was probably influential in making him a Nazi collaborator, many of his compositions have a strong local flavor and he has set to music the classic Old Norse poems *Vøluspá* and *Draumkvæe.*

Like the creative literature, the scholarship of the twentieth century has reflected both the new viewpoints of the industrialized era and—even more strongly—a warm national feeling. Much study by scholars of the very highest rank has been focused upon early times in Norway. The preeminent philologist Magnus Olsen, a brilliant and profound scholar, delved deeply into the dim past, illuminating many a dark corner mainly through the study of runic inscriptions and place names. Didrik Arup Seip's philological studies have been centered chiefly upon the history of the Norwegian language. A deep admiration for the Middle Ages finds expression in Harry Fett's studies of medieval art, and in Fr. Macody-Lund's works on the economic conditions during that epoch. The folklorist Knut Liestøl has devoted his learning to family sagas, folk songs, and legends, laying a scientific basis for the distinction between fact and fiction in the sagas. Building upon the work of Oluf Rygh and Ingvald Undset, prominent nineteenth century archaeologists, Haakon Shetelig and Anton W. Brøgger have brought that science into vital connection with history.

The twentieth century has been particularly rich in historical scholarship, in compensation, it might seem, for the dearth of the preceding decades. But no hard and fast line can be drawn between historians and literary critics. Prominent in the field of the history of literature, are Kristian Elster, who is also a novelist of rank, Francis Bull, and Fredrik Paasche. Less scientifically detached in his scholarship than Bull, Paasche wrote of the Middle Ages with a warm, deep appreciation of spiritual and cultural values. Thus, in a sense he supplemented the works of the historian Edvard Bull, who has also devoted himself mainly to the Middle Ages, but with emphasis on the economic phases of medieval life. Like Edvard Bull, Halvdan Koht has leaned heavily to a leftist economic interpretation of history; he finds in class conflict the central motif in Norwegian history, and emphasizes the prominent place that the common man has occupied in Norway through the ages. The scope of Koht's scholarship is enormous, several of his works being in the field of literary criticism. Jacob S. Worm-Müller is another historian whose chief interest is the economic development of his own country. Wilhelm Keilhau, who ranks among the great authorities on world economic problems, treats of modern history from a more conservative viewpoint.

Other distinguished scholars might be named, and it must be remembered that they did not confine themselves solely to the Norwegian field. But the few names mentioned indicate the extent to which the most distinguished modern scholarship has been devoted to the study of Norway's past.

In the fine arts, as in literature, the first years of the century were dominated by the great artists from the preceding decade who were still in their full vigor. But 1914 brought a revolution. At the centennial exposition of that year a special exhibit was held by a group of young artists, "The Fourteen," who were too radical to win the approbation of conventional tastes. The newer painting of the years that followed expressed the emotional and intellectual confusion of the time of the First World War. There was a hectic search for new avenues of expression, and for new forms. Artists experimented with all that was new in modern art: cubism and all forms of abstract art, expressionism in all its intensity, and unrestrained surrealism with its emphasis on the subconscious. But out of the confusion there developed in a remarkably brief space of time a new form of painting, largely through the influence of the French artist Henri Matisse. It was a restrained, purposeful, intellectual art. Composition, form, and decorative effect were paramount in this style. The firm drawing in black and the use of strong primary colors enhanced the monumental effect. This form was especially adapted to decorative fresco painting on a large scale, and much of real value has been achieved. The pioneer in this field was Axel Revold, but with him rank his pupils Alf Rolfsen and Per Krohg. These artists did not confine themselves to frescoes; especially Per Krohg, a worthy successor of his famous father, Christian Krohg, has produced a great variety of works. While these three men were the most prominent painters in the middle of the 'twenties, a number of new artists were also attracting attention. It is impossible to mention them all or pass judgment on the place of each in the history of Norway's art, but several trends are noticeably represented among them. Dagfin Werenskiold uses nationalistic peasant themes in a strong but unimaginative manner; Ridley Borchgrevink is noted for his drawings; and perhaps no one has expressed better than Henrik Sørensen the delicacy and the lyric element that were again entering into the work of the painters.

In the art of the sculptor Norway has achieved a greatness in our century unequaled in any earlier period of her history, unless it should be in the Gothic Age. The towering genius of this century, as of the 'nineties, has been Gustav Vigeland. During the first years of the century he chiseled a group of the finest portrait busts ever produced in Norway. As he began to concentrate upon the use of granite as his sole medium, his statues assumed a more monumental character. Between 1906 and his death in 1943 his chief efforts were concentrated upon his "Fountain," unquestionably the greatest work by any one Norwegian sculptor. It is more than a fountain and more than a piece of sculpture: it is a complex structure of vast proportions, too architectural and ponderous to seem typically Norwegian. While Vigeland's name has overshadowed all others, there are younger artists, notably Ingebrikt Vik and Gunnar Utsond, who have produced at least some work fully comparable to that of the great master.

In architecture the neo-romantic revival of Norway's traditional peasant forms of building received new impulses in 1905. An unrivaled opportunity to become acquainted with the old architecture has been offered by the open-air museums at Bygdøy, near Oslo, and at Maihaugen, in Lillehammer. The latter, which was formally opened in 1904, is primarily the result of the tireless efforts and enthusiasm of Dr. Anders Sandvig, who for years devoted himself to collecting historic buildings from all over the country and from all ages. Out of the neo-romantic impulses had arisen a "dragon style," which sometimes employed unsatisfactory, rather synthetic, copies of old forms. The further study of the old buildings, however, helped architects to find a way out of the somewhat chaotic state of their art. By 1910 or thereabouts they had evolved a fine national style, romantic in spirit, allowing a wide scope for the individuality of the artist as well as for adaptation to the locale. They used motifs from old buildings in the cities as well as in the country, but with discriminating adaptation to modern needs. In this school of architects the most noted are Magnus Poulsson, Arnstein Arneberg, and Olaf Nordhagen. Nordhagen's greatest work was the plan for the complete restoration of the Trondheim cathedral.

In the midst of national trends there were also discernible influences from all the greatest styles of the past, the Gothic, the Renaissance, and the Classic. But in 1927 modernistic architecture based on functionalism came to the fore. The idea of functionalism was, of course, as old in Norway as her oldest log hut, but in its modern application this principle meant a break with all old forms, as every detail that had no utilitarian purpose was sloughed off. The new style took a more rapid hold in Norway than in most countries, because at this time there was the greatest expansion in building that had ever occurred, and the old was not adequate to the new demands. At first aesthetics seemed to be disregarded in the new style, and solidity was neglected in an eagerness to satisfy immediate desires. Before long it was demonstrated, however, that the new materials, such as concrete, steel, and glass, lent themselves especially to large-scale buildings of substantial durability and real beauty. The modern style was employed in new public buildings such as the Oslo Town Hall, designed by Poulsson and Arneberg, and the University buildings at Blindern, planned by Finn Bryn and Johan Ellefsen. But more numerous are the large apartment buildings which have introduced a striking change in the appearance of the cities, especially of Oslo.

Functionalism has also had a great effect on the crafts, which in some cases have developed along extreme modernistic lines. Quite a number of men and women might be mentioned who have made notable contributions to Norway's high achievements in the crafts. Most gifted among them is Frøydis Haavardsholm, who has done distinguished work in glass painting, textiles, and illustrations of books.

There is an intimate relationship between the modern crafts and architecture. Painting and the plastic arts have also been more closely allied to architecture than in the past. Perhaps the near future will produce once more a harmonious blending of all the arts, with architecture occupying the central place. This will be in keeping with Norway's age-old traditions, which a brief interruption, however violent, has not been able to destroy.

CHAPTER 21

THE OCCUPATION AND LIBERATION, 1940-1945

"YOU MUST NOT SLEEP"[1] is the title of a poem by Arnulf Øverland which appeared in a Norwegian paper in 1936. It is a stirring, prophetic warning to the Norwegian people. While the author was not the only Norwegian who realized already at this time that Hitler was the greatest menace to the peace and security of the world, including even Norway, to most people the poet's vision—in so far as they noticed it—seemed a horrible nightmare, and any possible danger too remote to deserve serious consideration. As in our own country in the days of the Neutrality Act, opinions and even moral concepts were confused. Although only a very few individuals condoned Hitler's course, the incomplete news that came out of the totalitarian states and crafty German propaganda blurred the thinking of many—as in other countries. Besides, had not the Germans time and again professed special friendship for Norway? And who was to know that a fifth column was cunningly infiltrating the country through the German legation and consulates, and practically every representative of German business firms?

Moreover, Norway had a long tradition of peace, and the wars in which she had been engaged during the Danish Period were not of her making. The people had shown their faith in peace by active support of every peace movement of the nineteenth century and of the League of Nations and subsidiary efforts in the years after the First World War. Even when war came to other countries, it was confidently hoped that Norway's neutrality could be maintained as in the previous war; and yet after Italy's attack upon Ethiopia, there was great uneasiness in the whole North.

The task of guiding Norway through the critical years fell to the Labor government under Johan Nygaardsvold, which had been formed in March 1935. The heaviest responsibility had to be shouldered by

[1] *The American-Scandinavian Review*, 21:5 (March 1943), translation by Einar Haugen.

the minister of foreign affairs, the historian Halvdan Koht. The failure of Great Britain and France to carry out the sanctions against Italy caused great anxiety in the small countries which had pinned their faith to the League. Accordingly, in July 1936, the seven ex-neutrals—the three Scandinavian countries, Finland, the Netherlands, Spain, and Switzerland—issued a joint statement to the effect that, as the League followed no consistent policy against an aggressor, they did not consider themselves bound to participate in any future sanctions without a decision of their own in each case. The small countries had not yet abandoned all hope that the League might still be a force for peace, and when civil war broke out in Spain Koht backed the vain efforts which were made to get the League to interfere. Instead came the Non-Intervention Agreement of 1936, the full import of which was not clear at the time. The Japanese invasion of China and Hitler's assault upon Austria likewise brought only ineffectual expressions of disapproval in the Assembly of the League; and the Munich Agreement of September 1938, while it relieved the tension momentarily, seemed to justify the cynical statement that peace might be maintained as long as there were small countries that could be sacrificed. But after the invasion of Czechoslovakia in March 1939, general war seemed imminent indeed, and Koht warned his government that hostilities would break out in the autumn.

In order to cooperate more closely in supporting their policy of strict neutrality, Denmark, Finland, Iceland, Norway, and Sweden, by a declaration signed on May 27, 1938, agreed to adopt similar rules for neutrality which were not to be modified without informing the other four governments.[2] But while the northern states had machinery for common diplomatic action, this did not include any provision for backing their neutrality by force. Under the influence of the strong peace—even pacifist—sentiment of the 'twenties, Norway's defenses had fallen into a deplorable state. One little detail illustrates the prevailing sentiment: the sealed mobilization orders which had earlier been deposited in the churches throughout the land, ready to be opened in case of an emergency, had lately been removed. It now became the duty of a party with strong peace traditions to prepare the country for the difficulties that a European war were sure to bring. In 1936 measures for defense were inaugurated, which included not only armaments, but the storing of supplies against a possible blockade and the construction of

[2] *Norway's Rules of Neutrality* and other papers are found in *Documents of International Affairs: Norway and the War, September 1939-December 1940.*

a road of a thousand miles to the Finmark boundary—which the Germans later completed. At the best, it would have been impossible to build up an adequate army, navy, and air force in the brief time allotted, but how much could and should have been achieved, and to what extent the country should have concentrated its efforts on defense are questions difficult even for experts to answer.

In President Roosevelt's famous last-minute appeal to Hitler and Mussolini on April 14, 1939, he asked the two dictators to give assurance that they would not invade a number of countries specifically named. Among these was Norway. As a result, the German minister in Oslo inquired of the Norwegian foreign minister whether Norway felt that she was threatened by Germany, and whether she had been instrumental in having Roosevelt ask the question. To both queries Minister Koht naturally answered in the negative. Only a few days later, the northern governments were asked whether they were willing to make non-aggression pacts with Germany. After consultation among the foreign ministers, Denmark concluded such a pact, but the others refused to do so. Nor did Norway wish any special guarantee from the western powers, for as C. J. Hambro, the president of the Storthing, said, "a neutrality guaranteed from one quarter ceases to be neutral if the case arises."[3] On the last two days of August the governments of the four northern countries again issued a communiqué affirming their strict neutrality, and, on September 1, King Haakon formally proclaimed this to be his country's policy.

After the war had broken out, some pressure was brought to bear on Norway and other neutrals to ally themselves with the western powers for ideological reasons. While the earlier course even of Great Britain could not convince all neutrals that the motives for the war were purely idealistic, most Norwegians believed that the Allies were fighting for the cause of freedom and ardently hoped for Hitler's defeat. Yet public opinion was no doubt back of the government in its policy of strict neutrality. In view of the country's utter unpreparedness, this seemed the only possible course to follow, and Norway did not appear to be of sufficient military importance to warrant her occupation by any belligerent. It was clear, however, that the economic pressure would be more acute than in the First World War and the problems of maintaining a strict neutrality even more difficult.

As in the preceding war, Great Britain made an agreement with the Norwegian Shipowners' Association whereby Norwegian ships could

[3] *Le Nord*, 2:250 (August 1939).

be chartered to sail for Great Britain. Although this was not unneutral and in no wise hindered the trade with Germany, the Germans pursued their methods from the First World War, and in the seven months before Norway was invaded fifty-four Norwegian ships were sunk involving the loss of several hundred lives. Protest brought no reply. Germany ignored past international law by laying down rules of her own. Any ship, for example, which tried to evade being torpedoed by following a zigzag course, was liable to sinking without warning. Finally the Nazis declared all waters surrounding Great Britain a danger zone. On February 25, 1940, the three Scandinavian governments protested to Germany against the whole illegal warfare on the sea, but they were vouchsafed no reply.

Other less ruthless, but nevertheless unlawful violations of Norway's neutrality were occurring almost daily. The government was constantly engaged in negotiations with one or both of the belligerent parties, and was accused of leaning backwards in its efforts to offend neither. Most frequent were the violations of the rule prohibiting foreign airplanes from flying across the borders of neutrals. More serious, however, were the intrusions into Norwegian waters, and the vigilant little navy was constantly on guard to uphold the rights of Norway with firmness. The difficulties were especially great for Norway. Her extended coast—a shoreline as long as that of the whole continent of Africa—gave an excellent opportunity for German ships carrying Swedish iron ore from Narvik to escape from the English patrol by seeking refuge in the neutral fairway inside of the Norwegian skerries.

Two incidents were most spectacular and attracted a great deal of attention in the press. Early in the war the Germans captured an American ship, the *City of Flint,* and took her along the Norwegian coast toward Germany. When the vessel stopped at Haugesund, the German officers and crew were made prisoners and the *City of Flint* released to the American crew.[4] The Nazi government tried by dire threats to frighten the Norwegians into returning the ship and releasing the prisoners. When Norway would not scare, the matter was dropped. Later a German transport, the *Altmark,* came into Norwegian waters. When asked whether he carried other persons than the crew, the captain answered no, and, since the vessel was registered as a warship, it was not searched. The British, however, were well aware that the *Altmark* was carrying prisoners, and sent a cruiser and five destroyers in pursuit of the German ship. After a short battle in Norwegian waters,

[4] Florence Jaffray Harriman, *Mission to the North,* 229-245, Philadelphia, 1941.

the *Altmark* was boarded and the British prisoners set free. The two little Norwegian torpedo boats which were present could do nothing. Nevertheless, the Germans protested because the Norwegians had not done more to avert the incident. The British admitted that technically Norway's neutrality had been violated, but averred that their action was necessary and moreover justified because the *Altmark* was not confining itself to the type of passage allowed by international law. The incident had no important consequences and was about to be closed amicably when the war came to Norway.

The British continued to suspect that the Germans were making illegal use of Norwegian waters, and, while absolute proof was not obtainable, the sinking of several English ships just outside—in one case (the British claim three) inside—of Norwegian waters was strong circumstantial evidence. The German ore trade via Narvik was also becoming increasingly objectionable.

The most distressing problems that faced Norway during the months of neutrality were in connection with the Winter War between Finland and the Soviet Union. When Finland was faced with Russia's demands, it was made clear, at a meeting of the foreign ministers of the North, that the Scandinavian countries were not in a position to extend military aid and thus become involved in the war. The sense of impotence no doubt added to the sympathy for Finland's tragic fate, and every possible aid was extended to her. Volunteers from Norway and even more from Sweden flocked over the border, and material aid was sent to such an extent that, when war came to Norway, the housewives had to face their own problems with depleted larder and clothes press. Meanwhile the British were preparing to send assistance to Finland if a request should come. The force would have to be sent across Norway. The British government brought strong pressure to bear on Norway, even threatening to send soldiers through the country without permission. But the Norwegian government, as also the Swedish, clung to its policy of strict neutrality—albeit as friendly as possible. Knowing that Norway would refuse the passage of troops through her territory, Finland made no formal request for British aid. Before any help could have reached the scene of battle, the Winter War was over, and although Norway's policy was severely criticized at the time, subsequent events proved it to have been wise and a boon to the cause of the Allies. But their neutrality could not preserve the security of Norway and Sweden. "On the contrary," as Chamberlain said on March 19, "the danger has been brought closer to those two countries, till today it stands upon their doorsteps."

The war had been coming alarmingly near. Oslo became the center of increasing activity: foreign diplomatic staffs were enlarged; travelers, especially Americans, swarmed into the embassies seeking the earliest possible passage home; and refugees from here and there found safety in the neutral capital. At first it still seemed reasonable to expect that the policy of neutrality, to which the government clung tenaciously, would succeed. But the alarm was increasing and the question naturally arose as to whether, even within the frame of neutrality, more could be done to prepare for a possible German attack.

It is now known that in December, 1939, Vidkun Quisling had visited Hitler and told him that the western powers were planning, with her consent, to occupy bases of operation in Norway. He was very insistent and persuaded the Führer that to prevent this it was advisable to occupy Norway which, he claimed, was a point of vital importance in the war. Hitler was won over to the plan, thorough preparations were set on foot, and the date for the invasion was fixed for as early as February. But these measures were shrouded in absolute secrecy. Late in February a "fantastic" rumor leaked out in Berlin that Scandinavian ports were among places to be seized; but it was given no credence.[5] About a month later, March 28, William Shirer broadcast from Berlin: "From here it looks as if the neutrals, especially the Scandinavians, may be drawn into the conflict after all."

Some inklings of the danger had also reached the Norwegian government. It became known that a great force was being prepared in Stettin and Swinemünde. It was generally believed that the Nazis were preparing a great attack on the West, perhaps England, and it was thought that this might involve efforts to get bases in southern Norway. But by a people not yet inured to Nazi ways, it was taken for granted that an ultimatum would precede any action.[6] Both in February and in March reports from the legation in Berlin strengthened any suspicions the Norwegian government might have had, but nothing happened. Meanwhile an alarmingly large number of German "commercial representatives," who proved to be Nazi agents, were entering Norway. The Norwegian representative in Berlin, who had Nazi propensities, continued to hand out visas in spite of some misgivings on the part of his superiors at home.

[5] William L. Shirer, *Berlin Diary*, 291, New York, 1941.

[6] Halvdan Koht, *Norsk utenriks politikk fram til 9. april 1940*, pp. 47-51, Oslo, 1947.

The first days in April were tense indeed. The foreign office was worried about threats to Norway's neutrality from the western powers. On April 8 a broadcast from the British and French governments announced the mining of Norwegian territorial waters. The Norwegian government and Storthing at once protested. It seemed clear that the mining might furnish the Germans with an excuse for any course they planned to pursue. It was not known, of course—as now seems evident—that the mining was a result of Britain's knowledge of German plans.

In the meantime some indications of the danger from Germany had reached Norway, and one gruesome warning came from the Germans themselves. As a softening-up measure, there was a gala social function at the German embassy, on April 5, at which the diplomatic corps and high government officials were shown a horror film from the invasion of Poland, while on the same day the German minister invited Minister Koht and Mrs. Harriman, the American minister, to dine with him on April 19. On April 5, also, came a telegram from the legation in Berlin intimating the possibility of landings in southern Norway. The foreign minister was still skeptical; he believed the coast was sufficiently guarded and that no general mobilization was necessary, and his speech in the Storthing on the following day dealt with what seemed a more immediate problem—the plans of the Allies.

On the afternoon of April 8 came the first definite reports that German action was in progress, and the evening papers carried a story that the English had torpedoed, in Norwegian waters, a German transport bound for Bergen. Norwegian boats picked up 1,200 bodies, although their operations were hindered by countless floating carcasses of horses. The soldiers who came ashore thought they were going to Bergen to defend the city against the British. Even more alarming was news from the legation in London that the British navy had sighted German forces advancing northward, presumably toward Narvik. The Storthing held a secret meeting in the evening, and the government decided to take such precautions to strengthen the coast defenses as could be made effective at once. But there was no general call to arms by ringing the church bells. People went home and to bed as usual that night, although a few had a premonition that something evil might happen during the night, and that they might wake up in an occupied country. Those who lingered on the streets after dark were handed a little circular in which Vidkun Quisling announced that a great day was about to dawn for Norway.

¶ On April 9 the carefully laid plans for the attack on Norway were carried out with typical German precision and thoroughness. Although Norway had not been entirely without warning, the Germans had all the advantages of making a surprise attack. This was the first time the German advance was not preceded by some kind of ultimatum, and the first instance of the use of perfectly coordinated land, sea, and air forces. The Germans launched a simultaneous night attack on the seaport towns of Narvik, Trondheim, Bergen, Stavanger, Christiansand, and Oslo, and succeeded in getting possession of them all. Yet all did not go "according to plan." Norway's little fleet, which had largely been mobilized since the beginning of the war, put up an heroic fight and caused the Germans heavy losses. The first shot was fired by a little whaler with one small gun, which alone took on an enemy man-of-war. At Christiansand an enemy fleet sailed into the harbor under British and French colors, at Narvik Germans fought in Norwegian uniforms, and at Bergen freighters lying in the harbor unloaded soldiers as soon as the fighting had begun. While the game little fleet could not prevent German victory in every port, it did make the invaders pay a heavy price, and kept on fighting as long as the ships were afloat. When the armies in Norway had to give up, twelve ships remained to continue the fight with England as a base.

The most important action on April 9 was the attack on the capital. In Oslo the first air raid alarm sounded between 1:00 and 2:00 in the morning. Before long there was definite information that fighting was in progress in the Oslo Fjord, that four large warships and several smaller craft had reached the outer fortifications and been met with fire. The little fort of Oscarsborg not only inflicted injury on several ships, but sank the *Blücher*, and with it went down valuable material and men who were to have filled important posts in the occupation forces. The delay, moreover, prevented the Germans from capturing the king and government officials as they had planned. Several hours after the fighting had begun, the German minister, Bräuer, presented to Koht a note containing demands upon the government for a "cooperation" which in reality meant complete submission. Bräuer insisted on an immediate reply. After consulting the government, Koht refused the demands, reminding the German that the Führer had said that a people which meekly submits to aggression does not deserve to survive.

Meanwhile, the gold from the Bank of Norway was removed and started on its adventurous journey to England, and preparations were being made to carry out the proposal of C. J. Hambro that the royal family, the government, and the Storthing move to Hamar, in order that they might continue to function. Early in the morning general mobilization orders were issued, but before these could be carried out, the Germans were in possession of the military depots and supplies. There was air fighting over Oslo, which helped to swell the streams of evacuees who thronged every road out of the city. The little air force fought gallantly, supported by English planes, but the superior Nazi forces captured the air fields and at once established a ferry service to bring in more troops. It was evident that resistance in Oslo was futile. By noon the capital was completely in the hands of the invaders, and many a "commercial traveler" who had been staying at the Grand Hotel now appeared in full Nazi uniform. Even earlier they had taken over the radio and telephone system, and this added much to the inevitable confusion.

As dazed crowds watched the invaders march up Karl Johan Street, all seemed quiet. But one by one practically every young man was quietly leaving the city and joining any fighting force he could find, defying the announcement that if discovered he would be shot. In the late afternoon Quisling made a radio speech announcing that the government had been removed and that he had assumed power. He forbade mobilization and threatened to shoot any officer who took up arms against the forces of occupation. His plea that there must be "one kingdom, one people," contrary to his intention, really united the people in determination to resist. With remarkable speed forces gathered which delayed and inflicted heavy losses on the invaders that were pursuing the king and government. At Midtskogen, near Elverum, a contingent under Colonel Otto Ruge was able to defeat an armored German force and thus gain time for the evacuating government.

For a few hours the little city of Hamar was a diplomatic center, as the delegations at the embassies in Oslo, except the German and Italian, had followed the government. The foreign minister reported to the Storthing the German demands which had been refused and closed by declaring that the country was in a state of war. There was a spontaneous unanimity in that body, and a general agreement that party politics was out for the duration of the crisis. Nygaardsvold presented to the king the resignation of the cabinet. The king consulted Hambro, who declared in the Storthing that this was not the time to change leadership, but it was agreed to add to the cabinet three representatives of the other parties as ministers without portfolio. The session was interrupted by the news that the German forces were alarmingly near Hamar, and in short order the members were on their way to Elverum, where the meeting was resumed next day. But it was evident that conditions made it impossible for the Storthing to continue functioning. Under Hambro's experienced and courageous leadership, quick unanimous action was taken. Hambro advised that the government's resistance to the German demands be adhered to. He then proposed that the Storthing should give the government full power to "take any step and make any decision found necessary under the actual conditions of war." This was passed unanimously without discussion, and no objection was made when the president stated that it might be necessary for the government to continue its functions outside of Norway. The meeting was then adjourned *sine die*, and Hambro left for Stockholm, from where much of Norway's foreign policy would be carried out. Among those who left the country were Crown Princess Märtha and her children, who accepted President Roosevelt's offer of a haven in the United States.

A small delegation remained in the neighborhood, as Bräuer had asked for new negotiations. When Bräuer insisted on seeing the king, Haakon complied and returned to Elverum from a farm where he had been staying. After vainly trying to intimidate and flatter the king, Bräuer demanded that the Nygaardsvold cabinet be dismissed, and Quisling recognized as prime minister. Haakon answered that, as a constitutional king, he could not appoint a government which lacked the confidence of the people. Aware of the seriousness of his decision, Haakon told his ministry that as the final authority rested with them, he was willing to abdicate, but not to retract. From now on Haakon VII was more than a respected and beloved king, he was a national symbol and the rallying point for all patriots. The first appeal to the people to fight for their freedom took form at Nybergsund, a little hamlet in Trysil; but the radio station available could carry the message to only a small part of the country. When a last attempt to break the king's determination failed, the Germans bombed Nybergsund and then Elverum, thus inaugurating a pursuit of the king which was to continue as long as he remained in the country. This steeled the determination of the Norwegians that their king and government must under no circumstances fall into enemy hands.

The king appointed Otto Ruge commander-in-chief of the armed forces, and before long he had won a place second only to the king in the hearts of his countrymen. The task he faced seemed hopeless. He had little information and no way of getting a complete view, as telephone connections were broken off. But somehow companies and battalions gathered, with commissary and health departments, and took up the fight wherever there were Germans to be found. The chief conflict was in Gudbrandsdal where the king and government were taking temporary refuge. Utterly inadequate as the Norwegian forces were in equipment and military training, practically every man was a sportsman experienced in out-of-door life and an expert marksman and skier. Moreover, the Norwegians had learned guerrilla warfare from the Finnish Winter War and had valuable help from Finnish and some Swedish volunteers. For three weeks the small Norwegian forces, says Ruge, "fought without respite, day after day, night after night, without reserves, always in the front lines, against heavy artillery, tanks, and an overwhelming number of German bombers—to all of which we could oppose nothing, no armored cars, no anti-aircraft guns, no pursuit planes." Back of them were "stubborn, faithful men and women, . . . surgeons, nurses, Lottas, field laborers, workmen, railroad men and telegraph-functionaries, roadmenders, and so on."[7]

The troops protected landing places and held out until the Allied reinforcements began to arrive in sufficient numbers to begin operations against Trondheim. Then the English commander, on April 28, much to his disgust, received orders to retire from southern Norway and Trøndelag. Inadequate and disappointing as the Allied help had been, it might have been difficult for the government to withdraw to the North without the landing of British forces. Without them it was impossible to hold the South, all the more so as Nazi planes razed to the ground the seaboard towns, and warships were extending their operations far into the fjords. On May 7, Ruge had to withdraw from Trøndelag and all southern Norway. Some of the troops had to surrender, others escaped into the mountains to continue guerrilla fighting, but all who could accompanied Ruge and joined the forces in the North.

In the North the outlook seemed more hopeful. Ever since the Finnish war, some forces had been mobilized under the command of General Carl Gustav Fleischer. For almost three weeks after April 9 they fought alone, but later received good help from British, French, and Polish soldiers. On the sea the British were supreme, but the Nazis retained control of the air. Everywhere the tactics were offensive, and so successful that there seemed hope of driving the Germans out. Then came a staggering blow: shortly after the important battle of Narvik in late May the Allies found it necessary to withdraw all their forces

[7] Hambro, *I Saw It Happen in Norway*, 161.

including planes and ships, and abandon the whole campaign in Norway. As the little Norwegian army was isolated and cut off, further fighting was futile.

For the last four weeks Tromsø had been the capital of Norway, but now General Ruge informed the government that he could no longer be responsible for its safety. It was evident that the war could be continued only from a base outside of the country. It was therefore decided to accept the offer from England, and, on June 7, the king, the crown prince—who would have preferred to remain in Norway—the ministers, other officials, and many of the military staff boarded the British man-of-war *Devonshire* and set sail for London.

General Ruge, upon his own insistence, was left to negotiate with the Germans and help demobilize the army. On June 10 fighting stopped and in a few days all arrangements were made. The terms given the surrendering army were reasonable and in accord with military usage. The soldiers were to return home unmolested after delivering up their arms, and the officers were to be free if they signed a pledge not to fight any further against the Germans during this war. Later, however, the Nazis broke their promise and inflicted diverse penalties on many who had been in this campaign. Ruge refused to sign the pledge, and became a prisoner of the victors. Contrary to the promise that he would be treated with military honors, he was later sent to a concentration camp in Germany.

All of Norway was now in the hands of the enemy. The grief among the people was intense, the soldiers who for two months had put up a brave and successful resistance to the invaders were stunned, and it might seem that the war had been of no avail. But this was far from the truth. The morale and determination of the people had been strengthened, time had been gained, the king and government had been saved from falling into Nazi hands, and Norway had won the right to an honorable place in the counsel of the Allies. Moreover, the victory was costly for the Germans. They suffered heavy naval losses, and a German paper reported that 63,000 men had lost their lives. The Norwegians kept hundreds of thousands of soldiers tied up who otherwise might have made Dunkirk even more of a tragedy for the British than it was. And finally, for the Norwegians the fighting at home was only the first phase of the war, a preparation for a longer struggle.

¶ One of the serious handicaps during the early days of the war was the lack of communication among the different parts of the country and between Norway and the outside world, and the absence of true information about what was happening to the country. The Germans did all in their power to conceal or distort the facts, and wild rumors filled the air. This explains much that happened.

While the fighting was going on farther north, the problem of how to maintain civilian life faced the people in the occupied regions. GERMANY SAVES SCANDINAVIA! shrieked red headlines in Germany on April 9, and Ribbentrop announced to the foreign press that "the Führer has saved an ancient and respected part of Europe from that certain ruin and utter destruction to which our English and French enemies are clearly indifferent." In Norway, too, it was announced that the Germans came as protectors against England and defenders of the country's "true" neutrality. German soldiers seemed genuinely surprised that their "protection" was not welcome, and German authorities hoped and wished for "cooperation"—in other words, submission—on the part of the people.

Hardly had the government left Oslo on April 9 before Vidkun Quisling proclaimed himself head of the "national" government. He was leader of Nasjonal Samling (NS), the National Party, the small Nazi group in Norway. He sought an opportunity to satisfy his hitherto thwarted ambitions, and his proclamation no doubt had the approval of Hitler. But there were so many protests against this arrangement that his government was a complete fiasco, and chaos was threatening. The invaders were not prepared to take over the civil administration—the personnel intended for this purpose had gone down with the *Blücher*—and the commander-in-chief, General Falkenhorst, controlled both civil and military affairs. With his approval a committee known as the Administrative Council was appointed by the Supreme Court on April 15.

When the Storthing had adjourned and the executive authorities withdrawn, the only department of the government which remained in Oslo was the court. It was a non-political body composed of men of the very highest caliber. Chief Justice Paal Berg obtained King Haakon's approval of the Administrative Council, which, it was emphasized, was in no sense a government. It was insisted that the council would not function unless Quisling withdrew. Having no love for Quisling and believing the council useful, Falkenhorst agreed, but demanded that Quisling be publicly thanked for his "patriotic acts." Paal Berg accepted the inevitable, but, by a deft choice of words, in reality thanked the traitor for stepping out. The members of the council were men of affairs and of unquestioned patriotism and integrity who had the confidence of their countrymen. Besides the chairman, District Governor I. E. Christensen, perhaps the best known member was Didrik Arup Seip, rector of the University. This board did yeoman service of great value to the people, as it carried on a constant fight against the growing German encroachments on constitutional rights. On September 25, 1940, it was summarily dismissed by the Reich's commissar, who found the stiff-necked patriots of the Administrative Council a hindrance to his plans. On April 24 Hitler had appointed Josef Terboven, "the tough young Nazi *Gauleiter* of Cologne,"[8] as Reich's commissar for Norway, thus separating the military and civil authority. He organized his own administration all over the country, making the relations between Germans and Norwegians more and more difficult.

The Nazis did not wish, however, to establish a completely German administration, but believed it more to their advantage to have a Norwegian puppet government. When the king, to their great disappointment, had escaped, they wished for some Norwegian authority with which they could conclude an armistice. To do this it was necessary to get rid of the king and the Nygaardsvold government. As early as June 13 the Germans demanded that the Storthing be convened in order to depose the king and elect a new government to take the place of the Nygaardsvold cabinet. Paal Berg declared that any such method of removing the king was unconstitutional, and both the Supreme Court and the Administrative Council refused to have anything to do with it. There were meetings called of the party groups of members of the Storthing, but they took no decisive action. The Nazis then succeeded in persuading the members of the presidential board to send a letter to the king asking that, as he was not in a position to function, he resign the royal power for himself and his family. This committee consists of the presidents and vice presidents of the Storthing, the Odelsthing, and the Lagthing, but has no authority. The outstanding leader of the group, C. J. Hambro, was out of the country. The other five, approached individually, were not able to resist the Nazi threats and promises, though their act was ill-advised, not traitorous. Perhaps this might be a way to save their country, they thought: the outlook was dark, as the Germans were at the height of their power and even England in danger of falling. Moreover, while the intruders were becoming more hated every day, public opinion as to what ought to be done was hesitant; the underground, which was to spread information and unify action, had scarcely begun its work.

[8] Shirer, *Berlin Diary,* 321.

Fortunately the king's reply was an unequivocal no. He emphasized that the request was not a free expression of the will of the people; that to call a Storthing subjected to the duress of enemy occupation would violate the Constitution; that under prevailing conditions he could perform his duties as constitutional king only outside of Norway; and that the Constitution provided for just such a contingency as the present. The papers were not allowed to publish King Haakon's message, but were forced to print attacks upon him. Nothing further was done, however, to call a Storthing. Terboven continued to negotiate with the presidential board and party groups, but soon lost the little support he had had, and the Nazis were defeated in their effort to form a new Norwegian government.

Meanwhile Terboven was expanding his German administrative machinery until hundreds of functionaries were scattered over the country, becoming more and more obnoxious. The efforts of the Administrative Council to protect the people were stopped on September 25, when, in a rancorous speech, Terboven abolished the council and declared all political parties taboo except the Nazi.

With September 25, 1940, began a definite, completely German rule. Terboven appointed eight Norwegian "commissarian ministers," who, according to the Führer principle, were responsible individually to the commissar. They were his puppets, and they were all later found guilty of disloyalty to country and king. Quisling was not in the government, but as chief of the Nazi party his position was strong. A series of laws were promulgated which showed a clear-cut program of nazification. An attempt was made to fill the positions in the lower courts held by laymen with Nazis only, thus ensuring a Nazi majority, and a number of judges were arrested for anti-Nazi opinions. This flagrant violation of constitutional principles brought a protest from the Supreme Court, and a demand for the release of the imprisoned judges. Just then a case was coming up which involved the question of how far the court could test the legality of the acts of the occupation forces, that is, decide whether or not they were in accord with the Hague rules. When the judges refused to take orders, the Terboven government planned to get a Nazi majority by setting up a new age limit for judges. As a protest, the whole court resigned on December 23, and thus ended the last vestige of a legal central government. The Supreme Court had, however, pointed out the course and paved the way for the whole resistance movement which now was taking shape.

Terboven's minister of justice managed to find a few men of inferior caliber to serve as a court, and in 1941 they gave him the decision he wanted—that the court had no jurisdiction in cases involving the Hague rules. Thereafter international agreements were practically abolished as far as the administration of Norway was concerned.

When the Germans failed to secure cooperation from the people, they wished to make it appear that they had popular support, and brought as many Norwegian Nazis into their system as possible. These were given handsome uniforms and fine automobiles, but were mere stooges of the German authorities, who often employed them to carry out their most dastardly acts. Terboven's civil government was worse than the military, and his Norwegian helpers did not fall behind the foreigners. They were of necessity recruited largely from what was morally, if not intellectually, the scum of the population which made up the bulk of the little Nazi party.

The situation became particularly bad after February 1, 1942, when the Nazi organization was given its final form. On that day, Vidkun Quisling, with much fanfare and oratory, declared himself minister president, assumed the position of Führer in Norway, and surrounded himself with a typical Nazi ministry. Norway now really had two governments and two leaders, both greedy for power and intensely jealous of each other. The relation between the two is not clear, but the move of February 1 must have had the approval of Hitler. While Terboven held the superior authority, Quisling was allowed to do as he pleased in most internal affairs, and became more and more brutal and tyrannical. As he headed a "Norwegian" government and appointed his party men as a check on officials, a double administrative system resulted—one German and one Norwegian—with much confusion as to authority.

¶ The most immediate object of the German occupation was military—to make the best possible strategic use of the country and to obtain from it the sinews of war. This meant building up a war machine in Norway, and the maintenance of a military force much greater than allowed by the Hague Convention; efforts to recruit soldiers, which were doomed to failure; the use of civilian labor to fill the insatiable maw of the god of war; and the extortion from the country of all possible war supplies, including food. Economic exploitation was carried on also for the benefit of German civilians: not only was food sent to Germany, but thousands of Norwegians were driven from house and home to provide shelter for members of the *Herrenvolk* whose homes had been bombed or who needed to build up physically. While surreptitious thieving was a common practice, private looting was prohibited; but official plundering was carried on with Nazi ruthlessness and a German thoroughness, which had scientifically estimated the minimum on which the people could subsist.

The economic cost of the occupation was staggering. The national debt was increased ninefold, largely through the German appropriation of the funds of the national bank. More serious was the destruction of fixed capital—ruined industrial plants or worn-out machinery; depleted stocks; the deterioration of the means of communication; and wasteful cutting of timber. To this must be added not only the wholesale destruction of public and private property in warfare, but the stripping of valuables in every home or public building occupied by the Germans. Inflation also added to the hardships. Much of this cost was paid during the occupation through the lowered standard of living which brought great suffering and discomfort, not to mention disease and a general decline in health. If the war had caused no other economic difficulties, the severing of all trade with the West and the loss of all immediate benefits from the merchant marine would alone have been a devastating calamity.

The Nazis were not only utilizing Norway to satisfy their immediate wants; they were planning to incorporate the country into their economic system, with no thought for Norway's welfare. They entered into commercial arrangements in which the German commitments were paid with Norwegian products sorely needed at home, such as fish and fertilizer, and they brought the industrial plants under German control, destroying all competition.

¶ Even more serious than the material spoliation was the systematic effort to nazify the people. The press and radio were at once brought under strict control and access to new foreign books was limited to those from Germany. This was the beginning of the attempt to kill the soul of the nation. The Germans looked upon the Norwegians—except the few who had Jewish blood in their veins—as akin to the *Herrenvolk* and worthy of absorption into it. The Norwegians failed to appreciate this "distinction." With a naïve lack of psychological insight, the Nazis tried to force their *Kultur* upon an unwilling people by a continually growing use of imprisonment, torture, executions, concentration camps at home and in Germany, and a general policy of crafty, brutal terror. They were doomed to failure.

As the Nazi plans became evident it did not take long to weld the whole people, except the quislings, into a united home front of resistance. The political maturity of the people, its regard for justice and love of freedom, its irrepressible sense of humor, so irritating to the Germans, as well as its tenacious endurance and unquenchable courage, served it in good stead in the conflict. Almost every man, woman, and child made some contribution, however small, to the work of the home front. Every housewife helped to strengthen the morale, as she dressed up the meager meals, produced presentable clothing from the most unpromising remnants, and enabled her husband to show a brave front though his shirt might be backless.

The directive force for the whole home front was the underground. It was extremely effective and well organized, and from the first kept up communication with the Government in Exile. Through the illegal press, unknown men and women, at harrowing risk to themselves, circulated news, warned of danger, and gave directions about what to do under different circumstances. The heroic tales of escapes and adventures, but also of the dire consequences of being captured, have already filled volumes. But if one worker fell into the hand of the enemy, there was always another to take up his task.

The general principles of the opposition had been clarified by the course of the Supreme Court: to defend the rights of the individual under the Constitution and to emphasize that the "rights" of the occupying power should be defined according to the Hague Convention. The Nazis followed the policy of attacking certain strategic groups and requiring membership in Nazi organizations, which would lend support to Quisling's position; but in every case they met unyielding resistance from all kinds of associations whether composed of laborers, lawyers, or sportsmen.

When the children were to be trained in Nazi youth organizations, their parents refused to let them become members, and the children themselves learned to take their part in the active resistance movement.[9] They especially showed their mettle in supporting the teachers. These not only refused to use nazified texts as they were ordered to, but were willing to suffer for an idea rather than join a newly formed Nazi teacher's union. Their transportation to Finmark is one of the most savage incidents of German terrorism. In the University an equally unyielding opposition was carried on under the leadership of Rector Seip, as the government tried to force upon the faculty their own candi-

[9] Aase Gruda Skard, "Children of Conviction" in *Educational Leadership*, 1:106-109 (November 1943); and "Children with Responsibility" in *Childhood Education* (December 1944).

dates regardless of academic fitness. Before long many of the professors were forced to join the community of distinguished patriots at the concentration camp at Grini. Among them was the rector, who, with others, was later sent to Sachsenhausen. The unspeakable conditions there aroused in him a feeling of nostalgia as he thought of Grini.[10] The University was closed, and most of the students who did not flee the country were arrested and about 350 of them deported to Germany. At first they were treated fairly well in the vain hope that nazification, which had failed at home, might succeed on German soil. Later they were put to fortifying the frontiers of the Reich.

In its effort to save the people from the baneful influences of Nazism, the church was as zealous as the schools, and it rose from strength to strength in the face of persecution. Following the example of the Supreme Court, the bishops resigned their position in the state church. Somewhat later, at Easter time in 1942, the clergymen who had not already been removed resigned en masse, after reading in their churches a document entitled "*Kirkens grund*" ("The Foundations of the Church").[11] In defining the relations between the state and the church, this manifesto emphasized that in its main functions the church was not under the state, but was essentially a folk church. This event of Easter 1942 marks the separation of the church from the government then existing. The congregations stood loyally back of the clergy, who continued their work without cessation. When the primate of the church, Bishop Eivind Berggrav, who had been the moving spirit of the resistance, was placed under arrest, a temporary organization was effected under the leadership of O. Hallesby and Ludvig Hope. All that the Nazis controlled was the empty churches and pulpits filled by a motley array of their own creatures. The fight of the church produced a number of documents characterized not only by intense earnestness but also by remarkable restraint and intellectual acumen. As "the conscience of the state," the church not only resisted encroachments upon its own right, but also protested against other crimes, such as the persecution of the Jews. Between seven and eight hundred of these unfortunate people—the bulk of the Norwegian Jews—were transported to Germany, and with very few exceptions, all trace of them was lost.

One of the most notable manifestoes of the church came in May 1943. By this time the military situation of the Reich was precarious,

[10] Seip, *Hjemme og i fiendeland.*

[11] Bjarne Høye and Trygve M. Ager, *The Fight of the Norwegian Church against Nazism*, New York, 1943, contains this and earlier documents.

and it was therefore necessary to scrape the bottom of the barrel, so to speak, for war material and men. In Norway the year brought several ever-tightening measures for conscripting the youth, first for war production and then for military service. The protests from the church leadership and other representative men and women emphasized that a state of war between Norway and Germany still existed, and that to force people virtually to fight against their own country was the most flagrant violation of the Hague Convention imaginable. The Nazis took the stand that the two countries were allies fighting the common menace of communism. A plan was drawn up for a general mobilization and the training of Norwegians in Germany for use on the Russian front. This document, like many others, fell into the hands of the home front, the people were warned, and the Nazis were unable to carry out their schemes for recruiting military support in Norway.

They could and did, however, intensify the terrorism under which the people lived. The insecurity was harrowing. A late knock on the door might mean that some member of the family would be carried away to suffer imprisonment, torture, or even death for perhaps no offense at all. The most notorious example of mass terrorism was the ruthless destruction of the little community of Televaag—the Lidice of Norway. In daily life the corruption and inefficiency of little quislings who replaced earlier local functionaries caused constant irritation. Worst of all was the miscarriage of justice, as the severity of penalties varied with party affiliations. When the courts were ordered, if possible, to avoid the prosecution of members of the hird—a band of Quisling's young satellites—a rowdiness and lawlessness that knew no limit was let loose.

To the Norwegians the fact that the Germans could find willing tools in the country seemed a blot on the whole nation. It steeled the heroes of the underground—men and women, old and young, especially young, from all walks of life—to greater united efforts. It was necessary along the whole home front to adapt oneself to a new moral outlook which glorified acts which under normal conditions were contrary to all traditional conceptions of right. On the other hand, all the activities of the resistance were on a high plane, showing a most remarkable mental and psychological resistance to terrorism, while an unquenchable optimism and sense of humor baffled the enemy.

Practically the whole cultural life of the country had to go underground. During the early days of the occupation several books by distinguished authors appeared. After the publishing firms were subjected to Nazi control, however, they were boycotted and received no new manuscripts. But production did not cease, and there was a flood of books ready for publication as soon as the country was rid of its unwelcome visitors. The situation furnished the material and inspiration for countless books. Many of them were accounts of personal experiences and other stories full of human interest. Others were more exhaustive accounts and scholarly studies of the occupation, or carefully considered plans for the future. Scholarship did not confine itself to this narrow field. Even in the concentration camps, scholars and writers furtively continued their work under the noses of Nazi guards. A noteworthy book written at Grini is Francis Bull's memoirs, *Tradisjoner og minner.* Of more immediate significance were the lectures and other programs of wide cultural import which sustained the morale and comradeship in the camp.

The conditions during the occupation stimulated the demand for reading matter, and reprints of older Norwegian books and hasty translations of foreign books—often selected with little discrimination—flooded the country. The lack of new books was felt as keenly as the material shortages. The only means of spreading new literature was the illegal press and other underground channels, and obviously extensive works did not lend themselves to this method of circulation. Only a few novels grew out of the occupation, but lyric poetry flourished and met with warm appreciation, for it could best express the dominating emotions of the day. One new poet, Inger Hagerup, gained marked recognition. The leading poets were men who had won preeminence before the war but had grown in stature in the hour of trial. The whole home front was inspired by the stirring, patriotic poems of Øverland and Nordahl Grieg and moved by their martyrdom. Øverland was enduring the tortures of a German concentration camp, and Grieg met his death in a bomber crash over Berlin.

Music, too, had to go underground in its resistance to nazification. Hundreds of concerts were given in secret, often by the finest artists of the country, and before the evening was over, the audience joined in singing national songs, doubly dear now when forbidden. The war years were, moreover, a productive period in Norwegian music. So many composers, both old and new, added to the wealth of the national music that it is difficult to say who stands out most prominently, but names like Klaus Egge, Harald Sæverud, Finn Ludt, Sparre Olsen, and Harald Lie are representative of the best in the new music. In form it is decidedly modern, almost revolutionary, as was the development of the pre-war years. Yet there is no disruption of the continuity with the past, for the very newest compositions are as characteristically Norwegian and as close to the folk music as those of Edvard Grieg himself—one might be tempted to say even closer.

The brave resistance of the home front was strengthened by the knowledge that Norwegians abroad were also continuing to fight. Through the radio in London and other secret channels, news from abroad penetrated their isolation, greetings from the king and others strengthened their courage, and constant communication was maintained between the two fronts.

And finally, if conditions at home became too hazardous or the longing for service in the armed forces too strong, there might be a chance to join countrymen in exile. The exploits connected with the many escapes across the Swedish frontier were worthy of the Scarlet Pimpernel. Even more difficult and dangerous was the escape to England. Countless young men and women in small boats braved as great dangers on the treacherous North Sea as did their viking forbears. Some were captured, others—how many we shall never know—were lost on the way, but many joined the ranks of their compatriots in foreign lands.

¶ When its position in the North was untenable, the Norwegian government, accepting the hospitality of Great Britain, established headquarters in London, and, in accordance with the Constitution, the Government in Exile continued to be the only legal government of the country throughout the period of the occupation.[12] No other exile government had so large a staff or carried on such far-reaching activities as the Norwegian. Its tasks were many: to direct Norway's contribution to the Allied war efforts, to give the home front all possible support, to come to the aid of Norwegian citizens all over the world who suffered as a result of the occupation of the mother country, to prepare for the coming of peace, and to establish Norway's international position.

The government in London began at once to organize its military forces. Thousands of young Norwegians from all over the world entered the service, and they were joined by hundreds who managed to escape from Norway and reach their destination, often after encircling the globe by the most devious paths. The largest single contingent was 300 men who returned with the British warships after a raid on the Lofoten Islands, early in the war. This was the first of the naval and commando

[12] Hambro, *I Saw It Happen in Norway*, 182-202.

raids on the coast of Norway in which British and Norwegian forces cooperated. A Norwegian army, which was intended as a nucleus of the expeditionary force when an invasion of Norway should take place, was given first-class training in a camp in Scotland. Meanwhile an air force of high efficiency was developed in the training camp Little Norway, near Toronto, Canada, and Norwegian fliers made an honorable contribution to the successes of the British Royal Air Force. The little Norwegian fleet that escaped to England began at once to cooperate with the British navy, doing convoy duty, patrolling the shores, and taking some part in active combat. The navy very soon added to its manpower by recruiting, and acquired a number of additional ships.

Norway's greatest contribution to the war effort, however, was its merchant marine. "It is probably an understatement," said a British authority in 1941, "to say that at the present time this fleet is worth more to us than a million soldiers." When the war broke out, Norway had the most modern merchant fleet in the world, two-thirds of the 1,990 vessels being driven by Diesel engines. Especially valuable was the tanker fleet with a capacity almost equal to the British. The ships that were in German-dominated harbors on April 9, 1940, fell into German hands, of course, and the crews were interned. The others received orders via the Oslo radio to return home or put into the nearest Nazi-controlled port. But from London came directions that all ships should go to a neutral or Allied harbor, and not a single captain was led astray by the Nazi orders. Thus the government requisitioned all vessels and for the duration of the war administered the whole fleet through the Norwegian Shipping and Trade Mission, or Nortraship as it was called from its cable address. This largest shipping concern in the world had headquarters in London, but the New York office ranked with it, while the center at Montreal was also important. Norwegian boats were everywhere:[13] they helped evacuate the British forces at Dunkirk, to mention but one example, and by carrying supplies to Great Britain they were a decisive factor in winning the Battle of the Atlantic. The losses were enormous—about 50 per cent of the fleet—and the loss of life great, although the superior seamanship of the Norwegians kept down the casualties. In addition to its direct contributions to the war efforts, the merchant marine was a source of income which enabled the government to finance its far-reaching activities without touching the gold reserve which had been removed from Norway. Directly, as well as through Nortraship and other organizations, it

[13] Lise Lindbæk, *Tusen norske skip*, Brooklyn, 1943.

strove to keep all its citizens informed and united in loyal support of their country and to keep up their morale. Thus the director of shipping, Øivind Lorentzen, sent regular directives and news to all ships,[14] and the radio, both from America and London, was a powerful instrument not only in steeling the courage of the home front but in carrying on the fight of free Norway as well.

Equally important was the extensive welfare work, especially for seamen. Hostels, clubs, rest homes, and hospitals mitigated the hardships of the sailors' lot, supplementing the work of the seamen's mission which had been inaugurated earlier and was now expanded. Mention should also be made of the substantial contribution to the support of missionaries, whose means of subsistence had been cut off by the Nazi occupation.

Then there was the care of the refugees, which included even the establishment of a school in Scotland. But most of this work was done in and through Sweden, where thousands of refugees were welcomed. While the Norwegian government paid most—but by no means all—of the expenses, nothing could have been accomplished without the cooperation of Swedish officials and private organizations. Housing and feeding this influx of about 40,000 persons and caring for the sick was no mean task; and then came the problems of finding employment, supplying educational facilities, furnishing convalescent homes, and enabling the refugees to live as normal a life as possible while waiting for the opportunity to return home. To prepare for that day, 1,500 Norwegian policemen and 12,000 reserves were trained in Sweden.

Sweden was also the base of operations for relief work in Norway. This was organized through the Norwegian so-called Ditleff Commission, headed by the Norwegian minister to Sweden, whose name the committee bore. Its efforts were liberally supplemented by contributions from Sweden, America, and Denmark. Although only limited relief could be sent into the country, it was invaluable material aid and also an important part of the effort to keep in close touch with the homeland and to prepare for cooperation when the end of the war should come. In preparation for this happy event, the impatient army in Scotland was on the alert to go into Norway; supplies of food and clothing—largely from Norwegian-Americans whose love for their mother country had been intensified by the war—were stored in Great Britain ready for shipment, and close contact was maintained with the home front.

14 *Meddelelser fra skipsfartsdirektøren,* published in New York from August 1940 to May 1945.

Both the government in London and the embassy in Washington, under the able administration of Ambassador Wilhelm Morgenstierne, inaugurated extensive efforts to make Norway's share in the war known to the world. Scores of private Norwegian citizens in exile also contributed to this work. A great many books and articles appeared in English, many of them by capable journalists and eminent historians. But their interest was not confined to the immediate present. Equally significant were the increased cultural interchanges, especially in England, which strengthened the bonds between the Norwegians and the English-speaking peoples.

Norway gave wholehearted support to every move toward international cooperation. It was clear that neutrality was a thing of the past, and as the concept that an aggressor is a criminal was becoming an accepted principle of international law, neutrality would even be considered unethical. Moreover, in modern warfare Norway's position offered no security. In any discussion of regional groupings of nations, Norwegians felt that both ideologically and economically their country was closely bound to the North Atlantic states, especially to Great Britain and the United States.

The close cooperation among the countries in the North which had been developing, especially after 1914, was interrupted by the war. The suggestion which came from Swedish quarters that an alliance of the North be formed, met with no enthusiasm in Norway. Such an alliance, it was thought, would give neither military nor economic security in the future, and, moreover, the war had created considerable friction between the neighbors. Even before the war was over, however, a better understanding had once more been achieved. The common suffering created a close bond of sympathy between Danes and Norwegians, which was strengthened by the generous donations of food from Denmark to Norway and by constant underground communications between the two countries. When Finland declared war on Russia and virtually joined the enemies of Norway, it created considerable bitterness, but even this was assuaged through sympathy for Finland's unhappy fate.

Most involved were the relations with Sweden. The very fact that Sweden did not enter the war was a source of some resentment, although it came to be generally recognized that her neutrality was of much greater help to Norway than her participation in the war could have been. More widespread was the indignation because Sweden sometimes yielded to German demands that were detrimental to Norway, especially in allowing the transit of material, civilian personnel, and (when the fighting in Norway was over) even soldiers through Sweden. Thereby Sweden departed from strict neutrality and certainly from that friendly neutrality which, it seemed, Norway might have a right to expect. Since the liberation both governments have tried to clear up misunderstandings by publishing white books containing the documents relative to the situation.[15] But even earlier, the feeling against Sweden had been softened: her precarious position—the boundary between the two countries was totally unprotected—and the severe pressure upon her came to be more fully appreciated, and her frequent resistance to German demands and her repeated intercessions for Norway became known.[16] Moreover, the magnificent support given by Sweden, especially toward the close of the war, and the strengthening of cultural bonds during the years when so many Norwegians were residing in Sweden were not without effect.

No single achievement of the last days of the war did more to bind the three Scandinavian peoples together than their united efforts to free the Norwegian and Danish prisoners interned in Germany. As early as the spring of 1944 the Norwegian minister in Stockholm, Nils Chr. Ditleff, conceived the idea of getting these prisoners out before the final collapse of Germany. A rescue expedition was organized through the Swedish government and the Swedish Red Cross. Detailed preparatory work was done and careful plans laid through the cooperation of Norwegians, Danes, and Swedes, at home and abroad, even in Germany. Chief among them was Count Folke Bernadotte, who headed the expedition and carried out the plans with extraordinary skill and daring. It seems miraculous that he could obtain from Himmler himself the consent to carry out his mission. During April, 3,330 Norwegians were evacuated to Sweden, besides thousands of other prisoners, who were thus spared untold horrors in the final debacle of the Third Reich.[17]

¶ As the Second World War was approaching the final crisis, the Norwegians, too, shared in the intensified struggle on all fronts. The

[15] *Norges forhold til Sverige under krigen 1940-45: Aktstykker utgitt av det kgl. utenriksdepartement*, Oslo, 1946; *Aktstycken utgivna av kungl. utenrikesdepartementet: Handlingar rörande Sveriges politik under andra världskriget: transiteringsfrågan och därmed sammanhängande spörsmål april-juni 1940; transiteringsfrågan juni-december 1940*, Stockholm, 1946.

[16] Joakim Ihlen og Bertil Kugelberg, *Frendefolk: Streiflys over forholdet mellom Norge og Sverige under krigen 1940-45*, Oslo, 1945, gives a brief summary of the relations between the two countries.

[17] Folke Bernadotte, *The Curtain Falls; the Last Days of the Third Reich*, New York, 1945; Seip, *Hjemme og i fiendeland.*

merchant marine—busy everywhere—took a conspicuous part in the landing in Normandy, without the loss of a boat. Norway's warships, some contingents of the army, and the air force were taking an increasingly large part in the fighting. On the home front also, where the war had been in a comparatively passive state, the conflict entered a new acute stage—a terrific grapple between the underground and the Nazis.

When it became evident that the collapse of Germany was imminent, there was much uncertainty among Norwegians as to the part their country was destined to play in the final events. One thing was clear: liberation would not be attained without a cost. Hitler placed much emphasis on the strategic importance of "Fortress Norway." The Germans therefore made extensive military installations and built roads, notably a highway to the Finland border. Although an Allied attack through Norway, which had been considered early in the war, was abandoned as too costly, the Germans never felt sure that the enemy tactics might not be changed. They made effective use of air and naval bases in the North for attacks on the Allied convoys to the Murmansk Coast and on the Russians. The ore transportation from Narvik was also kept up with few losses until 1944, when the British went into serious action against the whole coastal traffic. The offensive force of the German fleet had, however, been broken long before this. Early in 1943 the nucleus of the German navy was withdrawn to the Alta Fjord in Northern Norway, and from there an overwhelming force made a raid on Svalbard. The reasons were probably the demoralization among the troops, and the desire to cover up an intended retreat from the Alta Fjord. Some units escaped, among them the *Scharnhorst*, which was later sunk in the Artic. Chief among the remaining ships was the *Tirpitz*. After repeated attacks, it was finally destroyed by the Royal Air Force while lying in Tromsø harbor, on November 12, 1944, and went down with 1200 men.

As the war developed, the military value of Norway to the Germans was losing its importance, and the morale of the troops in Norway had been on a steady decline ever since 1940. It is estimated that 2,000 recalcitrant German soldiers were kept in concentration camps in Norway, and they were given even worse treatment than the Russian captives. Although troops and supplies were moved to other fronts, especially after the invasion of Normandy, the Germans continued to strengthen the fortifications of Norway to the last. Carelessness in moving ammunition caused a serious explosion in the harbor of Oslo and an even more devastating catastrophe in Bergen, which took a toll of a hundred lives and made 4,000 homeless.

When Finland withdrew from the war, in September 1944, and ordered the German forces out of the country, it brought serious consequences for Norway, as German troops poured over the border into Finmark. Meanwhile the Russians were rounding out their Arctic campaign, bombing Kirkenes and other coastal towns, and invading eastern Finmark. The only possible course for the Germans was to evacuate the North, and in doing so they wanted to make the region useless to the Russians. Finmark was therefore subjected to all the horrors of a scorched-earth policy carried out with ruthless thoroughness, and the inhabitants were ordered to evacuate southward. In East Finmark most of the people managed to go into hiding or flee to the mountains, often with the help of the Russians; but farther west, where the Nazis held full sway, people were driven from their homes on short notice, on to the highways and down to the quays to be deported southward, crowded into open boats. The conditions among them were frightful, and the Nazis refused to allow the Swedish Red Cross to come to the aid of the evacuees.

Meanwhile, in the midst of the tragedy, the liberation of Norway had begun. In November the first contingent of Norwegian soldiers landed in Finmark, working with the Russians, and before long they were joined by a company of the police force trained in Sweden. Before the end of the year the Germans had withdrawn from most of Finmark without any important military action and the people were coming out of hiding to take up life among the ruins. The political reorganization was simple, and the free local government was reestablished as it had been in the past. Much more serious were the problems of mitigating suffering and rebuilding the economic life. Worst of all was the lack of houses—and most difficult to remedy. In other respects the situation was somewhat alleviated after a few critical weeks, as, through intensive efforts on the part of the government in London, food, clothing, medicine, fishing equipment, and the like were rushed northward.

For the whole nation the autumn of 1944 was depressing: the hopes for peace by the end of the year were doomed to disappointment and the country was facing the most trying winter of the war. The British practically stopped all coastal traffic, making any mass movement of troops out of the country impossible, and it was feared that the Germans would try their Finmark methods on the rest of the country. The Norwegians urged an Allied invasion with cooperation from Sweden, but in vain—fortunately. Then the home front girded itself for the final, great battle, and the history of the last months of the war is filled with thrilling tales of ingenuity, daring, great achievement, and narrow escapes.

The underground was working in close cooperation with the British and with the London government from which it received orders, and served as a liaison between the government and the people. The solidarity and loyalty of the people were manifested by the success of the home forces in carrying out their far-reaching program. Through the illegal press, which was more active than ever, the people were kept informed and given directions how to act in every eventuality. Repeatedly they were urged to refrain from any provocative act, which would only cause useless losses. As far as possible, help was extended to all who had suffered at the hands of the Nazis, and every effort was made to distribute equitably the dwindling food supplies and to steel the people against Nazi pressure.

Troops, equipped with arms made at home or obtained from England, were held ready for action. A few clashes with the Germans occurred, involving losses on both sides, but they were avoided when possible. First of all, precautions were taken to prevent the Germans from executing their plan to leave the country ruined if forced to retreat. Had the explosives planted under Oslo been ignited and the schemes for ruining industrial plants carried out, Norway's economic life would have been crippled for years. Aggressive sabotage against German war efforts was the most hazardous and difficult of home front operations, but also its chief contribution to the Allied cause. The illegal press emphasized that, even though sabotage involved some loss of life and destruction of property, it was the most effective and least costly mode of warfare. The work was carried on with great skill and care, with the assistance of experts brought over from Great Britain. The objectives were military installations, the central offices of the enemy, and bridges and railroads. Thus troops that might have been used in Germany were detained in Norway. An interesting episode was the carrying off of tons of Nazi documents, which later helped to convict many a quisling. The underground had become a people's organization in which men and women of all classes fought side by side, and its program was geared to the increasing Nazi terror.

The more desperate the Nazi situation became, the more relentless did the terror grow, as military authorities, the Gestapo, the hird, and the quisling police united their efforts. Mass arrests swelled the population of Grini and other concentration camps; death sentences became almost the order of the day; searching of houses and of individuals, even on the streets, became a mania of the police; and inhuman reprisals, even for rather minor offenses, were inflicted upon hundreds of innocent people. Above all, the Nazis were in search of arms. It seemed that they were preparing for a death struggle in Norway that might continue for months after the collapse of Germany—they had 400,000 fully equipped soldiers in Norway at the time of the capitulation.

The home front, too, was preparing for war, although there was a faint hope that the country might be spared this catastrophe. As the German collapse was approaching during the last days of April, panic seized Quisling and his cohorts. Quisling conceived the grotesque idea that he might head a transition government and "save the country from civil war." He even attempted to negotiate with the home front, but received a curt rebuff. After April 29, when Himmler's offer to surrender became known, a general unconditional surrender of all Nazi forces, those in Norway included, seemed not improbable. The next few days were the tensest of the whole five years of occupation. Yet the people obeyed implicitly the directives issued by the home front in conjunction with the London government. No violence, no provocative acts must mar the transition from terror to freedom. The watchword was, "Dignity—calm—discipline."

¶ One spontaneous outburst of joy swept over the country on May 7, 1945, when the news of the unconditional capitulation of all German forces was spread abroad. In the evening the German commander-in-chief announced over the Oslo radio that he would comply with the order to surrender. The same evening the home front leaders broadcast directions impressing on the people that capitulation did not mean peace, that there was still danger, and that "dignity—calm—discipline" was still the order of the day. In the night thousands of posters containing this proclamation were scattered over the country, and its warnings were heeded: the people showed admirable restraint, and the transition was made without untoward incidents.

The official day of liberation was May 8, when the "Big Three" formally accepted the German capitulation, and at three o'clock in the afternoon peace was solemnly proclaimed by the ringing of church bells throughout the land. On that day the underground army of the home front came out of hiding, as 40,000 men responded to mobilization orders. Everywhere soldiers appeared and without violence replaced the

German police, and took over as guards at power and industrial plants, bridges, and other important positions. Meanwhile the freeing of all Norwegian political prisoners was proceeding rapidly and in an orderly manner.

The members of the Gestapo, from whom some last outrages might have been expected, went to pieces and proved to be wretched cowards when deprived of the support of the Nazi system. Many followed the example of Terboven and committed suicide, others were arrested without difficulty. Yet the danger was not over, for the German army in Norway was ten times as large as that of the home front.

On the day of liberation the Allied Military Commission arrived and was greeted with wild enthusiasm. The capitulation agreement was signed at the German headquarters, at Lillehammer. War criminals and Gestapo men were to be delivered to the Allies, the soldiers were to gather in places designated and disarm themselves, leaving their weapons outside of the reservation. The discipline within the camps was in the hands of the German officers, who sometimes used the weapons they were allowed to keep for police purposes against any of their own men who expressed any anti-Nazi feelings. German soldiers were set to clearing away mines, and not a few moved freely about the streets without attracting any notice. Not before autumn was it possible to get them all transported back to Germany, and then only through help from Sweden.

The cooperation of Sweden was even more indispensable in solving the immediate problem of sending home Russian war prisoners and slave laborers, of whom there were about 80,000 in concentration camps in Norway. Some knowledge of the conditions in these camps had been noised abroad, and Norwegians, especially children, had often been able to help prisoners; but the horrors, exceeding those of Buchenwald, were not fully revealed before the liberation.

During the first weeks of peace the Allied Military Commission was the highest authority in the land. Before many days American and British military contingents arrived, and the Norwegian forces came home from Sweden and England. While the presence of Allied forces was a necessary precaution, the command followed the principle of interfering in civil affairs only when safety demanded. As its course of action had been mapped while war in Norway was still expected, some of the regulations were perhaps at first needlessly restrictive, and yet relations between the foreign troops and the people were most cordial. Although some foreign soldiers remained in the land until autumn, it was definitely substantiated on June 7 that the civil administration was once more wholly in Norwegian hands. On that day, exactly five years after his departure, King Haakon returned to his country, and was greeted with overwhelming ovations, as the people gave expression to their warm affection for the king.

¶ When the king arrived in Norway great steps had already been taken toward the return to normalcy. It was generally agreed that the principle of unity in action which had been adopted in April 1940 and strengthened through the war was to pervade also the critical years of reconstruction. The home front had laid detailed plans for the transition along all lines, and these were carried on with the authorization of the government. Temporary local officials were appointed for counties, communes, and cities; traitors were imprisoned and preparations made for their trial; the Supreme Court began to function as early as May 14; the church resumed its former relations to the government; organizations, political, cultural, and industrial, took up their old activities—purged of members of Quisling's National Party.

On May 14 the leaders of the underground, their work done, withdrew from their posts, and for the first time were revealed the names of the president, Chief Justice Paal Berg, and of the other key men. Prime Minister Nygaardsvold, who with tireless devotion and dauntless determination had carried on through the war, had repeatedly said that he would step aside as soon as Norway was free and allow those who had borne the brunt of the struggle at home to assume the lead. Accordingly he and his cabinet handed their resignation to the king on June 12. An interim government was formed under Einar Gerhardsen, the leader of the Labor Party. He had been mayor of Oslo in 1940, and had now returned to that post after a long stay in a German concentration camp. All but two members of his cabinet had been active on the home front. Among them was Kirsten Hansteen, the first woman to be a member of a Norwegian ministry. She was the wife of Viggo Hansteen, the first Norwegian to be executed by the Nazis.

Norway was the first of the liberated countries to have a parliamentary election. It was held on October 8, 1945. The result showed a definite trend to the left; the Labor Party won a clear majority, and the new regular government was also headed by Gerhardsen. He declared that his cabinet would cooperate with all six parties on the basis of an adopted unity program, and both government and people have been true to this pledge. In spite of many differences, it seemed to be the consensus that the Labor government performed its difficult task with sound judgment and wise moderation. On Haakon's seventy-fifth birthday, the prime minister paid a beautiful tribute to the contribution the king had made to the reconstruction through his tact, experience, and sage counsel.

Because Norway weathered the overwhelming calamity of the Second World War better, it seems safe to say, than any other country involved, the seriousness of the difficulties with which she was confronted must not be underestimated. But the innumerable problems connected with reconstruction and the methods of dealing with them, belonging to the present, are beyond the scope of history, and only the briefest mention of them is made here.

Within the government itself there were difficulties resulting from a greatly enlarged bureaucracy and the ensuing inefficiency. Indeed, the Labor ministry was fully aware of this. The presence of so many war prisoners and thousands of other displaced persons was a heavy drain on the depleted resources of the country. The problem of dealing with about 40,000 quislings was costly in money and time. But it was handled admirably, maintaining the traditional respect for the due process of law, yielding neither to revengeful impulse nor to pleas for softness. The death penalty was meted out to Vidkun Quisling and the other chief traitors, and various prison terms were imposed on thousands of other offenders. Most difficult was the task of ferreting out those who profited by the occupation. And there remained the long-range problem of absorbing into society the whole dissident group of collaborators.

In spite of the balanced Norwegian mentality, there were other psychological problems too, as prisoners who had suffered most cruelly in the war and thousands who had experienced the various vicissitudes of exile were reunited with the people at home who had borne the daily hardships of occupation. It is impossible to draw a balance between the losses and gains in the more intangible phases of life. There were evidences of an increased spiritual depth and mental strength, but on the other hand the effects of disruptive influences were noticeable, especially among the youth. The schools from the University down faced valiantly the problems of recuperating the losses of the past years.

Most exacting were the economic problems. The immediate need for food was met by supplies sent from the United States, Sweden, Denmark, and England, and the grain purchased by the government during the war and stored in England. Somewhat more slowly the most conspicuous demand for clothing was also alleviated, but the housing shortage continued to be acute. The task of rebuilding or reconditioning homes, public buildings, bridges, industrial plants, even whole towns, and—worst of all—the whole district of Finmark was staggering. Priority was given where the need was most glaring. Production capacity, which had been cut in half by the war, was rapidly brought back to normal, especially through the encouragement of small business; shipyards hummed with activity, for the merchant marine had to be restored if the country were to flourish. Building up foreign exchange in order to restore trade was but one of the financial problems with which the authorities were obliged to grapple.

A firm determination to restore the country through their own efforts, with the least possible dependence on others, pervaded people and government, both in the local communities and in the country as a whole. The spirit of collective action developed during the war was an admirable foil to the inherent Norwegian individualism. Strict rationing, as well as price, rent, and housing control, was maintained, and production was not hampered by strikes. Not only did all classes feel pledged to cooperation during the reconstruction, but labor was conscious that it had a large share in determining employer-employee relations as well as the policy of the government itself. This policy has been to promote private business, while always bearing in mind that public welfare takes precedence over private profit. With all that was accomplished, the business outlook did not, however, appear roseate. Agriculture was in an especially precarious condition, and had to be heavily subsidized in order to keep up production and maintain reasonable prices. The level in 1946 rose only three per cent above that of 1939. On the whole, Norway demonstrated in the years after the war a successful planned economy, but wisdom and self-denial were still needed to attain the high standard of living of pre-war days.

The Norwegians are keenly aware that the future of their country is perilously dependent on international developments. Situated between the East and the West, Norway desires to maintain connections with both, without becoming subservient to either, economically, politically, or ideologically. The people have shown their international spirit by sacrificing liberally to supply relief to those whose plight was worse than their own; by welcoming displaced persons to their shores; and by continuing to maintain the bonds of friendship and common cultural interests, especially with England and the United States, which the war had strengthened. Notable was the interest in the interchange of students. The close cooperation between the Scandinavian governments was resumed, emphasizing a certain unanimity—though not unity—of the North.

Even more importance has been attached to an active participation in all international activities of a world scope. On November 14, 1945, the Storthing by unanimous vote ratified the United Nations Charter, and on February 2, 1946, Trygve Lie took the oath of office as the first Secretary General of the United Nations. Lie was a man of the common people, who as foreign minister during the war and after the liberation did much to establish Norway's place among the Allies. His vigor, his forthrightness, and the wide scope of his international interests had won recognition in diplomatic circles, and his appointment was a tribute to the highly sensitive world consciousness which has pervaded his country in the twentieth century. But equally significant was the national spirit expressed in the last message from the leaders of the home front to their countrymen:

> "We have learned this, too, that there is something greater than our personal affairs and wishes: our country, our people, this Norway which has been sustained through adversity, ravaged, pillaged, and poor; but free—and our own in a deeper, more intimate sense than ever before."

RULERS

Harald I Fairhair	872- 930 (?)
Eirik Blood-Axe	930- 934 (?)
Haakon I the Good	934- 961 (?)
Harald II Graypelt	961- 970 (?)
Jarl Haakon of Lade	970- 995 (?)
Olaf I Tryggvason	995-1000
Jarls Eirik and Svein	1000-1016
Saint Olaf II	1015-1030
Canute the Great and Svein	1028-1035
Magnus I the Good	1035-1047
Harald III the Hard	1042-1066
Magnus II	1066-1069
Olaf III Kyrri (the Peaceful)	1066-1093
Magnus III Bareleg	1093-1103
Olaf IV	1103-1116
Eystein I	1103-1122
Sigurd I Jerusalemfarer	1103-1130
Magnus IV the Blind	1130-1135
Harald IV Gilchrist	1130-1136
Sigurd II Slembe	1136-1139
Ingi Hunchback	1136-1161
Sigurd III Mouth	1136-1155
Eystein II	1142-1157
Haakon II the Broad-Shouldered	1157-1162
Magnus V Erlingsson	1162-1184
Sverri	1177-1202
Haakon III	1202-1204
Ingi Baardsson	1204-1217
Haakon IV the Old	1217-1263
Magnus VI Lawmender	1263-1280
Eirik II Priesthater	1280-1299
Haakon V	1299-1319

Magnus VII	1319-1350
Haakon VI	1350-1380
Olaf V	1380-1387
Margaret	1388-1405
Erik of Pomerania	1389-1442
Christopher of Bavaria	1442-1448
Interregnum with Karl Knutsson and Christian of Oldenburg as rival claimants	1448-1450
Christian I	1450-1481
Interregnum	1481-1483
Hans	1483-1513
Christian II	1513-1524
Frederik I	1524-1533
Interregnum	1533-1536
Christian III	1536-1559
Frederik II	1559-1588
Christian IV	1588-1648
Frederik III	1648-1670
Christian V	1670-1699
Frederik IV	1699-1730
Christian VI	1730-1746
Frederik V	1746-1766
Christian VII	1766-1808
Frederik VI	1808-1814
Christian Frederik	1814
Karl XIII	1814-1818
Karl XIV Johan	1818-1844
Oscar I	1844-1859
Karl XV	1859-1872
Oscar II	1872-1905
Haakon VII	1905-

IMPORTANT DATES

793	First recorded Norwegian raid on England (Lindisfarne).
851	Olaf the White established in Dublin.
ca. 870	Settlement of Iceland.
872 (?)	Battle of Hafrsfjord, unification of Norway.
911	Normandy ceded to Rollo the Walker as a fief.
984	Settlement of Greenland.
995	Christianity introduced by Olaf Tryggvason.
1000	Leif Eiriksson visited America.
	Christianity introduced into Iceland and Greenland.
	September 9, Battle of Svold, disappearance of Olaf Tryggvason.
1014	Battle of Clontarf, Norwegian power in Ireland broken.
1030	July 29, Battle of Stiklestad, death of Saint Olaf.
1066	Battle of Stamford Bridge, last Norwegian attack on England repelled.
1101	Peace meeting of the three Scandinavian kings at Konungahella.
1152	Archbishopric of Nidaros created.
1163	First coronation in Norway.
1217	First commercial treaty with England.
1261-62	Greenland and Iceland formally incorporated into Norway's colonial empire.
1277	Concordat of Tønsberg.
1319	First dynastic union with Sweden.
1349	The Black Death.
1380	Dynastic union with Denmark (Olaf V).
1387	End of old Norwegian dynasty.
1397	Kalmar Union.
1450	First king of the Oldenburg house.
1468	Western Islands mortgaged to the Scottish king.
1523	Sweden seceded from the Kalmar Union.

1536	The Lutheran Reformation.
	Norway lost her national government.
1559	Hanseatic power broken.
1661	Absolutism established.
1688	King Christian the Fifth's Norwegian Law promulgated.
1720	End of the Great Northern War.
1763	The first newspaper.
1765	The Stril War.
1807	Denmark-Norway in the Napoleonic Wars.
1811	University in Oslo established.
1814	January 14, Treaty of Kiel terminated union with Denmark.
	May 17, Constitution adopted.
	November 4, Union with Sweden established.
1825	The sloop *Restoration* sailed for America.
1837	Law establishing local self-government.
1848	The Thrane movement.
1851	First railroad.
1869	The establishment of the Liberal Party.
1880	Resolution seating the ministers in the Storthing.
1887	The establishment of the Labor Party.
1892	The Factory Law of Emil Stang.
1895	Nansen farthest north.
1899	The Norwegian Federation of Labor.
1900	The Norwegian Employers' Association.
1901	Woman's suffrage in local elections.
1903-5	Roald Amundsen completed the Northwest Passage.
1905	June 7, Union with Sweden dissolved.
	November 18, Prince Carl of Denmark elected king of Norway.
	Norwegian whalers in the Antarctic.
	Norsk Hydro established.
1909	Christiania to Bergen railroad completed.
1911	December 15, Amundsen discovered the South Pole. (On May 12, 1926, he dropped the Norwegian flag on the North Pole.)
1913	Equal suffrage for men and women adopted.
1914	December 18, Malmö meeting of the three Scandinavian kings.

1917	Reform of *riksmaal. Landsmaal* also required for the University.
1920	February 9, Norwegian sovereignty over Svalbard recognized by signatory powers.
	March 4, Norway joined the League of Nations. Fridtjof Nansen delegate to and High Commissioner of the League.
1928	Norway's first Labor government.
1930	December 22, Convention of the "Oslo States."
1933	"The Greenland Case" decided in favor of Denmark by the World Court.
1935	The Nygaardsvold Labor government.
1940	April 9, German invasion of Norway.
	June 7, King Haakon left for England.
1945	May 7, Liberation from the Nazis.
	June 7, Return of King Haakon.
	November 14, Norway joined the United Nations.
1946	February 2, Secretary General Trygve Lie opened the United Nations at New York.
	April 18, Carl J. Hambro, President of the Assembly of the League of Nations, dissolved the League at Geneva.

A SELECTED BIBLIOGRAPHY

The American-Scandinavian Review. New York, 1913—.

Diplomatarium Norvegicum. Christiania, 1847—.

The Inter-Allied Review. A Monthly Summary of Documents on the Allied Fight for Freedom, 1941-42. Continued as *The United Nations Review,* 1943-45.

Kongeriget Norges Storthingsforhandlinger. Christiania, 1814—and *Forhandlinger i Stortinget.* Christiania, 1919—.

News of Norway, issued by Royal Norwegian Information Service. Washington, D.C., 1941-45.

The Norseman: An Independent Literary and Political Review. London, 1943—.

Bang, Anton Christian. *Den norske kirkes historie.* Kristiania, 1912.

Brandt, Willy. *Krigen i Norge.* 2 vols. Oslo, 1945.

Broch, Theodor. *The Mountains Wait.* Saint Paul, 1942.

Brøgger, Anton Wilhelm. *Ancient Emigrants, a History of the Norse Settlements of Scotland.* Oxford, 1929.

Bugge, Anders, and Steen, Sverre, eds. *Norsk kulturhistorie, billeder av folkets dagligliv gjennem årtusener.* 5 vols. Oslo, 1938-42.

Carlsen, Ingvald B. *Kirkefronten i Norge under okkupasjonen 1940-1945.* Oslo, 1945.

Elster, Kristian. *Illustreret norsk litteraturhistorie.* 2 vols. Kristiania, 1923-24.

Falnes, Oscar J. *National Romanticism in Norway.* New York, 1933.

Fiske, John. *The Discovery of America, with Some Account of Ancient America and the Spanish Conquest.* Boston, 1892.

Gathorne-Hardy, Geoffrey Malcolm. *The Norse Discoverers of America: The Wineland Sagas Translated and Discussed.* Oxford, 1921.

Gathorne-Hardy, Geoffrey Malcolm. *Norway.* London, 1925.

Gjerset, Knut. *History of the Norwegian People.* 2 vols. New York, 1915.

Grøndahl, Illit, and Raknes, Ola. *Chapters in Norwegian Literature.* Copenhagen, 1923.

Hambro, Carl J. *I Saw It Happen in Norway.* New York, 1940.

Haugen, Einar. *Voyages to Vinland; the First American Saga Newly Translated and Interpreted.* New York, 1942.

Hovde, Bryn J. *The Scandinavian Countries, 1720-1865; The Rise of the Middle Classes.* 2 vols. Boston, 1943.

Hovgaard, William. *The Voyages of the Norsemen to America*. New York, 1914.

Johnsen, Oscar Albert. *Noregsveldets undergang*. Kristiania, 1924.

Johnsen, Oscar Albert. *Norges bønder; utsyn over den norske bondestands historie*. Kristiania, 1919.

Johnsen, Oscar Albert. *De norske stænder*. Kristiania, 1906.

Jones, S. Shepard. *The Scandinavian States and the League of Nations*. New York, 1939.

Jorgenson, Theodore. *History of Norwegian Literature*. New York, 1933.

Jorgenson, Theodore. *Norway's Relation to Scandinavian Unionism, 1815-1871*. Northfield, Minn., 1935.

Keilhau, Wilhelm. *Det norske folks liv og historie i vår egen tid*. Oslo, 1938.

Keilhau, Wilhelm. *Norway and the World War*. (Economic and social history of the World War, Scandinavian series. Carnegie Endowment for International Peace. An abridged translation of *Norge og verdenskrigen*.) New Haven, 1930.

Keilhau, Wilhelm. *Norway in World History*. London, 1944.

Kendrick, Thomas Downing. *A History of the Vikings*. New York, 1930.

Koht, Halvdan. *1814: norsk dagbok hundre aar efterpaa*. Kristiania, 1914.

Koht, Halvdan. *Innhogg og utsyn i norsk historie*. Kristiania, 1921.

Koht, Halvdan. *Johan Sverdrup*. 4 vols. Kristiania, 1918-25.

Koht, Halvdan. *Norsk bondereising; fyrebuing til bondepolitikken*. Oslo, 1926.

Koht, Halvdan. *Norway: Neutral and Invaded*. New York, 1941.

Koht, Halvdan, and Skard, Sigmund. *The Voice of Norway*. New York, 1944.

Laurin, Carl, Hannover, Emil, and Thiis, Jens. *Scandinavian Art*. New York, 1922.

Leach, Henry Goddard. *Angevin Britain and Scandinavia*. Cambridge, 1921.

Leach, Henry Goddard, ed. *A Pageant of Old Scandinavia*. New York, 1946.

Lexow, Einar. *Norges kunst*. Oslo, 1926.

Lødrup, Hans P. *Det store oppgjør*. Oslo, 1945.

Mawer, Allen. *The Vikings*. Cambridge, 1930.

Munch, Peter Andreas. *Det norske folks historie*. 6 vols. Christiania, 1852-59.

Munch, Peter Andreas. *Norse Mythology*; in the revision of Magnus Olsen (translated from the Norwegian by S. B. Hustvedt). New York, 1926.

Myklebost, Tor. *They Came as Friends* (translated by Trygve M. Ager). New York, 1943.

Nansen, Fridtjof. *In Northern Mists; Arctic Exploration in Early Times*. 2 vols. New York, 1911.

Nielsen, Yngvar. *Lensgreve Johan Caspar Herman Wedel Jarlsberg*. 3 vols. Christiania, 1901-2.

Nielsen, Yngvar. *Norge i 1814*. Christiania, 1904.

Nordskog, John Eric. *Social Reform in Norway*. University of Southern California Press, Los Angeles, 1935.

Norges historie. 2 vols. Oslo, 1938-39. vol. 1, Andreas Holmsen. vol. 2, Magnus Jensen.

Norges historie fremstillet for det norske folk. 6 vols. Kristiania, 1909-17. vol. 1, Alexander Bugge. vol. 2, Ebbe Hertzberg and Alexander Bugge. vol. 3, Absalon Taranger. vol. 4, Yngvar Nielsen. vol. 5, Oscar Albert Johnsen. vol. 6, J. E. Sars.

Norsk litteraturhistorie. 5 vols. Oslo, 1923-37. vols. 1 and 3, Fredrik Paasche. vols. 2 and 4, Francis Bull. vol. 5, A. H. Winsnes.

Det norske folks liv og historie gjennem tidene. 10 vols. Oslo, 1929-35. vol. 1, Haakon Shetelig. vol. 2, Edvard Bull. vol. 3, S. Hasund. vols. 4-7, Sverre Steen. vols. 8-10, Wilhelm Keilhau.

Den norske sjøfarts historie fra de ældste tider til vore dage, med bidrag av Alexander Bugge, Fredrik Scheel, Roar Tank, Jacob S. Worm-Müller, et al. 3 vols. Kristiania, 1923-35.

Olrik, Axel. *Viking Civilization*. New York, 1930.

Østbye, Leif. *Norges kunsthistorie*. Oslo, 1938.

Paasche, Fredrik. *Kristendom og kvad: en studie i norrøn middelalder*. Kristiania, 1914.

The Poetic Edda, Translated from the Icelandic with an introduction and notes by Henry Adams Bellows. New York, 1936.

Schnitler, Carl W. *Slegten fra 1814*. Kristiania, 1911.

Seip, Didrik Arup. *Hjemme og i fiendeland, 1940-45*. Oslo, 1946.

Shetelig, Haakon, and Falk, Hjalmar. *Scandinavian Archaeology*. Oxford, 1937.

Snorri Sturlason. *Heimskringla; The Norse King Sagas*, Translated by Samuel Laing. New York, 1930.

Snorri Sturlason. *Heimskringla, or The Lives of the Norse Kings*, Edited with Notes by Erling Monsen and Translated into English with the Assistance of A. H. Smith. Cambridge, 1932.

Sørensen, Jon. *The Saga of Fridtjof Nansen* (translated from the Norwegian by J. B. C. Watkins). New York, 1932.

Sverrissaga. The Saga of King Sverri of Norway, Translated by John Sephton. London, 1899.

Topsøe-Jensen, Helge Gottlieb. *Scandinavian Literature from Brandes to Our Day* (translated from the Danish by Isaac Anderson). New York, 1929.

Vigness, Paul G. *Neutrality of Norway in the World War*. Stanford University, 1932.

Williams, Mary Wilhelmine. *Social Scandinavia in the Viking Age*. New York, 1920.

Worm-Müller, Jacob S. *Norge gjennem nødsaarene: den norske regjeringskommission, 1807-1810*. Kristiania, 1918.

Worm-Müller, Jacob S. *Norway Revolts against the Nazis*. London, 1941.

INDEX

INDEX

INDEX

INDEX

INDEX

COMMITTEE ON PUBLICATIONS
THE AMERICAN-SCANDINAVIAN FOUNDATION

PROFESSOR KENNETH BALLARD MURDOCK, *Chairman*
Harvard University

PROFESSOR MARGARET SCHLAUCH, *Secretary*
New York University

PROFESSOR ADOLPH BURNETT BENSON
Yale University

PRESIDENT JAMES CREESE
Drexel Institute of Technology

PROFESSOR ROBERT HERNDON FIFE
Columbia University

PROFESSOR CHESTER N. GOULD
University of Chicago

PROFESSOR HALLDOR HERMANSSON
Cornell University

PROFESSOR WILLIAM WITHERLE LAWRENCE
Columbia University

DR. HENRY GODDARD LEACH
The American-Scandinavian Foundation

MR. FREDERIC SCHAEFER
Carnegie Institute of Technology

PROFESSOR J. B. C. WATKINS
Canadian Department of External Affairs